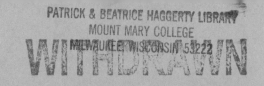

HUMAN SEXUALITY

HUMAN SEXUALITY

James Geer

*State University of New York
at Stony Brook*

Julia Heiman

*University of Washington
Harborview Community Mental Health Center*

Harold Leitenberg

University of Vermont

Prentice-Hall, Inc.
Englewood Cliffs
New Jersey   07632

Library of Congress Cataloging in Publication Data

Geer, James.
  HUMAN SEXUALITY.

  Bibliography.
  Includes indexes.
   1. Sex. 2. Sex crimes. 3. Sex instruction.
I. Heiman, Julia. II. Leitenberg, Harold. III. Title.
[DNLM: 1. Sex. 2. Sex behavior. 3. Sex disorders.
4. Psychosexual disorders. HQ 12 G298h]
HQ21.G333 1984   306.7   83-22889
ISBN 0-13-447516-X

Development Editor: Alison Gnerre
Production Editor: Jeanne Hoeting
Photo Research: Anita Duncan, Mira Schachne
Book Design and Page Layout: Meryl Sussman Levavi
Cover Photo: Fred Burrell
Cover Design: Linda Conway
Manufacturing Buyer: Ron Chapman

Illustrations: J & R Technical Services, Inc.
and Brown Ink

(Acknowledgments appear on p. 564, which constitutes
a continuation of the copyright page.)

ISBN 0-13-447516-X

Prentice-Hall International, Inc., *London*
Prentice-Hall of Australia Pty. Limited, *Sydney*
Editora Prentice-Hall do Brasil, Ltda., *Rio de Janeiro*
Prentice-Hall Canada Inc., *Toronto*
Prentice-Hall of India Private Limited, *New Delhi*
Prentice-Hall of Japan, Inc., *Tokyo*
Prentice-Hall of Southeast Asia Pte. Ltd., *Singapore*
Whitehall Books Limited, *Wellington, New Zealand*

*To Jean, Johan, and Barbara
and to our parents*

OVERVIEW CONTENTS

CONTENTS

PART ONE
Biology and Development

PART TWO
Sexual Expression

PART THREE
Sexual Problems

PART FOUR
Sexual Offenses

PART FIVE
Sex and Society

PREFACE

When we first started to work on this book, one thought was foremost in our minds: keep the writing as interesting as possible, but be sure to remember that human sexuality is a legitimate academic subject and deserves to be treated with the same respect for serious scholarship and research evidence as any other college or university subject. Of course, the topic of human sexuality has more personal significance to students than most other academic subjects, and any introductory textbook in this area must be keenly sensitive to this issue. The question is one of balance. Although we made every effort not to slight practical concerns, the primary mission of any introductory text, human sexuality included, should be to give the student a solid and authoritative grounding in what is known (and not known) about the subject.

Our goal was to build upon the intrinsic interest students have about sex. Since sex is such a fascinating area, we believe that students want more than a "gut course"; they want to learn something. We believe that just as we are excited and intrigued by specific research and clinical findings, so

too are our students. Again the issue is one of balance. Encyclopedic recitation of study after study and regurgitation of statistics can be exceedingly boring if presented uncritically and nonselectively. We try to avoid this kind of dullness by paying adequate attention to the broader implications of detailed findings.

In other words what we have tried to provide in this text is an up-to-date, comprehensive and in-depth introduction to the topic of human sexuality. We wanted to transmit the broad spectrum of information that is available about human sexuality, to be data based and thorough, but not obsessively so and not at the expense of clarity or interest. Topics are covered from a wide range of perspectives. We include not only information but, where appropriate and possible, we present integrative concepts from the many disciplines that contribute to the understanding of human sexuality. For that reason the reader will find data and ideas from anthropology, biology, psychology, and sociology. There will be information gleaned from the laboratory, from survey research, from clinical experience, and from historical sources. Any comprehensive and informative overview of human sexuality must be interdisciplinary in its perspective. This book accepts that premise and the challenge that it offers.

Following the introduction that examines the interdisciplinary nature of the field and the major methods for studying human sexuality, the book is organized into five sections. The chapters in these sections are not all of equal size. Instead we were guided by the importance and interest of the topic and the amount and quality of clinical and research literature that needed to be reviewed. The first section concerns the biological and reproductive aspects of sexuality. Although our general bias in this book was to devote much more space to sexual behavior than to sexual anatomy or physiology, fundamental and accurate information about the underlying biological system is essential. We then move to an indepth coverage of sexual expression throughout the life span including the topics of masturbation and fantasy, sexual attraction, love, and selection of partners, heterosexuality, and homosexuality. The third section concerns a variety of sexual problems, and deals more extensively than most other introductory texts with the topics of sexual dysfunctions, sexual deviations, and medical problems. In these chapters, we are responding to students' interest in these topics, and the fact that considerable clinical research has been published in these areas. The discussion of serious sexual offenses comes next. In this section we have chosen to treat sexual victimization of children and rape in separate chapters to highlight the importance of

each of these topics, and to reflect the growing research literature in each. The final section of the book deals with some of the broad issues that society must face concerning sexuality: pornography, prostitution, and sex education.

The book contains a number of teaching and student aids. The instructors' manual that accompanies this book provides suggested discussion topics and supplementary audio visual material as well as test materials. Each chapter also contains a judicious sprinkling of figures and tables, boxed items to highlight topics of special interest to students, case illustrations where appropriate, personal quotes, a chapter summary, and suggested further readings. Finally, we have included a glossary, and for the student who wishes to pursue a topic in greater detail, a more extensive bibliography than is usual in an introductory text.

A number of people contributed directly to the production of this book and we are pleased to have an opportunity to acknowledge their help. We are deeply indebted to the line-by-line editorial assistance of Barbara Leitenberg and Alison Gnerre. As they worked through various drafts of chapters, Barbara in the early stages and Alison in the later stages, the clarity of the writing was substantially improved. Left to our own devices, this book would have been twice as long and unreadable. John Isley, our editor at Prentice-Hall, provided needed encouragement and useful counter-point when we got too high up in the clouds. Jeanne Hoeting, our production editor, took us through the final steps of galleys, page proofs, graphs, and photo illustrations with grace, good humor, and gentle prodding. We also appreciated the helpful comments of the following reviewers:

John M. Allen, The University of Michigan
Michael D. Campbell, Highline Community
  College
Emily S. Davidson, Texas A & M University
Clive M. Davis, Syracuse University
Karen Duffy, State University of New York
  at Geneseo
Beverly I. Fagot, University of Oregon
Joseph R. Heller, California State University
Kathy Koser, California State University
Barry W. McCarthy, American University
Andrea Parrot, Cornell University
O'Neal Weeks, University of Kentucky

Our colleagues Jeff Holtmeier, Joseph LoPiccolo, and Jerry Vogt also provided useful feedback or encouragement as needed on several of the chapters.

We are tremendously grateful and lucky to have had the assistance of Jennie Bailey, Nina Fontana, Jackie Jochem, Virginia Lyman, Christine Psyk, Vivian Stabner, and Janet Woodford in the preparation of this book. We wish to thank these individuals for typing multiple drafts of chapters efficiently and without complaint, as well as providing unsolicited but much appreciated editorial advice and opinions.

J.G. J.H. H.L.

CHAPTER ONE

INTRODUCTION
Different Ways to Study Human Sexuality

It is a pity that sex is such an ugly little word, an ugly little word, and really almost incomprehensible. What is sex, after all? The more we think about it the less we know.
D. H. Lawrence, 1953

*W*hat do we know about human sexuality and how do we know it? Like any text in any academic course, the rest of this book is designed to answer these two basic questions. This introductory chapter provides a framework for approaching the more specific chapters that follow.

Each of us brings to the study and understanding of sexuality our own experiences and biases. What the professional knows and emphasizes depends, in part, on the academic discipline and the theoretical model to which he or she subscribes. The investigator who is trained as a biologist, for example, is likely to be interested in physiological events and reproduction and to view these as central to the understanding of sexuality. The psychologist, on the other hand, may feel that sexual behavior and the way it is learned and modified within each

individual is crucial. The sociologist, the historian, the anthropologist, the clinician, and the religious leader also bring unique perspectives to what should be examined and how the examination should be conducted. When we apply the different perspectives to an aspect of sexuality, we learn something different from each; to get a complete picture of human sexuality, we should examine all approaches and determine what each contributes.

In order to illustrate the range of these perspectives, we will offer some background information and describe the key incidents in a day in the life of two fictional college students, Susan and Bill, concentrating on those events that can be linked to their sexuality. Then we will examine these events according to various perspectives on human sexuality.

APPROACHES TO SEXUALITY

A Day in the Life of Susan and Bill

Susan is a 20-year-old college junior majoring in psychology with a minor in biology. She was raised in a small town in the Midwest and is the youngest of three children. The daughter of devout Roman Catholics, Susan has a strong religious background, but she does not regularly attend church while away at college. Susan's father owns and operates a small real estate agency, and her mother does most of the bookkeeping and records management for the business.

Bill is a 23-year-old senior in the premed program. He is an only child, his father is a physician, and his mother is the owner of a successful clothing boutique in the suburbs of a large metropolitan area. Bill was raised in a Protestant household, but religion has never been an important focus of his life or of the lives of his parents. Susan and Bill met this semester in a seminar, Social Problems in Biology. At the end of class today they made arrangements to meet at the library after dinner to study for an upcoming exam. This is the sixth time that Bill and Susan have dated; previously they have

kissed and enjoyed rather extensive sexplay, but they have not had intercourse. They are strongly attracted to one another, and they both realize that a more intense relationship is quite possible.

Susan's sexual experience prior to this day consisted mainly of extensive petting and sexplay, which led to intercourse only once. She has had several steady boyfriends and obviously gets along well with men. Bill, on the other hand, has had a somewhat more extensive sexual history. He has had several steady girlfriends and was engaged for about one year. The engagement ended almost a year ago, and he has dated only occasionally since that time. Bill has had intercourse with several different women. Intercourse with the woman to whom he was engaged was regular and frequent for about six months.

On this particular morning, Bill awoke quite early. He was aware that he had a partial erection when he got out of bed. He tried to recall if he had had a sexual dream, but he couldn't remember any. Later, while taking a shower, he found himself thinking about Susan and daydreaming about going to bed with her. When he imagined Susan lying naked beside him, he started to get sexually excited. Susan, on the other hand, did not have a clear sexual thought about Bill or anyone else after she awoke; she was hurriedly going over her notes in preparation for a lab quiz she had to take in her first class. Susan's first sexual thought occurred later in the morning when she went to the dining hall for breakfast. She met one of her friends, who told her about her recent date with a very attractive man. Clearly the evening had included sex, although there was no direct mention of it. This conversation led Susan to wonder whether she and Bill would get more sexually involved. She decided that they almost certainly would, an expectation that both excited and worried her a bit.

Periodically during the day, Bill thought of the evening that was to come in more explicit sexual terms than did Susan. He found himself thinking of ways to make certain that they would be alone and how he would begin making sexual advances. At one point, while thinking about what they might do together, Bill found that he was becoming quite aroused. When Susan thought about her developing relationship with Bill, she concentrated on the romantic aspects, such as how much she liked Bill. When she did think about sex, Susan wondered if Bill would think less of her if they did have intercourse. She also found herself worrying whether Bill found her attractive enough. Meanwhile, Bill was worried that Susan might reject him if he did try to initiate intercourse: Did *she* like *him* enough?

When Bill returned to his room between classes, he leafed through a copy of *Playboy*. He had the impulse to masturbate while looking at one of the pictures of a particularly sexy woman, but he didn't because he often felt he should resist masturbation.

On the other hand, during a typical week Bill would masturbate several times. Bill's other exposure to sexual stimuli during the day, other than seeing women on campus, was primarily in his conversations with male friends. It seemed as though talk about sexual experiences, both real and fantasized, dominated many of those conversations. Susan's conversations with same-sexed friends were often about men and relationships and were less often about sex itself.

After dinner both Susan and Bill focused their attention on the evening ahead. Susan admitted to herself that she would like to have sex with Bill. She thought he was very attractive, and both her friends and Bill saw intercourse as appropriate and expected in a relationship like theirs; but Susan herself had misgivings. Her religious training caused her to question the "rightness" of premarital intercourse, and she was concerned about the possibility of pregnancy. She resolved that she would not have sex without using some means of contraception, but she was uneasy about managing this. Although she had a diaphragm, taking it with her might appear calculating. Not as concerned as Susan about whether or not they should have sex, Bill was more concerned with making certain that it happened and that it was pleasurable for both of them.

After Susan and Bill met at the student center, they walked directly to the library. Each was pleased to be with the other, and their conversation was lively. They kissed lightly when they met and held hands as they walked to the library. While studying,

Bill found himself quite distracted from time to time by Susan's nearness. Susan felt Bill's attention and found herself being more aware of him than of what she was trying to study. By the end of the second hour in the library, they each began to feel more and more aroused, though neither made any direct sexual overtures. Bill and Susan left the library and stopped for a snack; after eating, they walked slowly back to Susan's room, stopping often along the way to kiss. Susan could feel that Bill had a partial erection when he held her closely, and she felt increasingly aroused by their caresses. Susan invited Bill into her room, and they lay down on the bed and began intense and intimate sexplay, which somehow "naturally" led into intercourse. All of this activity occurred without either Susan or Bill ever verbally asking for permission to move from one step to another and with both of them knowing what lay ahead.

Although sexual behavior can be studied from many points of view, in the interests of brevity and clarity we will describe only the most important approaches: (1) historical, (2) physiological, (3) learning, (4) actuarial, (5) psychoanalytical, (6) anthropological, (7) sociological, and (8) sociobiological. We will examine how each approach might look at, select, and emphasize different sets of data from the lives of Susan and Bill regarding their sexual relationship.

The Historical Approach

A *historical analysis* of sexual behavior not only examines the practices of the past but also looks for patterns, consistencies, influences, and cycles that have led to current practices. We know surprisingly little about the sexual practices of the past. One reason is that sexual activities usually occur in private and have not become part of the public record. Second, the existing historical documents that do describe sexual practices often reflect the interests and activities of a very limited part of society. For example, many people have heard or read that in ancient Greece male homosexuality not only was tolerated but also was presented as the ideal relationship. However, this "ideal" was limited to the educated and wealthy, and only if they chose adolescent partners. We know virtually nothing of the sexual practices of the masses in ancient Greece.

In Western society, sexual practices were profoundly influenced by the teachings of Christianity, with its Judaic roots. Although the emphasis has varied over the centuries, Christianity has always viewed sex, and especially women's role in it, as behavior that can be condoned for its reproductive function but not celebrated or encouraged for any other purpose. From the Middle Ages on through to the present time, sexual activity has been treated by church and state as a potential threat and as something that should be strictly controlled.

St. Paul was the first major figure in Christianity to connect sex and spirituality. He valued **celibacy,** which is abstinence from sexual relations, as the highest Christian ideal because the celibate would not be distracted from serving God. However, St. Paul recognized that celibacy was not possible for everyone; thus, his famous statement, "It is better to marry than to burn with passion" (I Cor. 7, 9). His view was not that marriage was bad, only that celibacy was more Christian. St. Augustine developed the position that intercourse was an expression of the original sin of Adam and Eve and, therefore, was evil. Interestingly, although St. Augustine held this view, he was very knowledgeable about the pleasures of sex. He admitted praying, "Give me chastity—but not yet" (Epistles XXII 7 and Confessions VIII 7, 17).

The interpreters of Christian doctrine have usually presented women in just two ways: the evil, sexual temptress on the one hand (Eve tempting Adam), and the virginal good woman on the other (Mary and the virgin birth). An interesting historical example of this unrealistic dichotomy of female sexuality occurred in the twelfth century among the upper classes. According to their concept of courtly love, women were seen as virtuous, pure, and worthy of honor and were not to be tainted with the physical side of love. The marital relationship during this time, however, had different rules—it was marked with obligations and sexual duties between the sexes.

These conflicting messages caused many in the church to take the position that women needed protection. Prostitution, therefore, was very popular during those times when women were viewed as pure and chaste; it was justified as an outlet for the "base" nature of men and a protection for the "honest" woman from the pressure to engage in sex. Brothels were sometimes even established on church property.

The Victorian Age, which began in the mid-nineteenth century and extended into the twentieth, continued to emphasize these opposing images of women. The "good" woman, one's wife, would naturally have a distaste for sex, except for its reproductive possibilities. Other interest in sexuality could be viewed as evidence of, if not proof of, questionable morals. In this context, it is not surprising that married men and women were inhibited in their sexual relations. During the Victorian years, prostitution flourished. In New York, a social reformer calculated that half of the adult males visited prostitutes two to three times per week (Rougoff, 1971).

Two relatively recent historical events that have greatly influenced sexuality are the discovery of effective, relatively safe contraception and an increased demand for women's rights. For many years infanticide (the murder of infants) was the only available method of population control. In fact, until the nineteenth century infanticide remained the principal method of regulating family size (Tannahill, 1980). Increasingly available contraceptive techniques precluded the need for, or use of, infanticide and simultaneously helped prepare the way for viewing sex as more than a procreative function. Of parallel importance, the traditional view of women as relatively passive sex objects whose function is only to satisfy men has changed drastically due to the work of the women's movement. Women now are acknowledged as having positive and healthy sexual interests. From a historical perspective, however, it is worth keeping in mind that:

the people of medieval Europe had 12 generations during which to adjust to the idea that women were worthy of respect, the Victorians three generations to accept that they were worthy of the vote. The modern world has had to adapt to almost complete legal and sexual equality in less than a decade. (Tannahill, 1980, p. 422)

Various aspects of Susan and Bill's experience become more understandable in light of historical analysis. A historical perspective would consider their sexual experience to be a consequence of complex sociocultural values—including attitudes toward the relationship between men and women—that might be characteristic of the time in which Bill and Susan live. Susan's hesitations about having sex and her conflict about taking responsibility for contraception, and Bill's concern over masturbation and his role of sexual leader, can be seen as consequences of lingering cultural and religious values carried into the present by society and by their parents. Their willingness to engage in premarital intercourse can be seen as an outgrowth of new views about women's sexuality and also about the nonprocreative function of sexuality in cementing relationships. We never really divorce ourselves, however, from ingrained and enduring past values, even though a particular decade may swing between very restrictive or very liberal values regarding "permissible" sexual activities.

The Physiological Approach

The *physiological approach* emphasizes the physical and biochemical aspects of sex-uality, including genetic, hormonal, neural, vascular, and anatomical factors. While the historical approach tries to understand sexuality within a broad perspective of sociocultural patterns over time, physiological data are restricted to the interaction of physical systems within a very immediate time frame. In order to gather relevant physiological data, the investigator might have to intrude directly upon the scene and perhaps influence the phenomena being studied. For example, a physiological investigator interested in the role of hormones in Susan and Bill's sexual encounter would have to take a number of blood samples, perhaps even while they were having intercourse. Or the physiologically oriented investigator might describe the mechanisms that result in erection and lubrication, showing what parts of the brain were active and what, if any, special neurochemical events were taking place during intercourse.

The best-known contemporary researchers and therapists in human sexuality, William Masters and Virginia Johnson have studied physiological responses during sexual activity in a laboratory setting. Masters, a physician, and Johnson, a psychologist, studied 694 individuals involved in sexual activities including masturbation and intercourse. The findings from their observations became the basis for their model of the sexual response cycle (Masters and Johnson, 1966). The importance of the model in this context is that Masters and Johnson focus on the physical changes during sexual encounters, especially those that are readily detected through either visual

William Masters and Virginia Johnson

observation or relatively simple measurements such as readings of pulse rate and blood pressure. Their findings were controversial, primarily because of the method they used to collect information—namely, direct observation of their subjects who were engaged in sexual activity. The idea of scientists observing others having sex was shocking to many and generated a storm of protest.

The Masters and Johnson approach would not consider why Susan and Bill were attracted to each other; nor would it attempt to describe how past experience influenced the evening's events. Instead, the points at which Susan or Bill experienced physical changes during sexual arousal would be of significance. For Susan, the first change to occur would most likely be vaginal lubrication, while Bill would experience penile erection. Thus, according to the framework devised by Masters and Johnson, the sexuality of the experience is identified by the presence of sexual arousal or excitement, which in turn is defined by physical responses, such as changes in the genitals. The approach would not, however, describe every physical change. It does not describe changes in the central nervous system; nor does it describe hormonal events.

The Learning Approach

The *learning approach* combines a group of individual points of view. What these views have in common is their focus on how past experiences affect present behavior. Although most of the other perspectives, with the exception of the physiological perspective, also concentrate on past experience, the learning approach especially emphasizes behavior—what a person does or says. The learning approach, unlike the psychoanalytic approach, does not include unconscious motivations, which may also be part of a person's past experience.

In the *social and cognitive learning approach* formulated by Gagnon and Simon (1973), sexual behavior is thought to follow a predictable sequence that is dictated by an internalized script. A *script* is a cognitive representation or guideline of a sequence of acts, learned both from others and by the specific experiences of the individual. According to this model, the scripts not only tell us how we are to act but also allow us to predict the behavior of others. The media, discussions with peers, and novels are just a few of the available tools that teach us how to act when in a sexual situation. Scripts are similar across members of a society because the sources that teach us our scripts are common to all or at least to most of us. That is, we read the same books, watch the same television shows, and hear from our friends the same stories about sex. The scripts differ somewhat depending on such things as one's sex, social class, age, and education.

The theory proposed by Gagnon and Simon predicts what specific acts Susan and Bill will engage in during intercourse. For example, it is almost certain that Bill will touch Susan's breasts before she touches his genitals and that both will caress their partner's genitals through clothing prior to touching them unclothed. This sequence is predictable because we all have been taught to behave in that manner, and so the order is incorporated into our script. The scripting notion is particularly useful because it helps to explain how Susan and Bill negotiate their way through the very complicated sequence of acts that result in intercourse. As shown in our description of Susan and Bill's experience, the absence of explicit directions and instructions is typical between sexual partners. The concept of a script explains how sexual behavior can be so predictable and stereotyped without being necessarily instinctive.

Gagnon and Simon are especially interested in the ways that scripts taught to men and women differ. For example, they note that in Western society women's scripts emphasize relationships and romance much more than do men's scripts. We have intentionally accentuated this different socialization process in describing how differently Susan and Bill thought about their relationship in the period of one day.

The Actuarial Approach

The *actuarial approach* relies on demographic statistics to describe and classify the sexual behaviors of individuals. Generally, these data are gathered in surveys or standardized interviews, the best known being those of Alfred Kinsey and his colleagues (see Box 1–1). Certain demographic categories have proven to be especially useful: Age, gender, marital status, educational level, and church attendance all have been found to be associated with both type and frequency of sexual activities. For example, these data would predict that Bill would have more masturbation experience than Susan, based on age and sex data, because males start masturbating at an earlier age and do so with greater frequency. Furthermore, this couple would probably prefer the male-above position for intercourse since this is the most common position used by couples in the United States.

The difficulty with the actuarial approach is that in spite of everything that we know, individual behavior is still very difficult to predict. The data are usually based

Box 1–1

ALFRED KINSEY

Alfred Kinsey (1894–1956), in the "Kinsey Reports," *Sexual Behavior in the Human Male*, and *Sexual Behavior in the Human Female*, presented the results of over 16,000 detailed interviews with individuals concerning their sex lives.

Kinsey, who held a Ph.D. in entomology, began his study of human sexuality in 1938 when he was selected to teach a noncredit course in marriage at Indiana University. He quickly found that there was little reliable information on sexual behavior. To offset that lack, he began to collect some data from class members and to interview off-campus subjects. It was not long before he was devoting his full energies to the study of human sexuality.

The Kinsey interview, the method by which all his data was collected, lasted anywhere from one to three hours. Subjects were asked from 350 to 521 questions. The first questions addressed nonpersonal matters such as age and years married; the later ones aimed at gaining detailed information about all aspects of an individual's sex life. The questions were direct and frank. Most important, the interviewer was totally nonjudgmental: Interviewees were not evaluated—they were only studied with the impartial eye of the natural scientist.

Sex research in Kinsey's day was highly controversial. Colleagues at his university questioned the project, and it took strong support by the president of the university to preserve Kinsey's research. Also, raising the funds to keep the project alive was difficult. The Rockefeller Foundation eventually supplied the money that allowed Kinsey and the Institute for Sex Research to press forward with its studies. During the McCarthy era, however, the institute came under attack from politicians who believed that the studies would weaken the moral fiber of the country. The Rockefeller Foundation withdrew its support because of this political pressure, and for a period of time the research was financed by monies raised from the sale of the "Reports." Kinsey became very defensive of the institute's work and began to consider attacks on the research as a personal affront (Gebhart, 1976).

on *means*, or the average behavior. Little attention is given to the range of behaviors (the high to low extremes), even though these data are gathered. The actuarial approach also usually does not assign causes or reasons for certain behaviors; rather, it is used to report statistical relationships only, leaving the interpretation of meanings and causes to other approaches. The value of the actuarial approach is that it provides a type of social bookkeeping by recording the frequencies of different sexual behaviors for different groups. It can be used to complement the short-term historical approach and to provide a context for interpreting sexual scripts since it provides a

Alfred Kinsey

statistical norm from which an individual can judge his or her own sexual behavior.

Psychoanalytic Approach

The *psychoanalytic approach,* originated by Sigmund Freud (1856–1939), focuses on sex-

uality as the major integrating factor of human personality. For Freud, **libido,** one's sexual drive or energy, was seen as the integrating life force that motivates all behavior. Freud himself had little to say specifically about sexual behavior; he was more interested in how sexual desires, conscious and unconscious, determine an individual's healthy or pathological personality characteristics.

In 1886 Freud began the practice of neurology. Quickly noticing that most of his neurological patients had no physical illness, he became interested in trying to understand the psychological roots of the problems that he encountered. Freud found that just by listening to his patients express their problems, they often improved, and he was determined to understand this phenomenon.

Freud felt that most of our psychological problems stem from issues surrounding sexuality, and especially sexual frustrations. This view led him to propose that masturbation, **nocturnal emissions** (wet dreams), the use of condoms, and withdrawal as a birth control technique all contributed to psychological disorders. Eventually he denied that these specific events were harmful, but he always viewed sexual frustrations as major factors in psychological disorders.

With the introduction of the psychoanalytic approach, three new ideas greatly influenced our views on sexual behavior: (1) children are sexual beings, (2) a critical period in a person's development is the successful resolution of sexual attraction toward the opposite-sexed parent, and (3) conscious and unconscious desires exist.

Sigmund Freud

According to psychoanalytic theory, the **Oedipal complex,** for boys, and the **Electra complex,** for girls, occur between the ages of 3 and 5 when all young children experience sexual attraction toward the parent of the opposite sex and thus are in competition with the same-sexed parent. Identification with the same-sexed parent marks the successful resolution of this phase. Without this resolution, later personality problems are supposedly bound to occur. It was Freud's opinion that because these conflicts became buried in the unconscious, people had no awareness of them without being psychoanalyzed. Freud's theories developed the view that the reasons for our actions are often, if not always, unknown to us.

Psychoanalytic theorists would concentrate on a variety of features of Susan's and Bill's past, including the basis of Susan's guilt about being sexual and the degree to which Bill might resemble Susan's father, or Susan resemble Bill's mother, in terms of appearance and personality. The psychoanalyst would explore whether feelings that Bill and Susan had toward each other were partly based on feelings they had for their parents. Understanding these factors, as well as exploring various dreams each might have that include the other, would help to interpret what Susan and Bill were unconsciously and consciously looking for in their sexual relationship.

The complexity of psychoanalytic theory, with all of the revisions since Freud, cannot be adequately represented here because of space limitations. In short, however, psychoanalysis attempts to go into more depth than other approaches by exploring unconscious motivations. Psychoanalytic views also see sex in extremely broad terms, defining sexuality far beyond sexual arousal and behavior. Its advantages are also its disadvantages: It traditionally requires lengthy consultations with a trained psychoanalyst, preferably for several years; it does not necessarily predict specifics about sexual functioning; and it offers a meaning to one's actions that may make sense emotionally but cannot be objectively confirmed in a laboratory or experimental sense. Confirmation, however, is not necessarily the goal of psychoanalytic thinking. Rather, it provides a way of interpreting our desires and conflicts.

The Anthropological Approach

According to the *anthropological approach,* sexual behavior must be considered in the light of the cultural context in which it occurs. Anthropologists have examined the sexual behavior of many cultures and have found wide variation in the patterns used to express sexuality. What becomes clear from these in-depth studies of different societies is that human sexuality, while limited in its biological expression, is relatively unlimited in the cultural meaning that it can take on.

Perhaps a few brief examples of the differing attitudes that some cultures have

surrounding sexuality will explain what we mean. In Tahiti during the nineteenth century, expression of sexual interests and pleasure by infants and preadolescents was not only permitted but also encouraged. The young were encouraged to masturbate, and premarital intercourse was readily accepted. Erotic themes were evident in the culture's dances and songs, and both marital and extramarital intercourse were openly discussed and practiced. These permissive attitudes can be compared with our own culture's more restrictive views on the same issues. Yet by examining other cultures, we can readily find views that are much more restricted than our own. For example, in the Gusii tribe of Kenya, women are expected to resist intercourse with their husbands. Husbands, in turn, expect to inflict pain and humiliation on their wives. Understandably, these women do not express any pleasure in coitus. What we learn from this example is that the emotional state that accompanies sexual activity varies widely from culture to culture.

Margaret Mead (1901–1978) was a distinguished anthropologist whose findings and writings have strongly affected our view of the nature of men and women. Her studies of cultures in the South Pacific certainly ensured her a place in the history of our understanding of sex differences. Mead found that differences in sex roles and behavior were determined by cultural influences. Stereotypes concerning the "basic" nature of men and women become unreasonable dogma in the light of her findings. Perhaps her own words written in the early 1930s best explain this:

Margaret Mead

If those temperamental attitudes which we have traditionally regarded as feminine — such as passivity, responsiveness, and a willingness to cherish children — can so easily be set up as the masculine pattern in one tribe, and in another be outlawed for the majority of women as well as the majority of men, we no longer have any basis for regarding such aspects of behavior as sex-linked. (Mead, 1935, pp. 279–280)

Let us now look at the relationship developing between Susan and Bill, as seen from the anthropological point of view. If we took this approach, we would believe that their behavior is conditioned by cultural factors. Accordingly, the culture defines who is an appropriate partner. It defines who is and who is not family, and the culture sets up the conditions that place

Susan and Bill in contact with each other. On a very concrete level, even when they kiss, Susan and Bill are reflecting cultural influences. In our culture lip kissing is the most widely practiced sexual act, and yet there are cultures in which kissing as we know it is unknown (Ford and Beach, 1951). The form of the kiss can also vary across cultures. In Oceania individuals lightly touch cheek to cheek or cheek to nose and inhale deeply in what has been called the "Oceanic kiss." This kiss functions much like our own lip kiss in that it is used to show affection between relatives and friends, and yet it also is always seen as a part of sexual interactions (Davenport, 1976). Thus, when Susan and Bill kiss, they are not expressing a stereotyped sexual pattern that is instinctive in all humans. Rather, lip kissing is identified as a sexual pattern because of cultural conditioning. The anthropologist repeatedly points out that the same may be said for most expressions of sexuality.

The anthropological perspective offers an appreciation of the richness and variety of human sexuality. One cannot examine the spectrum of cultural variations without becoming more tolerant of the sexuality of others, both within and outside of our own culture. The anthropological view forces us to recognize that a wide range of human experiences exists and that sexual behavior is adaptable.

Sociological Approach

The *sociological approach* deals with sexuality within the framework of an individual's social system. This perspective borrows heavily from historical, anthropological, and actuarial information to illustrate the role of sexuality within society. Generally, however, sociologists tend to describe sexual patterns within different subgroups of a society—for example, they will cite different ethnic or economic status groups, different educational levels, or different ages and sexes as the basis of their studies. The sociological perspective has often focused attention on the family, divorce, regulation of reproduction, and distribution of power in relationships as they influence and are in turn influenced by sexuality.

Gagnon and Simon (1973) point out that with few exceptions all of us have the

necessary physiological and physical foundations upon which sexuality depends. Therefore, the wide variety of behaviors that are seen must be the result of societal forces and structures as they affect the individual. For example, these researchers proposed several processes at work within contemporary society that are particularly important in determining sexual practices. The first process cited was the increase in material resources in contemporary society. Affluence permits increased flexibility in roles. They also noted that in affluent times consumption replaces production as the basis for society's norms. Second, they highlighted social movements that have sexual side effects. The importance of youth and the push for women's rights are two prime examples of social movements that greatly affect sexuality. Third, they noted social movements that are specifically sexual in nature. Here Gagnon and Simon refer to the Gay Liberation Movement and also the campaigns aimed at decriminalizing nonconventional sexuality such as prostitution. A fourth process has been the tendency toward reducing differences between the sexes. This is reflected in changes in dress styles, educational emphasis, and occupational roles in which gender differences are becoming less pronounced. Finally, Gagnon and Simon commented on how society has become increasingly erotic: The media are more explicit sexually, erotic materials are easily obtained, and nudity in movies and the theater is common.

Susan and Bill are undoubtedly influenced by societal forces. We noted how they were exposed to erotica. The fact that Susan attends college and that she had prepared for possible sexual activity by obtaining a diaphragm reflects changes in stereotyped sex roles. Societal change also is evident in Susan's reaction to peer pressure regarding sexual activity early in a dating relationship. For example, although she might not always accept it, she has come to expect certain behaviors from dates, which she can reject if she so desires. The sociological approach to sexuality concentrates on the examination of these influences and the ways that they interact.

The Sociobiological Approach

Sociobiologists attempt to describe how the social behavior of animals, including humans, can be understood through an evolutionary perspective. The *sociobiological approach* is interested in sexual behavior as determined by biological factors. Of the biological factors, sociobiologists are most interested in genetic influences on sexuality. Successful reproduction, according to this view, is the ultimate goal of all organisms and ultimately the directing force underlying sexual customs and behavior.

In studying Susan and Bill, the sociobiologist would note a fundamental conflict of interest between the sexes: For males, sexual promiscuity (having sex with many different women) is the best strategy for passing along genes, while for females, careful selection of a mate or mates will increase the likelihood of successful reproduction. Bill's best reproductive strategy, then, is to have intercourse with many different women in order to have as many surviving offspring as possible. Susan, on the other hand, is more limited in the number of potential offspring that she can have so she can less afford to take chances when choosing a partner. According to the sociobiological approach, it would make good evolutionary sense if Bill were the initiator of sexual activity while Susan delayed intercourse with him until she felt that Bill was a good and secure sexual partner (Barash, 1979).

According to sociobiological theory, these processes are automatic. They are based on genetic mechanisms and are not necessarily part of the individual's awareness. The sociobiologist would not be interested in either Susan's or Bill's thoughts about these matters, whether or not they used a contraceptive, or how "serious" they were about each other.

METHODS OF SEX RESEARCH

All of the approaches mentioned thus far have represented systematic or scientific methods that can be used for the study of human sexuality. Long before scientists began to study sexuality, however, writers and artists influenced people's feelings about love, romance, and sex. In poems, novels, plays, sculpture, paintings, and music, the full range of human sexual emotion has been explored and interpreted, often with great insight.

One might ask, then, Do we need to be concerned about whether or not the rules of science are followed in the study of human sexuality? In general, the answer we would give is a qualified "yes." Because any good scientific approach tests its own predictions, incorrect ideas will be rejected and progress toward increasingly objective and thorough formulations will be made. Without self-correction, we would only be able to hope that nonscientific theories are correct.

Methods of collecting information concerning sexuality include surveys, participant-observer studies, clinical observations, laboratory research and animal research. The following sections describe the strengths and weaknesses of each of these sex research methods.

Surveys

Most of the information concerning human sexuality that is recorded comes from data obtained with different kinds of *surveys*. The range of surveys that have been used include the tear-out-and-mail-in types such as those found in popular magazines, and also extremely detailed and standardized interviews such as the Kinsey interviews.

A basic weakness of surveys is that they are easily distorted. Respondents can deliberately lie when they answer questions concerning their sexual practices. They can brag and exaggerate about some aspect of their behavior, or they can deny or under-report activities they may wish to keep secret. Although researchers can do little to guarantee truthfulness, they can assure anonymity to the respondents, which hopefully encourages honesty.

In some surveys there are checks on distortions, such as the same questions asked in different forms and at different places to determine consistency. Kinsey occasionally assessed the consistency of his respondents' answers by interviewing sexually intimate couples, asking both parties the same questions, or interviewing the same individual on two occasions. That most people are honest in their answers to surveys can be supported by the high degree of agreement in findings across surveys. For example, all reported surveys that deal with the topic have reported higher levels of masturbation among males than among females. Thus, we can have considerable confidence in that finding.

The most serious problem with surveys, and one that is less commonly recognized, is *sample bias*. A biased sample is one that inadequately represents the population that it is designed to describe. Typical sample biases are those that include too many people of a specific age, income, social class, marital status, or sex, beyond their occurrence in the population. For example, a weakness of the Kinsey reports was the overrepresentation of whites and people from higher educational levels.

In some surveys only a special population is contacted, and yet the implication is made that the sample represents the general population. For example, in the *Redbook* survey conducted by Tavris and Sadd (1975), only married *Redbook* readers who bothered to read the survey, complete it, and return it to *Redbook* were included. The fact that 100,000 people responded does not reduce the bias; it only assures a large biased sample. We cannot know to what degree this survey and others like it represent the general population, and so the findings must be interpreted cautiously.

Biased samples are even more common when the survey method is used with relatively small, selected populations; sex offenders and people involved in extramarital affairs are examples of such populations. These special groups are often difficult to locate and evaluate because they fear disclosure. Gebhard, Gagnon, Pomeroy, and Christenson (1965) surveyed a group of convicted and imprisoned sex offenders; that group almost certainly would differ considerably from the offender who has not been apprehended, convicted, and sent to jail. Yet studying the nonconvicted sex offender is virtually impossible, since these individuals are naturally reluctant to identify themselves. Clearly, as surveys examine smaller and often increasingly deviant populations, the likelihood of sample bias distortion increases. Even so, the majority of sex research includes data on selective rather than random samples, simply because they are more accessible.

Associated with the sample bias problem is the bias involved in the self-selection of respondents, or the problem of *volunteerism.* Those who volunteer to participate in a survey concerned with sexual behavior are more likely to hold liberal views about sexuality than are those who refuse to participate (Maslow and Sakoda, 1952). Bauman (1973), however, did not find differences between volunteers and others in sexual attitudes and behavior. Thus the issue is not resolved at this time, but researchers need to be aware of the possible bias of volunteerism.

Interpreting survey research is also problematic. Survey research allows us to describe populations in terms of their attitudes or behavior. It does not, however, allow us to make cause-and-effect statements. Surveys describe correlations, not causes. For example, from one survey we may learn that a relationship exists between educational level and extramarital affairs. What is not revealed is why this is the case. Is it really because of education, or because of some other variable associated with education, such as income level? Further experimental research would be needed to answer this question.

Let's look at another example. If we asked Susan and Bill to complete a questionnaire that measured whether or not they found sex more or less pleasurable after drinking alcohol, they might respond that they felt more easily aroused when they had been drinking. Many other people might give the same response. We could subsequently conduct an experiment to test that suggestion. In such an experiment we might be interested in learning whether or not the reported effect was really due to alcohol consumption or due to the *expectation* that alcohol would have such an effect. This could be studied by having people assume that they are consuming alcohol when in reality they are not, and vice versa. As you will learn in Chapter Nine, drinking moderate amounts of alcohol appears to enhance sexual feelings only if one expects such an effect (Marlatt and Rohsenow, 1980). In this case, if we were to rely only on survey data, we would be misled into assuming that alcohol produced the effect. Keep in mind, though, that it was the survey information that led to the experimental study.

Participant-Observer Studies

In *participant-observer research,* the investigator becomes part of the scene being observed. This method is generally used when the researcher believes that any other method of study will distort the situation. Aside from some "field" anthropological research, however, the few existing studies using participant-observer techniques to investigate human sexuality are limited to the study of "swinging" and "group sex." Because the sexual practices being investigated usually are controversial, nonparticipant observers might be seen as threatening by the group under study, and these observers might have an inhibiting influence.

On the other hand, it is impossible for the participant-observer not to be influenced by his or her participation. If an observer finds an experience distasteful, preventing those feelings from coloring any observations made would be difficult. In most cases, however, the opposite is true. Since participant-observers tend to observe those phenomena in which they are interested, they might feel obliged to "accentuate the positive."

Another source of bias in participant-observer studies (though not limited to this type of research) is the influence of any observer on a testing situation. If the participants know that someone is observing, they are very likely to alter their behavior as a result, even though they had agreed earlier to the observer's presence. This is known as *reactivity.* Reactivity is difficult to assess and control, and its influence in a given situation is hard to predict.

Clinical Observations

Clinical observations usually refer to detailed case histories or descriptions of patients receiving treatment. This method contrasts with clinical outcome research, in which accepted scientific practices — including the use of comparison or control groups or conditions — are employed to evaluate some aspect of treatment. After survey information, clinical observations probably provide our largest body of information about human sexual behavior. Conclusions drawn from this information, however, must be carefully examined for the following reasons:

1. There are major problems with assuming that what we learn through the study of one or a limited number of cases can be applied to an entire class of situations or

individuals. Although it is possible that the findings from clinical examinations apply only to those cases studied, it is all too often assumed that what is true for one case is true for all cases. Furthermore, evidence derived from patients may apply only to other patients and may be completely irrelevant to the non-patient population.

2. Published cases are often nonrepresentative. Unusual events or cases of successful treatments are often published, and the mundane and/or unsuccessful treatments are typically not reported. This introduces a special type of sample bias.

3. Clinical case studies are also particularly susceptible to observer bias. Although all researchers are biased in the sense that they select the material to be examined and the questions to be asked, in clinical reports the clinician and the client are personally involved in how the case turns out. Quite understandably, the clinician may try to present the case in only positive terms.

4. Information obtained from the case histories may be misinterpreted in the absence of an appropriate control group. For example, in early clinical reports of male homosexuals who were being treated by psychoanalysts, researchers noted that a large number recalled that their mothers were domineering and their fathers were passive. As a result, it was argued that this pattern contributed to the development of male homosexuality. However, many heterosexual males also had domineering mothers and passive fathers, and comparisons of non-patient samples of homosexual and heterosexual males often failed to show any differences in the mothers.

In spite of these problems, the clinical investigator's detailed examination of cases offers an excellent opportunity to develop hypotheses that can then be tested more rigorously.

Laboratory Research

Laboratory research has one major advantage over other methods of study: control over conditions. The application of clearly defined conditions and the objective examination of the effect of applying those conditions permit the laboratory investigator to make cause-and-effect statements.

The major weakness of laboratory research, however, is directly related to its strength: How can we know that what happens in the laboratory is relevant to the outside world? The laboratory is by definition an unnatural environment in which events are carefully controlled. Because of this, does what we learn in the laboratory generalize to nonlaboratory settings? The answer seems to be, "It depends." In some instances, laboratory findings are directly relevant, while in other cases the relevance is questionable, if not nonexistent. It is important to test the question of relevance in all cases. One can neither assume relevance nor deny it without testing directly. For example, although Morokoff (1980) surprisingly found that sexually inhibited women are more responsive in the laboratory to erotic stimuli than are less inhibited women, determining whether that holds true in the "real" world is still necessary.

Laboratory research is also plagued by sample problems. As in survey research, clearly not everyone feels comfortable enough to participate in laboratory studies on sexuality (Farkas, Sine, and Evans, 1978). The effects of this bias will vary from case to case. For example, an investigator looking at a biochemical aspect of hormone activity would not likely consider bias to be a serious problem. However, interpersonal sex in the laboratory would be subject to considerable bias, since we would expect that only unique individuals would agree to participate in such research. What is less clear is how the bias would affect results.

A final problem with laboratory research is that many important variables cannot be brought into the lab for study because of time limitations and the complexity of the phenomena. For example, child-rearing practices are thought by many to influence sexuality. Setting ethical considerations aside, providing a laboratory study of different forms of child rearing is impossible, because the manipulation of parental practices would be too complex and would require years of application.

Animal Research

The use of animals in research on sexuality has a long and substantial history. Much of our knowledge concerning the functioning of hormones and brain mechanisms comes from animal research. The question re-

mains, Is animal research relevant to the study of human sexuality? The problem with the use of the animal model is most obvious when we are examining sexual behavior per se. As Frank Beach (1979) has carefully pointed out, to assume that similar behaviors across species are the result of the same causes or serve the same functions is often a serious mistake. For example, Calhoun (1962) reported that under crowded conditions male rats are more likely to mount other male rats (as well as any other objects that are handy). This finding does not mean that male homosexuality in humans would result from similar conditions.

A common assumption is that the closer on the phylogenetic scale a species is to humans, the more valid are the generalizations made from one to the other. Consequently, it follows that findings from nonhuman primates are more likely to be relevant to the human than are those from rodents. For instance, Herbert (1977) notes that the male sex hormone testosterone works differently in primates than it does in the lower nonprimate; therefore, on a biochemical level, primates, including humans, have characteristics in common that are not shared by lower animals. This fact suggests, though it does not prove, that information gained from primate research is more likely to be relevant to humans than are data from studies of lower animals. However, some researchers believe that the differences among species are so great that to generalize even among primates is impossible. For example, researchers found that in the Rhesus monkey a vasectomy results in the development of hardening of the arteries (Alexander and Clarkson, 1978). This correlation has not been found in humans and indicates that differences do exist between two primates.

There is, of course, interest and value in understanding the sexual behavior of animals for its own sake. In this book we present animal data for both its interest value alone as well as for the opportunity to uncover interesting hypotheses concerning the causes and function of human sexual behavior. What is important, however, is that we always remain cautious and selective in accepting animal findings as relevant to humans.

ETHICAL ISSUES IN SEX RESEARCH

Ethical issues are a constant consideration in sex research. In part, these issues, like confidentiality and privacy, are no different from those faced by anyone who studies any aspect of human behavior. However, due to the often highly emotional nature of sexuality and the personal importance placed on it by the individual, issues of confidentiality and privacy are heavily stressed in sexual studies. Subjects in research studies pertaining to sexual behavior require special assurance that personal information will not be disclosed. To invade the privacy of others in the name of research is unwarranted and unethical, and subjects have the right to expect that their privacy will be protected.

Federal guidelines for research with human subjects require that investigators describe the precautions that are taken to ensure confidentiality and fully informed voluntary consent. Any deception that is a necessary part of research has to be justified to the government funding agency, and detailed descriptions of how subjects will be "debriefed" after the study is completed must be provided. In addition, researchers seeking federal funds must make a statement concerning risk-benefit ratios. That is, they must describe how the benefit to either or both the subject or society exceeds any risk to which the subject may be exposed. This requirement is very difficult to comply with in practice. Risks are not always dramatic or obvious, and to project a study's immediate benefits to society is also difficult. In research on specific sexual problems, the potential benefits are usually clear, but in basic research benefits are often less obvious. Box 1–2 provides an example of how potential benefits can be overlooked or de-emphasized.

Researchers have other ethical concerns, including the determination of what should be studied. For example, puberty is apparently an important time in the development of sexuality. However, because the study of sexuality during puberty is very controversial, only indirect research is currently possible. Ethical issues preclude direct observation and measurement of sex-

IS LOVE A DOMAIN FOR SCIENTISTS?

Elaine Hatfield Walster and Ellen Berscheid have conducted a number of studies on love. In the mid-1970s their research came under attack. Senator William Proxmire, well known for his Golden Fleece awards for research that he feels is a waste of taxpayers' money, found that the National Science Foundation had given Ellen Berscheid a grant to study why people fall in love. Berscheid's study was Proxmire's choice for the "biggest waste of taxpayers' money for the month of March 1975." Soon afterward Walster's work was similarly criticized. In a press release Proxmire said:

> I believe that 250 million other Americans want to leave some things in life a mystery, and right at the top of things we don't want to know is why a man falls in love with a woman and vice versa. . . . So National Science Foundation—get out of the love racket. Leave that to Elizabeth Barrett Browning and Irving Berlin. Here, if anywhere, Alexander Pope was right when he observed, "If ignorance is bliss, 'tis folly to be wise." (*Time,* March 24, 1975)

The two issues raised by Proxmire are that (1) certain human experiences should not be studied but should be protected by ignorance; and (2) taxpayers' money should not be spent on certain kinds of research. These are, in fact, important issues that lead to further questions. Some of the more obvious ones are: Can knowledge spoil our appreciation of things that we experience? How do we decide what research is worthy of taxpayers' money, and who decides?

ual behavior in puberty, yet because of these limitations we shall undoubtedly remain ignorant about an important aspect of sexuality.

Our intention is not to suggest that ethical limitations are inappropriate. Without a solid ethical framework research in any field runs the risk of harming individuals and perhaps society itself. It is interesting to note, however, that ethical standards are not absolutes. For example, the survey research of today is considered quite acceptable and can appear in widely read magazines; yet publication of such research would have been unthinkable seventy-five years ago. It is not clear what changes will

develop in the next seventy-five years, but we can be assured that there will be changes.

Ethical limits also vary within the same time frame. When one of the authors of this text requested permission to conduct psychophysiological research on genital arousal at a major university in England, permission was refused because of the "unsuitable" nature of the topic. Yet the same research was already being conducted in the United States. Certainly, similar variations would occur *within* the United States and reflect the fact that ethical considerations are not constant and vary both from time to time and from place to place.

SUMMARY

1. The study of human sexual behavior is particularly complex because it cannot be separated from other aspects of human behavior. For humans, sex is not only physiological, it is also cultural, psychological, intellectual, and emotional.

2. Various approaches, in addition to emphasizing certain aspects of sexuality, can complement each other. By recognizing that a wide range of factors influence sexuality, it is possible to gain a broader and more comprehensive picture. The approaches to the study of sexuality include (a) historical, (b) physiological, (c) learning, (d) actuarial, (e) psychoanalytic, (f) anthropological, (g) sociological, and (h) sociobiological.

3. There are many ways to collect information concerning sexuality. The principal ones used are surveys, participant-observer studies, clinical observations, laboratory research, and animal research. There are strengths and weaknesses with all of these methods.

4. Ethical concerns are prominent in sex research. Subjects' rights, particularly those involving confidentiality, privacy, and the need for fully informed voluntary consent, should be part of all considerations when designing research. Ethical concerns also play an important role in determining what questions may be asked. Political and cultural values often dictate what is appropriate for study. This is particularly true in the study of sexuality, a topic that is identified with a full range of emotions and moral values.

SUGGESTED READINGS

Brecher, E. *The sex researchers.* Boston: Little-Brown, 1969. Biographical sketches of influential sex researchers in the nineteenth and twentieth centuries.

Ford, C. S., & Beach, F. A. *Patterns of sexual behavior.* New York: Harper & Row, 1951. A classic text of sexual behavior in different cultures and different species.

Gagnon, J., & Simon, W. *Sexual conduct,* Chicago: Aldine, 1973. A review of the social origins of human sexual behavior.

Tannahill, R. *Sex in history.* New York: Stein & Day, 1980. A review of sexual behavior and attitudes throughout recorded history.

CHAPTER TWO

BIOLOGICAL FOUNDATIONS
Structure, Function, and Development

Love's mysteries in souls do grow,
But yet the body is his book.
Donne, *The Extasie*

*U*nderstanding human sexuality requires familiarity with the underlying biological system. Too often we lose sight of the manner in which biology and behavioral science work together. This chapter describes the anatomy of both sexual and reproductive organs, as well as how these organs respond during sexual activity. Some of the important physiological events that underlie sexual behavior are then described, and the chapter concludes with a description of hormones and their role in sexuality. Chapter Three takes the discussion one step further by explaining the reproductive functions of the biological system and the implications for sexuality. In our description, we divide sexual anatomy into external and internal organs. In addition, we describe some of the **secondary sex characteristics.** Secondary sex characteristics, such as breasts and hair patterns, develop during puberty because of the effects of sex hormones.

And so we begin with anatomy. Human genitals vary greatly in size and shape, as do all other body parts. As you study any crowd of people, whether they be in a classroom or supermarket, you will notice that no one looks the same (except twins, of course). You will see both short and tall people, a few with noticeably odd-shaped noses, and perhaps a person with exceptionally large eyes. This same variation can also be found in genitals. Consider, too, that while the reproductive organs are vital to sexual functioning, nonreproductive organs also contribute to sexual encounters. Kissing, for example, can be highly erotic, and yet it involves nongenital organs—the lips, mouth, and tongue.

FEMALE ANATOMY

For many, the female anatomy is a mystery. With most of the genital parts "undercover," many people do not know what these structures look like. Knowledge of the sexual organs is necessary for a female to feel comfortable with herself and with others. Males should become familiar with the female body so that they are better able to appreciate and to understand their female partners.

External Genitals

The female genital area is known as the **vulva.** In the mature woman, much of the vulva is covered by pubic hair. The sexes differ in the general distribution of genital hair (see Figure 2–1). For most women, the upper border of genital hair is relatively straight across so that the genital hair distribution is shaped like an inverted triangle. In contrast, males tend to have an upper border that extends toward the umbilicus (the "belly button") (see Figure 2–6). Not all individuals are alike, and the differences have no known physiological importance.

To obtain an unobstructed view of the external genitals, the external lips must be parted (see Figure 2–2). The layer of fatty tissue that covers the place where the pubic

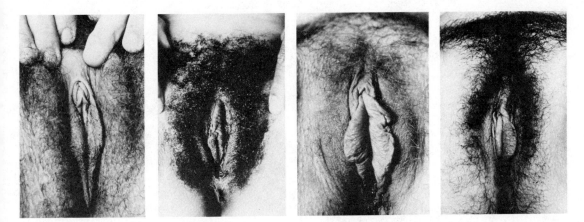

Figure 2-1. *The external genitals of four women who differ in age and race.*

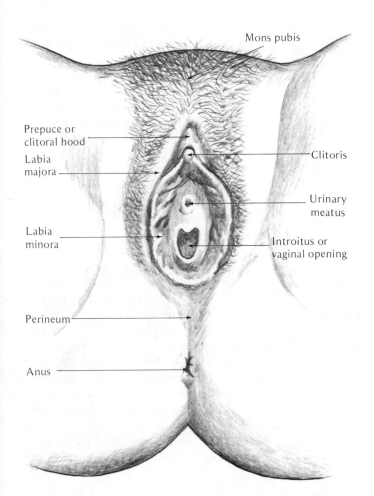

Mons pubis

Prepuce or clitoral hood

Labia majora

Labia minora

Perineum

Anus

Clitoris

Urinary meatus

Introitus or vaginal opening

Figure 2-2. *Female external genitals; Labia parted to facilitate viewing.*

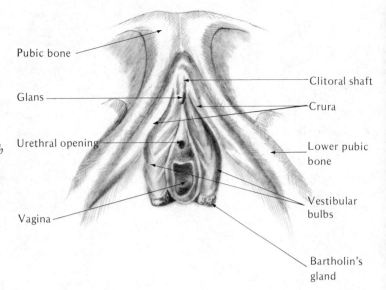

Figure 2-3. Female external genitals with labia minora removed to reveal the structures.

Labels in figure: Pubic bone, Glans, Urethral opening, Vagina, Clitoral shaft, Crura, Lower pubic bone, Vestibular bulbs, Bartholin's gland

bones join at the top of the vulva is called the **mons pubis** or **mons veneris** (the mound of Venus). The mons is covered with pubic hair and is rich in nerve endings. Two large folds of tissue extend downward from the mons and surround the rest of the genitals. These are called the **labia majora,** also known as the outer lips. Some pubic hair appears on their outer portions, but the sides toward the center are hairless and smooth; when the lips are not parted, these smooth sides touch each other. The labia majora protect the inner structures from direct contact with the environment. They are heavily supplied with blood vessels and contain several types of nerve endings. The labia majora merge into the **perineum,** which is the area between the most posterior portion of the genitals and the **anus,** or rectal opening. Because the anus and perineum have many nerve endings, people often find this area sensitive to sexual stimulation.

Inside the labia majora are the **labia minora,** the inner lips. These smaller, hairless structures enclose an area called the *vestibule,* that contains the clitoris, the urethral opening, and the vaginal opening. The

urethral opening, or the **urinary meatus,** is the external opening of the urethra through which urine is discharged. The portion of the labia minora that covers the clitoris is known as the *prepuce,* or the *clitoral hood.* The *vestibular bulbs* are composed of erectile tissue and lie within the labia minora. This tissue surrounds the vaginal and urethral openings. The labia minora also contain many nerve endings and blood vessels.

The **clitoris** is made up of several parts (see Figure 2-3, which shows the genital area with skin and labia majora removed). The body of the clitoris, known as the *clitoral shaft,* is an elongated structure that is about 1 inch long by ¼ inch wide. At the base of the shaft the clitoris divides in two, forming the *crura.* They are attached to the pelvic bone and engorge with blood when a woman is sexually stimulated. The head, or *glans,* of the clitoris normally is its only visible portion, as the clitoral hood covers most of the clitoral shaft. The glans is richly endowed with pressure-sensory nerves and an abundant blood supply. The erectile tissue of the clitoris can become engorged with blood; the tissue usually increases in size with engorgement. The clitoris appears

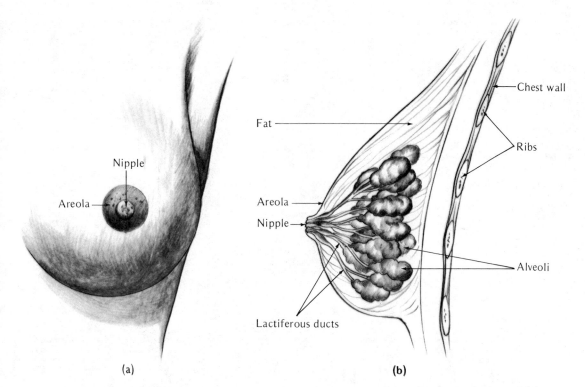

Nipple

Areola

(a)

Fat

Chest wall

Ribs

Areola

Nipple

Alveoli

Lactiferous ducts

(b)

Figure 2-4. External and internal anatomy of the female breast.

to serve only as a source of sexual enjoyment, being very sensitive to any stimulation and serving no known reproductive function.

On the innerside of the labia minora and lying next to the vestibular bulbs are the **Bartholin's glands.** These glands discharge small amounts of mucus into the vestibule. At one time this secretion was believed to lubricate the vagina; however, this is not true. There is no known purpose for this fluid.

Just below the urinary meatus lies the **introitus,** or vaginal opening. This opening may be partially covered by a thin membrane called the **hymen.** Although the rupture of the hymen is traditionally associated with the first time a woman experiences sexual intercourse, rupture may result from vigorous activity, such as encountered in active sports. On the other hand, the hymen may remain intact, even though a tampon or a finger has been inserted into the vagina. The presence or ab-

sence of the hymen is not a true indicator of the occurrence of coitus.

Breasts

The **breasts** are not considered genitals; rather, they are among the secondary sex characteristics distinguishing males from females. Breasts consist primarily of fatty tissue, and also *mammary glands,* or **alveoli,** which are capable of producing milk following childbirth (see Figure 2–4). The *lactiferous ducts* (milk ducts) transport the milk to the nipple. The **nipple,** which is located externally in the lower and outer part of the breast, has small muscles underlying it that erect the nipple by contracting. Nipple erection results from being touched, cold temperatures, and other stimulation, including sexual arousal. The nipple is sur-

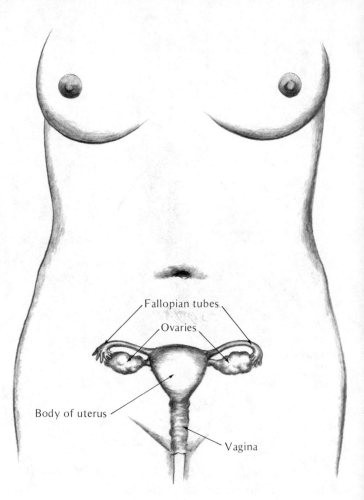

Figure 2-5a. Front view of female internal reproductive organs.

Fallopian tubes

Ovaries

Body of uterus

Vagina

rounded by the **areola,** a pink- to dark-colored circle of tissue that contains a number of elevations or bumps called *Montgomery's tubercles.* These structures release an oily secretion that keeps the nipple supple and prevents it from drying out and cracking.

Female breasts vary greatly. In addition to differences in overall size and shape, the nipple and areola also show great variation. In our society the breast has been emphasized as a sex object, which may be a source of concern for the developing young woman. "We all were either too small or too big, too pear shaped or grape shaped or melon shaped or boy shaped or cow

shaped; no matter what we simply *didn't measure up"* (Lear, 1974). Cultural standards, not biological needs, result in the emphasis that has been placed on a woman's breasts.

Internal Reproductive Organs

A female's reproductive organs are located within the lower abdominal area and are encased within the bones of the pelvis. The male pelvis is heavier and narrower than the female pelvis. One group of researchers points out that, "the female pelvis has sacrificed much of its strength and has become

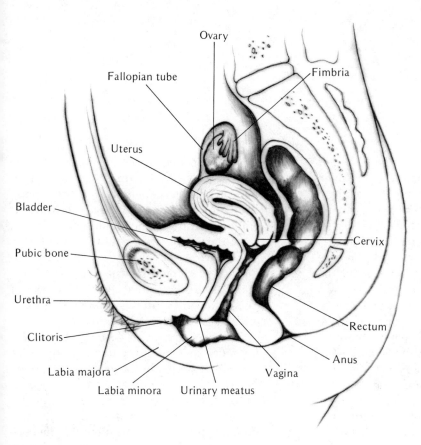

Ovary

Fallopian tube

Fimbria

Uterus

Bladder

Pubic bone

Urethra

Clitoris

Cervix

Labia majora

Rectum

Labia minora · Urinary meatus

Vagina

Anus

Figure 2–5b. Side view of female internal reproductive organs.

wider so that it may function as a birth canal" (Smout, Jacoby, & Lillie, 1969, p. 30). The reproductive organs are attached to the pelvis by both muscle and ligaments. Figures 2–5(a & b) show a diagrammatic representation of the reproductive organs, from both a front view and as they appear from the side.

The **vagina** extends from the vaginal opening in the vestibule to the uterus. The vagina averages about 3 inches in length in the nonaroused state, and when the woman is sexually aroused, the vagina increases at least 50 percent in diameter and length. The inner surface of the vagina is made up of many folds of tissue called *rugae*. During intercourse, the penis presses against the walls of the vagina, and the folds smooth out, permitting the normal vagina to ex-

pand and accommodate any size penis. The vagina itself has only smooth muscles that are not controlled voluntarily. In contrast, the **pubococcygeus muscle** surrounding the outer third to one-half of the vagina can be tensed voluntarily. Although the vagina has relatively few nerve endings, it does have a rich supply of blood vessels. The cells of the lining of the vagina slough off into the canal where bacteria convert the chemicals in the cells into lactic acid. This acid helps protect the vagina from infections.

At the end of the vagina is the **uterus,** the organ that holds a developing fetus during pregnancy. The uterus lies between the *bladder* and the *rectum,* and its position shifts whenever the bladder or rectum is full. A pear-shaped organ, the uterus measures approximately 2 by 3 inches in the woman who has not had a child, and is slightly larger in the woman who has given birth. The uterus is suspended by six ligaments that hold it within the pelvic cavity. The uterus is composed of three layers: (1) the perimetrium, or the outer layer, which is also known as the *serosa;* (2) the middle layer of thick, smooth muscle called the *myometrium;* and (3) the inner layer, known as the *endometrium.* The endometrium changes throughout the menstrual cycle and provides the proper environment in which a fertilized ova can develop. The muscle layer of the uterus provides the strength for the contractions that deliver a child.

The **cervix** is the part of the uterus that connects the vagina with the uterus. Sperm must travel through the **cervical canal** for fertilization to occur. The openings of the canal are called the *internal os,* which is inside the uterus, and the *external os,* which opens to the vagina. The cervical canal varies in diameter from 3 mm during ovulation to 1 mm at other times. Glands in the cervix secrete mucus that forms a plug. This plug restricts the transport of material from the vagina to the uterus, changing consistency during ovulation so that sperm can travel into the uterus. The cervix and its role in reproduction will be discussed further in Chapter Three.

The **Fallopian tubes,** or oviducts, are two muscular tubes that join the uterus on the sides just below the top of the uterus and extend out toward the ovaries (see Figure 2–5). The Fallopian tubes are about 4 inches long and are held in place by ligaments. The outer end of each Fallopian tube has fingerlike projections called *fimbria.* The fimbria are believed to direct the ovum toward the Fallopian tubes, although no one is certain how the ovum successfully completes its journey from the ovaries. The inner surface of each Fallopian tube is lined with *cilia,* hairlike structures that aid the passage of the ovum to the uterus. Conception takes place inside the Fallopian tubes.

The **ovaries** are two flattened bodies lying on either side of the uterus at the ends of the Fallopian tubes. They measure about ¾ inch by 1½ inches and are attached to the uterus and the pelvic wall by ligaments. The ovary is comprised of two parts, the *medulla* and the *cortex.* The medulla, the center, is made up of connective tissue, blood vessels, and lymph vessels, and supports the developing ova that migrate from the cortex, where they originate.

In the cortex are the **follicles;** these tissues hold the ova. In the sexually mature woman, the cortex of the ovary is pitted and scarred from the healing of follicles that have erupted during ovulation. Following ovulation, the follicle enlarges and becomes a yellowish structure called the **corpus luteum,** a major source of hormones. If pregnancy occurs, the corpus luteum is maintained beyond its usual two-week life span and provides the hormones necessary in early pregnancy. The ovaries themselves produce the female hormones, estrogen and progesterone, and small amounts of some male hormones.

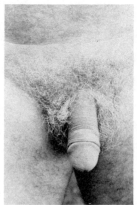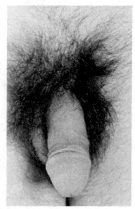

Figure 2-6. *The external genitals of four men who differ in age and race.*

MALE ANATOMY

The male anatomy is not as simple as it appears to be at first glance. As Figure 2–6 illustrates, males like females differ in the size and shape of their genitals. The penis itself is a highly complex organ, as are the testicles and the internal genitals. Along with the complexity of the male genitals, also of interest to note are the similarities between the male and female parts. (Pages 58–61 contain a discussion of how embryos differentiate and develop into males and females, although they begin as the same embryonic structure. The differentiation process can help explain the similarities that exist.)

External Genitals

The most obvious external genital structure in males is the **penis,** an elongated shaft that contains erectile tissue, a dense supply of nerves, many blood vessels, and the urethra. In the flaccid, or limp state, adult penises can measure from 3.33 inches to 4.5 inches in length, with the average being about 3.75 inches long. The range for erect penises is from 4.7 inches to 9.2 inches, with a few rare extremes. The average diameter of the flaccid penis is 1.25 inches, which increases about one-quarter of an inch when erect. Penile size does not correlate with individual body build or size (Masters & Johnson, 1966). Nor is size an indication of male sexual ability.

The penis is certainly a complex organ, as can be seen in Figure 2–7. For the sake of clarity, we can consider the penis as having three parts: (1) the base, or root, (2) the shaft, and (3) the glans. At the base of the penis are the *crura,* which are attached to the bones of the pelvis and are covered by muscle. This part of the penis actually extends into the body. The second section of the penis is the body, or *shaft,* which begins where the penis is joined to the body. In the shaft, the crura become the *corpus cavernosa,* which lie side by side on the top part of the shaft, and the *corpus spongiosum,* which expands until, at the end, it becomes the glans. The *glans,* separated from the shaft by a ridge of tissue called the *corona,*

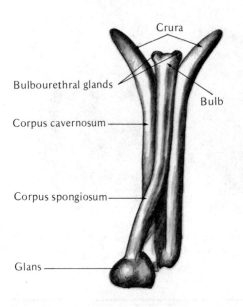

Crura

Bulbourethral glands

Bulb

Corpus cavernosum

Corpus spongiosum

Glans

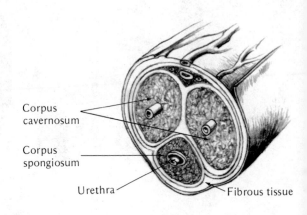

Corpus
cavernosum

Corpus
spongiosum

Urethra

Fibrous tissue

Figure 2-7. *Internal structures of the penis.*

forms a cap over the tapered end of the corpus cavernosa. Both the corpus cavernosa and the corpus spongiosum are made up of spongy tissue surrounded by a dense fibrous coat. The *urethra* runs through the corpus spongiosum and terminates at the tip of the glans in the *external urethral meatus* (the urinary opening). The penis is well supplied with blood vessels and is covered by thin, loose skin. On uncircumcised males a portion of this loose skin forms the *foreskin,* or *prepuce,* which covers the glans of the nonerect penis. The foreskin is what is removed during circumcision.

The **scrotum** is a pouch of skin made of connective tissue and muscles that contain the *testicles* (testes), the *spermatic cord,* and the *epididymis.* (These terms will be defined later.) The thin skin of the scrotum contains a light supply of hair and many sweat glands. When the smooth muscles of the scrotum contract, the scrotum has a wrinkled appearance. A sheath of connective tissue separates the enclosed testicles. In most men, the left testicle hangs lower than the right, although why this is so is not known.

The penis and scrotum are heavily endowed with sensory nerves. However, since they are not uniformly distributed, the degree of sensitivity of the different parts to touch varies. For most men, the glans, the corona, and the underside of the shaft are, in that order, the most sensitive parts. The top side of the shaft is typically the least sensitive. The scrotum is quite sensitive, usually being somewhat more sensitive than the top of the shaft, but less so than the rest of the penis. As with any aspect of anatomy, these sensitivities may vary from one person to another.

Internal Reproductive Organs

The best way to understand the internal reproductive system in males is to trace the path of sperm from the testes to the urinary opening of the penis (see Figure 2–8). The first organ in this system is the testis. The **testes** are two oval-shaped organs located in the scrotum; they usually measure about 1 inch by 1.75 inches. The testes, being located outside the body cavity, are maintained at about 5.5° F lower than the nor-

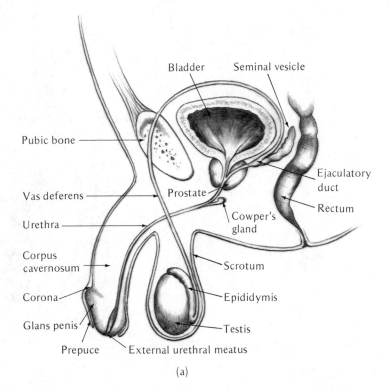

Figure 2-8. *Side view of male internal reproductive organs.*

Bladder

Seminal vesicle

Pubic bone

Ejaculatory duct

Vas deferens

Prostate

Rectum

Urethra

Cowper's gland

Corpus cavernosum

Scrotum

Corona

Epididymis

Glans penis

Testis

Prepuce

External urethral meatus

(a)

mal body temperature. The belief is that lower temperatures result in fewer changes in the sperm's genetic material and greater sperm health.

The testes are divided into compartments; each compartment contains a coiled **seminiferous tubule** in which sperm cells are produced. Each tube, if stretched out, is 1 to 3 feet long, with an estimated total of half a mile's worth of tubing in each testis (see Figure 2-9). The *interstitial cells* lie between the seminiferous tubules; they produce testosterone, the principal male hormone. The seminiferous tubules meet at the top of the testes in a network of ducts called the *rete testis*. The sperm travel through the rete testis duct system to reach the **epididymis,** a structure that is positioned alongside the testes. The epididymis is approximately 2 inches long and is made up of a twisted passage; stretched out, it would be from 10 to 20 feet long. Sperm

take about 2 weeks to travel through the epididymis, the time necessary for the sperm cells to mature.

The epididymis runs into the **vas deferens,** a muscular tube that travels upward from the epididymis through the scrotum, and then over the rear surface of the bladder. In the scrotum the vas deferens is part of the **spermatic cord.** In addition to the vas deferens the spermatic cord contains a network of arteries, veins, lymph vessels, nerves, and the cremaster muscle. The *cremaster muscle* is responsible for the raising and lowering of the testes that occur in response to temperature changes and sexual excitement.

The **seminal vesicle,** a gland located behind the bladder, secretes a fluid material that is essential for the survival of sperm. The seminal vesicle joins the vas deferens and supplies about 60 percent of the fluid to the traveling sperm. The sperm then en-

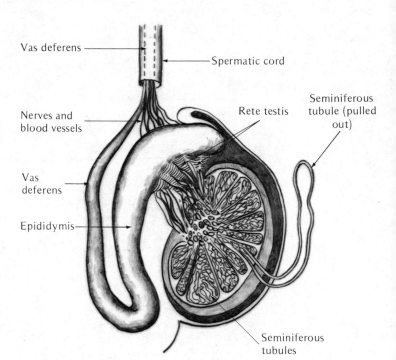

Figure 2-9. Internal structure of the testes.

Vas deferens

Spermatic cord

Nerves and blood vessels

Rete testis

Seminiferous tubule (pulled out)

Vas deferens

Epididymis

Seminiferous tubules

ter the *ejaculatory duct,* through which they pass to get to the urethra. The ejaculatory duct runs through the center of the **prostate gland,** which is located at the base of the bladder. About 0.75 inch in diameter, this gland is made up of three lobes that contain thirty to forty individual glands that produce and discharge fluid directly into the ejaculatory duct. The prostate provides about 30 percent of the fluid that is discharged during ejaculation.

The ejaculatory duct eventually enters the **urethra,** which is the duct through which urine leaves the bladder. Two small glands are positioned directly below the prostate gland and to the left and right of the urethra, each connected to the urethra by small ducts. These glands, called the *bulbourethral glands,* or the **Cowper's glands,** secrete into the urethra a small amount of fluid that neutralizes the acid environment of this canal. The clear drops of sticky fluid that often appear at the urethral opening during sexual arousal (but before ejaculation) are produced by these glands. This fluid may contain some sperm and can account for pregnancies that occur in the absence of ejaculation.

THE HUMAN SEXUAL RESPONSE

Alfred Kinsey and his colleagues (1948, 1953) were the first researchers to provide some frame of reference for describing the human sexual response. After the Kinsey reports were released, attitudes toward human sexuality were never quite the same. Although the work of Kinsey and his colleagues has been criticized, their contribu-

TABLE 2-1 THREE MODELS OF THE SEXUAL RESPONSE CYCLE		
KINSEY (1953)	MASTERS AND JOHNSON (1966)	KAPLAN (1979)
—	—	Desire phase
The buildup	Excitement phase	Excitement phase
—	Plateau phase	—
Orgasm	Orgasm	Orgasm
Aftereffects of orgasm	Resolution phase	—

tions cannot be overlooked. Almost hidden among the mass of data that was accumulated on sexual behavior was a description of the human sexual response.

Masters and Johnson, as we mentioned in Chapter One, deserve the credit for conducting the most extensive research on the human sexual response. They studied 382 women and 312 men and observed at least 10,000 sexual response cycles, about three-fourths of which were female response cycles. From the mass of information gathered by interview, visual observation, and physiological recordings, Masters and Johnson (1966) provided both a model to help describe the human sexual response cycle and a detailed description of the physical changes that occur. They published their findings in *Human Sexual Response*. The book received a great deal of publicity and attention, in part because it presented information gathered from the direct observation of sexual activity. Although many people were offended by the nature of the research and the method of data collection, Masters and Johnson demonstrated that ethical and responsible scientists can study sexual behavior directly and provide valuable information.

Another model of human sexual response that differs from the ones identified by the Kinsey group and by Masters and Johnson has been proposed by Helen Singer Kaplan, a well-known psychiatrist whose research and writings on sex therapy have been very influential. She presents this

model in her book, *Disorders of Sexual Desire* (1979). Table 2-1 contains an outline of the three models, illustrating their similarities and differences.

All of the models have a phase describing an increase in sexual excitement or arousal. Kinsey called this the "buildup"; Masters and Johnson and Kaplan have labeled this phase the "excitement phase." Each model describes orgasm following the buildup, or excitement, phase. Finally, each researcher observed that sexual excitement returns to prestimulation levels following orgasm, although Kaplan does not give this phase a separate label.

The models differ in that the Kinsey model contains only three phases, while the Masters and Johnson model adds a plateau phase, a period during which reactions to the sexual excitement phase level off just before the occurrence of orgasm. Kaplan's model differs from the others in two respects. First, she describes a desire phase, which precedes the excitement phase. This desire phase, not differing between the sexes, consists of activity in the brain that produces a sexual appetite or drive. "When this system is active, a person is 'horny' " (Kaplan, 1979, p. 10). Second, Kaplan does not describe the return to prestimulation levels. She says that such a phase is just the "absence of sexual arousal" (p. 5). Kaplan does not deny that the body returns to the prestimulation state following orgasm, but she feels it is of little or no importance.

Body Changes during the Sexual Response Cycle

In 1948, Kinsey and his colleagues described the bodily changes that occur during sexual activity in this way:

> Erotic stimulation, whatever its source, effects a series of physiologic changes which, as far as we yet know, appear to involve adrenal secretion, typically autonomic reactions, increased pulse rate, increased blood pressure, an increase in peripheral circulation and a consequent rise in the surface temperature of the body; a flow of blood into such distensible organs as the eyes, the lips, the lobes of the ears, the nipples of the breast, the penis of the male, and the clitoris, the genital labia and the vaginal walls of the female; a partial but often considerable loss of perceptive capacity (sight, hearing, touch, taste, smell); an increase in so-called nervous tension, some degree of rigidity of some part or of the whole of the body at the moment of maximum tension; and then a sudden release which produces local spasms or more extensive or all-consuming convulsions. The moment of sudden release is the point commonly recognized among biologists as orgasm. (Kinsey, 1948, p. 158)

The description provided by Kinsey and his colleagues was basically accurate, but in 1966 Masters and Johnson offered a more detailed and accurate description of physiological changes that occur during sexual response. Although dramatic changes do occur in the genitals, Masters and Johnson emphasize the fact that *the entire body is involved in sexual arousal.* For example, muscle tension, or **myotonia,** increases throughout the body, and blood pooling in

tissues increases the size of many parts of the body. This increase in the amount of blood in certain organs, **vasocongestion,** is the first bodily response that occurs during sexual excitement. In both males and females the genitals become increasingly engorged with blood, resulting in the initial signs of an erection in men, and a swelling of the genitals in women, accompanied by the lubrication of the vagina. Myotonia also begins early in the cycle and is a reaction common to both men and women.

Many of the specific bodily responses that occur during sexual excitement are based on vasocongestion and myotonia, and the reactions of men and women are often similar, although genital and reproductive organs differ. Physical changes, their sequence, and the degree to which they occur are not fixed, however. Individuals can and do vary from the sequence described, and variations should not necessarily be considered a sign of a problem. For example, while nipple erection occurs later for men than for women most of the time, for a particular couple the male might show signs of this response much sooner than the female.

In the review of the sexual response phases that follow, we will not present the plateau phase separately. Masters and Johnson (1966) define this phase as a leveling off in the excitement phase that precedes orgasm. No studies independently confirm the existence of a plateau phase; rather, sexual arousal seems to rise continuously during the excitement phase until it peaks, which is the point at which orgasm occurs. We will thus include the plateau phase in the excitement phase. Also, because there is currently no available physical measure of Kaplan's desire phase, we will begin with the excitement, or buildup, phase.

☐ *The Excitement Phase* The **excitement phase** begins with initial sexual stimulation and ends with orgasm. This phase is characterized by increasing feelings of arousal and may last only a few minutes or may be prolonged for several hours. Should sexual stimulation stop or either (or both) partners become distracted there is a reversal of the phase with a return to the prestimulation level of nonexcitement. Innumerable distractions can occur, ranging from a loud argument in a neighboring apartment to the sudden remembrance by one partner that he or she has an exam scheduled for the following day. Brief or weak distractions do not return arousal to prestimulation levels. The rate of increase in sexual excitement is affected by many psychological and physical variables and will change from time to time for any individual. A description of the bodily changes in the excitement phase categorized by sex and location is provided in Table 2-2 and illustrated in Figure 2-10. The description offered is a composite and may not totally match the experience of any given individual.

☐ *The Orgasm Phase* **Orgasm** is an event that is clearly different from the excitement phase that precedes it. Characterized by a peaking in sexual excitement, orgasm is experienced as a sudden release and is usually reported to be an extremely pleasurable event. (See Box 2-1 for some personal accounts of the orgasmic experience.) According to studies that have recorded subjective descriptions of orgasms (e.g., Hite 1976; Proctor, Wagner, & Butler, 1974), the experience varies both for individuals from time to time and among individuals. One group of researchers reported that there are different types of male orgasms as recorded physiologically (Bohlen, Held, & Sanderson, 1980). They reported that males differ in the duration of orgasm and in the number of pelvic contractions experienced. According to this report, the pattern and duration of orgasm appear to be quite stable for the individual male across several orgasms.

Some attempts to describe different types of orgasms in women have also been made. Freud (1933) spoke of vaginal versus clitoral orgasms and suggested that they differed in their psychological importance. Vulval, uterine, and blended orgasms have been offered as orgasmic variations by Singer and Singer (1973). They suggest that the differences are both anatomical and psychological. Their view is derived from the Freudian model and appears to be based on largely anecdotal or clinical observations. On the other hand, Masters and Johnson (1966) unequivocally reject the notion of a separation of female orgasm as suggested by Freud. What is the truth? In fact, we don't know for certain. Using measures of genital contractions, Bohlen, et al. (1982) found evidence for patterns of individual differences in women's orgasms.

Masters and Johnson (1966) analyzed the subjective reports of 487 women concerning their sensations of orgasm. (Because the

TABLE 2-2 THE HUMAN SEXUAL RESPONSE: THE EXCITEMENT, OR BUILDUP, PHASE

GENITAL CHANGES

FEMALES	MALES
Clitoris: increases in size early in phase and appears to withdraw under clitoral hood as arousal increases. Vagina: begins lubricating rapidly, becomes longer and wider, and color changes to a darker purple. The outer one-third (called the *orgasmic platform*) fills with blood. Uterus: starts elevating and by the end of the phase is pulled up from vagina, providing a "tenting," or open area, at the inner one-third of the vagina. Labia majora: become increasingly filled with blood, move somewhat away from midline where they normally touch. Labia minora: become somewhat larger; they become much more deeply colored due to vasocongestion. Bartholin's glands: may secrete a few drops of fluid late in this phase.	Penis: rapid beginning of erection; size increases throughout most of this phase. Scrotum: becomes thicker and elevates toward body. Testes: elevate toward body wall and increase in size as much as 50 percent. Cowper's gland: may secrete two or three drops of fluid, which may contain viable sperm.

EXTRA-GENITAL CHANGES

FEMALES	MALES
Breasts: nipples erect and breasts increase in size, up to 25 percent larger. Sex flush: a measlelike rash may develop over the upper abdomen and spread over the body. Breathing: may increase in rate late in this phase. Heart rate: slows early, then begins to increase up to as high as 175 beats per minute. Blood pressure: elevates as phase progresses. Myotonia: both voluntary and involuntary muscle activity increases as phase progresses.	Breasts: nipples erect in some males. Sex flush: typically develops later and less frequently than in females. Rectum: some voluntary contractions late in the phase. Breathing: may increase in rate late in phase. Heart rate: slows early, then begins to increase as phase develops, as high as 180 beats per minute. Blood pressure: elevates as the phase progresses. Myotonia: both voluntary and involuntary muscle activity increases as phase progresses.

women were all multiorgasmic and comfortable enough concerning their sexuality to participate in laboratory research, we must be cautious before assuming that the findings from this study are applicable to women in general.) Masters and Johnson reported that orgasm could be separated into three stages. The first stage begins with a brief feeling that time stops, a "sensation of suspension or stoppage" (p. 135), which is then followed by strong genital sensations and a loss of sensory awareness. The second stage is characterized by a feeling of spreading warmth throughout the pelvic region. The third and final stage is described as a throbbing or pulsating experience ap-

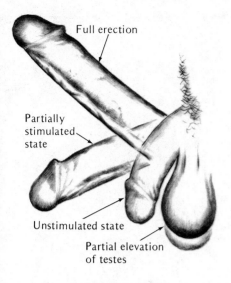

Full erection

Partially
stimulated
state

Unstimulated state

Partial elevation
of testes

EARLY EXCITEMENT

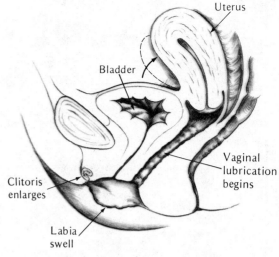

Uterus

Bladder

Clitoris
enlarges

Labia
swell

Vaginal
lubrication
begins

EARLY EXCITEMENT

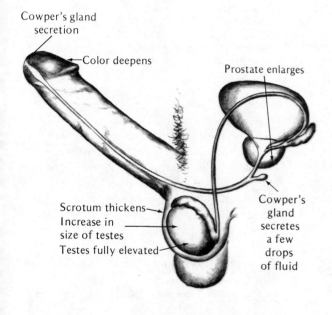

Cowper's gland
secretion

Color deepens

Prostate enlarges

Scrotum thickens
Increase in
size of testes
Testes fully elevated

Cowper's
gland
secretes
a few
drops
of fluid

LATE EXCITEMENT

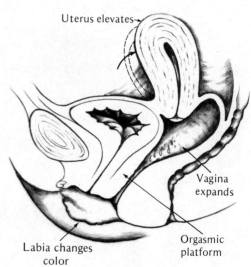

Uterus elevates

Vagina
expands

Labia changes
color

Orgasmic
platform

LATE EXCITEMENT

Figure 2–10. Genital changes during early and late excitement phase.

parently related to the contractions that occur in the genital structures. These contractions reportedly occur every 0.8 seconds, with the time between becoming longer with successive contractions.

For males, orgasm was described by Masters and Johnson as consisting of two

stages. The first stage, which occurs when the seminal fluid moves toward the urethra, is experienced as "a sensation of ejaculatory inevitability" (Masters & Johnson, 1966, p. 215). That is, at this point, the male

THE EXPERIENCE OF ORGASM

We offer here some individual reflections on the experience of orgasm. Their purpose is to illustrate that orgasms differ from one person to another and from one experience to another. Perhaps you have sexually responded in one of the ways described below, and yet your experience may be totally different.

Has a buildup of pressure in genitals with involuntary thrusting of hips and twitching of thigh muscles. Also contracting and releasing of the genital muscles. The pressure becomes quite intense—like there is something underneath the skin of the genitals pushing out. Then there is a sudden release of the tension with contraction of genitals with a feeling of release and relaxation.

They vary a great deal depending on circumstances. If it's just a physical need or release it's OK, but it takes more effort to "get there." If you're really very much in love (at least in my case) it's so close at hand that the least physical expression by your partner, or slightest touch on the genitals brings it on. And then if the love-making is continued it repeats again and again. It's about 90% cortical or emotional and the rest physical. But one has to have the emotion or (in my case) I don't even want to begin or try.

feels that ejaculation is sure to occur and cannot be prevented. The second stage consists of the propulsion of the semen through the urethra and its ejaculation through the urinary opening. Masters and Johnson report that semen may be ejaculated as far as 12 to 24 inches during orgasm. The second part of the male orgasm is experienced as contractions or pulsations. As with women, contractions initially occur at 0.8 second intervals. The contractions are quite intense at first and subsequently level off. Masters and Johnson note that when a brief time occurs between successive orgasms, males generally report that the second orgasm is less intense, while women report it as being more intense than the first.

The differences between male and female orgasm, as presented by Masters and Johnson (1966), are not consistent with the findings of Vance and Wagner (1976), who found that even experts could not distin-guish between descriptions of orgasm written by men from those written by women. The major difference between the reports may be that Masters and Johnson recorded the reactions of their subjects immediately after they had experienced orgasm, while the subjects in the Vance and Wagner study recalled orgasms that they had had in the past.

Most of us assume that male ejaculation occurs simultaneously with the experience of orgasm. However, this is not necessarily true. For example, men with damaged spinal cords can ejaculate without experiencing an orgasm. Also, some men with spinal cord damage have experienced orgasm without ejaculating (Higgins, 1978). Kinsey's group (1948) reported that prepubescent boys can reach an orgasm, yet are unable to ejaculate. These are special conditions, but they do illustrate that orgasm and ejaculation are not inevitably bound together.

There is a great release of tensions that have built up in the prior stages of sexual activity. This release is extremely pleasurable and exciting. The feeling seems to be centered in the genital region. It is extremely intense and exhilarating. There is a loss of muscular control as the pleasure mounts and you almost cannot go on. You almost don't want to go on. This is followed by the climax and refractory states!

Begins with tensing and tingling in anticipation, rectal contractions starting series of chills up spine. Tingling and buzzing sensations grow suddenly to explosion in genital area, some sensation of dizzying and weakening—almost loss of conscious sensation, but not really. Explosion sort of flowers out to varying distance from genital area, depending on intensity.

I think that there are a variety of orgasms that I experience. I have noted a shallow "orgasm" which consists of a brief period which is characterized by an urge to thrust but which passes quickly. On the other hand, I have also experienced what I call a hard climax, characterized by a mounting, building tension and strong thrusting movements which increase in strength and frequency until the tension is relieved.

A feeling where nothing much else enters the mind other than that which relates to the present, oh sooo enjoyable and fulfilling sensation. It's like jumping into a cool swimming pool after hours of sweating turmoil. "Ahh Relief! What a great feeling it was, so ecstatically wild and alright!"

Source: Vance & Wagner, 1976.

It has been reported that some women during orgasm ejaculate. The original report of this phenomenon was contained in a case study (Addiego et al, 1981). It was reported that the subject ejaculated when a particular spot on her vagina was stimulated. They named the area, located a few centimeters inside the vagina on the anterior wall, the Graffenberg spot after the individual who reported that this location contained glands and structures that were homologous to the male prostate. In another study (Perry and Whipple, 1981), it was reported that this spot could be located in forty-seven women and that these women reported that stimulation of the spot was pleasurable. In this larger study ejaculation was not evaluated although many of the women, selected because of this characteristic, reported that they did ejaculate. The reports both of female ejaculation and of a particular spot that is extremely sensitive to stimulation are controversial and have been subjected to criticism. Of particular importance are the criticisms that note that there are many problems involved in the way the information and data are collected (Bohlen, 1982). There is a need for further study to either verify or to refute this challenging report. Regardless of the outcome, orgasm for most women is not accompanied by an event as clearly identifiable as ejaculation is in men. The implication is that both the female subject and the investigator have a greater chance of uncertainty in determining whether or not orgasm has occurred. In research or clinical situations, a woman's report is usually accepted, but a few women have trouble identifying an orgasmic response and other women may feel pressured to claim they have had an orgasm even if they have not.

Men and women appear to differ in the

TABLE 2-3 THE HUMAN SEXUAL RESPONSE: THE ORGASM PHASE	
GENITAL CHANGES	
FEMALES	MALES
Vagina: orgasmic platform (see Table 2–2) contracts from five to twelve times; the contractions occur slightly faster than one per second, with the time between contractions becoming longer and the strength of the contractions decreasing. Uterus: contractions of the uterus, which are similar to those that accompany labor.	Penis: contractions of the penile urethra timed as in females, but typically being fewer in number in males. Prostate and seminal vessels: contractions occur, moving semen to the exterior.
EXTRA-GENITAL CHANGES	
FEMALES	MALES
Sex flush: its intensity is related to the subjective experience and is more widespread than in other phases. Rectum: contractions linked in time to vaginal contractions, but usually fewer. Breathing: maximum change; some individuals uttering sounds. Heart rate: maximum change, with rate of up to 180 beats per minute recorded. Blood pressure: greatest elevation. Myotonia: some loss of voluntary control, with spasms and contractions of many muscle groups.	Sex flush: in those males where it occurs (twenty-five percent), maximum development. Rectum: contractions linked to genital contractions. Breathing: maximum change; some individuals uttering sounds. Heart rate: maximum change, with rate of up to 180 beats per minute recorded. Blood pressure: greatest elevation, generally somewhat greater than females. Myotonia: some loss of voluntary control with spasms and contractions of many muscle groups.

capacity to have multiple orgasms. Multiple orgasms are not precisely defined, but they are said to occur when the time between orgasms is brief and sexual excitement does not return to low or prestimulation levels between orgasms. Many women experience multiple orgasms, and Sherfey (1973) suggests that all women have the potential to have multiple orgasms. In general, men are not able to experience multiple orgasms. The reason for this difference between the sexes is unknown. It is not that men are "drained" by an ejaculation and must build up more semen before another can occur. The fact that there are cross-cultural differences in how long men delay between successive intercourse experiences suggests that at least part of the longer

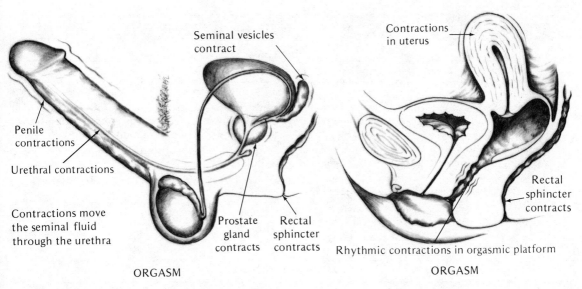

Seminal vesicles contract

Contractions in uterus

Penile contractions

Urethral contractions

Contractions move the seminal fluid through the urethra

Prostate gland contracts

Rectal sphincter contracts

Rectal sphincter contracts

Rhythmic contractions in orgasmic platform

ORGASM

ORGASM

Figure 2-11. Genital changes during orgasm phase.

delay in males is determined by expectations about their own sexual performance (Ford & Beach, 1951).

Table 2-3 lists the bodily responses that occur during orgasm. These responses are diagrammed in Figure 2-11.

☐ *The Resolution, or "After Effects," Phase* The **resolution phase** of the sexual response cycle begins when the orgasm is complete and continues until sexual excitement returns to resting or unstimulated levels. In general, this phase is simply the reverse of the excitement phase. The resolution phase may last for 30 minutes or longer, with many of the changes taking place within the first 5 or 10 minutes. The return to prestimulation levels occurs more rapidly when an orgasm has occurred than

when a person has reached a high level of excitement but has not been orgasmic. Apparently, males often complete the resolution phase more rapidly than females. While Kaplan does not describe this phase in her model, it is clearly part of the response cycle. Table 2-4 contains a summary of the changes that occur during the resolution phase, and Figure 2-12 illustrates those changes.

Sexual Response in the Aging Individual

The only extensive study of the sexual response cycle in an aging population was

TABLE 2-4 THE HUMAN SEXUAL RESPONSE: THE RESOLUTION OR AFTEREFFECTS PHASE	
GENITAL CHANGES	
FEMALES	MALES
Clitoris: returns to prestimulation position within 5 to 10 seconds; loss of vasocongestion takes longer. Vagina: rapid loss of orgasmic platform; loss of vasocongestion in walls takes much longer—15 minutes or more. Uterus: returns to prestimulation condition within 20 to 30 minutes. Labia majora: returns to prestimulation condition. Labia minora: returns to prestimulation color within 15 seconds; size returns more slowly.	Penis: loss of erection occurs in two stages, with a rapid loss of 50 percent of the erection, followed by a slower return to prestimulation condition. Scrotum: rapid loss of swelling and return to prestimulation state. Testes: loss of swelling and lowering of testes into scrotum.
EXTRA-GENITAL CHANGES	
FEMALES	MALES
Breasts: rapid loss of nipple erection, with slower loss of breast volume. Sex flush: rapid return to original state. Breathing: rapid return to normal. Heart rate: rapid return to prestimulation level. Blood pressure: rapid return to prestimulation level. Myotonia: loss of tension over a 5-minute period.	Breasts: loss of nipple erection if it occurred in excitement phase. Sex flush: rapid return to original state. Breathing: rapid return to normal. Heart rate: rapid return to prestimulation level. Blood pressure: rapid return to prestimulation level. Myotonia: loss of tension over about a 5-minute period.

that reported by Masters and Johnson (1966). They studied in detail 61 women between the ages of 40 and 78, with 34 women over 50 years of age, and 39 males between 51 and 89 years of age. They established several important points about sexual response and aging. First, people of all ages respond sexually, and this response does not cease at menopause or at any given age. According to Masters and Johnson, "There seems to be no physiologic reason why the frequency of sexual expression found satisfactory for the younger woman should not be carried over into the postmenopausal years" (Masters & Johnson, 1966, p. 246). Second, if both men and women have ac-

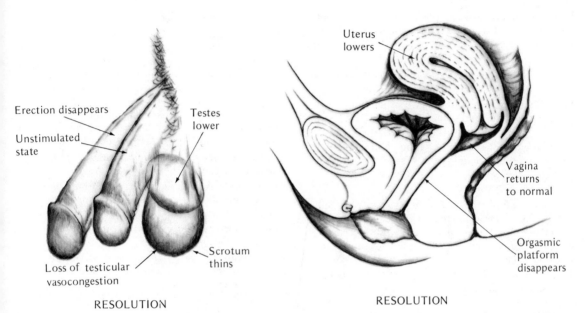

RESOLUTION

RESOLUTION

Figure 2-12. Genital changes during resolution phase.

tive sex lives when they are young, they are more likely to have a continued ability to respond both psychologically and physiologically as they age. For example, the penis becomes less sensitive to tactile stimulation with age, but the change is less distinct in the male who is sexually active (Edwards & Hurted, 1976; Newman, 1970). According to Masters and Johnson (1966), "The most important factor in the maintenance of effective sexuality for the aging male is consistency of active sexual expression" (p. 262). The same statement is true for women.

In most cases, the difference between younger and older people appears to be a matter of degree rather than an absolute change. For example, Solnick and Birren (1977) found that men between the ages of 48 and 65 reacted more slowly and with smaller increases in penis size to an erotic movie than did men between the ages of 19 and 30. While in general younger men were more responsive, some older men were more responsive than some of the younger subjects. Table 2-5 summarizes the sexual response of the aging individual by pointing out those differences that have been identified. Keep in mind, however, that there are also many similarities. More research is needed in this area because our aging population is growing. (Chapter Six reviews other aspects of the sexual behavior of the aging individual.)

TABLE 2–5   CHANGES IN THE SEXUAL RESPONSE WITH AGE

FEMALES	MALES
Breasts: the response of the nipple is relatively unaffected except that loss of erection takes longer. The increases in breast size occur less frequently in the older female.	Breasts: nipple erection reaction happens less often, but when it occurs it lasts longer after orgasm.
Sex flush: occurs less frequently in the aging individual and spreads less widely when it occurs.	Sex flush: it is even less common and less intense in the older male.
Myotonia: decreases with age, but much less so in women who continue regular sexual activity.	Myotonia: decreases with age but much less so in males who experience regular sexual activity.
Clitoris: response is quite similar at all ages with somewhat less tumescence in the glans.	Penis: the speed of attainment of an erection is slowed, but erection is maintained for longer periods. The aging male will experience more difficulty in reacquiring an erection if lost before orgasm, the refractory period is longer, and loss of erection is more rapid. The force of ejaculation and intensity of contractions is reduced.
Labia majora: this structure loses its ability to move away from midline.	
Labia minora: these structures lose their response of enlargement and the color change becomes less pronounced.	
Bartholin's glands: very gradual loss of production of secretion.	Scrotum: reduced vasocongestion and less frequent lifting toward the body wall.
Vagina: lubrication occurs at a slower rate, but lubrication can be extensive in sexually active older women. The vagina's ability to increase in width and depth decreases, and its return to prestimulation levels occurs rapidly.	Testes: less elevation of the testes, and increase in size is not as evident. The return to prestimulation levels is very rapid in the aging male.
	Prostate and ejaculatory ducts: appear to respond less in the aging male.
Uterus: elevation less pronounced in the aging individual, and contractions may be uncomfortable.	Ejaculation: volume and force are less intense, and sensations are different for the older male. Less of a phase of inevitability and less feeling of expulsion of semen so that experience is more like a single stage.
The intensity of the subjective experience of orgasm decreases.	The intensity of the subjective experience of orgasm decreases.

Measurement of Sexual Response

While research in the field of human sexuality has depended heavily on the use of questionnaires or interviews to collect data, some investigators have measured physiological reactions in order to broaden our knowledge of sexuality. The early studies of this type measured nongenital responses such as blood pressure, heart rate, or sweat gland activity. These studies were severely limited by the fact that such measures are only weakly associated with reports of the experience of sexual excitement, and they change under emotional states other than sexual arousal (Zuckerman, 1971). The difficulty in such studies is to tell if the subjects are embarrassed, disgusted, angry, or frightened rather than sexually aroused. In reaction to this problem, a number of techniques have been developed to measure genital activity directly.

The first report published in the English language on the development of a technique to measure genital responses during sexual arousal was based on studies conducted by Kurt Freund, a Czechoslovakian researcher (Freund, 1963). Freund developed a hollow, glass, cylinder-shaped device that enclosed the penis and, by detecting changes in air pressure, accurately measured changes in the size of the penis. He reported that sexual interest and preferences were successfully measured using his device and that at least some people who were attempting to hide their sexual interests were unable to do so. Since that time, researchers have developed less complicated devices that fit around the penis and expand and contract as the penis changes size. These *penile strain gauges,* made of either rubber tubing filled with mercury or some type of flexible metal, make the measurement of changes in penile size relatively simple, and they are highly reliable (Geer, 1980; Rosen & Keefe, 1978).

The first instrument that successfully measured genital responses in women was devised in 1971 by Cohen and Shapiro (1971). They mounted temperature-sensing units, called *thermistors,* on the rim of a vaginal diaphragm. The device recorded changes in blood flow in the vaginal walls. (A diaphragm is a contraceptive device that blocks the entrance to the cervix; see Chapter Three for further information on this and other methods of contraception.) They found that vaginal blood flow was altered by sexual arousal. Due to its complex nature, and particularly the fact that each woman must be individually fitted for a diaphragm, this device has not been widely used in research. An instrument that has met with greater success is the *vaginal photometer,* which detects changes in vasocongestion in the walls of the vagina (Geer, 1980; Geer, Morokoff, & Greenwood, 1974; Hatch, 1979). This device works on the principle that increased amounts of blood act

to alter the amount of red light that can be transmitted through the tissue. Henson, Rubin, and Henson (1978) reported the successful use of a measure of labial temperature, and other researchers developed a way to measure the absolute amount of blood in the vaginal walls (Levin & Wagner, 1978). These methods of monitoring female genital response are based on the observation that sexual arousal is accompanied by increases in the amount of blood in the genitals. The vaginal photometer and the device used by Henson and his colleagues have the advantage of being positioned in private. The photometer detects vaginal changes that occur very quickly; it may be most valuable in the study of moderate to low levels of sexual arousal.

Since Masters and Johnson reported extensively on genital changes during sexual activity, one would expect their measures to set the standard for the field. Unfortunately, this isn't so. In *Human Sexual Response,* they report only the use of visual observations, and their judgments are made on the basis of those observations. Masters and Johnson do report the development of an artificial penis made of clear plastic that allows for the direct observation of intravaginal events. However, since they provide no details concerning its operation, it is not possible to verify or replicate their findings (Bancroft, 1980).

The findings from the male and female tests cannot be compared because they measure different events. Of value would be to have a way of measuring similar physiological events in order to compare the reactions of men and women with identical stimuli. There is considerable speculation that the sexes differ in terms of what "turns them on" (Gagnon & Simon, 1973; Kinsey et al., 1953). In fact, what research we have on genital measures suggests that the sexes are much more alike than anyone had assumed (Heiman, 1977). Comparable measures would also permit research on whether or not dysfunctional men and women are alike in their sexual responsiveness. These and many other questions can be fully answered only when genital measures are developed to evaluate similar events in males and females.

One process that attempts an equivalent measure for both sexes is *thermography* (Seeley et al., 1980). In thermography, heat-sensing cameras scan the body and detect temperature changes. The color of the photo taken can be used to determine temperature changes resulting from increased vasocongestion. Temperature changes during arousal occur in both sexes, and so thermography may permit some form of direct comparison between the sexes.

The development of an anal probe that measures vasocongestion and pressure changes in the rectum is another procedure for use by both sexes (Bohlen & Held, 1979). The researchers, however, report that this device is uncomfortable and thus finding subjects willing to use it may be difficult. Because anal and rectal changes are common in both males and females during the sexual excitement phase, this technique may be worth pursuing.

Finally, several investigators have used photometry in measuring penile response in males (Bancroft, 1980; Hatch, Heiman, &

Hahn, 1980). Further development of this method may also allow for direct comparisons between the sexes.

Events That Produce Bodily Changes

The entire nervous system is involved with sexual arousal and response; thus one must know how it works to fully understand sexual behavior. There are two major divisions: the **central nervous system** (CNS) and the **peripheral nervous system** (PNS). The brain and the spinal cord make up the CNS. The job of the PNS is to link the CNS to the outside world through the sense organs and also to connect the CNS to the muscles, glands, and all other bodily tissues affected by the nervous system. Figure 2–13 illustrates the relationship among the divisions of the nervous system.

The output side of the PNS, when messages are sent from the CNS to the rest of the body via the PNS, is divided further into the *somatic* and *autonomic* branches. The **somatic** branch of the PNS brings impulses in from the sense organs, and it also transmits impulses from the CNS to striate (voluntary) muscles like those in the arms and legs. The **autonomic** branch connects to smooth muscles, such as stomach muscles, and to glands, and is often associated with involuntary reactions such as sweating or heart palpitations. Another division occurs in the autonomic branch of the nervous system, resulting in the sympathetic and parasympathetic branches. These divisions are quite different, both anatomically and physiologically: They seem to act in opposite

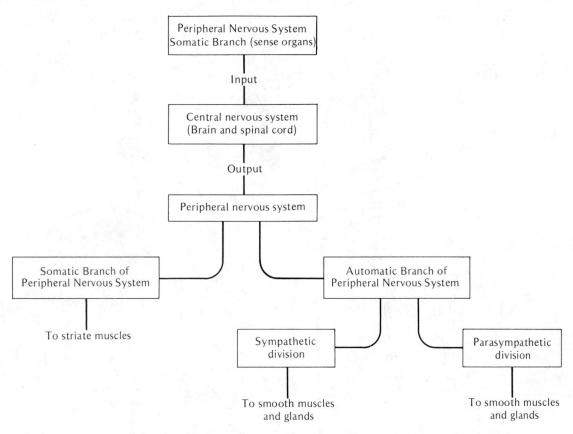

Figure 2-13. *Divisions of the nervous system.*

directions. The **sympathetic** branch increases activity, while the **parasympathetic** branch decreases activity in the organs that are affected. Most organs are dominated by only one of the branches. Figure 2–14 shows the organs and systems that are affected by the two divisions; it also shows where the nerves leave the CNS. Note that the sex organs receive signals from both sympathetic and parasympathetic nerves. In males, for example, erection appears to be under parasympathetic control and ejaculation under sympathetic control. In females, however, vasocongestion and orgasm appear to be under sympathetic control. No explanation for this odd assignment of control has yet been uncovered.

The parts of the body that respond during the sexual response cycle include facial, abdominal, pelvic, back, leg, and arm mus-

cles; they all show increased activity and tension. The tension shown in these muscles is beyond that accompanying any deliberate sexual activity such as pelvic thrusting. These muscle responses, myotonia, are controlled by the somatic branch of the PNS.

The response of vasocongestion is less obvious than myotonia. Tissue may become engorged with blood through two mechanisms. Vasocongestion in *erectile tissue* results from blood filling specially constructed spaces. The second and more common type occurs when blood vessels engorge with blood. Each *capillary,* the smallest of the blood vessels, is surrounded by smooth muscle. When these muscles are stimulated by the sympathetic division of

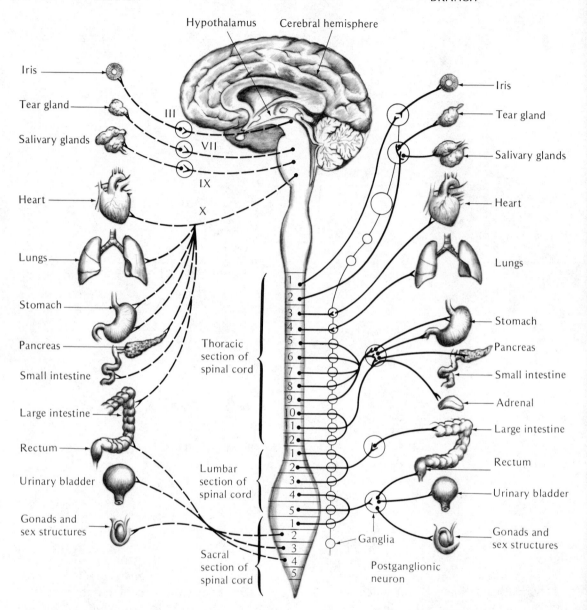

PARASYMPATHETIC BRANCH

SYMPATHETIC BRANCH

Hypothalamus   Cerebral hemisphere

Iris

Tear gland

Salivary glands

III

VII

IX

X

Heart

Lungs

Stomach

Pancreas

Small intestine

Large intestine

Rectum

Urinary bladder

Gonads and sex structures

Thoracic section of spinal cord

Lumbar section of spinal cord

Sacral section of spinal cord

Iris

Tear gland

Salivary glands

Heart

Lungs

Stomach

Pancreas

Small intestine

Adrenal

Large intestine

Rectum

Urinary bladder

Gonads and sex structures

Ganglia

Postganglionic neuron

Figure 2–14. The autonomic nervous system, its branches and organs affected.

the autonomic nervous system, they contract and the vessel shrinks. On the other hand, when the degree of sympathetic stimulation decreases, the blood pressure in the vessels causes them to expand because the smooth muscles relax. This expansion, occurring in many vessels at one time, is the

cause of vasocongestion in nonerectile tissue. Blood does not seep out into the tissue; instead the vessels become larger so they can hold more blood. The increased size of structures such as the breast and labia result from this type of vasocongestion. Tissue color often changes because tissue containing a lot of blood will have a color different from tissue with less blood, as when a person blushes.

The major genital responses, vaginal lubrication and penile erection, are based on vasocongestion. Vaginal lubrication occurs because the capillaries in the vagina increase in size and alter the fluid pressures in the walls of the vagina, resulting in an increased amount of fluid passing through the cell layers and into the vagina. This lubrication is the by-product of vasocongestion and has both sexual and reproductive value. The lubricated vagina more comfortably accommodates penile thrusting because friction is reduced. The additional moisture on the external genitals often heightens a woman's sensory experience, and the tendency of the lubrication fluid to reduce the natural acidity level of the vagina may act to prolong sperm life.

Penile erection appears to be primarily a parasympathetic response; ejaculation and the subsequent loss of erection appear to be sympathetic responses. Erection, as opposed to vaginal lubrication, is the result of blood filling erectile tissue, not capillaries. The erectile tissue in the shaft of the penis is made up of many irregular spaces and cavities, much like a sponge. A layer of fibrous tissue surrounds the erectile tissue. During sexual stimulation the blood vessels leading into the encased tissue dilate (probably because of increased parasympathetic stimulation and/or decreased sympathetic stimulation), and that dilation permits an in-creased inflow of blood. Because the out-flow is not increased, and may even be inhibited, the spaces in the erectile tissue fill with blood, and the spongy tissue increases in size and fills the space enclosed by the fibrous cover. Thus, the erection is the result of erectile tissue becoming "inflated" with blood, making it larger and rigid. This process can be compared with inflating an inner tube, which is made of thick rubber. When inflating the tube, a limit will be reached and the pressure will maintain a rigid structure, but the tube will not expand any further because the pressure can be easily contained by the thick walls. Similarly, the size of the penis can increase only so much because the fibrous coat surrounding the erectile tissue limits the expansion.

Loss of erection occurs when the arterioles that channel blood into the erectile tissue decrease in size. The blood leaving the tissue now exceeds the amount that flows in. As the blood leaves the spaces in the spongy tissue, there is no longer any pressure against the fibrous cover, and the tissue resumes its noninflated state. Keep in mind that loss of erection is not only caused by a decrease in stimulation, but also possibly by the inappropriate signaling of the sympathetic nervous system mechanism that reduces erection.

Undoubtedly, all parts of the CNS have some effect on sexual responses. Certain portions, however, have been identified as being more directly or more importantly involved than others. For example, in the spinal cord is an "erection center." If the spinal cord in that region is damaged, a person will not be able to have an erection. (Some men with damaged cords, however, have reported that they have ejaculated with little or no erection.)

The brain itself has many parts that have been identified with sexual behavior, and many of these sections are also associated with other emotional behaviors. The *limbic system,* a group of phylogenetically old structures lying beneath the cortex, is a good example. This system is involved in sexual behavior as well as many other emotional states, such as aggression and fear. Damage to the limbic system in nonhuman species can result in rage, and stimulation of the hypothalamus, which is part of the limbic system, can cause a cat to become violent (Gellhorn & Loofbourrow, 1963).

In other studies the stimulation of an animal's limbic system has produced a sexual response such as ejaculation (Vaughan & Fisher, 1962). In humans tumors of the limbic system have been associated with changes in sexual interest (Blumer & Walken, 1967). One researcher reported that chemical stimulation of the system caused a subject to experience an orgasm,

and electrical stimulation produced erections (Heath, 1972). These and other studies clearly point toward involvement of the limbic system in human sexual behavior.

Special chemical reactions in the brain occur during sexual activity, and these biochemical reactions are currently being studied extensively. Researchers know that certain nerve cells are affected by sex hormones, while others are not, and that these effects play a role in determining adult sexual behavior in animals (Brower & Naftolin, 1979). For example, when male and female hormones are directly implanted into the brain of rats and cats, they affect sexual behavior at some sites but not others (Davidson, 1966; Michael, 1965). Such results indicate that chemicals, particularly hormones, affect brain systems that organize or control sexual behavior. The hormonal effects in the CNS are very complex. Most investigators believe that the brain does not have a "sex center" but rather complex systems of various parts and activities upon which adequate sexual response depends.

HORMONES AND SEXUALITY

A **hormone** is a chemical secreted or produced by an endocrine gland; it enters the bloodstream and affects some specific target tissue. In general, hormones have the effect of increasing or decreasing metabolic activity. The sex hormones, also known as **gonadal hormones,** act to produce changes in specific target tissues, namely those in-

volved in reproduction and those that produce the secondary sex characteristics, such as hair and fat distribution.

All hormones exist in both sexes, although the levels vary between the sexes and within the same individual from time to time. **Estrogen, progesterone,** and **testosterone** are the sex hormones that the gonads produce. Males produce low levels of the ovarian hormones, estrogen and progesterone, and conversely, females produce low levels of **androgens,** the male sex hormones. "Androgen" is used to name any hormone that has a masculinizing effect, such as producing excessive facial hair growth. In addition to testosterone, two other male hormones, **aldosterone** and **androsterone,** are included in this category. They are produced in the adrenal cortex, which is discussed later.

Quite similar in their chemical structure, the various gonadal hormones allow metabolic processes to occur through which hormones can readily be changed from one to another. For example, in both males and females progesterone can be changed into testosterone, which, in turn, can become an estrogen. Figure 2–15 shows the typical concentrations of hormones in adults of both sexes. For the woman the luteal and follicular phases of the menstrual cycle are shown separately because hormone levels change considerably during the cycle. (See pp. 65–67 for a further discussion on the menstrual cycle and its phases.)

Figure 2–16, a schematic representation of the sex hormone system, highlights the structures that are involved and the hormones that are produced. This complete system is sometimes referred to as the *hypothalamic-pituitary-gonadal axis.* The hypothalamus, which is the part of the brain that helps regulate basic body functions, upon receiving input from various portions of the brain, is stimulated to produce hormones called **releasing factors.** These releasing factors are transported via a network of blood vessels, called the *portal system,* to the pituitary gland, where they stimulate the production of the hormones **LH** (luteinizing hormone), **FSH** (follicle-stimulating hormone), and **corticotrophin.** There is a specific releasing factor for each pituitary hormone.

Both sexes produce the same pituitary hormones. In men, however, LH is sometimes called ICSH (interstitial-cell-stimulating hormone), although it is chemically identical to LH. LH and FSH are known as **gonadotrophins** because they affect the gonads (the ovaries and testes). FSH stimulates the ovaries to develop ova and to produce estrogen, and the testes to develop sperm. LH induces the ovaries to ovulate or release the ova, while the testes are stimulated to produce testosterone. Corticotrophin, also known as ACTH, is not a gonadotrophin because it stimulates the cortex of the adrenal gland, which is located near the kidneys. **Prolactin** is a hormone that acts to stimulate the production of milk in the breasts, but also acts to stimulate the corpus luteum to produce progesterone. (You will recall that the corpus luteum is an ovarian structure that develops after ovulation.) Prolactin's production is controlled by *PIF,* the prolactin-inhibiting factor. This substance acts to inhibit the pituitary gland from producing the hormone prolactin. PIF's action is the reverse of the releasing factors.

Built-in regulatory systems control the production of the various hormones. These regulatory systems are the inhibitory and stimulatory feedback mechanisms. An inhibitory feedback system is one in which a

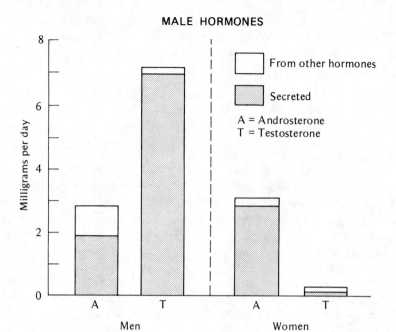

MALE HORMONES

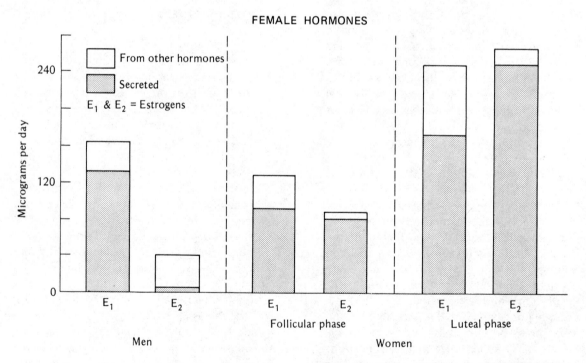

FEMALE HORMONES

Figure 2-15. Amounts of hormones produced daily by both sexes.

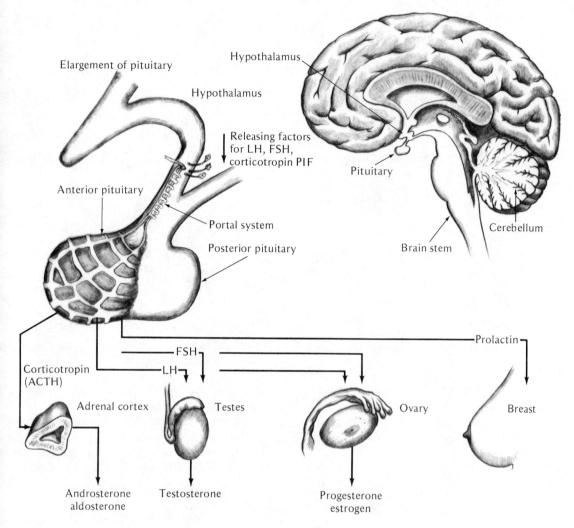

Figure 2-16. *The structures involved in the sex hormone system.*

high level of one hormone results in the low output of another, and vice versa. This system can be compared to the way in which a household thermostat regulates temperature: It shuts off the furnace when the temperature is too high and turns it on when the temperature is too low, in accordance with the setting on the thermostat.

An example of an inhibitory feedback system at work in the human body is the effect of the sex hormones on the production of LH and FSH. If the gonads are removed, the level of sex hormones in the body drops, which stimulates the production of high

levels of LH and FSH. If sex hormones are then introduced into the body, the production of LH and FSH slows. This system efficiently regulates the amount of sex hormones that are produced.

Stimulating feedback systems are those in which the presence of one hormone results in the increased production of another hormone. For example, if a woman were given additional progesterone or estrogen early in her menstrual cycle, ovulation

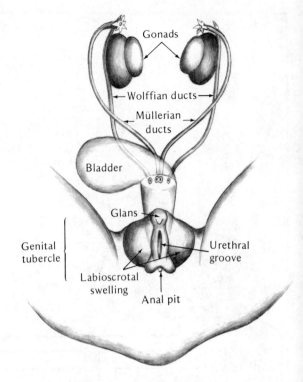

Figure 2-17. Embryonic structures before differentiation.

Developmental Effects of Hormones

The effects of sex hormones can be described as being either developmental or concurrent (Beach, 1978). Developmental effects are those that occur at a specific time in a person's life and cannot be produced at other times. The results of these effects are permanent, although developmental effects do not show up immediately. Concurrent effects are those that occur only while the hormone is present.

The developmental effects of sex hormones are most pronounced during two phases of a person's life: the period from six to twelve weeks after conception and during puberty. From conception until about

would be accelerated because of the increased production of LH and FSH. Why a sex hormone acts as an inhibitor in one instance and as a stimulating agent in another is as yet unknown.

the sixth or seventh week of development, male or female embryos look the same. This period is called the *predifferentiation stage,* and embryos have neither ovaries nor testes, only undeveloped gonads. The two structures that have the potential to develop into parts of the reproductive system are (1) the *Mullerian duct system,* which can develop into oviducts, uterus, and part of the vagina and (2) the *Wolffian duct system,* which can develop into the epididymis, vas deferens, and seminal vessels. Figure 2–17 illustrates the predifferentiated genital structures that have the potential for either male or female development. The predifferentiated embryo, while anatomically undifferentiated, is genetically male or female.

The *period of differentiation* begins when the undifferentiated gonadal tissue changes into either ovarian or testicular tissue because of genetic factors. Embryos with two X chromosomes become female, whereas an XY combination will be a male. The presence of a single Y chromosome will result in

Box 2-2

SEXUAL RESPONSE DURING SLEEP

Some aspects of sexual behavior continue during a person's sleeping hours. Most people have sexual dreams at some time in their lives, and sexual arousal and orgasm occasionally accompany such dreams. This experience, *nocturnal orgasm,* seems to occur more often in males than in females. By the age of 40, about 80 percent of all males and 40 percent of all females have experienced orgasm during sleep (Kinsey et al., 1953).

Although evidence supports the statement that males have more nocturnal orgasms than females (Kinsey et al., 1953) and although the popular view is that this is so (note the well-known terms "wet dreams" and "nocturnal emission," which refer only to male nocturnal dreams), no one is absolutely certain. One of the problems is that people often do not wake up during a nocturnal orgasm and then sometimes do not remember the experience when they are conscious. For males, the presence of semen is a reminder. Females, however, usually have no "physical" evidence of orgasm. A woman will know if she has had a nocturnal orgasm if she remembers it, if she has been awakened by the experience, or if she notices some swelling and lubrication of her genitals when she wakes from an orgasmic dream. Uncertainty is quite common; for example, a woman might wake up after a particularly vivid sexual dream in which she imagined she was aroused, even though there were no physical signs of arousal. Had she had an orgasm or was her dream so vivid that she felt that she had experienced orgasm? There really is no answer.

Sexual arousal during sleep may not even be dependent upon having a sexual dream. Numerous studies on sleep patterns have shown that people dream approximately every 90 minutes during sleep. These periods are called *REM* (Rapid Eye Movement) sleep and are characterized by the movements of the eyeballs and other signs of physiological activity, including movement and rapid, irregular pulse and respiration.

Among males, partial or full erections accompany 80 to 90 percent of the REM periods (Dement, 1965; Fisher et al., 1965; Kleitman, 1953). Teenage males have erections for nearly 40 percent of their total sleeping time, but duration and hardness of erection decrease with advancing age (Karacan, et al. 1976). Since these periods are not necessarily associated with sexual dreams, researchers are still uncertain about the significance of erections during REM sleep. The fact that erections and REM sleep occur in infant males (Langfeldt, 1982) adds further doubt to the assumption that an erection during sleep means that a sexual dream is occurring.

Women have also been found to have changes in vaginal vasocongestion (Abel et al., 1979; Cohen & Shapiro, 1970; Shapiro et al., 1972) and clitoral vasocongestion (Koracan, Rosenbloom, & Williams, 1970) during REM sleep cycles. However, at this time there is not enough evidence to determine if this activity is associated with waking sexuality or with sexual dreams.

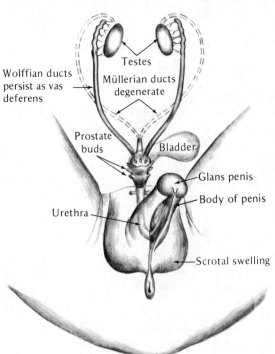

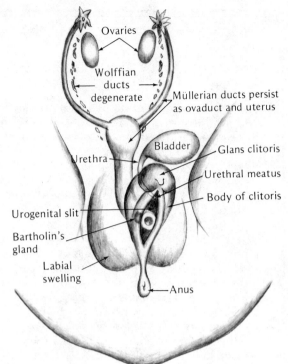

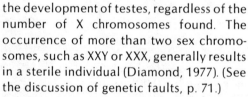

Figure 2-18(a). Embryonic differentiation of genital structures partially completed.

the development of testes, regardless of the number of X chromosomes found. The occurrence of more than two sex chromosomes, such as XXY or XXX, generally results in a sterile individual (Diamond, 1977). (See the discussion of genetic faults, p. 71.)

When the gonad develops into testicular tissue, an as yet unidentified hormone is produced that is sometimes called MIS, the *Mullerian-inhibiting substance*. This substance induces the Wolffian duct system to develop male structures and simultaneously inhibits the development of the Mullerian duct system, which eventually disappears. In females, the Mullerian duct system and the associated female structures develop because there is no MIS due to the absence of a Y chromosome. The Wolffian duct system is then inhibited.

Following the differentiation of the internal structures, the external genitals begin a similar process. Around the end of the third month of embryonic development, the ex-

ternal genitals begin to differentiate. The presence or absence of androgens, particularly testosterone, determines the development of the external genitals. If androgens are present, the *genital tubercle*, undifferentiated embryonic genital tissue, becomes longer and takes within it the *urethral groove* (see Figure 2-17). This structure now becomes the penis. The *labioscrotal swelling* enlarges to become the scrotum. In the absence of androgens, however, the urethral folds on either side of the urethral tube do not fuse but rather remain separated and become the labia minora; the labioscrotal swellings develop into the labia majora. Figure 2-18(a) shows this differentiation phase partially completed for both sexes. In Figure 2-18(b), the differentiation is complete. For female differentiation, estrogens are not necessary. In addition, the

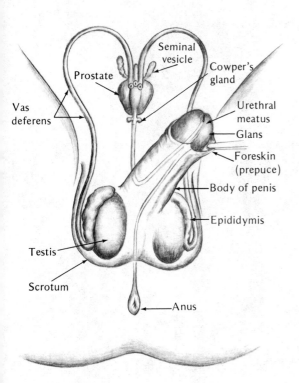

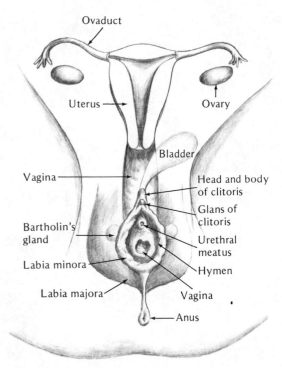

Figure 2-18(b). Embryonic differentiation of genital structures completed.

presence of androgens before or after the sixth to twelfth week of fetal development has little or no effect on the anatomical development of genital structures.

Researchers have suggested that the presence of androgens might affect the developing brain tissue in other ways (Beach, 1979; Hines, 1982; Imperato-McGinley, et al., 1981). For example, perhaps the presence or absence of androgens strongly influences the *behavior* of the individual throughout his or her life. The evidence for this position, however, is not as solid as that of anatomical differentiation being caused by hormones, and the implication that there are biologically based differences in behavior between the sexes is controversial.

From the differentiation period until birth, the genitals, both internal and external, continue to grow and to move toward their final location. This development is most obvious in the male when the testes descend from the abdominal cavity into the

scrotum during the seventh or eighth month of fetal development. In about 2 percent of all males, the testes fail to descend into the scrotum. This condition is called **cryptorchidism** and is associated with sterility and an increased risk of cancer in the undescended testis (Krabbe et al., 1979).

From birth to puberty, development resulting from the production of sex hormones continues. Males are slightly heavier and taller until puberty, when females catch up and momentarily pass them. The subtle changes that occur during the time before puberty are slow to develop. They include thickening skin and fat layers in girls and greater muscle development and sustained energy output in boys.

The next major developmental period that is affected by sex hormones is puberty. **Puberty** is the beginning of sexual maturity of males and females. What causes the on-

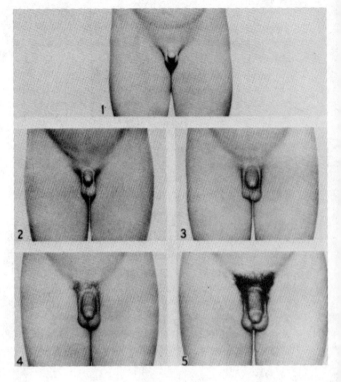

Figure 2-19. Changes in the external genitals of a pubescent male.

set of puberty is unclear. We do know that for some reason the hypothalamus becomes active and starts producing releasing factors (Guyton, 1976). At around 9 to 10 years of age boys experience an increase in androgen secretion, which is triggered by an increase in LH and FSH production. The additional LH and FSH result in the growth of the testicles as the seminiferous tubules increase in size.

The first physical evidence of puberty in males is the growth of the testicles. At this time the penis also begins to enlarge, and the first sign of pubic hair is noticed; both events are caused by increased production of testosterone. Figure 2-19 illustrates the changes in the external genitalia that occur as the pubescent male develops. In time the voice deepens, a growth spurt in both height and weight takes place, *spermatogenesis,* the production of sperm, begins, and the first ejaculation is commonly experienced. Of interest is Niesschlag's report

(1979) that deeper-voiced male singers have high levels of androgens throughout their life. Baldness, combined with a genetic trait for this condition, also results from high levels of androgens.

In females the onset of puberty occurs about two years earlier than it does for males. At around 11 years of age most females begin to show breast development, which is followed by the growth of pubic hair (see Figure 2-20). The areola begins to darken, and there is an increase in height and weight. Sometime during the second year of puberty, menstruation begins. For the next year or two the periods are irregular, and most cycles are *anovulatory,* which means that ovulation has not taken place. Breast development and pubic and underarm hair development are generally complete by age 14, and most young women have experienced **menarche** by age 15.

The hormones responsible for the pubertal changes in females are different from

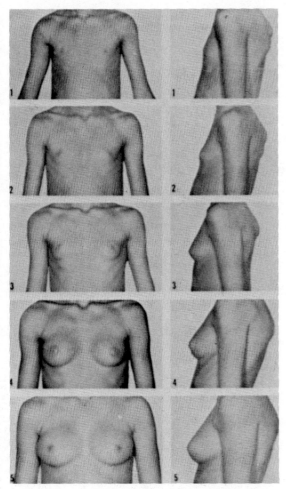

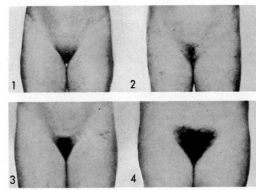

Figure 2-20. *Changes in the breast and genital hair distribution of the pubescent female.*

those for males. The adrenal glands produce androgens that are responsible for the enlargement of the clitoris and the development of pubic and underarm hair. Estrogen released from the ovaries is responsible for most of the remaining changes, such as increase in breast size and genital development. The presence of estrogen inhibits long bone growth, thereby lessening the period in which the height of females increases, as compared with males.

Figure 2-21 shows the average weight gain in successive years for developing males and females. This figure clearly illustrates the earlier pubertal development of

females. The spurt in weight gain begins around age 10 for females, but it is delayed about two years for males. Figure 2-22 shows how breast sensitivity to touch changes for the sexes following puberty. Males do not show a change, but females' breasts are more sensitive following puberty. Such data illustrate how hormones can prepare individuals for sexual activity without necessarily having a direct effect upon sexual behavior.

The final developmental period that we wish to note is the *climacteric,* or **menopause.** Between puberty and menopause, developmental changes are gradual. At menopause (usually between the ages of 45 and 55) the female reproduction function ceases. In males, until ages 17 to 20, androgen production is high. The testosterone level then lowers gradually but steadily over time, with little effect on adequate sperm production. Some researchers theorize that the problems experienced by men during their mid-40s are more likely to reflect psychological factors rather than physiological ones (Hafez, 1980a).

In women, the most obvious effect of the hormonal changes at menopause is the cessation of menstruation. At about age 50,

Average weight gain

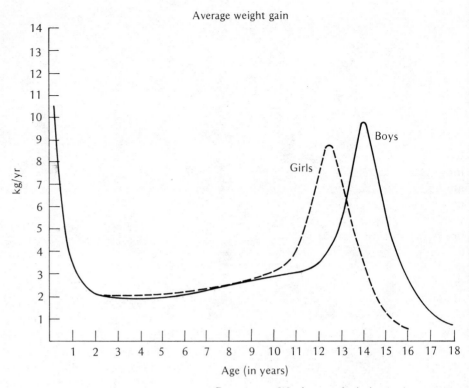

Figure 2-21. Weight gains for both sexes by age.

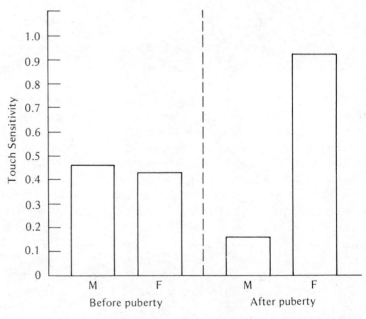

Figure 2-22. Breast sensitivity to touch before and after puberty for both sexes.

women begin having irregular periods, with more time between periods, and the amount of material that is discharged decreases. It usually takes from one to three years for menstrual periods to cease entirely. Vaginal dryness and "hot flushes" are common symptoms that accompany female menopause. The hormonal change that produces most of the effects is the loss of estrogen. Of interest to note is that females are now beginning puberty earlier than at the start of this century, and that the average age of menopause is being delayed (Witter & Jones-Witter, 1980). Low, relatively constant levels of estrogen accompany menopause. In women, LH and FSH levels increase dramatically when estrogen output decreases at menopause. These levels then gradually return to premenopause levels (Hafez, 1980).

Concurrent Effects of Hormones

Concurrent effects are relatively transitory in nature and disappear when the hormone is no longer present. The most obvious of these in humans is the female menstrual cycle. This periodic cycle consists of a series of hormone-induced changes that occur repeatedly during a woman's reproductive span.

☐ *The Menstrual Cycle* The first day of menstrual flow marks the first day in the menstrual cycle. The average cycle lasts twenty-eight days, with the first three to five days distinguished by menstrual flow. The cycle can be divided into three principal phases: (1) the **follicular,** or proliferation, stage, during which the follicle develops prior to ovulation and the wall of the uterus prepares to receive a fertilized ovum; (2) the **ovulatory** stage, named for the fact that the ovum is released from the ovary; and (3) the **luteal,** or secretory stage, during which the corpus luteum is present. Figure 2–23 shows the changes in hormones that produce the events in the menstrual cycle. At the beginning of the cycle there is a gradual buildup of estrogen. Throughout this early portion of the follicular stage, estrogen is maintained at a relatively constant but low level. This apparently is the result of negative feedback interaction with FSH and LH. Toward the end of the follicular phase, the estrogen level starts to increase and now reverses its actions and becomes a positive feedback mechanism (Keyes et al., 1980).

The cycle now enters the ovulatory phase, and at about the twelfth day of the cycle, the positive feedback loop triggers a rapid increase in the production of FSH, followed in 8 to 18 hours by a surge in LH production. These surges result in ovulation within 24 to 36 hours. At this point, the production of FSH and LH lowers, and the cycle enters the luteal phase. The place on the ovary that released the ovum changes its physical makeup and becomes the **corpus luteum.**

The corpus luteum, now acting as an endocrine gland, secretes high levels of estrogen and progesterone. The progesterone released by the corpus luteum prepares the lining of the uterus to receive a fertilized ovum. LH maintains the corpus luteum for

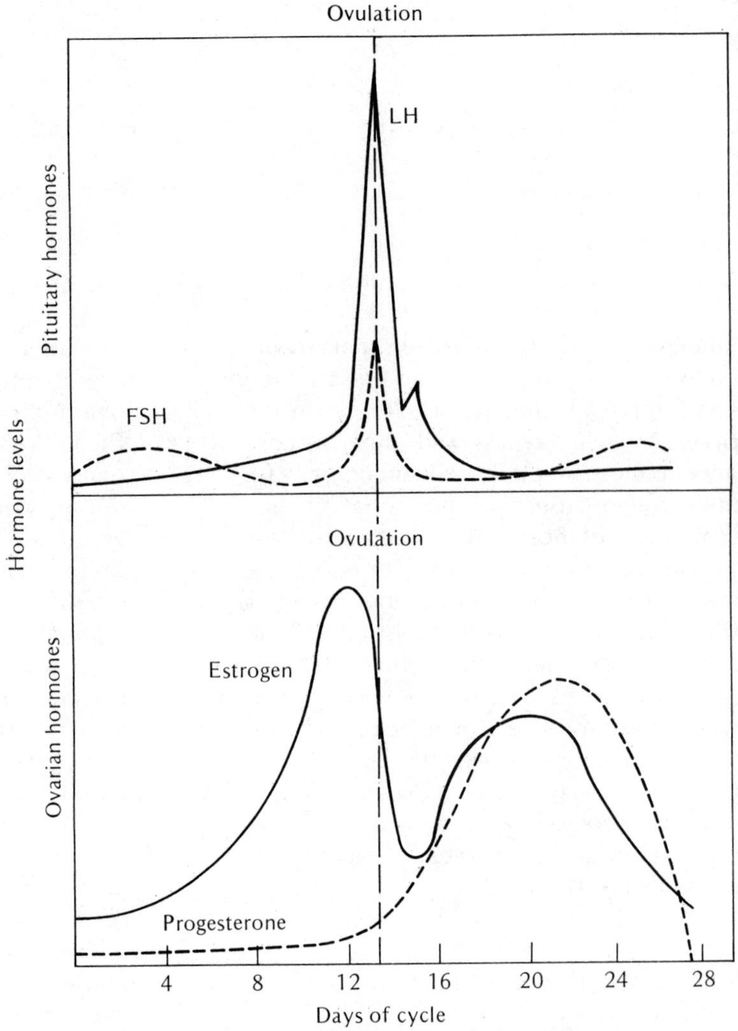

Figure 2-23. Change in hormone levels across the menstrual cycle.

a period of time (Hafez, 1980b; Keyes et al., 1980) and stimulates it to secrete its hormones (Guyton, 1976).

After several days the corpus luteum begins to degenerate and is replaced by scar tissue; the cause is unknown. As this scarring occurs, the corpus luteum produces less estrogen and progesterone, and, when progesterone levels become quite low, the blood vessels of the uterine lining constrict. The cells in the lining of the uterus die as a result of having their blood supply cut, and the uterine lining starts to slough off. The resulting fluid is discharged from the uterus through the vagina. Clotting is usually minimal because of the action of enzymes present in the uterus. Just before menstruation begins, the lowest levels of both gonadotrophins and sex hormones are experienced. Menstruation starts about two weeks after ovulation.

Shortly before menstruation begins, the levels of FSH and LH rise slightly and may trigger the rise in estrogen that occurs in the follicular phase of the next cycle. The cycle is repeated, except during pregnancy, throughout a woman's reproductive years. If no pregnancies intervene, a woman will

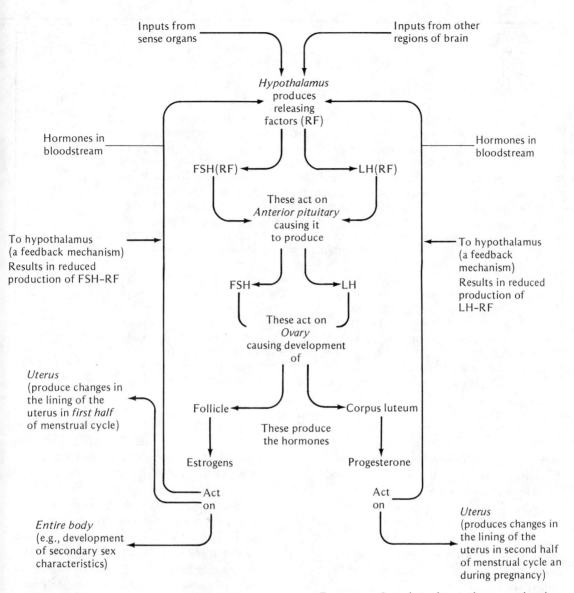

Inputs from
sense organs

Inputs from other
regions of brain

Hypothalamus
produces
releasing
factors (RF)

Hormones in
bloodstream

Hormones in
bloodstream

FSH(RF)

LH(RF)

These act on
Anterior pituitary
causing it
to produce

To hypothalamus
(a feedback mechanism)
Results in reduced
production of FSH–RF

To hypothalamus
(a feedback
mechanism)
Results in reduced
production of
LH–RF

FSH

LH

These act on
Ovary
causing development
of

Uterus
(produce changes in
the lining of the
uterus in *first half*
of menstrual cycle)

Follicle

Corpus luteum

These produce
the hormones

Estrogens

Progesterone

Act
on

Act
on

Entire body
(e.g., development
of secondary sex
characteristics)

Uterus
(produces changes in
the lining of the
uterus in second half
of menstrual cycle an
during pregnancy)

Figure 2-24. Interrelationships in the menstrual cycle.

ovulate about 400 times throughout her life. As is discussed in greater detail in the next chapter, the implantation of a fertilized ovum in the wall of the uterus releases a hormone that maintains the corpus luteum with its production of high levels of progesterone and estrogen. The high levels of these hormones block the deterioration of the uterine wall, and thus menstruation does not occur. Figure 2-24 illustrates the interrelationships in the menstrual cycle.

Effects of Hormones on Sexual Behavior

Researchers generally agree that sexual behavior in humans is relatively free from the influences of sex hormones. That is not to say that hormonal influences are nonexistent but rather that they are not as pronounced as in lower animals. Some hor-

THE DES SYNDROME

In the 1940s a report was issued that claimed that the synthetic estrogen DES was effective in reducing the threat of habitual or threatened spontaneous abortion. As a result, many pregnant women were given the drug. Estimates are that in the 1950s in the United States 4 to 7 percent of all pregnant women received DES (Page et al., 1981). The use of DES declined in the 1960s as its effectiveness in preventing spontaneous abortions was questioned. In the early 1970s researchers learned that female offspring of women who had been given DES during pregnancy showed changes in the cellular structure of the cervix and vagina. Further, a rare form of genital cancer appeared to occur more in these same offspring.

Since the original studies, considerable research has been directed at examining the effect of DES exposure on the developing embryo. Several findings have emerged. In addition to the clearly demonstrated cellular changes, women exposed to DES in the embryonic stage have higher rates of giving birth prematurely, higher rates of pregnancies that terminate with stillbirths, and in general more problems in their pregnancies. Problems common to males exposed to DES in the embryonic state include smaller testes, an increased number of malformations of the

monal effects have been identified that may or may not influence sexual behavior directly. For example, the female's sense of smell changes across the menstrual cycle (Vierling & Rock, 1967), and touch sensitivity of both the penis and the nipple is affected by levels of sex hormones (Beach, 1977). These responses most likely affect sexual behavior, but as yet there is no direct evidence.

Mood is widely recognized for its ability to fluctuate across the menstrual cycle. For example, some women experience increased psychological disturbances associated with the menstrual cycle, known as *premenstrual distress* (Dalton, 1964; Moos, 1969). Unfortunately, most researchers do not look for positive behavioral changes related to the menstrual cycle (Heimen, 1983). Many women report positive feelings concerning the menstrual cycle (Brooks,

Ruble, & Clark, 1977), and researchers should be careful not to be blinded by cultural attitudes and myths. Undoubtedly, some of the mood changes that occur in association with the menstrual cycle result from hormonal changes; the dramatic rise and fall of progesterone is one such change.

The question remains, Does sexual behavior rely upon hormonal activity? Generally speaking, the answer is "yes." Although the search for a hormone that underlies the "sex drive" has been largely unsuccessful, androgens appear to be necessary for normal sexual activity in males.

In both males and females the picture is incomplete. There is little evidence that short-term hormonal changes influence male sexuality. Rather, the evidence is that after castration (the removal of the testes), when testosterone production is eliminated, sexual activity slows gradually.

urethra, and a lower quality of semen (Robboy et al., 1978). All in all, DES exposure has resulted in a wide range of embryonic developmental problems that are quite serious.

There is no evidence that the DES-induced cell changes found in women lead to the development of cancer. However, some investigators believe that the cell changes coupled with exposure to cancer-producing agents may increase a woman's chances of developing cancer (Page et al., 1981). These women are urged to have yearly checkups to detect any problems early, when treatment is most likely to be effective (Robboy et al., 1978).

What is particularly frustrating about the DES problem is that it could have been avoided. In the early 1960s, experimental biologists had shown that exposure of embryos to estrogens resulted in developmental defects. Unfortunately, these findings were not widely publicized, and physicians used the synthetic estrogen DES, unaware of the problems that were being created. Care must be taken to see that such an incident does not happen again, but apparently that is easier said than done. For example, in 1978, physicians were prescribing progesterone to prolong pregnancy (Cunha, 1978), when, in fact, evidence was beginning to accumulate that, like estrogen, progesterone also may have an adverse effect on developing embryos. Extreme caution must be used when any medication is given to pregnant women. The DES story graphically illustrates the dangers involved.

More than ten years may pass before sexual activity ceases in men who are castrated (Leshner, 1978). Learning plays an important role: The sexually experienced male only gradually ceases sexual activity, while a male who is castrated before he has had sexual experiences will be apathetic about sex (Leshner, 1978). One group of researchers noted an example of a short-term hormonal effect in males (Reinberg et al., 1978). They found that testosterone levels increase during the summer and peak in September; this peak is accompanied by a surge in sexual activity. Additional evidence is needed, however, to establish that the relationship is one in which hormonal changes "cause" changes in sexual behavior.

In women, sex and pituitary hormonal levels change throughout the menstrual cycle. Udry and Morris (1968) reported that the highest rate of intercourse occurs at about the time of ovulation, with another increase occurring just before menstruation begins. Other researchers did not find a midcycle peak, but reported that sexual activity increased both pre- and post-menses (Money & Ehrhardt, 1972). The reasons underlying any change in sexual activity across the menstrual cycle are unclear. Any change could be caused by a female's sexual interest at any given time, or it could be that individual women are more sexually attractive at certain times, causing others to react differently toward them.

At least two other findings suggest that sex hormones affect human sexual behavior: Oral contraceptives, which contain estrogens and progestin, seem to affect sexual activity (Melges & Hamburg, 1977); and individuals with abnormal sex hormone production often have altered sex lives, frequently being uninterested in sex (Money, 1977). The reported effects in both cases, however, are not predictable, as the findings in one study often contradict the results of a similar one. These discrepancies raise the question of the relative importance of experience versus biological factors in human sexuality. If effects of the pill and abnormal hormone production are not predictable, then we can argue that learning and experience are as important as hormones in determining sexual behavior.

How Do Hormones Have These Effects?

Frank Beach (1977) has tried to reconcile the roles of learning and hormones in his explanation of the effects of hormones on sexual behavior. According to his theory, the brain is programmed to respond as a result of both genetic factors and the influence of prenatal hormones with males responding to male hormones, females responding to female hormones. Beach further suggests that, ". . . the basic mechanisms for both female-related and for male-related behavior are present in all normal individuals of each sex" (p. 261). This model suggests that androgens will activate male patterns in both sexes, but that in males the patterns are more intense; on the other hand, ovarian hormones will activate feminine activity in both sexes, but the activity will be more predominant in females. Most importantly,

however, the behaviors shown can occur only after exposure to various social learning experiences.

According to Beach's view, hormones act to release the sexual behavior, but learning determines which behavior is released. Thus, while we might need a certain hormonal level to engage in intercourse, we would not do so unless some degree of prior learning about intercourse had occurred. As Beach notes, the powerful influence of learning in the human obscures but does not eliminate the role of hormones in human sexual behavior. Beach suggests that social learning must occur before hormones can have a modifying influence, since the hormone by itself will not produce behavior.

Disorders of Hormonal Functioning

Abnormal hormonal functioning during the key developmental periods can lead to various disorders or problems. These disorders have been studied to learn the role of hormones in the development of sexual interests and **gender identity** — an individual's private sense of being male or female — and the cultural roles assigned to the sexes (Money & Ehrhardt, 1972). A person's gender identity may or may not be identical with his or her genetic sex. The difference between biological sex and one's concept of gender is made obvious in those instances where hormonal problems lead to errors in genital formation or ambiguity in determining the biological sex of a person.

☐ *Problems during Prenatal Development*
As the genitals start to develop during the
second and third month following conception, genetic faults can lead to malformations. One of the most common is *Klinefelter's syndrome* (XXY), which occurs once
in about every 500 male births. Born with an
extra X chromosome, Klinefelter victims often appear normal at birth. As development
proceeds, however, their genitals become
small and atrophied. In addition to being
sterile, they usually experience delayed
puberty and are often mentally retarded.
The male with Klinefelter's syndrome frequently complains of low sex interest.

About one out of 2,500 females is born
with *Turner's syndrome* (XO), which is
caused by one missing X chromosome. The
external genitals of a female with Turner's
syndrome are normal, but the ovaries do
not develop normally. Turner's syndrome
victims can receive hormones in order to
develop secondary sex characteristics, but
they will always remain sterile.

Genetic factors sometimes lead to faulty
hormone production. In the *congenital
adrenal hyperplasia syndrome* (CAH), the
developing female embryo's adrenal gland
produces high levels of androgens, which
affect the formation of the external genitals
making them more masculine. The genital
malformations associated with CAH range
from a mild enlargement of the clitoris to a
completely masculine appearance of the
external genitals. Some of these individuals
have been incorrectly, but understandably,
identified at birth as males. In a few rare instances the mother of a developing female
may produce high levels of androgens due
to an adrenal disorder, or she may have
been given androgens during the critical period of her unborn child's differentiation
period. The results of those conditions are
similar to those listed for CAH. Evidence
suggests that after two and a half to three
years, sex reassignment is impossible for
these misassigned children (Money & Ehrhardt, 1972). In other words, once a young
child has been raised to age 2½ to 3, he or
she will not accept a change in sex roles.

In the rare *androgen insensitivity syndrome,* a genetic male develops testes, but
he is insensitive or unresponsive to his own
androgen. As a result of this condition, the
male's external genitals look like female
genitals, although no uterus or ovaries are
present internally and there are internal testicles. Testosterone is produced, but a male
with this insensitivity does not react to it.
Surgery and hormonal treatment are prescribed for these genetic males, and they
are raised as females. The surgery removes
the internal masculine organs, and the administration of female hormones aids in developing feminine secondary sex characteristics at puberty.

☐ *Problems of Puberty*   During puberty,
genetic or hormonal problems can either
hasten development or delay it. Figure 2–25
is a photograph of a 5-year-old female with
precocious puberty, which is signaled by
unusually early sexual development. This
young girl's breasts are developing, and she
has the uterus and oviducts of a post-pu-
berty woman. Such a condition can be
caused by tumors or other diseases of the
pituitary and/or hypothalamus, which re-

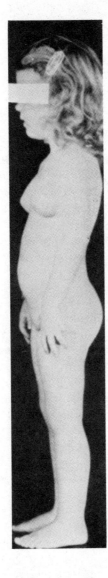

Figure 2-25. Precocious puberty in a five-year-old female.

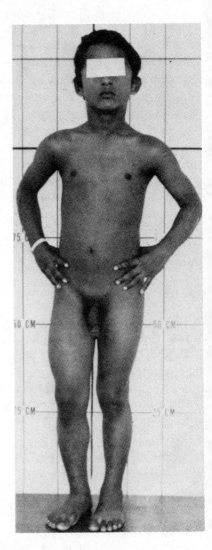

Figure 2-26. Precocious puberty in a four-and-a-half year-old male.

sult in high levels of gonadotrophins that force early production of sex hormones (Hafez, 1980b). Figure 2-26 shows a 4½-year-old boy with precocious puberty. He has both the muscle development and the genital development of a post-pubescent male. Precocious puberty in males also results from the early production of sex hormones due to pituitary disease. In both sexes the affected individuals are quite short because long bone growth stops very early.

Delayed puberty is defined by a lack of evidence of the onset of sexual maturity beyond 13 to 16 years of age. Causes for the delay of puberty are numerous. In females, the condition identified by a failure to menstruate by age 18 is called *primary amenorrhea*. Slight breast enlargement and scanty pubic and underarm hair growth are usually associated with primary amenorrhea. In

Box 2–4

PROBLEMS OF MENSTRUATION:
AMENORRHEA AND DYSMENORRHEA

Amenorrhea is the absence of menstrual flow. When the conditions of pregnancy, prepuberty, and menopause are excluded, the principal causes of amenorrhea are hormonal (Kistner, 1979). The reasons underlying disturbed endocrine functioning widely differ; they range from psychological factors, such as fear or anxiety, to nutritional problems, such as a sudden and severe weight loss. For example, women who suffer from anorexia nervosa, a behavior disorder characterized by symptoms such as obsessive concern about weight and an inability to eat, generally experience extreme weight loss, and often fail to menstruate because of it. Women who are long-distance runners often do not menstruate, although the reasons are unknown. The woman who stops menstruating and is not pregnant or menopausal should seek medical advice. For example, acute infections, anemia, tuberculosis, and disorders of the endocrine system can result in amenorrhea. In general, failure to menstruate is associated with a failure to ovulate and thus also is often associated with sterility.

Some women suffer from pain and cramps when they menstruate. Called *dysmenorrhea,* this condition may arise from a number of physical conditions. These include endometriosis (a disease in which the lining of the uterus grows inside the body cavity), pelvic inflammatory disease, and malformations of the uterus. However, in about 80 percent of all cases, there is no obvious physical reason for dysmenorrhea.

In cases with no observable physical cause, psychological disturbances such as anxiety are often assigned as the cause. However, the production of prostaglandins, a substance that induces uterine contractions, has proved to be the physiological basis of painful menstruation. Dysmenorrhea is now treated with drugs that reduce the output of prostaglandins or with mild pain relievers. Aspirin, which is a weak prostaglandin blocker, often is effective in relieving dysmenorrhea. Masters and Johnson (1966) reported that for some women the occurrence of orgasm was associated with the relief of dysmenorrhea. At least now, less and less is the illness viewed as "psychological," nor are the sufferers dismissed so often as chronic complainers.

males, delayed puberty is characterized by a lack of genital development and little evidence of secondary sex characteristics. In both males and females the lack of normal hormone production is the problem. The causes vary widely from problems in pituitary and hypothalamic functioning to some of the genetic syndromes noted previously. Hormone supplements are often administered to help manage these disorders.

SUMMARY

1. Human sex and reproductive organs can be divided into two groups: external and internal organs. **Secondary sex characteristics** form a category of their own. These characteristics, which develop during puberty, further distinguish males from females. Female breast development is an example of a secondary sex characteristic.

2. The external female genital area is called the **vulva.** The **mons pubis, labia majora, labia minora, clitoris, introitus** and **urethral meatus,** make up the vulva. The **perineum** and **anus** are located in close proximity. The clitoris is the structure that is most sensitive to sexual stimulation in females.

3. Female **breasts** develop during puberty. The breasts contain the **alveoli** or milk glands, fatty tissue, and the **nipple** is surrounded by darker tissue called the **areola.** Breasts vary greatly in size and shape. Their primary function is to supply nourishment to offspring, but they are also sexual organs that respond to stimulation. Male breasts sometimes show change during sexual arousal as well.

4. The internal reproductive organs are located within the lower female abdominal area. The internal organs are the **vagina,** the **uterus,** the **cervix,** the **Fallopian tubes,** and the **ovaries;** they are attached to the pelvis by muscles and ligaments. The **pubococcygeus muscle** surrounds the outer one-third of the vagina.

5. The **penis** and the **scrotum** are the external male organs. They are highly sensitive to sexual stimulation, with different parts on each structure being more sensitive than others.

6. A man's internal reproductive organs include the **testes, seminiferous tubules, epididymis, vas deferens, spermatic cord, seminal vesicle, ejaculatory duct, prostate gland, urethra,** and **Cowper's glands.** The journey of the sperm through the reproductive organs is quite complex.

7. Alfred Kinsey and his associates were the first to attempt to describe the human sexual response. The release of the Kinsey reports in the late

1940s and early 1950s met with much criticism, but his contributions to the study of sexuality cannot be overrated. Masters and Johnson began in the 1960s to produce their own research on sexual response in humans. They observed the response cycle in their subjects rather than questioning the individuals about it. This innovative approach changed the study of sexuality and gave more validity to the research.

8. The phases in the human sexual response cycle are the **excitement phase,** the **orgasm phase,** and the **resolution phase.** The two major physiological reactions during sexual arousal are **myotonia,** muscle tension, and **vasocongestion,** the pooling of blood in tissue.

9. Masters and Johnson were the first to conduct any type of in-depth research on sexuality and the aging. They reported that people of all ages respond sexually, and that people who have active sex lives when they are young are more likely to respond as they grow older.

10. Various instruments have been used to measure the physiological reaction of the genitals to sexual stimulation. Some attempts have been made to develop a means of measuring similar physiological events in both sexes in order to be able to compare responses.

11. The entire nervous system is involved in the response of humans to sexual stimulation. The nervous system can be divided into the **central nervous system** (CNS), which consists of the brain and the spinal cord, and the **peripheral nervous system** (PNS), which connects the CNS to the rest of the body. The output side of the PNS, in turn, divides into the **somatic** and **autonomic** branches. The autonomic branch has two subdivisions, the **sympathetic** and **parasympathetic** divisions.

12. A **hormone** is a chemical secreted or produced by an endocrine gland. Sex hormones, or **gonadal hormones,** are secreted by the ovaries or testes and act to produce changes in specific target tissues that are involved in reproduction and the development of secondary sex characteristics.

13. The female sex hormones are the **estrogens** and **progesterone.** The principal **androgens,** the male sex hormones, are **testosterone,** and also **aldosterone** and **androsterone.**

14. **LH** (luteinizing hormone) and **FSH** (follicle-stimulating hormone) are known as **gonadotrophins** because they affect the gonads (the ovaries and the testes). Their production by the pituitary is stimulated by **releasing factors** produced by the hypothalamus. **Corticotrophin,** also produced by the pituitary, stimulates the adrenal gland of both sexes to release weak androgens.

15. Hormones are involved in the differentiation stage that embryos go through when the undifferentiated gonadal tissue develops into either masculine or feminine structures.

16. In **puberty**, the period of sexual maturation for males and females, sex hormones once again become very active. The sexual and reproductive organs grow and the secondary sex characteristics develop. There is also a height and weight growth spurt. All of these changes are brought about by hormonal action. During **menopause** hormone production in women is lowered and ceases monthly fluctuations.

17. The menstrual cycle lasts an average of twenty-eight days. During the **follicular** stage the ova develops and the uterus becomes prepared to support a fertilized egg. The ovum is released during the **ovulatory** stage and the **corpus luteum** produces hormones during the **luteal** phase.

18. Abnormal hormone functioning can result in disorders associated with embryonic development. Both genetic males and females can be born with genitals that appear like those of the opposite sex. Hormone problems also can result in early or delayed puberty.

SUGGESTED READINGS

Brecher, R., and Brecher, E., *An Analysis of Human Sexual Response*. New York: New American Library, 1966. A clear description of the Masters and Johnson work on the sexual response written for the interested nonprofessional.

Guyton, A. C., *Textbook of Medical Physiology*, 6th Ed. Philadelphia: W. B. Saunders, 1981. A very large and imposing text with the highest standards of scholarship. Nevertheless written at a level surprisingly comprehensible to the interested beginning student in physiology.

Sex, Hormones, and Behavior: Ciba Foundation Symposium 62. New York: Excerpta Medica, 1979. An array of current research on biological aspects of sexuality. Often quite technical but a good sample of the varied problems that are approached from a biological perspective.

CHAPTER THREE

REPRODUCTION
Conception, Pregnancy, and Contraception

We are vulnerable because of our very intricacy and complexity. We are systems of mechanisms, subject to all the small disturbances, tiny monkey wrenches, that can, in the end, produce the wracking and unhinging of interminable chains of coordinated, meticulously tuned interaction.
Lewis Thomas, *The Medusa and the Snail*

Although one of the themes of this book is that sexual behavior is a complicated social pattern that can have both communicative and recreational value, sexual behavior also functions to ensure reproduction of the species: The mature sperm and egg meet, the egg is fertilized and implanted, and the human fetus starts to develop. Reproduction in itself is a complex process, and what precedes the meeting of sperm and egg (the journeys of each) is truly amazing.

The discussion does not end with conception, pregnancy, and childbirth, however, because very much related to these life processes is their regulation. As soon as humans began to understand how reproduction occurs, they set out to control it. We will review the devices used to avoid pregnancy—contraceptives—and the ways in which pregnancy is terminated—abortion.

As in all aspects of human sexuality, a description of biological events leads to social, emotional, and moral implications. It is no different here. In particular, the regulation of reproduction is at the center of considerable controversy. We will consider these aspects of reproduction as well. Personal choice on these issues can be most readily and appropriately made when the individual is aware of the issues and has the most up-to-date information on them.

In this chapter, we offer an extensive review of reproductive difficulties. This emphasis occurs because a good deal of research has been aimed at coping with the problems, and a knowledge of the problems can often result in their avoidance. The reader should not be misled or frightened by the material on reproductive problems. Most pregnancies are uneventful, most offspring healthy, and most contraceptive practices quite safe.

REPRODUCTION

Spermatogenesis: The Development of Sperm

Spermatogenesis, the process of sperm production, takes place in the seminiferous tubules of the testes. Two types of cells are present: the *spermatogenetic cells,* from which sperm arise, and *Sertoli cells,* which provide structure and support for the spermatogenetic cells. Sperm development takes between seventy and seventy-eight days, during which time the spermatogenetic cells go through a series of changes (Heller & Clermont, 1964). First, the spermatogenetic cell divides via *mitosis* into several copies of itself called *primary spermatocytes.* These copies then divide by *meiosis* to produce *secondary spermatocytes.* The spermatocytes are transformed through a second meiotic division into *spermatids,* which develop a head and a tail. (Meiosis is a two-stage cell division process by which the original forty-six chromosomes in the primary spermatocytes are reduced to twenty-three in the spermatids.) The spermatids then develop into mature sperm, which are freed into the seminiferous tubules. Figure 3–1 illustrates these changes.

A number of factors affect spermatogenesis and influence its course. Without the hormones FSH and LH, for example, sperm production ceases (see Chapter Two). However, the role of the hormone testosterone in spermatogenesis is unclear (Vilar, 1973). The male's age is another factor in spermatogenesis. In preadolescents sperm are not produced, and as males age spermatogenesis declines. Yet at age 60, 20 percent of all males still experience normal sperm development.

The fluid ejaculated by males is called **semen.** Semen is a complex substance made up of, in addition to sperm, products of the epididymis, seminal vesicles, and prostate, and of other structures as well. About 95 percent of the fluid ejaculated during orgasm is the transporting fluid, with 5 percent being sperm (Hafez, 1980). The transporting fluid carries many substances that are similar to those found in blood plasma, but it also has prostaglandins, enzymes, enzyme inhibitors, acid phosphatases, fruc-

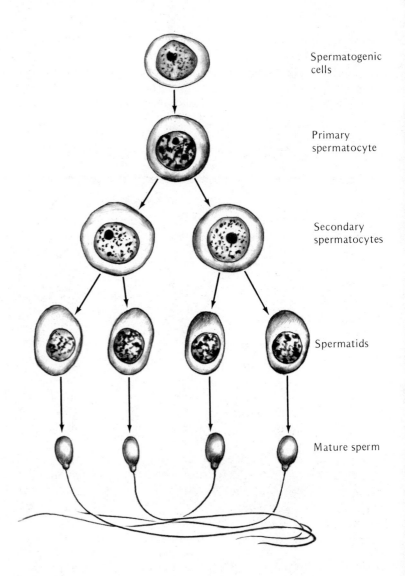

Figure 3-1. Formation of sperm.

Spermatogenic cells

Primary spermatocyte

Secondary spermatocytes

Spermatids

Mature sperm

tose, citric acid, spermine, and the hormones FSH, LH, and testosterone (Hafez, 1980). The roles of each of these substances, as well as others whose roles are not yet known, are still being examined.

In the typical ejaculation, the volume of semen averages 3 ml. and contains about 120 million sperm/ml. In addition to providing nutrients for the sperm, the carrying fluid also counters the acidic environment of the male urethra and the female vagina (Hafez, 1980). This latter function is crucial because sperm motility is reduced in such an environment.

Some remarkable discoveries have been made in the area of reproduction. One such discovery is that semen can be frozen, and some sperm can retain their viability for several years. Sperm can now be stored in *sperm banks,* where men have their sperm frozen and saved for later use. The freezing and storing of sperm may interest the male who is considering sterilization, or the female who wishes to become pregnant, but who is not in a committed relationship that offers her the opportunity. Researchers report that conceptions from frozen sperm result in lower rates of malformed offspring, but why this is so has not yet been determined (Page, Villee, & Villee, 1976). Perhaps only healthy sperm survive the freezing process.

The Repository for Germinal Choice, recently established by Dr. Robert Graham, is a different kind of sperm bank. It accepts sperm only from those men who are considered highly intelligent by the institution and who have a record of achievement in science. Two women, inseminated with sperm from this bank, have conceived and delivered children as of early 1983. The founder claims that many more women are waiting (Davis, 1982). The ethical considerations surrounding the criteria for "suitability," including who makes such decisions, raise many questions, especially concerning racism and elitism.

Oogenesis: The Development of Ova

In women the ovary is the site of development of the *ovum,* or egg. The process by which the ovum is formed is called **oogenesis.** The developing ova go through stages that are similar to those of the developing sperm. These developmental changes, which are under hormonal control, occur over the female life span. In the second month following conception, approximately 700,000 oogonia are in the female embryo. *Oogonia* are the cells from which the eggs are derived. These cells continue to divide mitotically until about five months after conception, when about 7 million oogonia are on hand. For the remainder of the female's life, these first-stage cells decline steadily. At birth a female's ovaries contain approximately 2,000,000 oocytes, and at age 7 there are about 300,000. The primary oocytes remain in a resting state unless ovulation is about to take place. About thirty-six to forty-eight hours prior to ovulation, a surge of the hormone LH is released from the pituitary gland; the release of LH signals the beginning of the first of two meiotic divisions for a number of oocytes (Edwards, 1980). During each menstrual cycle, three to thirty oocytes and their associated follicles begin this last stage of development, reducing to two just before ovulation. When the follicle ruptures, typically only one secondary oocyte, a mature egg, is released from the ovary. The released egg contains twenty-three unpaired chromosomes. Perhaps those oocytes that begin development but are not ovulated provide hormonal activity for the

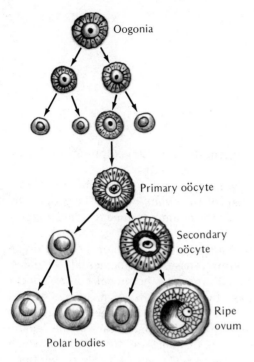

Oogonia

Primary oöcyte

Secondary oöcyte

Ripe ovum

Polar bodies

Figure 3-2. Formation of ovum.

completion of ovulation. In 99 percent of all ovulations, only one egg is released. Figure 3-2 illustrates the changes in the oogonia.

Sperm and Egg Transport: How Do They Get Together?

For conception to occur, sperm and egg must join together in the Fallopian tube, or oviduct. Sperm are deposited in the vagina, and they head toward the uterus; meanwhile, the egg journeys from the surface of the ovary. The transportation and union of the sperm and egg are involved procedures, primarily because they must travel in opposite directions. Most of the information gathered describing the paths of both sperm and egg comes from studies of animals. Possibly, variations will occur when these studies are applied to humans.

Usually a substantial gap separates the surface of the ovary where the egg is released and the entrance into the oviduct. Around the time of ovulation, however, muscular activity in the tissue supporting the ovary causes the ovary to move closer to the opening of the oviduct. When the egg is released, it is rapidly directed toward the opening by cilia on the fimbria of the oviduct. The process is more involved than it sounds, however, since women with only one functioning ovary and one functioning Fallopian tube, on opposite sides, have become pregnant. In fact, one woman in this situation became pregnant four times (Guyton, 1971). How the egg crosses from one side of the uterus to the other remains a mystery.

Once in the oviduct, the egg moves toward a narrow section of the duct called the *ampullary isthmic junction* by means of muscular contractions of the oviduct and further cilia activity. The muscular movement of the oviduct is under the control of the autonomic nervous system and, thus, potentially under the influence of emotions. The egg is in the oviduct about three to four days, spending most of that time at the ampullary isthmic junction. The oviduct, because of its own secretions, provides a supportive environment for the egg (Guyton, 1971). The egg remains at this junction due to the reduced size of the duct and because of a decrease in oviduct muscular activity at that point. If the egg fails to enter the oviduct, it simply floats free in the abdomen and rapidly degenerates. If fertilization does not occur, the egg continues through the oviduct and enters the uterus, where it either degenerates or is discharged through the vagina.

The transport of sperm through the female reproductive system is far more complex. Just one ejaculation releases 200 to 400 million sperm into the vagina, but only one is needed to fertilize the egg (Hafez, 1980). During the process of sperm transport, millions of sperm are eliminated. The female reproductive tract is not simply a receptacle for sperm; in fact, it plays a major role in selecting which sperm will fertilize the egg.

Semen undergoes several rapid changes after it is ejaculated into the vagina. Within one minute it coagulates; during the next several minutes it liquefies completely as a result of the action of enzymes contained in the semen. The sperm contained in the semen are not fully motile until the liquefication is complete. Since vaginal secretions will immobilize sperm in one to two hours after ejaculation, sperm must be transported to the uterus quickly if conception is to occur (Hafez, 1980).

The first barrier to sperm is a mucus plug in the cervix. Around the time of ovulation the plug develops openings that permit sperm to enter the uterus, leaving the transporting fluid behind. This plug appears to filter out dead and defective sperm, a clear example of the female's active role in sperm transport and selection (Hafez, 1980).

Once in the uterus, sperm confront other barriers and aids. First of all, the walls of the uterus contain many fissures and folds that seem to select against weak or defective sperm and also act as reservoirs for the re-maining sperm, keeping them alive for several days (Hafez, 1980). This latter feature helps explain why fertilization can occur several days following intercourse.

Sperm move themselves toward the oviduct by thrashing their tails, but estimates are that through tail movement alone sperm can travel only 1 to 5 mm. per minute (Guyton, 1971). The distance from the vagina to the point of fertilization in the oviduct averages 100 mm. (Gardner, Gray, & O'Rahilly, 1975). Under ideal circumstances, then, sperm could reach the oviduct in about twenty minutes if they had only themselves to depend on. However, sperm have been found in the oviduct within five minutes after being placed in the vagina (Settlage, Motoshima, and Tredway, 1975), and inactive and dead sperm have been found in the oviduct. Therefore, some feature of the female reproductive system obviously further aids in sperm transport. That feature is contractile movements of the vagina and uterus (Hafez, 1980).

Semen contains **prostaglandins,** chemicals which are known to stimulate uterine contractions. Perhaps the presence of semen in the reproductive system stimulates the uterus to contract (Hafez, 1980). Another theory suggests that because uterine contractions occur during orgasm, sperm transport might be indirectly supported by orgasmic response. This proposal, however, has been criticized (compare Fox, 1977, and Masters & Johnson, 1966).

The picture is not yet complete. Cilia in the uterus continue the filtering process and move sperm away from the oviduct.

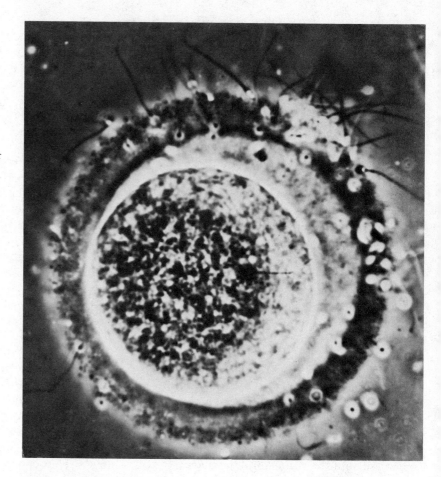

Figure 3-3. A photograph of the sperm penetrating the ova.

Also, leukocytes in the uterus attack and destroy sperm as they would any invading microorganism. Finally, some women develop antibodies in their reproductive tract that destroy sperm. Thus the female's reproductive system both facilitates sperm transport and helps select the sperm for fertilization.

The changes in the sperm, from their relative inactivity at the time of ejaculation to the point at which they become capable of fertilization, is called **capacitation.** Capacitation occurs because of characteristics of the sperm themselves and also because of specific agents in the female system (Hafez, 1980). Without this process, sperm would be unable to penetrate ova. The end result of successful sperm transport is a capacitated sperm present in the ampullary isthmic junction of the oviduct at the same time that an egg is present.

Fertilization and Implantation

The meeting in the oviduct of a viable, capacitated sperm and an egg is necessary before fertilization can take place. The exact details of the fertilization process are still unknown, but several interesting features are understood. First, penetration occurs through several layers surrounding the egg (see Figure 3–3).

As a result of penetration, the egg undergoes changes in its outer layers. These changes in the egg inhibit penetration of all sperm except the first (Guyton, 1971), ensuring that only one sperm fertilizes the egg. Twins result from either the penetration of two eggs by two sperm (*dizygotic twins*) or of one egg by one sperm, followed by a special type of cell division (*monozygotic twins*). The process of penetration takes about three hours to complete, and the period beginning with penetration and ending with the first cell *cleavage,* or division, lasts about twelve hours. When the sperm enters the egg, the two sets of unpaired chromosomes, twenty-three from the sperm and twenty-three from the ovum, align themselves to form a complete set of forty-six chromosomes. In this alignment, each parent supplies half of the genetic material needed to determine the characteristics of the individual. From this point on, cell division can take place.

The fertilized egg normally remains in the oviduct for three to four days, until it reaches the *blastocyst* stage of development. At this stage the initial cell has divided many times, and a hollow cavity has formed. In the prior stage the developing embryo is called a *morula,* which means a mass of cells without a cavity. The blastocyte is apparently large enough to stimulate wavelike movements in the oviduct; these movements send the blastocyte through the rest of the oviduct to the uterus, where it adheres to the midpoint of the uterine walls. Within a short period of time a series of changes occur, and the developing **conceptus** (a term used to describe the egg in all of its forms throughout the development of the offspring) becomes imbedded in the uterine wall by digesting the cells in the wall. For the first eight to twelve weeks these digested cells provide nutrients for the developing conceptus (Guyton, 1971). By this time the placenta has formed; it provides further nutrients necessary for the continuation of the pregnancy. During the first two months of pregnancy the developing offspring is referred to as the **embryo;** from the third month until delivery, it is called the **fetus.**

The **placenta** is the structure that is attached to the uterine wall. It is also attached to the **umbilical cord**—a cord that connects the placenta to the developing offspring. The placenta serves a number of functions: It supplies nourishment through the umbilical cord for the embryo, and later for the fetus; it transports oxygen from the mother's blood to the fetus; it removes the fetus's waste products; it acts as a barrier to infection; and it produces hormones (estrogens and progesterone) necessary for the maintenance of pregnancy.

Fertility and Infertility

The likelihood of pregnancy is very high when a couple engages in sexual intercourse without contraception. Estimates are that 25 percent conceive in the first month of unprotected intercourse, 60 percent within the first six months of unprotected intercourse, and 80 percent within a year. The ability to conceive and produce a child increases until age 25 for both sexes. After age 30, for women, there is a decline, which becomes rapid after age 40 (Page, Villee, & Villee, 1981). For males the decline is more gradual.

Some people have trouble conceiving: A reported 15 to 25 percent of all couples have fertility problems (Page et al., 1981; Witters & Jones-Witters, 1980). The cause of infertility can be identified in only about 50 percent of the cases, and an estimated 10 percent of all married couples remain completely sterile regardless of treatment. Among cases in which the cause can be identified, 60 percent involve problems related specifically to the woman, with the remainder related to male problems (Speroff, Glass, & Case, 1978). Currently, the correction of fertility is generally easier in women than in men, perhaps in part because more reproductive research has been done with women.

Although the subject has not been extensively researched, sexual behavior may be implicated in low fertility rates. For example, if the frequency of sexual intercourse is less than three times per week, the likelihood of pregnancy is reduced. Increased ejaculation, on the other hand, does not greatly affect fertility. Freund (1963) estimates that males would have to ejaculate at least two and one-half times a day for over ten days to reduce their fertility significantly. The chances of impregnation are apparently greatest when intercourse occurs about four times per week (Page et al., 1976).

Other features related to sexual behavior can influence the likelihood of conception.

The use of a substance for artificial lubrication, for example, may act as a spermicide. Douching, a method of cleansing the vagina, can also reduce fertility, although it is not a reliable means of contraception. And if a woman takes a position immediately following ejaculation that results in sperm being rapidly drained from the vagina, again the likelihood of conception is reduced. All of these factors are of relatively minor importance in reducing fertility, but they should be considered if conception is a problem.

☐ *Female Infertility*   For women, the major cause of infertility is failure to ovulate (Edwards, 1980). In general, women fail to ovulate because of insufficient production of gonadotrophins. The occurrence of ovulation is detectable by either hormonal analysis or by the careful charting of the woman's temperature over the period of the menstrual cycle. A woman who does not ovulate may be given the drug Clomiphene citrate for the purpose of stimulating the pituitary to produce gonadotrophins. Approximately 70 percent of nonovulating women reportedly do ovulate after being treated with this drug, with successful pregnancies occurring in about 40 percent of those treated (Kistner, 1968). Gonadotrophins can be administered directly, but, at the present time, the procedure is expensive.

One of the problems with stimulating ovulation by direct LH administration is that the procedure generally results in "super" ovulation—that is, a woman so treated will often produce multiple ova and, as a result, multiple births are relatively common. Progesterone levels must be monitored during this treatment because, as you will recall, progesterone stimulates development of the uterine wall so that a fertilized egg can implant and begin development.

The second most common cause of sterility in women is obstruction of the Fallopian tubes. There is a 70 to 90 percent success rate for removing the blocks in the Fallopian tubes that are imposed by microsurgery for sterilization purposes (Hatcher, et al., 1980). If, however, a blockage is the result of infection, caused by gonorrhea, for example, the likelihood of successful surgery is greatly reduced.

Another cause of infertility in women is the failure of the mucus plug in the cervix to change its physical makeup around the time of ovulation. The estrogen levels just prior to ovulation result in the structural change of the cervical mucus that facilitates sperm transport (Hafez, 1980). In some women this change does not occur, even though the appropriate estrogen levels are present. A common cause of this problem is cervical infection, and treatment for this infection often eliminates infertility (Edwards, 1980).

Some women produce antibodies that destroy sperm. The reported rate of this phenomenon has varied from 5 percent to 35 percent of infertile women across different studies (Haas, Cines, & Schreiber, 1980; Menge & Behrman, 1980). Treatment of this condition is rather simple. The male is advised to use condoms for a period of time so that sperm are not deposited in the vagina and new antibodies are not formed. In one study, twenty-five out of twenty-nine women showed reduced antibody formation as the result of this procedure, and subsequently, 20 percent became pregnant (Franklin & Dukes, 1964). A somewhat lower success rate was reported by Behrman (1968).

☐ *Male Infertility* One extensive study on male fertility problems reviewed 1,294 cases (Amelar & Dubin, 1973). The conditions noted in this study reduce fertility by lowering the sperm count. The most common problem, affecting 39 percent of the men studied, is **varicocele**. This condition is characterized by an enlarged vein in the spermatic cord that blocks sperm transport from the testes to the rest of the ejaculatory system. Varicocele can be surgically corrected; the procedure is successful about 75 percent of the time. The second most common problem reported by these researchers is **testicular failure** (14 percent). Testicular failure means that the testes do not produce sperm. A number of possible causes are responsible for this problem. For example, sperm production may be lowered because of an infection in the testes, as a result of radiation treatment of testicular tumors, or because of a poorly functioning endocrine system.

Another condition resulting in low sperm count is the obstruction of the ejaculatory duct system. The blocking of the epididymis often is caused by scarring resulting from gonorrhea or tuberculosis. The scars prevent the transport of sperm from the testes to the ejaculatory duct system, resulting in infertility in 7 percent of the cases reported in the Amelar and Dubin study.

Low semen volume, defined as ejaculate being less than 1 cc., is the third-ranking cause of male sterility and was reported in 12 percent of the cases in the Amelar and Dubin study. This condition has been treated with some success by administering gonadotrophins. Since the greatest concentration of sperm occurs in the first portion of the ejaculate, the ejaculate can be collected on several occasions and the first portion of it extracted. Thus sperm concentration is increased in a sample that can be used for artificial insemination.

The Amelar and Dubin study also identified endocrine imbalance as the cause of infertility in almost 9 percent of the cases. In some instances, hormonal treatment has been successful in treating the problem. However, failure rates in treating cases involving endocrine imbalance are still quite high.

Erectile difficulty and cryptorchidism were responsible for a small percentage of the infertility problems experienced in the Amelar and Dubin study. Five percent attributed their infertility disorder to sexual problems, or erectile difficulty. Problems with erection may be the result of psychological and/or organic dysfunctions, which we will further explore in Chapter Eight. **Cryptorchidism,** as mentioned in Chapter Two, is the condition in which the testes have not descended from the abdominal cavity into the scrotum. If the testes remain outside the scrotum and inside the abdominal wall, the male is sterile because the higher body temperature prevents sperm production. However, secretion of testosterone is not prevented; therefore, the individual will show all of the appropriate secondary sex characteristics that result from testosterone production. Treatment of an undescended testicle should be started at around age 2, beginning with the administration of hormones. If that treatment does not work, surgery is recommended (Fonkalsrud & Mengel, 1981).

Although not included in the Amelar and Dubin research, evidence does exist that males may experience infertility due to an immunity factor. That is, some males produce antibodies against their own sperm (Menge & Behrman, 1980). Estimates are that in 4 percent of infertile couples, the males produce antibodies that destroy their own sperm (Fjallbrant, 1968). This condition can be treated in several ways. First, hormonal treatment may be used that suppresses the manufacture of sperm for a period of time and allows the antibodies to disappear. When sperm production is reinstituted, the individual may be fertile. Attempts have also been made to reduce the male's own immune response by administering corticosteroids, which suppress antibody formation long enough for viable sperm to be ejaculated and for pregnancy to occur.

Interestingly, among men who have had vasectomies, 50 to 70 percent have developed sperm antibodies (Menge & Behrman, 1980). This finding has implications for the male who wishes to have surgery to repair the vasectomy. Many vasectomized males will now be sterile because of the immune response, even though surgical repair of the vasectomy is possible. As yet, the effects of long-term formation of antibodies resulting from absorption of sperm in the testes are unknown (Menge & Behrman, 1980).

Although many of the specific infertility causes are physically based and medically treated, no one knows the extent of psychological influences. Further research is needed in this area.

☐ *Artificial Insemination* **Artificial insemination** is the process of placing sperm in the vagina or uterus through means other than sexual intercourse. Artificial insemination is categorized in two ways. In one category, the male partner is sterile, and the sperm from a donor is used. In the second instance, when the male's sperm density is too low, techniques are used to increase sperm concentration and to assure its placement at the optimal time. Estimates are that in the United States at least 250,000 pregnancies have resulted from artificial insemination, and in most cases the husband's sperm was used for insemination (Witters & Jones-Witters, 1980). Legal issues, however, still surround the use of donor's sperm. For example, in some states children conceived from a donor's sperm are ruled illegitimate (Davis, 1982).

Recently some women have consented to become surrogate mothers. A **surrogate mother** will receive, by means of artificial insemination, the sperm of a male whose spouse is infertile. The surrogate will carry and deliver the child, who is then given to the childless couple. This option is for couples who are unable to produce children together, but there are certain considerations. For one thing, giving up her child when the time comes to do so can be difficult for a woman. Also, laws vary from state to state concerning the legal status of the offspring carried by a surrogate mother. All the legal requirements should be investigated before becoming involved in such a procedure.

Pregnancy

The length of pregnancy averages 267 days from conception. Naegele's rule for calculating the most probable delivery date is to count back three months from the final day of the last menstrual period, and then to add seven days to that date. For example, if a pregnant woman's last menstrual period ended on September 27, you would count back three months to June 27, and then add seven days. Thus, July 4 would be the most likely date of delivery. The pregnancy period is divided into *trimesters:* months 1 to 3 are the first trimester; 4 to 6 are the second trimester; and months 7 to 9 make up the third trimester.

For most women the first sign of pregnancy is a missed menstrual period. Physicians group the signs of pregnancy into three categories: presumptive, probable, and positive (Page, Villee, & Villee, 1980). Table 3-1 lists the signs of pregnancy according to these categories; you will see that the probable and positive signs can be

TABLE 3-1   THE SIGNS OF PREGNANCY

PRESUMPTIVE

Missed menstrual period.
Morning sickness, which can occur at times other than in the morning.
Frequent need to urinate.
Breast soreness.
(If lack of menses plus two other presumptive signs occur, the odds are two to one that a woman is pregnant.)

PROBABLE

An increase in the size of the uterus.
A softening of the uterus.
A change in the color of the cervix and upper vagina from pink to a dark-bluish tint.
A positive test for the presence of human chorionic hormone.
A change in the shape of the uterus.
(Each of these signs accurately predicts pregnancy 80 to 95 percent of the time.)

POSITIVE

The detection of a fetal heart beat.
The objective detection of fetal movements; if reported by a woman who has never previously been pregnant, a medical professional should verify because movement of the bowel and/or gas can be mistaken for fetal activity.
X-ray or ultrasonic detection of the fetus.

(From Page, Villee, and Villee, 1976.)

detected only by a medical examination and tests.

Throughout pregnancy, the developing offspring grows tremendously, as illustrated in Figure 3-4. The rate of growth is much more rapid in the early stages; in fact, during the first month of pregnancy the weight of the embryo increases one million times (Page et al., 1981). By the end of the embryonic period, all primary systems have begun to develop. Table 3-2 presents average fetal growth for weeks 9 to 40, showing

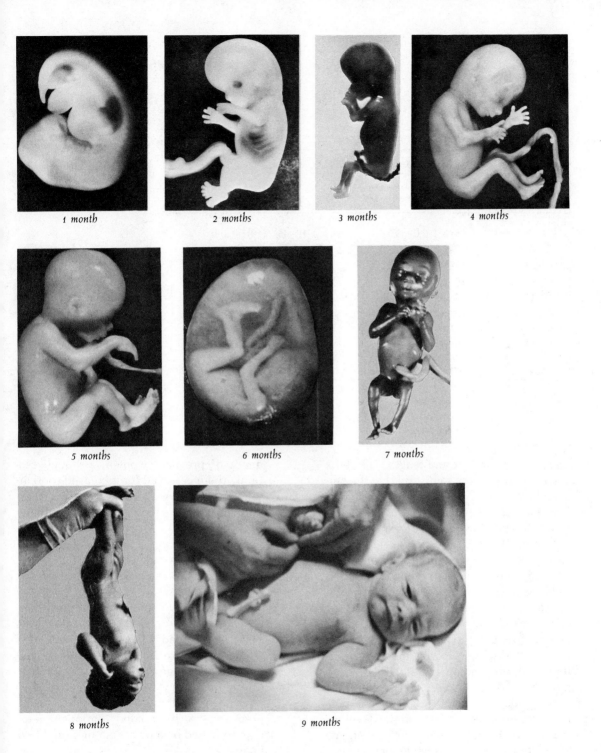

1 month

2 months

3 months

4 months

5 months

6 months

7 months

8 months

9 months

Figure 3-4. The appearance of the embryo or fetus at various times following conception.

TABLE 3-2 TYPICAL FETAL GROWTH IN LENGTH AND WEIGHT		
AGE (WEEKS)	CROWN-RUMP LENGTH CENTIMETERS (IN.)	WEIGHT GRAMS (LBS.)
9–12	5–8 (2.0– 3.1)	10–45 (.03– .09)
13–16	9–14(3.5– 5.5)	60–200 (.12– .43)
17–20	15–19(5.9– 7.5)	250–450 (.56–1.0)
21–24	20–23(7.9– 9.1)	500–820 (1.06–1.81)
25–28	24–27(9.4–10.6)	900–1300(2.0 –2.75)
29–32	28–30(11.0–11.8)	1400–2100(3.06–4.63)
33–36	31–34(12.2–13.4)	2200–2900(4.88–6.38)
37–40	35–36(13.8–14.2)	3000–3400(6.63–7.50)

(From J. Langman, 1973.)

gains in both weight and length. The fetus does not grow at the same rate that the embryo does.

A number of factors are associated with reduced fetal growth, including (1) multiple births, which result in lower weight per offspring; (2) smoking during pregnancy; (3) malnourishment during pregnancy; and (4) reduced oxygen intake, which can be caused by living at high altitudes or by some heart disorders (Page et al., 1981). Low-birthweight offspring run a much greater risk of developing medical problems both pre- and postnatally (Ciba Foundation, 1974).

A well-balanced diet is of utmost importance for both the mother and the developing fetus (e.g., Aladjem, 1975; Wiggins, 1979). Considerable disagreement continues, however, over the exact nutritional needs of pregnant women, although certainly there is a need for increased food intake (Kaminetzky and Baker, 1980). We do know that while a woman is breast-feeding, the requirements for many nutrients are greater than during pregnancy. At the present time, prescribing vitamin supplements for pregnant women is a routine matter for many physicians.

Optimal weight gain during pregnancy is a controversial topic. The average amount of weight gained is 23 pounds, but anywhere from 13 to 35 pounds is still considered normal (Page et al., 1981). Weight loss during pregnancy is also a matter of concern. In general, many of the problems of pregnancy can be avoided by good prenatal care provided by a physician or a qualified health adviser.

For pregnant women to experience

Children are often fascinated by pregnancy.

changes in how they feel is normal. For example, common and natural conditions are the frequent urge to urinate and increased respiration rate and depth. Some women experience breast secretions and, of course, as the fetus becomes larger many women have problems finding comfortable positions for sitting and sleeping. As a general rule, physicians expect that vague complaints like sleeplessness, fatigue, and minor headaches will disappear by mid-pregnancy (Nesbitt, 1980). Any severe or continuing problem should be medically evaluated.

☐ *Intercourse during Pregnancy and the Postpartum Period*   Whether or not to continue sexual intercourse during pregnancy is a question that concerns most sexually active couples. Taboos against sexual activity during pregnancy have been quite common across cultures. Ford and Beach (1951) found that in about one-third of the preliterate societies they studied, intercourse was not allowed during most, if not all, of pregnancy. Concerning our own society, the suggestion has been made that, "It may well be that the feeling of inappropriateness of intercourse late in pregnancy was fostered in

Box 3–1

TEST-TUBE BABIES

On July 25, 1978, Mrs. Lesley Brown gave birth to a baby girl, the famous English test-tube baby who was the product of the first documented case of in vitro fertilization. Drs. Robert Edwards and Patrick Steptoe were the research physicians involved in this historical event. Mrs. Brown was first given hormones, which caused her ovaries to produce many ova. The eggs were collected and placed in a culture plate, where they were mixed with the husband's sperm. One of the eggs became fertilized and was kept in the culture for two days, until it reached the blastocyst stage. At this point it was transferred to Mrs. Brown's uterus, which had been hormonally prepared for implantation. The blastocyst attached itself to the walls of the uterus, and a normal pregnancy and delivery ensued. Since that time, successful in vitro fertilizations resulting in live births have been recorded in Australia, England, India, and the United States.

In vitro fertilization is being tried with women who are infertile because their oviducts are unable, for various reasons, to transport ova and unable to serve as the site for fertilization. The procedure is successful for about 6 percent of those women who receive fertilized ova (Edwards, Steptoe, & Purdy, 1980). However, success rates are steadily climbing. Thus, while the technique offers hope to some childless couples, as yet only a very few can actually have a child in this manner.

A number of interesting ethical and legal issues are raised by this procedure. For example, if a defective child is born, should the physician be liable? Even more complex problems arise when we but briefly note the various options that are now possible. For example, while there are no

medical teachings, not so much from the desire to diminish maternal infection, but as an expression of a societal taboo" (Butler & Wagner, 1975 p. 135).

The data that are available all point to a general decrease in intercourse as preg-

nancy progresses. This decrease continues throughout pregnancy, but it becomes most pronounced during the third trimester (Morris, 1975; Tolor & DiGrazia, 1976; Masters & Johnson, 1966; Kinny, 1973; Solberg, Butler, & Wagner, 1973). In one study of 216

Louise Brown, the first test-tube baby.

reported cases, an ovum could be taken from one woman and implanted in another. Who then is the legal mother? The issues are similar to those raised by the use of a donor's sperm in artificial insemination. Legal, legislative, medical, and religious bodies have begun to discuss these issues, and it is important that they be resolved because of rapid advances in the bio-technological field.

women, the median frequency per week of intercourse was reported to be 2.25 during the first trimester, 2.39 during the second, and 1.08 during the third (Tolor & DiGrazia, 1976). Women offer a variety of reasons for the changes in intercourse frequency dur- ing pregnancy. Solberg, Butler, and Wagner (1973) report that the most common reason given is physical discomfort, followed by fear of injuring the baby, loss of interest, awkwardness of intercourse, physician's recommendation, reasons unrelated to pregnancy, feelings of unattractiveness, and the suggestion of someone other than a physician. LaRossa (1979) disagrees with these findings and instead suggests that excuses such as the "woman feels less attractive" are more frequent than justifications based on physiological and anatomic factors. Regardless of the explanations given, clearly intercourse frequency declines as pregnancy proceeds.

Is this decline justified on the basis of increased risk to the mother or the fetus? The general medical consensus is that if there are no complications in the pregnancy, intercourse does not have to be restricted (Anderson, Clancy, & Quirk, 1978). A controversy, however, does surround the possibility that intercourse and orgasm may trigger premature labor. Some researchers report no complications resulting from intercourse and orgasm (Pugh & Fernendez, 1963; Butler & Wagner, 1975), whereas others express concern that orgasm, because of the uterine contractions it causes, may trigger premature labor (Goodlin, 1969; Javert, 1957). A recent report suggests that intercourse during pregnancy increases the risk that the fetus will develop amniotic fluid infections (Naeye, 1979). According to this study, the risk is greater early in pregnancy and represents an increase in infection of around 40 cases per 1,000 births. Fetal mortality increases from about 2 percent to 11 percent in those fetuses that were infected. As Naeye points out, however, these data were collected in the early 1960s when prenatal death rates were higher in general; today the risk may be lower.

Most medical authorities do not believe that the risk from intercourse during pregnancy is sufficiently great to warrant recommending that healthy pregnant women abstain. There is, however, one serious caution concerning sex during pregnancy. Aronson (1969) has documented a number of cases of maternal deaths where, during cunnilingus, air was forced into the pregnant woman's vagina. Evidence shows that this practice permits the air to enter the woman's bloodstream, forming an air embolism that could result in her death.

Several other considerations are relevant to the discussion of intercourse during pregnancy. As the fetus grows, the woman may be more comfortable with intercourse either in the side-by-side or rear-entry position. The suggestion has been made that noncoital sexual activity can be safely enjoyed in instances in which coitus is not desirable (Butler & Wagner, 1975). Tolor and DiGrazia (1976) report that the desire for physical contact, independent of intercourse, remains high throughout pregnancy.

Following birth, intercourse can be safely resumed as soon as any minor tearing around the vaginal opening or the **episiotomy** (minor surgery to facilitate delivery) has healed, generally within seven days. Even though physicians often recommend longer delays, there is no medical reason to abstain for more than a week, particularly if care is taken not to strain the site of the episiotomy (Anderson et al., 1978). For most women sexual interest returns about four weeks after delivery (Kinny, 1973), frequently before the woman feels that intercourse can safely be resumed (Tolor & Di-Grazia, 1976). Ford and Beach (1951) note that in some American Indian and African tribes the postpartum taboo against intercourse lasts until breast-feeding ceases, in some cases as long as three years.

☐ *Labor and Delivery* The natural end of pregnancy is the birth of the child. Although Caesarean sections have been performed a great deal in the past decade, most births still occur vaginally (Page et al., 1976). (For more information on Caesarean births see Box 3–2.)

The onset of labor may be accompanied by any of several physical changes. In about 15 percent of pregnant women, the placental membranes rupture and there is a loss of amniotic fluid before contractions begin (Page et al., 1981); the mucus plug in the cervix may be expelled before labor commences; and the pregnant woman experiences nonpainful contractions, which are best described as pressure sensations, at widely spaced intervals. The reason that labor starts is not well understood. It seems to commence after stimulation from steroids that are produced by the fetus and from the stretching of the uterus. Probably because they stretch the uterus, twins are born, on the average, nineteen days before their full-term due date (Guyton, 1971). Whatever the initiating events may be, labor progresses through three stages (see Figure 3–5 on p. 98). The stages can be described as follows:

■ *First stage:* Begins with dilation of the cervix and the concurrent development of

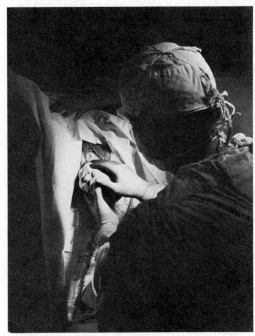

A child's head appears just before birth.

regular contractions of the uterus, which are about ten minutes apart. The first stage ends when the cervix is fully dilated. In an uncomplicated labor, this stage lasts from three to twelve hours for the first birth, and from two to seven hours for the woman who has had previous children.

■ *Second stage:* Begins when the cervix is fully dilated (about 10 cm.) and ends when the child is delivered. This stage lasts about fifty minutes for first births and about twenty minutes for subsequent births.

■ *Third stage:* Begins when the child is born and ends with the delivery of the placenta. Normally the final stage lasts about ten minutes. The uterus vigorously constricts, which acts to stop bleeding (Page et al., 1981).

In 95 percent of all nonsurgical births, the delivery of the child follows a regular

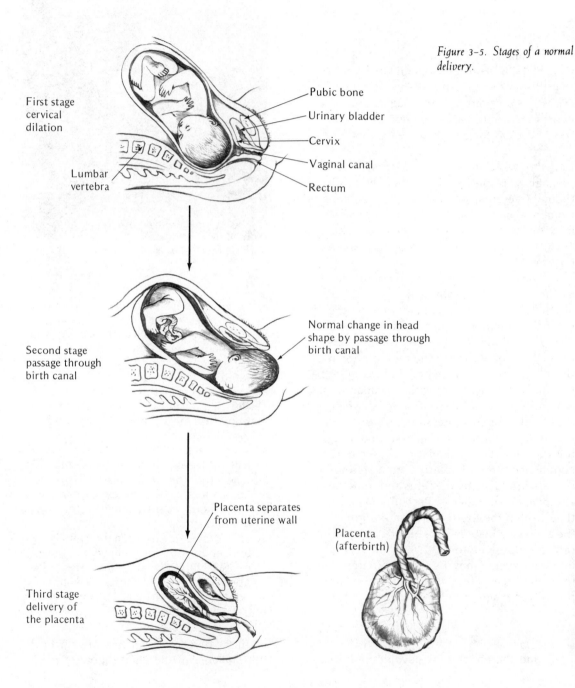

Figure 3-5. *Stages of a normal delivery.*

First stage cervical dilation

Pubic bone

Urinary bladder

Cervix

Vaginal canal

Rectum

Lumbar vertebra

Second stage passage through birth canal

Normal change in head shape by passage through birth canal

Placenta separates from uterine wall

Placenta (afterbirth)

Third stage delivery of the placenta

pattern. The child's head goes through several positional changes to maneuver successfully through the bony structures of the pelvis while moving from the uterus, through the vagina, and to the outside. Forceps are used in about one-third of all deliveries to help guide the fetus through the birth canal (Page et al., 1981).

In about 4 percent of all deliveries, the child occupies a position other than the head-down which is called the **vertex presentation** position (Page et al., 1981). The abnormal positioning of the fetus is called a **breech presentation.** Depending on a number of factors, including the particular variety of breech presentation, the incidence of both premature births and infant mortality increases with breech presentations. The Caesarean method of delivery may be used if the fetus is in a breech position. Following the birth of the child, the uterus undergoes many changes before returning to the non-pregnant state within approximately six weeks.

□ *Controversies in Delivery Practices* A number of controversies surround the conditions and practices that accompany the birth process. One issue is where labor and delivery should take place. On the one hand, the medical profession believes that a hospital is the best location because of the sterile conditions and the availability of specialized facilities in case of an unexpected emergency. On the other hand, advocates of home births or deliveries in alternative birth centers argue that in hospitals the mother's feelings tend to be ignored, that drugs and anesthetics are

more widely used, and that risks may be taken just because special facilities are available (Stewart & Stewart, 1976). Very little objective evidence is available to support these arguments. Clearly, costs are lower outside the hospital setting, but whether or not the birthing alternatives cause increased or decreased risks is still unknown.

Controversy also surrounds the use of specialized childbirth techniques such as natural childbirth and the **Lamaze method.** These alternative delivery practices are generally acknowledged to result in lowered levels of subjective distress on the part of the mother. When these techniques are practiced, the tendency is to avoid the use of drugs, and the rate of spontaneous delivery is higher (Friedman, 1978). However, no well-controlled studies have been done to explore the reasons for these findings. Since mothers in these programs are self-selected, older, and more educated, such factors may be responsible for the positive findings. There is currently no evidence to support claims that time spent in labor is cut short when one of the alternative birth procedures is used (Friedman, 1978).

Medical practices that are followed in delivery have been reevaluated in recent years. Since drugs and anesthetics are known to affect the neonate adversely, the widespread use of medications is often criticized (Page et al., 1981). In Box 3-2 we noted that many physicians are concerned about the increased use of the Caesarean section because of its obvious risks. Other controversies involve the routine use of minor surgery (e.g., episiotomy) to ease deliv-

Box 3–2

THE CAESAREAN BIRTH

The *Caesarean section* is the surgical method of childbirth in which an incision is made in the walls of the abdomen and uterus. The first Caesarean section performed on a living woman occurred about 1500 A.D.

Evidence points toward a dramatic increase in the number of Caesarean births: In 1970 the percentage of all births delivered in this way was 5.5 percent; in 1978 this figure jumped to 15.8 percent. Physicians are debating the justification for this increase and have not yet resolved the many issues that surround the controversy (Ledger, 1980).

The following conditions are noted as being responsible for the decision to perform a Caesarean section (Amirikia, Zarewych, & Evans, 1981).

1. Dystocia (difficult labor).
2. Fetal distress (the fetus is in jeopardy, often due to insufficient oxygen supply).
3. Breech presentation.
4. Placenta ruptures without delivery within a short time.
5. Blood pressure disease in the mother.
6. Placenta previa (the placenta develops in the zone of dilation in the uterus, signaled by painless bleeding).
7. Abrupto placenta (premature separation of the placenta from the uterus, typically accompanied by bleeding and shock in the mother).
8. Malpresentation of the fetus (other than breech).
9. Diabetes in the mother.

The Caesarean section can be quite stressful for the mother, particularly when it is unplanned. The woman may not be able to have the support of her husband during the birth process, and the physical stresses of surgery and anesthesia typically exceed those of vaginal births. Some investigators believe that delivering a child vaginally may facilitate the bonding of mother and infant in the first week or so after birth (Keverne, personal communication). Despite the negative aspects, however, the Caesarean section is a necessary and valuable birthing alternative.

ery, the widespread use of forceps, and the deliberate induction of labor. Although the decision concerning appropriate delivery procedures to follow depends primarily on the medical facts involved, whenever possible, medical personnel should include the mother in the decision-making process. All too often the mother, who is most vitally involved, is treated as a disinterested participant.

As a final point, psychological processes also play a role in the birth process. For example, obstetricians know that in some cases labor will stop when the physician enters the pregnant woman's room (Friedman, 1978). The emotional well-being of the mother plays a central role in the personal comfort that she experiences. Therefore, medical personnel must be sensitive to the psychological needs and condition of the woman during delivery. To ignore them can only be viewed as poor medical practice.

☐ *The Premature Infant* A **premature birth** may be defined in two ways. The most common definition is that any birth occurring before thirty-seven weeks from the last menstrual period is premature. In addition, many physicians suggest that the weight of the child be included, and that an infant who weighs 5.5 lbs. or less be considered premature by weight. Often the diagnosis is made only when both features are present (Page et al., 1981). Premature births may be caused by any condition that stimulates uterine contractions, interferes with the normal course of pregnancy, or makes the uterus unable to retain its contents (Vaughn et al., 1979).

The premature infant is at risk since many of the systems necessary to support life outside the uterus are only partially formed or functioning. The amniotic fluid in which the fetus is developing can be tested to determine fetal maturity for the purpose of selecting the best time if it is necessary to perform a Caesarean section. Once born, the premature child's condition can be rapidly evaluated. If physiological activity is depressed, the child is placed at once in an incubator, which controls temperature, humidity, and oxygen content of the air. In addition, special feeding diets and procedures are followed (Vaughn et al., 1979). The use of these specialized techniques has resulted in a much more favorable prognosis and outcome for premature babies.

☐ *Milk Production and Breast-Feeding* Should childbirth occur, a sequence under hormone control occurs that begins **lactation,** or milk production. The high levels of estrogen and progesterone present during pregnancy stimulate the development of the alveoli (milk glands) of the breasts. Pregnant women may secrete **colostrum,** sometimes called the first milk, during this period, well before giving birth. The high estrogen and progesterone levels stimulate the production of the **prolactin** inhibiting factor. Once the estrogen and progesterone levels drop following birth, the prolactin inhibiting factor level drops, and the pituitary secretes relatively high levels of prolactin. This increased secretion of prolactin stimulates the alveoli to produce milk

Box 3–3

CAN PARENTS DETERMINE THE SEX OF THEIR CHILD?

Throughout much of history, people have been fascinated by the idea of controlling the sex of their children. Figure 3–6 illustrates a good example of this interest. It shows a patent issued in 1922 by the U.S. Patent Office for a sex calculator devised to allow people to determine the sex of developing offspring (Whelan, 1977). The calculator was based on the incorrect belief that one ovary produced male ova and the other produced female ova, and that the ovaries produced their eggs in alternate months.

Indeed, people do seem to have a desire to choose the sex of their children. One researcher investigated parental wishes concerning the sex of their first child and found that one-half would prefer males, one-third females, and one-fifth had no preference (Coombs, 1977). These figures have been verified by some social scientists, who estimate that there would be a seven to ten percent increase in the number of male births if sex determination were possible (Markel & Nam, 1971). Of course, speculations on the effects of sex determination, while "thought provoking," often fail to consider the possible effects of either government regulation or alterations of societal norms resulting from changes in sex ratio (Largey, 1980). Regardless of the potential effect of sex determination, the question still remains, "Can it be done?"

The data on the effectiveness of determining the sex of children are controversial. Some studies indicate that the timing of sexual intercourse in relation to the day of ovulation influences the sex of the offspring (Guerrero, 1970, 1974; Harlap, 1979). These data suggest that intercourse that occurs about three days before ovulation is more likely to produce a female child than conceptions that occur when coitus is simultaneous with ovulation. Harlap studied Jewish women in Israel, who, for religious reasons, abstained from coitus for a certain period of time following their menses. Harlap reported that in this group the proportion of males born increased when conception occurred following ovulation. Although Harlap's data did not completely agree with Guerrero's data, both studies suggest that the timing of intercourse has an effect on the sex of the offspring. In a popular book on the subject, *Boy or Girl?*, Whelan (1977) suggests that the use of acid-based douches can also affect the sex of children. This suggestion is based on the still unproven hypothesis that

Figure 3-6.

Patented Sept. 5, 1922.   **1,428,065**

UNITED STATES PATENT OFFICE.

HUBERT ROYDS TIDSWELL, OF WINNINGTON, ENGLAND.

SEX CALCULATOR.

Application filed March 30, 1920. Serial No. 369,927.

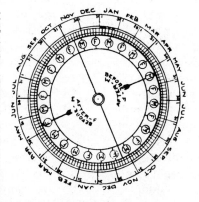

To all whom it may concern:

Be it known that I, HUBERT ROYDS TIDS-
WELL, a subject of the King of Great Britain and Ireland, residing at 46 Winnington
5 Lane, Winnington, Cheshire, England, have
invented certain new and useful Improve-
ments in Sex Calculators; and I do hereby
declare the following to be a full, clear, and
exact description of the invention, such as
10 will enable others skilled in the art to which
it appertains to make and use the same.

A device for finding the sex of all children, born to the same woman, after the first
child has been born, when one knows the
15 approximate dates of births of the expected
children and the sex of the child previously
born. The device also shows when fertilization must take place for a particular sex
to be born.

20 This invention is based on the well-known
and proved theory that in normal women
the ovaries ovulate alternately, and that one
ovary always produces male ova and the
other female ova, and that this action oc-
25 curs at regular intervals, the sequence not
being disturbed by gestation or lactation.
Consequently if the date of birth and sex
of first child born be known, one can predict or determine the sex of subsequent chil-
30 dren. The device consists of two or more
parts of any regular geometrical form, and

PATENT OFFICE HAS ACCEPTED "SEX-DETERMINATION"

That "the well known and proved theory" on which this calculator is based is a
proven fallacy has not prevented this inventor from displaying considerable ingenuity
in the development of this device. It is not difficult to cite instances of women with
only one ovary producing children of both sexes, and reference may also be made to
the birds, which consistently produce the sexes in approximately equal numbers with
only one functional ovary.

male sperm are more sensitive to acid solutions. The effectiveness of
douches in sex determination has been strongly questioned by Downing
and Black (1976).

The isolation of both the X and Y sperm by a filtering process has been
successfully completed (Dmowski, 1979). Although such technology has
not yet been used to determine a child's sex, it would indicate that the
possibility is close at hand. We can speculate that in the near future
parents will be able, if they wish, to determine the sex of their children.

within two or three days after delivery. The nursing newborn at first ingests colostrum, which is present immediately. High in antibodies, colostrum gives the newborn some protection against disease. As the newborn continues to nurse, colostrum is replaced by milk.

As the infant sucks on the nipple, another hormone control sequence occurs. Sucking, via direct nervous system paths, sends impulses to the hypothalamus, which in turn sends nerve fibers to the pituitary where the hormone **oxytocin** is released to the blood stream. Oxytocin produces contractions in the milk glands, which forces milk into the duct system that leads to the nipple. The infant lowers the pressure outside the nipple by sucking, then receives milk from the breast. After birth, prolactin levels gradually lower, and FSH and LH are released, allowing the menstrual cycle to begin again. The woman who breast-feeds her infant has higher prolactin levels for longer periods, thus menstrual cycles are delayed relative to the non-breast-feeding woman. The effect of breast-feeding on reproduction control will be discussed later in this chapter.

The La Leche League, begun in 1959, is an organization that encourages women to breast-feed their children. The league publishes a periodically revised book, *The Womanly Art of Breastfeeding* (La Leche League International, 1978), in which the benefits of breast-feeding are emphasized: breast milk is superior to prepared milk; infants are never allergic to mothers' milk; breast-fed babies are healthier; women who breast-feed have lower rates of breast cancer; breast-feeding helps mother get back into shape after giving birth; and breast-feeding saves both time and money.

Ultimately, each woman who gives birth must decide whether or not to breast-feed her child. While, as noted above, arguments can be made in favor of breast-feeding, they are not so strong as to suggest that this is the only course to follow (MacKeith and Wood, 1977). For example, certain conditions, such as illness in the mother or infant, may be cause to avoid breast-feeding (MacKeith & Wood, 1977). Of course, in the final analysis the mother's personal feelings should determine the choice.

☐ *Maternal Risks in Pregnancy*   Risks to the mother during pregnancy range from minor discomfort to death. The mortality rate for women in 1978 in the United States resulting from complications of pregnancy was 9.6 deaths per 100,000 births. This figure represents a dramatic decrease from the 620 deaths per 100,000 births reported in 1933 (Page et al., 1981). The decrease is due almost entirely to better medical care during pregnancy and childbirth. The need for good prenatal care cannot be overemphasized as a crucial factor, and all women should seek medical care as soon as they recognize or suspect that they are pregnant. We will now describe the more common major complications that can accompany pregnancy (adapted from Page et al., 1981).

An increase in the mother's blood pressure during pregnancy is a common occurrence that can be very serious. A mother whose blood pressure was high before the pregnancy may find it elevated even more during the pregnancy. **Preeclampsia** and **eclampsia** are syndromes common during pregnancy that include as a major symptom greatly raised blood pressure. In preeclampsia, a major rise in blood pressure is found following a rapid weight gain. The weight gain is caused by water and sodium retention. The kidneys fail to function properly, and if the syndrome is not treated, maternal death can result from cardiac failure, stroke, or irreversible liver damage. Eclampsia is the same disorder, but, in addition, the mother suffers convulsions. Rest and medication are successful treatments in most cases of eclampsia and preeclampsia, but Caesarean section or labor induction may be necessary in the most severe instances.

During pregnancy several problems can occur with the placenta. In **abruptio placentae** a premature separation of the placenta from the uterus occurs. Depending on the degree of separation, the attendant bleeding and shock can pose a serious threat to the mother. Abruptio placentae occurs in about 1 percent of all pregnancies and is the cause of 15 percent of fetal deaths. In cases diagnosed as being severe, a Caesarean section is recommended. In **placenta previa** the placenta develops its attachment to the uterine wall partially or completely over the cervical canal leading to the vagina. This condition results in painless bleeding during the last trimester. Placenta previa occurs in about .05 percent of all pregnancies. In severe cases the mother is ordered to bed until the fetus is able to survive outside of the womb, at which time it is delivered by Caesarean section.

Hydramnios is a condition in which excess fluid accumulates within the placenta. The cause is generally unknown, but hydramnios may result in severe damage to the developing fetus. Most cases result in premature labor. Removal of excess fluid has been attempted.

If, after twenty weeks into a pregnancy, fetal movement cannot be detected or the size of the uterus has not increased, fetal death is a possibility. With further tests a positive diagnosis can be made. Spontaneous abortions occur about 90 percent of the time within three weeks of the death; if the fetus does not abort, however, labor must be induced due to an increased threat to the mother.

Following birth the uterus undergoes contractions that not only return it to the nonpregnant state but also act to stop bleeding. Excessive bleeding results if there are no contractions. In addition, surgery or tearing of the birth canal may contribute to bleeding. The use of transfusions and other procedures has been successful in the treatment of serious bleeding during birth. Page and his associates (1981) believe that proper medical intervention could prevent essentially all deaths from bleeding after birth even though bleeding remains one of the major causes of maternal mortality.

Infections during pregnancy and following birth were the major causes of maternal death in the past. Childbed fever, an infection that develops following delivery, was once terminal; it has been all but eradicated by bringing sterile conditions to the delivery room—a fact that opponents of home births like to emphasize. Treatment of infection with antibiotics has further decreased the seriousness of the condition.

The pregnancy in which more than one embryo develops is a source of complications during pregnancy, including premature births, preeclampsia, placenta previa, anemia, and postpartum hemorrhage. The mother who expects multiple births is usually advised to reduce activity and to rest.

An **ectopic pregnancy** occurs when a fertilized ova begins development outside of the uterus. Over 90 percent occur within the Fallopian tube. An ectopic pregnancy happens in 1 out of every 80 to 250 pregnancies and is responsible for about 8 percent of all maternal deaths. Bleeding and shock in the mother are often the first indications of an ectopic pregnancy. In very rare cases, the fetus fully develops in the abdominal cavity. These extremely rare successful abdominal pregnancies are discovered accidentally when a Caesarean section is performed.

Almost any disease may be present when a woman is pregnant. In fact, the symptoms of a few diseases such as rheumatoid arthritis and endometriosis lessen during pregnancy. Several diseases, however, are of particular importance because their symptoms may be aggravated by pregnancy or because the disease may affect the developing embryo or fetus. Diabetes mellitus was associated with high rates of maternal and fetal mortality before the advent of insulin. The diabetic mother continues to be at risk but at a greatly reduced rate. The mother with heart disease is at greater risk and needs careful medical attention throughout pregnancy and particularly dur-

ing the birth process. The same is true of pregnant women who are anemic or who have an infection of the urinary tract.

A number of complications that are not life threatening are usually handled by minor treatment or simple reassurance to make the woman more comfortable. These complications include excessive weight gain, nausea, heartburn, constipation, hemorrhoids, vaginitis, leg cramps, swelling in the legs, and varicose veins.

Many studies have examined the circumstances that lead to or are associated with complications during pregnancy. As a result, systems for assessing risks have been developed. One such system, developed by Morrison and Olsen (1979), isolates several factors that are associated with increased risk of complications during pregnancy, including age (either under 16 or over 35), having had no children or more than five children, problems with previous pregnancies, the presence of illness in the mother, and, of course, problems with the current pregnancy. After having weighed and combined these various features, the likelihood of serious complications can be determined and preventative steps taken. Finally, although many risk factors and risks are present, we should not lose sight of the fact that most pregnancies are uncomplicated and that real risks are infrequent.

☐ *Spontaneous Abortions* Pregnancies that terminate or abort due to natural causes are called **spontaneous abortions.** Estimates are that only one-third of all fertilizations of ova result in live births (Grobstein, 1981). Many spontaneous abortions occur early in pregnancy, but they often go undetected because women do not realize they are pregnant (Page et al., 1981). About 15 percent of all pregnancies spontaneously abort between four and twenty-two weeks following the last menses. Examination in these cases has revealed that over one-half the aborted embryos have developmental defects. In later stages of pregnancy, many of the spontaneous abortions of healthy fetuses are due to uterine anomalies (Page et al., 1981). Almost any serious illness or injury to the mother can result in a spontaneous abortion at any phase of her pregnancy.

☐ *Postpartum Psychological Disturbances*
The rates of psychological disturbances in women during the first three months following the birth of a child increase four- to fivefold. Furthermore, two-thirds of all women reportedly experience at least a brief period of emotional instability after giving birth, and the rates of psychosis following birth are between one and two per thousand (Melges & Hamburg, 1977). This psychological state is called **postpartum depression.**

Meares, Grimwade, and Wood (1976) have suggested the following three categories of postpartum disturbances: (1) depressive disorders that last for at least one month; (2) profound mood changes that last at least one month but do not have the characteristics of guilt, self-depreciation, and helplessness that are common in the first category; and (3) transient postpartum blues. These categories reveal the fact that postpartum disturbances vary widely among individuals and do not represent a single, clearcut disturbance. Many women find that they cry for no apparent reason or because they are happy; others report that while normally they are not weepy, they do cry during the postpartum period (Yalom et al., 1968).

One reason that many women experience postpartum disturbances may be the drastic change in hormone levels that occurs very rapidly after birth. These changes result primarily from the loss of the placenta that produces high levels of hormones. For example, large amounts of the chorionic gonadotrophin can be found in the pregnant woman, but it drops to undetectable levels three days after birth. Estrogen levels are much greater at the end of pregnancy than during the luteal phase of the menstrual cycle, but this high level returns to normal very rapidly following delivery. Figure 3–7 shows the drop in progesterone and estradiol after giving birth. Some researchers suggest that the rapid drop in hormone levels produces a withdrawal response that is the basis of these psychological disturbances. One hormone, prolactin, which is necessary for lactation, rises gradually throughout pregnancy then drops rapidly at the onset of labor and then rises quickly to high levels in the nursing mother (Tulchinsky, 1980). In nonpregnant women and men, elevated prolactin levels have been found to be associated with stress (Melges & Hamburg, 1977). In addition to these hormonal changes, the woman's metabolic system undergoes major changes in fluid and water balance.

These dramatic physiological changes undoubtedly have an impact on the emo-

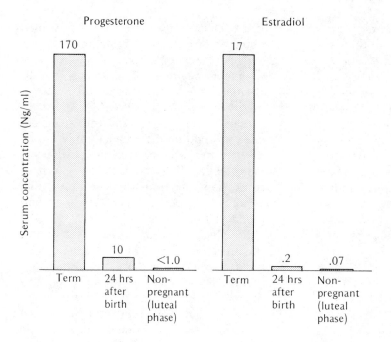

Figure 3-7. Change in the mother's hormone levels following giving birth. Source: D. Tulchinsky, 1980.

tional state and the psychological experiences of the individual. Although no one has yet been able to pinpoint the exact hormonal and/or body chemistry changes that predispose some women to psychological disturbances following delivery, the hypothesis that such changes are related to the dramatic hormonal shifts seems quite reasonable (Melges & Hamburg, 1977).

In addition to dramatic hormonal changes, a number of nonphysiological features of the postpartum period might contribute to the development of psychological disturbances for new mothers. These

have been summarized by Magnus (1980), who proposes that their importance should not be overlooked when considering the causes of the postpartum blues. Magnus's summary of possible stresses during the postpartum period is presented in Table 3-3. She suggests that the reason some women experience postpartum disturbances while others do not is the result of environmental factors that can either intensify or relieve the degree of stress. These factors are listed in Table 3-4. How they influence the degree of stress experienced is unknown. Magnus concludes that the ac-

TABLE 3-3 STRESSES IN THE POSTPARTUM PERIOD

1. *Inadequacy of caretaking:* The mother feels she is unable to take proper care of her infant.
2. *Estrangement from the infant:* Early in infancy babies give few positive responses and little feedback to the mother.
3. *Guilt:* The mother feels guilty over not being able to provide as much care or love as she feels she should.
4. *Entrapment:* The mother feels tied down by the infant and is unable to pursue her own interests as she would desire.
5. *Worries about responsibility:* The mother expresses great concern over having total responsibility for the infant.
6. *Exhaustion:* Many mothers experience considerable fatigue and feel unable to cope with the infant along with other responsibilities.

(From Magnus, 1980.)

TABLE 3-4 ENVIRONMENTAL FACTORS THAT CAN INCREASE OR RELIEVE STRESS

1. *Characteristics of the infant:* Infants vary in the degree to which they are irritable, and they differ in the amount of responsiveness they express.
2. *Hospital practices:* The use of medications, such as anesthetics, can affect mother-infant interactions, as well as variations in the amount of early mother-infant contact that hospitals allow, or the encouragement versus discouragement of breast-feeding that the mother receives.
3. *Lack of assistance and support for caretaking:* Families, friends, and partners differ widely in the amount and kind of help and support given to the new mother.
4. *Unplanned or unwanted pregnancy:* The attitudes and feelings attendant upon unwanted or unplanned pregnancy can adversely affect the mother's psychological state.
5. *Internalized cultural attitudes about mothering:* Adverse effects may also result if the woman feels that success in mothering is the ultimate test of her value and worth.

(From Magnus, 1980.)

ceptance of society's definition of the role of the mother is what produces the conflict: "The more women accept cultural expectations of the mothering role, the more likely they are to react with anxiety, guilt, feelings of inferiority, and depression when their experiences of the postpartum period do not fit with cultural expectations" (Magnus, 1980, p. 203). She suggests that an increased sharing of child-care responsibilities and changes in the expectations of motherhood are necessary if postpartum disturbances are to be reduced.

Birth Defects

About 6 percent of all children are born with some type of birth defect (Polani, 1974), and about 25 percent of all children in hospitals are there for treatment of genetic disorders (Bolognese & Corson, 1975). Birth defects fall into two general categories: those caused by the genetic makeup of the developing fetus and those caused by environmental factors. The study of environmental influences has expanded in recent years and is currently demanding a good deal of attention. The occurrence of birth defects can be categorized in a number of ways. We have adopted the scheme proposed by Bolognese and Corson (1975) to describe some of the more common birth defects.

☐ *Chromosomal Disorders* Around 20,000 infants are born each year in the United States with chromosomal abnormalities. These abnormalities occur in approximately one out of every two hundred live births. Perhaps the best known of these disorders is **Down's syndrome,** sometimes still referred to as mongolism. This disorder occurs when the child has an extra chromosome. The Down's syndrome victim exhibits the following characteristics: mental retardation; facial changes in eyelids, nose, and ears; defects in hands and feet; and defective heart structures. Approximately 96 per-

cent of all Down's syndrome cases are of the nonhereditary type. Maternal age is known to be closely related to the likelihood of producing a Down's syndrome child. For example, mothers aged 35 and over make up only about 13.5 percent of all pregnancies; yet that same group is responsible for more than 50 percent of all Down's syndrome births. Maternal age is associated with other chromosomal disorders as well: The likelihood that an offspring will experience chromosomal anomalies triples when the mother is between ages 35 and 45 (Bolognese & Corson, 1975).

☐ *Sex-linked Disorders* A large number of hereditary diseases are sex-linked. We are most familiar with *hemophilia,* which is characterized by a defect in blood clotting. The carrier of the disease is female, yet the male offspring is the one affected by the disease. The gene for hemophilia is carried on an X chromosome of a female, and there is a 50 percent chance that a hemophiliac son will be born to a mother who carries the gene. Other sex-linked disorders include the Duchenne type of muscular dystrophy (the progressive degeneration of muscles, particularly in the legs); testicular feminization; Fabrys disease, which causes skin, kidney, heart, and eye defects; and Hunter's syndrome, which leads to mental retardation, visual problems, and other complications.

☐ *Hereditary Biochemical Disorders* Bolognese and Corson (1975) report that approximately one out of every hundred children born have some sort of metabolic

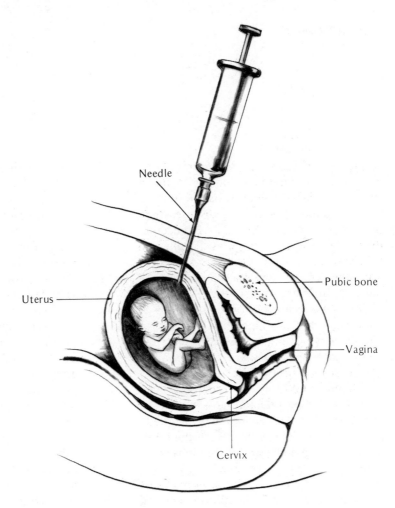

Figure 3-8. The technique used in amniocentesis.

Needle

Uterus

Pubic bone

Vagina

Cervix

biochemical disorder based on inherited factors. Some of these disorders present no obvious symptoms, while others result in severe problems ranging from mental retardation to death. Most of these disorders are genetically recessive so that two carriers must mate to produce offspring with these problems.

Perhaps two of the best-known hereditary biochemical disorders are *Tay-Sachs disease* and *sickle-cell anemia*. Tay-Sachs disease, a fatal disorder in which nerve cells are destroyed, is chiefly a problem among Jewish people who have descended from families in northeastern Europe. Sickle-cell

anemia, a disease of the red blood cells that impairs circulation, most frequently affects blacks.

□ *Diagnosis of Prenatal Disorder* Some diseases and defects can be identified before the child is born, principally through the use of the diagnostic technique known as **amniocentesis**. In this procedure a needle is inserted through the lower abdominal wall of the uterus and placenta in order to withdraw some of the amniotic fluid for chemical analysis (see Figure 3–8). The procedure is relatively simple and minimally risky for the mother and the fetus. The offspring's sex can be readily determined by analysis of the fetal cells found floating in the fluid. This technique is useful in diagnosing sex-linked hereditary diseases such as hemophilia and Duchenne's muscular dystrophy. The chromosomes in cells can be analyzed to detect Down's syndrome and other chromosomal abnormalities. Finally, if sufficient fetal cells are obtained, they may be examined for the presence of enzymes, which will permit diagnosis of certain enzyme deficiencies. As research in amniocentesis progresses, a greater number of diseases will be identifiable early in fetal development. With this information, decisions concerning prenatal care and/or termination of the pregnancy can be made (Gerbie & Friedman, 1980). Once the information is obtained, parents should receive genetic counseling. The counselor informs the parents of any problems that may exist and helps them reach a decision concerning their desired course of action. The genetic counselor also helps parents deal with their strong emotional reactions to the discovery that their developing offspring has a genetic disorder.

Ultrasonic examination is another method of identifying some major defects in the developing fetus. The technique is called **sonography.** When ultrasonic waves are directed toward the uterus, the pattern that registers on specialized equipment can be used to detect such problems as major defects in growth of the nervous system or abnormalities of the digestive system or kidneys. Some professionals feel that this technique is just coming into its own and will provide increasingly sophisticated and

complex diagnoses with no risk to mother or fetus (Page et al., 1981).

□ *Birth Defects Resulting from Noninherited Causes* About 4 percent of all children born have malformations caused by factors other than those that are inherited. These birth defects are responsible for about 14 percent of all infant deaths during the first year of life and also for many cases of severe mental retardation (Bolognese & Corson, 1975). The cause of these congenital defects is often not known, but among the more common causes are infections that are acquired during pregnancy, radiation exposure, drug use, and exposure to adverse environmental chemicals. The term **teratogen** is used to identify any substance or condition that will produce a defect in the developing embryo or fetus. Malformations are not consistently related to contraceptive practices (Vessey et al., 1976), nor are they related to previously induced abortion (Bracken & Holford, 1979).

VIRAL INFECTIONS OF THE MOTHER THAT CAN AFFECT THE FETUS Pregnant women can contract a number of viral diseases that can have powerful adverse effects on the developing fetus (Sever & Fuccillo, 1977). *Hepatitis,* a viral infection that attacks the liver of the mother, is associated with a high mortality rate (20 percent) among fetuses and can result in hydroencephaly (enlargement of the ventricles of the brain typically resulting in mental retardation) and low birth weight in the offspring. *Herpes simplex,* a common sexually transmitted disease (see Chapter Nine) results in up to a 90 percent fatality rate for the developing fetus if the mother has the disease. Children born to herpes simplex victims often show malformations of the central nervous system. *Influenza* is associated with spontaneous abortions and malformations of the central nervous system. If *mumps* are contracted during the first trimester of pregnancy, fetal death will result in 25 percent of those cases. Cardiac problems and low birth weight can also develop in children born to mothers who had the mumps early in pregnancy. *Rubella,* sometimes called "German measles," is widely known to cause congenital malformations in the offspring of women who contract the disease while pregnant. The malformation rate for this disease runs from 10 to 50 percent in the first month of pregnancy, 14 to 24 percent during the second month, and 6 to 17 percent in the third month. Rubella also causes spontaneous abortions during the first trimester among 12 to 15 percent of all affected pregnancies. Those children who are born are often afflicted with congenital heart disease, cataracts, deafness, microcephaly (very small heads), and/or mental retardation (Bolognese & Corson, 1975).

TERATOGENIC AGENTS   The thalidomide catastrophe of the 1960s, during which the administration of the tranquilizing drug thalidomide to pregnant women resulted in the subsequent birth of children with missing arms and legs, provided the impetus for the study of *teratogenic agents.* Because the average woman takes five different drugs during her pregnancy and is exposed to many environmental chemicals, the study

of teratogens is vital (Aladjem, 1975). Table 3-5 lists some of the more important teratogenetic agents and their effects. Unfortunately, certain widely available and frequently used substances are potential teratogens. For example, recent evidence suggests that among mothers who smoke twenty or more cigarettes a day, there is an increase in birth defects, particularly among male offspring (Christianson, 1980). The use of alcohol during pregnancy, particularly in excessive quantities, also may have powerful effects on the developing offspring (Abel, 1981).

THE RH FACTOR   One of the real success stories of medicine has been the identification of problems related to the Rh factor and their treatment. Until the 1940s this disorder was the cause of about 10 percent of all cerebral palsy victims, and around 50 percent of all Rh babies died (Page et al., 1981). The infant born with this incompatibility may be only slightly affected or could be fatally damaged. Problems encountered with the **Rh baby** include severe anemia, jaundice, liver damage, and brain damage (Reid, Ryan, & Benirschke, 1972).

Often during the birth process some of the infant's blood passes into the mother's bloodstream. If there is an Rh incompatibility, the mother will develop antibodies that destroy the foreign blood. From that time on the mother will be immune to that blood factor in the sense that she continues to produce the antibodies. If in a subsequent pregnancy the developing fetus has a blood type with the incompatible Rh factor, the mother's antibodies cross the placenta and

TABLE 3-5 A PARTIAL LIST OF TERATOGENS	
AGENT	*TERATOGENETIC EFFECTS*
Streptomycin (used in treating infections)	Hearing loss.
Anticoagulants (used to treat certain vascular diseases)	Skull anomalies.
Alcohol	Fetal alcohol syndrome (symptomized by developmental delay, microcephaly, lymph and cardiovascular anomalies).
Smoking	Reduced birth weight; increased infant mortality; increased number of still-born deliveries; at age 7 offspring of smoking mothers are three months behind in reading, math, and general ability.
Barbituates	Cleft palate, cleft lip.
Meprobanate (a tranquilizer)	Congenital heart disease.
Androgens (sometimes used in treatments of pregnancy problems)	Masculinization of fetus.
Estrogens (a component of many birth control pills)	Anomalies of the genital organs of both sexes.
Mercury	Fetal damage occurs before mother shows symptoms of mercury poisoning.
Lead	Associated with anemia and retarded development.

(This list is compiled from data from Aaldjem, 1975, and Bolognese & Corson, 1975.)

attack the fetal blood cells, greatly shortening their life (Queenan, 1977). The result is anemia and possible widespread damage to the fetus.

Pregnant women can be tested for Rh antibodies, and if they exist, further testing can determine if the developing fetus is at risk. Treatment can include a transfusion while the fetus is in the uterus or the possibility of early delivery via a Caesarean section. Once delivered, whether naturally or via Caesarean section, the baby's blood is replaced with compatible blood from a donor who does not have the antibodies. This transfusion immediately relieves the anemia, and if the damage has not been great, the child will recover quickly and develop normally (Queenan, 1977).

REGULATION OF REPRODUCTION: A BRIEF HISTORY

Humans have been concerned with regulating reproduction throughout the course of history. Many of the early contraceptive practices were based on magical ideas. For example, peasants in eastern Europe would turn a grain-threshing wheel backwards four times at midnight to prevent conception (Gordon, 1976). In Hungary, women reportedly drank a mixture of gunpowder and vinegar in an effort to "blast" any conceptus from their system (Himes, 1963). People have tried many different methods in the past, and some proved to be successful, while others failed. Today a number of effective alternatives are available.

Birth control is still a major issue today, with many unresolved conflicts. The main areas of conflict focus on contraceptive use and the religious community, abortion as a means of birth control, the opinion of minority groups that reproduction regulation is aimed at them, and the question of societal morality in light of the availability of contraceptives.

The conflict between contraception and religion stems principally from the teachings of Roman Catholicism. The church argues that most types of contraception interfere with the "natural order" and thus go against God's will. Catholicism teaches that conception is sacred and life giving; thus, any interference other than some form of sexual abstinence is contrary to one of the basic beliefs of the church. This negative viewpoint is not shared by all members of the Christian faith, Catholics included. The Catholic church maintains its position on contraception, however, in spite of evidence that "there has been a spectacular increase in non-conformity in Catholic women in the youngest age groups" (Westoff & Ryder, 1977, p. 24).

The anti-abortion position is based on the assumption that from conception onward the fetus is a person who should be granted the full rights of a human being. The conclusion drawn from this theory is that abortion is murder. All people who support the pro-abortion position do not necessarily favor abortion; rather, many believe that the decision should be a matter of individual choice. This issue generates extremely powerful emotions in supporters on both sides, and it has become a national political priority.

Another concern over contraception and regulation of reproduction centers on some individuals within the minority communities who believe that contraceptive information and practices are aimed most heavily at minority group members and are deliberately designed to control the reproduction of minority groups. Although many family planning services do address lower-income groups that have a disproportionate percentage of minority group members, these agencies do not necessarily have as their goal the suppression of minority birth rates.

Finally, how the availability of contraceptives will affect the morality of the country is of concern to some people. These people worry that because the fear of pregnancy is eliminated, the youth of our country will become totally uninhibited. According to this theory, family life will suffer greatly, which will lead to the breakdown of the moral structure and fiber of society (see also Chapter Fourteen). No studies, however, support this concept.

Individuals and groups advocate the regulation of reproduction for a number of reasons, including issues on human rights, population concerns, the effects of large families, and the occurrence of unwanted pregnancies. On a human values level, many have argued that individuals should have the right to choose their reproductive pattern. For example, ir the 1962 United Nations Declaration of Human Rights, the following statement appears: "We believe that the objective of family planning is the enrichment of human life, not its restriction; that family planning, by asserting greater opportunity to each person, frees man to attain his individual dignity and reach his full potential."

World population control is an important consideration because of limited world resources. On a more immediate level, family size in relation to other social conditions is also an issue that deserves attention. The larger the family, for example, the lower the probability of higher education within that family. Physical growth and development of individual family members are affected by the number of people in the family; child mortality rates increase with family size, regardless of the socioeconomic class from

which the family originates; and there is an increase in the likelihood of childhood illness for each child as family size increases (Garcia & Rosenfeld, 1977). Due to the nature of correlational data, to say that large families cause these adverse consequences is difficult, but to say that these consequences cause large families is certainly unreasonable. What may be concluded is that factors that lead to large families are associated with these adverse conditions.

All babies born should be wanted and loved; unfortunately, the facts are that a great many pregnancies are unplanned, and a fair number of infants are unwanted. Table 3–6 shows the percentage of unwanted births as a function of the education level of the mother. As educational level rises, the number of unwanted pregnancies decreases. This finding would correlate with the high number of unwanted teenage pregnancies, as estimates are that 80 percent of female teenagers who drop out of high school do so because they are pregnant. Each year 30,000 young women under the age of 15 become pregnant, with over 75 percent of these pregnancies unintended (Alan Guttmacher Institute, 1981). As you will learn in Box 3–4, unwanted pregnancies among females in this age group is a particularly serious problem — not just for those involved but for society in general. Unwanted pregnancies result in a heavy drain on resources for both the family and for society. The costs of hospital and physician services alone are extensive, to say nothing of the emotional and physical cost of unwanted children.

The economic impact of family-planning

Counseling on contraceptive use.

programs that help reduce unwanted births is considerable. To put this statement in perspective, estimates are that family-planning services have prevented over 1,000,000 pregnancies in the years from 1970–1975. In terms of money, it means that the government saved over $1 billion in welfare and medical support payments during that same period (Cutright & Jaffe, 1977). Family-planning services not only reduce the personal suffering of unwanted births but also make sound economic sense.

Clearly, the teenager who becomes pregnant is faced with consequences that extend far beyond the immediate experience. With a high degree of predictability, teenage pregnancy interferes dramatically with

TABLE 3-6 MOTHER'S LEVEL OF EDUCATION IN RELATION TO UNWANTED BIRTHS	
EDUCATIONAL LEVEL	*PERCENT UNWANTED BIRTHS*
Less than high school	17.4
One to three years of high school	15.5
Four years of high school	11.2
One to three years of college	9.3
Four or more years of college	4.7
(From the *Statistical Abstracts of the United States,* 1981.)	

PREGNANCY AND THE TEENAGER

Hatcher and his colleagues (1980), make the following statement
concerning teenage pregnancies:

> Teenage pregnancy increases the incidence of premature births and child abuse,
> halts the educational process for many young people, leads to one-third of all
> abortions, and contributes mightily to the United States' divorce rate, now the
> highest in the world; yet, teenage pregnancy still remains a very low priority in
> our society today.

The research on teenage pregnancy provides evidence of these severe
societal problems. Over 1 million teenagers between the ages of 15 and
19 become pregnant each year, and the birthrate among unmarrieds
continues to rise (Alan Guttmacher Institute, 1981). In the years from 1970
to 1978 the overall rate of pregnancy for women had declined in the
United States; however, among younger mothers, the decline was less
than for older women, and for 15-year-olds there was no decline (National
Center for Health Statistics, 1980). Lyle and Segal (1979) note that

the economic and social position of the young woman throughout the rest of her life. Since teenage parents are likely to have had a teenage parent themselves (Alan Guttmacher Institute, 1981), the problem tends to be passed along from generation to generation. The sum of the findings related to teenage pregnancy is that unwanted teenage pregnancy is a serious problem that deserves attention and consideration for future preventative measures.

CONTRACEPTIVE TECHNIQUES

A wide range of contraceptive techniques are available, with most methods aimed at interfering with the female reproductive role. Table 3-7 summarizes some information on the use of contraceptive techniques among married couples (Mosher, 1983). The table shows that roughly 70 percent of all married couples used some form of contraception. In this group the most common contraceptive technique is the pill, and the second most common is the condom. Recent evidence, however, suggests that use of the pill is declining (Zelnick & Kantner, 1980).

The effectiveness of various contraceptive techniques is summarized in Table 3-8. In this table the first column of figures reflects the number of pregnancies that are teenagers have higher failure rates for all types of contraceptives than do older women.

The pregnant teenager faces a greater health risk. Teenage mothers have more complications during and after pregnancy than do women in their 20s (Menken, 1972). The child of the teenage mother tends to be smaller, and more neurological abnormalities occur among children born to teenagers than among children born to women between the ages of 20 and 24. Six percent of the first-born and 10 percent of the second-born children born to women 15 years old or under die. This mortality rate far exceeds that of offspring born to older mothers. Problems apparently occur not because of age per se, but rather because of poor prenatal and postnatal care. Seventy percent of women under 19 years of age receive no prenatal care (Hatcher et al., 1980).

Teenage parents are at a higher risk for unemployment, and the mean family income in families in which the mother is age 16 or younger at the time of the first birth has been reported to be one-half of that earned in families in which the mother is 25 to 29 years of age when the first child is born. Families headed by young mothers between 14 and 25 years of age average an annual income of just under $4,000—about one-fifth of the national average income (Alan Guttmacher Institute, 1981). In addition, the suicide attempt rate for teenage mothers is ten times greater than that of the general population, the divorce rate is very high in teen marriages, and the rate of child abuse and neglect by teenage mothers increases.

TABLE 3–7   BIRTH CONTROL PRACTICES AMONG MARRIED WOMEN (WOMEN IN SAMPLE WERE ALL UNDER AGE 45)

	PERCENT
Women not using contraception	**50.4**
Sterile	30.0
Surgical	28.2
Nonsurgical	1.8
Pregnant	6.8
Seeking pregnancy	6.8
Nonusers of contraception	7.6
Nonsurgical contraception	**49.6**
Birth control pill	22.5
IUD	6.3
Diaphragm	2.9
Condom	7.3
Spermicidal foam	3.0
Rhythm method	3.4
Withdrawal	2.0
Douching	.7
Other	1.0

(From Mosher, 1983.)

TABLE 3-8 EFFECTIVENESS OF VARIOUS CONTRACEPTIVE TECHNIQUES		
Number of Pregnancies during First Year of Use, per Thousand Women		
TECHNIQUE	THEORETICAL PREGNANCY RATE	ACTUAL PREGNANCY RATE
Combination pill	3.4	40–100
Intramuscular progestin shot	2.5	50–100
Condom plus spermicide	less than 10	50
Low-dose oral contraceptive	10–5	50–100
IUD	10–30	50
Condom	30	100
Diaphragm with spermicide	30	170
Spermicidal foam	30	220
Spermicidal suppository	30	200–250
Coitus interruptus	90	200–250
Rhythm method, temperature only	70	200
Rhythm method, calendar only	130	210
Cervical cap	20	250
Douching	unknown	400
Lactation	150	400
No protection	900	900

(Adapted from Hatcher et al., 1980.)

likely to occur in the first year of usage among one thousand heterosexually active women; the second is the actual rate per thousand. In all instances the actual rate of pregnancy is higher than the estimated rate (see column 2). These figures reflect improper use of the procedures. The point, however, is that no birth control method, short of abstinence, is completely effective.

For women there is a mortality risk associated with contraceptive practices. Tietze (1978) summarized these risks for three categories of contraceptive methods by the age of the women as compared with mortality risks associated with unwanted pregnancy (see Figure 3–9). Two major points can be made based on the findings presented in Figure 3–9. First, for all contraceptive techniques, as well as unwanted pregnancies, the risk increases with age. Second, risk of death from unwanted pregnancy is

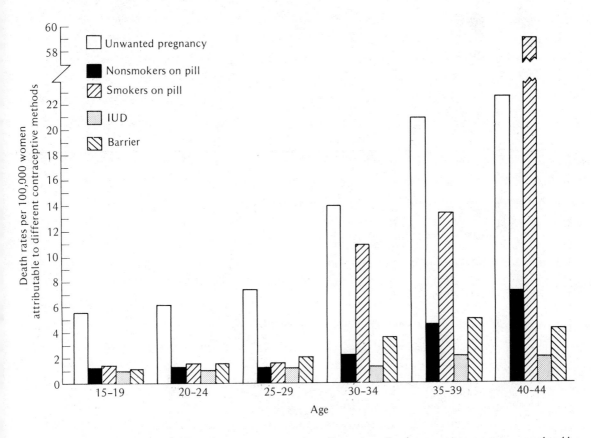

Death rates per 100,000 women
attributable to different contraceptive methods

Legend:
- Unwanted pregnancy
- Nonsmokers on pill
- Smokers on pill
- IUD
- Barrier

Age groups: 15–19, 20–24, 25–29, 30–34, 35–39, 40–44

greater than that associated with contraceptive use at all times except for smokers on the pill who are 40 years of age or older.

Hormone Contraceptives (The Pills)

Birth control pills contain hormones that modify the female reproductive cycle. These pills do not contain natural hormones but rather laboratory-produced hormones. Thus pills vary from manufacturer to manufacturer in their chemical (i.e., hormonal) content. The most common pill, called the *combination pill,* contains between 30 to 50 mg. of estrogen compounds and .5 to 10 mg. of progestin (Dickey, 1980). The *mini-pill* contains no estrogen and typically less than 1 mg. of progestin. Hormones are used for contraceptive purposes,

Figure 3-9. Death rates per 100,000 women attributable to different contraceptive methods. From Tietze, 1978.

although less frequently, in the following ways: Progestin is injected or implanted under the surface of the skin, IUDs are inserted that have progestin as part of their makeup, and the postcoital or "morning after" pill is sometimes prescribed.

Even though there are several accepted descriptions of how female birth control pills prevent conception, some mystery still surrounds the exact process. The estrogen in the pill inhibits ovulation (Speroff, Glass & Case, 1979). Hatcher and his associates suggest that the progestin in the pill may also slow sperm transport (Hatcher et al., 1980). Apparently, however, the principal function of the pill is to interfere with ovulation.

Box 3–5

THE BIRTH CONTROL PILL: CONDITIONS THAT SIGNAL "STOP" OR "CAUTION"

Women should not, under any circumstances, use the pill or should discontinue using it immediately if the following conditions exist or develop while taking it:

1. Blood-clotting disorder or history thereof
2. Cerebral vascular accident or history thereof
3. Coronary or artery disease
4. Impaired liver function
5. Malignancy of reproductive system or history thereof
6. Pregnancy

It is strongly suggested that women not use the pill if any of these conditions exist:

1. Termination of pregnancy within last 2 weeks
2. Cerebral vascular or migraine headaches
3. Hypertension
4. Diabetes or strong family history of diabetes
5. Gall bladder disease
6. Mononucleosis

The chances are unlikely that any type of male pill will be available until at least the late 1980s due to a number of complicating factors (Hatcher et al., 1980). Among these are the side effects of currently studied compounds: Some compounds appear to be slow in taking effect, and problems exist with administration of the medications. In 1978, China reported tests on a male birth control substance, gossypol, that is derived from cotton plants (National Coordinating Group on Male Anti-Fertility Agents, 1978). Men who were being given gossypol yielded very low sperm counts after two months. Research continues, and the development of a male contraceptive pill is anticipated.

7. Sickle-cell disease
8. Undiagnosed vaginal bleeding
9. Elective surgery due within four weeks
10. Full leg cast or major injury to lower leg
11. Age over 35 to 40
12. Fibrocystic breast disease

Use of the pill is not recommended if the conditions listed below are present:

1. Failure to have regular menstrual cycles
2. History of cardiac or kidney disease
3. History of heavy smoking
4. Lactation (breast feeding)

The following diseases may be worsened or, in some instances, improved, by use of the pill, but careful medical monitoring is needed:

1. Depression
2. Asthma
3. Epilepsy
4. Acne
5. Varicose veins
6. History of hepatitis with normal liver functioning at current time

(Adapted from Hatcher et al., 1977, 1980.)

☐ *The Combination Pill*   Between 5 and 8 million women in the United States are on the combination pill. Of women who start on the pill, between 45 to 75 percent continue to use it for more than one year. Women often discontinue using the pill because of a number of side effects. Physicians also discourage the use of birth control pills by women with certain health problems that might be aggravated by the chemical makeup of the pill. The conditions that should be considered before deciding to use this means of contraception and while taking it are highlighted in Box 3–5.

Side effects of the combination pill vary

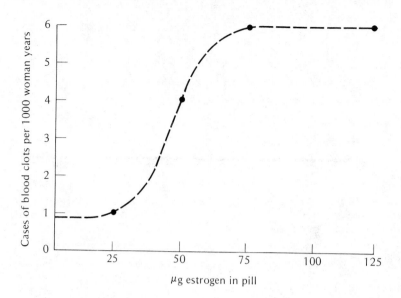

Figure 3–10. Estrogen content and rate of thromboembolic disorders. From Speroff, Glass & Case, 1978.

according to the amount and kind of estrogen and progestin contained in the pill. Possible side effects can be grouped according to the following categories: life threatening, serious, and fairly minor (Hatcher et al., 1980).

LIFE-THREATENING SIDE EFFECTS   Blood clots in the legs, lower abdomen, lungs, heart, or brain are side effects of the pill that are life threatening. Clots in the brain generally yield prior warning signs of headaches, blurred vision, and pain. A woman on the pill who experiences any of these symptoms should notify her physician immediately. The risk of a heart attack among pill users also increases, particularly in women over 40 who smoke. In addition, pill users have an increased risk of bleeding in the liver resulting from the development of benign (noncancerous) tumors, which could be a very serious condition (Sturtevant, 1979). Speroff (1979) noted about a sixfold increase in thrombosis, or blood clotting, in the leg in the pill user over the non–pill user. Figure 3–10 shows the relationship between the amount of estrogen in the pill and the occurrence of blood clots (Speroff

et al., 1979). One researcher noted that there is an increased chance of fetal abnormalities among pregnant women who are also using birth control pills (Sarto, 1979). The relationship between taking the pill and the development of cancer is still quite controversial. However, the individual who has a malignant growth and takes the pill may aggravate the condition and cause the cancer to grow more rapidly (Bibbo, Bartels, & Wied, 1979).

SERIOUS SIDE EFFECTS   Non–life-threatening but serious complications of the pill include gall bladder disease and hypertension. The latter is typically reversible when pill use is discontinued (Hatcher et al., 1980).

MINOR SIDE EFFECTS   Nausea, weight gain, mild headaches, light bleeding between periods, increased likelihood of vaginal infections, mood changes, and acne are considered minor side effects of the pill. Because of some of these side effects, many doctors recommend that the lowest possible dosage levels be administered (Speroff et al., 1979). An unusual type of side effect reported is that women who discontinue the pill have an increased likelihood of having twins once they go off the pill and conceive (Bracken & Holford, 1979).

POSITIVE SIDE EFFECTS   Certain benefits have been identified with taking the combination pill. One researcher, for example, notes: "A woman within a pill-taking group is as safe, or safer, from dying as a woman in a group using no contraception or using a less effective contraceptive" (Hatcher, 1978, p. 50). In addition, pill use has been associated with relief of some unpleasant symptoms of menstruation such as cramping and heavy menstrual flow. The pill has been used for the treatment of certain medical conditions, such as endometriosis, which is reviewed in Chapter Two. Pill usage is also associated with a decrease in ovarian cysts and fibrocystic breast disease. Finally, some women report that acne conditions improve when taking oral contraceptives.

☐ *The Mini-Pill*   The mini-pill contains no estrogen and only small amounts of progestin (1 mg. or less). The effects of the mini-pill are somewhat less predictable than the combination pill, but the mini-pill's major advantage is the reduction of side effects that are related to the estrogen content in the combination pill. Data indicate that 40 percent of the women on the mini-pill ovulate regularly, 40 percent do not ovulate, and 20 percent shift back and forth between ovulatory and anovulatory cycles (Hatcher et al., 1980). During the first six months of mini-pill use the risk of pregnancy continues; therefore, during that period an additional method of contraception is recommended, such as a diaphragm or condom (Hatcher et al., 1980).

The mini-pill is suggested as the pill of choice for women over 35 years of age and for those who have frequent headaches or hypertension, as those conditions are reduced with mini-pill use (Hatcher et al., 1980). Not known at this time is whether the mini-pill reduces the threat of thrombosis. Women on the mini-pill report irregular menses and more spotting between menses than do women on the combination pill. Therefore, women who have undiagnosed genital bleeding should avoid the mini-pill because a physician may assume that the bleeding is pill related, and an illness may remain untreated. The mini-pill has been available in the United States since 1973, but its long-term effects are still unknown. Although mini-pills contain no estrogen and less progestins than the combination pills, long-term scientific studies are necessary before mini-pills can be declared safer than combination pills (Hatcher et al., 1980, p. 45).

☐ *The Shot*   An injection of progestin that is given approximately once every three months is theoretically similar in effectiveness to the combination pill. The shot, however, has not yet been approved for use in the United States because of concerns over breast tumors and fetal damage found in test animals. Although it provides protection for three to four months, the shot is often associated with irregular menstrual bleeding and, therefore, as with the mini pill, can mask other abnormalities of the reproduction system (Brenner & Mishell, 1979). The shot appears to inhibit the LH surge and thus prevents ovulation (Brenner & Mishell, 1979). Quite often women using this method of birth control report that menstrual bleeding ceases after nine to twelve months of using this technique. Another common complaint is that its use causes a significant weight gain. The shot could be valuable for women who might not have access to regular supplies of oral contraceptives, are likely to forget to take them, or are irregular in pill taking (Toppozada & Hafez, 1980). Researchers note that very often there is a delay in return to fertility following administration of the shot; therefore, it might not be the choice for women who eventually want to become pregnant (Brenner & Mishell, 1979).

☐ *Hormone Implant* A new technique being developed and studied employs the implantation under the skin of a silastic capsule, which is made of inert silicone rubber. This capsule contains progestin, which is released gradually in controlled amounts over long periods of time. The silastic implant can last up to five years, and its hormone release apparently suppresses ovulation (Brenner & Mishell, 1979). As yet the implant is not available in the United States. Women using the silastic implant have reported problems with irregularity in menstrual bleeding, and there have been some reports of ectopic pregnancies. The implant provides long-term contraceptive protection, but research to date does not provide us with enough information to determine conclusively its possible side effects or complications.

☐ *Postcoital Pill* The postcoital or "morning after" pill is unique in that it prevents implantation of the egg in the uterine wall by somehow altering the fertilized ovum's transport to the uterus. It might also prevent implantation by affecting the lining of the uterus. At the present time, the exact method by which the postcoital pill works is unknown (Aref & Hafez, 1980). The postcoital pill is used when unprotected midcycle intercourse occurs and a woman does not want to become pregnant. The pill should be taken as soon as possible but no later than seventy-two hours after coitus (Aref & Hafez, 1980). It should be viewed as an emergency treatment only and not as a substitute for more usual and less dramatic contraceptive practices. The postcoital pill contains high dosages of estrogen, progestin, or a combination of the two. Its administration is about 97 percent effective when using estrogen and apparently somewhat less effective when using progestin or a combination. The estrogen pill causes nausea in about 50 percent of the cases. Bleeding is the most common side effect of the progestin technique, and there appears to be an increased risk of ectopic pregnancy when this method is used (Aref & Hafez, 1980). Postcoital contraception can be most useful in instances of rape or incest or when other techniques such as the condom fail. Whether or not the postcoital pill can be considered a method of abortion or a

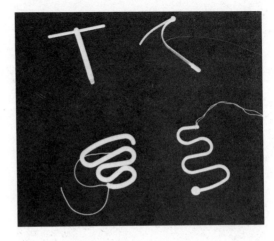

IUDs of differing designs.

means of contraception depends on one's definition of conception (Aref & Hafez, 1980).

IUD

The **intrauterine device**, or **IUD**, is an object that is inserted into the uterus to prevent pregnancy. Hippocrates, the "Father of Medicine," is credited with noting that foreign bodies in the uterus reduce fertility. In 1909, one of the earliest reports on this device described using silkworm gut to make an IUD. Not much was heard about IUDs until 1959 when Oppenheimer reported a study of 793 women in Israel who had been using IUDs (Oppenheimer, 1959). The study showed a low failure rate of only 2.5 pregnancies for every hundred sexually active women over the course of one year. That finding led to extensive studies on the IUD in the United States, with the subsequent appearance of a number of devices on the market. The best known were the Margulies spiral, the Lippes loop, and the Saf-T coil series. In the 1960s, IUDs that contained copper appeared on the market, and in the 1970s IUDs that released hormones were produced. Estimates are that currently 60 million IUDs are in use around the world, with the Lippes loop being the most popular (Hatcher et al., 1980).

One accepted function of the IUD in relation to the inhibition of conception is that it sets up an inflammatory response, independent of any temporary infection, that changes the uterine environment (Moyer,

Shaw, & Fu, 1980). Immobilization of sperm, mechanical dislodging of fertilized ova in the endometrium, and effects on the transport of sperm and ova are also possible factors that affect conception. The larger the IUD, the more successful it is in preventing pregnancy (Edelman, Berger, & Keith, 1979).

A physician places the IUD by inserting a tube that holds the device into the uterine cavity and then withdrawing the tube but leaving the IUD in the cavity (see Figure 3–11). Penetration of the uterine wall can result from this procedure if a careful pelvic examination has not been completed beforehand to identify the shape of the woman's uterus. The complication of uterine or cervical perforation by the IUD occurs in 1.2 women per thousand (Hatcher et al., 1980). The seriousness of this complication varies from case to case.

IUDs differ in both effectiveness and in expulsion rates. One research group reports that copper IUDs are more effective than similar ones without copper (Moyer, et al., 1980). Expulsion rates of up to about sixteen per one hundred insertions have been reported for some IUDs (Moyer, et al., 1980),

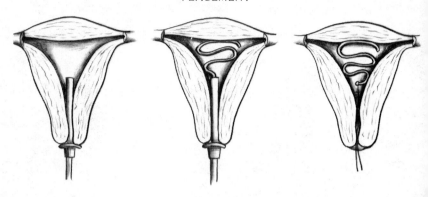

Figure 3-11. The steps in placement and removal of an IUD.

REMOVAL

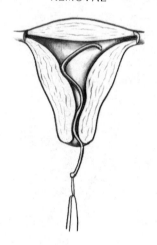

and rates are even higher when the IUD is placed within six weeks following childbirth (Edelman et al., 1979). IUDs should never be placed in women who are pregnant or who have pelvic infections. Women with recent or recurring infections, vaginitis, abnormal pap smears, a history of ectopic pregnancies, and certain anatomical anomalies of the reproductive organs are advised to consider seriously another means of contraception (Edelman, et al., 1979; Hatcher et al., 1980).

Besides perforation of the uterine wall and expulsion, other complications are as-

sociated with the IUD. Approximately 15 percent of women with an inserted IUD seek its removal because of increased menstrual bleeding or mid-cycle spotting (Hatcher et al., 1980). Interestingly, requests for removal decrease over time. Some women report pain and cramping at the time of insertion, at the time of menstruation, or when the IUD is expelled or removed. Under normal circumstances, a physician can use the strings attached to the IUD that extend into the vagina to remove the device. However, removal of the IUD sometimes can be a difficult procedure and may require hospitalization and anesthesia. When pregnancy does occur with an IUD in place, there is a threefold increase in spontaneous abortions (Cates & Ory, 1979). There is a six- to twenty-fold increase in ectopic pregnancies, and the risk of death from infection also increases dramatically (Cates & Ory, 1979). One-third of the pregnancies that occur with an IUD in the uterus are associated with the partial or complete expulsion of the IUD (Hatcher et al., 1980). A therapeutic abortion is advised if pregnancy occurs with the IUD in place because of increased risks to the woman (Hatcher et al., 1980). Other researchers report no increase in birth defects if pregnancy occurs with a copper IUD in place (Moyer, et al., 1980).

The occurrence of *pelvic inflammatory disease* is three times greater in a woman who has an IUD; unfortunately, pelvic inflammatory disease is a very serious complication that can result in death (Cates & Ory, 1979). The risk of infection associated with the IUD is one reason that it is not used as often as it had been, although newer materials and medical techniques have lowered the risk somewhat (Moyer, et al., 1980).

The IUD has, of course, the advantage of not requiring the individual to perform a daily act such as taking a pill or positioning a diaphragm, and it has been successfully kept in place for long periods of time with no complications by many women. In addition, there is no evidence that using an IUD interferes with subsequent fertility (Edelman et al., 1979). However, although the IUD is second only to oral contraceptives in effectiveness, its numerous side effects have hindered its acceptance.

Diaphragm

The **diaphragm** is a dome-shaped rubber cap with a thickened ring as an outer edge. The diaphragm is inserted into the vagina, and the ring fits over the cervix. The diaphragm is kept in place by the internal anatomy of the woman. It is most effective when a spermicide is placed in the dome before the diaphragm is positioned. The diaphragm covers the cervix so that sperm cannot enter the uterus, and the spermicidal agent kills sperm.

When used correctly, the diaphragm has a success rate of 98 percent (Lane, 1976). This high rate occurred in an unmarried, young population, with 80 percent of the group continuing to use the device. This effectiveness rate is higher than the rates reported in other studies and probably reflects the careful counseling that users received in this study. Figure 3–12 illustrates proper placement of the diaphragm, which is vital to its success.

Diaphragms vary in rim size and construction, and each woman needs to be fitted for her appropriate size. The diaphragm and spermicide should be inserted no earlier than six hours before coitus and left in place six to eight hours following coitus. It is left in place so that the spermicide can continue to work. A diaphragm should not be used by anyone who has allergies either to the rubber or the spermicide. Dia-

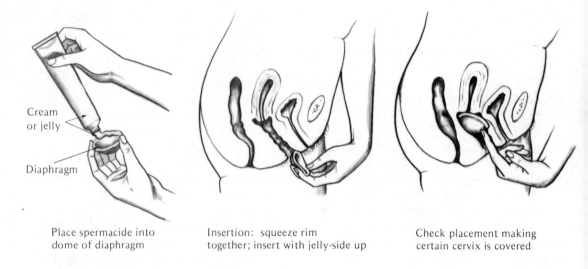

Place spermacide into
dome of diaphragm

Insertion: squeeze rim
together; insert with jelly-side up

Check placement making
certain cervix is covered

Figure 3-12. Proper use and placement of a diaphragm.

phragms also are not recommended for individuals who have recurrent urinary tract infections; nor are they suggested for use by women for whom fitting is difficult. Also, women who are concerned about interrupting the spontaneity of sex or about placing the device should probably not choose the diaphragm as a means of contraception.

A device closely related to the diaphragm is the **cervical cap.** Not as yet commercially available in the United States, the cervical cap is a thimble-shaped plastic device that fits over the cervix and blocks the entrance to the uterus. A suction effect keeps it in place. The cervical cap is not removed for a period of three to four weeks, and thus the problem of insertion before each intercourse experience is avoided. Reports on its effectiveness are not readily available, but Hatcher and his colleagues state that it appears to be less effective

than the diaphragm as a contraceptive technique (Hatcher et al., 1980).

Condom

The Egyptians were using the condom as a contraceptive device as early as 1350 B.C. (Hatcher et al., 1980). Made most commonly of rubber or a rubberlike material, **condoms** are thin sheaths that fit over the erect penis and function as a barrier to keep sperm from being deposited in the vagina. The condom is a very effective contraceptive device, especially if a spermicide is inserted into the vagina first, and there are essentially no complaints of side effects. Breakage is unlikely if a space is provided

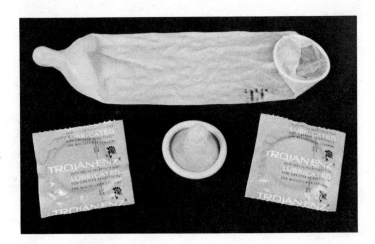

The condom—rolled up and unrolled. Note the reservoir at the tip.

at the tip of the condom to act as a reservoir for the ejaculate. Effectiveness is very high if care is taken to ensure that ejaculate does not escape or that the condom does not slip off the penis upon withdrawal. A major complaint about the condom is decreased sensitivity for males, and some people express concern about having to interrupt sexual activity to put the condom on the penis. A major advantage of the condom is that it is effective in reducing the transmission of venereal disease.

Vaginal Spermicides

Spermicides function in two ways. First, as their name implies, they kill sperm, thus preventing conception. Second, spermicide in the vagina actually blocks the os (the opening into the uterus) so that sperm cannot enter the uterus. Vaginal spermicides are classified by method of application: The three types are *foam, suppository,* and *cream* or *jelly.* Some researchers believe that spermicidal foam is the most effective of the three types (Hatcher et al., 1980). Spermicidal foam is placed deep in the vagina and is often used as a backup for other contraceptive procedures such as the condom (see Figure 3–13). Hatcher and his

group report that failures with this form of contraception result typically from its careless application. After the foam has been placed, women should wait at least eight hours before douching. The only known side effect is possible allergic reaction to the chemical. When using spermicides in suppository form, the suppository is placed in the vagina, and the fluids that are naturally present react with the suppository to produce a foaming action. The resulting foam distributes the spermicide throughout the vaginal canal. Suppository effectiveness is not as well established as is the effectiveness of spermicidal foam. Spermicidal creams and jellies are also available. Although not as effective as foams, creams and jellies used in combination with the diaphragm provide effective protection.

The Sponge

During April of 1983 the Food and Drug Administration approved the use of a new form of vaginal birth control, the contraceptive sponge. The sponge, made of polyurethane, is formed into a soft disposable pad that is saturated with the spermicide nonoxynol-9. This pad is placed deep within the vagina and is said to be an effective

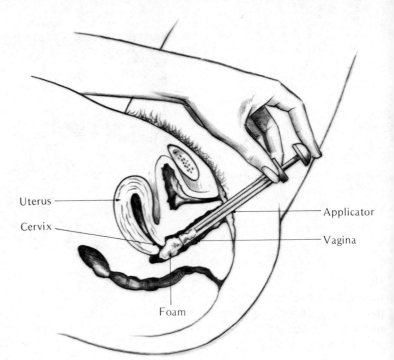

Figure 3-13. Placing the spermicide within the vagina.

Uterus

Cervix

Applicator

Vagina

Foam

contraceptive for at least 24 hours. Its effectiveness is based upon three modes of action. First, it absorbs sperm; second, it blocks sperm from entering the uterus; and third, the spermicide acts to destroy sperm. While the data on its effectiveness are not yet completed, it appears similar to the diaphragm in its ability to prevent conception (Pear, 1983).

There are several major advantages to the sponge over other vaginal contraceptives. Unlike the diaphragm it can be purchased across the counter in drug stores and does not require a medical examination for fitting. Its relatively long time of effectiveness (24 hours) means that the sponge can be placed well before an anticipated sexual interaction and thus not interfere with sexual spontaneity. Finally, it is not as "messy" as spermicidal creams and jellys. Failures with the sponge seem to result primarily from failure to follow instructions such as inserting the sponge incorrectly or removing it too soon.

Rhythm

Use of the **rhythm** technique relies on signs of ovulation that signal when to avoid intercourse or when to use additional contraceptive techniques. The appropriate use of the rhythm method requires that women keep personal records. Some women report that irregular menstrual patterns make the rhythm method difficult to use. Other people complain that sexual spontaneity is interfered with when the times for intercourse are decided in advance. Most failures with any rhythm technique are due to intercourse that occurs before the fertile period, and the pregnancies often result from sperm that have prolonged life. One researcher raises the possibility that use of the rhythm method increases birth defects because conception is likely to involve ova that are relatively old (Jongbloet, 1974). Data on this issue are sparse, and the suggestion remains highly speculative.

There are three basic rhythm techniques:

the calendar method, tracking of body temperature, and observance of cervical mucus.

☐ *Calendar Technique*   The following steps are recommended if a woman is using the calendar technique to determine the period of likely conception. To avoid pregnancy, unprotected intercourse should be avoided during the fertile period.

1. Record the length, in days, of at least eight successive menstrual cycles. Count the first day of flow as day 1.
2. Calculate the fertile period by determining (a) the earliest day in the cycle on which conception can occur, and (b) the latest day in the cycle on which conception is possible.
3. The earliest day on which conception is likely to occur is computed by subtracting 18 from the number of days in the shortest cycle, as determined in step 1. For example, if the shortest cycle was twenty-three days, 23 − 18 = 5. This means that the earliest that conception is likely to occur is five days into the cycle.
4. The latest day on which conception is likely to occur is computed by subtracting 11 from the number of days in the longest cycle, as determined in step 1. For example, if the longest cycle was twenty-nine days, 29 − 11 = 18. This means that the last day on which conception is likely to occur is eighteen days into the cycle.
5. Unprotected intercourse should be avoided from the earliest to the latest day. In our example, this would mean from day 5 to day 18, counting the first day of flow as day 1.

The calendar technique is based on the assumptions that the ova can survive up to twenty-four hours, that sperm are viable for only two or three days following ejaculation, and that ovulation occurs on day 14, plus or minus two days. In general, the more regular a woman's cycles, the more effective this method is in determining fertility (Hatcher et al., 1980).

☐ *Body Temperature Technique*   Hatcher and his colleagues recommend the following steps be taken if one is to use the temperature technique to determine the period of likely conception (Hatcher et al., 1980). To avoid pregnancy, unprotected intercourse should be avoided during the fertile period.

1. For two to three months the woman should take her body temperature each morning before rising. The same body site and conditions should be followed each day when recording her temperature. She should note when the temperature has risen 0.4 to 0.8 degrees.
2. Once the woman has learned to identify the temperature rise that is associated with ovulation, she can apply the technique.
3. The fertile period is from the fourth day of the cycle (counting the first day of flow as day 1) until three days after the

temperature has risen the 0.4 to 0.8 degrees.

The woman must be careful to watch out for infections that might raise body temperature, and she should also know that electric blankets can raise body temperature. Body temperature will rise twenty-four to seventy-two hours after ovulation and will remain there until the beginning of the next menstrual period.

☐ *Cervical Mucus Technique* Cervical mucus changes its consistency just before ovulation, and the cervical mucus technique is based on detection of that change. Cervical mucus changes from a yellow viscous consistency to a "slippery, clear discharge, much like a raw egg white" (Hatcher et al., 1980, p. 108). A drop of this clear discharge can be stretched into a strand of 6 or more centimeters (about 2.5 inches). This stretching will not occur in mucus obtained at any time other than the period around ovulation. The woman using this technique is counseled to examine herself by touching her cervix with a finger to obtain some of the mucus and determine its consistency and appearance. "As ovulation nears, the mucus usually becomes more abundant. You can notice an increasingly *wet* sensation. Mucus becomes clear, slippery, and very stretchable. You might be able to stretch it three or more inches between your thumb and forefinger. *Consider yourself very fertile when you have found this kind of mucus*" (Hatcher et al., 1980, p. 110). The mucus technique does not always give enough warning, however, and it is of-

ten recommended only as a supplement to the other rhythm methods.

Lactation

When women are breast-feeding and producing milk (lactating), fertility is reduced. The apparent reason is that a surplus of gonadotrophins are released when women are breast-feeding. A woman is less likely to conceive during this period as ovulation is suppressed. However, as a contraceptive procedure, this method is ineffective. In cultures in which contraception is not practiced and breast-feeding is common, there is about a 20 percent reduction in the number of anticipated births (Jain et al., 1970). Menstrual cycles when a woman is breast-feeding seem to be poorly related to ovulation so that the combination of lactation and rhythm methods is not very satisfactory. For anyone in our society to use lactation as a contraceptive technique is unusual.

Coitus Interruptus

Many couples use **coitus interruptus** (withdrawal) as a birth control technique. In this method the penis is withdrawn prior to ejaculation so that sperm are not deposited in the vagina. Despite widespread use, withdrawal is a poor contraceptive practice. One problem is that the individual may have difficulty withdrawing early enough, and a second is that fluid containing sperm is often discharged prior to ejaculation.

STERILIZATION PROCEDURES

Sterilization refers to surgical procedures that leave men and women incapable of reproducing. Due to its relative nonreversibility, it raises serious ethical and practical concerns. Sterilization procedures must be accompanied by fully informed voluntary consent and, to that end, some governmental regulations require a waiting period between counseling and the subsequent decision to be sterilized. Since 1969, the number of voluntary female sterilizations has risen steadily, and the number of voluntary male sterilizations rose abruptly and subsequently has declined during that same period (Hatcher et al., 1980).

The principal advantage of sterilization is that it is permanent. Once the sterilization procedure has been successfully completed, the individual does not need to be concerned about unwanted pregnancies. On the other hand, side effects have been reported in relation to most of the surgical procedures, and there is also the slight chance that the patient might die. These methods also are more expensive, at least in the short run, than other contraceptive techniques. The most common sterilization procedures involve removal of part of the reproductive system involved in sperm or ova transport (vasectomy and tubal ligation, respectively) or in the removal of the receptor organ (hysterectomy). There are no consistent changes in the hormonal patterns of individuals who undergo sterilization (Johnsonbaugh et al., 1975; Rosenberg et al., 1974). Reportedly, about 5 percent of individuals who undergo sterilization procedures subsequently regret the decision and, therefore, medical professionals are seeking to discover dependable means of reversing the procedures (Peel & Potts, 1969).

Vasectomy

The **vasectomy,** the surgical removal of the vas deferens' obstructing the transport of sperm, has been in use for a fairly long period of time. For example, in 1909 there is a report of 176 males who were vasectomized as a treatment for the "habit of masturbation" (Sharp, 1909). Also, in the early part of this century literally thousands of vasectomies were performed because the surgical procedure was considered a "rejuvenation operation" that would restore youthfulness.

Surgical techniques vary somewhat, but they all involve the sectioning and removal of the vas deferens, typically done under local anesthesia. Figure 3–14 illustrates one of the techniques employed. A failure rate of approximately 1.2 percent over twenty-one months has been reported (Kaplan & Huether, 1975). The failures of the vasectomy can be due to a number of factors, including (1) unprotected coitus occurring shortly after the surgical operation when viable sperm are still in the system, (2) the re-

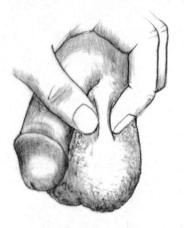

(1) Locating vas deferens

(2) Vas deferens exposed by small incision in scrotum

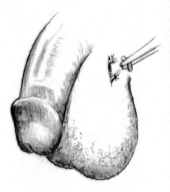

(3) A small section of vas deferens removed and ends tied and/or cauterized

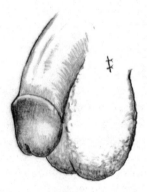

(4) Incision in scrotum closed

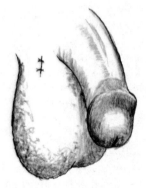

(5) Steps 1-4 repeated on right side

Figure 3-14. Vasectomy

development of a passage for the sperm, and (3) the inadvertent cutting of the wrong structure. All of these failures, particularly those having to do with the redevelopment of the sperm transport system, reportedly decrease as the length of the vas deferens that is removed is increased (Lipshultz & Benson, 1980).

Although there are minor disagreements concerning the length of time between surgery and the occurrence of absolute sterility, most physicians recommend that at least twelve weeks with a minimum of two ejaculations per week occur between surgery and unprotected intercourse (Lipshultz & Benson, 1980). Following the delay a sample of ejaculate should be examined to make certain that no viable sperm are present.

Vasectomy surgery can cause a number of transient side effects. For example, swelling, pain, and bruising occur in approximately 50 percent of the operations, although treatment with aspirin and ice seems to be sufficient to handle these minor complications. More extensive bleeding is reported in up to 18 percent of the cases. Infection anywhere except the epididymis occurs in up to 6 percent of the cases, and infection of the epididymis in 0.5 to 6.1 percent of the cases. *Sperm granuloma,* swellings that result from sperm leaking into the scrotal tissues, occur in 5 to 10 percent of the cases (Leader et al., 1974). Schmidt and Morris (1973) report sperm granuloma to be the most common of the complications following vasectomy.

A substantial number of men who have had vasectomies develop sperm antibodies subsequent to the surgery. As noted previously, these antibody formations are reported to occur in 50 to 70 percent of vasectomized men (Menge & Behrman, 1980). At the current time, there is no evidence that the body's immunity system is adversely affected by the development of a specific immunity to one's own sperm. Possibly, however, this immunologic response could interfere with attempts to reverse the sterilization procedure. In respect to vasectomy reversal, microsurgical techniques have been developed that successfully reverse vasectomies, with the subsequent pregnancy of the partner occurring in between 20 and 60 percent of the cases (Hatcher et al., 1980). Attempts have been made to develop various types of valves that could be implanted in the vas deferens, but to date none have met with success (Lipshultz & Benson, 1980). Valves would make reversal much simpler.

In general, the vasectomy is less invasive and surgically less risky than the female alternatives (Hafez, 1980).

Tubal Methods

For women, the most common sterilization procedure involves the interference of ova transport by destroying portions of the Fallopian tubes. This surgery is generally called **tubal ligation.** A range of surgical procedures are used that have varying success rates and varying levels of complications. In the *culpotomy* the physician reaches the Fallopian tubes through a small incision made in the vaginal wall. A *culdoscopy* is performed with the aid of a tube called a laparoscope that provides both light and access to the illuminated area. The tube is inserted through a small incision in the abdomen, and it locates the oviducts. The surgeon, reaching the oviducts with surgical instruments through another small incision nearby, is thus able to see as he or she performs surgery upon the Fallopian tubes. Recent developments in microsurgery have permitted culdoscopy to be done through one small incision. The culdoscopy is, in general, safer and results in fewer complications than the culpotomy. It does, however, require a greater level of expertise; complications reportedly arise four times more often among less experienced surgeons (Keith et al., 1976). Sometimes the culdoscopy is called a "bandaid" operation, as the incision is so small that it can literally be covered by a bandaid. This procedure does not require hospitalization.

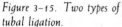

Figure 3-15. Two types of tubal ligation.

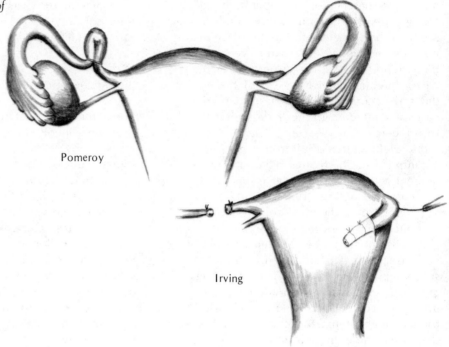

Pomeroy

Irving

Once the Fallopian tubes are made accessible, the physician has the option to use one of many surgical techniques. Figure 3-15 shows two of the better-known procedures, the Pomeroy and Irving methods. Physicians have found that simply tying the tubes is generally not sufficient, since approximately 20 percent of all women whose tubes have been tied subsequently become pregnant. When tying the tube is combined with crushing the area between the ties, the failure rate drops, and when a section of the tube is removed along with tying, the fail-

ure rate is almost nonexistent (Evans, 1980).

In one study, the failure rate was reported to be 0.19 percent for 3,600 culdoscopic procedures. The more extensive surgical procedure that includes removal of a portion of the tube, the *laparotomy,* is reported to have a 0 percent failure rate. However, because the laparotomy requires that the abdominal wall be opened for an unaided view, complications are more frequent and serious. In general, with the development of more precise and adequate methods of microsurgery, between 50 and

70 percent of tubal surgical procedures are reversible (Hatcher et al., 1980).

Hysterectomy

A *hysterectomy* is the surgical removal of the uterus. Until very recently this operation was the most common form of sterilization available in the United States (Hatcher et al., 1980). Hysterectomies performed for sterilization purposes, however, have become uncommon because of adverse consequences resulting from the surgery. The rates of both adverse side effects and mortality among hysterectomy patients range from ten to one hundred times greater than for a similar group undergoing tubal ligation (Hatcher et al., 1980). In addition, the hysterectomy is a more expensive procedure that requires hospitalization and a relatively long recovery period. Furthermore, the surgical trauma resulting from tubal surgery is less severe than the trauma experienced following a hysterectomy. Nor are psychological problems following sterilization procedures as likely to occur if tubal ligation is the type of surgery performed (Hatcher et al., 1980).

New Directions in Contraception

At the 1980 conference, "Frontiers of Contraceptive Research," perhaps the most promising development revealed was the manufacture and use of a synthetic luteinizing hormone-releasing hormone, LHRH (Benditt, 1980). LHRH apparently functions as a contraceptive in both men and women. Synthetic LHRH appears to be much more powerful than the natural hormone, and it seems to be effective because of "paradoxical inhibition" which seems to reduce rather than raise the LH and FSH levels in both sexes. In women, this reduction of FSH and LH levels inhibits ovulation and probably reduces the luteal phase of the menstrual cycle, thus preventing implantation of any fertilized ova. Casper and Yen (1979) report some preliminary studies that found no change in estrogen levels for women who were taking the synthetic LHRH. Should that finding be replicated and further information uncovered, this new substance may possibly provide a means of birth control with fewer side effects than the current hormonal methods offer. In men, the substance seems to reduce sperm production, but does not seem to reduce the production of testosterone. How it achieves the reduction is not understood at this time, but perhaps the availability of a male contraceptive pill will soon be a reality. So far, no side effects have been reported by the individuals taking the synthetic LHRH.

At the conference it was noted that injectible, long-lasting hormones were being increasingly used worldwide and that research in this field is moving ahead. At this time the pregnancy rate is an unacceptable 3.6 percent with the injection of progestin, and there is a fair amount of breakthrough or mid-cycle bleeding and irregularity of menstrual cycles. Hopefully, these side effects can be controlled with regulation of dosages. Testosterone injections in men have been shown to reduce sperm counts, but they have thus far been accompanied by unwanted side effects such as acne and weight gain. Inserts such as vaginal rings with hormone-releasing factors and the use of devices that are placed within the cervix rather than within the uterus are also being explored.

ABORTION

Few issues related to sexuality generate more intense feelings or more fixed views than does abortion. **Abortion,** defined as the expulsion or removal of a fetus or embryo from the uterus before it is sufficiently developed to survive, goes back to ancient times. The earliest medical reference to induced abortion can be found in Chinese history dated around 2700 B.C. (Zimmerman, 1977). The first U.S. law concerning abortion was passed in Connecticut in 1821. That law forbade the deliberate termination of a pregnancy after "quickening," the first fetal movements felt by the mother. Subsequently, various laws were passed in other states concerning the termination of pregnancy. The current controversy began when, on January 22, 1973, the U.S. Supreme Court ruled in two induced abortion cases. Three principal points were established in the first ruling. First, until approximately the end of the first trimester of pregnancy, the decision concerning termination of a pregnancy is left exclusively to a woman and her physician. Second, the state may regulate or pass legislation limiting abortion until the end of the second trimester as long as those regulations are concerned with the health of the woman and reflect safe medical practices. Third, during the last trimester, states may prohibit abortion except in those instances in which the life or health of the woman is at stake. On July 1, 1976, a second important decision concerning abortion was reached by the Supreme Court. In that decision, the Court ruled that third parties, such as parents or a spouse, cannot be given the legal right to interfere with an otherwise legal abortion decision. The early 1980s has been marked by political efforts to reverse the court decisions on abortion.

Who obtains legal abortions? Table 3–9 shows the relationship between the age of women and the number of abortions, and the percentage of pregnancies terminated. The figures highlighted are for the years 1978 and 1975, but the same relationships hold for the previous years as well. The number of abortions per woman increases until age 25 and then decreases. However, the probability that any pregnancy will be

TABLE 3-9 ABORTIONS BY MOTHER'S AGE

AGE	NUMBER PER 1000 WOMEN (1978)	PERCENTAGE OF PREGNANCIES TERMINATED BY ABORTION (1975)
less than 15	1.1	51
15–19	29.7	32
20–24	34.7	20
25–29	18.8	14
30–34	9.5	18
35–39	4.7	28
40	1.5	37

(From the *Statistical Abstracts of the United States,* 1981.)

aborted shows a somewhat different pattern. The probability of abortions per birth is higher in the younger population, declines for those between the ages of 25 and 30, and then increases until age 40 and above. Thirty-two percent of all abortions are performed on blacks and other minority group members, and about 75 percent of all pregnancy terminations are performed on unmarried women. In 1977 there was approximately one legal abortion for every three live births in the United States (Zimmerman, 1977). Worldwide, between 30 and 55 million abortions are performed each year (Tietze and Lewit, 1977).

The various ways that legal abortions are performed can be divided into two groups: surgical techniques and nonsurgical techniques. The second group is distinguished by the fact that abortion is induced by administering some type of substance into the uterus.

Surgical Abortion Techniques

☐ *Vacuum Curettage* When using the *vacuum curettage* technique, a slender hollow probe, typically made of flexible plastic, is introduced into the uterus through the cervix. This probe is attached to a vacuum source, which removes the contents of the uterus through this slender probe. The probe is rotated within the uterus to ensure full contact with the walls of the uterus. The more advanced the pregnancy, the larger the probe. Following this vacuum procedure, a sharp curette is placed within the uterus, and the walls are gently scraped to make sure they are cleared. This procedure, partially illustrated in Figure 3–16, can be performed under a local anesthetic. Typically, a woman is able to undergo vacuum curettage on an out-patient basis. Following the procedure a woman will need to

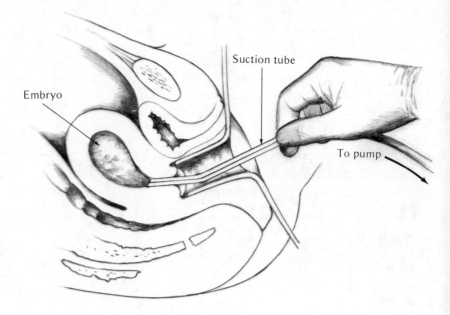

Embryo

Suction tube

To pump

Figure 3-16. Vacuum
aspiration abortion.

rest, but, in general, the recovery period is brief.

Vacuum curettage is sometimes used following intercourse but prior to menses for the individual who is concerned about pregnancy yet wishes to alleviate possible psychological feelings of guilt by having the vacuum curettage performed before a pregnancy is confirmed. When performed this early, the technique is called *menstrual extraction* (Bolognese & Corson, 1975). Two major disadvantages are associated with this procedure. One is that because the use of the sharp curette is often not employed, there is a higher than usual chance of failure to remove the embryo. Second, because it is performed prior to confirmed pregnancy, the procedure is often performed unnecessarily at the expense and distress of the woman.

□ *Dilation and Curettage* A *Dilation and Curettage,* more commonly known as a D & C, is less commonly employed for terminating pregnancy, as compared with vacuum curettage. A sharp curette is used to scrape the walls of the uterus: Typically, a larger cervical dilation is needed, and general anesthesia is used. The D & C is used to treat a variety of gynecological complaints.

□ *Dilation and Evacuation* A *Dilation and Evacuation,* or a D & E, is an abortion procedure used in the second trimester of pregnancy. By this time fetal development has progressed considerably; the technique thus requires larger surgical instruments, including forceps and a suction with a larger probe. The D & E procedure is performed under general anesthesia and lasts less than thirty minutes (Grimes & Cates, 1980).

□ *Hysterotomy* The *hysterotomy* is similar to a small Caesarean section in that the embryo or fetus is removed through incisions made in the abdominal wall and the uterus. With safer and less expensive means of pregnancy termination available, the hysterotomy has all but disappeared as an abortion procedure.

Nonsurgical Abortion Techniques

☐ *Prostaglandins F₂* This abortion procedure takes place in the second trimester of pregnancy. Prostaglandins F_2 is injected into the amnionic fluid, and shortly thereafter the uterus begins to contract and forces an abortion. The prostaglandin procedure is associated with a high level of gastrointestinal distress, including pain, diarrhea, and vomiting. An ethical and legal concern that surrounds the use of this procedure is that in some instances a live fetus is delivered (Hatcher et al., 1980).

☐ *Prostaglandins E₂* A vaginal suppository containing prostaglandins is used in this method of abortion (Hatcher et al., 1980). Following the placement of the suppository, in a manner similar to the injection described above, the uterus begins contracting, and the conceptus is aborted. As with the previous procedure, there is the problem of gastrointestinal discomfort and there is concern about the delivery of a live fetus.

☐ *Hypertonic Saline and/or Urea* As with the use of the prostaglandins, this procedure generally is used in the second trimester of pregnancy. A saline or urea solution is injected into the amnionic cavity, the fetus dies, and delivery is induced (Potts, Diggory, & Peely, 1972). Approximately thirty to thirty-six hours after injection the woman will abort (Bolognese & Corson, 1975). This procedure does not result in delivery of a live fetus and, in general, is associated with somewhat fewer side effects than prostaglandin administration. With the saline injection there is a report of approximately 5 percent failure rate. Typically, the woman is able to leave the medical setting as early as four to six hours later, but sometimes an overnight stay is recommended (Bolognese & Corson, 1975). The risk, should the solution inadvertently enter the woman's bloodstream, is less for urea than for saline (Potts et al., 1977).

Complications of Abortion

Because of the controversy surrounding the voluntary termination of pregnancy, abortions have been extensively studied for side effects and risks. One of the serious risks of abortion is failure to terminate the pregnancy. This problem occurs relatively infrequently in legal abortions, however. Very little information is available on the effects of an unsuccessful abortion attempt. Damage to the embryo or fetus seems possible.

A number of complications can occur as a result of abortion. For example, the walls of the uterus may be perforated by the curettes used in some of the procedures. The complication rate is a function of the technique used. The more extensive surgical procedures provide a much higher risk of complications, such as extensive bleeding, infection, and embolisms or blood clots.

A risk of maternal mortality is also asso-

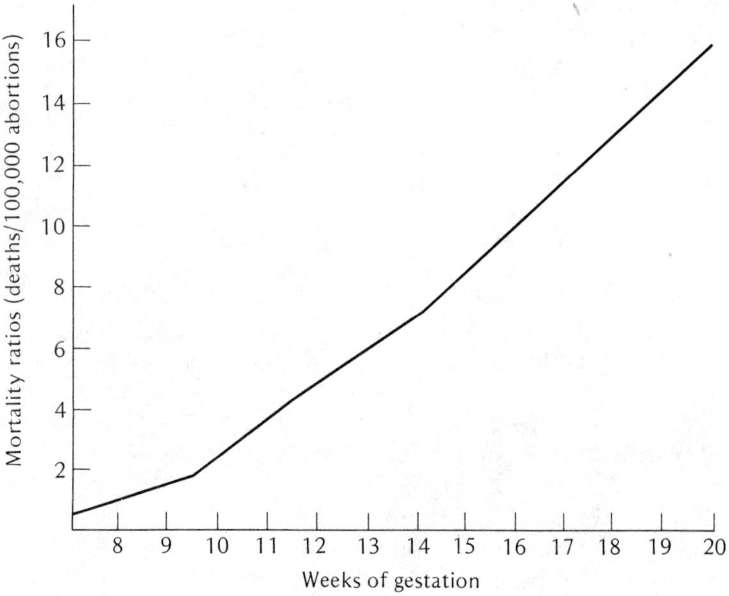

Figure 3-17. The risk of maternal death from legal abortion as a function of the length of pregnancy. Institute of Medicine, Academy of Sciences, 1975

ciated with abortion procedures. Figure 3-17 shows that the risk of death increases dramatically when an abortion is performed beyond the first trimester of pregnancy (Institute of Medicine, Academy of Sciences, 1975). When comparing the risk of abortion with the risk of birth, the following information is available. Overall, for the years between 1972 and 1975, there were approximately 14 deaths per every 100,000 live births (National Center for Health Statistics, 1976). Deaths from legal abortions throughout the fifteenth week of gestation were approximately 2 per every 100,000 (Grimes & Cates, 1980). Thus, while abortions certainly have attendant risks, at least through the fifteenth week of pregnancy, the risks associated with full-term pregnancies are much greater (Grimes & Cates, 1980).

In one study, infection accounted for 27 percent of all abortion deaths, 26 percent

were caused by an embolus in the bloodstream, complications of anesthesia accounted for 15 percent, 10 percent were brought on by bleeding, and all other causes of mortality from abortion combined to form approximately 22 percent of the deaths (Grimes & Cates, 1980). The data indicate that the decision to terminate pregnancy should be made as early as possible: Fewer deaths and complications result because abortion procedures are less stressful early in pregnancy.

Many women fear that having an abortion may reduce their chances of being able to conceive a child at some later time. In one study about 80 percent of a group of women who had had abortions ovulated within six weeks following the procedure (Lahteenmaki et al., 1980). In a controlled study of over 2,000 women who had had abortions, it was noted that, "women with a previous induced abortion showed a small but statistically significant increase in the incidence of subsequent pregnancy failure" (Madrone et al., 1981). These researchers stress, however, that the reduced ability to conceive because of a previous abortion was less than that found as a result of social and economic factors. These two reports indicate that very shortly after having an abortion a woman can become pregnant and that the abortion only slightly lowers the ability to have children at a later time. The effect of multiple abortions, however, is as yet unknown.

SUMMARY

1. **Spermatogenesis,** sperm production, takes place in the male's seminiferous tubules. **Oogenesis** is the development of ova in the female. While sperm production continues throughout the male life cycle, all of a woman's eggs are formed by the time she is born.

2. The sperm and egg must meet in the oviduct for fertilization to occur. The fertilized egg then travels to the uterus and implants itself in the uterine lining. On rare occasions the fertilized ovum will develop outside of the uterus, most commonly in the Fallopian tube, resulting in an **ectopic pregnancy.** Many serious complications are possible with an ectopic pregnancy.

3. The prenatal period is divided into *trimesters:* The first trimester lasts from month 1 to month 3; months 4 to 6 mark the second trimester; and months 7 to 9 make up the third. During the first two months of pregnancy the developing offspring is referred to as an **embryo;** from the third month until delivery it is called a **fetus.**

4. The signs of pregnancy are classified into three groups: presumptive, probable, and positive. A missed menstrual period is generally a woman's first indication of a possible pregnancy.

5. Fetal growth is influenced by a number of factors, and the following contribute to reduced fetal growth: multiple births, smoking during pregnancy, maternal malnourishment, and reduced oxygen intake.

6. Professionals generally agree that if no complications exist, sexual intercourse during pregnancy does not have to be restricted.

7. Labor and normal vaginal delivery take place in three stages: The first stage begins with dilation of the cervix and uterine contractions and ends when the cervix is fully dilated; the second stage begins from this

point and ends with the delivery of the baby; and the third stage involves the delivery of the **placenta.** A **Caesarean section** is the surgical method of delivery through incisions in the abdominal and uterine walls.

8. Female infertility is primarily caused either by failure to ovulate or by blockage of the Fallopian tubes. The major cause of male infertility is low sperm count, which is triggered by a number of conditions, including **varicocele** and **testicular failure.**

9. The placement of sperm (**semen**) in the vagina or uterus by means other than sexual intercourse is called **artificial insemination.** Within the last few years we have seen the development of in vitro fertilization, in which the fertilization process takes place on a culture plate. The fertilized egg is then transplanted into a woman's uterus. The babies that result from this process of fertilization are called test-tube babies.

10. **Down's syndrome,** a result of chromosomal abnormalities, causes severe consequences to the child. Its occurrence is closely related to maternal age at the time of conception.

11. **Amniocentesis** is a diagnostic technique used to identify fetal diseases and defects. A needle is inserted through the abdominal and uterine walls into the placenta, and amniotic fluid is withdrawn for analysis.

12. A **teratogen** is any substance or condition that produces deformities in the developing fetus. Teratogenic agents include infections, drugs, exposure to radiation, and environmental chemicals.

13. Contraceptive devices interfere with conception. A variety of types are available, including *hormonal contraceptives* (the Pill), **IUDs, condoms, spermicides, diaphragms,** and the **rhythm method** (natural birth control method). **Sterilization** is a permanent form of contraception. The **vasectomy** is the sterilization procedure for men, and **tubal ligation** is the most common method of female sterilization. Many factors must be considered when choosing a contraceptive method — it is a highly individual choice.

14. **Abortion** is the termination of pregnancy before the embryo or fetus is sufficiently developed to survive. Induced abortion is an issue that is currently causing a great deal of controversy. A number of techniques are available, and their use primarily depends on the stage a pregnancy is at when the decision is made to abort. The most common methods are vacuum curettage, D & C, D & E, hormonal injections and suppositories, and saline or urea solution injections.

SUGGESTED READINGS

Hafez, E. S. E. (Ed.). *Human reproduction: Conception and contraception.* New York: Harper & Row, 1980. A very up-to-date text that offers wide coverage of the technical knowledge on conception and contraception. For advanced students.

Moghissi, K. S. (Ed.), *Controversies in contraception.* Baltimore: Williams & Wilkins, 1979. A technical text on the current status of many of the issues in contraception with an emphasis on side effects and complications of various techniques.

Page, E. W., Villee, C. A. & Villee, D. B., *Human reproduction: The core content of obstetrics, gynecology, and prenatal medicine, 3rd ed.* Philadelphia: Saunders, 1981. A medical text of up-to-date information on all aspects of reproduction. It can be understood by the serious student who lacks medical training.

CHAPTER FOUR

MASTURBATION AND FANTASY
Patterns of Arousal by and for One's Self

The subject of masturbation is quite inexhaustible.
Sigmund Freud, Collected Works

*I*f we were to walk around a college campus and ask people about their first sexual experience, most everyone would assume we were asking about the first time they were involved with another person. "Sex" is usually thought to involve two people. Yet, as we are growing up, our first sexual activities are frequently experiences that occur when we are by ourselves. Such solitary activities may include **masturbation,** which is the physical stimulation of one's own genitals and other erogenous areas for the purpose of sexual gratification, or they may consist of sexual fantasies, erotic dreams, or the reading of erotic literature.

In these expressions of sexuality, sexual arousal results from thoughts or activities that can occur in the absence of any interpersonal contact. Traditionally, they have been categorized as "autoeroticism," a word coined by Havelock Ellis at the turn of the twentieth century. Other researchers have used the label **"self-stimulation"** (Ford & Beach, 1951). For clarity, we will use the term self-stimulation to cover all varieties of solitary sexual arousal in all species, and reserve autoeroticism for humans, since "erotic" seems to be a word with particularly human reference.

Two further points on the definition of self-stimulation are important. One is that masturbation, fantasies, and erotic dreams can also occur in the presence of someone else. In this chapter, however, we restrict our discussion to solitary sexual activities, and thus we will not be concerned with the use of fantasy during intercourse. Similarly, we classify the manual stimulation of a partner's genitals as foreplay or sexplay rather than mutual masturbation. A second important point is that orgasm does not have to occur for an activity to be identified as self-stimulation.

Self-stimulation is a nonsocial activity. Because of this distinction, we wish to consider in this chapter the extent to which self-stimulation has social implications, and to determine its psychological value. Historically, in Western societies, masturbators have been persecuted, threatened with everything from eternal damnation to epilepsy, feeblemindedness, and sterility. Even today, in spite of more open and accepting attitudes regarding sexuality in general, many people still have negative feelings about masturbation. The fact that shifting attitudes regarding autoeroticism have lagged behind attitudes toward other sexual activities is curious. Examining the negative attitudes and their shift will help illustrate different views about sexual patterns in general. For example, masturbation was believed to cause physical deformities and disease in the 1700s and 1800s, but by the 1900s it was more likely to be blamed for psychosocial maladjustment.

We will explore a kind of defiance—that of individual person's masturbation and fantasy practices in the face of strong social disapproval. Researchers such as Davis in the 1920s and Kinsey and Terman in the 1930s and 1940s revealed that over 50 percent of the women and 90 percent of the men they surveyed masturbated at some time in their lives. Judging from these results, no other sexual practice has apparently been so universally practiced and at the same time so pervasively condemned. So that we might understand such contradictory behaviors, we must try to identify the factors that have made our social and religious institutions label self-stimulation such an undesirable sexual activity; we must also determine if there is any truth to the belief that autoerotic activities are harmful.

A TROUBLED HISTORY

Antimasturbation attitudes have persisted for a very long time. The condemnation of masturbation was recorded as far back as the *Egyptian Book of the Dead,* c. 1550–950 B.C. In early Jewish scriptures, masturbation was regarded as the most severe sin one could commit, and at times throughout history, Jewish Orthodox codes have regarded masturbation as a capital offense, punishable by death (Epstein, 1948; May, 1931). Over the centuries, Jewish literature on masturbation has stressed the severity of this sin, pointed out its health dangers, and threatened fearful punishments. Regulations from the Talmud—the basis of religious law for traditional Judaism—offer obsessive details on how to prevent accidental ejaculation: Males were warned not to sleep on their backs, not to wear tight trousers, and to avoid touching their penis while urinating (Epstein, 1948). All of these orders were aimed not only at preventing masturbation but also at preventing potentially sexually arousing situations.

The Christian Church shaped the sexual ideals of the Middle Ages and set up an elaborate code of regulations to govern sexual behavior. Masturbation was regarded as sinful—perhaps as sinful as *bestiality* (sex with animals) and homosexuality (May, 1931). Moreover, ecclesiastical chastisement was not limited to sexual *acts.* Even thinking about fornication (which was any sexual activity except intercourse with one's spouse for the purpose of procreation) was punishable by forty days of penance.

From the Middle Ages have come some of the more derogatory terms referring to autoeroticism. Wet dreams were once known as **nocturnal pollution,** which effectively conveys a sense of contamination and filth. **Onanism,** still used as a synonym for masturbation, was based on the interpretation of the Biblical story of Onan. Onan was put to death after "spilling his seed" on the ground because he violated the law that specified that a man was to provide his brother's widow with offspring (Genesis 38:7–10). Rather than masturbation, the act of **coitus interruptus,** or withdrawal before ejaculation, is now generally believed to be the act for which Onan was punished. A careful reading of the passage does suggest the latter interpretation; however, onanism may conceptually include any activity that is not procreative. At any rate, some critics believe that the

Church writers deliberately sought Biblical justification for banning masturbation and altered the interpretation of the story of Onan to suit their purpose (Taylor, 1954). In fact, masturbation is never mentioned in the Bible; its sinfulness is based on interpretations of certain passages such as Onan's story (Ginder, 1975).

Why should the prohibitions against masturbation have been so strong? One possibility is that to ensure population growth, strict rules concerning sexual activity had to be enforced. Another related explanation is that any nonsocial sexual activity was disturbing to the Church. These ideas are tied together in the following passage:

> Masturbation tended to exempt the practitioners from their social obligations and shifted the sexual instinct beyond its teleological implication, the procreation of children. It was in the interests of the priests to promote and foster the greatest degree of fertility among its congregants and to encourage them to follow the ancient rule: "Like the sands of the sea shall you increase and therefore you must not waste your seed." (Gordon, 1972, p. 20)

According to the Catholic code, female masturbation was a crime against nature but not as sinful as male masturbation. Gordon (1972) also mentions that Church rules permitted married women to reach orgasm through masturbation either before or after intercourse, perhaps because of the belief that a woman's orgasm was essential for conception to occur. The leniency granted females supports the idea that the concern over masturbation was aimed at solidifying the family structure and increasing family size. Alternatively, more permissive attitudes toward female masturbation may have reflected the belief that most women would not be tempted to masturbate because women were not expected to be very sexual.

From evil and sin, the emphasis by the eighteenth century had shifted to concerns over the dangerous psychological and physical consequences of masturbation. A book written in the early 1700s, *Onania, or the Heinous Sin of Self-Pollution,* had great influence among the general public. In 1760 an infamous work, *Onania, or A Treatise on the Diseases Produced by Onanism,* repeated many of the ideas of the earlier volume on masturbation and was readily accepted by the medical community. S. A. Tissot, its author, was a respected Swiss physician who attributed most human ills to loss of seminal fluid; he believed that the loss of one ounce of semen weakened a man more than the loss of at least 40 ounces of blood. Tissot's theory was that masturbation resulted in increased blood flow to the brain, which in turn could produce insanity (Hare, 1962). Subsequent writers came to similar conclusions. By the 1800s the masturbatory theory of insanity was firmly established in the mainstream of medical practice. For instance, Benjamin Rush, the "father" of American psychiatry, listed masturbation as a cause of insanity. These views of masturbation have continued well into the twentieth century (see Box 4–2).

When moral arguments failed to persuade individuals to cease this "solitary

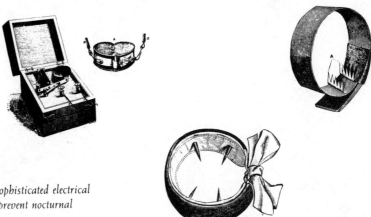

From the simple mechanical to the more sophisticated electrical versions, the devices historically used to prevent nocturnal emissions were a young man's nightmare.

vice," more radical treatments were advocated up until the early 1900s. One such treatment involved having young boys wear, at night, girdlelike structures lined with spikes, or constructed so that a bell would ring in the parents' room at the least suggestion of an erection (Milton, 1881). Chastity belts to prevent "self-abuse" were also available for women. Applying camphor to the genitals was another technique; it was based on the premise that pain in the genital area would cause an individual to avoid masturbating. Recommended treatment for mental patients included placing a silver ring through the prepuce, the loose fold of skin that covers the glans of the uncircumcised penis, to prevent the individual from retracting the foreskin to masturbate. Even more radical treatments such as clitoridectomies (removal of the clitoris) were performed in the late 1800s to reduce such activity in women, and castrations were performed on men. Surgical methods were rather quickly abandoned, primarily because they were unsuccessful.

Francis Cooke (1870, 1974) expanded the list of ill effects of "excessive" masturbation to include paleness and feeblemindedness, fever, muscular convulsions, weak backs, and loss of appetite. Women who masturbated, Cooke grimly observed, would suffer gastric and uterine disorders, a loss of flesh, and a loss of freshness and beauty. He also believed that they would become emaciated, pale and filthy, have bad breath, and eventually become nymphomaniacs and die a lingering death. One of the most important early figures in the study of sexuality, Havelock Ellis (1906), who otherwise had a liberal view of sexual practices, also believed in the dangerous results of too much masturbation—deafness, epilepsy, acne, asthma, insanity, and criminality were among the disorders he attributed to self-stimulation.

Gradually, toward the end of the nineteenth century, masturbation was increasingly associated with general psychological disturbances. Richard von Krafft-Ebing, for instance, a psychiatrist who was influential in shaping the attitudes of both professionals and nonprofessionals concerning the basic nature of sexuality, frequently mentioned the masturbation histories of individuals with very atypical sexual practices. He claimed that masturbation would "contaminate and . . . exhaust the source of all noble and ideal sentiments" and leave behind only the "coarse animal desire for sexual satisfaction" (Krafft-Ebing, 1886, pp.

In his book, Psychopatia Sexualis, *Richard von Krafft-Ebing (1840–1902) claimed that masturbation was one of two major causes (the other being genetics) of sexual variations.*

188–189). Krafft-Ebing actually believed that masturbation was the root of all evil, including criminal acts and murder.

Almost all of these early books on masturbation were written in complete ignorance of psychology, physiology, and biology. From a late twentieth-century vantage point, we can easily see from the titles of books on masturbation as well as from the synonyms used to describe the act ("self-abuse," "pollution," "solitary vice") that authoritative theories of masturbation were riddled with assumptions that masturbation was shameful and dirty. Why was there such feverish disgust and so much one-sided condemnation?

One important factor seems to be the cultural *Zeitgeist,* the intellectual and emotional climate of the times. Social institutions, including religious ones, were opposed to masturbation because it was viewed as a threat to sacred values—especially procreation and solidarity of the family structure. Fears were that masturbation would cause a loss of interest in and decreased dependency on intercourse. Such an attitude provided a receptive atmosphere for whatever antimasturbation theory came along.

At the broadest level, masturbation, especially by adults, was seen in an overwhelmingly negative light because it was believed to lead to a decay of human virtues and qualities. Because the development of Western civilization often depended on social cooperation, postponement of immediate pleasure, family responsibility, and religious commitment, this form of asocial

sexual indulgence was considered dangerous and something that should be eliminated. In this context, those who masturbated were undoubtedly seen as less godly, and more animalistic, depraved, unfit, ill, or mad.

Freud's views on the effects of masturbation were both positive and negative. His theories of masturbation were based more on interpretation than systematic investigations of large samples of people, and his opinions changed somewhat over the course of his twenty-three volumes. Freud and his followers generally viewed masturbation to be as critical in the development of the healthy personality as it is to the potential development of neuroses. Freud saw masturbation progressing through four phases: (1) infancy, with stimulation in the form of genital play; (2) childhood (from ages 4 to 10), a critical period when the child learns to suppress masturbation and to use fantasy; (3) latency, when masturbation urges and fantasies are repressed as the child learns to control instinctive desires; and (4) adolescence, when masturbation and fantasies again surface. Freud believed that if the adolescent successfully passed through the various developmental stages, then masturbatory practices would be helpful in becoming a heterosexual adult.

Freud thus brought masturbation, and sexuality in general, back into a framework of "natural" human development. Masturbation and fantasy were considered normal, depending on an individual's level of maturation. However, early Freudian theory proposed that this process of maturation was unstable and could easily result in fixation or arrested development at an infantile level. For instance, girls were expected to switch from clitoral to vaginal masturbation at puberty if they were to be considered mature; also, inadequate suppression of masturbation or the continued experience of certain fantasies during childhood was likely, according to the Freudian

theory, to lead to personality disorders.

Later modifications of Freud's theory suggested that masturbation was harmful only when it produced guilt or was preferred to heterosexual intercourse. However, social and parental sources of guilt were so common that emerging from adolescence free from personality scars caused by masturbation was difficult. This was particularly true for women, who were made to feel immature if they enjoyed clitoral stimulation, or masturbation, more than vaginal stimulation.

We have learned that masturbation was viewed as sinful in the Middle Ages, that Tissot and Ellis claimed that it results in insanity and physical depravity, and finally that Freud was convinced that autoeroticism threatened one's personality and character development. This overview of the history of masturbation will help you to better understand more current opinions of the subject based on the biological, sociological, and cultural data that have accumulated in recent times.

CROSS-CULTURAL PERSPECTIVE

Information on autoeroticism in other cultures does exist, but it is rather sparse. Generally, the majority of preliterate or nonindustrialized cultures have strong, negative sanctions against the *adult* practice of masturbation, perhaps even more so than Western industrialized societies. Individuals

who masturbate are usually thought to be sexually inadequate or immature. For instance, the Crow Indians believed that the only people who masturbated were those unable to attract partners of the opposite sex. Similarly, the Lesu, inhabitants of a small South Pacific island, allowed masturbation for women who did not have access to approved heterosexual outlets (Ford & Beach, 1951). Although the Trobriand Islanders reportedly were much more tolerant about autoerotic behaviors, such behavior was viewed as inappropriate for adult men and women:

> Masturbation (ikivanyni kwila: "he manipulates penis," isulumomoni: "he makes semen boil over") is a recognized practice often referred to in jokes. The natives maintain however that it would be done only by an idiot (tonagowa), or one of the unfortunate albinos, or one defective in speech; in other words, only by those who cannot obtain favors from women. The practice is therefore regarded as undignified and unworthy of a man, but in a rather amused and entirely indulgent manner. Exactly the same attitude is adopted toward female masturbation (ikivayni wila: "she manipulates cunnus," ibasi wila o yamala: "she pierces vagina with her hand"). (Malinowski, 1932, pp. 400–401)

Although masturbation is nearly universally frowned on for adults, there is a greater range of cross-cultural tolerance toward childhood masturbation. Some cultures permit and even encourage genital self-play in children, while others enforce strict limitations. The Kwoma of New Guinea were not allowed to masturbate, nor were they permitted even to touch their own genitals. The genital taboo of this culture was so pervasive that men and women were not allowed to handle their own genitals at all, even during urination (Ford & Beach, 1951). A small Irish folk community fictitiously called "Inis Beag" severely punishes childhood masturbation, as it does almost any (direct or indirect) form of sexual expression, such as nakedness or mutual body exploration (Messenger, 1971).

In contrast to these highly restrictive attitudes, the Hopi (Southwestern American Indian) and Siriono (Bolivian nomad) tribes reportedly manually stimulated the genitals of their children and, in addition, permitted self-stimulation until the age of puberty (Ford & Beach, 1951). Some cultures permit children to masturbate in public (the Pukapukans of Polynesia, for instance). In several cultures the boys are likely to masturbate in small groups, while the girls tend to be more private; the Bala or Basogyne of Africa (Merriam, 1971) and the Samoans (Mead, 1928) follow this pattern. And yet, anthropologist Donald Marshall (1971) reports exactly the opposite tendency among the Polynesian people of Mangaia, where masturbation is a more private activity for boys than it is for girls.

We have almost no information on how often masturbation occurs in those cultures that permit such activity. Marshall (1971) estimates that the Mangaian boys masturbate two to three times a week, and that nocturnal orgasms increase in adult men when access to women is denied. Similarly, almost nothing is known about masturbation techniques except that the use of vaginal objects by females seems to be quite common. The type of object varies considerably and includes dildos made of wood, reindeer muscles, bananas, and manioc roots.

Generally, although cultures vary widely in their attitude toward childhood masturbation, from puberty onward most cultures enforce negative sanctions regarding masturbation and at the same time increase their expectations for males and females to seek out heterosexual relationships. A few exceptions can be drawn from exceedingly restrictive cultures, such as Inis Beag, where masturbation tends to occur at high frequency in adolescence because premarital sex is even more forbidden than is masturbation.

The fact that masturbation seems to be more common in industrial than nonindustrial cultures is interesting. Similar statistics occur in West Germany, Denmark, and the United States. Industrial societies tend to prolong the shift from childhood to adulthood. Unlike less technological societies that acknowledge a sudden transformation to adulthood at puberty, technologically sophisticated cultures provide for an extended adolescence during which people continue their education rather than join the adult work force. One aspect of this slow transition is that interpersonal sexual outlets are restricted. Adolescents do have sexual feelings, however, and masturbation offers an outlet.

Equally important in contrasting the two general types of societies is the degree of control that an individual culture is able to maintain over its population. Certainly, the control in a large and complex society is loosely exercised, a point easily illustrated by the discrepancy between formal laws governing sexuality and the rates of unlawful activities committed in the United States. A smaller nonindustrial society may be able to enforce its laws more strictly or pressure individuals' conformity to norms. The relaxation of societal and familial controls, combined with the lengthened transition from childhood to adult status, probably are major influences in sustaining masturbation as an important sexual outlet in our society.

Overall, cross-cultural information on masturbation is very limited or very dated, in part because people are often reluctant to answer questions on masturbation (Gondonneau et al., 1972; Wilson, 1975). One can imagine the difficulties encountered in attempting to retrieve such information from a foreign group whose culture is very different from ours. Since most of the anthropologists are from Western cultures, with Western industrial values that do not, to say the least, wholeheartedly embrace masturbation, the phrasing of questions and the attitudes expressed could very well influence the openness and quality of the responses. Also, it is not always clear how anthropologists get their information or how integrated into the culture they become. If information is dependent on one or two "informants" or confidants, as is sometimes the case, the relationship between the informant and the rest of the society may be a factor in retrieving reliable information about sex.

MASTURBATION IN NONHUMAN SPECIES

Although masturbation has been observed in many species, it is not frequently reported (Ford & Beach, 1951). Animals may stimulate their genitals by rubbing against other objects or by using sticks, paws, a tail, or a tree trunk. However, determining whether this activity is random, an effort to relieve genital irritation, or an intentionally sexual behavior is often impossible to tell.

The conditions that foster masturbation seem to be a combination of biological and learned factors. Learned factors include space availability and early social deprivation. Learning may be especially important to primate species. For example, in a study of zoo animals, one chimpanzee pair that were imported at a very young age were unable to breed successfully, but frequently masturbated (Hediger, 1968). Young primates have been observed to masturbate more than older ones, and primates who are reared in social isolation may be unable to engage in successful coitus but still may be able to masturbate (Harlow, 1965). These studies suggest that masturbation, unlike coitus, requires little social learning or practice.

SOCIAL FACTORS AND PSYCHOSOCIAL PERSPECTIVE

Genital self-stimulation occurs at all ages; it has been observed in children under 1 year and in men and women over 70. Yet, if we asked 4-year-olds why they were playing with their genitals, the answer would probably be "because it feels good," with little, if any, knowledge on their part about the sexual meaning of their activity. The sexual meaning of masturbation is taught to the child, usually in a very haphazard way.

I can still vividly remember being three or four, and naked in my crib, and having my mother come in and fly completely off the handle. I was playing with myself at the time, and it shocked the living daylights out of her. When I was an adolescent and would get an erection, I'd want to grab it and do things to it—I'd be almost sick wanting to—but I felt too terrified. Finally one time I did, and for days I lived with a sense that something terrible was going to happen to me. (Hunt, 1974, p. 78)

While masturbation initially is an activity that is engaged in primarily for pleasure, it later becomes an activity that has sociosexual significance attached to it. From this perspective, we shall try to identify what factors are important in the discovery and practice of masturbation, how these factors might interact with a person's social identity, and the effect of masturbation on other areas of a person's sexuality.

Discovery and Techniques of Masturbation

I was 14 or 15 years old and a virgin. I was sitting cross-legged on my bed one day, and became aroused by memories of petting with my boyfriend and having orgasms. I was also aroused by the sex smell I was exuding. I suddenly realized that I could do to my clitoris what he had done. I masturbated for the first time, I had an orgasm, and wasn't so sure what I had done was right. (Boston Women's Health Collective, 1971, p. 31)

How do people learn to masturbate? Given our discussion of biological factors in Chapter Two, we might expect that males, be-

cause their genitals are fully exposed, would be more likely to learn about masturbation accidentally while handling their genitals. However, Kinsey's group reported that only 28 percent of the males they surveyed, compared with 55 percent of the females, said that they learned to masturbate through self-discovery. Instead, far more males (75 percent) than females (43 percent) found out about masturbation through verbal or printed sources. One explanation offered for this difference is that males in our culture have access to more information about sex and at an earlier age than do females. Girls must discover masturbation more independently. Data show that in the 1970s, with more information on sexual patterns available to both sexes, an increasing number of females were experimenting with masturbation, and men and women were reporting similar amounts of experience (Hunt, 1974; Miller & Lief, 1976).

In fact, the greater availability of information for males is probably not the whole story. Attitudes about sexuality have a strong impact on whether masturbation is practiced. Since masturbation involves initiating and being responsible for one's own sexual feelings, it is not surprising that fewer females than males take up masturbation. Females, during early adolescence, are likely to be encouraged to inhibit sexual feelings, to dissociate their genitals from pleasure (and connect them to menstruation), and to defend their bodies from sexual advances (e.g., Gagnon & Simon, 1973). This type of encouragement does not promote positive feelings about seeking sexual self-satisfaction. For young boys, however, the seeking of sexual stimuli is accepted and expected, whether they read erotic books or are sexually aggressive with girls. Masturbation is a more predictable "discovery" within this social context. The social setting of the young male reinforces a masculine image that is active, aggressive, and interested in physical expressions and expertise.

A female's introduction to her genitals is usually through menstruation. Though many girls look forward to their first period, it is usually not a truly celebrated event, and it even tends to be marked by annoyance and discomfort rather than by sexual pleasure. Additionally, the adolescent social climate tends to demand responsible but nonautonomous sexual behavior from females. In other words, a girl is supposed to avoid pregnancy, but she must always experience her sexuality with others. To make the jump to autonomous sexual behavior, whether by masturbating or by enjoying some other activity, is difficult for females because it counters the social and sexual expectations of their subculture. The opinion that females should achieve sexual satisfaction only through a committed, emotional relationship with a male has not shifted notably (Gagnon, Simon, & Berger, 1970).

Orgasm through masturbation does seem more likely for females from the late teens and into adulthood. Kinsey's data show that 50 percent of the women who masturbate to orgasm did so after their first heterosexual or homosexual experience. Another researcher made a more general observation: Because some women viewed masturba-

tion and intercourse as related events, knowledge of one provided greater enjoyment of the other (Clifford, 1978a).

How does one masturbate? Many people believe that there are only certain methods of masturbation, with little variation across individuals, but that is not the case. For both sexes, although a fairly basic pattern can provide sexual satisfaction, the variations that are possible are limited only by one's imagination (Lea, 1967).

Most males masturbate by rubbing the shaft and glans of their penis with their fingers. Usually the thumb and index finger are formed into a circle, and the penis is rapidly stroked in an up-and-down motion. Some men find pleasure in stroking their scrotal and anal areas. A less common means of masturbating involves rubbing the penis against pillows, beds, chairs, or bottles. Sometimes unusual items such as hairpins, nailfiles, thermometers, toothbrush handles, and shoelaces have been inserted in the anus or, more rarely, the urethra, as a source of stimulation. However, these objects are not recommended as they can damage the urethra, bladder, and anal sphincter muscles. Last of all, a small number of men (0.02 to 0.03 percent) are agile enough to stimulate themselves to orgasm by inserting their penises into their mouths (Kinsey et al., 1948).

Women use a greater variety of masturbating techniques than do men (DeMartino, 1979). Variety in self-stimulation has a long and interesting history for women. Havelock Ellis (1906) gives a historical and cross-cultural account of inventions, ranging from a leather artificial penis mentioned in

Lysistrata by Aristophanes to Japanese *rin-no-tama,* which are metal balls that produce vibrations when inserted in a woman's vagina. There is also a foot-pedaled masturbation machine in the Dresden Museum on which different-sized penis structures could be attached (Lea, 1967).

The more typical masturbatory pattern for women consists of manual stimulation of the genitals by rubbing, stroking, or just pressing on the labia minora and around the clitoris. A majority of women who masturbate do so using this method (Dickinson & Beam, 1931; Kinsey et al., 1953). An additional 10 percent masturbate by squeezing their thighs together in a rhythmic pattern (Kinsey et al., 1953). Some women combine general body tension with pelvic thrusting, while others enjoy having flowing water come in contact with their genitals. A few women (Kinsey reported about 2 percent) are able to experience orgasm through fantasy alone. Breast stimulation is sometimes used to enhance genital stimulation while women masturbate, and a small percentage of women are able to have orgasm through breast stimulation alone. Vaginal insertions such as fingers, candles, dildos, vibrators, or even bananas and cucumbers are sometimes used. Rubbing the vulvular area against objects, including pillows, towels, blankets, and furniture has also been reported (Hite, 1976). Recently, electric vibrators have become popular, providing a very intense and steady form of stimulation (DeMartino, 1979).

Body tension, movement, and rapid breathing are arousal responses to sexual stimulation as well as stimulation for further arousal and orgasm. Also, body position can be important. In one study, for example, college women most often masturbated while lying on their backs (Clifford, 1978a). However, women in this sample who masturbated while on their stomachs were found to be more orgasmic in intercourse than women whose preferred position was on their back with their legs bent. Clifford (1978a) speculates that in the stomach position a woman may experience more stimulation overall than when using direct genital stimulation while lying on her back. Such stimulation may most resemble the sensations usually experienced during intercourse.

While there is little question that the penis is the focus of sexual stimulation during male masturbation, there has been a longstanding argument about the best method of stimulation for women. Clitoral stimulation, whether direct or indirect, seems to be necessary for many women to become aroused and to experience orgasm (Clifford, 1978a; Dickinson & Beam, 1931; Hite, 1977; Kinsey et al., 1953). However, as can be seen from the types of stimulation already mentioned, a significant percentage of women experience psychological and physical pleasure from vaginal stimulation.

Most people assume that women are much slower to reach orgasm than men. This belief is not supported by the data. Men and women have similar ranges of masturbation times—stimulation may be necessary for only 20 seconds for some people; others may deliberately prolong masturbation for hours. Although almost all of

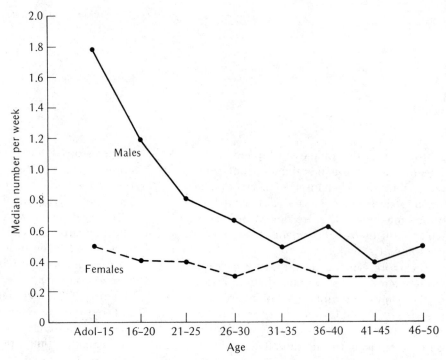

Figure 4–1. Frequency of masturbation activity (median number per week) for single males and females.

the data are based on self-reports, there seems to be very little difference between the sexes in time needed to achieve orgasm via masturbation (Kinsey et al., 1953). Research by Masters and Johnson (1966), which included observations of male and female patterns of masturbation, supports Kinsey's figures.

Factors Relating to the Occurrence of Masturbation

Kinsey and his colleagues isolated several important features about an individual's development that were related to masturbation experience (Kinsey et al., 1948, 1953). The principal categories were sex, age, age at puberty, whether a person was raised in an urban or rural setting, religious involvement, socioeconomic class, educational level, and marital status. In spite of

the fact that Kinsey's figures are dated, several of his categories are still relevant for discussing different masturbation practices.

The data presented here are reported in two ways: in terms of the percentage of the whole sample who have ever masturbated, and in terms of the subsample who currently masturbate.

□ *Age: For him, the Younger the Better; For Her, the Older the Better, at Least for Now.* Not surprisingly, the frequency of masturbation varies over a person's lifetime. Kinsey found dramatic differences between the rates of single males and females on this variable (married individuals will be considered separately). As Figure 4–1 demonstrates, the frequency of masturbation activity declines markedly for males between adolescence and age 30, while staying relatively constant but considerably lower for females.

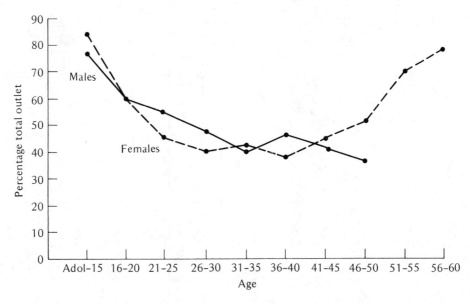

Figure 4-2. *Percentage of orgasms resulting from masturbation for single males and females.*

More revealing is the importance of masturbation to the unmarried individual at different ages. Figure 4-2 shows the percentage of orgasms (or to use Kinsey's term, "total outlet") that results from masturbation. Apparently, masturbation becomes a less important source of orgasm for both sexes until about age 40, when it begins to take on increasing importance for women.

Prepubertal masturbation has been minimally studied; we can be assured, however, that autoerotic activities are clearly present prior to puberty. Kinsey's group (1948, 1953) found that 45 percent of their male sample reported having masturbated by age 13. A study conducted prior to Kinsey's found that 85 percent of the sample had tried masturbation by age 13 (Ramsey, 1943). Ramsey's study did not rely on adult recollection, as did Kinsey's, and his sample was made up of urban middle-class males only.

Several recent studies have examined autoerotic patterns in college students, showing less pronounced sex differences than previously had been found. Seventy-four percent of Clifford's (1978a) female sample (mean age 19.6) had masturbated, with 49 percent reaching orgasm. A sample of high school, college, graduate school, and medical school students revealed that 97 percent of the males and 78 percent of the females had masturbated (Miller & Lief, 1976). Hunt's (1974) survey showed a similar trend: During the late teens and early twenties the percentage of males masturbating and their frequency of masturbation were comparable with Kinsey's figures. Females of the same age, however, showed several changes. Hunt's results showed that 50 percent of the females in his study, compared with about 35 percent of Kinsey's females, were currently masturbating. A closer look at the female pattern (Figure 4-3), clearly shows that during adolescence females are generally inactive in terms of masturbatory experience.

Information on masturbation in middle-aged and elderly men and women is almost nonexistent. These groups have been signif-

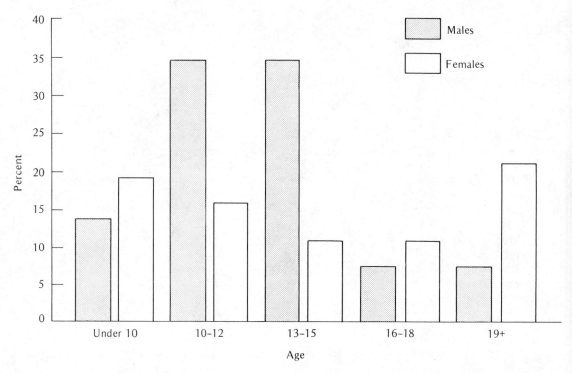

Figure 4–3. *Age of first masturbation adapted from a study by Miller and Lief, 1976, on 556 students.*

icantly overlooked, except by Kinsey and also by researchers who have focused on sexual activities other than masturbation (George & Weiler, 1981; Newman & Nichols, 1960). Masturbation has been acknowledged as an important psychological and physical sexual release for older people because partners are not always readily available (Masters & Johnson, 1970). Masturbation can also help prevent the mature female's genitals from experiencing thinning and dryness due to hormonal changes (Masters & Johnson, 1966). Helen Kaplan (1974) has noted that "in sharp contrast to men, elderly women remain capable of enjoying multiple orgasms" (p. 112). In fact, studies indicate that 25 percent of 70-year-old men and women with sexual partners still masturbate (Christenson & Gagnon, 1965; Rubin, 1963). Masturbation is more

likely in older *single* women (Christenson & Gagnon, 1965), and we presume the same to be true for older men without partners. Future research hopefully will reveal more about the importance of autoeroticism throughout the life span.

☐ *Marital Status: Masturbation Survives.* Many people assume that masturbation does stop and should stop when a person marries. Kinsey and his colleagues found that masturbation usually occurred less frequently after marriage, but that it still accounted for 6 to 13 percent of the total sexual outlet for women and 10 to 20 percent of the total outlet for men. In fact, for some people marriage did not change their frequency of masturbation (Kinsey et al., 1948, 1953).

More recent data on the relationship between masturbation and marital status come from Hunt (1974). Hunt's results suggest an increase in marital masturbation. Seventy-two percent of the married males in their late twenties and early thirties mas-

---

Box 4–1

MASTURBATION IS NOT ALWAYS FOR SEX

Clifford (1978*a*) noted that at the time of their first masturbation, "approximately one-half of the women [in her study] were aware that their behavior had sexual meaning" (p. 565). The following anecdote taken from our own case records illustrates this point:

A young woman disclosed to one of the authors that she had been worried and was seeking an explanation for a puzzling part of her life. She reported that she had been bothered by a chronic sinus condition that often resulted in painful headaches. The sinus problem had existed for as long as she could remember and dated at least from age 3 or 4.

Around age 5 or 6 Ms. B. reported that during exploration of and playing with her genitals, she experienced some kind of a body reaction that was accompanied by the clearing of her sinuses and the alleviation of the associated pain. Quite rapidly she learned to repeat the experience as a technique for clearing her nasal condition. She reported continuing this practice at frequent intervals over the next 15 years. For many years she did not perceive her actions as being sexual. She kept this information secret from her parents since she knew that touching her genitals was disapproved of, but the entire experience was viewed as a self-help for her sinuses and not related to sex. In fact, when her brother once complained of a head cold with sinus ache, she tried to tell him how to relieve his discomfort. They were both preteenagers at that time, and her brother never did understand what she was talking about.

On a date, at around age 17, Ms. B said that she and her partner were involved in heavy petting including his manually caressing her genitals. After some intense and prolonged sexplay she had an orgasm. She suddenly realized that she had just had the same experience that for years she had been providing to herself as a sinus treatment.

---

turbated occasionally, as compared with 40 percent in Kinsey's study, while 68 percent of the comparable sample of married women (versus 32 percent of the Kinsey sample) masturbated. Allowing for the fact that Hunt's sample is probably less repre- sentative of the average population than was Kinsey's, these results do suggest that masturbation may be more freely acknowl- edged or more freely practiced, or both, forty years after Kinsey's study was com- pleted. As one woman observed:

I heard some women talk about masturbating. Just the openness of the talk shocked me at first. They said it was fun, pleasurable! And many of them were women who were married or with men. I was stunned. I had so many questions that I didn't dare ask. How do you do it? Do you do it when you are alone? Do you do it in bed with your lover or husband there? Do you let him watch? Do you let your children know? (Boston Women's Health Collective, 1971, p. 31)

Although a number of studies have shown that married people masturbate, the frequency of masturbation during marriage appears to be very low. Hunt (1974) found that husbands in their twenties and thirties masturbated about twenty-four times a year. Although he considers this to be a "remarkable" increase over Kinsey's figures, which indicate that his male sample masturbated about six times a year, the frequency is still rather low. For wives of the same age, both Kinsey and Hunt cite a frequency of ten times a year, a rare example of *no* change, in spite of the fairly noticeable changes in other areas of female sexuality.

Are people who masturbate after marriage usually more unhappy with their marital relationship? Fisher (1973) found that masturbation in married women was not correlated with orgasmic consistency or intercourse frequency, actual or preferred. Masturbation, according to Fisher, is not a form of "compensation" for deficiencies in other areas of sexual activity. Instead, masturbation frequency is likely to be higher for a woman who feels that sex is important to her life, enjoys sexual movies or novels,

believes that sexual freedom should be increased in our culture, spends more time thinking about sex, and has a greater frequency of intercourse during menstruation.

Overall, masturbation seems to occur in marriage, whether or not a particular couple is happily married. DeMartino (1974) found that most women believed masturbation had no effect on their marriage, and Hessellund (1976) discovered that masturbation frequency had little to do with the satisfaction of husbands or wives with regard to intercourse frequency.

□ *Religion: Strong Beliefs, Less Masturbation*   Kinsey found religion to be a major influence in sexual patterns. For single men, as participation in religious activity increased, masturbation frequency decreased. (Kinsey based his definition of "devout," a term he used often in his study to identify the very religious, on frequency of church attendance.) Orthodox Jews and devout Roman Catholics had the lowest rates, while inactive Protestants had the highest rates of masturbation. The same pattern was generally true for single women, although in their case the particular religious sect was of little importance. Interestingly, although fewer devout women masturbated (41 versus 67 percent), masturbation represented a greater percentage (80 versus 63 percent) of total sexual activity among devout than among nondevout women. Thus religious involvement seems to be an inhibitory factor on the likelihood of a woman having tried masturbation, but if she has, and continues the activity, she tends to depend on masturbation as a major form of sexual expression. Possibly, for the devout single woman, the idea of masturbation may seem less sinful than premarital petting or intercourse.

More recently, however, Fisher (1973) found that conventional religious involvement was not consistently correlated with masturbation among women. Masturbation was not linked to church membership, self-ratings of religiosity, or frequency of church attendance. However, what did seem to be negatively correlated with frequency of and satisfaction with masturbation was a scale that measured how committed a person was to religious ideals and the belief in the existence of God (Allport, Vernon, & Lindzey, 1960).

Orgasm and Relative Satisfaction

Women are more likely to experience orgasm in masturbation than in coitus. Kinsey and his colleagues (1953) found that 96 percent of the women who had ever masturbated were orgasmic, while only 83 percent of the women were orgasmic during sexual experiences with their husbands, even after five years of marriage. Clifford (1978b) also found that the modal rate (the most frequently reported rate) for orgasm in masturbation was 100 percent, which was much higher than the rate for orgasm in coitus. For most of these women, however, intercourse was the preferred sexual activity. One interesting result from Clifford's study is that orgasm ability and the frequency of feeling satisfied were not correlated for masturbatory activity, but were correlated for intercourse and oral sex. This means that although a person is orgasmic while masturbating, it does not automatically follow that she will be sexually satisfied. Orgasms may simply be more satisfying when shared with a partner. Masters and Johnson (1966) also pointed out that masturbation provides more intense, but not necessarily more psychologically satisfying, orgasmic releases for men and women.

Current Attitudes about Masturbation

At the beginning of our discussion of masturbation, we mentioned the overwhelming negative sanctions against masturbation. What, we might ask, are current attitudes toward masturbation?

Feelings are mixed, to be sure. Overall, acceptance of masturbation is greater now than in previous generations, yet it still retains a taboo quality. For instance, Sorensen (1973) said of his teenage sample:

> There seems to be no sex practice discussed in this study about which young people feel more defensive or private than masturbation. Superstition is seldom a factor. Self-esteem, embarrassment, and personal disgust seem to be the major inhibiting factors. (Sorensen, 1973, p. 144)

Sorensen discovered that 65 percent of the boys and 49 percent of the girls in his survey enjoyed masturbating somewhat or a great deal, and 51 percent of the total sample (both sexes) were rarely or never guilty about masturbating. However, examining the negative side of these percentages is also important: Between 35 and 50 percent of this group *did not* enjoy masturbating, and almost half felt guilty about it at least some of the time. Furthermore, younger girls were more likely than older girls to feel guilty, anxious, or concerned about masturbating.

Hunt (1974) notes that, except for pubescent boys, most people remain somewhat guilt-ridden and very secretive about masturbation. These feelings are common in spite of the fact that only 15 to 29 percent of the males and 14 to 36 percent of the females agreed to the statement, "Masturbation is wrong." As is often the case, people seem to separate their objective intellectual attitudes about sexual matters from their feelings about their personal behavior; therefore, while people believe that masturbation is permissible for others, they often find it unacceptable for themselves.

Attitudes and knowledge (psychological, physiological, and social) about masturbation have been shown to be related to masturbation experience. Generally speaking, there is an increase in both knowledge of and liberalized attitudes about masturbation as education levels increase. Miller and Lief's (1976) study shows some interesting patterns in attitudes concerning masturbation:

1. In high school and college, males have more liberal attitudes than females; in graduate school, the females are more liberal.
2. People who have never masturbated are more conservative, and they are less knowledgeable about masturbation than are people who masturbate.
3. Mental and emotional instability are believed to be caused by masturbation according to 18 percent of first-year, but only 2 percent of fourth-year medical students. However, 10 percent of the medical residents surveyed believe in this connection.
4. Women who begin masturbating at an early age have less heterosexual experience than late masturbators, and they have liberal views about premarital heterosexual experiences for males, but conservative views about premarital experiences for females.
5. Seventy-six percent of the entire sample felt that masturbation was a healthy practice.

Indeed, notions about the undesirability of masturbation are still with us. We would like to mention several of the more common assumptions and review their validity in light of what has been learned about the practice of autoerotic activities:

1. *Masturbation is immature.* Although masturbation decreases substantially when people marry, it still occupies at least 10 percent of the total sexual outlet for men and women. The sheer numbers of well-functioning adults who masturbate make the labeling of the act as "immature" seem unreasonable.

2. *Masturbation leads to an aversion toward heterosexual activities, and it encourages social isolation.* There is no evidence that supports this view. What might be true is that people turn to masturbation

THE BOY SCOUT HANDBOOK ON CONSERVATION

The following quotation is from the 1934 edition of the *Handbook for Boys,* published by The Boy Scouts of America. How do the attitudes expressed here (and, in fact, no longer espoused by the B.S.A.) compare with current attitudes on masturbation?

CONSERVATION

In this chapter much has been said of the active measures which a boy should take in order to become strong and well. We should be equally concerned in saving and storing up natural forces we already have. In the body of every boy who has reached his teens, the Creator of the universe has sown a very important fluid. This fluid is the most wonderful material in all the physical world. Some parts of it find their way into the blood, and through the blood give tone to the muscles, power to the brain, and strength to the nerves. This fluid is the sex fluid. When this fluid appears in a boy's body, it works a wonderful change in him. His chest deepens, his shoulders broaden, his voice changes, his ideals are changed and enlarged. It gives him the capacity for deep feeling, for rich emotion. Pity the boy, therefore, who has wrong ideas of this important function, because they will lower his ideals of life. These organs actually secrete into the blood material that makes a boy manly, strong, and noble. Any habit which a boy has that causes this fluid to be discharged from the body tends to weaken his strength, to make him less able to resist disease, and often unfortunately fastens upon him habits which later in life can be broken only with great difficulty. Even several years before this fluid appears in the body such habits are harmful to a growing boy.

To become strong, therefore, one must be pure in thought and clean in habit. This power which I have spoken of must be conserved, because this sex function is so deep and strong that there will come times when temptation to wrong habits will be very powerful. But remember that to yield means to sacrifice strength and power and manliness.

because they are fearful of heterosexual situations. Perhaps the social isolation is what leads people to masturbate, but the reverse is not true.

3. *Masturbation encourages "perverted" fantasies.* Many people occasionally do fantasize about a broad range of socially unacceptable activities that may be categorized as "perverted"; however, they not only do so while masturbating but also when involved in other sexual activities. Thus, masturbation no more encourages these fantasies than does sexual intercourse.

4. *Masturbation is sexually unsatisfying.* It may be fair to say that masturbation is less satisfying to most people than interpersonal sexual experiences, but it is not unsatisfying, to be sure. It fulfills a physical need and can even fulfill an emotional need under certain circumstances.

5. *Masturbation exhausts the sexual drive.* Within the typical range of masturbation frequencies, people do not experience a depletion of energy.

6. *Masturbation will impair a person's sexual response in marriage.* No data sup-

port this myth. In fact, Kinsey's report on the positive effect of masturbation on orgasmic potential is evidence to the contrary.

7. *Masturbation may lead to an excessive interest in sex.* Interest in sex, whether excessive or not, is again independent of any sexual activity. The differences between high and low desires and frequencies are not determined by the occurrence of masturbation but by the general level of an individual's sexual and social needs.

Masturbation: Reasons and Rationales

> It is unsafe to generalize about the genesis and desirable or undesirable consequences of a habit which is so common that by a familiar method of reasoning even fallen arches may be ascribed to it. (Hamilton, 1929, p. 423)

Masturbation, as we have seen, is a common sexual pattern. The majority of both men and women try it at some point in their lives, and many people continue to masturbate throughout their lifetimes, with varying frequency. Why?

Kinsey viewed masturbation as a means of reducing physical and psychological sexual tension. Indeed, if people have no sexual contact for a period of time, or if they are sexually aroused but are inhibited or prevented from satisfying themselves in interpersonal ways, a natural outlet would be masturbation. Thus, single people are found to depend more on masturbation, as are married people whose spouses are absent, ill, or temporarily uninterested in having intercourse (Hunt, 1974).

Masturbation has other "practical" advantages. An important one is that premarital experience with masturbation may actually contribute to a woman's capacity to respond sexually during intercourse. Kinsey found that women who were orgasmic prior to marriage were three times more likely to be orgasmic after marriage than were women with no premarital orgasmic experience. The type of premarital activity (intercourse, petting, homosexual relations, or masturbation) was less important than whether or not orgasm occurred and, "since masturbation was the activity in which the largest number of females had reached orgasm, it was of particular significance in these correlations" (Kinsey et al., 1953, p. 172).

However, Kinsey's data must be considered carefully, since he also found that even among women who had a great deal of experience with masturbation before marriage, 16 percent did not reach orgasm during the first year of marriage. Other studies have also found little or no relationship between masturbatory experience and orgasmic consistency in coitus, whether preceding or following marriage (Clifford, 1978a; Fisher, 1973).

Since 1960, masturbation has been used quite successfully in sex therapy to teach women to become orgasmic (Annon, 1974; Barbach, 1975; Hastings, 1963; Heiman, LoPiccolo & LoPiccolo, 1976; LoPiccolo & Lobitz, 1972). More about this therapy procedure will be discussed in Chapter 8. Masturbation may also help reduce general physical or nervous tension (Davis, 1929; Hunt, 1974), and it may reduce the discomfort of menstrual cramps as well (Clifford, 1975).

Beginning in the 1970s, there has been an increasing trend to regard masturbation as valuable in its own right, not necessarily as only a poor substitute for sexual relations with another person. In this context, masturbation, particularly when used with fantasy, may provide a source of pleasure and sexual variety, while not necessarily causing a person to reject a sexual partner or spouse. In addition, it allows people increased freedom to be sexually spontaneous. Many sexual disagreements arise from the fact that one person wants to have sex more than the other. This imbalance can make the low-interest person feel hounded and resentful, and sometimes "used," and the high-interest person feel unloved and rejected. Masturbation is not the only solution, of course, but it is an alternative that increases options for sexual expression.

Can masturbation ever be done too often or prove to be harmful? If a person masturbates because of fear of seeking out other sexual outlets, it can interfere with psychosexual development, but not because masturbation itself causes problems. Instead, negative attitudes toward masturbation can make the person who masturbates feel less worthwhile and less able to attempt more social forms of sex. On the other hand, for a person who feels compelled and driven to masturbate all the time, even when other outlets are available or potentially available, it may be an indication of other conflicts that are confining the person's social and sexual growth. For someone who is afraid to make any effort to enjoy interpersonal sexual activities, a steady diet of fantasy and masturbation alone is not likely to get him or her closer to interacting with others. But again, such people are not slaves to masturbation; they are, in fact, usually imprisoned by their own insecurity about sociosexual contacts. The key is personal choice. A person with a healthy attitude masturbates by choice but does not experience a driving compulsion to do so or a fear of interpersonal alternatives.

THE ROLE OF FANTASY IN MASTURBATION

Fantasies, which are mental images often focusing on fulfilled or unfulfilled desires, are presumed to be a uniquely human sexual activity. A fantasy allows a person to create or recreate a highly erotic sexual experience with any number of people and activities, even though he or she is alone. Fantasies can serve many purposes, not the least of which is achieving personal satisfaction, facilitating arousal during masturbation, and increasing sexual variety. Fantasy is important for another reason: It can help us to understand the role of masturbation in a person's sexual development.

For instance, assume that Kinsey's figures are still valid—that is, only 50 percent of the females he surveyed as compared with 72 percent of the males used fantasy during masturbation. This means that if you were the average college male who matured at 14, married at 22, and masturbated about twice a week prior to marriage, you would enter marriage having masturbated about 850 times. Further, you would have fantasized during those experiences, practicing in your imagination many varieties of sexual activities. On the other hand, if you were the average college female, entering pubescence at 12, masturbating about once every two weeks, and marrying at 22, you would be starting marriage having fantasized and masturbated to orgasm about 210 times. Actually, this female and this male are not necessarily typical, but are merely illustrative of the fact that males and females usually enter heterosexual relationships with different degrees of imagined sexual experience gained during masturbatory experiences.

Whether sheer quantity alone is important to a person's emerging sexuality is questionable, particularly after the first year or so of masturbation. What does seem to be meaningful is the learning that can take place in fantasy associated with masturbation. Early masturbation and fantasy might be viewed as rehearsals for what is eventually to occur with a partner.

Fantasy is probably far more common for women than Kinsey's figures imply. One study found that only 14 percent of its normal sample of women between 15 and 35 years of age never used fantasy during masturbation (Landis et al., 1940, cited in Kinsey et al., 1948); Kinsey's figure for the "never" category was 35 percent. More startling is Robert Sorensen's (1973) report,

which was based on a sample of over 400 adolescents. Although Sorensen's adolescents were not randomly selected and probably came from families with liberal sexual attitudes, he found that, of those adolescents who were currently masturbating, 7 percent of the females and 11 percent of the males never used fantasy, while 46 percent of the females and 57 percent of the males fantasized most of the time. DeMartino (1974) found that between 50 and 70 percent of the women he sampled used fantasy during masturbation, with younger women using fantasy far less often than older women. One of the most carefully constructed studies of women's fantasies found that 65 percent of 141 married, upper-middle class women fantasized during coitus (Hariton and Singer, 1974). Clifford (1978a) reported the same percentage (65 percent) of college women using masturbatory fantasies.

The use of fantasy does differ between men and women on another dimension, however: Women generally start to use fantasies years after they have been masturbating without them (Hamilton, 1929; Kinsey et al., 1953; Schaefer, 1973). According to Kinsey, older women tend to use fantasies more often than younger women, which DeMartino (1974) also found, and the content of women's fantasies is more likely than males' to be based on past experiences. Earlier we suggested that females get sexual information later than males. It should not be surprising, then, that females do not use fantasy at the early ages that males do—where would they get their material for their fantasies? When fantasy use

Women surrendering and being overpowered, and the wickedness and danger of sexuality are common themes reported by both women and men.

does finally become a part of female masturbation, it is usually after some sexual experiences.

What sorts of things do people fantasize about? In Kinsey's sample, the majority of females who fantasized (60 percent) based their images on some kind of heterosexual theme, while under 10 percent included homosexual, bestial, sadomasochistic, or other themes. Gagnon and Simon (1973) similarly summarized the content of most women's fantasies as including past sexual experiences, thoughts of love and marriage, and what they called mild masochism, while male fantasies are richer in specific sexual behavior such as oral-genital sex and specific techniques. And married women, according to one study, most frequently use coital fantasy themes of an "imaginary romantic lover," "being overpowered and forced to surrender," or doing something "wicked and forbidden" (Hariton & Singer, 1974). Popular books also have summarized and quoted personal fantasies of men and women (Friday, 1973, 1980).

More detailed, though less systematic, discussions of fantasy content came from Sorensen (1973) and Hunt (1974). Hunt found that the most commonly mentioned type of masturbation fantasy centers around thoughts of intercourse with a loved person. Table 4-1 lists this theme and less conventional ones used by males and females at least some of the time (Hunt, 1974).

Sorensen (1973) informally reported on the major fantasy themes of sexually inexperienced teenagers. For boys, the more common categories were sex with more

TABLE 4-1 COMMONLY MENTIONED THEMES OF MASTURBATION		
	MALE	FEMALE
	(percent)	
Intercourse with a loved person	75	80
Intercourse with strangers	47	21
Sex with more than one person of the opposite sex	33	18
Doing sexual things you would never do in reality	19	28
Being forced to have sex	10	18
Forcing someone to have sex	13	3
Homosexual themes	7	11
(From Hunt 1974)		

than one girl, group sex, sex when one partner is forced to submit, varying degrees of violence to a sexual partner, and oral or anal sex. Themes for girls included sex with a much-admired male, sex with one or more males when she is forced to submit, mild violence inflicted on another person, and oral sex.

Another study, which sampled midwestern college students, revealed that love and commitment themes occurred more often in the fantasies of young women, while seduction domination themes were more common for the men (Heyman, 1979). Likewise, 70 to 85 percent of the college women fantasized about attractive men they knew or were involved with, but only 10 to 30 percent used fantasies in which they were forced to submit, were being harmed, or were watched while involved in some type of sexual activity (Clifford, 1978a). The suggestion that males and females differ according to the themes of their fantasies seems to reflect early sociosexual scripts: Males are aggressors and females are relationship seekers in the sexual sphere (Gagnon & Simon, 1973). It would be interesting to test this idea by evaluating a group according to their ideals of a sexual encounter, their real-life experiences, and their fantasy themes. By looking at changes in fantasy, personal values, and experiences over time, we would have a clearer idea of what purposes fantasy serves.

Fantasy certainly can be a substitute for a desired but unavailable sexual activity. For instance, the theme of intercourse with a loved one may be used by someone who is not involved in a sexual relationship or whose partner is away or ill. Fantasy is also a way of experimenting with new or forbidden sexual experiences, providing a means of broadening a person's sexual interests or fulfilling needs that people have for variety. Included here are the less conventional themes, such as fantasies of sex with strangers or of being forced to have sex, which provide a safe and acceptable substitute for the real-life situation. While fantasy themes may reflect a person's hopes or experiences, some fantasies are self-contained images that a person would never be able to or never want to act upon.

Some people believe that fantasizing is "unhealthy" (Hollender, 1963; Shainess & Geenwald, 1971). Although fantasy use can be interpreted in this way, there is also plenty of information to suggest positive values of using sexual images. Fantasies have been noted to correspond to heightened interest and enthusiasm in a satisfying sex life, and may play a part in increasing one's positive feelings toward sexuality (Heiman, LoPiccolo, & LoPiccolo, 1976). They also can enhance the enjoyment of sex (Hariton & Singer, 1974). However, although there is some evidence that people who fantasize more frequently are more sexually experienced (Heyman, 1979), frequent fantasizers are not necessarily more or less sexually satisfied (Hariton & Singer, 1974).

A number of people have reported negative aspects of sexual fantasizing, and as a result some research has examined the concept of sex guilt. *Sex guilt* is defined as a "generalized expectancy for self-mediated punishment for violating or for anticipating violating standards of proper sexual conduct" (Mosher & Cross, 1971, p. 27). People have different ideas about what it means to breach standards of "proper sexual conduct." Sometimes, regardless of the fantasy content, people just feel guilty when they think about sex. Thus, not surprisingly, people who do not often experience sex guilt tend to have more diverse and more frequent fantasies and are probably more likely to admit to their fantasies in a research project (Heyman, 1979).

Special mention should be made of one study that dealt with attitudes and sex guilt in masturbation (Abramson and Mosher, 1979). Subjects of both sexes were shown a

film of either a male or female masturbating. After viewing the film, each person completed forms on their reactions and then wrote fantasies about what occurred in the film. Subjects high in sex guilt were more likely to express negative motives (for example, rejection, anxiety, depression) to explain why the people in the film were masturbating, and they were more likely to fantasize about sexual behavior that was beyond their own prior experience. Furthermore, both men and women with more positive attitudes toward masturbation were more positive about the orgasmic responses of the film's subjects. One of the most valuable aspects of this study is that it underscores the fact that masturbation, fantasy, and sexual attitudes, both negative and positive, are interrelated. When a person fantasizes, it is not an activity that is removed from a larger set of sexual values and social meanings.

SUMMARY

1. Solitary sexual activities are often a person's first sexual experiences. **Masturbation,** the manual stimulation of one's genitals and other erogenous areas for the purpose of sexual pleasure, is the primary form of solitary sexual activity; sexual fantasies and dreams, and the use of erotic literature and films, also enable a person to be sexually stimulated without the aid of another person.

2. The history of masturbation is troubled and complex. Masturbation was condemned as early as 950 B.C. Early on, religious groups strongly rejected masturbation. One possible explanation is that in order to ensure

population growth, any form of sexual activity that did not result in procreation was prohibited.

3. By the eighteenth century, the concerns about masturbation centered on its psychological and physical consequences. Various treatments were developed, ranging from spiked-lined devices to be worn by young boys to more radical treatments, such as clitoridectomies and castrations.

4. Freud suggested four stages of development regarding masturbation. He considered masturbation normal in an individual as long as he or she was properly progressing through the stages he described. He believed, however, that personality disorders would develop if a person was unable to resolve developmental conflicts of each stage.

5. In preliterate or nonindustrialized societies, masturbation is generally taboo for adults but often accepted in children. Puberty is the turning point for acceptability in most cultures.

6. Masturbation seems to be more common in industrial cultures. One possible explanation is that adolescence is extended in these cultures, which limits the availability of interpersonal outlets for sexual activity and the acceptability of such actions. Also, the larger, more complex cultures have a harder time controlling individual activity.

7. More women learn about masturbation through self-discovery than do males, who learn about it through verbal and printed sources. Also, differing social expectations for males and females influence the practice of masturbation. For example, adolescent females are encouraged to repress sexual feelings and to avoid sexual encounters, whereas males of the same age group are encouraged to be sexually aggressive and are given approval, though sometimes unspoken, to seek stimulation.

8. Techniques for masturbating vary greatly, especially with women. The most common method for both men and women involves the manual stimulation of the genitals. Less frequently other techniques are used; for instance, men may rub their penises against a mattress or pillow, while women may use vibrators.

9. A somewhat greater percentage of females and slightly more males are masturbating earlier than people were forty years ago. Males masturbate a great deal more than females, but while males begin to masturbate in their early teens and peak in their late teens, females only begin to stimulate themselves in their late teens and maintain more of a consistent pattern through adulthood. Unfortunately, we know very little about masturbation patterns among older adults.

10. Although people generally do not masturbate as frequently after marriage, some do not alter their pattern at all. Masturbation in marriage does not seem to hinge on whether or not a couple is happily married.

11. Religious convictions strongly influence the incidence of masturbation. Those who strictly practice their faith are least likely to masturbate.

12. People masturbate for several reasons. First, Kinsey believed that masturbation is a means for people to reduce physical and psychological tension. For instance, a person with no interpersonal contact for an extended period of time could use masturbation as a type of release. Second, masturbation is used as a therapeutic device to help women become orgasmic. Third, masturbation may be valuable in itself and not only as a substitute for interpersonal relations.

13. Whether or not a person is masturbating to an unhealthy extent is determined by attitude. The reasons that first motivate a person to masturbate, as well as the degree of compulsion one feels to carry out the act, are more indicative of whether or not a person has a "healthy" attitude.

14. **Fantasies,** which are mental images often focused on fulfilled or unfulfilled desires, are unique to humans. They allow people to achieve personal satisfaction, enable them to facilitate arousal during masturbation, offer them sexual variety, and aid them in understanding the effect of masturbation on sexual development. As in other areas of sexual activity, males fantasize more frequently than females, and women usually start fantasizing years after they first begin masturbating.

15. Fantasies take a variety of forms: images of intercourse with loved ones, intercourse with strangers, and being forced into sexual activity are just a few of the fantasy themes used.

SUGGESTED READINGS

Ginder, R. *Binding with briars: Sex and sin in the Catholic church.* Englewood Cliffs, N. J.: Prentice-Hall, 1975. Deals with conflicts of conscience in being Catholic and being sexual. The author is a Roman Catholic priest.

Gordon, D. C. *Self-love.* Baltimore: Penguin, 1972. A brief essay attempting to understand the shame surrounding masturbation and to place the practice in a more humanistic framework.

Taylor, G. R. *Sex in history.* New York: Harper & Row, 1954. An introductory overview of sexual attitudes and behaviors, including masturbation, dating from the Middle Ages. Restricted to Western Civilization.

CHAPTER FIVE

THE SELECTION OF PARTNERS
Attraction, Courtship, and Love

A woman walking in a sagging dress, with a heavy walk, and her hair—this above all—not conforming to the prints made by fashion, is not "set" to attract men's sex. The same woman in a dress cut this or that way, walking with her inner thermostat set just so—and click, she's fitting the pattern.
Doris Lessing, *The Summer Before the Dark*

Suppose, for a moment, that you are sitting in a cafe or in an airport, casually watching people as they pass by. What is it about an individual that might catch your attention and make that person seem attractive? The face? Body? Hair? Or is it a movement, a certain expression when a person talks, or some undefinable combination of qualities? Now imagine that the person you were noticing comes over, sits down next to you, and begins a conversation. As you talk, what makes your interest increase or decrease? Does your interest feel primarily sexual (would you like to touch him or her)? Or nonsexual (are you interested in what the person has to say and would you like to get to know him or her better)? And how does the other person communicate his or her own interest and attraction to you?

Rarely does just one characteristic make someone sexually attractive, and most people have difficulty identifying exactly what attracts them to others. Some people are sexually interested in almost all males or females, while others rarely are drawn to someone else. A general cultural belief is that men are more attracted by physical features than are women, who, instead, measure attraction based on personality characteristics. The reality of this belief and others is explored in Chapter Five, along with research and ideas about interpersonal sexual attraction and courtship.

Sexual attraction and love have long fascinated poets, novelists, songwriters, film producers, and, more recently, scientists. An air of mystery surrounds the topic, for no one really knows what is essential in making a relationship click. In this chapter, we present research and theory about the ingredients that are important in getting two people together: attraction, the courtship process, partner selection, and the beginning of sexual activity. Different types of communication go on at different distances—visual, kinesthetic, nonverbal, and verbal—and the complexity of these "signals" becomes evident in our discussion. Communication is the subtheme of this chapter, because getting two individuals interested in one another simultaneously involves an exchange of messages. This communication is discussed in terms of nonhuman species as well, for although other species do not have singles bars, romantic restaurants, and cocktail parties, often they have evolved intricate and sometimes flamboyant patterns of their own to attract a mate.

Getting two individuals together first involves **attraction.** Attraction may take the form of sending or receiving specifically sexual signals, which may be expressed in one's style of dress or way of walking or by presenting one's self in a culturally defined sexual way. Attraction may also take the form of a more general kind of liking, with sexual interest not the primary feature, at least initially. Most researchers, however, have focused on the importance of sexual attraction as the first step in partner selection. *Sexual attraction* means defining a person as a potential sexual partner, and perhaps finding that person arousing.

Very early in the attraction process some form of courting occurs. **Courtship** is a continual communication process by which

one or both people assess their interest in the other. Courtship may be brief or lengthy, and the outcome is not always predictable. Courtship may result in increased closeness and intensified sexual interest, or, alternatively, in a breaking off of contact. At some point during the development of the attraction and courtship individuals may experience love or falling in love. **Love** cannot be simply defined, as it has been used to describe too many different kinds of relationships. But the experience of love, however defined by an individual or couple, may be the essential element in understanding the depth of attachment, the level of intimacy, the power a relationship has over the participants, and the degree of joy or pain possible in the development of an intimate relationship.

BIOLOGICAL PERSPECTIVE

A common thread unites all species that reproduce sexually: There must be reliable ways of getting the two sexes together. Organisms such as the *hydra* simply "bud" new offspring, and the single cell *parame-cium* splits in two to reproduce; neither has to discover the methods of attracting, courting, or arousing prospective mates that are part of sexual reproduction. (We should note, however, that both of these species can also reproduce sexually under certain conditions.) Because a major biological goal is the continuation of the species, we might expect that substantial biological influences operate to optimize the likelihood that gametes (male sperm and female ova) will meet. On another level, certain social activities help to ensure that two individuals are in the right place at the right time, and are attuned to each other's mating signals.

Natural Selection and Sexual Selection

A biological perspective depends on an evolutionary perspective. The theory of evolution that Charles Darwin proposed in the *Origin of Species* (1859) stated that evolution proceeds primarily through a mechanism of **natural selection:** Those animals that best meet the demands of their environment will survive and reproduce. Thus certain characteristics — such as the ability to camouflage one's self from predators, as deer do, or the ability to see prey from a great distance, as hawks are able to do — would be selected for. Adaptability to the environment depends on a certain amount of within-species variability because over time the environment changes. If the species cannot react to the change, extinction will follow. The natural selection of observable characteristics (and some behaviors) occurs by way of selecting for particular genetic combinations that transmit the information (characteristics and predisposition for behavioral patterns) between generations.

While natural selection is a matter of life and death, **sexual selection** is important for the continuation of the species because it determines the production or lack of production of offspring. Darwin defined sexual selection as the process that shapes physiological, anatomical, and behavioral characteristics, which, in turn, attract mates. He did not include primary reproductive characteristics such as genital formation. Rather, he focused on traits that were the result of the competition for mates, including (1) the ability to attract members of the opposite sex and (2) the power to fight off other members of the same sex when competing for a mate. Darwin saw both kinds of competition as male dominated, since of the species he observed, generally the males courted the females and competed with other males for the attention of a female (see Wilson, 1975).

Darwin credited sexual selection as the reason for male-female differences in appearance and behavior. In most species of birds, for instance, the male is more colorful than the female. The display of the male's coloration is used to attract females and, at the same time, to repel other males. The courting male must demonstrate to the female his vigor, his fitness, and in some cases his resources, such as territory or food. The courted sex, in this case the female, selects from the most fit of males. Her behavior is often cautious, forcing the male to continue his courtship, presumably in order for her to decide who would be the best mate. Thus, in some species, the sight of nest building is an essential part of the courting process. For instance, the male three-spined stickleback fish establishes his

Figure 5-1. *A female fly* (H. Sartor) *accepts the courtship silk balloon, as three other males tempt her with their own creations.* (Source: Alcock, 1979)

territory and builds a nest. When a female enters his territory, he does a zigzag dance—zigging toward the female and zagging away toward the nest, in order to lure the female to it. He prods her with his nose to lay her eggs in the nest, after which he fertilizes and cares for them. Niko Tinbergen (1951), who has done a great deal of work with sticklebacks, has demonstrated that there are crucial "courting signs" for both males and females. The female is attracted to the male's red belly, which only turns red during the breeding season, and the male is attracted to the female's egg-swollen belly. The male stickleback will fiercely fight off another red-bellied fish, even if it is only a model, and vigorously court a swollen grey-bellied fish.

Functions of Courtship

The most obvious function of courtship is attracting a mate. However, if males and females of a species are already paired off when the female is ready to mate, courtship patterns are almost nonexistent. In some species of seals, for instance, the female locates a place to bear young in an area defended by a male. During the breeding season the male simply mates with females available in his territory.

With other species more complicated signals are necessary during courtship because the males and females live independently of each other. Signals as diverse as the songbird's song, the monarch butterfly's chemical secretions, or perhaps the facial expressions of humans communicate sexual interest. Such communication depends on the ecology as well as the social structure of the group. Visual signals would not work for grassland floor species, for example, because individuals are typically out of each other's sight. Also, the signals can change with decreasing distance; many primates often begin with a visual courting sequence and progress to tactile communication.

A second function of courting practices is to limit individuals to mating only with members of their own species. In evolutionary theory this restriction is called **reproductive isolation.** Although other factors help guarantee reproductive isolation (size, shape, color, genitalia compatibility, and survival of offspring), in many cases the species-specific courtship pattern serves as a major reproductive isolating mechanism. A classic example is the courtship display of three species of fiddler crabs. Subtle differences in the speed, smoothness, arc, and elevation of the crab's claw movements help the female to recognize her own species as well as signal a warning to other males (Bermant & Davison, 1974).

In most species the female decides which courting male she will accept. The female rat, for example, will usually accept most males. In other species, such as the chimpanzees, a female will always refuse certain males, and yet always accept others. Also, in some species one male may be the exclusive suitor throughout a female's fertile periods; he will drive other males out of his territory.

An important variable with regard to the female's degree of choosiness and the male's degree of possessiveness has to do with what biologists call the theory of **parental investment** (see Trivers, 1972; Williams, 1975; Wilson, 1975). Parental investment is defined as "any behavior toward an offspring that increases the chances of the offspring's survival at the cost of the parent's ability to invest in other offspring" (Wilson, 1975, p. 337). Among birds and animals, the female generally has the greatest parental investment for two reasons. First, she contributes the eggs, which are in more limited supply than sperm. Once an egg is fertilized, her ability to produce more eggs stops or slows during the gestation period. Regardless of whether or not the male sperm fertilizes an egg, the male's parental investment is less because he is able to produce sperm continuously and inseminate other females. Second, the female typically is the most involved in parental care, thus making the immediate production of more offspring difficult (costly in time, energy, and resources).

One version of the biological argument concludes that because most females have a greater investment, they must be careful about their choice of partners. The competitive sex, generally the male, thus evolved secondary sex characteristics or courtship displays to attract the discriminating female. The more limited the resource, the more likely that competition within a species will be fierce (thus, more dramatic courtship displays); further, some of the competitive sex will have multiple mates and others will not mate at all, but almost all members with the scarce resources will be mated.

What biologists have found is that in those species in which the male does take on his share of parental care, the females are the competitive sex and have more conspicuous courtship displays. If the male does have more investment in the offspring, he should have a courting pattern that ensures he is the father—that is, he should keep other males out of his territory, control access to females with a dominance hierarchy, or, more generally, be part of a seasonally monogamous species (Barash, 1977).

What are human patterns and how do they relate to these evolutionary ideas of courtship and mate selection? This question sparks an old but recently reopened debate. Those in favor of a sociobiological argument claim that part of being human includes being an animal, and thus we share certain behavioral patterns seen in other species. This means that genetic influences on human behavior patterns are strong. The following examples show how sociobiological principles can be extended to include interpretations of mate selection in humans (see Barash, 1977 and Symons, 1979 for further details).

1. *Good health is a primary feature of attractiveness for both men and women, across cultures.* Health is one indicator of "fitness"—the ability to survive, reproduce, and care for young. Therefore, that this would be a predominant factor in partner selection makes evolutionary sense.
2. *Younger women are cross-culturally considered to be more sexually attractive than older women. Youth is less important for men; they are considered to be sexually attractive long after women start to lose their appeal.* The fact that age appears to be a crucial element of women's attractiveness has been viewed by the biologically inclined as being connected in a very essential way to the fact that women have a reproductive time limit after which they are no longer fertile (menopause).
3. *For men, status may play a more important role than physical characteristics* (Ford & Beach, 1951). Sociobiologists find that this observation agrees with the idea of males showing off their resources to prospective female partners, whether it be with dinner, gifts, or some other symbols. Often wealth and status are connected with older rather than younger males, and thus an older man is more likely to have a younger woman or several women attached to him if he has acquired status and resources.
4. *Women's physical attractiveness is the focus of much attention in various cultures. Breasts, buttocks, or hips are often emphasized by clothes or other adornments.* One reason may be that these body areas are connected to reproduction and may be biologically determined symbols of a woman's fertility.

Perhaps sociobiologists are correct in their theory that a great deal of human behavior is genetically linked, as suggested in the above examples. Each of these points, however, could also be accounted for with a sociocultural rather than a biological framework. For instance, health facilitates social interaction in that a healthy person has the interest and energy to mix and interact with others.

Age and its importance to sexual attraction makes sense as a biological factor only if we assume that reproduction is the primary reason for male-female human bonding. In humans, if we consider the dependency demands of young children, childbearing is somewhat less of an issue than child rearing. Child rearing is easier if both parents are involved, which means continued mutual attraction of some sort between these individuals. From this point of view, increasing age should not lead to a loss of attraction, at least until one's children are independent.

The importance of women's youth as a characteristic of sexual attractiveness may be reflective of more general social and traditional roles beyond the younger woman's ability to have children. In industrialized countries, women always have been the childbearers and raisers, and men have supplied the resources necessary for family survival. A woman's culturally prescribed role was to find a man who was a good provider at the earliest possible opportunity, marry him, and have children with him. Men, on the other hand, select a mate later. From this perspective, a high amount of seduc-

tiveness displayed by females should coincide with early adulthood since this period is generally their prime mating time. If youth is the period when the greatest degree of mate selection is occurring, more likely the youthful subculture will set the standards for sexual attractiveness. In the last two decades economic independence of women has become more common. This shift, however, is recent, and its effects on sexual attractiveness cannot be expected to be seen as yet. This economic change may lead to some expansion of the age range of female attractiveness, coinciding with economic and sex-role changes throughout the society.

In sum, no simple or single explanation can account for our current standards of sexual attractiveness. In spite of considerable speculation, we do not know the extent of biology's influence on culture, or vice versa.

COMMUNICATION OF SEXUAL INTEREST

Visual Sexual Signals: The Language of the Body

For nonhuman primates most courting occurs in response to the female's estrus cycle. Humans differ in this respect since they do not have a breeding season or an observable estrus cycle. Desmond Morris (1967) believed that this constant state of receptivity for sexual activity, which is only inter-

rupted for a short period surrounding childbirth, makes humans the most sexual of all primates.

Humans do attach social significance to a variety of body features for which other primates show less interest. The human female breast is more rounded and enlarged than that of any other primate, though the same maternal function is served adequately in each case. The human breast is also emphasized by a contrasting darker nipple. Fleshy, rounded buttocks are not found in any other primate. These features, of course, are more noticeable because humans are "naked"—they are without the usual primate fur covering most of their bodies. The hair that is there, pubic and armpit hair, may contribute to a person's sexual appeal, and it also retains sexual smells. The many frontal sexual "signals"— breasts, pubic hair, and even noticeable navels—evolved along with the upright posture of the early hominids. These signals may be related to the human preference for a face-to-face intercourse position, which has been observed only rarely in certain other primates, such as the gorilla and the pygmy chimpanzee. This position keeps the face, a highly expressive transmitter of emotional information, in view as well.

Certain male-female differences in body characteristics may also hold communicative value. The smooth female shape that develops during puberty, with fatty tissue in the hips, thighs, and breasts, is distinctly different from the muscular development of the male. Body hair is distributed differently on the male, and, of course, the male's genitalia are exposed. These differences are constant signals—that is, they do not appear and then vanish, as is the case with sexual signals that appear during the estrus cycle of other primates. Additionally, different cultures adorn the bodies of males and females in a way that maximizes the impact of the signals. Depending on the cultural importance or taboos associated with various body parts, sexual features may be emphasized (for instance, Renaissance codpieces, which are flaps that fit over the tight pants of men, emphasized male genitals), or deemphasized (loose-fitting Roman togas or religious robes disguised body parts).

Postures and gestures can also be used as sexual signals and often differ markedly between males and females. In what are supposed to be nonsexual social situations—office or classroom situations, for instance—many gestures and postures can have sexually communicative significance. Typical examples for Western societies include a hand placed on a hip, a displaying or caressing of the thigh area, a female thrusting her breast forward, the tilt of someone's head, slow wrist or finger motions, or an open presentation of the palm. The person displaying these signals may have no intention of communicating a sexual message; as some researchers have pointed out, the function of the behaviors seems to be general mutual attraction and an invitation to establish a relationship (Birdwhistle, 1960; Scheflen, 1964, 1972).

The most important visual signals for humans are those involving the face. Primate faces are generally more expressive (at least to other primates) than those of other mammals, and they are able to communicate a variety of moods and feelings. The use of eyes is particularly valuable. Most primates, including humans, use the direction of the glance in dominance-subordinate encounters—for example, a direct eye-to-eye gaze is potentially threatening. But humans are the only species to use eyes in sexual flirting (Ekman, 1972), and there is cross-cultural evidence to support this statement (Eibl-Eibesfeldt, 1970). A gaze met or held can indicate sexual interest and may be

Interest, communication, and companionship continue well past late adolescence.

very important as one of the first signals of attraction. As one young man recalled:

> I think I noticed Sue and felt physically attracted the minute I entered the room that evening. When I saw her dance I was also impressed with her extraordinary talent. At that point I was ripe and when she gave me that look, I succumbed totally. (Tennov, 1979, p. 18)

Visual expression depends on several characteristics. Pupil size increases involuntarily with certain emotional states, including general and sexual interest or arousal (Hess, 1965). Pupil dilation makes eyes more noticeable. Additionally, the human eye is unusual with respect to the amount of white, or sclera, surrounding the iris, a fact that increases one's ability to tell the direction of someone else's glance (Hewes, 1973). Even cosmetics that accent the eyes, brows, and lashes tend to enhance the eyes and probably their communicative intensity (Argyle & Cook, 1976).

The ears and nose do not play much of a role in the communication of sexual interest. Both areas, however, do have some erotic value since they have erectile tissue that can swell with blood during sexual arousal. For many people the ears are particularly erogenous when swollen during sexual arousal; in fact, instances of males

and females who have reached orgasm as a result of earlobe stimulation have been recorded (Kinsey et al., 1953).

Additionally, human lips are turned "inside out." Chimpanzee lips are very flexible and thin instead of fleshy and protruding like ours. Women also tend to have fuller lips than men. The visual noticeability of the lips' mucous membranes and the ability of people to be expressive with their lips, both visually and by kissing (lips, too, have many sensitive nerve endings), make them a potentially important means of sexual and nonsexual human communication (Morris, 1967).

Sexual Communication by Touch

A great deal of sensitivity to touch that is particular to humans has to do with our "nakedness." Most of the human body lacks fur or hair, as we have mentioned, and many areas are rich with sensitive nerve endings. Smooth and sensitive hands (relative to other animals) provide the important means of exchanging *tactile communication,* or communication by touching.

In other primates, grooming provides a powerful bonding mechanism between infants and mothers, as well as between

Box 5–1

THE SEXUAL COMMUNICATION OF SMELLS

Although body smells are generally camouflaged in our society with soaps, deodorants, mouthwashes, lotions, or perfumes, they have attraction value in other cultures as well as among other primates. Indeed, artificial fragrances have taken on sexual meaning in our own culture, which is evident in the many sensual ads we see for perfumes and colognes for both men and women. The natural areas where human bodily odors generally develop, the armpits and genitals, are both decorated with pubic hair and are equipped for producing and retaining odors (apocrine sweat glands, unique to these areas, produce more solids than ordinary sweat glands, which are then trapped by the surrounding hair). Thus, visual and olfactory attention is drawn to these areas. This is particularly true for the human female, who has 75 percent more apocrine glands than does the male (Morris, 1967). It is puzzling that the underarm area, like the genital area, traps odors. One theory is that because humans favor face-to-face courtship and sexplay, the upper body may be an additional lure in our species.

Secretions that prove sexually stimulating odors or tastes are called sexual **pheromones.** Some research has shown that vaginal secretions have a sexually stimulating value for other primates. The males of many species often smell or taste the female's vaginal secretions prior to mounting and copulation. E. B. Keverne (1976) did an experimental study with rhesus monkeys in which he applied natural and artificial vaginal secretions to each female's hindquarters and observed the response in the males. With eleven pairs of animals he recorded the following responses:

1. In some cases these olfactory stimulants increased male mounting, masturbation, and ejaculation.
2. In other cases the male displayed no real sexual behavior but rather a decreased amount of aggression or increased amount of grooming.
3. Males did not always respond in the same way to the same odor cue, but they did show partner preferences.

Keverne concluded that the variability in response of the male rhesus monkeys suggests that perhaps human pheromones do not exist. Nevertheless, some researchers are actively looking for a pheromone in humans that might be correlated with increased male sexual interest during ovulation, which is the time when fertilization can occur (see Doty, et al., 1975).

adults. Humans engage in a parallel "grooming" response that can be considered a prelude to and part of sexplay. Rubbing, caressing, massaging, and stroking are all considered variants of mutual grooming.

Self-grooming is also a part of or preparation for sexual communication; it occurs in other mammals as well as in humans. Psychiatrist Albert Scheflen (1972) and his colleagues (e.g., Birdwhistle, 1960, 1961) have observed "preening" in individuals who anticipate meeting a person of the opposite sex, a situation they label as "quasi-courtship." Beyond straightening ties and pulling up socks (men) or checking makeup and hair (women), Scheflen noted another characteristic of courtship readiness—that is, individuals anticipating the possibility of meeting new partners often have improved muscle tone, making for tauter faces, improved posture, a more assured walk, and tighter abdominal muscles—all generally conveying an impression of youthful vigor. People even report a change in the glow of a person's skin and eyes, which may "defy objective analysis but which most of us have probably experienced" (Hewes, 1973, p. 85).

Verbal Expression

By far the most extensive form of human sexual communication is language. Words entice, attract, arouse, reveal a potential partner, arrange for a sexual encounter, create an emotional atmosphere, direct sexual activities, give feedback as to how aroused someone is, and set rules for who is and who is not a viable sexual partner. As Gorden Hewes remarks, most strangers "do not start to copulate after an interchange of some facial expressions, whiffs of perfume, or seductive posturing" (Hewes, 1973, p. 91). Language, in fact, strongly influences one's choice of sexual partners; it transmits information about where a partner is from, about the person's social status and education, and about the person's emotional and psychological qualities.

CROSS-CULTURAL PERSPECTIVE

Different cultures favor different parts of the female body. American males appear to be more obsessed with the female breast than Europeans, who have long been attracted to the woman's buttocks (Kinsey et al., 1953). Some cultures find the navel sexually arousing. Most cultures require some type of genital covering, which marks the difference between modest and immodest dress.

In cultures that feature few fashion adornments, the body and face still occupy primary importance as sexual attractions. One example is offered in Malinowski's (1929) detailed study of the Trobriand Islanders. According to Malinowski, "regular delicate features, well-built lithe bodies, clear skins, and that personal charm ..." are characteristics of both male and female Trobriand beauty (Malinowski, 1929, p. 242). Old age, deformity, mental or physical disease, albinism, and baldness all were beyond erotic interest. Attractive people conveyed vigor, vitality, strength, well-proportioned bodies, and youthful grace. While Trobrianders had strong preferences regarding body structure of potential partners, a majority of attention was focused on

Young shepherdess pair, members of the Senbury tribe in Kenya

High fashion model, Halston Show, New York, USA

the face: To be attractive, the face had to be well rounded ("imiliyapila" — like a full moon), the forehead was to be small and smooth, and there was to be no facial hair, but a full crop on the scalp. Red, black, or white facial paint was used. Attractive eyes were small but shining, eyebrows were shaved, and eyelashes were often bitten off during lovemaking. The mouth, reddened with betel nut, was most desirable when it was full but not protruding. Likewise, a full and fleshy nose was preferred. Ears were pierced and adorned with turtle shell rings, and teeth were blackened. If we compare these characteristics to 1929 American standards of sexual appeal, we can see quite clearly that cultures define attractiveness and provide the conditions that permit the members to enhance their sexual charm.

191

Box 5–2

FASHION AND NUDITY: AN HISTORICAL GLIMPSE

Fashion and nudity go together. We can assume that the way fashions adorn or form the body is related to how attractive or seductive the whole body and its parts are considered to be. Let's take a look at some historical patterns:

—In early medieval days, good Christians, the church fathers felt, should express the certainty of sins and uncertainty of salvation with a simple, somber appearance. As a result, the dress of the Middle Ages tended to be sober and subdued.

—In fourteenth-century England, men and women wore clothes that accentuated their breasts and genitals. During this period, attitudes about sexuality were quite liberal, at least in the early days, and such attitudes were expressed in the fashions of the day. Sexual abstinence was regarded as unhealthy, and incest, homosexuality, and prostitution were well established, the latter being tolerated and in many cases supported by the church (Sanger, 1910). In addition, there were few restrictions on nudity. People could walk through the streets to the baths nude, or nearly so; warriors usually went naked except for their weapons. Historian G. Rattray Taylor (1954) reports that the Queen of Ulster and the 610 ladies of the court met Charlemagne naked from the waist up and with raised skirts to expose their bodies in honor of him. On the European continent, rich and colorful clothes, cosmetics, false hair, and perfumes were used extensively. In France, in the fourteenth and fifteenth centuries, men were dressing in silk and lace, and styles (skirted coats and lace collars) that were quite similar to women's fashions.

In the 1600s, clothing styles and ideology changed again, becoming much more in line with early medieval customs. At this time, the Puritans had gained political strength in the English Church and managed to make pleasure in any form both a sin and a severe legal transgression. Not surprisingly, the Puritans objected to rich decoration and color, both in fashion and in church decor.

—More striking and familiar was the extensive modesty of the Victorian era. Prodded by the post-Puritanical fear of sex and its power, sex and the body in general were regarded with extreme prudery. Even piano legs were fitted with crinolines, lest anyone be sexually stimulated by the mere sight of their curves. There was an attempt to view women as sexless, with any area of the body between the neck and the knees referred to as the "liver." A doctor would often give a female patient a doll to use to point out the area of her discomfort. And as women's undergarments were beginning to be advertised in Victorian papers, those that might have suggested that women had legs (such as panties or bloomers) were illustrated folded, rather than open (Taylor, 1954).

—Since the 1890s in the United States, we can see general alterations in fashion that conceal and/or reveal body parts. The bustle of the turn of the century, combined with corsets that were tightly laced around the waist, emphasized female breasts and hips. After World War I, on the other hand, the ideal feminine figure was flat and straight, neither too hippy nor too busty, and bras were designed to achieve the latter. While women's clothes were relatively colorful, men's were subdued and simple,

Fourteenth century

Early 1600s

1800s

changing little between 1910 and 1950. Men's coats tended to be long enough to conceal any reference to buttocks and genitalia, with sufficiently loose fitting pants achieving the same effect if the coat was removed. From World War II through the early 1950s, women's dress clothes became tighter, lower cut, slit up the side—in other words, more revealing and seductive. Yet the "on-the-street-look" remained prim and rather tailored. However, in the 1960s, several changes took place. Men's fashions became more similar to women's fashions and more casual; and, if women were not wearing men's pants, they were at least wearing "pant suits." Men's clothes became more colorful, decorative, and ruffled, and by the early 1970s were more form fitting. More parts of the body were visible, either with, without, or through the clothes. Bras were occasionally, and then more frequently, absent. The smooth breast of the 1940s and 1950s became outlined, nipples included, by the 1970s.

All of these fashion changes, here suggested in their most general form, were accompanied by economic and social changes. As sensuality became more accepted, fashion reflected the attitude; or as women gained social or public recognition, their clothing styles tended to either downplay their femaleness or converge with men's styles toward a less distinctly feminine style.

1800s

1970

1920s

1920s

Courtship:
Sexual Attraction Lures

In many cultures courtship demands a demonstration of expertise or courage on the part of the male. Sometimes acts of true valor (or foolhardiness) are required to demonstrate one's readiness for marriage. Earlier in this century, a young male from the Mascusis group of Guyana might have found himself sewn up in a hammock full of fire ants (Westermarck, 1921). Bolivian youth had it no easier:

> Ordinarily young people of nubile age are supposed to be shy of one another, and while tending herds, pass one another by many times without apparently seeing each other. Around Camata, if a boy in such a situation wishes to take notice of a girl, he picks up a handful of fine earth or dust and throws it at her. This is a first step of courtship in the Jesus de Machaca region. The next time they meet, the boy picks up some fine gravel, and the girl may do likewise. If they continue to be interested this goes on until finally they throw rocks at each other. Informants told me that there were two cases of deaths in Camata during the last four years from such a cause; one woman received a fractured skull and the other a broken back. (LaBarre, 1948, p. 129)

If men have usually been viewed as the pursuers, women have usually been described as the ones with the power, the allurers. An often-quoted piece of legislation from the British Parliament in 1700 illustrates the latter:

> All women of whatever age, rank, profession or degree, whether virgin maid or widow, that shall from and after such Act impose upon, seduce and betray into matrimony any of His Majesty's subjects by means of scent, paints, cosmetic washes, artificial teeth, false hair, Spanish wool, iron stays, hoops, high heeled shoes or bolstered hips, shall incur the penalty of the law now in force against witchcraft and like misdemeanors, and that the marriage upon conviction shall stand null and void. (quoted in James, 1908, p. 318)

Courtship throughout much of the Western world can be characterized as *entrepreneurial,* meaning that mate selection is a kind of free market with every person on his or her own (Wiseman, 1976). Family and friends have little control over a person's selection of a partner.

Such is not the case in many other societies; in traditional China and Japan, as well as modern day India, marital arrangements are the responsibility of parents and relatives. In India many children are betrothed at birth and are married before they are nine or ten years old (Stephens, 1963). In such cultures boys more often are able to choose a partner than are girls. For instance, in Polynesia, if a boy is interested in a girl, he offers general assistance and gifts to the parents and, if the parents accept his efforts, they must allow him to marry their daughter, whether she likes him or not.

Although the American style of partner seeking seems to optimize the opportunity for freedom of choice, it also introduces problems that more controlled planning avoids. First, there must be places to meet potential partners and there must be mutually understood ways of communicating sociosexual interest. Schools, and particularly the college campus, provide the most convenient and comfortable of locations for partner searching. When people are no longer in school, meeting potential partners becomes more difficult. Jobs, athletic events, social affairs, and parties can serve this function. Since the 1960s, singles bars and singles apartment complexes have catered to the searching crowd. So too have UNIVAC and other computer services gotten into the act; they offer an opportunity to match preferences as diverse as personal attractiveness and smoking habits. Attractiveness is often tricky to determine. One computer match of college students found that 97 percent described themselves as either "average" looking or "better" looking than most.

So even though there are no direct controls over courtship selections, Americans have invented their own ways of matchmaking *ex machina*. In part these American ways must reflect the inadequacy of allowing complete freedom of choice; narrowing the field or at least defining it does increase a person's chances of selecting an appropriate partner. For all of its attempted efficiency and technology, however, the American meeting and selection system is still cumbersome; it is based on chance and is often full of trial, error, and anxiety. Many people like it for those very reasons. It is part of the excitement of discovering other people as well as learning about one's own qualities and values. Yet for other people, the whole process is a dreary one, with different problems at different ages. Certainly, the demands for making the system work are harsh. The young, good-looking, self-confident, and financially independent individuals often have an easier time of it, but for those "with ravaged faces, lacking in the social graces" (Janis Ian), being ignored or refused is a frequent reality. These cultural pressures are heavy and, even though their importance may decrease somewhat as people mature, they take their toll on those who feel socially isolated. Cultural pressure also causes problems for the "beautiful people," who tend to be appreciated and seduced for their superficial qualities, which may mean that they themselves have trouble relating to other people except at this distant level, and desperately cling to their looks as their only identity over the years.

SOCIOCULTURAL PERSPECTIVE

Social Influences on Physical Attraction

Getting to know someone is like a steeplechase, and the good-looking have the advantage of being among those who start beyond the first hurdle. (Cook & McHenry, 1978, p. 74)

Physical appearance often marks the beginning, our "first hurdle," of interpersonal attraction. People form impressions about others based on facial and bodily appeal and also according to how approachable and available other people seem to be.

When studies are done on physical attractiveness, raters of "good looks" can, surprisingly, often agree on evaluations of the attractiveness of someone else. Walster and her colleagues (1966) reported correlations measuring agreement between raters of 0.49 and 0.55. Later Berscheid and Walster (1974) claimed that correlation averaged about 0.70. Two qualifications on these figures are worth considering. First, the majority of raters and those rated were from college populations, where standards and values may be far more homogeneous than in an over-30 age group. Second, ratings are never in complete agreement, thus suggesting that individual preference plays a role.

What facial features people prefer is a complex issue. Some studies have shown that most people prefer features that are babylike (sometimes called the "Bambi effect"): a large rounded forehead, large eyes, and rounded features. All groups except preadolescents seem to prefer these features (Fullard & Reiling, 1976). Other features of facial attractiveness are difficult to agree on. Leonardo da Vinci clearly saw beauty as a matter of proportions: ear length should be equal to nose length and to the distance from the bottom of the nose to the eyelid; the space from the nose to the forehead should equal the distance from the chin to the bottom of the nose. However, few beautiful women or handsome men, whether in da Vinci portraits or *Vogue* magazine, conform to such strict rules of proportion and symmetry. Furthermore, beauty itself does not always seem to be a qualification for sexual attraction.

One type of study examining body shape preference involves the presentation of slides of silhouettes that systematically vary the size of different body parts. In one study with college men, there were indeed "breast," "leg," and "buttocks" men who preferred one part of the female body over another (Wiggins, Wiggins, & Conger, 1968). Preferences also may be based on the overall body proportions (e.g., Cook & McHenry, 1978). Similarly, other researchers have found that a person's total impression of another, including body and facial features and expressions such as smiling (Holstein, Goldstein, & Bem, 1971), and whether or not a person spends time gazing at someone else (Kleinke, Staneski, & Berger, 1975) are important elements of attraction.

Women who were shown silhouettes or photos of men (Lavrakas, 1975; Beck, Ward-Hull, & McLear, 1976) preferred men of average build, usually with broad chests and narrow hips. Sporty, outgoing women, as well as those who were older and more conventionally sex-typed, liked muscular men. Younger, more liberated women preferred tall, slim men (Lavrakas, 1975; Wilson & Nias, 1976). In Britain, women and men were shown color photos that varied in how fully dressed the featured male or female was (Mathews et al., 1972). Men and women of different social classes were asked to rate the attractiveness of the photos. Some differences emerged by class, others by occupation. Male psychologists generally liked women who were dressed and who appeared unconventional or provocative. Soldiers and porters preferred large-breasted women who were posed in bedroom shots and/or looked sexy. One especially interesting finding was that when selecting women as potential marriage partner types, *all men,* regardless of class, preferred conventionally dressed and attractive women rather than the sexy and provocative ones. In other words, men distinguished between sexy women and "proper" women, between those one only has sex with and those whom one marries.

Women also showed different preferences according to their occupational class. Professional women, psychologists and psychiatrists, were repulsed by the "muscle man" image, which was the body of choice for the cleaning staff and nurses. Professional women instead preferred mostly dressed, slim, dark, and sensitive-looking men (Mathews et al., 1972).

☐ *To Be Beautiful Is to Be Good* The fact that people may be differentially evaluated in terms of physical attractiveness may be less important than the associated attributes of good looks. Study after study has shown that attractiveness signifies goodness to many people.

A classic piece of research on the meaning of good looks was done by Dion, Berscheid, and Walster (1972). College students gave their impressions of a series of photographs of men and women, preselected to be low, average, or high in physical attractiveness. Both male and female subjects formed remarkably consistent beliefs about people based on physical attractiveness. Good-looking men and women were thought to be more poised, self-assertive,

kind, likable, sociable, sexually warm, and interesting. Attractive people were also thought to be better dates or spouses, happier, and more occupationally successful. This "positive halo" effect does not seem to be limited to impressions about young men and women. Attractive middle-aged people were judged by subjects of different ages to be more socially outgoing, more pleasant, higher in self-esteem, and to have higher occupational status than were unattractive people (Adams & Huston, 1975). In fact, the stereotype that success is equal to attractiveness often is upheld. For instance, attractive college students have more sexual and dating experience and less dating anxiety than unattractive students (Curran & Lippold, 1975).

Height is an important characteristic when measuring the attractiveness of males (Cook & McHenry, 1978). The expectation of socially desirable characteristics increases with male height. In one study, researchers found that as authority level increased, so did the tendency to estimate a person as being taller (Wilson, 1968). People also tend to believe that the men they choose to vote for are taller (Feldman, 1971). On a more concrete level, height may make a difference in income: Starting salaries were reported to be 12.4 percent higher for tall graduates (6 feet 2 inches and over) than for students under 6 feet tall (Feldman, 1971).

To be fair, attractive people are not always described in a positive light. They are more likely to be seen as egotistical, vain, and participants in extramarital affairs (Dermer & Theil, 1975). While attractive defendants are seen as less guilty and are less severely punished for exam cheating or burglary (Efran, 1974), misbehavior such as swindling, in which attractiveness may be part of the crime, brings on harsher judgment and punishment (Sigall & Ostrove, 1975). In dating situations, people who are extremely attractive may be somewhat frightening to potential partners (e.g., Berscheid et al., 1971).

One study done with first-year Canadian college students found, as expected, that the more popular students were more attractive (Krebs & Adinioff, 1975). However, the *most* attractive students were rated as unpopular. Keep in mind that the ratings were given by members of the same sex, which may influence the results. Highly attractive people of the same sex may incite jealousy or competitive feelings.

☐ *Sex Differences and the Value of Attractiveness* Physical attractiveness seems to have a greater impact on women than on men. One study has found that attractive women are less neurotic, happier, more assertive, and higher in self-esteem than unattractive women. No such differences emerged in comparing the two levels of attractiveness in men (Mathes & Kahn, 1975). In couples, there does not seem to be an enhanced social evaluation of the female who is seen with an attractive male companion. However, men are evaluated more favorably if seen with an attractive woman (Bar-Tal & Saxe, 1976). Men accompanied by good-looking women have been evaluated as more self-confident, friendly, and likable than men accompanied by unattractive women (Sigall & Landy, 1973). Men may

also be more guilty of believing the "beauty equals goodness" stereotype than are women (Janda, O'Grady, & Barnhart, 1981).

The problem for attractive women whose lives are directly controlled by their beauty is that they must eventually deal with the effects of aging. There is some evidence that males who were more or less attractive as teenagers did not differ in happiness at middle age; on the other hand, women who were more attractive as teenagers reported more depression and less life satisfaction at middle age than did their less attractive counterparts (Berscheid & Walster, 1974).

☐ *When the Sexes Meet* The time when physical attractiveness seems to be particularly important is when a male and female first meet. In the study by Walster and her colleagues (1966), 752 college freshmen were matched according to information received from and about the students. Students filled out forms on their self-rated popularity, attractiveness, and self-esteem, and they indicated how attractive and considerate they expected their dates to be. Academic and personality records were also available on all students. All students were then randomly assigned partners, by computer, and instructed to attend a dance held in an armory. During intermission, students' impressions of their dates were assessed.

The results were interesting. First, the more attractive the subjects were, the more they expected their dates to be attractive and personable. Second, more attractive students consistently judged their dates more harshly than did less attractive subjects. Third, everyone preferred the most attractive date possible, regardless of their own attractiveness. And finally, how much a person liked his or her date was most strongly determined by physical attractiveness rather than by intelligence or personality. We should note, too, that physical attractiveness was of equal importance to the response of both males and females. Other research has found physical attractiveness to be as important on the fifth date as it is on the first (Mathes, 1975).

What about people who have already formed long-term relationships? In a study conducted over fifty years ago, married couples were asked what changes they would make in their spouses (Hamilton, 1929). Of the 100 couples questioned, 38 men and 45 women reported that they would make no changes in the physical qualities of their mates. In fact, only three characteristics generated any noticeable dissatisfaction. The major one for women was desiring that their spouses be taller (29 women). Between 25 and 30 men and women would have preferred their spouses to be a different weight, with a nearly equal number of both sexes wanting a heavier or thinner spouse. The other category in which a number of males reported a desired change was skin texture—14 males wished their spouse's skin texture was finer. Although recent research on long-term relationships has not focused on physical attractiveness, one investigator has shown that the attractiveness of husbands and wives, rated by independent judges, was similar even in middle age (Murstein, 1972, 1976). These studies suggest that attractiveness is perhaps most important in the selection of sexual partners and mates, and becomes less important after mate selection unless there is a drastic physical change in one partner or the other.

□ *Matching for the Sake of Equity* We have learned that physical attractiveness is most important when relationships are forming. The next question we might ask is, Do people select and date others who are equal in attractiveness to themselves? It turns out that yes, they usually do (e.g., Walster, Walster, & Berscheid, 1977). The attractiveness of a couple and the degree to which the partners are "equal" are influenced by who arranges the date. In studies where partners are assigned (by computer, for example) matching of attractiveness does not always occur. On the other hand, when the individual must choose the date, matching of attractiveness does occur (Berscheid et al., 1971; Huston, 1973).

The interpretation of these results is based on equity theory. People select dates according to who they feel will not be too different in terms of appearance. The reason they do this is not completely clear, although equity theorists refer to the importance of similarity as an initial means of attracting someone. In other words, physical appearance is the first cue, and comparable attractiveness may be interpreted on some level as "something in common." Possibly, this pattern is related to the potential meaning of rejection: If a less or more desirable person rejects an advance, such a rebuke may negatively influence one's own sense of desirability, one's own self-esteem. A person of similar attractiveness may be less threatening. Additionally, rejection from someone of equal attractiveness may be more easily attributed to nonattractiveness variables: The rejector is a snob, is shy, is nervous, hates the opposite sex, and so on. One wonders what reasons for rejection (looks, values, ideas) hurt people the most. Given the value placed on physical attractiveness, it would seem that people are sensitive to being rejected for the way they look. Thus, self-protection may mean being cautious, or choosing dates or potential partners who are equally attractive.

Kiesler and Baral (1970) examined the effect of self-esteem on men's romantic interest in a more, or less, appealing woman. Self-esteem was varied by telling one group of men (lowered self-esteem) that they were doing poorly on a new intelligence test and telling a second group (raised self-esteem) that they were doing very well. During a break in testing, the experimenter took each man to the snack bar to relax. There they met a woman, a confederate, who was actually part of the experiment, although the subject was not aware of her role. The woman was either made up to look very attractive or very unattractive, but in either case she acted friendly, accepting, and interested. The degree of interest shown by the men — asking for a date or phone number, offering to buy coffee, and so on — was scored on a "romantic behavior" index. In support of the equity theory, men in the raised self-esteem condition behaved more romantically toward the more attractively groomed confederate, whereas men whose self-esteem had been lowered behaved more romantically toward the less appealing confederate.

The Kiesler and Baral study illustrates that a person's internal cognitive-emotional state may influence his or her perceived freedom of behavior and thus any choices made by that person. It also illustrates that feelings about our psychological or social attractiveness can interact with our physical attractiveness to round out the matching equation. On a more objective level, a large group of men and women were interviewed about their dating or marital relationships (Berscheid et al., 1973). Of interest to the researchers was how people balanced inequities in different spheres of their relationships. All participants were asked to judge their own attractiveness and that of their partners. As expected, when people rated themselves as more attractive than their partners, they then rated their partners as more loving, self-sacrificing, and wealthy.

Interestingly, people tend to label such relationships as compensatory, as if something has to be going on to make up for a difference in attractiveness: "What does that handsome man/beautiful woman see in her/him?" Quite clearly there is more to be "seen" than meets the eye. Apart from the enormous importance of physical appearance in initiating a relationship, maintaining a relationship goes beyond physical attractiveness.

Psychological Factors in Attraction

In discussing physical attractiveness, we are actually talking about the association between good looks and their psychological meaning to individuals. We focus now on the psychological features that are likely to increase our attraction to others.

☐ *Reciprocity: The Potency of Mutual Admiration* In the second century B.C., philosopher Hecato wrote, "I will show you a potion without drug or herb or any witch's spell; if you wish to be loved, love" (quoted in Berscheid & Walster, 1978, p. 40). Indeed, a lot of popular advice for people wishing to make friends and influence people (see Dale Carnagie, 1937) embraces the idea of impressing other people with how wonderful they are in your eyes.

The reciprocity-of-liking proposition—if someone likes you, you are more likely to return the feelings—is accurate, but only some of the time. A typical study on this idea might involve telling several people in a group that according to predetermined tests or interviews, certain other people like them. Later, data are collected on who likes whom. To summarize the results of these studies, let's use a hypothetical couple, Sam and Judy. Let's say that Sam has knowledge (we do not know if it is true or false) that Judy likes him. He is more inclined to like Judy if any one of the following is true:

1. He has just met her, and he assumes that the information is correct until it is confirmed or disconfirmed (e.g., Backman & Secord, 1959).
2. Sam has been feeling socially isolated or badly about himself, especially if he has just broken up from a relationship or been told that he is incompetent at work (Dittes, 1959; Jacobs et al., 1971; Walster, 1965). However, Sam's current

mood must not be a chronic one; in other words, he must not always feel negatively about himself, in which case he is likely to be suspicious and mistrustful of anyone who shows interest in him (Deutsch & Solomon, 1959).
3. Sam feels that Judy is accurately assessing the qualities she claims to like about him—for example, his superior intelligence, his sexy body, and his sensitivity (Berscheid, Walster, & Walster, 1969).
4. Judy can also tell him some negative feelings she has about him, assuming he is in agreement with her evaluation (Berscheid et al., 1969).
5. Sam does not feel manipulated. If Sam feels that Judy is ingratiating herself—trying to win favors by complimenting falsely—his affection is unlikely to be won (Jones, 1964; Dickoff, 1961; Lowe & Goldstein, 1970).

What exceptions are there to the reciprocity-of-liking rule? We all have experienced situations where others do not like us, but we do not dislike them, or where others like us, but we do not have similar feelings. If, for example, Sam *always* feels he is unlikable or unworthy (rather than just momentarily so after a bad day, a poor grade, or a fight with a friend), he may very well dislike someone who likes him. Sharauger (1975) summarized the results of the reciprocity versus nonreciprocity research, concluding that people do like to think favorably of themselves and feel better toward people who praise them rather than criticize them. However, people have more respect for evaluations that are consistent with their own view of themselves.

Some additional considerations on the topic of reciprocity of liking remain. First, people who are too flattering or full of praise may lose some of their initial credibility, but overall, people are tempted to believe anything positive someone might say about them. If praise initially feels "inaccurate" ("I'm not really that good of a guitar player" or "I'm not really that bright"), people are very flexible in updating their personal self-evaluations in a positive direction. The research seems to suggest that when in doubt, use flattery.

Second, research has also revealed that the accuracy of flattery may not be crucial because we hope to be appreciated for qualities that we would like to have. As Lord Chesterfield bluntly stated:

> Very ugly or very beautiful women . . . should be flattered on their understanding, and mediocre ones on their beauty. (Finck, 1891, p. 245, quoted in Berscheid & Walster, 1978)

> Men . . . are most and best flattered upon those points where they wish to excel, and yet doubtful whether they do or not. (Jones, 1964, p. 24, quoted in Berscheid & Walster, 1978)

Third, the process of liking and disliking seems to be enhanced by changes in feelings. People are particularly fond of others who had initially disliked them, but who then changed their feelings, while people more intensely dislike someone whose affection they have lost (Aronson & Linder, 1965; Clore, Wiggins, & Itkin, 1975).

Most of the research on the mutuality of liking has been done with college students, whose interaction rules may not hold up for other populations. Also surprising is that researchers seem to treat the flatterer, praiser, or ingratiator as a two-dimensional entity, with no other characteristics except for the person's sex and his or her attraction for someone else. In the real world, this singlemindedness rarely occurs. People have many other reasons for liking or disliking someone else.

□ *Proximity: Nearness Becomes Dearness*   Not surprisingly, geographical closeness increases the likelihood of attraction. People tend to become friends with or marry someone living near to them. One of the earliest studies on proximity and marital partners was carried out by James Bossard (1932), who found that 34 percent of his large sample of 5,000 married couples lived within four city blocks of one another prior to marriage. Similar findings were collected in England (Pond, Ryle, & Hamilton, 1963).

Even friendship patterns are, to some extent, determined by where one lives. Festinger and his colleagues found that in a new housing development, the probability of "best friends" living next door was 0.41, two doors away was 0.23, three doors away was 0.16, and four doors away was 0.10 (Festinger, Schacter, & Back, 1950). Students in the same class or those sharing living quarters tend to form closer friendships than students with less daily contact (Festinger, 1954; Byrne, 1961a). Even working in small groups, such as in a department of a large store or on board an airplane, enhances closer relationships within that group (Kipnis, 1957; Zander & Havelin, 1960).

Although proximity does not qualify on its own as a condition for attraction, it does tend to contribute to positive rather than negative relationships. One theory regarding this phenomenon says that when two people are thrown together by circumstance, a feeling of an anticipated close interaction surfaces and causes the people to like each other more. People tend to set up harmonious relationships, probably because such relationships are more reinforcing and pleasant, and they make close contact easier to sustain (Heider, 1958). An equally plausible theory is that proximity allows people to find out about each other, during which time more favorable than unfavorable information is likely to be exchanged, thus promoting the exchange of positive rather than negative feelings (Newcomb, 1956).

☐ *Similarity: Likes Attract*   Most of the research on interpersonal attraction has focused on the importance of attitude similarity to mutual liking. Two basic hypotheses have been tested: (1) When people like/dislike one another, they *perceive* their attitudes as more similar/dissimilar than they really are; (2) People tend to like others who possess similar attitudes.

In support of the idea that liking precedes and influences the perception of attitude similarity, studies have shown that husbands and wives often perceive their attitudes to be more alike than they really are (Byrne & Blaylock, 1963). Also of interest is a study in which college students were asked to fill out a number of attitude scales (Schoedel, Frederickson, & Knight, 1975). They were first asked to complete one on themselves, and then to look at pictures of a previously rated "attractive" person and "unattractive" person of the opposite sex

and to fill out scales for them. Both male and female subjects rated the attractive person's attitudes, in contrast to the unattractive person's attitudes, as being significantly more similar to their own.

The majority of research has pursued the alternative hypothesis—namely, that similar attitudes elicit and enhance attraction. If people are asked to evaluate a stranger about whom they know nothing except his or her attitudes on various topics, attraction will be greater when the stranger is described as having a greater proportion of attitudes that are similar to those held by the subject (Byrne & Nelson, 1975). Why should like attitudes foster attraction? For one thing, people who like similar activities can anticipate rewarding interactions. For example, two people who share an interest in outdoor sports and who don't enjoy going to a lot of parties can anticipate the pleasure of spending time together.

Another reason why we might be attracted to people with similar attitudes is that a similarity of ideas is reinforcing, a position advanced by the *Byrne-Clore Reinforcement-Affect* model (Clore & Byrne, 1974). Such agreement tells both people that they are "correct," in a sense, in how they interpret the world. Or, said another way, attitude agreement is a form of social validation (Festinger, 1954). Disagreement raises the possibility that "we are to some degree stupid, uninformed, immoral, or insane" (Byrne, 1961, p. 713). Or, possibly, disagreement might make people feel less attractive (see Schoedel et al., 1975).

Several attempts have been made to refine and qualify the "similarity law." One obvious limiting condition is the impor-

A mixture of similarities and differences makes up the chemistry of attraction.

tance of the particular attitude. Sharing a cherished attitude, such as common religious beliefs, may be more vital to liking another person than common trivial attitudes (Byrne, 1961). However, there is also evidence that pure agreement, and not importance, is the critical factor (Clore & Baldridge, 1968). How interested someone is in a topic influences the importance of another person's attitude about it. An avid art historian, for example, may not be able to tolerate indifference to or dislike of primitive art, even though the topic is not central to the daily function of a friendship. The quality and category of the interpersonal relationship may also be a factor. Centers (1975a) found that attitude similarity was present only in couples who were least involved. Couples who dated on a regular basis ("going steady"), were engaged, or were married showed no agreement. In fact, couples who were living together reported many disagreements (Centers, 1975a,b).

□ *Complementarity: Do Opposites Attract?* Perhaps because many people view the sexes as "opposite," there is a tendency to believe that certain personality differences actually increase interpersonal attraction. "Need" theories—and especially the instrumental theory—claim that people select mates in an attempt to maximize their gratification of needs. Thus people seek qualities in others that complement their own needs.

Complementarity of needs is hardly a recent idea. In Plato's *The Symposium,* Socrates explained how Zeus, who was angry at the insolence of humans, originally a single sex, fashioned two sexes. He condemned them to seek one another in order to be whole again: "And whenever half was left alone . . . it wandered about questioning and clasping in the hope of finding a spare half-woman—or whole woman as we should call her nowadays—or half a man" (Plato, 1961, p. 544).

Freud (1922) implied a kind of complementarity when he divided love into two types: **dependent love** was to derive gratification from reverence and submissiveness to loved ones, and egotistical or **narcissistic love** was to derive gratification from the approval and adoration of loved ones. More generally, Freud suggested that one reason for falling in love is related to a quest for perfection, whereby the lover exemplifies what one person has tried to attain but cannot. Expanding on the idea that complementarity is the result of seeking ego completion, other theorists have proposed that seeking one's ego ideal (to compensate for failing to attain an ego ideal) is such a strong need that it distorts our perception of our loved one (Benedek, 1946; Reik, 1944). Although this idea has not been proved, it corresponds to the clichés surrounding the process of strong attraction, such as "beauty is in the eye of the beholder" or "love is blind."

From a different theoretical perspective, Adlerian theory states that a balance between basic life patterns is vital to a relationship:

> Two individuals each of whom want to be dominant hardly fit together. Neither would two martyrs. The distinction must be made, however, between psychologically insignificant qualities and the all important life-style. Husband and wife may both be ambitious or resentful and yet may get along: their identical qualities may unite them more closely. But the decisive point is neither the qualities nor, we may add, the common interests, as many believe, but—the basic pattern of life, the method by which they strive for superiority or suffering, for success or security. This explains why so often an oldest child marries a youngest one; why the brute finds a saint, and the rogue his protective victim. (Dreikurs, 1946, p. 83–84)

No one has successfully determined how similarity *and* complementarity might be important to a relationship. One study that examined engaged college students over a seven-month period did note that similarity and complementarity both played a part in the relationships, but each was prominent at a different time (Kerckhoff & Davis, 1962). The results suggested that early in a relationship consensus on certain values (similarity), based on religion, socioeconomic class, and other status variables, was an important determinant in whether the couple would continue to date. According to these researchers, complementarity only becomes important much later in the relationship. The inability to find a good deal of evidence to support the need-complementarity hypothesis does not mean that the theory is necessarily wrong. Possibly the relevant needs for a long-term, committed marital relationship have not been singled out, and neither has a system been developed within which to track the changing needs of individuals throughout the course of a relationship.

Love: Delightful Potion and Dread Disease

☐ *A Historical Sketch of Love*   Sappho's description of being in love, which follows, was used for some time by Greek physicians to diagnose the "being in love" condition. Although Sappho was describing her love for another woman in these lines, the feelings portrayed are not restricted to same-sex or opposite-sex experiences.

> For should I but see thee a little moment,
>   Straight is my voice hushed;
> Yea my tongue is broken, — through and
>   through me
> 'Neath the flesh, impalpable fire runs
>   tingling;
> Nothing see mine eyes, and a voice of roar-
>   ing
>   Waves in my ear sounds;
> Sweat runs down in rivers, a tremor seizes
> All my limbs, are paler than grass in
>   autumn,
> Caught by pains of menacing death, I falter,
>   Lost in the love trance.
>   Sappho, Ode to Atthis

Most people seem to know what being in love is like, but few seem able to define the term. Throughout the centuries people have tried to organize love into categories. Plato, in Greece during the fifth century B.C., saw love as central to humanity and divisible into "common" and "heavenly" categories. Common love was that concerned with physical pleasures, and was often identified with homosexual love. Heavenly love was the love of the soul, which was supposed to inspire virtue and spiritual pleasure. The Greeks are known, in fact, for giving love two names: **eros** (carnal love) and **agape** (spiritual love).

It was Ovid, a Roman poet of the first century B.C., who wrote the first textbook devoted to educating lovers; for example, he explained how to attract lovers, how to flirt, and how to manage adultery success-

fully, the latter of which seemed to be a favorite Roman pastime. Ovid's *Ars Amatoria* (*The Art of Love*) counseled men to write love letters, to offer intense covert looks, subtle gestures, and secret touches of feet under tables, to run errands, and to flatter "with feeling." He advised men and women to be clean and fresh and women to remove the hair from their legs with pumice stone. Fidelity was not part of Ovid's vision of sexual love: "As to men, so to women is stolen love the more pleasant." Ovid also discussed sexual techniques based on patience and mutual satisfaction.

A new, unique form of male-female love was introduced at the end of the eleventh century A.D. *L'amour courtois,* or **courtly love,** began as

> . . . a playful exercise in flattery, but became a spiritual force guiding the flatterers; it was first a private sport of the feudal aristocracy, but became finally the ideal of the middle classes; and with wonderfully consistent inconsistency, it exalted at one and the same time adultery and chastity, duplicity and faithfulness, self-indulgence and austerity, suffering and delight. (Hunt, 1959, p. 131)

The setting of courtly love—feudal barbarism, male domination, and religious asceticism—certainly did not encourage this form of love. Women were property, husbands had canon and civil permission to beat their wives, and prostitution in some cities was legal. Courtly love was not between husbands and wives, nor between single lovers; in fact, both parties were usually married. It was characterized by gallant acts performed to please a woman, usually of noble birth, which might include fighting in crusades or slaying enemies. Usually the love and adoration began from afar. A man did not marry his lady love; instead, he wooed her, wrote songs and sang for her, and went through extreme hardships for her, risking money and health. If lucky, a man eventually became his lady's suitor, and finally her accepted lover. But even as lover, the rules were curious. "Pure love" was the ideal, which included kissing, fondling, and touching in the nude but not final consummation by intercourse. Consummation was thought to be a fall from the higher spiritual union. That pure love was rigorously practiced is unlikely, but it apparently did exist, and few children were born out of such liaisons.

Courtly love followed the rule that love and lust could not be combined in the same person. The precedents for it were Greek agape, Manichean chaste and spiritual marriages, and the separation of sex and love in Christian writings. By the eleventh century there were also the beginnings of cults that worshipped Mary, the Mother of God; she was the sacred female image, separate from the profane image of Eve. Proclamations were made concerning the separation of love and marital bonds. For example, in 1174 the Countess of Champagne proclaimed:

> We declare and we hold firmly established that love cannot exert its powers between two who are married to each other. For lovers give to each other fully, under no compulsion of necessity, but married people are duty bound to give to each others' desires and deny themselves to each other in nothing. (quoted in Hunt, 1959, p. 144)

The image of women has changed a number of times since courtly love was popular. The glamorous and high-status Renaissance lady (a parallel to Greek Heterae, who were intellectual as well as love companions) was quickly supplanted by another image—woman as witch. Witches were supposedly sexually united with the Devil, and they were blamed and burned for a variety of social ills, many of them of sexual origin.

By the middle of the seventeenth century, the Age of Reason had ushered in a new version of love, which focused on gallantry. Gallantry was not only noted for its intimate, ritualistic, and socially supported routine of flirtation and seduction, but also for its acceptance of adultery. During this period love was not to be ruled by passion but by rational thought and arrangement. The ruthless and heartless seducer became popular during the Age of Reason. Giovanni Jacopo Cassanova, a Venetian who had as many as 116 mistresses and sexual affairs with many more women, certainly took the role of seducer seriously. He recounted making love to all kinds of women in a variety of settings, doing anything to woo them to bed; soon after he had succeeded, he would move on to find his next prey.

The Victorians of the nineteenth century again separated love and sex. Love and women were pure. Women were not to be flirtatious or seductive, and courtship was formal and male orchestrated. Married women were to keep men's base desires under control and leave sexual desire and intercourse to prostitutes. Although women were apparently worshipped, many faced subjugation, the marital relationship suf-

Box 5–3

SHYNESS: ATTRACTION WITH INHIBITIONS

To some extent, attraction can be decreased or enhanced by all of the factors mentioned thus far: physical appearance, degree of proximity, amount and type of reciprocation, similarity, and complementarity. In addition, there may be social constraints on the degree of attraction expressed; for example, student-teacher, employer-employee, married-nonmarried, or married-married role combinations can be so problematic that individuals resist fully expressing their feelings of attraction.

However, sometimes two people find one another mutually attractive and could act on it, but do not do so. The most likely inhibiting factors are social anxiety, lack of the appropriate social skills, and cognitive distortions (Arkowitz, 1977; Curran, 1977; Perri, 1977). These three factors can be part of a common reaction to sociosexual situations called shyness.

Shyness refers to a tendency in social interactions to feel distressed, anxious, and self-conscious; it can also include feeling inhibited or wanting to avoid interpersonal relations. Survey research tells us that 40 percent of both men and women described themselves as currently shy, and over 80 percent reported being shy at some point in their lives. Feeling shy is not bad in itself, and it can provide a person with greater privacy, less responsibility, and fewer chances of facing direct rejection. Nevertheless, missing out on the risks of social interactions also means missing the benefits. Shy people can become socially isolated, with increased susceptibility to depression and loneliness.

Table 5–1 lists situations in which college students commonly feel shy and also what their cognitive, physiological, and behavioral responses are, based on Zimbardo's research (Zimbardo, 1977; Zimbardo et al., 1974).

If we observe the behavior of shy people, we might misinterpret their shyness as something else. Someone who is quiet and avoids others may be considered reserved, modest, conceited, aloof, or disinterested. In fact, what may be going on inside the shy person is social anxiety so extreme that he or she is frightened—frightened of not being accepted and liked, frightened of being seen as inadequate or of being ridiculed, and frightened of pure rejection. The extremely shy person (as opposed to the person who just experiences some initial nervousness in strange social situations) is so terrified of other people's evaluations that he or she cannot focus on what that other person wants or feels. As a result, the shy person cannot act appropriately, even if he or she knows how, and as a result will try to avoid or escape uncomfortable situations. About 40 percent of all shy people overcome their shyness with age; others simply

TABLE 5-1   COMMON SITUATIONS AND REACTIONS SURROUNDING SHYNESS

ELICITORS OF SHYNESS	PERCENTAGE OF SHY STUDENTS	REACTIONS OF SHYNESS	PERCENTAGE OF SHY STUDENTS
Situations		*Physiological Reactions*	
Being the focus of attention in a large group (as when giving a speech)	73	Increased pulse	54
Large groups	68	Blushing	53
Being of lower status	56	Perspiring	49
Social situations in general	55	Butterflies in stomach	48
New situations in general	55	Heart pounding	48
Situations requiring assertiveness	54	*Cognitive and Affective Reactions*	
Being evaluated	53	Self-consciousness	85
Being the focus of attention (in a small group)	52	Concern about managing impression	67
Small social groups	48	Concern about social evaluation	63
One-to-one different-sex interactions	48	Unpleasantness of situation	56
Vulnerability, needing help	48	*Behaviors*	
		Silence	80
People		No eye contact	51
Strangers	70	Avoidance of others	44
Opposite sex	64	Avoidance of action	42
Authorities by virtue of their knowledge	55	Low speaking voice	40
Authorities by virtue of their role	40		
Relatives	21		

(Adapted from Zimbardo, 1977; and Zimbardo, Pilkonis, & Norwood, 1974.)

develop a small circle of stable friends and never venture beyond; still others remain miserable within their shyness; and a few become so socially isolated that they become angry, desperate, and sometimes destructive (Girodo, 1978).

fered, and prostitution was widely practiced. As a result, women gradually began to revolt against the social structure.

In the twentieth century, new categories of love have emerged, rearranging and restating the older ideas. Abraham Maslow (1954) distinguished *D-love,* which he defined as deficiency love arising from needs of security and belongingness, from *B-love,* in which another person is appreciated only for him- or herself rather than for what he or she can provide to satisfy another's needs. Freud (1925) had distinguished between dependent love and egotistical love, which were defined earlier in the chapter. Erich Fromm (1956) saw love as a way to reduce the isolation in human existence. From his standpoint, love could be either *symbiotic,* with two people locked into mutual dependence at the loss of individuality, or *productive,* so that caring, respect, knowledge, and responsibility between people would help to maintain individuality.

☐ *Passionate Love*   Walster and Walster (1978) have recognized two kinds of love, passionate and companionate, which will be useful categories in the discussion of research results. *Passionate* or *romantic love* is

> a state of intense absorption in another. Sometimes "lovers" are those who long for their partners and for complete fulfillment. Sometimes "lovers" are those who are ecstatic at finally having attained their partner's love, and, momentarily, complete fulfillment. A state of intense physiological arousal. (Walster & Walster, 1978, p. 9)

Passionate love is more than intense liking. One of its qualities is the tendency for people to idealize and to fantasize about the object of their desire. A related example is a study in which men evaluated the photo of a woman who was described as active, intelligent, and liberal, after they had read either an erotic seduction story or a treatise on the sex life of herring gulls (Stephen et al., 1971). The men who read the erotic story emphasized the woman's sexual desirability and her receptivity: She was more beautiful, more amorous, more immoral, more unwholesome, more nasty, more careless, more desirable, and less inhibited. Fantasy was indeed set into motion. Also of interest is that the earlier-mentioned distinctions between good (loving) women and bad (sexy) women were intimated in this study. History is clearly still with us.

Another difference between romantic love and liking is that liking seems to increase or stabilize across time, while intense passion seems to be a temporary phenomenon. For example, couples who had been married for various amounts of time were asked by researchers to rate their degree of liking and loving (Cimbalo, Faling, & Mousan, 1976). Liking remained high, but romantic love faded.

Dorothy Tennov (1979) talks about what she calls **limerence,** her word for passionate love, as typically lasting a maximum of two years. In an interview survey of people of all ages who had been in love, Tennov identified several other characteristics that make limerence unique:

- intrusive thoughts about the object of desire.
- Strong longing for reciprocation.
- Dependency of mood on love object's actions.
- Inability to be in limerence with more than one person at a time.
- Relief from unrequited passion through fantasy.
- Fear of rejection, along with almost incapacitating shyness.
- Intensification of limerent feelings through troubled times.
- Sharp sensitivity to interpret desired person's actions favorably, and ability to interpret *any* signs from the other as hidden passion.
- An aching of the "heart" (a physical tightening of the chest or stomach) when uncertainty is intense.
- Buoyancy, walking-on-air feeling when reciprocation is evident.
- Intensity of feelings that leaves other concerns in the background.
- Ability to emphasize what is admirable in the love object and to avoid dwelling on the negative or even to reconceptualize the negative into a positive attribute.

Not everyone falls in love. Sensation seekers—those who require novelty and excitement—seem more drawn to passionate relationships (Walster & Walster, 1978; Zuckerman, 1974). So are people who see their lives as controlled more by external factors than by internal factors (Dion & Dion, 1973).

Certain conditions may facilitate passion. Surprisingly, fear may be one such emotion. A dramatic example of this idea was demonstrated by Dutton and Aron

(1974). The reactions of two groups of men were measured after they crossed one of two bridges in North Vancouver, British Columbia. One was a suspension bridge that swayed and trembled over a 230-foot drop to rocks below. The other bridge was nearby but was solidly built and only 10 feet above a small inlet leading to the river. Prior to crossing, a male or female experimenter asked each man to fill out a questionnaire; following the crossing the experimenter asked subjects to fill out an imagery questionnaire (Thematic Apperception Test) and offered his or her phone number in order to explain the study in greater detail. As Figure 5-2 indicates, more men called the female than the male experimenter, and more calls to the female experimenter were made by the males who had crossed the river on the high suspension bridge. Also, men in the high suspension bridge group showed a greater amount of sexual imagery if the experimenter was female (Dutton & Aron, 1974).

Some researchers use what is called a two-component theory of emotional arousal to explain these results. According to this theory, a person feels a particular emotion based on the appropriateness of that emotion for the context in which it is experienced and also based on physiological arousal (Schacter & Singer, 1962). Both body and mind are involved and can be manipulated. If we are experiencing arousal from fear but the situation tells us that sexual arousal is appropriate, the situation can be relabeled as sexual.

One of the unusual features of love is

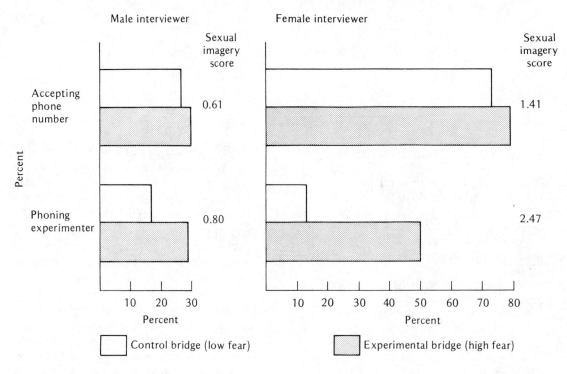

Male interviewer Female interviewer

Figure 5-2. Sexual imagery and attraction under low- and high-fear conditions. (From Dutton and Aron, 1974)

that obstacles may heighten passionate feelings:

> Some obstacle is necessary to swell the tide of libido to its height; and at all periods of history wherever natural barriers in the way of satisfaction have not sufficed, mankind has erected conventional ones in order to enjoy love. (Freud, 1925, p. 213)

Love can also be heightened by rejection, as illustrated by the courtly love escapades of the twelfth and thirteenth centuries. Unrequited love, with its emotional suffering and sexual and emotional frustration, may also feed the early fire of love. Sometimes the obstacle can be as mundane as interference by family members, or what can be called the Romeo-and-Juliet effect. The feud between the Montague and the Capulet families did not weaken but seemed to intensify the passion that Romeo and Juliet

shared. Research has supported this idea. One study evaluated the relationship between parental interference and degree of romantic love in 91 married couples and 49 dating couples (Driscoll, Davis, & Lipetz, 1972). Positive correlations were noted for both the committed and noncommitted couples. Additionally, the researchers checked back with couples in six to ten months and found that increases in parental interference were associated with intensified feelings of love, while decreases of parental objections were associated with waning relationships. Whether the parents are reacting to the seriousness of the relationship or whether the relationship intensifies in reaction to the parental barriers is not clear.

Jealousy, the condition characterized by feelings of rivalry regarding one's real or imagined competition for one's partner, can both fan the fires of love and put them out. According to Clanton and Smith (1977), men and women experience jealousy differently: Men are more apt to deny their own jealousy and to externalize the cause and blame their partner, a third partner, or other circumstances. Women are more apt to acknowledge jealous feelings and to internalize the cause—namely, they blame themselves. Thus, women may react by becoming more possessive, whereas men are more likely to become competitive and even express rage and violence. Jealous provocation seems to have two different outcomes: Some people try to protect their own egos by angrily protesting and scolding their partner, while others attempt to get even with their partner (more typically a male strategy). Women usually try to improve the relationship by changing their physical appearance and talking things out (Bryson, 1977).

Generally, jealousy is accompanied by an onslaught of negative feelings, including the feeling of being "dethroned" from the number one spot in someone's life, a sense of powerlessness, feeling unable to predict what will happen next, being emotionally and sexually deprived, and feeling a loss of privacy and exclusive access to one's mate (Constantine, 1977). Sometimes, however, jealousy can create emotions that are channeled into positive relationship changes and increased love.

Before leaving the topic of passionate love, let us return to some of the distinctions made earlier in our discussion of types of love. From Maslow and Tennov, we saw evidence that love comes in healthy and unhealthy forms. In one study this aspect of love was described in terms of love versus addiction (Peele & Brodsky, 1976). Distinguishing criteria separating love from addiction include the following:

1. Is each person confident in his or her own value?
2. Are the lovers improved by the relationship? Do they value the relationship in part because it makes them better, more attractive, or more sensitive individuals?
3. Do the lovers maintain serious outside interests, including meaningful relationships with other people?
4. Is the relationship one aspect of the lovers' lives that joins with other aspects, or is it completely isolated?
5. Are the lovers beyond possessiveness or jealousy of each other's growth and expression of interests?
6. Are they also friends and would they continue to want to know each other if their love relationship ceased?

Most people can find some addictive elements in their love relationships. The more there are, however, the more likely the "love" will become poisoned and kill the relationship or halt the individual's chance to develop personally. The major characteristics of addictive love are the desire to sacrifice the other person's happiness in order to keep him or her involved in the relationship and an attempt to keep the relationship as is no matter what the cost. Jealousy in this situation is ferocious and destructive. Some interesting parallels to drug addiction, including tolerance and withdrawal, are discussed by Peele and Brodsky (1976).

☐ *Companionate Love*   Walster and Walster have defined **companionate love** as follows:

The affection we feel for those with whom our lives are deeply entwined. The only real difference between liking and companionate love is the depth of our feelings and the degree of involvement with the other person. (Walster & Walster, 1978, p. 9)

Sometimes companionate love develops without people ever being romantically involved, and sometimes companionship is the next stage after romantic involvement. While romantic love is more difficult to fit into the theories and processes involved in interpersonal attraction, companionate love fits this framework more smoothly.

Murstein (1970) has proposed a simple system for describing mate selection. In the initial phase, the *stimulus* stage, first impressions are important: Physical attractiveness is concentrated on, mannerisms are observed, and cues are both given and noted in order to get some idea of each other's interests. Next, in the *value* stage, a couple begins to discover similar attitudes and to complement and satisfy each other's needs. Finally, if the prior stages are survived, the couple tests out the *role* stage, sharing in different role experiences at work, school, and/or socially. This final phase usually precedes marriage.

Other than the research already mentioned in our discussion of interpersonal attraction, few studies have concentrated specifically on companionate love. Some studies on partner selection, however, can be of use. One theory that has been explored in this area is the equity theory. In a study of male and female college students who were either casually or steadily dating, the degree of equitability in their relationships was evaluated by asking how much in the way of personal, emotional, and day-to-day contributions they thought they and their partners made to the relationship (Berscheid & Walster, 1978). The results showed that equity characterized intact relationships that were expected to last. Men and women who were getting far less or far more than they felt they deserved from the relationship did not expect the relationship to last.

Equity, or at least matching, also seems to be important in the sexual sphere. A survey of courting couples found evidence for matching on estimated sex drive (Murstein, 1970). In couples where the man had a higher sex drive, the likelihood of marriage six months later was decreased. Men may consider similar sex interests to be more important than do women. Centers (1971) reported that men found "erotic ability" in their mate to be very important, and their estimates of their own and their fiancee's ability were highly correlated, while the women's estimates of their own and their fiance's ability were lower.

Another factor that relates to companionate love and mate selection has to do with family background. While Freudian theory has given the most attention to this perspective, a variety of other theories do take familial experience into account. The basis for this type of thinking is that in the family environment we first experience the potential for deep emotional involvement with members of the same and opposite sexes. Our involvement occurs at important periods in our lives. It begins when we are totally dependent on our parents or parent substitutes and progresses through the life stages as we mature sexually and socially. Our emotional history with attachment and separation is heavily influenced by these early and repeated experiences.

Whether or not we truly seek a reincarnation of our opposite-sexed (or for homosexuals, same-sexed) parents, as strict Freudian theory would have it, has not been demonstrated. In fact this idea is not easily testable, since Freudian theory deals heavily with unconscious desires. However, the familial patterns do seem to be important. For example, in one study, men who had younger sisters and women with older brothers were happier in their marriages than men who had older sisters and women with younger brothers (Kemper, 1966). The interpretation of these results is not straightforward, but one could imagine that the dominance associated with being first born more easily fits into the socially accepted stereotype of male roles than female roles. A great deal of clinical evidence, primarily of couples experiencing marital or sexual distress, suggests that the family does, in fact, have a substantial impact on the quality of relationships.

ATTRACTION IN PERSPECTIVE

We have seen that there are a few universal features of sexual attraction. Forms of attraction and courtship have biological importance; through these functions the chances are optimized for (1) getting two individuals of good reproductive potential sexually interested, or (2) in those cases where reproduction is not the goal, getting two individuals to share satisfying sexual contact, thereby strengthening the interpersonal bond and decreasing aggression.

And yet we have also pointed out that even among animals of the same species, sexual attraction and courtship patterns are not identical; for example, certain groups that are geographically separated have variations in courtship elements. Furthermore, what is sexually arousing in one culture is of little interest in another, and what is arousing to one person is unpleasant for another, in spite of similar "erogenous zones."

Sexual behavior, in other words, has both a biological, or genetic, base and a social, or learning, base. Learning is a crucial ingredient in the individual's development of interpersonal sexuality. While certain features of sexual attraction may carry a biological predisposition, they are also shaped, refined, expanded, and developed as the individual gains contact with parents, siblings, friends, and the other media channels of society.

Neither social nor biological scientists have answers to some of our most obvious questions. Why, for instance, are people differentially attracted to others? Idiosyncratic preferences are particularly difficult to ascribe to a genetic predisposition, although some sociobiologists are inclined to do so. Learning seems to be the more likely foundation, and yet the exact process by which this learning might occur is theoretical. Some behavioral psychologists talk about the pairing of stimuli and responses. Other psychologists also believe that accidental conditioning is important. For instance, if a young boy is wrestling with another boy and has an erection and ejaculates, he may develop a sexual preference for other males, or for violence. Some people report exactly this situation, but others with a very similar "accidental conditioning" do not.

The cultural variations in preferences suggest that learning is usually based on more than a one-time experience. Discovering which types of people and situations are particularly arousing is probably based on what Gagnon and Simon (1973) call a social "script"; that is, the ideas of masculinity and femininity, sexual behavior, fantasies, and sexual attraction that have evolved as society's norms. People learn, as they grow up in a culture, a general set of scenes, lines, and activities, and also likes and dislikes. But the script is not a prescription in the sense that everyone learns exactly the same things at the same time. People pick up bits and pieces along the way, often omitting or ignoring parts, while being exposed to others. People also learn by *imita-tion*—that is, watching what others do and trying new things based on what they have heard.

Whether trying to explain heterosexual or homosexual attraction, science has a difficult time showing how the process works. We are still in the descriptive phase of trying to chronicle what we see happening and what individuals experience in sexual attraction (Hinde, 1976, 1978; Hinde and Stevenson-Hinde, 1976). While the choices of theoretical frameworks are numerous, each one seems to explain too much with too little or to be tested only against itself. Many people believe that reading a good novel or seeing a film portrays human sexual attraction more clearly. If such is the case—and it is difficult to dispute—perhaps a scientific framework will have to devote itself more to the process of attraction in multiple levels of complexity rather than examination of only a few variables at one or two points in time. Some inroads have been made in this direction, but there is still a long way to go if the goal is to enrich our understanding of interpersonal attraction and courtship patterns.

SUMMARY

1. Darwin, in his theory of evolution, distinguished between natural selection and sexual selection. **Natural selection** is the process by which those animals that best meet the demands of their environment will survive and reproduce; those who do not will eventually be eliminated. **Sexual selection,** according to Darwin, is concerned with the production or lack of production of offspring. It is a process that chooses the

physiological, anatomical, and behavioral characteristics that will be most beneficial for the attraction of mates.

2. **Courtship** is a communication process by which one or both sexes express their interest in the other. Its most obvious function is mate attraction. Another function is **reproductive isolation,** which acts to ensure that species do not mate with other species. Courtship patterns vary tremendously across species and may include nest building, complex mating songs, changes in bodily coloration or appearance, and special courting movements or dances. In most species, males are the courting sex, the aggressors, and females do the selecting.

3. Both sociobiological principles and a sociocultural perspective can help explain what is important in mate selection: good health, youthfulness in females, status for men, and physical attractiveness of women.

4. Sexuality is communicated by humans in a number of ways. Differences in male and female physical development, such as the fatty tissue that develops in female breasts, hips, and thighs, and the distribution of body hair are two examples of steady sexual signals.

5. People communicate sexual interest by looking, touching, smelling, and talking. Although **pheromones,** body secretions that produce sexually stimulating odors, are found in other primates, researchers have not yet discovered evidence to indicate that such secretions are very important to human sexuality. Language is the most-often used method of human sexual communication.

6. Cultures vary greatly in their types of courtship rituals and practices, and also in their attitudes about the human body, especially the female body. Although people in the Western world generally are free to make their own mate selections, in other societies conditions are quite different. In India, for example, children are often betrothed at birth.

7. In general, good-looking people have the initial advantage in many situations. Physical attractiveness appears to be of particular importance when a male and female first meet.

8. The equity theory, as applied to relationships, suggests that people, both males and females, select and date others who are equal in attractiveness to themselves. Along with similarity in attractiveness, attitude similarity also seems to be important in selecting a mate.

9. According to the reciprocity theory, people will be more apt to like someone if they think or know that the person likes them.

10. Proximity, or geographical closeness, increases the likelihood of people being attracted to each other.

11. Complementarity, as opposed to similarity, also has been suggested as a factor that influences attraction. Rather than seeking partners who

are similar, people would seek those who have qualities that complement their own needs—qualities that the seeker may, in fact, be lacking.

12. The tendency to feel distressed, anxious, and self-conscious in social interactions is known as **shyness.** It is a common problem that most people overcome enough to be able to function socially.

13. Love is a difficult concept to define. The Greeks distinguished between **eros** (carnal love) and **agape** (spiritual love). **Courtly love,** popular in the eleventh century A.D., was an interesting male-female relationship, the main premise being that love and lust could not be experienced with one person. According to Victorian standards, love and women were pure; sexuality, to the contrary, was a base desire. Prostitution was widely practiced during this period, and sex in marriage was acceptable for procreative reasons only.

14. *Passionate love,* or **limerence,** is "a state of intense absorption in another;" it is the romantic form of love. **Companionate love** is defined as "the affection we feel for those with whom our lives are deeply entwined."

SUGGESTED READINGS

Berscheid, E., & Walster, E. *Interpersonal attraction* (2nd ed.). Reading, Mass.: Addison-Wesley, 1978. A good summary of much of the research, especially from social psychology, on interpersonal attraction.

Cook, M. *The bases of human sexual attraction.* New York: Academic Press, 1981. An edited book of major theorists and researchers on sexual interest and attraction.

Murstein, B. *Love, sex and marriage throughout the ages.* New York: Springer, 1974. A good coverage, with research, on the major themes in sexual relationships across the centuries.

Tennov, D. *Love and limerence.* New York: Stein & Day, 1979. Reporting on a variety of individuals who describe what "being in love" means, this is one of the few books that describes the experiential side of love. Also some theory development included.

CHAPTER SIX

HETEROSEXUAL BEHAVIOR
Patterns across the Life Span

A young girl and a young boy is a tormented tangle, a seething confusion of sexual feelings and sexual thoughts which only the years will disentangle. Years of honest thoughts of sex, and years of struggling action in sex will bring us at last where we want to get. . .
D. H. Lawrence 1953

*H*eterosexuality refers to the sexual preference that a person has for members of the opposite sex. In this chapter we examine heterosexual patterns of behavior throughout the life span, with a primary focus on adolescents and adults.

Coitus is the most preferred form of sexual expression in all known cultures, and, of course, it remains the "ultimate" sexual activity in terms of its potential for procreation. When sex is mentioned, most people think of coitus, or **intercourse.** Although terms such as oral-genital intercourse, anal intercourse, and inter-femoral (between the thighs) intercourse are sometimes found in the technical literature, we prefer in this chapter to restrict intercourse to its more common usage as a synonym for coitus. The term coitus is derived from the Latin word *coire,* meaning to go together, and

conventionally refers to penile-vaginal sex. All other forms of sexual activity and stimulation between opposite-sexed partners are categorized under heterosexual *petting* and *foreplay.*

Most of our knowledge about patterns of heterosexual behavior—positions used during intercourse, frequency, duration, types of genital and nongenital stimulation employed, satisfaction, and so forth—is derived from survey data. Frequently, this information is presented in terms of premarital, marital, and extramarital sexual behavior. We will use a slightly different format: First we will describe petting/foreplay activity and coitus in general, and then we will focus on special issues involved in premarital sexual intercourse and extramarital sexual intercourse. Two additional sections briefly review sexual behavior in two specific age groups, young children and the elderly.

Who does what with whom, how often, when, where, and with what degree of satisfaction are not easy questions to answer. Survey research is plagued with methodological problems, as described in the introductory chapter. In addition to the issues discussed in that chapter, one important question to ask concerning survey data is whether dry statistics can ever come close to explaining the nuances that are so much a part of human sexuality. Surveys that ask women questions such as, How long must foreplay go on for you to achieve orgasm during intercourse? illustrate the

problem beautifully. No doubt, the answer "depends"—it depends on mood, on type of stimulation, on the partner involved, on feelings of closeness and excitement, and on a host of other current circumstances and past history factors. All that surveys can reveal are average numbers. Subtleties and feelings are usually lost in the statistics game. However, despite these and other methodological concerns, surveys, especially when considered in combination, do yield considerable information and at least provide a framework for understanding contemporary patterns of heterosexual behavior.

PETTING AND FORELPAY

Neither term, *petting* nor *foreplay,* does adequate justice to the type of sexual behavior we wish to discuss in this section. "Petting" sounds juvenile, and many use "foreplay" to refer to a secondary form of sexual stimulation, only relevant insofar as it prepares us for actual intercourse. The truth of the matter is that simple body contact, as well as manual and oral stimulation of various parts of the body, need not stop once intercourse has begun. Unlike bike riding, when making love there is nothing great about saying, "Look Ma, no hands." Physical touching not only before but also *during and after* intercourse is stimulating and gratifying. Furthermore, various forms of sexual interaction between two partners

need not progress to intercourse in order for people to experience a great amount of sexual satisfaction. In fact, orgasm may be more likely to occur and to be more intense when achieved through forms of stimulation other than intercourse (Masters & Johnson, 1966). Although for most people intercourse may be the most satisfying aspect of interpersonal sexual activity, it need not be so for all individuals at all times. Also, intercourse is seldom attempted unless it has been preceded by a certain amount of other sexual activity. Thus, intercourse and other sexual activity cannot be separated very well in terms of either importance or satisfaction.

Petting and foreplay refer to the same

type of sexual activity. The distinction between the two is primarily based on the purpose behind the activity. **Petting** commonly refers to sexual contact that is not intended to lead to intercourse, whereas **foreplay** simply means petting that precedes intercourse. A secondary means of distinguishing petting from other forms of sexual activity is in its relation to the age of the couples. Petting is sometimes used synonymously with terms such as "necking" or "making out," referring to those forms of sexual activity that typically occur during adolescence and before couples have started to engage in actual intercourse. In this context, petting serves as a socially acceptable substitute for premarital intercourse and is the first heterosexual experience for most people. According to Sorensen's 1973 survey of a national probability sample of adolescents in the United States, only 20 percent of all boys and 25 percent of all girls between the ages of 13 and 19 had *not* had any heterosexual petting experience (Sorensen, 1973).

Every conceivable form of noncoital petting known to modern youth has been known throughout history. The earliest art and writing samples on human sexual behavior include everything from kissing and hugging to oral-genital techniques. Petting involves a variety of physical contacts deliberately engaged in to produce sexual arousal. Of course, petting also includes nonsexual motives, among them curiosity, learning to trust a partner, attempts to be popular, and obtaining and keeping the friendship of a prospective partner.

In our society petting tends to follow a natural progression. Hugging and simple kissing are the initial acts. Deep kissing (with mouth open) and manual stimulation of a woman's breasts (first over and then under the clothing) are introduced next. Manual stimulation of the female and male genitalia is the third stage, and the final act is oral-genital stimulation, which often is introduced *after* rather than before an individual's experience with intercourse (Bentler, 1968 *a, b*). Not everybody proceeds "in order" through all of these stages all of the time. Nevertheless, this sort of general progression is interesting in several respects.

First, note that kissing and being held occur earliest. In our society these acts also occur in nonsexual contexts. For example, parents kiss and hug children as a way of expressing affection. Perhaps, then, these forms of petting occur first because they are least directly sexual and because they also satisfy other needs—the need for intimacy, caring, and showing approval and affection. Such needs are probably as important, if not more important, than are sexual needs. (This latter point is probably as true in marital and other long-term relationships as it is in premarital relationships.)

A second feature of the petting progression is that hand stimulation of the female's body, particularly of the breasts and genitalia, tends to occur prior to similar stimulation by the female of the male genitalia. This pattern probably reflects the still prevalent dating pattern in Western society that calls for the male to pursue the

18th Century lockets: An example of erotic art.

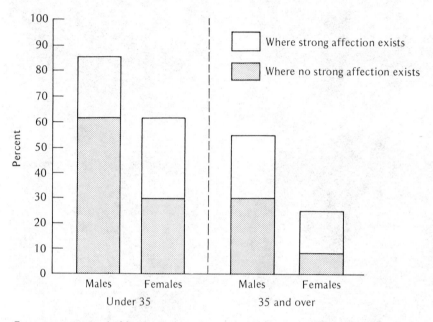

Figure 6-1. Approval of heavy petting with and without strong affection. Adapted from Hunt, 1974, p. 133.

female and initiate sex, while the female is expected to set limits on the couple's sexual intimacy (Peplau, Rubin, & Hill, 1977).

Deciding "how far to go" in petting is a decision that adolescent couples in this country must make in the early phases of new premarital relationships. Hunt describes the traditional rules of the game in twentieth-century America:

> The more deeply a boy and girl cared about each other, the further they considered it all right to go. The standard enforced by the girl and grudgingly accepted by the boy held, in a general way, that kissing was all right if the two merely liked each other; "deep" or "French" kissing if they felt romantic about

each other; breast touching through the clothing if they were halfway "serious" about each other, and with the bra off if they were somewhat more serious than that; and explorations "below the waist" or exposure of the naked penis to the girl's touch only if the couple considered themselves really in love. (Hunt, 1974, pp. 132–133)

These social scripts of premarital petting have not changed all that dramatically in the past ten to twenty years. Figure 6-1 compares the attitudes of those under and over age 35 in the Hunt (1974) survey. Although the figures indicate that approval of premarital petting is higher than it used to be, they also show that people are still influenced by the perceived presence or absence of mutual affection. In both age groups females more than males consider this variable important. The evidence suggests that females still fulfill the policing role by determining what is allowed and not allowed.

Petting and Foreplay Techniques

Erogenous zones are parts of the body that produce sexual arousal when caressed and, therefore, are the center of attention in petting and foreplay. The genitals, breasts, lips, buttocks, and thighs are usually regarded as the erogenous zones. Individual differences do exist, however, and other parts of the body, such as the neck, shoulders, ears, and palms of the hands, are often sensitive to sexual stimulation as well. Also, at different stages of arousal, some forms of stimulation are more pleasurable than others. Finally, mood and other factors can influence when and what form of physical stimulation is exciting. For example, prior to menstruation many women may not find breast caressing particularly pleasurable because of increased breast sensitivity.

One general point about gender differences should be noted before going on to describe specific stimulation techniques. Men seem to be more responsive to genital stimulation earlier in the sequence of sexplay than are women. The most frequent sexual complaint one hears from women about men is that the male directs his attention to the woman's genitals too soon,

without adequate hugging and caressing of other parts of the body first.

☐ *Kissing* Stimulation from kissing may involve simple contact of the lips, thrusting of the tongue inside the partner's mouth, nibbling of lips, or other mouth-to-mouth variations. In addition, plenty of other parts of the body can be kissed—the face, nose, neck, and so forth.

☐ *Breast Stimulation* Although some males are aroused when their breasts are stimulated, more often than not the male is the one who strokes and caresses the female's breasts and nipples. Some women, of course, enjoy breast stimulation more than others. Most people use their hands and mouth to stimulate a partner's breasts, but other methods are just as effective, rubbing with the penis or softly brushing the nipples with hair are two of the more common alternatives. Personal preferences (e.g., gentle or hard stroking) need to be communicated between partners.

☐ *Manual Stimulation of the Female Genitals* Generally, the clitoris is the most sensitive part of the female genitals. A man who rushes directly to the clitoris, however, may find his partner reacting negatively. Light stroking of the thighs, the mons area, and the outer lips are usually preferred in the earlier stages of sexual contact. Furthermore, at the height of sexual arousal, direct stimulation of the clitoris may be painful. Therefore, a woman should communicate to her partner if, when, and how she likes this form of stimulation. An actual demonstration, either by using her own hands or by guiding her partner's, is probably the clearest way to do this. One common misconception among males is that all women enjoy having men insert their fingers into the vagina. For many women this practice is less pleasurable than are other forms of genital stimulation. The timing is also a factor. For example, early in sexplay, before a woman is aroused and has begun to lubricate, a finger probing the vagina can be particularly uncomfortable.

☐ *Manual Stimulation of the Male Genitals*   The areas of the penis that are most sensitive to stimulation are the coronal ridge and the glans area. A man can express his preferences regarding penile stimulation either by demonstration or by guiding his partner's hands; he can also communicate what parts of his penis are most sexually excited when touched and stroked. Again, the desired tempo of stroking, the exact location of the most sensitive areas, and how firm a grip to use while stroking are going to vary somewhat from person to person, and also from time to time for the same person. Note also that many men enjoy stimulation of the scrotum.

☐ *Oral-Genital Stimulation*   **Cunnilingus** is the oral stimulation of the female genital area. In Latin, *cunnus* means vulva and *lingere* means lick. The man can suck, nibble, and flick his tongue around the clitoris and the outer and inner lips of the vagina. The method used depends on what feels good to the female partner, a sensation that not only varies from one woman to the next, but also from one minute to the next for the same woman during the course of petting and/or foreplay. As we mentioned in Chapter Three, blowing air into the vagina is dangerous, particularly if a woman is pregnant, for it can cause a fatal air embolism.

Oral stimulation of the male genitals is known as **fellatio.** *Fellare,* in Latin, means to suck. Various techniques are used, just as in the case of cunnilingus. The woman may lick the glans of the penis, as well as the testicles. She can insert the penis into her mouth and suck it as she strokes the shaft of the penis or the scrotum with her hand. Once the penis is erect, she may move her mouth up and down on the penis while at the same time moving her tongue around the glans of the penis. A woman may wish to be in a position where she can control how far she slides the penis into her mouth, thus avoiding possible gagging reactions. Kneeling over the man is one such position. A couple may take turns stimulating each other orally, or they may engage in mutual oral-genital stimulation. Figure 6–2 illustrates the so-called "69" position, which is one way that mutual stimulation can be achieved.

Some people want to know if they are "normal" if they *don't* enjoy oral-genital stimulation, and others want to know if they are "normal" if they *do.* Because these acts are sometimes carried out to the point of orgasm—without subsequent intercourse—traditional Judeo-Christian teachings have condemned them. According to

Figure 6–2. Oral-genital stimulation

this view, any sexual activity that is not directed toward procreation is immoral. However, if procreation were the only acceptable motive for sexual relations, intercourse would also have to be considered immoral when contraceptive devices are used, when a woman is past menopause, or when either partner is sterile.

Some people object to oral-genital stimulation more for psychological reasons than for religious beliefs. The reasons for such objections are often vague, but if pressed, these people will say that sexual organs are somehow "dirty" or "shameful." Women in particular are concerned about their own genital smells, which, barring the presence of a yeast vaginal infection, many men find arousing. Odor is also of concern in fellatio. The simple suggestion that one can wash prior to oral-genital activity will not resolve this issue: The repulsion is more deeply rooted. Another reason that fellatio is avoided is that many women dislike the

prospect of the man ejaculating in their mouths.

In any case, if the question of normality is to be answered on statistical grounds, then the answer is relatively easy: Any individual can feel secure that he or she is *not* abnormal for either liking *or* disliking oral-genital stimulation. Currently, although more married and unmarried heterosexual partners are engaging in oral-genital sex than not, there are still many people on both sides. The following two comments are representative of both views:

I feel that sex is something beautiful and good, but oral sex makes it seem dirty. Animals go around licking each other. Human beings are supposed to be more intelligent. Also, oral sex is unsanitary. (Tavris & Sadd, 1975, p. 89)

I usually have an orgasm from oral sex, then another during intercourse. For a long time I felt abnormal and deficient because of this. Finally I realized that I enjoyed the orgasms

227

which happened according to this pattern more than those which happened at the "right" time. It seemed silly to be trying to have my orgasms during intercourse just because other people liked theirs then. Foreplay, intercourse, and afterplay are all a part of lovemaking, so there should be no reason to make sharp distinctions about what happens when. (Tavris & Sadd, 1975, p. 79)

Oral-genital sex is apparently gaining more widespread acceptance in the United States. Figure 6–3 shows that higher percentages of married people reported experience with fellatio and cunnilingus in the Hunt survey of the 1970s as compared with the reports given in the earlier Kinsey survey. Both studies related higher levels of education to the increased use of these techniques. A breakdown according to the age of respondents also reveals the increasing practice in recent times of oral-genital techniques. Hunt reported that 80 percent

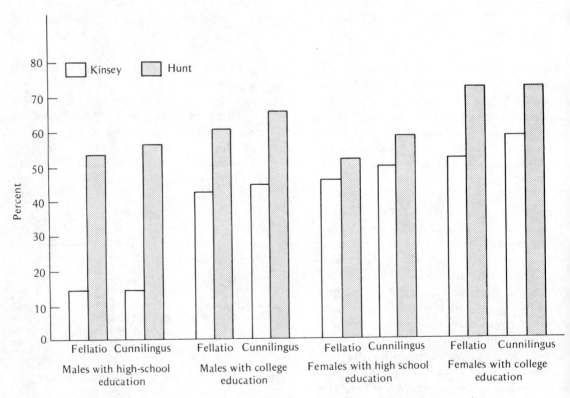

Figure 6–3. Oral-genital techniques used in marital sexual relations: Comparison of Kinsey (1938–1949) and Hunt (1972) samples. Adaped from Hunt, 1974, p. 198.

of married males and females under age 35 and 90 percent of those under age 25 use oral-genital methods of sexual stimulation. The *Redbook* survey (Tavris & Sadd, 1975) of female sexuality found that less than 10 percent of the married women said they never had experienced cunnilingus or fellatio. On the other hand, only 40 percent said they engaged in these techniques "often," and 15 percent of the women found fellatio either "unpleasant" or "repulsive."

As we stated earlier, during adolescence oral-genital contact is less common in individuals who have not yet engaged in sexual intercourse as compared with those who have (Curran, Neff, & Lippold, 1973). For example, Kinsey and his colleagues (1953) found that of the younger females in their sample without coital experience, only 3 percent had engaged in cunnilingus and even a smaller percentage had performed fellatio. On the other hand, 20 per-

cent of this age group who had some experience with premarital intercourse had also engaged in oral sex, while the figure increased to 50 percent for those with extensive premarital experience. The frequency of oral-genital sex among unmarried couples has also increased since the time of Kinsey's study (see Table 6-1).

☐ *Anal Stimulation* The buttocks and the perineal area are erogenous zones for most people. However, manual stimulation, especially insertion of the fingers into the anus of the partner, may be psychologically repulsive and thus avoided. Insertion of the penis into the partner's rectum—**anal intercourse**—is also problematic for most couples. Unlike the vagina, the rectum has no natural lubrication. Thus, if anal intercourse is to be attempted, some sterile moisturizing agent such as K-Y jelly needs to be used. The penis has to be inserted gently and slowly into the

TABLE 6-1 SELECTED TECHNIQUES OF FOREPLAY USED PREMARITALLY		
	KINSEY STUDY, 1938–1949 (ADOLESCENT TO 25)	HUNT STUDY, 1972 (18 TO 24)
Male manual play with female genitals	91	90
Female manual play with male genitals	75	89
Fellatio	33	72
Cunnilingus	14	69

Adapted from Hunt, 1974, p. 166.

rectum because the sphincter muscles surrounding the anal opening are rather tight, and sudden thrusting can be painful. Another word of caution: If vaginal contact takes place after rectal contact, serious infection can occur. Care needs to be taken so that bowel contents do not contaminate the vagina.

Oral stimulation of the anal area is primarily done with the tongue, but health issues have to be considered here as well, including the danger of hepatitis. In one sample of married men and women under age 35, approximately half had experienced at least some manual-anal foreplay (Hunt, 1974). Anal intercourse, according to this survey, is more rare, occurring in less than 25 percent of those under 35. Most of these people had tried it on only a few occasions. In the *Redbook* survey, 43 percent of the women had tried anal intercourse at least once; only 2 percent said they engaged in anal intercourse often (Tavris & Sadd, 1975).

Foreplay Duration

Kinsey and his colleagues (1953) reported on the length of time married couples usually devote to foreplay (see Table 6–2). Not contained in their results, however, are any data on how much foreplay men and women prefer. The impression is that men are generally interested in proceeding to intercourse sooner than women.

An interesting relationship between social class and educational level and foreplay duration was also noted by Kinsey. The

TABLE 6-2 FOREPLAY DURATION: FEMALE SAMPLE	
TIME	PERCENTAGE
under 3 minutes	11
4–10 minutes	36
11–20 minutes	31
over 20 minutes	22

Adapted from Kinsey, et al, 1953, p. 364.

total time of foreplay tended to be higher in the middle- and upper-socioeconomic groups. One possible explanation is that at the time of Kinsey's survey (1938 to 1949) men played a more dominant role in lower-class marital relationships and may not have been concerned about their partner's feelings. Another hypothesis is that the majority of women in poverty cultures did not know that they could experience any type of sexual pleasure (Rainwater, 1965). Finally, in a related hypothesis, the poorly educated couples in Kinsey's sample may simply not have known that foreplay duration can make a difference in a female's sexual response patterns. Unfortunately, recent objective data are not available to determine if social class differences still prevail.

Foreplay: Cross-cultural Perspective

The extent to which noncoital foreplay techniques are used obviously is influenced by cultural forces. Some societies encourage erotic sexuality more than others.

SEXUAL REPRESSION IN INIS BEAG

John Messenger, an anthropologist, spent nineteen months between the years 1958 and 1966 studying the community and culture of a small island off the coast of Ireland. In his study he named the island, fictitiously, Inis Beag. The major livelihood for the 350 people residing in this community was agriculture. At the time of this study, there was no electricity or running water and no motorized vehicles on the island. A small steamer delivered supplies and mail once a week, and Messenger observed that the inhabitants seldom visited the mainland. The following quotes from Messenger provide a flavor of the attitude toward sex that existed in this small folk community.

> A considerable amount of evidence indicates . . . that foreplay is limited to kissing and rough fondling of the lower body, especially the buttocks. Sexual activity invariably is initiated by the husband. Only the male superior position is employed; intercourse takes place with underclothes not removed; the orgasm, for the man, is achieved quickly, almost immediately after which he falls asleep.

> Women have been taught . . . that sexual relations with their husbands are a duty which must be rendered, for to refuse coitus is a mortal sin. A frequently encountered assertion affixes the guilt for male sexual strivings on the enormous intake of potatoes of the Inis Beag male. Asked to compare the sexual proclivities of Inis Beag men and women, one mother of nine said, "Men can wait a long time before wanting it, but we can wait a lot longer." There is much evidence that the female orgasm is unknown—or at least doubted or considered a deviant response

Messenger, 1971, p. 16

For example, the famous Hindu treatise on sexual practices, Vatsyana's *Kama Sutra,* describes in detail eight forms of oral-genital contact (Ellis, 1973). By contrast, some societies are quite repressive in their attitudes and sexual practices (see the example provided in Box 6–1).

Foreplay, Cross-species Perspective

Behavior that is ostensibly comparable to "petting" in humans has been observed among almost all species of mammals, sometimes leading to coitus and sometimes not. (Note that courtship displays and courtship rituals are not discussed here but can be found in Chapter Five). Activity such as rubbing, playful nipping, grooming of fur, and nuzzling and licking of genitals can occur for seconds or hours, depending on the species. Because many of these behaviors occur in nonsexual situations (for example, mothers often groom their offspring) as well as in sexual situations, determining which have a purely sexual function can be difficult. Moreover, one runs the risk of ascribing purpose or intentionality where it may not be present. Nonetheless, animals do seem to share similar foreplay behaviors with humans. Physical contact that precedes copulation and seems to be linked to increased readiness for intercourse does not seem to be in any way unique to human beings. Horses do it, sheep do it, pigs do it, and skunks, dogs, porcupines, rabbits, monkeys, and chimpanzees do it—apparently we all do it.

INTERCOURSE

Positions of Intercourse

Theoretically, people can assume an infinite number of intercourse positions, limited only by imagination and physical dexterity. In reality, however, certain "standard" positions predominate, most likely because they are comfortable, enjoyable, and/or socially acceptable. Presumably, couples use those positions and movements that they find mutually pleasurable and acceptable. Although variety may be occasionally exotic, most people develop stable preferences for position and movement. Because two people may disagree on what they each prefer, some sort of exchange and open communication is usually necessary to keep each partner sexually interested and satisfied. This kind of communication is more easily prescribed, however, than carried out. Even though people may be intent on pleasing both themselves and their partners during lovemaking, many are still amazingly inhibited about saying directly and specifically what they like or don't like at the moment.

Couples in the United States today seem to be using a greater variety of positions than they did twenty to thirty years ago, with younger people more freely experimenting (Kinsey, et al., 1949, 1953; Hunt, 1974). Although the male-superior position is still the one most commonly employed, many people are trying some of the other positions. Let's investigate the "standards," starting with the face-to-face positions, which are the ones most commonly used. The face-to-face positions allow partners to look at each other (though many people prefer to close their eyes in order to concentrate on the physical sensations), as well as to kiss and use their hands to caress those parts of each other's body that are accessible. For example, depending on whether a couple lies side by side or one on top, the man can kiss the women's breasts, reach around to her buttocks, and easily caress her shoulders and neck, with the same being true for the woman.

☐ *Face-to-Face, Man-on-Top Position* This position, sometimes referred to as the "male-superior" or "missionary" position, is illustrated in Figure 6–4. (Oceanic Islanders coined the term "missionary position" after discovering that missionaries engaged in sexual intercourse in this way, whereas the islanders were used to the woman being on top.) The woman lies on her back with her legs parted. She may have her legs completely extended, slightly bent at the knees, or raised toward the chest to allow for deeper penetration. The man lies between her legs and can vary the amount of weight and complete body contact by supporting himself with his arms and knees. The rhythm of moving, the extent of pausing, and the amount the penis is withdrawn during thrusting will vary with different couples, depending on what they find pleasurable as they experiment with each other. The man-on-top position has several physical disadvantages. For example, it is not ideal for women who enjoy direct manual clitoral stimulation during intercourse. Another possible disadvantage is that the woman's movement is somewhat restricted, and thus she may feel that the tempo is too controlled by the man.

Figure 6–4. Face-to-face, man-on-top position.

Figure 6–5. Face-to-face, woman-on-top position.

No one knows for sure why the face-to-face, man-on-top position is the most popular position in Western society. One biological hypothesis that has been suggested for the human preference of some variant of the face-to-face position over the rear-entry position is that the vaginal opening of the human female is located farther forward than it is in other mammals (Ford & Beach, 1951). A second hypothesis is both psychological and physical, namely that the face-to-face, man-on-top position permits the fullest body contact for both partners. Another possible contributing factor is that the man-on-top position provides the male with a greater psychological and physical sense of being in control.

☐ *Face-to-Face, Woman-on-Top Position* This position is sometimes referred to as the "female-superior" position, and variations are possible (see Figure 6–5). Some women prefer to sit upright, using their knees and arms to support the body, because they can control their own movements and monitor the overall pace. Another advantage to this position is that the female's clitoris is more accessible. The woman can also lie in a semiprone position to increase the amount of body-to-body contact. Nearly 75 percent of the married couples in the Hunt survey (1974) reported using the female-above position with varying frequency, as compared with only about 35 percent in Kinsey's surveys (Kinsey et al., 1948, 1953).

Figure 6–6. Face-to-face, side-by-side position.

☐ *Face-to-Face, Side-by-Side Position* The variations available for this position are principally limited to how the legs are intertwined, with either the man's outer leg resting on the woman's thigh, or vice versa (see Figure 6–6). The major advantages of this position are that it allows both partners to move freely and to have some control, and it provides ample opportunity for mutual caressing of neck, shoulders, and buttocks. The major disadvantage is that deep penetration is difficult; neither partner has as much individual control as in the superior position. More than 50 percent of Hunt's sample, compared with 25 percent of Kinsey's, said that they sometimes or often use the face-to-face, side-by-side position.

☐ *Rear-Entry Position* Various positions allow for rear-entry intercourse (see Figure 6–7). The woman can be kneeling, lying on her side, or lying on her stomach. She can also sit on the man's lap facing away from him. When both partners lie on their sides,

the male's front presses against the female's back. With rear-entry positions, the man's hands are generally free to caress his partner, and the clitoral area is easily accessible. This position is the least preferred of the standard positions, with only 10 percent of Kinsey's sample and 40 percent of Hunt's sample having engaged in it. One disadvantage is that the rear-entry positions lessen full body contact, causing a feeling of distance. Some individuals are also repelled because the position resembles that used by animals during copulation.

☐ *Cross-cultural Perspective on Positions of Intercourse* The male-on-top position is not the preferred position in all cultures. For example, the conventional position for members of the Bala tribe in the Congo is the side-by-side, face-to-face position, with the man lying on his right side and the woman on her left side (Merriam, 1971). "The position in which the man lies on top of the woman is also recognized, but that in which the man is on his back and the wo-

Figure 6-7. Rear-entry position.

man on top is considered strange, funny and not used at all" (p. 85). By contrast, in some Pacific Islands, the most common position is for the woman to sit astride the man (Ford & Beach, 1951).

☐ *Cross-species Perspective on Positions of Intercourse* A fascinating variety of copulation patterns exist across the "animal kingdom." We provide here only a brief overview of some patterns observed in mammalian species, focusing primarily on coital positions in primates. Before doing so, however, keep in mind one general factor: Sex is clearly a type of social behavior; therefore, not surprisingly, behavior asso-

ciated with copulation can have other social meanings as well, especially among primates.

Copulation in nonhuman primates occurs when the female is sexually receptive, or in *estrus*. Such sexual receptivity is closely tied to the occurrence of ovulation (Bermant & Davidson, 1972). In many primate species, some external swelling and increased coloration of the hindquarter genital, or perineal, area takes place during the female's estrus period. The female baboon, for example, shows swelling and bright pinkish-red coloration of the hindquarter genital area. To attract a male baboon, she will present this area to him. He may explore her genitals, mount her, or do nothing.

This pattern of female presentation is a very common behavior among primates. In those same species where it has a sexual meaning, it has other social meanings as well. In particular, it is used to reduce the threat of attack from another animal in the group. For instance, a less dominant animal that may be smaller, younger, or weaker than the others may present his or her perineal area to a more dominant animal in an effort to make peace. The one who is dominant almost never attacks the presenting animal but will often mount (rarely with intromission) or touch the subordinate's hindquarters. This behavior can occur between two males, two females, or a male and a female.

In general, the rear-entry position predominates for all primates, especially in the wild. Why is it, then, that humans tend to use the face-to-face position, while nonhuman primates and most other mammals use the rear-entry position? Perhaps the anatomical differences mentioned earlier can account for this disparity. Also evolutionary pressures may have favored the rear-entry position in most animals because of its survival value; the all-fours, rear-entry position allows for optimal "readiness of flight" for both females and males, particularly in comparison with the front-to-front position. This is particularly important for animals in the wild that need to be prepared to flee from a situation if threatened by a predator or other danger. Another possibility is that psychological factors override biological ones in humans.

Just as the occurrence of intercourse in humans is not completely governed by physiological changes in the female, choice of position is probably less biologically determined than in other primates.

Frequency of Intercourse

Statistics on frequency of intercourse are mainly derived from married couples. Some surveys have observed that when husbands and wives are interviewed separately, estimates of coital frequency are not always in agreement. When these estimates are correlated with the desire expressed by the partners, people who want intercourse to occur more often tend to underreport actual frequency, whereas those who prefer intercourse to occur less often tend to overstate actual frequency (Levinger, 1966). On the whole, however, correspondence between partners' reports is surprisingly good (James, 1971).

Hunt (1974) compared the frequency of marital intercourse reported by respondents in his and in Kinsey's samples; two conclusions are obvious (see Figure 6–8). First, both samples showed that frequency of intercourse declines with age. However, the separate contributions of age and number of years married cannot be judged from these data. For example, will a newly married couple in their 30s have a frequency that more closely approximates that of the younger age group? Undoubtedly both age *and* years married contribute to the declining frequency observed in both the Kinsey and Hunt surveys. The decrease

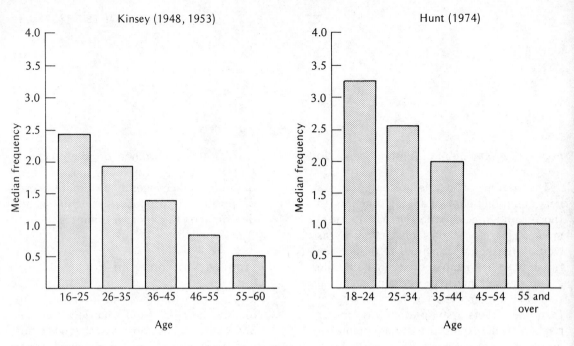

Figure 6-8. Marital coitus: Frequency per week, male and female estimates combined. Adapted from Hunt, 1974, p. 191.

in the frequency of intercourse per week or per month as a function of age has been repeatedly corroborated in other surveys as well (e.g., Pearlman, 1972; Westoff, 1974; Wilson, 1975). The second conclusion that can be drawn from Figure 6-8 is that the average frequency of intercourse has increased in recent times. Across every age group, the median frequency of intercourse was higher in the Hunt survey of the early 1970s than in the Kinsey survey conducted during the period from 1938 to 1949.

We cannot assume that the numbers presented in Figure 6-8 reflect what is "normal." These particular figures are *medians*—that is, half the sample in any one of the age groups had a higher frequency and half a lower frequency than the number presented in the figure. Therefore, at any given age the range will vary considerably. Some couples may engage in sexual intercourse nearly every day, while others may do so only once a month.

What factors other than age and years of marriage influence frequency of intercourse? Aside from such obvious factors as marital discord and poor health, not much has been found to be systematically related to marital coital frequency. For example, neither education, socioeconomic levels, nor religious conviction have been shown to have any consistent or striking effects.

Are couples engaging in intercourse as often as they like? Early surveys revealed that of those who were unhappy with their current activity rate, men usually wanted it increased whereas women wanted it decreased (Davis, 1929). By contrast, in a study conducted in the 1970s, only 2 percent of the wives surveyed said it was "too frequent," while 32 percent thought it was "too infrequent" (Bell & Bell, 1972). These figures may reflect changing social attitudes about relative sex drives of men and women. Fifty years ago women were not supposed to be interested in sex, whereas now women are expected to have sexual desires, just as men do. In any case, these figures suggest that in recent times married women often want sexual intercourse to occur more often.

Intercourse during Menstruation

One of the more pervasive taboos in human sexuality has to do with the question of intercourse during menstruation. Most preindustrial societies avoid sexual intercourse during menstruation. In fact, many primitive societies insist that menstruating women stay in separate huts (Delaney, Lupton, & Toth, 1976). Although we don't go this far, we still harbor prohibitions against intercourse when a woman is menstruating even though there is no medical reason (except possibly for concurrent venereal or vaginal infections) why intercourse should be banned. In one study of married women, 52 percent reported that they never had sex when they were menstruating (Paige, 1977). This statistic is very close to that reported by male respondents in the Pietropinto and Simenauer (1977) survey, namely that 49 percent said they did not engage in intercourse when their partners were menstruating.

Duration of Intercourse

Detailed information about the duration of intercourse—time from intromission to time of withdrawal of the penis from the vagina—is scarce. More often, people report the time devoted to foreplay, or the total time, starting with first foreplay advances and ending with orgasm either in the male or female, without separating actual intercourse from foreplay. Also, time estimates are obviously of questionable accuracy, and no one has attempted to obtain objective measures using stopwatches or more sophisticated technology for large samples of couples. Kinsey's group estimated that 75 percent of all males reach orgasm in approximately 2 minutes following intromission (Kinsey et al., 1948). Another researcher estimated the median intercourse duration to be 10 minutes (Hunt, 1974). Do the differences in these two studies reflect an actual change in duration of intercourse or do they reflect a change in what people perceive to be a socially desirable response? With so few data, no one really knows. People in our society today are much more conscious of the fact that most women need extended sexual stimulation to be aroused and to reach orgasm; this awareness may affect the actual duration of intercourse or the estimates given.

☐ *Cross-cultural Perspective on Duration of Intercourse* Studies conducted by anthropologists on preindustrial societies indicate that not only position but also the duration of intercourse is affected by cultural dictates. For example, the Balinese believe that brief intercourse experiences will result in a deformed child; they thus make a special effort to extend the duration of intercourse. On the other hand, men from Ifugao report that prolonging the time of intercourse is unnecessary and unpleasant (Ford & Beach, 1951). Clearly, these variations in intercourse duration across different cultures or even within cultures over time indicate that biological factors alone are not the sole determinants of even such "basic" aspects of sexual behavior as intercourse duration.

☐ *Cross-species Perspective on Duration of Intercourse*   Many large animals copulate and ejaculate very quickly, usually within 30 seconds. A dramatic example is the ferenuk antelope, which copulates for a fraction of a second while still in motion. Ford and Beach (1951) claim that the longest mammalian matings occur in the sable and mink, with time from intromission to withdrawal sometimes lasting 8 hours. In general, copulation time tends to be longer in carnivores (meat eaters) than in herbivores (vegetation eaters), suggesting that animals who are preyed upon are more likely to have shorter copulatory times.

Fantasy during Intercourse

During intercourse a large number of men and women fantasize at least occasionally about other sexual activity, such as having sex with different partners. Some people are troubled by these fantasies and believe that they somehow reflect sexual shortcomings. They may also be fearful that such fantasy during intercourse signifies that they are not sufficiently attracted to their partner—"Why else would I need to do this?" Still other people experience guilt because

they believe they are somehow deceiving their partner by engaging in fantasy during intercourse. Clinical and research evidence suggests that such fears and guilt feelings may be unwarranted. Sexual arousal is a function of a number of factors other than simple sexual attraction to one's partner (e.g., familiarity, physical fatigue, psychological comfort, and relaxation). Evidence increasingly points to sexual arousal being more a function of the mind than of bodily stimulation alone. Thus, to rule out completely any use of fantasy to facilitate arousal during intercourse is to rule out an important part of human sexuality. It should be reassuring to know that many people occasionally make use of fantasy during intercourse; in fact, some people intentionally act out certain fantasies to heighten arousal. On the other hand, many people are embarrassed to even speak about their fantasies with their partners.

> Bill brought my fantasies back into the open again from those depths where I had prudently decided they must live—vigorous and vivid as ever, yes, but never to be spoken aloud again. I'll never forget his reaction when timidly, vulnerable, and partially ashamed, I decided to risk telling him what I *had* been thinking.
>
> "What an imagination!" he said. "I could never have dreamed that up. Were you really thinking *that?*" (Friday, 1973, p. 4)

In one of the first studies conducted on the topic of sexual fantasies, a sample of 141 married women drawn from a middle-class New York suburb were evaluated

TABLE 6-3   OCCURRENCE OF FIFTEEN FANTASIES DURING INTERCOURSE: FEMALE SAMPLE

ITEM	PERCENTAGE
Thoughts of an imaginary romantic lover enter my mind.	56.0
I relive a previous sexual experience.	52.0
I enjoy pretending that I am doing something wicked or forbidden.	49.6
I imagine that I am being overpowered or forced to surrender.	48.9
I am in a different place like a car, motel, beach, woods, etc.	46.8
I imagine myself delighting many men.	43.2
I pretend that I struggle and resist before being aroused to surrender.	39.7
I imagine that I am observing myself or others having sex.	38.3
I pretend that I am another irresistibly sexy female.	37.6
I daydream that I am being made love to by more than one man at a time.	35.5
My thoughts center about feelings of weakness or helplessness.	33.3
I see myself as a striptease dancer, harem girl, or other performer.	28.4
I pretend that I am a whore or a prostitute.	24.9
I imagine that I am forced to expose my body to a seducer.	19.1
My fantasies center around urination or defecation.	2.1

Adapted from Hariton & Singer, 1974, p. 317.

(Hariton & Singer, 1974). The major finding of this study was that 65 percent of the sample reported moderate to high levels of erotic fantasy during intercourse. Furthermore, other measures indicated that such use of fantasy was generally not related to sexual or marital difficulty but was instead a simple device for enhancing arousal. There also was no evidence that women who made use of these fantasies were in any way "neurotic." Table 6-3 summarizes the relative frequency of the fifteen most common fantasy themes reported by these women.

David Sue (1979) performed a similar study with male and female unmarried undergraduates who had engaged in sexual intercourse. Nearly identical percentages of men and women—58.6 percent and 59.4 percent, respectively—reported using fantasy during intercourse either "sometimes" or "almost always." The three most frequently cited reasons for using fantasy were to facilitate sexual arousal, to imagine activities that a couple does not engage in, and to increase a partner's attractiveness. The conclusion drawn from both these studies is that fantasy during intercourse is a normal process for increasing sexual excitement and pleasure. Fantasy, however, can also decrease arousal by distracting the individual from the immediate situation to the point where the person does not react to it.

FACTORS RELATED TO FEMALE ORGASM IN INTERCOURSE

The orgasm issue is raised for women and not for men because orgasm during heterosexual intercourse is much less frequent in women than in men. (Men experience orgasm almost 100 percent of the time.) What do normative data reveal about the number of women in the United States who are orgasmic during intercourse? Do factors such as age, years married, quality of a relationship, sexual techniques, education, childhood experiences, and general personality have any effect on the likelihood of a woman experiencing orgasm during intercourse?

Frequency of female orgasm during coitus as reported in four different surveys is shown in Table 6-4. In the years between Kinsey's survey and the three more recent surveys, the percentage of women who indicate that they are "never or almost never" orgasmic declined, and the percentage who indicate that they are orgasmic "all or most of the time" stayed about the same.

Female Orgasm: Length of Marriage and Interaction with Age, Quality of Marriage, and Practice

One of the more interesting discoveries the Kinsey group made about female sexuality was that the likelihood of orgasm increased as a direct function of the number of years married. In the first year of marriage, 25 percent were nonorgasmic, whereas by the twentieth year of marriage, only 10 percent of the women were nonorgasmic during intercourse. For all of the women in Kinsey's sample, in the first year of marriage coitus resulted in orgasm 63 percent of the time; in the fifth year of marriage coitus resulted in orgasm 71 percent of the time; and by the twentieth year coitus resulted in orgasm 85 percent of the time during intercourse.

Why should this be the case? There is no single answer because lots of different factors that occur concurrently with length of

TABLE 6-4 FREQUENCY OF FEMALE ORGASM DURING COITUS: FOUR SURVEYS		
	NEVER OR ALMOST NONE OF THE TIME	ALWAYS OR MOST OF THE TIME
Kinsey et al., 1953	17%	65%
Bell & Bell, 1972	9	59
Hunt, 1974	7	74
Tavris & Sadd, 1975	7	63

marriage have been shown to have some independent influence on orgasm. *Age* is one such factor. For whatever pyschological, sociological, or biological reasons, women tend to be at the peak of sexual responsivity between the ages of 30 and 45, whereas men are at their peak between the ages of 16 and 25 (Kinsey et al., 1948, 1953). The quality of marital relationships is also probably involved. For example, a positive relationship between orgasmic frequency and marital happiness has been noted in several studies (Bell & Bell, 1972; Clark & Wallin, 1965; Gebhard, 1966). Thus, it would seem that more people who were happy with their marriages were likely to be in Kinsey's sample of twenty years married than in his sample of first or fifth year married. Another qualitative factor presumably associated with increased number of years married is *trust in one's partner*. Of all the personality characteristics examined by one researcher, the only one that could be said to predict female orgasm was the woman's feelings that her partner was dependable (Fisher, 1973).

A final factor obviously related to years in marriage is *increased sexual practice*. Women generally have had much less premarital orgasmic experience, as compared with men, either from masturbation, petting, or from petting combined with premarital intercourse. The Kinsey group reported that during early adolescence, when 95 percent of the males of corresponding age were experiencing orgasm with an average frequency of 2.3 times per week, only 22 percent of the females were reaching orgasm (Kinsey et al., 1953).

Female Orgasm and Religious Adherence

Although anecdotal reports from clinical samples of women who are not orgasmic suggest that devout religious beliefs may be responsible, survey data fail to provide any supporting evidence for this common impression. Many researchers found no correlation between various indicators of religious adherence (e.g., church attendance, devoutness of parents, and strong endorsement of religious values) and orgasm (Fisher, 1973; Hunt, 1974; Kinsey, 1953; Terman, 1938). The *Redbook* survey of female sexuality actually found just the reverse of what might be expected from clinical reports (Tavris & Sadd, 1975). Those women who characterized themselves as "very religious" were also more likely to say they "are almost always orgasmic," as compared with those who were moderately religious or not religious at all.

Female Orgasm and Duration of Foreplay and Intercourse

Some evidence links the likelihood of orgasm with the duration of foreplay and intercourse. One investigator summarized the results of a subsample of the women originally surveyed by Kinsey and his colleagues in 1953; these were women who had intact marriages at the time of the interview and who expressed no intention of terminating their marriage (Gebhard, 1966). When intercourse lasted an average of less than a minute, only 27.5 percent reported being orgasmic on 90 to 100 percent of intercourse occasions. When intromission lasted 1 to 1.9 minutes, the proportion of women reporting orgasm "nearly all the time" jumped to 51.2 percent, with little change for succeeding time increments until intercourse lasted 12 to 15 minutes; at this point, 61.6 percent of the women reported the occurrence of orgasm. These data generally suggest the existence of an optimal stimulation time, after which additional stimulation does not contribute to the likelihood of orgasm.

In another study, the average intercourse time reported for attainment of orgasm was about 8 minutes (Fisher, 1973). Fisher also provided some statistics on the type and sequence of stimulation associated with orgasm, which leads to the conclusion that manual stimulation of the clitoral region is often needed as a supplement to intercourse for many women to achieve orgasm.

Exaggerating the importance of the mechanical techniques used to achieve orgasm can be misleading. As previously noted, length of marriage, age, quality of the relationship, practice, communication, and trust in one's partner are also involved and are probably of greater importance. Furthermore, all sorts of other experiences enter into the picture, even though these are documented less often. Job anxiety or preoccupation, fatigue, fears of "letting go," residues of anger with a spouse, and poor health are examples of variables that obviously cannot be ignored. In this regard, a recent study of a sample of 619 well-educated, upper-middle-class women being treated for various sexual dysfunctions, foreplay and intercourse durations did not differ between those who were and those who were not orgasmic (Huey, Kline-Graber, & Graber, 1981).

Female Orgasm: Cross-cultural Perspective

Societies differ markedly in their expectations about and the actual occurrence of female orgasm. Margaret Mead (1935) noted a fascinating contrast between the Mundugumor and the Arapesh, two primitive South Seas societies. The Mundugumor expect women to be orgasmic just as men are, whereas in the Arapesh, female orgasm doesn't even have a name. On the Polynesian Island of Mangiai, the cultural goal is for a woman to have multiple orgasms, and all Mangiain women report that they are orgasmic (Marshall & Suggs, 1971). In fact, the Mangiains believe that women must be taught to have orgasms. By contrast, on the island of Inis Beag, which was highlighted in Box 6-1, orgasm is practically unheard of, and the cultural belief is that women do not enjoy sex.

Female Orgasm: Cross-species Perspective

Because the overt behavioral signs of female orgasm are sometimes ambiguous, until recently researchers were uncertain as to whether or not female, nonhuman primates experienced orgasm during sexual activity. This question was finally resolved in a 1980 study of female stump-tailed macaques conducted in the Netherlands (Goldfoot, Westerborg-Van Loon, Groene-veld & Slob, 1980). Using sophisticated physiological measurement techniques, uterine contractions were recorded during copulation. Other physiological events and behavioral manifestations also suggested that this response was comparable to female orgasm in humans.

SEXUAL SATISFACTION

Before considering specific factors that have been shown to be related to sexual satisfaction in marriage, we first need to address the more general question of how many married men and women in the United States are happy or unhappy with their sex lives. Unfortunately, this question has no clear answer. In the Hunt survey, only 3 percent of the males and 7 percent of the females rated intercourse in the past year as either neutral or mostly unpleasurable (Hunt, 1974). Yet other studies have estimated that in about one-third of all marriages, sexual relationships are somewhat unsatisfactory (Bell & Bell, 1972).

Closely tied to the issue of female orgasm is the question of whether orgasm is always essential for realization of sexual satisfaction. A widespread assumption is that a woman *must* climax to be satisfied. Survey data suggest that this is not always the case. Sexual interaction can afford considerable satisfaction with or without orgasm. For example, in a study by Butler (1976), 73 percent of the women reported that orgasm was not necessary to enjoy sexual relations. For many women, being held,

"cuddling," and feeling close to one's partner are apparently as satisfying as orgasm, if not more so (Bell & Bell, 1972). We are not, of course, suggesting that orgasm for women is unimportant. Without question, a sexual experience is more likely to be rated as satisfying if an orgasm does occur than if it does not occur (Clifford, 1978). Nevertheless, what must be stressed is that a woman is not invariably dissatisfied if she does not have an orgasm.

The reason some women report being dissatisfied if they don't experience an orgasm during intercourse is not because of physical frustration but because they fear their partner's reaction, thinking *he* will feel disappointed or inadequate. As a result of this pressure, 58 percent of the women in one study reported that they sometimes fake an orgasm (Butler, 1976). Another reason some women are dissatisfied when orgasm does not occur has to do with their expectations; they may believe that they are abnormal if they are not consistently orgasmic during intercourse.

Surprisingly, ratings of general sexual satisfaction and dissatisfaction do not seem to be tied very closely to the presence or absence of specific sexual problems. In a study of a nonclinic sample of one hundred couples, only 14 percent of the women and 15 percent of the men considered their sexual relations to be "not very satisfying" or "not satisfying at all" (Frank, Anderson, & Rubenstein, 1978). Yet, in this same sample, the percentage who reported having occasional sexual problems and dysfunctions was much higher. For example, 48 percent of the women reported some difficulty in getting excited, and 36 percent of the men reported ejaculating too quickly. This study is not the only one to discover that sporadic sexual problems are *commonly* reported by married couples, and much more so than reports of general sexual dissatisfaction (see also Nettelbladt & Uddenberg, 1979).

What other sexual and nonsexual variables seem to be pertinent to whether a person reports being satisfied with the sexual aspects of his or her life? In the sexual sphere, frequency of intercourse is probably the most important factor to consider. In one survey, women who reported the most satisfaction were also those who reported the highest intercourse frequency (Bell & Bell, 1972). In another study researchers found that women who were most satisfied had frequent intercourse, experienced orgasm consistently, and enjoyed gentle and seductive erotic activities, including breast stimulation, but were unresponsive to erotic literature and media (Hoon & Hoon, 1978).

In the nonsexual sphere, factors that have been shown to be highly related to sexual satisfaction are general marital happiness, years married, social class, and self-esteem. That sexual happiness and marital happiness are linked should come as no great surprise. The results from Hunt's survey document this connection in a rather clear fashion. For example, if one looks at the men and women who characterize their marriage as "very close," over 70 percent of these individuals also rated their sex life as "very pleasurable." On the other hand, only 12 percent of the men and 10 percent of the women who felt their marriage was "not too close" rated their sexual interaction as "very pleasurable" (Hunt, 1974). It also seems that, on the average, sexual satisfaction declines somewhat after the first year of marriage (Tavris and Sadd, 1975).

In a classic study of the effects of social class on sexual satisfaction, Lee Rainwater (1968) found that sexual enjoyment for both husbands and wives was less in the lower socioeconomic class. These class differences were particularly pronounced in the female sample, where 54 percent of the lowest class as compared with only 14 percent of the middle-class women reported being either slightly negative toward sex or outright rejecting of sexual relations. Why should this be the case? The possible answers are many, not the least of which is that people preoccupied by poverty and stress may find concentrating on sex to be difficult.

How one sees oneself—a person's *self-esteem*—is also important. For example, women who dislike their bodies, for whatever reason, often find themselves at odds with their sexuality (Heiman, LoPiccolo, & LoPiccolo, 1976). Similarly, women who generally judge themselves negatively often report less sexual satisfaction (Frank et al., 1979). In summary, sexual satisfaction is obviously a complex measure and is influenced by a host of interpersonal relationship factors that go far beyond a sequence of mechanical sexual acts.

PREMARITAL SEXUAL INTERCOURSE

At least since the late 1950s, if not earlier, the media has paid a great deal of attention to the "sexual revolution." The radical changes suggested center mainly on the occurrence of coitus in adolescence and to **premarital intercourse** in general. (A formal distinction between premarital intercourse and nonmarital intercourse should be mentioned, although they are often presented together. Premarital sexual activity refers only to those past experiences of people who have since been married. Nonmarital refers to sex between single individuals who have never been married.) Changes have occurred in both attitude about and experience with premarital intercourse during this century. In fact, some dramatic shifts have taken place, particularly in the female population, as better contraception has developed, as the double standard has become more relaxed, and as the battle for equality between the sexes in all areas has been pursued.

Some people strongly support premarital sexual intercourse and its benefits to marriage, and others believe that it can only have destructive consequences. However, neither one of these positions is well supported with objective data. In most instances people tend to endorse as desirable *whichever* course of action they actually pursued prior to marriage (Ard, 1974). Seemingly, if one's choice of action causes no regrets, then there is likely to be no negative impact on ratings of marital adjustment. Those who support premarital sexual intercourse use Kinsey's correlation between premarital orgasmic experience and the experience of orgasm in the first year of marriage—"practice makes perfect." However, the argument in favor of premarital sexual training is suspect since no one has ever shown that premarital orgasmic experience is related to long-term sexual satisfaction or happiness with the marital relationship (Shope & Broderick, 1967), or that happiness hinges on whether or not a woman is orgasmic during the first year of marriage.

An issue related to premarital intercourse is the phenomenon of **cohabitation,** a living arrangement characterized by sexual intimacy without the sanction of marriage. Such an arrangement was once considered rather scandalous behavior; now it is relatively commonplace. It is astonishing that social conventions taken for granted today were practically nonexistent just twenty-five years ago. Even coed dorms were unheard of in the 1950s. In the United States, various campus surveys indicate that somewhere between 10 percent and 35 percent of male and female students have established such living arrangements (Macklin, 1976). In the general population, estimates are that between 1960 and 1977 the number of unmarried couples living together more than doubled.

A couple may have many personal and social reasons for living together without getting married. The usual reasons are convenience, desire for sexual fulfillment, need for a more meaningful and complete relationship with another person; escape from loneliness; dissatisfaction with frenzied bar scenes and dating games; and search for security. In addition to these reasons, many couples are wary of the long-term commitment implied by marriage.

Incidence of Premarital Intercourse

The best way to assess what percentage of men and women have experienced premarital intercourse (as distinguished from nonmarital intercourse) is through the reported histories of people who are or have been married. Major surveys of the married population conducted in the United States suggest that the vast majority of both males and females have experienced intercourse before marriage (Burgess and Wallin, 1953;

Hunt, 1974; Kinsey et al., 1948, 1953; Tavris & Sadd, 1975). Each of these surveys, however, also reveals a consistent sex difference: More married males than females have engaged in premarital intercourse. Despite this difference, the increase in premarital intercourse experience for women during the past half-century has been dramatic. Kinsey's group found that over twice as many women born between 1900 and 1910 as compared with those born before 1900 experienced sexual intercourse before marriage (Kinsey et al., 1953). Contemporary studies show similar trends. Hunt, for example, found that only 31 percent of married women aged 55 or over in his survey had experienced premarital intercourse, as compared with 81 percent of those in the 18- to 24-year-old bracket (Hunt, 1974). The same pattern was observed in a recent study of 1,600 black and 1,600 white women who had ever been married sampled from low-income neighborhoods in sixteen cities (Udry, Bauman, & Morris, 1975). Both races had a higher incidence of premarital intercourse in each successive decade of birth.

These survey findings have led investigators to conclude that attitudes toward premarital intercourse most drastically changed during two time periods: the early 1920s right after World War I and the 1960s to the 1970s. Both periods are considered times of general social upheaval and rebellion against established social values.

☐ *Incidence of Intercourse during Adolescence* Excluding the numerous campus surveys of college students, three major surveys of adolescent sexual behavior in the United States have been conducted in the past decade (Miller & Simon, 1974; Sorensen, 1973; Zelnick & Kantner, 1980). Sorensen attempted to obtain a national probability sample that would be representative of the general population. However, his original sample was altered somewhat, due to parental objection, and also unwillingness on the part of some of the youths to participate. Although the remainder still were appropriately distributed demographically, they are likely to over represent those with more "liberal" sexual attitudes or more extensive sexual backgrounds. Sorensen found that 59 percent of all males and 45 percent of all females aged 13 to 19 had experienced premarital intercourse on at least one occasion.

Very different results were reported by Miller and Simon (1974). By age 16 or 17, 21 percent of the males in this sample had engaged in intercourse. This figure for males is not only substantially less than that reported by Sorensen, but also less than that originally reported by Kinsey. The proportion of females in the Miller and Simon study who had some premarital coital experience was 22 percent. These investigators recalculated Kinsey's original raw data for females in this age range and found that only 8.2 percent had reported coitus by the end of their sixteenth or seventeenth year. These differences in estimates of mid-adolescent experience with intercourse could be a function of the different geographic locations of the samples. Miller and Simon drew their sample from Illinois,

a midwestern state; sexual practices there may not be representative of the wider range of localities included in either the Sorensen or Kinsey surveys. Perhaps the most interesting finding of the Miller and Simon study was that the percentages of adolescent males and females who had had intercourse were very similar. These figures offer the most striking support ever presented that finds males and females experiencing premarital sex at approximately the same age and at the same rate.

Zelnick and Kantner (1980) surveyed adolescent females residing in metropolitan areas in the United States during 1971, 1976, and 1979. According to the results of this comparison study, sexual intercourse among unmarried teenage girls rose from 27 percent to 46 percent during this period. The increase was almost entirely attributable to the unmarried white sample. (For a related discussion of the topic of teenage pregnancy, see Chapters Three and Fourteen.)

□ *Reactions to First Intercourse* Most people in our society view the loss of virginity as a landmark event. Thus the decision to engage in intercourse for the first time and the actual experience of first intercourse are acts that are often met with mixed emotions. Individual reactions vary, of course. Some people are relieved and some are overjoyed, while others are afraid, guilt-ridden, and full of regret. In one study, when adolescents were asked which words best described how they felt the first time they engaged in intercourse, a striking difference was revealed between the way males and females responded. As can be seen in Table 6–5, a much higher percentage of girls, as compared with boys, expressed negative, self-doubting feelings after their first experience (Sorensen, 1973). Perhaps the best way to convey the range of feelings is through personal commentary. Box 6–2 contains quotations excerpted

---

Box 6–2

PERSONAL ACCOUNTS BY ADOLESCENTS OF FIRST PREMARITAL INTERCOURSE EXPERIENCE

I felt really guilty. Like, I thought, I wondered if my mother really knew. Like when I came in from the drive-in, I felt I had guilt, just guilt, written all over my face. (p. 187)

An 18-year-old girl

Once you've had sex, you know, you're really like trying to justify it in your own mind. I mean, so you change your views really drastically. (p. 187)

A 17-year-old girl

I was 15 and he was 26 or 27. I was a virgin, and I was horny and curious and all of that. So I balled him and I didn't like it and I didn't dislike it. But he didn't try to make it nice for me. (p. 187)

A 17-year-old girl

We went with each other for a couple of years before we did anything except necking. I'll never forget that evening. We were at a friend of a friend's house—they were real rich, twelve bedrooms and all that bit. We were talking about an hour. And then we just kind of got into things. I don't know—it was the way we felt about each other and everything. I didn't even need any lessons or anything. It just came natural. We talked about it before, but we never made any specific time or anything like that. I was a scared one all along, and I was the one who balked. It wasn't that we didn't have a place. But I kind of sat down and thought everything over a lot, and it didn't seem terribly wrong if two people really loved each other. I just can't go with any guy, you know. Like I really have a feeling for him. Yes, it was his idea but we both agreed. I had to agree, because I wasn't scared anymore. (p. 194)

A 16-year-old girl

from Sorensen's survey of adolescent sexual behavior (Sorensen, 1973).

☐ *Campus Surveys of the Incidence of*

Premarital Sexual Intercourse Nowhere has the pursuit of sexual bookkeeping been carried out more persistently than on the college campus. Dormitory surveys, class-

---

I never kissed a girl before, but I just kissed her, you know, the only way I knew how. And that's what happened. I just kept right on going. One thing followed the other and the other and the other. I remember being very nervous but the more I got into it. . . . I took her clothes off and I felt her and I felt my body against hers and I realized that this isn't really that complicated or that unusual. It relieved my tensions. It was like a big question I had that was finally answered. The question was how, where, and when. Like I say, as it progressed I became less and less nervous and more able to enjoy what was happening. In the beginning I must have been pretty numb, I guess, because I was too self-conscious, and I suppose it might have been a small let down in the beginning. This had been built up to be a very great thing. In a way, I was expecting the world to tumble down. I just knew it was going to be something great, but I didn't know how. (p. 194)

A 14-year-old boy

We slept on the floor because there weren't any couches or anything. We only did it so that we could make love. So it was like unplanned, and I hadn't used any kind of contraceptive. So we were on the floor and we smoked a joint and as gross as it sounds we just fucked. And it was just as I thought it would be. And he also didn't know I was a virgin, and he never knew. And that was it. It was over. I had known him about four weeks, which was longer than I have known anybody else.

It was the first time that I had made love, but it wasn't the first time that anybody had touched me. I knew what it was going to feel like. I always know things like that. I always know how things are going to be. Something like that I've waited for. And I really enjoyed it. It was fun. It was something new to do. I didn't think about getting pregnant, because my period—since I got it so young—had stopped. I didn't get it for about a year, and then the next year I got it about five times, and it's always been super mixed up since then. So I didn't care. I wasn't thinking about it and he wasn't thinking about it, which made me resent him later. I went into the kitchen and took a clean towel and I cleaned myself with it and put it in the hamper. And that's all I remember. I saw him after that for a few months. And it was very natural you know. We used to make love in my room after school all the time. And we used to park and get it on all the time. I never slept with him any place after that. (pp. 202–203)

A 17-year-old girl

Sorenson, 1973.

TABLE 6-5 ADOLESCENTS' IMMEDIATE REACTIONS TO THEIR FIRST INTERCOURSE		
	BOYS	GIRLS
Excited	46%	26%
Afraid	17	63
Happy	42	26
Satisfied	43	20
Thrilled	43	13
Curious	23	30
Joyful	31	12
Mature	29	14
Fulfilled	29	8
Worried	9	35
Guilty	3	36
Embarrassed	7	31
Tired	15	14
Relieved	19	8
Sorry	1	25
Hurt	0	25
Powerful	15	1
Foolish	7	9
Used	0	16
Disappointed	3	10
Raped	0	6

Note: Percentages add to more than 100% because most respondents reported more than one reaction.

Adapted from Sorenson, 1973, p. 203.

room surveys, cohabitation surveys — the college student is the most captive and most receptive "guinea pig" available for research of this kind. Such studies conducted in the mid-sixties indicate that approximately 50 to 60 percent of the male student body and 30 to 40 percent of the female student body reported having engaged in premarital intercourse. There is reason to believe that the greatest changes in recent times have taken place in the female population (Christensen & Gregg, 1970; Robinson et al., 1972).

Factors Affecting the Likelihood of Premarital Intercourse

We have already encountered a number of factors that influence the likelihood of premarital intercourse. One is generational: People born in recent decades are more likely to have engaged in premarital intercourse than those born in earlier periods. Gender is a second factor. Males have more premarital intercourse experience than do females, although evidence is mounting of a growing convergence between the two sexes in more recent times. A third consideration is age. Premarital intercourse is more likely to occur when people are in their twenties than when they are in their teens. A fourth factor reflects regional influences. For example, premarital intercourse for both males and females is less likely in the Midwest than in other parts of the country. Also college-aged males in the South are more likely to experience premarital intercourse than are their contemporaries in the East; for college-aged females, just the reverse is true (Packard, 1968). A number of other factors seem to be influential, including how close one is to getting married, religion, and education.

Number and Type of Premarital Intercourse Partners

The proportion of women whose only lover before marriage is their future spouse has not shown any dramatic change over the past thirty years. In Kinsey's study, slightly more than half of the women with premarital intercourse experience had had only one partner. This figure was much the same in the Hunt and *Redbook* surveys (Hunt, 1974; Tavris & Sadd, 1975). Less than 10 percent of the women in these two samples report having more than five premarital sexual partners in their lives.

Men with premarital intercourse experience seem to have a somewhat greater number of partners, but the numbers are still not substantial. The median number reported in the Hunt survey was six. In fact, there is reason to believe that the number of different premarital sexual partners is declining for males. In a college student population, one investigator found that although the proportion of males who had premarital coital experience had increased from the mid-1940s to the late 1960s and early 1970s, the number of partners with whom they were active had decreased (Finger, 1975). And in a related vein, the evidence is overwhelming that premarital sexual encounters with prostitutes has declined. The most recent studies of college men estimate that of those males surveyed, about 5 percent have had premarital experience with prostitutes, a substantially lower figure than the 28 percent reported by the Kinsey group (Kinsey et al., 1948).

The information on number and type of premarital partners strongly supports the notion that in one respect attitudes regarding premarital sexual behavior have not really changed all that much: Casual sex outside of an affectionate, committed relationship is not accepted by most people. Although the incidence of premarital intercourse has increased in recent decades, the conclusion that this increase represents a radical shift toward libertarian values, casual promiscuity, moral decay, and so on is just not true. Most females still engage in premarital intercourse only with their future spouse; the number of premarital partners for both men and women has not increased in the past thirty years; and strong affection and a committed relationship are still considered important criteria for becoming sexually involved. In sum, contemporary standards differ from the past only in being more permissive toward premarital intercourse *within* a romantic and close relationship.

Premarital Intercourse: Cross-cultural Perspective

A review of anthropological studies reveals that most cultures have been more lenient than ours about permitting nonmarital and premarital intercourse. In one study, data compiled from a worldwide sample of 250 nonindustrial societies were reviewed (Murdock, 1949). Premarital intercourse was prohibited in only 30 percent of the cases. Also, in many societies formal objections to premarital sexual intercourse are not taken seriously or enforced (Ford & Beach, 1951).

Several of the societies that permit free sexplay also allow children to observe explicit adult sexual behavior (although they usually do not observe their parents) and to participate openly in discussions of sexuality. The attitudes in these societies seems to be that appropriate sexual development should be taught, and that the best way to learn is via direct observation, instruction, and practice. For example, among the Lepcha of India early sexplay between boys and girls involves various forms of mutual masturbation and usually ends in attempted intercourse. By the time they are 11 or 12 years old, most girls regularly engage in complete intercourse. Among the Trobrianders, 6- to 8-year-old girls and 10- to 12-year-old boys receive explicit instruction about sexual behavior from older companions. Their sexplay includes masturbation and oral stimulation of the genitals. During early adolescence, heterosexual intercourse is a matter of course; at any time a couple may retire to a convenient place with the full knowledge and approval of their parents (Ford & Beach, 1951).

Although many societies allow far greater sexual freedom for their unmarried population than we allow for ours, others have more negative attitudes toward premarital sexual behavior. Modern China, where nearly one-quarter of the earth's population lives, has a very prudish and harsh policy toward premarital sexual behavior, even for people in their late teens. For example, girls are often sent to reformatories for having "affairs" with boys (Rosenthal, 1981).

EXTRAMARITAL INTERCOURSE

"What is your opinion about a *married* person having sexual relations with someone *other* than the marriage partner — Is it always wrong, almost always wrong, wrong only sometimes, or not wrong at all?" This question regarding **extramarital sex** — that is, sexual relations with someone other than one's spouse — was included in surveys conducted by the National Opinion Research Center in 1973, 1974, 1976, and 1977 (Glenn & Weaver, 1979). During this time period, about 70 percent of those surveyed answered "always wrong" to the above question. By contrast, in these same years only about 30 percent believed that premarital sexual relations were "always wrong." Not surprisingly, attitudes about extramarital sex are much more negative than those about premarital sex: Adultery violates one of the Ten Commandments and is perceived as a direct threat to the family unit. As late as the seventeenth century, the penalty for adultery in most of the New England colonies was death. Although this sentence was not often carried out, whippings, fines, brandings, and other severe punishments were common. Though we ob- viously view extramarital affairs more lightly now, reminders of such harsh condemnation still remain. In fact, adultery is still a criminal offense in many states and, although not often done, can still be cited as grounds for divorce.

In the last two decades the popular press has been filled with sensational articles and stories of open marriage, free love, mate swapping, group marriage, and other forms of consensual extramarital sexual relations. Monogamy is sometimes portrayed by liberal social commentators as an outdated, unnatural convention. Conservatives, partly in reaction to these stories, decry the moral dissolution of our society, claiming that marriage is seriously threatened by "loose morals." Both these views, however, take the issue to the extreme, distorting the actual facts.

In 1970, 96 percent of all Americans said they were committed to the idea of two people sharing a life and home together; a decade later the percentage was the same (Yankelovich, 1981). Despite the rising divorce rate in the United States, three out of every four divorced women, and five out of every six divorced men, remarry (Yankelovich, 1981). Furthermore, in various surveys conducted during the 1970s, over 75 percent of respondents disapproved of married men or women having affairs (Yankelovich, 1981). As you will learn in the following sections, the proportion of men and women who have actually had extramarital coital experience has not shown very much change in recent decades. The values of marriage and fidelity are ap- parently alive and well, much stronger than one would ever gather from the divorce statistics and the public debate about this topic in the mass media.

Incidence of Extramarital Intercourse

Kinsey found that about 50 percent of the men and 26 percent of the women in his sample had had at least one extramarital sexual affair (Kinsey et al., 1948, 1953). In more recent surveys, the overall percentages have not substantially changed. For example, the percentage of females who have had extramarital experience range from 18 percent in the Hunt (1974) survey to 29 percent in the *Redbook* survey (Tavris & Sadd, 1975). The total percentage of males in Hunt's sample who had engaged in extramarital intercourse was only 41 percent, a figure lower than that reported by Kinsey. If one looks solely at the youngest age groups, however, some evidence supports the notion of a growing similarity in the incidence of extramarital affairs between men and women. For instance, in Hunt's study, the proportion of married females under age 25 who had already had some extramarital sexual experience was 24 percent, compared with 32 percent for males in the same age group.

The number of different extramarital sexual partners (for those who have had any extramarital experience) also runs counter to the myth of rampant promiscuity and casual sex in our society. In Kinsey's female sample, of those with extramarital experience, 41 percent had only one partner, and

40 percent had between two and five partners; Hunt reported nearly identical figures (Hunt, 1974; Kinsey et al., 1953). These figures, along with the incidence figures, indicate that attitudes regarding extramarital relationships have not changed drastically.

Why Should I Get Involved? Why Shouldn't I?

The reasons for engaging or not engaging in an extramarital relationship are very complex. Love, adventure, excitement, curiosity, desire for variety, opportunity, restoration of self-esteem, vanity, tendency toward rebellion from conventions, emotional gratification, sexual gratification, fear of aging, fear of missing out on a new experience, dissatisfaction with marriage, boredom, sexual dissatisfaction, and escape from general unhappiness with life are *some* of the reasons why people become involved in extramarital relationships. Fear of spouse reaction if discoverd, fear of potential destructive effects on marriage, fear of pregnancy, fear of venereal disease, guilt, anxiety, and religious beliefs are contributing factors that discourage such involvements. Obviously, some people in our society rule out extramarital sexual relationships, and others do not. But because the context for such a decision is so multifaceted, no single factor alone, whether it pertains to the current quality of the marital relationship or to personality variables, demographic factors, general background history, or prior sexual experience, can predict with any degree of certainty the likelihood of an extramarital sexual relationship occurring during a person's lifetime.

Surveys have highlighted several general factors, however, that influence the likelihood of an extramarital sexual relationship. The first factor to consider is gender. As already indicated, the incidence of extramarital coitus is somewhat higher among males as compared with females. We can only speculate on the reasons. One obvious possibility is that historically women were considered the property of men. Males were thus in a more powerful social and economic position; they could restrict the activities of women more easily than women could control men. In general, men are also more powerful, and they have used this strength to control female activity of all kinds. In addition, women have been traditionally more likely than men to limit their sexual activity to partners for whom they feel an emotional bond. Interest in casual sex is much more rare for women than for men. We suspect that the reasons have less to do with differences in biological drives than with differences in social values taught from an early age.

A second factor related to the development of extramarital relationships is number of years married. For example, in the *Redbook* survey, only 12 percent of those women married less than a year compared with 38 percent of those married ten years or more had experienced extramarital coitus (Tavris & Sadd, 1975). These figures could be affected by such factors as opportunity and changes in the quality of the marital relationship.

A third factor, and the one most people think of first, is rating of marital satisfaction. A number of studies have shown that the incidence of extramarital coitus is higher in troubled than in trouble-free marriages (Bell & Peltz, 1974; Edwards & Booth, 1976; Johnson, 1970; Tavris & Sadd, 1975.). In the Bell and Peltz study, 55 percent of the women who considered their marriages fair to bad had had an affair, compared with only 20 percent of the wives who said that they were happily married. Furthermore, survey results tentatively suggest that the relationship between marital distress and extramarital affairs is stronger for men than it is for women (Edwards & Booth, 1976; Johnson, 1970). To assume, however, that extramarital sex will occur only if something is amiss in the marriage is incorrect. No doubt unhappiness with the marriage is often a contributing factor, but by no means a necessary factor. In the *Redbook* survey, slightly more than one-half of those wives who reported an extramarital affair also stated that they were perfectly happy with their marriage and with marital sex (Tavris & Sadd, 1975).

Considerable interest has been expressed recently as to whether the surge in female employment will increase the likelihood of extramarital affairs in the female population, either because of increased opportunity, increased financial and personal independence, or increased self-esteem. While the *Redbook* survey strongly suggests that an increase is likely (Tavris & Sadd, 1975), other researchers have found no such relationship (Edwards & Booth, 1976). Further research in this area is required before any conclusions can be drawn.

Finally, religious conviction, regardless of denomination, is often cited in connection with extramarital intercourse in women. Kinsey's figures for active versus inactive Protestant, Catholic, and Jewish women were quite similar, indicating a higher frequency in each case in the inactive samples (Kinsey et al., 1953).

Effect of Infidelity on Marriage

In most cases spouses are unaware of a partner's extramarital affairs. In Hunt's sample only 20 percent of the married women or married men reported that their spouses knew of their affairs (Hunt, 1974). The general consensus is that less harm results if the marital partner remains uninformed. However, this view is no more than an impression and has never been objectively confirmed. Deception could very well be more destructive. Certainly more research on this topic is needed.

Do extramarital relations play a part in separation and divorce? Again, not enough research has been conducted to answer this question properly. Though surveys such as Hunt's indicate that a much smaller percentage of the presently married population reports having had extramarital experience (17 percent) compared with the presently divorced or separated population (52 percent), these surveys do not tell us anything about cause and effect (Hunt, 1974). Poor marital relations could have been the cause for both establishing extramarital relationships and divorce, or each event could have developed independently of the others.

Consensual Extramarital Relationships: Beyond Monogamy?

Consensual extramarital relationships refer to situations in which both spouses are aware of, agree to, and usually mutually participate in extramarital sexual encounters. The three most common varieties are open marriage, mate swapping or "swinging," and group marriage. Despite the publicity surrounding these activities, they are all still relatively rare. Existing statistics, for example, suggest that no more than 2 percent of the married population has ever been been involved in swinging (Hunt, 1974; Spanier & Cole, 1975). Furthermore, attempts to overthrow the confines of sexual exclusivity are not particularly new or revolutionary. Many utopian communes formed in the mid-1800s in America subscribed to the same philosophy. (Note also that one of the most socially conservative religious groups in this country—the Mormons—condoned polygamy for many years, and some contemporary branches still practice it.) The one striking difference in present practices as compared with earlier ones is that they are somewhat less male dominated.

☐ *Open Marriage* Both partners in an **open marriage** agree that each is free to develop intimate but secondary sexual relationships with someone else. The notion here is to avoid secrecy or deception, and the usual arrangement presumably involves letting one's spouse know when such a relationship is in effect. However, couples can simply agree that each partner is equally free to participate in adulterous encounters and still prefer not to be told when it is happening. Also, the concept of an open marriage does not necessarily mean that both partners must be simultaneously involved in extramarital sexual relationships.

There are no statistics regarding how many and what kinds of couples in the population have entered into such open-marriage agreements or how they work out. The basic premise is perfectly rational: Since people now have average life expectancies into their 70s, for one person to totally satisfy another for, say, fifty years may be difficult. But the question remains whether jealousy and emotional conflict can truly be avoided when the concept of an open marriage is introduced.

> Shelley: It turned out to be a one-time thing. It wasn't a particularly gratifying experience. And I didn't do it again for years—for two years. Of course I told Jeff about it. He was fine. He wasn't upset by it.
>
> Jeff: I felt a twinge of the old jealousy. The feeling was that the guy was an intruder into the closeness and the bond between Shelley and me. You are socialized toward feeling that possessiveness. You are programmed to feel that sickening emotional response. I knew exactly what was bothering me. I was hurt on an emotional level.
>
> But there was a difference between my emotional response and what I rationally believed. So I had to figure out rationally what was really happening. And I was never angry with Shelley. I didn't brood about it. But it took me a while to get over it. (Annobile & Annobile, 1979, p. 99)

☐ *Swinging* The defining characteristic of **swinging** is that husband and wife are involved together and simultaneously in extramarital relationship(s). This activity is sometimes known as *mate swapping* or *comarital sex,* and couples generally make contact with each other through swingers' clubs, swingers' magazines, and advertisements in "underground" publications. Swinging can involve just two couples or a larger group. Couples meet, and then husbands and wives separate and pair off with the other people present. The newly formed pairs can remain together in one common room or they can go to separate rooms. The purpose is purely recreational sex. "True" swingers are willing to swap mates with a couple with whom they are not well acquainted, and/or to engage in sexual intercourse with relative strangers at a "swinging" party (Symonds, 1971).

Researchers have found that swingers are generally middle-class people, often in their thirties, who, aside from swinging, lead highly conventional lives (Bartell, 1970; Breedlove & Breedlove, 1964; Denfield & Gorden, 1975; Palson & Palson, 1974; Smith & Smith, 1970; Symonds, 1971; Varni, 1974). In almost all cases the husband is the one who instigates the initial involvement. In general, wives go along, at least in the beginning, mainly to please their husbands. The big fear for both partners is that the marital relationship will be threatened. One way swingers try to assure that this will not happen is to always go together and to avoid emotional involvement with other swingers. Based solely on interviews with participants, who are obviously biased in a positive direction, there is no evidence to date that swinging is harmful to marital stability (Cole & Spanier, 1974).

☐ *Group Marriage* In a **group marriage,** or multilateral marriage, each member considers himself or herself married or committed in an essentially equivalent manner to at least two other members of the group (Constantine & Constantine, 1971). Three people form a group, or several couples can live together and share each other sexually. The number of verified group marriages is very small—probably no more than 1,000 in the entire country (Salsberg, 1973). Unlike swinging, the purpose of a group marriage is not simply to occasionally have a different sexual partner, but rather to develop a committed emotional and sexual relationship with several people at once. The survival rate of group marriages is very low. Jealousy is one problem, but, in addition, all sorts of interpersonal conflicts are more likely to occur when a number of people live together and try to share labor, money, child-rearing responsibilities, and decision making in an equitable fashion, along with having sexual access to each other as well.

Extramarital Intercourse: Cross-cultural Perspective

In Ford and Beach's review of the anthropological literature, they noted that of 139 different societies for whom evidence was available, 39 percent approved of some form of extramarital liaison (Ford & Beach, 1951). Among the Toda of India, for example, a married woman may have several lovers as well as several husbands; there are no limitations whatsoever. More often, however, even in so-called permissive societies, certain limits are set. Some groups generally forbid extramarital relationships except between siblings-in-law. Among the Siriono, for example, the man may have sexual contact with his wife's sisters and with his brothers' wives and their sisters, but with no one else. Similarly, the woman can engage in sex with her husband's brothers and the husbands of her sisters. In some societies, mate swapping is a form of hospitality, while in still others, explicit permission for extramarital sexual activity is limited to ceremonial occasions. During a harvest feast, for example, prohibitions are lifted for a short time, and everyone is expected to have sexual intercourse with someone other than a spouse.

In societies considered restrictive, there is a wide range in the intensity of disapproval. In some, the punishment can be quite severe, while in others extramarital affairs are somewhat expected and only seriously frowned on if they are conducted in a flagrant manner.

SEXUAL BEHAVIOR IN YOUNG CHILDREN

This section briefly reviews certain aspects of sexual behavior in prepubescent children. (Other topics relevant to childhood sexuality are covered in Chapters Two, Ten, and Eleven). Although much still has to be learned about the frequency of various sexual behaviors in young children, no longer is there any question that children are capable of physical sexual response from a very early age. Even at birth, as many medical students discover to their surprise, male infants often are delivered with an obviously erect penis. Erections in male infants appear to occur reflexively throughout infancy (Halverson, 1940). Masturbation has also been observed in infants under 1 year of age, and Kinsey and his colleagues (1948; 1953) reported evidence of orgasm in children this young (see also Bakwin, 1973). Moreover, there is little question that sexual arousal in young infants results also from genital stimulation that is not self-induced. In fact, in some societies parents intentionally stimulate the genitals of their infants to soothe them (Martinson, 1980).

Genital self-stimulation in prepubescent children is not restricted, of course, to infants under 1 year of age. Fifty years ago, when a sample of parents in the United States were interviewed, they reported that approximately 50 percent of the boys and 20 percent of the girls engaged in rhythmic self-stimulation of the genitals (Levy, 1928). More recently, researchers have reported the results of interviews with young children themselves (Elias & Gebhard,

1973). Among these prepubescent children, 56 percent of the boys and 30 percent of the girls reported masturbating.

When socially permitted, sexplay between young children is also a frequently observed phenomenon. In all likelihood, however, such behavior may often have no erotic intent. Instead, it may be motivated by a natural curiosity to explore another child's anatomy. In a study of prepubescent children in the United States, 34 percent of the boys and 37 percent of the girls reported peer heterosexual activity involving either the exhibition or the manual or oral exploration of the genitals of playmates (Elias & Gebhard, 1973). Similar activity between same-sexed playmates was at least as frequent, occurring in 53 percent of the prepubescent boys and 35 percent of the prepubescent girls.

In our society strong attachments can develop between boys and girls when they are around three to six years of age. After this time, however, during middle childhood when children are attending elementary school, boys and girls seem to do everything they can to avoid each other. Freud called this behavior the *latency* period in sexual development. This stage is usually followed by a reawakened sexual interest as puberty blooms in junior high school and high school. The point that needs to be stressed about these supposed stages of sexual development is that they are *not* universal across cultures or even within our own culture. As one authority on childhood sexuality puts it: "Rather than passing through a set series of sexual stages determined by physical growth, children develop at different rates in a wide variety of directions depending on how they are raised" (Martinson, 1980, p. 31). For example, in some societies children are encouraged and instructed in how to engage in sexual activity, sometimes having sexual relations with each other even before puberty (Ford & Beach, 1951). Even in the United States, one investigator of childhood sexual behavior found communities in which children eight and nine years of age played kissing games, and by ten and eleven nearly half had begun to date and almost all of the children reported having "crushes" on other adolescents and adults (Broderick, 1966).

Considerable uncertainty remains concerning what factors during early childhood are necessary for, or detrimental to, heterosexual development. Studies with monkeys have demonstrated that being reared in extreme isolation from contact with adults and peers results in a permanent inability to mate as an adult (Harlow, 1962). Presumably, extreme social and parental deprivation would have the same effect in humans. Beyond this, however, the question has primarily been dealt with in a speculative rather than in an experimental manner. According to one investigator, the following conditions are essential in laying the foundation for adult heterosexual attachments (Broderick, 1968):

1. The same-sexed parent must be neither so punishing nor so weak as to prevent the child from identifying with him or her.

2. The opposite-sexed parent must not be so seductive, punishing, or emotionally unstable as to prevent the child from trusting members of the other sex.
3. The parents must not systematically re-

ject the child's biological sex by constant denigration or cross-dressing.
4. The parents need to establish in the child a positive view of marriage as an eventual goal.

SEXUAL BEHAVIOR IN THE ELDERLY

Social attitudes concerning the sexual activity of older people are generally marked by prejudice, denial, and repulsion. In one study college students were asked to complete the sentence: "Sex for most old people is . . ."; the prevailing responses were "unimportant," "negligible," or "past" (Golde & Kogan, 1959). Students also typically underestimate the frequency of sexual activity of older generations, and particularly of their parents.

Life-styles established in nursing homes are a good indication of general societal views of sex among the elderly. These institutions do their best to eliminate the opportunity for sexual expression. They characteristically have segregated rather than co-ed sleeping arrangements—even married couples may be separated. Sexual activity requires privacy, but little effort is made to provide an atmosphere of privacy because of the assumption that the elderly have no sexual interest or capacity.

We have previously described the physiological changes in sexual response that occur with aging (see Chapter Two). The present section is therefore concerned only with sexual behavior. Although older people, in general, are less sexually active than

younger people, sexual interest does not disappear. Research conducted at Duke University's Center for the Study of Aging and Human Development indicates that at ages 66 to 71, about 62 percent of all men, regardless of marital status, were still sexually active, with the vast majority engaging in intercourse no less than once a month. At ages 72 to 77, the proportion of men still sexually active on a regular basis declined to about 50 percent. Finally, for those men in their sample who survived into their 80s and 90s, approximately 20 percent reported that they still had intercourse (Verwoerdt, Pfeiffer, & Wang, 1969).

The pattern for elderly women differed somewhat in the Duke University study, with marital status playing an important role. Those who were not married engaged in sexual intercourse much less often than those who were married. Very few unmarried women over age 65 (less than 5 percent) reported any degree of regular heterosexual activity, primarily because the widowed elderly woman has few available sexual partners. The average life expectancy of women in the United States is about seven years longer than for men, and so elderly single women far outnumber elderly single

Physical affection and sexual activity continue to be a part of life, regardless of age.

men. This imbalance in available partners among the elderly is further magnified by the social convention of men marrying women younger than themselves.

For elderly women who do have spouses, however, the statistics are similar to those reported for older men (Christenson & Gagnon, 1965; Verwoerdt, Pfeiffer, and Wang, 1969). To a large extent, sexual activity of aging women is determined not only by the availability of a sexual partner but also by the partner's interest and capacity. Women in their 60s who are married to younger men engage in intercourse more frequently than those who are married to older men. Moreover, when asked why sexual relations ceased, women overwhelmingly stated that their husbands were responsible, and their husbands generally agreed (Pfeiffer, Verwoerdt, & Davis, 1972).

In addition to marital status for women, there are a number of other reasons why some men and women continue to be active sexually in their advancing years while others do not. Physical health is a contributing factor, especially for men. Both objective and subjective health ratings seem to play a lesser role for women (Pfeiffer & Davis, 1972). Prior sexual history is another important consideration. Those who engage in sex frequently and enjoy it throughout their earlier years are likely to continue to do so as they get older (Pfeiffer & Davis, 1972). How much of this effect is due to physical rather than psychological reasons is unknown, since repeated use of one's sexual organs seems to enhance their physical functioning (Masters & Johnson, 1970).

On the basis of their clinical work with older males, Masters and Johnson list the following factors that they believe to be generally responsible for the wane in sexual activity that occurs with increasing age:

1. Monotony with a repetitious sexual pattern, including loss of physical attractiveness of one's partner (most people feel that the aged body is less beautiful, or erotic, than a young body).
2. Preoccupation with career or economic pursuits.
3. Mental or physical fatigue.

4. Excessive alcohol consumption.
5. Physical and mental infirmities of the individual, or of his or her spouse.
6. Fear of not performing well.

Women's negative attitudes about their body and about menopause may also be destructive to their sexuality. If they no longer feel they are attractive, women may fear rejection or their own interest may be affected. Similarly, if they believe menopause means the end of sexuality, they may just make it happen.

The myth of "sexlessness" in the elderly is destructive. Sex not only symbolizes vigor and what it means to be a woman and a man to many people; it also provides a feeling of being wanted, of being capable of giving and receiving love and affection, and of being close to another person. Because sexuality is not only influenced by physical capabilities but also by social and psychological factors, many elderly people may be dropping this "life giving" activity when it isn't necessary, and when, in fact, it may be harmful to do so.

SUMMARY

1. **Heterosexuality** refers to the sexual attraction a person has for members of the opposite sex.

2. There are two types of sexual activity: intercourse, or coitus, and noncoital activity. **Intercourse** is limited to penile-vaginal sex, and all other sexual activity is classified under petting and foreplay. **Petting** refers to sexual contact not intended to lead to intercourse, whereas **foreplay** is petting that precedes intercourse.

3. A certain order of events generally defines petting: hugging and simple kissing, deep kissing and manual stimulation of the female's breasts, manual stimulation of the female and male genitals, and oral-genital stimulation.

4. **Cunnilingus** is the oral stimulation of the female genitals, and the oral stimulation of the male genitals is called **fellatio.** In recent times, oral-genital sex has become more commonplace in petting and foreplay. Psychological as well as religious reasons influence individual acceptance of these acts.

5. The standard intercourse positions include face-to-face, man-on-top; face-to-face, woman-on-top; face-to-face, side by side; and the rear-entry position.

6. Open communication between partners is vital both in petting and

foreplay and in intercourse so that sexual intimacy can be enjoyable for both people involved. Partners should communicate what they do and do not enjoy, either verbally or nonverbally.

7. Some of the factors related to the occurrence of female orgasm include length of time married, the quality of marriage, and the amount of sexual practice one has had. Duration of foreplay and intercourse also seems to have an effect. Sexual satisfaction, however, is not solely dependent on the incidence of orgasm.

8. **Premarital intercourse,** which is intercourse between partners who are not married, is on the rise, although not to the extent suggested by some groups.

9. Living together and sharing a sexual relationship without the sanction of marriage is known as **cohabitation.** Although quite common today, it was considered scandalous in the not too distant past.

10. The incidence of **extramarital sex** has not increased drastically in recent decades, although women have apparently become somewhat more active extramaritally within the last few years.

11. **Open marriage, swinging,** and **group marriage** are consensual extramarital relationships—that is, relationships outside of marriage that both spouses are aware of, agree to, and usually participate in together.

12. Although the double standard in sexual behavior between females and males seems to be on the decline in recent decades in the United States, the following sex differences still remain:

- More males than females initiate sexual overtures.
- During adolescence females more than males set limits on "how far to go."
- More females than males consider mutual affection a necessary precursor for sexual intimacy.
- More males than females engage in premarital and extramarital intercourse, although the differences are not as extreme as they once were.
- More males are consistently orgasmic during intercourse than are females.
- Males seem to be more responsive to genital stimulation earlier in the sequence of sex play than females, and they are generally ready to proceed from foreplay to intercourse sooner than females.
- More females than males experience multiple orgasm.

13. Doubt no longer exists that children from birth onward are capable

of physical sexual response. Long before puberty boys have erections and girls lubricate. Orgasm can even occur during infancy.

14. Social attitudes regarding the sexuality of the elderly population are unfortunately marked by prejudice, denial, and repulsion. Elderly people are generally quite capable of enjoying sexual activity, and given the opportunity many do.

SUGGESTED READINGS

Hunt, M. *Sexual behavior in the 1970s.* Chicago: Playboy Press, 1974. Next to the Kinsey surveys, the Hunt survey is probably the most well-known survey of adult human sexuality.

Kinsey, A. C., Pomeroy, W. B., & Martin, C. E. *Sexual behavior in the human male.* Philadelphia: Saunders, 1948. Classic survey of male sexuality.

Kinsey, A. C., Pomeroy, W. B., Martin, C. E., & Gebhard, P. H. *Sexual behavior in the human female.* Philadelphia: Saunders, 1953. Classic survey of female sexuality.

Marshall, D. S., & Suggs, R. C. (Eds.). *Human sexual behavior.* Englewood Cliffs, N.J.: Prentice-Hall, 1972. A collection of anthropological studies of sexual behavior in different societies.

Rubin, I. *Sexual life after sixty.* New York: Basic Books, 1965. An excellent introduction to understanding sexuality in the elderly.

Smith, J. R., & Smith, L. G. (Eds.). *Beyond monogamy.* Baltimore: Johns Hopkins University Press, 1974. A collection of studies on different kinds of extramarital consensual sexual arrangements.

Sorensen, R. C. *Adolescent sexuality in contemporary America.* New York: World Publishing Co., 1973. Results of a survey study of sexual behavior in adolescence.

CHAPTER SEVEN

HOMOSEXUALITY
Physical and Emotional Bonds
Between People of the Same Sex

. . . considering the physiology of sexual response and the mammalian backgrounds of human behavior, it is not so difficult to explain why a human animal does a particular thing sexually. It is more difficult to explain why each and every individual is not involved in every type of sexual activity.
Kinsey, et al., 1953, p. 451

*H*ow would *you* answer the following question: Do you think that sexual relations between two adults of the same sex is always wrong, almost always wrong, wrong only sometimes, or not wrong at all? Examine your feelings about homosexuality. Would you be upset if a friend recently let it be known that he or she is homosexual? Have you had some homosexual fantasies or homosexual experiences that have made you wonder if you are gay or, possibly, if you are "normal"? Your experiences may have seemed natural to you or they may have scared you a lot. To say that, in general, our society "frowns" on homosexual relationships is an understatement, and most religions similarly consider sex between women or between men "unseemly" and "against God's laws." On the other hand, some people believe that homosexuals are unjustly persecuted. Certainly, our primary intention in this chapter is neither advocacy nor condemnation of homosexuality. Instead, we wish to describe in as objective a manner as possible the research that has been done and to develop an understanding of what it means to be homosexual.

Before we attempt to do this, we should establish what we mean by **homosexuality.** In considering a definition, three components need to be distinguished: (1) homosexual behavior, (2) homosexual attraction or desire, and (3) homosexual identity. Homosexual *behavior* refers to sexual activity with another person of the same anatomic sex. Homosexual *attraction* refers to erotic and emotional interest in members of the same sex. Homosexual *identity* refers to a person's self-acknowledged preference for sexual partners of the same sex. None of these components has to exist simultaneously. For example, some people may engage exclusively in heterosexual relations but still predominantly fantasize and have an erotic preference for homosexual activity. Such individuals may be married and simply choose not to act on their homosexual preference. Other people may at some stage have particular desires that are either heterosexual or homosexual but choose not to engage in any overt sexual activity because of lack of opportunity, preoccupation with other aspects in life, or for other reasons. Matters could certainly be simplified if sexual behavior, psychosexual desires, and self-professed sexual identity were always in perfect agreement and remained constant over time. However, that human sexuality is not so simple should come as no great surprise.

A common misconception is that homosexuality and heterosexuality are mutually exclusive phenomena. Not so; even though some people throughout their lives are interested only in members of the same sex (exclusive homosexuality) or in the opposite sex (exclusive heterosexuality), a large number fall somewhere in between. People in this "gray" area are called **bisexuals,** meaning that their sexual interests are not limited to just one sex. Men and women who characterize themselves as bisexuals are people who have had more than incidental or transient sexual experiences with both same-sexed and opposite-sexed partners. A study of 156 self-identified bisexuals showed that sexual attraction to

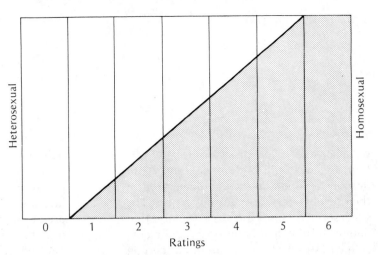

Figure 7-1. Kinsey Heterosexual-Homosexual Rating Scale.

Ratings

Based on both psychological reactions and overt experience, individuals rate as follows:

0. Exclusively heterosexual with no homosexual
1. Predominantly heterosexual, only incidentally homosexual
2. Predominantly heterosexual, but more than incidentally homosexual
3. Equally heterosexual and homosexual
4. Predominantly homosexual, but more than incidentally heterosexual
5. Predominantly homosexual, but incidentally heterosexual
6. Exclusively homosexual

and enjoyable sexual experience with both sexes were the factors most responsible for adopting a bisexual identity (Blumstein and Schwartz, 1977). As a matter of fact more people fall into this category than do people who consider themselves exclusive homosexuals. Heterosexuals and homosexuals alike seem to feel that being bisexual is impossible, an act of bad faith, hypocritical, a "cop-out," or denial of true homosexual identity. Many heterosexuals simply fail to make a distinction and consider all bisexuals equivalent to predominant or exclusive homosexuals. Similarly, members of the homosexual community reject bisexuals, taking an "either you are with us or you are against us" attitude. However, neither view seems to be accurate. Although perfect ambisexuality (complete neutrality in partner preference or exactly equal psychosexual attraction to both sexes) is probably rare, a person may still

enjoy both experiences. The desire of both groups to look at sexuality in pure categories is conceptually and politically easier to grasp but does not accurately represent the way many people behave and feel.

Even this type of classification (homosexuality, bisexuality, and heterosexuality) is misleading because it implies three completely separate categories. As Kinsey, Pomeroy, and Martin (1948) noted, nature rarely deals in terms of absolutes. Accordingly, these investigators developed a 7-point scale of sexual preference based on the idea that exclusive homosexuality and heterosexuality are two extremes of a continuum (see Figure 7-1).

The Kinsey scale of sexual preference can be used in several ways: (1) to describe a person's current or past preference, (2) to summarize a person's cumulative sexual experience, (3) to describe both overt sexual behavior and covert processes (sexual fantasy, feelings, and preference), and (4) to describe a population of people in terms of their sexual interests at any given time. The suggestion of Kinsey and his associates that heterosexuality and homosexuality be considered as part of a continuum has certain implications, the most important of which is that these two orientations are related. Thus, homosexuality and heterosexuality can be expected to share certain common properties. Also, shifting gradations in degree of homosexual or heterosexual interest can be expected, depending on a person's age, environment, training, and circumstances. These basic themes will be repeated and developed as this chapter progresses.

The use of the word "homosexual" as a singular noun, as in "the homosexual male" or "she is a homosexual," typically refers to people who would receive ratings of 5 or 6 on the Kinsey scale—that is, predominantly or exclusively homosexual. Because such usage is conventional and convenient, we employ it throughout this chapter, but we do so with reservations. Labeling someone as homosexual may exaggerate the sexual aspect of their lives: An individual's occupation, interests, personality, physical and mental health, and social adjustment are not governed solely by his or her sexual orientation. Aside from sharing a preference for same-sexed partners, the diversity among homosexuals is incredible in terms of early sexual experience, number of sexual partners, duration of relationships, preferred sexual life-styles, heterosexual history, choice of sexual techniques, the degree to which they reveal their homosexual interests to others, and so on. Thus talking about *the* homosexual in some uniform, stereotyped manner does not make sense.

Researchers are in general agreement that not all heterosexuals are alike, and not all homosexuals are alike either. As Bell and Weinberg (1979) point out, no wonder so many homosexual men and women reject the label "homosexual" and prefer, instead, such terms as **gay** or **homophile** or **lesbian** (female homosexual). (The term *lesbian* is based on the reported characteristics of the ancient inhabitants of the Greek island of Lesbos.)

INCIDENCE AND PREVALENCE OF HOMOSEXUALITY IN THE UNITED STATES

Determining precisely how many people engage in or are psychologically aroused by different sexual activities is not an easy task, especially when some of those behaviors are still sometimes referred to as "crimes against nature." Since homosexuality has long been the object of social disapproval, scorn, and legal sanctions, not many people readily admit to homosexual experiences. Thus statistics from various surveys must be considered as no more than estimates.

Male Homosexuality

In 1948, when Kinsey and his colleagues published their monumental book on sexual behavior in the human male, the most shocking statistics concerned homosexuality (Kinsey et al., 1948). In plain terms, Kinsey's data indicated that one out of every three males on the street had performed a homosexual act to the point of orgasm, and one out of every two males had had homosexual desires at least once. These figures were startling because they suggested that male homosexuality was an incredibly widespread phenomenon. In some ways, however, the findings of Kinsey and his associates were misleading. First, the findings included masturbation in the presence of other males, which does not have to be considered homosexual behavior at all. More importantly, one-half of the males had had homosexual experience between the ages of 12 and 14 and then never again; another one-third had experienced it by age 18 but never as an adult (Karlen, 1971). The other statistics reported by Kinsey's group are probably of greater relevance. For example, 25 percent had more than incidental homosexual experience or reactions (ratings of 2 through 6 on the Kinsey scale) for a period of at least three years between the ages of 16 and 55, and 4 percent were exclusively or nearly exclusively homosexual throughout their entire lives. Clearly, male homosexuality is not an insignificant, rare occurrence. The 4 percent figure of predominant or exclusive homosexuals alone translates into millions of American men.

No study since Kinsey's suggests any increase in homosexuality. If anything, other surveys imply that Kinsey's figures somewhat exaggerated the prevalence of male homosexual experience (Gagnon and Simon, 1973; Hunt, 1974; Finger, 1975). One study indicates that Kinsey's statistics were based on a population sample that included an excessive number of criminal and delinquent males (Gagnon and Simon, 1973). These researchers reanalyzed Kinsey's data, concentrating on a subsample of 2,900 men who were in college between the years 1938 and 1950. Of the 30 percent who reported some homosexual experience, three-fourths of the cases were confined to early adolescence, with a few isolated incidents occurring up to the age of 20. Three percent were exclusively homosexual, and another 3 percent had substantial homosexual as well as heterosexual histories.

Hunt (1974) found that only 7 percent of the males in his total national sample had homosexual experiences during more than three years of their lives, and only 2 to 3 percent of the males were predominantly or exclusively homosexually oriented throughout their lifetimes. In addition, many studies report that a high percentage of homosexual experiences occur in adolescence; Finger's (1975) findings indicate, however, that the incidence of preadolescent and early adolescent homosexual experience has declined over the past thirty years. If confirmed by additional research, one could speculate that such a change might be a function of increased opportunity and a more permissive attitude toward premarital heterosexual experience.

Female Homosexuality

Female homosexuality appears to be less prevalent than male homosexuality. Of the 5,940 women that Kinsey and his group interviewed, only 28 percent reported some homosexual response, and only 13 percent, compared with 37 percent for males, had experienced homosexual contact to the point of orgasm (Kinsey et al., 1953). Additionally, only 2 to 3 percent of the total female sample were predominantly homosexual at any age period. Even this statistic may be slightly overestimated because there was an overrepresentation of single women in the sample. The data, as might be expected, showed homosexuality to be more common among single women than among those who were married. In Hunt's national survey, less than 2 percent of the total sample rated themselves as predominantly or exclusively homosexual (Hunt, 1974).

What Do the Numbers Mean?

Estimates of the number of people involved in homosexuality can have a tremendous impact on personal and social attitudes. Of course, just because a large number of people engage in a particular behavior does not mean anything in terms of moral judgments. Millions of people in the United States may gamble on sports events. This does not mean that gambling is either "right" or "wrong." Millions of men and women in the United States may eat too much. This does not mean that overeating is "good" or "bad." Numbers alone cannot justify any behavior, but when the numbers are known to be sufficiently large, there are certain natural consequences. First, strict enforcement of legal sanctions is impossible. This reality, in turn, provides support for decriminalization—as was the case with alcohol prohibition in the twenties and as is currently an issue surrounding the use of marijuana. Second, if a behavior is sufficiently common, its continued status as deviant and/or psychopathological is automatically questioned. Third, when estimates are small or unknown, those who perform the behavior feel more isolated and threatened. To learn that you share a behavior with millions of other people lessens the tremendous burden of self-doubt and alienation. There is less need, then, to hide continually behind a mask. Finally, if, as research shows, approximately 25 percent of the population engages in homosexual behavior at least in an incidental manner at some point in their lives, and close to 10 percent of all males pursue homosexual experiences in a substantive manner during adulthood, then the odds are that some friend, colleague, or relative is likely to be among them. As a result, harsh condemnation is more likely to be replaced, over time, by tolerance.

According to the surveys that have been performed, we can conclude that for the greatest percentage of males and females, homosexual activity is a temporary experience. Only a small fraction of those with homosexual experience in early adolescence will exclusively or even predominantly engage in homosexual activity in adulthood. Also, of those with homosexual experience, only a small percentage have an exclusively homosexual orientation for an entire lifetime (approximately 3 to 4 percent of males and 1 to 2 percent of females). Most people who have engaged in homosexual acts also have had heterosexual experience, and far more have experienced both than have been exclusively homosexual. Therefore, contrary to popular opinion, degree of preference for same-sexed or opposite-sexed partners for many people may fluctuate over time.

CROSS-CULTURAL AND HISTORICAL PERSPECTIVE

Most cross-cultural studies of homosexual behavior have examined "primitive" societies, with more attention paid to male than to female homosexuality. In Ford and Beach's (1951) study of seventy-six preindustrial cultures, forty-nine permitted some form of male homosexuality, while female homosexual practices were noted in seventeen cultures. In those cultures in which male homosexuality was accepted, persistent and exclusive homosexuality was still quite rare. Instead, homosexuality was usually regarded as suitable primarily for the young. In fact, in some cultures all members of the male community took part in some type of homosexual activity during their transition to adulthood. For example, among the Keraki of New Guinea and the Kiwai Papuans, young men participated in anal intercourse as part of their initiation rites. In some societies only a certain type of homosexual act was considered acceptable; the Batak people of Sumatra, for example, permitted mutual masturbation and anal intercourse, but not fellatio (West, 1977). Age of partners has also been prescribed. In most cultures homosexual relationships between only older and younger males or between only same-aged adolescents were approved, and homosexual activities were to be abandoned in adulthood when heterosexual relations and responsibilities were assumed (Churchill, 1967).

Homosexual behavior has always been a fact of life in just about every country, but few, if any, have ever promoted exclusive homosexuality between adults. Even in ancient Greece, where homosexual relationships flourished to a degree that has never been seen since, there were still limitations. Masculine love affairs were only celebrated if they occurred between an adult male and an adolescent boy, known as **pederasty,** or between two soldiers. Exclusive homosexuality was still considered somewhat ridiculous, if not repulsive (Karlen, 1971). Similarly, although the term "lesbianism" is derived from the romantic poetry of Sappho on the Greek island of Lesbos, there is little other evidence to suggest that female homosexuality was particularly popular at that time.

Extreme antagonism to male homosexu-

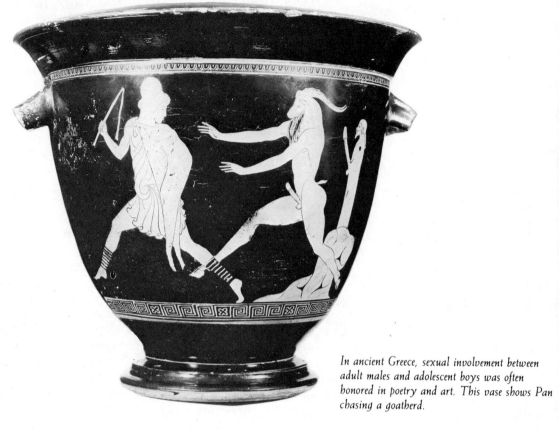

In ancient Greece, sexual involvement between adult males and adolescent boys was often honored in poetry and art. This vase shows Pan chasing a goatherd.

ality in Judeo-Christian civilizations can be traced back to the seventh century B.C. (Weinberg and Williams, 1974). Indeed, the Bible condemnation of male homosexuality is quite explicit and severe:

> If a man lies with a man as with a woman, both of them have committed an abomination; they shall be put to death, their blood is upon them. (Leviticus 20)

The contrast in early Judaic feelings about male and female homosexuality is striking. Whereas male homosexuals were sentenced to death, the penalty for female homosexuals was not being allowed to marry a Rabbi (Szasz, 1965). Clearly, in male-dominated societies female homosexual behavior has never been a matter of much concern. Even in recent times lesbians do not get as much attention as their male counterparts.

With the spread of Christianity, male homosexuality continued to be considered a major crime, at first by church law and then by civil law. In the Middle Ages the legal definition of homosexuality in Christian countries was "*pectactum illud horrible inter Christianas non nominadum*—a sin so horrible that it should not be put into words" (Bancroft, 1976, p. 173). Despite these ill feelings, however, homosexuality has persisted through to modern times.

Male homosexuality in non-Western, non–Judeo-Christian cultures historically was more prevalent, or at least far less severely censured. According to Karlen (1971), in medieval Japan the warrior class took boys as pages and lovers following a pattern similar to that of the ancient

Greeks. In the nineteenth century, Western travelers also noted that male brothels featuring adolescent boys were easily found in Southern Europe, North Africa, Turkey, Persia, the Arab Near-East, Kashmir, Moslem India (but not the Hindus), Indo-China, China, and Japan (Karlen, 1971).

CROSS-SPECIES PERSPECTIVE

The fact that homosexual behavior of one form or another has been described as being relatively common for almost every species of nonhuman mammals and primates is often cited as proof that homosexuality is biologically "normal" or "natural" for humans as well. This conclusion may or may not be correct, but, as Beach (1976) points out, surface similarities in behavior between different species does not mean that the behavior has the same meaning, function, or causal properties for the different species. For example, male animals of some species will mount even inanimate objects when they are aroused. Female-female mounting behavior during estrus is also quite common among nonprimates. In short, homosexual activity in the non-primate groups often seems to be an indiscriminate response to arousal. In the absence of a receptive heterosexual partner, both males and females will mount whatever is available.

With primates homosexual activity seems to be less governed by immediate drive states. Instead, the most common homosexual activity—that taking place between adult males and younger males—seems to serve a complex function aside from a sexual one; it involves the expression of dominance. Homosexuality also seems to be a form of practice, part of a normal developmental sequence for immature animals.

Probably the closest replica to human homosexual behavior has been observed in stumptail macaque monkeys (Chevalier-Skolnikoff, 1976). Male homosexual encounters involved prolonged manual-genital stimulation, oral-genital stimulation, rear mountings with pelvic thrusts, and, occasionally, anal intromission. Chevalier-Skolnikoff described "affectional" ties between pairs of male monkeys who engaged in such homosexual activity; generally an adult male monkey paired with a young male. Once the younger partner began to show evidence of sexual maturity, the intense relationship between the two males lessened and eventually ceased, although they remained "friendly."

An interesting observation is that in no case has preferential, exclusive homosexuality been described in adult nonhuman primates (or any other mammal) when receptive heterosexual partners were available, nor has homosexual behavior ever completely replaced or supplanted heterosexual behavior (Beach, 1976; Gadpaille, 1980).

ORIGINS OF HOMOSEXUALITY

Obviously, in our culture heterosexuality is encouraged, and homosexuality is discouraged. Through cues all around us—advertisements, behavior of others, verbal comments—boys are taught that directing their sexual interests toward girls is appropriate, and girls are taught that being interested in boys is appropriate. To act otherwise is to be "queer." Why, then, do some people develop a sexual preference for members of their own sex? What follows is a brief evaluation of some of the major hypotheses that have been proposed to answer this question. Like most aspects of human behavior, theories of the cause of homosexuality fall into two general categories: those claiming that homosexual interests are a function of genetic, or biological, factors, and those claiming that homosexual interests are a function of social learning or environmental factors.

Genetic Hypothesis

At the outset, it should be noted that men and women who engage in homosexual behavior, whether exclusively or not, have no abnormal chromosomal pattern (Pare, 1956). A few studies have suggested, however, a genetic influence for homosexuality. In 1952 Kallman published a twin study that suggested a rather strong genetic predisposition for homosexuality. He compared the monozygotic, or identical, twin brothers of homosexual men with the dyzygotic, or fraternal, twin brothers of homosexual men. Of the identical twin pairs, all the brothers had some homosexual experience, and more than half were rated by Kallman as exclusive homosexuals. Of the nonidentical twins, half had no homosexual experience, and only three were considered to be predominantly homosexual. The finding of 100 percent agreement for identical twins compared with 12 percent for fraternal twins was astonishing, and almost too perfect.

Since its publication, Kallman's study has been greeted with considerable skepticism. More importantly, Kallman's results have never been replicated by any other investigator. In addition a high concordance rate for identical twins who are raised together does not necessarily mean that common behavioral characteristics (e.g., homosexuality) are a function of genetic factors; the social and parental environment is likely to be the same as well. Further, because of their similar appearance, age, sex, and so forth, people who come in contact with identical twins during their formative years are likely to react to them in a similar manner. There is another obvious reason to be skeptical of a simple genetic hypothesis: Since homosexuals are seldom the offspring of other homosexuals, why hasn't homosexuality been substantially reduced through the evolutionary process of natural selection?

Hormonal Hypothesis

The possible role of hormones in the development of homosexual behavior has received considerable attention. Researchers have tried to determine whether or not a hormonal imbalance exists in adults with a predominantly homosexual orientation as compared with adults with a predominantly heterosexual orientation. Most of these studies have been performed with males, mainly by examination of testosterone levels in blood and urine samples. The findings are contradictory from one experiment to the next: Some investigators have found lower testosterone levels in homosexual males as compared with heterosexual males (Loraine, Adamopoulous, Kirkham, Ismail, and Dove, 1971; Kolodny, Masters, Hendryx, and Toro, 1971), whereas others have reported just the opposite (Brodie, Gartrell, Doering, and Rhue, 1974; Doerr, Pirke, Kockoff, and Dittmar, 1976). In still other studies no difference or considerable overlap in plasma testosterone levels was found between homosexual and heterosexual males (Barlow, Abel, Blanchard, and Mavissakalian, 1974; Pillard, Rose, and Sherwood, 1974). Moreover, although the use of androgens or anti-androgens has been shown to affect overall sex drive, such drugs have not been found to change sexual orientation.

Sex hormone studies with adult female homosexuals have also yielded contradictory findings. Gartrell, Loriaux, and Chase (1977) compared plasma testosterone levels of homosexual and heterosexual women.

Although values for the two groups overlapped considerably, testosterone concentrations were reported to average 38 percent higher in the homosexual sample than in the heterosexual sample. On the other hand, another study reported no difference between the hormone levels of homosexual and heterosexual women (Seyler, Canalis, Spare, and Reichlin, 1978).

Even if the hormonal levels of homosexuals consistently differed from the levels reported by heterosexuals, what would such a result mean? Hormonal levels are influenced by a number of different factors. Low levels of testosterone are also correlated with stress, low sexual desire, depression, low aggression, and other mood states. Similarly, high levels of testosterone could mean high sexual desire, high sexual activity, low stress reactions, or very aggressive feelings. The homosexual and heterosexual groups may differ on these dimensions as well as on sexual preference; for example, perhaps the homosexual sample in one study was more depressed than was the heterosexual sample or vice versa. Thus, testosterone levels may have nothing to do with differences in sexual orientation. Furthermore, if testosterone levels differed between homosexuals and heterosexuals, one could still not say whether or not such a hormonal difference was the cause or the consequence of differences in sexual orientation.

Is it possible that subtle changes in androgen levels during the prenatal period (reduced levels for genetic males and increased levels for genetic females) can predispose humans to adult homosexual behavior? Dörner and his colleagues (1975) answer "yes," with male homosexuals supposedly possessing a predominantly "female-differentiated brain" and female homosexuals a "male-differentiated brain." Studies with animals indicate that this is possible (Meyer-Bahlburg, 1977, 1979). However, there is no direct evidence to support such a hypothesis with humans; in fact, research has suggested that hormonal levels have no effect. Even in the case of gross hormonal disturbances during pregnancy, researchers have found that the way a child is subsequently reared, either as a boy or as a girl, is the overriding influence on both gender identity and sexual preference (Money and Erhardt, 1972). For example, in the adrenogenital syndrome, the fetal female is exposed to large amounts of androgen. Although genetic females, with internal female reproductive organs, these children are born with external male genitals. Money observed a number of such females as they matured, during which time they underwent corrective surgery and continued estrogen treatment. None exhibited homosexual preferences. Yalom, Green, and Fisk (1973) reported similar findings for male fetuses who were exposed to opposite-sex hormones. Studies with other known prenatal hormonal abnormalities in humans all yield the same results. Hormonal factors during the prenatal period may be found someday to play a contributing role in the development of human homosexual behavior, but as yet this possibility has not been established to be the case for either males or females.

Early Psychoanalytic Theory

Freudian theory suggests that the unresolved *Oedipal complex* is the cause of male homosexuality. For example, a boy who attempts to deal with his incestuous feelings for his mother by avoiding all contact with women may eventually find himself more comfortable in homosexual relationships.

Freud's view of lesbianism, though less clearcut and more variable, was based on a similar viewpoint. A young girl having difficulty resolving her attraction for her father, a syndrome known as the *Electra complex,* while also competing with her mother for the father's attention, may be encouraged, according to Freud, to choose a homosexual life-style. Becoming a lesbian could be an avenue of revenge for her, as well as a way of retiring from sexual competition with her mother.

The two major implications of Freudian theory are that (1) homosexuality represents either arrested sexual development or regression caused by disturbed relationships with parents and (2) homosexuality is a result of *heterosexual aversion.* Let us now turn to data that are relevant to each hypothesis to see if they have any empirical support.

☐ *Family Dynamics*   Irving Bieber and his colleagues (1962) performed one of the earliest studies on the relationship between parents and homosexuals. The study compared the family histories of 106 homosexual male patients and 100 heterosexual male patients. According to the information provided by the psychoanalysts, 69 percent of the homosexual patients as compared with 32 percent of the heterosexual patients could be described as having "close, binding, and intimate" (CBI) relationships with their mothers. According to Bieber, the CBI mother was simultaneously seductive and restrictive. She would smother the child in protectiveness and be inappropriately sexual, while at the same time conveying puritanical and rigid attitudes regarding sexual behavior and "masculine" assertiveness. Bieber characterized the CBI mother as favoring the prehomosexual son over the other children and her husband, behavior that would alienate the son from his sources of masculine identification. In Bieber's study, 80 percent of the mothers of homosexuals were described as dominating, 60 percent as overprotective, and 60 percent as preferring the son to the husband and encouraging the child to side with her against the husband.

Bieber felt that the "pathological" effects of such a mother could be neutralized by a warm, affectionate relationship with the father. However, over 80 percent of the fathers of the homosexual patients as compared with 50 percent of the fathers of the heterosexual patients were described as detached and hostile to their sons. Bieber concluded that the *combination* of a CBI mother with a distant, passive, humiliating father increases the tendency for homosexuality in the male child.

In two studies of nonpatient groups, only a portion of Bieber's initial findings were supported (Saghir and Robins, 1973; Siegelman, 1974). Fathers of male homosexuals were reported to be more rejecting and distant than were fathers of male heterosexuals. However, support for the dominant-seductive-over-protective mother was nonexistent. On the other hand, some of the studies comparing nonpatient samples of male homosexuals and heterosexuals are more consistent with Bieber's description of the CBI mother (Evans, 1969; Thompson, Schwartz, McCandless, and Edwards, 1973). In summary, while support for the distant and rejecting father is consistent, results in regard to the mother are contradictory. Why, then, one might ask, is the same-sexed parent more influential? One possible explanation is that a boy who feels rejected by his father has greater difficulty accepting and incorporating his father's model of sexuality.

The family histories of female homosexuals have also been examined. Saghir and Robins (1973) reported one of the most startling differences in parental background between lesbians and matched heterosexual female controls: 39 percent of homosexual women compared with only 5 percent of heterosexual women had lost one or both of their parents due to death or divorce prior to age 10. Lesbians who were raised by both parents also often had poor ties with their same-sexed parent. Only 23 percent of the lesbians as compared with 85 percent of the heterosexuals reported a positive relationship with their mothers (see also Wolff, 1971; Poole, 1972). That lesbians are reporting more disturbed family backgrounds than are women in the heterosexual control groups seems apparent.

Before concluding this section on parental backgrounds of homosexuals, certain methodological cautions should be noted. First, all of the studies cited have relied on retrospective reports by adults of childhood experiences. These may or may not be accurate reflections of what actually took place. Second, although poor family relationships might be associated with homosexuality, existing findings do not allow one to conclude that they are the sole cause of homosexuality. For one thing, a substantial percentage of homosexuals do not report such disturbances, and an equally substantial percentage of heterosexuals do. Thus, family dynamics may be considered as only one of many contributing factors.

☐ *Heterosexual Aversion*   Psychoanalytic theory suggests that a homosexual orientation, especially in males, is always associated with anxiety regarding heterosexual activity. Although studies on homosexuals in therapy support this idea, data on nonpatient samples indicate that heterosexual aversion is not typical. Numerous surveys of male homosexuals reveal that a substantial percentage have experienced heterosexual intercourse sometime in their lives (see Table 7–1).

The usual self-report is not that heterosexual activity was aversive, but simply that it was less satisfying than was homosexual activity. Anxiety and/or revulsion in response to heterosexual situations is much less common than is mild disinterest or even mild interest.

TABLE 7–1   PERCENTAGE OF MALE HOMOSEXUALS WHO HAVE HAD HETEROSEXUAL INTERCOURSE

STUDY	PERCENTAGE
Westwood (1960)	42
Schofield (1965)	34
Manosevitz (1970)	57
Saghir & Robins (1973)	48
Bell & Weinberg (1979)	66

The figures in Table 7–2 indicate that female homosexuals, as compared with male homosexuals, are even less apt to have avoided heterosexual activity. The women reported that much of their heterosexual experience was obtained as a result of curiosity, social pressure, and the desire to have a family. Looking back on these experiences, most lesbians do not report associated anxiety or repulsion. Rather,

TABLE 7–2   PERCENTAGE OF LESBIANS WHO HAVE HAD HETEROSEXUAL INTERCOURSE

STUDY	PERCENTAGE
Gundlach (1967)	75
Kenyon (1968)	58
Saghir & Robins (1973)	79
Bell & Weinberg (1979)	85*

*Only refers to a subsample of white homosexual females with a Kinsey rating of 5 or 6.

heterosexual activity was simply not as enjoyable or as emotionally gratifying as their homosexual experiences. Such data should help dispel the belief that the only reason a woman would be homosexually involved is because she cannot attract a man. This theory may boost male egos, but it has no factual basis.

Sex-Role Pressure

Some studies have suggested that by choosing a homosexual orientation, the male may be withdrawing from competition with other males (e.g., Thompson, 1947). Rather rigid stereotypes of masculine aggressive behavior have long been a part of almost every contemporary society. No matter where one looks—Europe, Asia, Africa, North and South America—this pattern prevails. In the United States, for example, males are under unmistakable pressure to compete and win and to be successful, brave, strong, and dominant. Perhaps cultures with exaggerated sex differences, which place special emphasis on male supremacy, may produce males who do not have the temperaments to meet these strong role expectations (West, 1977). Homosexuality may be a means of escape for these men.

Sex-role stereotypes of masculinity can encourage homosexuality in another way: Boys who prefer toys and activities that are usually associated with girls are often labeled "sissies," a classification that can be damaging. A boy may begin to feel like an "oddball" because he doesn't like sports and rough and tumble play, and he may experience isolation among his peers. A young boy approaching adolescence may think such unconventional play preferences, timidity, and fear of violence mean that he is homosexually inclined; eventually he may act on this belief. Social reaction to his personality traits may further influence his behavior. The effects of peer pressure on the development of one's sexual orientation is examined in Box 7-1.

Several recent studies support the theory that early childhood behavior contributes to adult homosexuality. Saghir and Robins (1973) found that 67 percent of the male homosexuals in their sample, in contrast with only 3 percent of the male heterosexuals, considered themselves to be effeminate during preadolescence; in general, they had no male buddies; played more with girls than with boys; participated little, if at all, in sports; and were called "sissy" by others.

It seems safe to conclude that a clear failure to pursue traditional masculine patterns of behavior during preadolescence is sometimes associated with male homosexuality in adulthood. Of course, such childhood indicators do not cause all instances of male homosexuality. Indeed, a substantial percentage of male homosexuals do not show such childhood characteristics, and a larger percentage of boys who do engage in such behavior do not turn out to be homosexual. In addition, some other common factors (e.g., temperament or parental rearing patterns) could underlie both atypical childhood behavior patterns and adult homosexuality. Furthermore,

ADOLESCENT PEER RELATIONSHIPS: A VIGNETTE

Walter is a 47-year-old business executive. His view of his homosexuality (with which I agree) is that a crucial factor in its development was the problems he had during adolescence with his schoolmates, especially his male peers. He came from a family not like those described by Bieber as typical for homosexuality. His mother was the passive parent and was quite devoted to her husband. Walter's relationship with his father was close and, he feels, quite satisfactory. He says his childhood was very happy.

When he entered high school, however, he began to have troubles. He was rather clumsy and never good at athletics, in which he had no interest anyway. (It might be added that neither did his father, so even if his father was a good role model, Walter certainly wouldn't have picked up any such interests from him.) As a result of this disinterest and inability at sports, he became isolated from his age-mates, who all considered athletic interest a sine qua non for social acceptance and gave the greatest prestige to athletic stars. As a complicating factor, Walter had a fairly severe case of acne during his early teens, and so was considered unattractive by the good-looking girls at school.

As a result of all this, he began to feel that maybe there was something amiss in his masculinity. He formed a friendship with another outcast who, unlike Walter, had effeminate mannerisms. They finally engaged in some homosexual experiences, which were not at first defined as such, but which they later came to regard as gay. (Unlike most of their classmates, both were interested in reading, and they eventually discovered that there was such a thing as homosexuality. They then had to admit to themselves that they were engaging in homosexual acts.)

From this point in his life, Walter's sexual development took a definitely homosexual course. By the time he got to college he was ready and eager to enter the gay world. He feels that if he had been accepted socially by his high school peers he might have developed in a more "normal" direction. While this cannot be proved, it is hard to imagine that his adolescent problems did not have a profound effect on his sexual orientation.

From Hoffman, 1968, pp. 150–151.

since retrospective self-reports are the major source of these findings, one cannot rule out the possibility of distortion. An accurate recollection of childhood experiences is never easy, and for a variety of reasons professed homosexuals tend to convey the impression that "I was always this way." All that has been shown to date is that some predictive, not causative, link between these self-reports and later homosexual practices is present in a certain percentage of male homosexuals.

As yet, similar links have not been as clearly demonstrated for female homosexuals, perhaps because there is somewhat less pressure on fulfilling stereotyped sex-role expectations in young girls by comparison with young boys. In one study, however, 70 percent of a lesbian sample in contrast to only 16 percent of a heterosexual female control group reported that they were tomboys as children (Saghir and Robins, 1973). As with males, such retrospective self-reports need to be interpreted with caution.

Early Sexual Experience

Some studies comparing the early sexual development of adult male homosexuals and heterosexuals provide support for the notion that homosexuals tend to be somewhat sexually precocious. For example, more homosexual men reported having experienced sexual arousal prior to age 14 than did heterosexual males (Manosevitz, 1970; Saghir and Robins, 1973). Furthermore, for the vast majority, first homosexual encounters resulting in arousal involved genital contact with a male, whereas heterosexual males report that in their initial sexual contacts arousal was usually the result of nongenital contact with a female (e.g., kissing and necking). Psychosexual responses such as sexual fantasy and romantic attraction were also reported to occur more often in preadolescence for homosexuals than for heterosexuals.

Based on these results, one has to consider seriously the possibility that males

who become sexually mature at an earlier age are more likely to experience gratifying homosexual encounters and, as a result, have an increased likelihood of maintaining a homosexual orientation. On the other hand, studies show that a large percentage of adult male heterosexuals also had early homosexual experiences (Kinsey et al., 1948; Brady and Levitt, 1965; Schofield, 1965). These findings indicate that early homosexual behavior does not automatically mean that as an adult a man will be homosexual. Obviously, people follow different patterns of development. The evidence is sufficient, however, to conclude that satisfactory homosexual experiences in adolescence and adulthood can contribute to the development and maintenance of a homosexual orientation.

Survey studies of lesbians suggest a somewhat different pattern of development. Sexual activity usually occurs later for most lesbians than it does for male homosexuals and is typically a gradual outgrowth of an intense emotional attachment to another female (Saghir and Robins, 1973). In addition, female homosexuals often delay any overt expression of their homosexuality, with first physical contact taking place about five years after they have become aware of their homoerotic feelings.

Despite this difference in age of onset, most lesbians surveyed described their first sexual encounter with a same-sexed peer in positive terms (Hedblom, 1973; Hogan, Fox, and Kirchner, 1977). As in the case of males, sexual arousal occurred at an earlier age for prehomosexual females than for preheterosexual females (Saghir and Robins, 1973). Therefore, although female homosexuals do not get involved in sexual activity as early as do male homosexuals, they may still develop sexual interests earlier than their heterosexual counterparts; the positive nature of their earliest homosexual experience undoubtedly determines whether or not some females continue with this activity.

Conclusions Regarding the Origins of Homosexuality

Most researchers agree that human behavior is usually an outgrowth of an interaction between biological and environmental factors. Evidence collected to date certainly supports this interactionist model in regard to the development of homosexuality.

No single, overriding cause of homosexuality has been discovered, nor is it likely that any will be discovered in the future. Homosexuality is a very complex pattern of human behavior, and research suggests that what predisposes any single individual to prefer one orientation over another is probably determined by a number of factors: genetic and hormonal influences, relationships with same-sexed and/or opposite-sexed parents, failure to conform to masculine and feminine pressures during childhood, peer relationships, and earliest sexual experiences. Not all of these factors remain unchanged over a person's lifetime, and how they interact to account for homosexuality (or heterosexuality) is unknown. As with a jigsaw puzzle, even if all the pieces are handy, fitting them together is not an easy task. Furthermore, we have only described what appear to be the major pieces in this "puzzle." Undoubtedly, for any given individual, several other factors play a part.

HOMOSEXUAL IDENTITY AND "COMING OUT"

At some point we all become aware of our sexual interests. We begin to like, feel attracted to, or imagine enjoying a sexual experience with someone else. In our society, these stirrings usually occur during adolescence, and they are usually tolerated or even encouraged.

This point of self-awareness is far more traumatic if a person is attracted to someone of the same sex. Societal forces, including family, peers, and the broader culture, work against homosexual interests.

The consequences of letting homosexual inclinations be known may be complete or partial rejection from people who were previously sources of support—namely, friends and family. Simply to admit to oneself a homosexual orientation can be frightening. The only terms a young adolescent may have to apply to his or her feelings are extremely negative—for example, "fag," "queer," "fairy," "pansy," or "dyke." Understandably, the years that precede full-fledged acceptance of the homosexual label are often ones of internal turmoil and self-doubt. Accepting for oneself a socially unacceptable form of sexuality is not easy, and some people in fact never do.

Coming out is a term that can have several meanings. It can refer to that period in a person's life when complete self-recognition and acceptance of one's homosexuality takes place. It can also refer to the first public identification with the gay community. Warren (1974) distinguishes between a "homosexual identity" and a "gay identity." The former simply describes one's sexual orientation, whereas the latter implies overt affiliation with other homosexuals.

"Coming out" in the sense of openly admitting one's homosexual interest both to one's self and to others means coming out of the "closet." It can also mean *coming into* an alternative means of defense against the public attitude toward homosexuality and all of the sources of rejection that homosexuals face. That defense, or shelter against social prohibitions, is the gay subculture, or homosexual community. A homosexual community generally can be defined as a loosely knit group of people who share common interests and have a social life that revolves around being homosexual. One clear function of this community is to help neutralize the stigma of homosexuality.

For many homosexuals, restricting leisure time activity to interactions with other homosexuals results in greater self-acceptance (Weinberg and Williams, 1974). The subculture can provide a sense of belonging and support for being part of a minority subgroup. Like ethnic, racial, and religious minorities, homosexuals, by joining together and by sharing beliefs and attitudes, can develop a feeling of unity. A dramatic reconceptualization can take place in which a homosexual life-style is portrayed as being desirable rather than undesirable, something to be proud of rather than to conceal in shame. Many homosexuals no longer question whether they are "sick" or deviant; rather, they have adopted a positive ideology characterized by the slogan, "Gay is Good."

Homophile organizations and the Gay Liberation Movement have been important forces in fostering a sense of community and legitimacy for homosexuals. Homosexual organizations range from the more conservative groups such as the Mattachine Society and the Daughters of Bilitis to the more radical groups such as the Gay Liberation Front and the Gay Activists Alliance. More than just support groups, the homophile organizations provide legal advice and referral services, lobby on behalf of homosexual civil liberties, and publish newspapers and magazines. Such activities can have a powerful effect on the beliefs and behavior of the homosexual subcommunity. For example, the *Advocate,* a national homophile newspaper based in Los Angeles, publicized the fact that the Metropolitan Community Church was welcoming gays and wished to serve the religious interests of homosexuals in the area. As a result, church attendance grew phenomenally.

Self-identification as a homosexual and even open participation in the gay com-

Gay pride parade; a mother and son demonstrating in support of gay rights.

munity does not necessarily mean that an individual will voluntarily reveal his or her homosexuality to people in the "straight" world. Because they fear rejection, ridicule, or the possibility of losing a job, many homosexuals are cautious when it comes to revealing the social-sexual side of their lives. The decision regarding how open to be about one's sexual preference—whether to tell no one in the heterosexual community, to tell just one or two people, or to be completely open about it—is often a difficult one.

Deciding whether or not to tell parents about one's homosexuality is a particularly stressful dilemma. In not telling them, the young homosexual must often silently accept parents' constant prodding about heterosexual relationships and marriage. Lesbians probably suffer from this kind of parental pressure, especially pressure to marry, more often than their male counterparts because women, in general, are expected to seek approval from and to be more open with their parents (Weinberg, 1972). More important, trying to maintain secrecy often provokes anxiety, and a sense of hypocrisy can threaten a person's feelings of self-esteem. Yet telling parents also can be very frightening because there is a good possibility that they will react with disappointment, confusion, guilt, and even rejection. Here is how one homosexual felt:

> My mother asked me if I was gay and I told her. It was a very painful experience and I cried all day because I didn't want her to find out and was afraid she would reject me forever. She and I get along quite well now and she no longer hassles me about my friends or activities. I have introduced her to a lot of my friends and she seemed to like them. They are all very level-headed people and very straight-acting. Now that my mother knows about me I don't worry about anyone else, because I feel that the worst is over. I'm not sure if my father knows or not. (Jay and Young, 1977, p. 150)

If parental bonds have been weak and marked by indifference and hostility or if the child has moved out of the house previous to admitting his or her homosexuality, the possibility of parental rejection may be less painful. But if a homosexual is living at home and/or values close parental ties, the subject of "coming out" may be traumatic.

Opening up to heterosexual friends and co-workers can also be difficult. Although peer bonds may be less intense than those that exist between child and parents, their meaning and importance to a person's current life-style may be far more crucial.

Some friends, like some parents, react negatively when a person admits to being gay. They might experience concern about their own reputation (especially if they are same-sexed friends). Friends may also have an unclear idea of what homosexuality is and be afraid that their gay friend may try to "convert" or proposition them. Such concerns have little basis, mainly because most homosexuals avoid sexual overtures out of respect for their friends and fear of rejection.

For married homosexuals to reveal homosexual interests is particularly stressful, for both husband and wife. The spouse of the homosexual feels betrayed, rejected, and often questions his or her own attractiveness. The anguish of one married homosexual is evident in the following statement:

> I dislike the dishonesty of presenting one face to the world and another to my gay acquaintances. However, I dislike much, much more the mindless abuse and resulting misery that comes with complete sexual revelations. Very little would be gained for the cause by my "coming out." The damage done to my parents and my wife and boys would be horrendous and far-reaching in their devastation. It would not be fair to them nor to myself. It is relatively easy for a single gay living in a big city to declare himself. It is impossible for a family and community man to let it be known to everyone that he is gay, even in 1977. At least that's my opinion. (Jay and Young, 1977, p. 146)

Although recent media attention and open discussion of homosexuality might suggest that fewer homosexuals need be concerned about disclosing their homosexuality to others, there is still considerable variation in how candid most homosexuals choose to be. In the most recent survey conducted, the majority of homosexuals were found to be relatively secretive about their homosexual preferences (Bell and Weinberg, 1979).

Obviously, many homosexuals continue to be discreet when it comes to revealing their sexual preferences to the heterosexual community. Perhaps maintaining two separate identities is not as stressful as many professionals have assumed. To some extent, heterosexuals also compartmentalize their sexual behavior. Although one's sexual choices are very important, they do not have to affect all aspects of life.

THE SEXUAL BEHAVIOR OF HOMOSEXUAL MALES

Stimulation Techniques

What do male homosexuals do in bed? The simplest and most direct answer is that homosexuals do everything heterosexuals do, except vaginal intercourse. According to a recent U.S. survey, the four most common sexual practices are oral-genital stimulation (fellatio), manual-genital stimulation, anal intercourse, and full body contact (genital apposition) (Bell and Weinberg, 1979). Although there are different preferences among individuals, the old stereotype that some only take the passive (insertee) role while others the active (inserter) role applies only to a small number. Instead, the vast majority of male homosexuals engage in both roles.

In a laboratory setting, when comparing sexual interaction among heterosexual and homosexual couples who had been partners for some time and had a committed relationship to each other, Masters and Johnson, (1979) found complete overlap in the physiological response to genital stimulation in homosexual and heterosexual males. They did observe several differences in behavior, however, the most notable being greater prior verbal communication of likes and dislikes and more prolonged and gradual sexual stimulation among homosexual couples than among heterosexual couples. In their words, "More time was taken in low-key, non-demanding genital play in male-male interactions than in female-male genital stimulation" (Masters and Johnson, 1979, p. 72).

As we learned in Chapter Six, open communication is essential in sexual relationships. Partners of the same sex may already have an edge on knowing what each other will enjoy, judging from their own preferences, and they may find it easier to discuss sexual techniques with each other.

Number of Sexual Partners

Casual, transient relationships with a large number of different partners is much more common among homosexual males than among heterosexual males. For example, in the most extensive, up-to-date, and probably most representative survey of male homosexuals ever done, Bell and Weinberg (1979) reported that of 574 white homosexual males, 84 percent had experienced sexual relations with 50 or more partners, and 43 percent with 500 or more partners. For the black homosexual male sample the comparable percentages were 77 percent with 50 or more different partners and 33 percent with 500 or more different partners. To a heterosexually oriented male these statistics are incredible; they are completely outside of his experience and perhaps even beyond his wildest fantasies.

Why is there such a difference? Are male homosexuals by nature more **promiscuous,** or do they have higher sex drives than heterosexual males? Or, are all males similarly inclined, with the limiting factor being different degrees of opportunity, different social support systems, and different life-styles? Are the decisive factors the availability of female partners and female preferences? In fact, this issue is a very complex one with no single explanation.

We must understand that while one person may have had sexual relations with 1,000 partners, the frequency of sex may be less than that of a person who has had only one partner in a lifetime. Kinsey and his associates found that at any age, only one homosexual in twenty had as much sex as the average married, young, heterosexual male (Kinsey et al., 1948). Although more recent studies suggest that the number of homosexual contacts per week has increased, the general direction of Kinsey's findings has been confirmed. Because of the difficulty in finding acceptable partners and sustaining an intimate relationship with a given partner for a long period of time, homosexual men tend to have a lower frequency of sexual activity than do heterosexual men.

Even though promiscuity at some stage is common, a significant percentage of male homosexuals do establish sustained relationships. Why don't more do so? And why don't these relationships last longer? The following is the perspective of one male homosexual.

The beginning of a homosexual relationship is just the opposite of heterosexual courtship. There you start out with a common social background and have emotional rapport in a mild pleasant recreational sense, then you gradually work up to more intense relationships. You start out with a community of interests. Theoretically you meet these girls in a situation where you have something in common with this girl (e.g., same school, neighborhood club); if things go well, then you build up to an intimate sexual relationship. Homosexuality, this is the opposite. You start out with sex and it may be the most sensual, hedonistic, animalistic thing you can think of. First you think of your partners as objects, then you get to know them as persons. And if you have a very strong promiscuous background and there is some point about the sexual behavior you don't like, then you go on and get something else which is more interesting. You have to work at building a friendship, it just doesn't happen. Although it's not a necessity, I usually don't consider a person my friend until I've known him a year. You have to see him in a variety of situations, and you have to try to get out of a sexual dead end where you're just seeing him as a bed partner. That's not an easy thing to do. Living in a city, where friendships can easily be replaced, the temptation for anonymity and running around irresponsibly is so great that the urge to build a friendship has to be cultivated. (Gagnon and Simon, 1973, p. 147)

"Promiscuity" has negative connotations when applied to either heterosexual or homosexual relations. It implies lack of commitment, love, and intimacy. Sex without obligation and emotional involvement, however, can provide excitement, freedom, and sexual variety. Perhaps many male homosexuals simply do not agree that to have frequent sexual encounters with relative strangers is wrong. Such an outlook is hard to accept. Most people, regardless of sexual orientation, want to establish close, affectionate ties with others. An unending or exclusive pattern of one-time sexual encounters is just as likely to be damaging for homosexuals as it is for heterosexuals. In fact, few homosexuals ever report wanting to limit their sexual experiences to impersonal contacts (Bell and Weinberg, 1979).

Frequent shifts in male homosexual partners can be explained in a variety of ways. An often heard argument is that heterosexual couples would break up as readily if it were not for the pressures of parental responsibility, economic and legal constraints, and social tradition. Another explanation is that the gay male community contains a network of public facilities (gay bars, baths, and restrooms) that encourage brief sexual encounters. It is also noteworthy that lesbians do not tend to exhibit the same promiscuous sexual pattern as do male homosexuals. Thus, promiscuity is not a homosexual "problem" per se, but, instead, a male "problem." Although this is speculative, perhaps if heterosexual males were not limited by the tendency of many females to avoid impersonal, brief sexual relationships they too might have as many partners as homosexual males.

Seeking Sexual Partners

Male homosexuals have established a subculture in which casual sexual partners can be found with relative ease in places such as gay bars, gay baths, public restrooms, certain areas of parks, on certain streets, and at highway rest stops that have an established homosexual reputation. The term **cruising** is sometimes used to describe the process of seeking a sexual partner in bars, parks, and so forth.

The most frequented of these public locations is the gay bar. The sexual emphasis may vary; some fulfill the social functions of a neighborhood bar, while others serve almost exclusively as sexual meeting places (Hoffman, 1968; see also Hooker, 1965). In this environment, homosexuals need not hide their homosexuality; a known homosexual clientele eliminates any need to dread rejection and prejudicial reactions.

Gay baths are similar to gay bars in that sexual partners are easily found in both settings. Gay baths are licensed "health clubs" that provide the male homosexual community with a setting in which impersonal sex can take place (Weinberg and Williams,

A gay naval officer and his lover in 1982, one of the few instances where a dishonorable discharge based on sexual preference was later reversed.

1975). Operated as private clubs, they offer some protection against police intrusion and inadvertent attendance by naive heterosexuals. The baths also protect their clientele by encouraging anonymity and by reducing the chance of theft or assault, which is otherwise an ever-present danger in the pursuit of impersonal sexual encounters.

Other locations for seeking out sexual contacts are more public, such as restrooms in bus terminals, parks, streets, and highway rest stops. While they are all public locations in the sense that anyone can enter the area, an underground grape-vine pinpoints the "hot spots." The restroom encounter provides what is sometimes referred to as "instant" sex. The sexual interchange is brief, completely anonymous, and carried out in silence. One investigator found that a large number of participants were actually predominantly heterosexual — over half were married — and were using restrooms as meeting places to obtain quick, free oral-genital sex (Humphreys, 1970). The remainder were either bisexuals or homosexuals ("closet queens") who did not want to jeopardize their reputations by appearing in obvious homosexual settings such as gay bars.

THE SEXUAL BEHAVIOR OF HOMOSEXUAL FEMALES

Stimulation Techniques

Adult female homosexuals in the United States prefer three major kinds of sexual stimulation: manual-genital stimulation, oral-genital stimulation (cunnilingus), and full body contact (genital apposition or body rubbing). Insertion of a **dildo** or other inanimate object into the vagina of one partner by the other appears to be a relatively uncommon practice (Saghir and Robins, 1973). Although most research points to manual-genital stimulation as being the most frequently used sexual technique, the one most preferred by about half of the female homosexuals in the Bell and Weinberg (1979) study is cunnilingus.

Contrary to popular assumptions, sexual behavior between women seldom reflects any distinct "butch-femme" sex-role stereotypes. Instead, women typically alternate giving and receiving each form of stimulation preferred by their partner. For example, Saghir and Robins (1973) report that 91 percent of their lesbian sample had orally stimulated their partners, while 96 percent had received oral-genital stimulation.

Kinsey and his associates (1953) compared orgasmic response in women married five years with equally experienced lesbians. Among married heterosexual women, 30 percent reported that on most occasions they did not achieve orgasm during sexual relations. By comparison, the figure for homosexual women, 14 percent, was lower. If these self-reports are accurate, one possible reason lesbians may be more orgasmic during homosexual activity is that more sexual stimulation is provided by a homosexual female partner than by a heterosexual male partner. Masters and Johnson (1979) reported that committed lesbian couples spent a great deal of time holding, kissing, and caressing the total body area before any specific approach was made to breasts or genitals. In contrast, males in heterosexual interactions rarely waited longer than 30 seconds to 1 minute before directly stimulating their partners breasts and/or genitals. Genital stimulation also differed. The lesbians almost always stimulated the labia, mons, inner thighs, and vaginal outlet *before* the clitoris was stimulated directly; this sequence only happened in about 50 percent of the heterosexual interactions (Masters and Johnson, 1979).

Number of Sexual Partners

The number of sexual partners reported by lesbians is much more comparable to the number reported by heterosexually inclined women and nowhere near the number reported by male homosexuals. In the 1979 study by Bell and Weinberg, only 7 percent of the white homosexual females as compared with 84 percent of the males reported having had fifty or more homosexual partners. Furthermore, only 6 percent of

In our society isn't it more common to see two women rather than two men hugging each other? Why do you think this is?

the female homosexuals as compared with 79 percent of the male homosexuals reported that more than half of their partners were strangers.

Some of the other differences in sexual patterns of female and male homosexuals are striking. For example, lesbians are more likely than are male homosexuals to be involved in long-standing affairs. In the 20- to 29-year-old age group, Saghir and Robins (1973) found that 82 percent of the lesbians but only 41 percent of the homosexual males were involved in a relationship that had lasted for more than a year, and a larger number of homosexual women than men lived with their partners. In keeping with these findings, researchers further reported that fidelity was characteristically found in long-lasting female homosexual relationships but not in long-lasting male relationships (Saghir and Robins, 1973; Bell and Weinberg, 1979).

Why do female homosexuals have so many fewer sexual partners than do male homosexuals, and such different relationships? Perhaps a basic difference in biological drives between the two genders is partially responsible. Gagnon and Simon

(1973), however, suggest that cultural factors may play an even more important role, as "for most women, including most lesbians, the pursuit of sexual gratification as something separate from emotional or romantic involvement is not particularly attractive; indeed, for many, it is an idea so strange as to be impossible" (p. 182). These authors believe that women—whether homosexually or heterosexually inclined—have been socialized to deemphasize the sexual aspects of a relationship and to emphasize the emotional ones. It should also be noted that Western society is more tolerant of women living together, dancing together, showing affection for one another (e.g., hugging and kissing) than it is of similar behavior exhibited by males. Thus, lesbians are less driven by social prohibitions into fleeting and furtive sexual encounters.

Seeking Sexual Partners

Lesbians are most likely to find sexual partners through friends, at informal social gatherings, at meetings of feminist groups, or at work. There is little counterpart to the cruising behavior of male homosexuals: gay baths and restroom, street, and park activity are not part of the lesbian life-style. In addition, although gay bars for women can be found in many cities, they are fewer, less frequently attended, and do not serve the same sexual marketplace function as they so often do for male homosexuals. The obvious sexual trafficking that characterizes many male gay bars is seldom seen. Instead, the lesbian bars serve primarily as a social meeting place where gay women can relax together in a somewhat protected environment.

I'm probably most comfortable meeting other lesbians through mutual friends as opposed to the bar scene as I'm not into cruising, and I think a lot of bar women are. I should say I'm a novice to the singles scene, as my first relationship evolved ideally, with her moving from co-worker to friend to close friend to lover over a period of time. I'm not by nature a shy person, once I've had a chance to observe a person for a while. Of course some women are easier to relate to than others. (Jay and Young, 1977, p. 221)

PSYCHOLOGICAL AND SOCIAL ADJUSTMENT

Throughout most of the twentieth century homosexuality was considered by definition a sign of mental illness. Perhaps the following exchange tells the story best. One psychiatrist supposedly said to another, "All my homosexual patients are quite sick," whereupon the second psychiatrist retorted, "So are all my heterosexual patients." The moral: Professional perspectives can be easily distorted by limited experience with nonrepresentative samples. In 1973, however, the American Psychiatric Association (APA) declassified homosexuality from its list of disorders. This action was taken in part because data accumulated from nonclinical samples of homosexuals failed to substantiate its mental illness classification, and in part as a conciliatory response to mounting political pressure from the Gay Liberation Movement.

The two specific clinical problems that seem to occur more often among homosexuals than among matched heterosexuals are alcohol abuse and suicide attempts (Saghir and Robins, 1973; Bell and Weinberg, 1979). What causes this difference is unknown. It may simply stem from negative societal pressure, which heterosexuals do not have to endure. Another possibility, in the case of males, is that a heavy reliance on bars as social meeting places, combined with an unrelenting pursuit of sexual activity without emotional involvement, may also be mentally taxing. In this regard, Bell and Weinberg (1979) found that male homosexuals with stable partnerships were less likely to exhibit psychological problems.

Studies using standard psychological tests and rating scales suggest that there is little difference in scores of personal or psychological adjustment between homosexual and heterosexual male samples (Manosevitz, 1970; Siegelman, 1972a, 1978; Thompson, McCandless, and Strickland, 1971). In addition, a number of studies have found that lesbian samples were either no more or were *less* neurotic according to test scores than were heterosexual controls (Gundlach and Riess, 1968; Hopkins, 1969; Wilson and Green, 1971; Siegelman, 1972b; Adelman, 1977). These studies also found that lesbians were more dominant, self-accepting, self-sufficient, independent, and resilient than were their heterosexual counterparts.

One flaw in almost all of these studies is that homosexual subjects are recruited from homophile organizations and other parts of the accessible gay community (e.g., gay bars). Whether or not these samples are representative of the general homosexual population cannot be determined. Despite this qualification, the vast majority of homosexuals apparently suffer no severe psychopathology, and the following conclusion still seems to be accurate: "Many homosexuals are neither as maladjusted as many psychiatrists have suggested nor as well adjusted as many homosexuals would like the public to think" (Weinberg and Williams, 1974, p. 100).

Aging is often described as a time of exceptional stress for male homosexuals. The homosexual subculture is supposedly even more youth oriented than is the heterosexual culture, and the aging, homosexually oriented male is less likely than the heterosexual male to have a family or a stable partnership to rely on. Consequently, the belief is widespread that the elderly homosexual is likely to be lonely and disillusioned. This assumption may be exaggerated. For example, although Weinberg and Williams (1974) found that older homosexual males were more likely to be living alone, having less sex, and frequenting gay bars less, they were *not* more likely to report psychological problems such as anxiety, depression, or loneliness. Older male homosexuals did not have to be as concerned about exposure of their homosexuality, they had more stable self-concepts, and they were less effeminate; interestingly, each of these concerns in the younger homosexual is correlated with greater psychological distress. In another study of aging male homosexuals, the number of persons involved in stable liaisons seemed to increase with age, reaching a peak in this sample of 59 percent for those between 46 and 55 years of age and then declining rapidly thereafter, partly due to death of a partner (Kelly, 1980).

THERAPY AND HOMOSEXUALITY

Psychotherapy with homosexuals has typically followed two different tracks: Either to enhance homosexual adjustment or to initiate or broaden heterosexual activity. These goals are usually perceived as being mutually exclusive, although there is no logical reason why this should always be the case.

Box 7-2 contains a reproduction of a famous letter written by Freud to an American mother in 1935. Once again, he was way ahead of his contemporaries. The opinions expressed in this letter are more in line with present views than with any previous time period.

Surveys indicate that a substantial number of homosexuals have at some time in their lives sought therapeutic counseling. The most typical reasons are (1) to deal with distressing feelings of depression, anxiety and so forth, (2) to gain insight into past and present behavior, and (3) to be better able to deal with a homosexual orientation. Therapy in these instances is designed to improve one's adjustment to homosexuality, to reduce conflicts, guilt, and fear about homosexuality, and to alleviate psychological disturbances that may be an outgrowth of the conflict between a homosexual orientation and a hostile society. Nowadays these goals are relatively noncontroversial—except to those who have strong religious beliefs opposed to homosexuality. Saghir and Robins (1973) reported that although the majority of homosexual males and females who sought therapy felt they gained from it, many also had negative experiences.

Much greater controversy arises—especially in the homosexual community and among professionals—if the aim of therapy is to promote change in a person's sexual orientation. Just the prospect of such a "conversion" or a reversal to a predominant or exclusive heterosexual orientation stirs deep feelings of outrage. Assuming for the moment that a homosexual orientation could be modified, many object even to making the attempt (e.g., Davison, 1976). These people believe that any homosexual who desires a change in sex preference is responding to negative social pressure. Furthermore, they argue that the mental health professional's job is

Box 7–2

A LETTER FROM FREUD

Dear Mrs. X:

I gather from your letter that your son is a homosexual. I am most impressed by the fact that you do not mention this term yourself in your information about him. May I question you, why do you avoid it? Homosexuality is assuredly no advantage, but it is nothing to be ashamed of, no vice, no degradation, it cannot be classified as an illness; we consider it to be a variation of the sexual function produced by a certain arrest of sexual development. Many highly respectable individuals of ancient and modern times have been homosexuals, several of the greatest men among them (Plato, Michelangelo, Leonardo da Vinci, etc.). It is a great injustice to persecute homosexuality as a crime, and cruelty too. If you do not believe me, read the books of Havelock Ellis.

By asking me if I can help you, you mean, I suppose, if I can abolish homosexuality and make normal heterosexuality take its place. The answer is, in a general way, we cannot promise to achieve it. In a certain number of cases we succeed in developing the heterosexual tendencies which are present in every homosexual, in the majority of cases it is no more possible. It is a question of the quality and the age of the individual. The result of the treatment cannot be predicted.

What analysis can do for your son runs in a different line. If he is unhappy, neurotic, torn by conflicts, inhibited in his social life, analysis may bring him harmony, peace of mind, full efficiency, whether he remains a homosexual or gets changed. If you make up your mind he should have analysis with me!! I don't expect you will!! He has to come over to Vienna. I have no intention of leaving here. However, don't neglect to give me your answer.

Sincerely yours with kind wishes,

Freud

P.S. I did not find it difficult to read your handwriting. Hope you will not find my writing and my English a harder task.

From Freud, 1935, as reprinted in *American Journal of Psychiatry,* 1951.

always to help the individual withstand such pressure, not to give in to it. Others question the wisdom of this strong advocacy position; they believe that the professional is there to help the individual achieve his or her goals, not the therapist's social goals. Motivation is an important aspect to consider, but it can be questioned only so far. A strong desire to abide by social convention or to respect religious teachings should not be dismissed. Furthermore, negative pressure may not be the only motivation for seeking change. Some homosexuals sincerely desire children and a stable heterosexual family life-style.

Considering the ideological commitment associated with assuming a gay identity, a surprisingly high percentage of male homosexuals admit to some regret about their homosexuality. Different studies offer different figures on the percentage of male homosexuals who at one time or another seriously wished to make a change in their sexual orientation; the figures range from slightly over 25 percent in the Bell and Weinberg (1979) study to 62 percent in the Saghir and Robins (1973) report. (Female homosexuals have been found to express less regret and less desire for change in sexual orientation than do male homosexuals. Lesbians are possibly more content because they are not faced with as much social condemnation as are male homosexuals, and they have fewer social restrictions, thus resulting in a greater degree of self-acceptance and psychological adjustment.)

Despite occasional feelings of regret, the majority of homosexuals who seek psycho-

therapeutic assistance do not do so to change their homosexual preference. Even of those who do want to change, few believe change is possible, and they therefore do not seriously consider it. The vast majority of homosexuals seem to believe that a homosexual orientation is a fixed characteristic, something established either by genetics or by some early set of developmental experiences. Such pessimism about the possibility of changing one's sexual orientation is echoed by the professional community, and its roots can be traced back to Freud, as we learned in his letter highlighted in Box 7-2. Is this view still justified? What does the evidence suggest? (We can only consider the male homosexual because outcome statistics on treatment studies with substantial samples of female homosexuals have never been reported. Therapists rarely encounter female homosexuals who are seeking to change their sexual orientation.)

Simple age-specific incidence figures indicate that regardless of treatment, changes in orientation do take place. Although one-quarter to one-third of the male population in the United States has had some homosexual experience in their lifetimes, this experience is mostly confined to adolescence (Gebhard, 1972). In other words, they change orientation as they become adults.

Numerous treatment studies have been reported in the past twenty-five years, and to review them in any detail here would be impossible. One of the major problems with these studies is determining the appropriate measure of successful outcome: Do all homosexual desires have to be suppressed or is a complete cessation of overt homosexual behavior sufficient? For how long? Why try to suppress homosexual behavior in the first place? Is it sufficient simply to increase heterosexual experience, especially when this behavior was completely absent at the outset of treatment? What is meant by "successful" heterosexual experiences? Is intercourse the major criterion? If so, does the number of times define success? Or is success measured by the time spent in heterosexual relationships — say six months, one year, two years, or five years? If the goal is sustained suppression of all homosexual desires and behavior plus complete involvement in a full heterosexual life-style, the results of most treatment studies suggest that, at best, moderate success rates can be expected.

Most of the early outcome studies (e.g., Bieber, 1962; Curran and Parr, 1957; Freund, 1960; Woodward, 1958) reported "successful" outcomes in 30 percent or less of the homosexuals treated. More recent studies, especially those using a variety of behavioral techniques, are reporting somewhat better results, ranging around 50 percent (Birk, Huddleston, Miller, and Cohler, 1971; Feldman and MacCulloch, 1971; Freeman and Meyer, 1975; McConaghy, 1975). In each of these studies, however, the homosexuals who were most apt to show substantial decreases in homosexual interests combined with an increase in heterosexual arousal and behavior were those who had prior histories of positive heterosexual experiences. The outcomes for formerly exclusive homosexuals were much poorer (success rates for this sub-population usually range between 0 and 20 percent). The most recent outcome study to appear in the literature reports the most positive findings ever: Of the fifty-four male homosexuals treated by Masters and Johnson (1979), approximately 67 percent reversed their sexual orientation completely, according to self-reports made five years after treatment concluded. However, less than 20 percent of this sample were originally exclusively homosexual, and more than half were married at the time they underwent treatment. This sample certainly does not represent a typical population of homosexuals, although it may be more representative of those who are motivated to seek out therapy for the purpose of changing sexual preference.

Some homosexuals seek out professional assistance for entirely different reasons than problems associated with acceptance or change of homosexual orientation. Like heterosexuals, they are not immune to more "mundane" concerns such as difficulty finding a partner or maintaining a stable relationship. They also exhibit sexual dysfunctions such as impotence, difficulty in becoming aroused, or lack of orgasm. In their recent book describing the treatment of such sexual dysfunctions in homosexuals, Masters and Johnson (1979) were dismayed to find a history of repeated unwillingness by other professionals to attempt to deal with these problems. Of twenty-six male homosexuals who had sought therapeutic assistance because of a sexual dysfunction, twenty-three had been refused treatment at least once. Female homosexuals were no luckier. Of fourteen lesbians who had requested professional help because of a sexual dysfunction, eleven had been turned down at least once, and eight had been refused assistance more than once. Furthermore, not a single one of these men or women who had been refused treatment were referred elsewhere. Such obvious disregard of people's needs should not be excused. One implication is that

homosexuals might do better initially to seek assistance at gay counseling centers. The same therapeutic approaches that have been developed for treatment of sexual dysfunctions in heterosexual males and females are applicable to homosexuals as well, and the prognosis for a successful outcome is equally good.   .

HOMOSEXUALITY IN PRISONS

No discussion of homosexuality would be complete without at least some mention of the special problem of prison homosexuality. Newspapers and magazines often report sensational stories of gang rapes in prisons, and there is a widespread belief that these violent and repulsive incidents typify the usual and customary patterns of homosexual sex in prison. Actually, sexual assaults, although common enough, are still the exception rather than the rule (Davis, 1970). They occur primarily in male institutions, especially in those that are providing a temporary, custodial function with the added problem of overcrowded conditions. Prison life, like other extremely stressful situations such as war, in which normal patterns of sexual relationships are prevented by unusual circumstances, illustrates in an important way two basic truths about human sexual behavior: It is surprisingly malleable and very often tied to other emotions and motivations.

Contrary to general opinion, sexual release per se may not be the major motiva-

tion for engaging in homosexual relations in prison settings. In male prisons many experts believe that homosexual activity serves at least several other important functions, including providing an outlet for aggression, establishing dominance-submission hierarchies, and allowing younger and weaker inmates to trade sexual access for protection against other inmate assaults. In total, approximately 30 to 45 percent of male inmates are estimated to be involved in homosexual activity while in prison, although only a small percentage of these men would consider themselves homosexual (Sagarin, 1976).

Estimates of the number of female inmates who become involved in homosexual activity tend to be higher than are estimates for male inmates. Approximately 50 to 75 percent of female prisoners engage in homosexual activity (Giallambardo, 1966; Ward and Kassebaum, 1965). Most are "turnouts," women who had not been homosexual prior to entering prison.

Motivations for homosexual involvement in prison differ for males and females. Giallambardo (1966), in a study of a women's prison in West Virginia, was struck by the pseudo-familial function that homosexual alliances seem to serve for the inmates. Affection and romantic attachments — the psychological and emotionally tinged aspects of intimate relationships — were of paramount importance, not sexual gratification. Perhaps this difference in male and female homosexual patterns in prisons should come as no surprise. Male prisoners may be reflecting values of power and aggression that they are familiar with outside of prison; women, on the other hand, fall back on the relationship model to which they are socialized, namely marriage and the family.

ATTITUDES TOWARD HOMOSEXUALITY

Although people are more knowledgeable regarding homosexual motivations, practices, and life-styles than ever before, and certain opinions have changed (the declassification of homosexuality as a mental disorder by the APA is one example), negative attitudes still abound. For example, the National Opinion Research Center has conducted general social surveys each year from 1972 to 1978. One of the questions asked was the following:

> What about sexual relations between two adults of the same sex — do you think it is always wrong, almost always wrong, wrong only sometimes, or not wrong at all?

How would you answer this question now that we are at the end of Chapter Seven? Is your response the same as in the beginning of the chapter? If different, what did you read that caused you to change your opinion? The percentage of those surveyed who felt that sex between two same-sexed adults was "always wrong" hovered between 70 and 75 percent across the years (Glenn and Weaver, 1979). In another survey over 75 percent of a nationwide sample felt that homosexuals should not be allowed to work as judges, teachers, or ministers, and 67 percent felt that they should not be employed as physicians or government officials (Levitt and Klassen, 1974). Although Nyberg and Alston (1976) report several segments of the general population with somewhat less negative attitudes — namely those who are under age 30, live in an urban environment, have been to college, and espouse no religious affiliation — the major finding is quite consistent: The vast majority of the people in the United States strongly disapprove of homosexuality. Notwithstanding increased media exposure, the public relations efforts of gay organizations, and the more liberal views held by sexologists and of late by mental health professionals, the public's traditional hostility has not substantially modified.

The term **homophobia** is sometimes used to refer to strong negative attitudes toward homosexuality, the assumption being that people's hostility is based on a fear of their

*Protestor demonstrating against
the Miss Gay America
Pageant, 1982.*

own homosexual inclinations (Weinberg 1972). The danger with this concept is that by explaining all antigay feelings in terms of psychological constructs such as uncon-scious fantasies and defenses, it ignores the many other reasons, political and religious among them, of why some people hold such prejudicial views about homosexuality.

LEGAL STATUS OF HOMOSEXUALITY

Throughout its history, the United States has always harbored a fascinating contradiction between constitutional support for individual liberties and separation of church and state on the one hand, and the attempt to legislate private morality on the other. Homosexuality is an excellent example of how these opposing values collide.

Compared with almost every other major country in the world, the United States has the most severe laws against homosexual activity. Archaic laws containing phrases such as "whoever commits the abominable and detestable crime against nature . . ." are still to be found in the majority of states. The "unnatural acts" referred to in these so-called "**sodomy** statutes" are oral and/or anal intercourse. These laws are based on Judeo-Christian limitations that define any sexual act not directly involved in the procreative process as sinful.

Although the American Bar Association passed a resolution in 1973 calling for repeal of all state laws against sex between consenting adults, excluding prostitution, most of the states have been unwilling to do so (West, 1977). The first state to follow these recommendations was Illinois in 1962. By the mid-1970s, however, only six additional states had followed suit (Connecticut, Colorado, Delaware, Hawaii, Ohio, and Oregon). Meanwhile, countries such as France, Belgium, Spain, and Italy have not had any criminal penalties for homosexual acts between consenting adults for more than a century. Nor currently does Japan, East or West Germany, Austria, Czechoslovakia, Poland, the Netherlands, Denmark, Finland, Sweden, Norway, or Greece. A noteworthy exception to this list, in addition to the United States, is the Soviet Union, where, as of 1934, sex acts between males were made a criminal offense (West, 1977).

In actuality, the United States does not outlaw homosexuality per se; instead, sodomy laws prohibit certain sexual acts associated with homosexuality. The presence or absence of such laws seems to have little bearing on actual behavior; public attitudes are more important. For example, aside from perhaps Amsterdam, in no city in the world is homosexuality more common and visible than in San Francisco. Estimates are that one out of every ten people in San Francisco is gay, and yet California still has laws opposing homosexual acts.

Even though police harassment of homosexuals has been on the wane for about a decade, other legal issues and discriminatory practices have come to the forefront. For example, do private or public employers have the right to fire someone solely on the grounds of an individual's known homosexual orientation? Lower court rulings have been contradictory. Some indicate that unlike blacks and women, homosexuals are not considered a minority group subject to the equal protection clause of the Fourteenth Amendment. Certain court opinions in California and the District of Columbia, on the other hand, suggest that a person's homosexual orientation is insufficient grounds for dismissal (Knutson, 1979).

Employment is not the only area in the United States in which discrimination is a problem for homosexuals. For instance, people have been subject to discharge from the armed services solely on the basis of known homosexual activity; no proof of impaired military performance was required. Similarly, the Immigration and Naturalization Act of 1952 can be used to forbid entry or to force deportation from this country of known homosexuals who are not citizens. Also, formerly married homosexuals are often at odds with the court in child custody decisions. Few judges consider homosexuals to be fit parents.

Local or federal laws designed to protect the homosexual against discriminatory practices are hard to pass. In fact, there is a movement afoot to repeal those few local ordinances that have been previously passed. The eventual outcome of these legal and legislative battles concerning minority rights based on sexual preference is hard to predict. Given the unrelenting nature of public attitudes, however, homosexuals have little reason to feel particularly secure or hopeful about the future.

SUMMARY

1. **Homosexuality** is not just a word used to define sexual acts; rather, three aspects of homosexuality must be considered: Homosexual *behavior* refers to the sexual activity that same-sexed partners share; homosexual *attraction* is the erotic-emotional interest one has for members of the same sex; homosexual *identity* refers to a person's self-acknowledged preference for same-sexed partners. These three components can be separate from one another. For example, homosexual behavior does not always imply homosexual identity.

2. Female homosexuals are often referred to as **lesbians,** a name that can be attributed to the poetry of Sappho. Sappho was a poet and teacher who lived on the island of Lesbos in ancient Greece. Although female homosexuality is referred to in her poetry, there is little evidence that homosexuality was popular at that time.

3. Although homosexual behavior is common, cross-species, cross-cultural, historical, and contemporary perspectives suggest that a lifetime, exclusive homosexual orientation is relatively rare. Present estimates in the United States indicate that only about 3 to 4 percent of all adult males and 1 to 2 percent of all adult females have an exclusive homosexual orientation.

4. Contrary to myth, most people with homosexual experiences in their history have also engaged in heterosexual activity. The two are not mutually exclusive. In fact, most homosexual experience is confined to the adolescent period, and more people can be considered **bisexual** than homosexual. Even among people who are predominantly homosexual, minimal evidence of an aversion to heterosexual activity is exhibited. Rather, in most cases homosexuality is just a decided preference.

5. Considerable effort has gone into the search for the cause of a homosexual orientation. However, no single, common pathway has been found. Instead, a number of different contributing factors—biological, cultural, developmental, familial, psychodynamic, and situational—have been implicated. Homosexuals are not a homogeneous group in terms of current behavior; not surprisingly homosexual preferences cannot be linked to any one common source.

6. **Coming out** can mean that a person is finally accepting his or her homosexuality, or it can refer to the first public association one makes with the **gay** community. Revealing one's homosexuality to family, friends, and co-workers can be terrifying; a person often risks a great deal because of the uncertainty of how the admission will be accepted.

7. Social condemnation is one reason why the gay community is so important for the young homosexual who is at the "coming out" stage. The gay community serves as a sanctuary and as a social support system, and promotes self-acceptance. It also provides a network in which sexual partners can be more easily located.

8. A number of differences in sexual experience and life-styles have been observed between male and female homosexuals. The most important distinction has to do with overt sexual activity. Impersonal sex with many different partners is common among male homosexuals but virtually unheard of in the lesbian subculture. Whether or not different socialization patterns or different biological predispositions are responsible is a matter of dispute, but unquestionably the drive for casual sexual encounters as distinguished from close, sustained attachments is much more central to established life-styles of male homosexuals than it is to life-styles of lesbians.

9. A vast majority of both male and female homosexuals show no evidence of physical or mental abnormality. Nevertheless, the incidence of suicide attempts, alcohol abuse, and regret about one's sexual orientation is higher among homosexuals than among heterosexuals, especially in males. In large measure, whatever unique despondency, guilt, or fear homosexuals may experience can be attributed to the negative attitudes and rejection they anticipate and, to some extent, experience from society.

10. Most homosexuals who seek therapeutic assistance do so in order to gain insight into their behavior, to relieve distressing feelings of anxiety and/or depression, and to come to better terms with their sexuality. A minority, especially those who are married, those who want to have children, and those with religious scruples and strong fears of an unconventional life-style, seek therapy in order to change their sexual preference. Although prevailing opinion in the homosexual and professional community is that therapy designed to promote a change in orientation is futile, recent evidence suggests that the situation is not quite so hopeless.

11. Homosexuals exhibit vast individual differences in sexual behavior, psychological and social adjustment, occupational and recreational interests, education, intelligence, physical appearance, tastes in food, dress, music, art, developmental histories, interpersonal styles, personality characteristics, and so on. Because human beings and human behavior are so complex and so situation specific, type casting of any kind is probably doomed to failure.

12. Since the advent of Judeo-Christian civilizations, attitudes toward male homosexuality, and to a lesser degree female homosexuality, have been condemnatory. Legal and social oppression, however, is not nearly as severe now as it once was. Whether or not this portends complete acceptance of homosexuality in the future, however, is questionable. In the United States, laws against homosexual behavior between consenting adults remain on the books even if they are seldom enforced. And more importantly, whether justified or not, public opinion remains strongly in favor of discriminatory practices against homosexuals.

SUGGESTED READINGS

Bell, A. P., & Weinberg, M. S. *Homosexualities.* New York: Simon & Schuster, 1978. An excellent survey study emphasizing the variety of sexual experiences and lifestyles of homosexual men and women.

Karlen, A. *Sexuality and homosexuality.* New York: W. W. Norton, 1971. A comprehensive historical and cultural analysis of homosexuality.

Marmor, J. (Ed.). *Homosexual behavior: A modern reappraisal.* New York: Basic Books, 1980. Chapters on homosexuality written by experts in different disciplines.

Paul, W., Weinreich, J. D., Gonsiorek, J. C., & Hotvedt, M. E. (Eds.). *Homosexuality.* Beverly Hills, Calif.: Sage Publications, 1982. A collection of original chapters covering mental health and biological, sociological, and legal aspects of homosexuality.

CHAPTER EIGHT

SEXUAL PROBLEMS
Description and Treatment

The history of sex in the West, according to Owen Barfield: Sex in the head, sex in the heart, sex in the loins—and what next?
John L. Mood, *Consciousness*

It is not always necessary to use words to communicate conflict.

One can easily develop the impression that sexual response is so natural that it always progresses more or less automatically from arousal through orgasm. Similarly, one can assume that people who respond adequately are also people who find sex satisfying and enjoyable.

Human sexuality does not conform to these assumptions. As we have learned from previous chapters, sexuality is a combination of physiological, psychological, and sociocultural factors, which should give us a clue about the intricacy of satisfactory sexual relationships. If something — increased pressure at work or a bad cold, perhaps — is not quite right in any of these broad spheres, a person may have difficulty functioning sexually. Conversely, sexual problems may contribute to an individual's personal or social problems. These interacting factors will become clearer in this chapter as we examine the more common sexual dysfunctions and their treatment.

The extent to which any particular sexual pattern is called "a problem" is very much determined by whatever is defined at the time as good sexual functioning. As was already discussed, couples may have a variety of sexual problems — lack of orgasm, ejaculating too quickly, lack of arousal — but still find that their sexual relationship is satisfying (Frank, Anderson, & Rubinstein, 1978).

In fact, the definition of sexual problems

is determined not only by the individual or couple but also by the sociocultural climate. For example, in late nineteenth-century England and America, good marital sexuality was restricted to the duty of procreation. A "good" woman was not expected to be orgasmic or even to enjoy sex, and men were expected to seek pleasurable sex with prostitutes rather than burden their spouses. Frequent intercourse was considered to be a health hazard:

> Many married people give themselves up to the embrace daily. . . . But not only its frequency, but the manner in which it is performed, are so unnatural and studiously licentious, that the most desperate cases of paralysis and epilepsy are frequently the direct and immediate result. (MacFadden, 1900, p. 34)

Sexual problems of the late 1800s were expressed in terms of excess—of intercourse, oral sex, and particularly masturbation (Robinson, 1976). Not surprisingly, sexual problems were most likely to be met with restraints and punishment of a mechanical, religious, psychological, or legal nature. In stark contrast, sexual problems today are primarily expressed in terms of inhibitions or lacks—of desire, of arousal, and of orgasm (e.g., Kaplan, 1979)—and their treatment a matter of disinhibition.

CLASSIFICATION OF SEXUAL DYSFUNCTION

The current classification of sexual dysfunctions is based on the conceptualization that adequate sexual functioning includes appropriate levels of desire, arousal, and orgasmic response, without pain or discomfort. Until the mid-1970s, the major categories of dysfunction centered on physical symptoms: ejaculating too quickly, lack of erection, infrequent or absent orgasmic response, and painful or incomplete intercourse. In addition, sexual desire, and particularly inhibited sexual desire, has become an area of clinical concern only recently (e.g., Kaplan, 1979).

As each of these dysfunctions is discussed, keep in mind that there are degrees of functioning. For example, most people have a sexual "dysfunction" at some point in their lives, perhaps during a period of stress or life change. These experiences are not cause for alarm or even for therapeutic intervention. Additionally, a sexual problem for one couple is not necessarily a sexual problem for another couple, especially in the case of premature ejaculation and sexual desire. Therefore, the current dysfunctions are usually evaluated according to both *temporal* dimensions (whether a person has always or only periodically had the sexual problem) and *situational* dimensions (whether the problem occurs in all sexual situations or only under certain conditions). Finally, the major categories of sexual dysfunctions often overlap. For instance, orgasm inhibition may occur along with desire problems, and arousal obviously influences the likelihood of orgasm. As has been suggested by a recent proposal for classification, a person should be evaluated on the degree of dysfunction he or she experiences within each category—including desire, arousal, orgasm, and pain—in order to develop a more complete picture of the level of sexual distress being suffered (Shover et al., 1982).

INCIDENCE OF SEXUAL DYSFUNCTIONS

Since there has not been a substantial demographic study reporting the frequency of sexual dysfunctions or dissatisfactions, we can only estimate the incidence of sexual problems. Research has reported figures ranging from 14 percent (Rainwater, 1964) to 77 percent (Frank et al., 1978), with the majority of estimates hovering around 20 to 50 percent (Frank et al., 1978; Masters & Johnson, 1970).

Accurately reporting the incidence of sexual problems is difficult because sexual *functioning* (the extent to which the sexual arousal cycle "works") can be a very separate dimension from sexual *satisfaction* (see Chapter 6). For this reason some people report being sexually satisfied although they do not experience orgasm—a point clearly made by one recent study on marital sexuality (Frank et al., 1978). In this study, women experienced sexual problems and dysfunctions far more often than did men. In spite of the prevalence of reported sexual difficulties, however, the researchers found surprisingly high levels of sexual and marital satisfaction. Although limited in size and scope, this study does raise the following questions on issues that influence our understanding of sexual problems:

1. Do married people, and particularly women, have low expectations about their sexual relationships? This theory would help explain the high degree of satisfaction often reported by those with sexual problems. On the other hand, such a pattern may also point out that more important factors determine sexual satisfaction.
2. Do women experience sexual problems more often than men? Possibly they do. Another possibility is that women are somewhat more comfortable than men in acknowledging sexual problems.

The relationship between sex and marital satisfaction is complex. For example, a study that examined a variety of potential differences between two extreme groups — very unhappily married couples versus very happily married couples — found that sexual problems ranked as the most frequently reported problem in the very happily married group; sex ranked only eighth or ninth in importance in the unhappily married group, while "expressing one's emotions" clearly ranked first (Birchler & Webb, 1975).

GENERAL ETIOLOGICAL FACTORS

There is little agreement about the causes of sexual dysfunction, as indicated by the remarks of well-known clinicians in the field:

> On one level, the sexual dysfunctions, as well as the sexual phobias, are caused by a single factor: anxiety. (Kaplan, 1979, p. 24)

> Despite the availability of different theoretical interpretations, we are at a loss to specify in any meaningful way the actual developmental and/or traumatic events that lead to the [sexual] difficulty. . . . Anxiety is often mentioned as an important factor, but anxiety can lead to excessive sexual desire or lack of desire, and to premature ejaculation or retarded ejaculation. (Pervin & Leiblum, 1980, p. 380)

The etiological factors to be discussed in the following sections have not been proved to cause sexual dysfunction. They have been observed by clinicians to be part of the history of dysfunctional people, and they are best viewed as hypothesized influences, the knowledge of which can be useful in treatment.

Organic Influences

Four major organic, or physical, factors can interfere with sexual functioning. One is illness, to the extent that fatigue, pain, chronic depression, or poor nutrition may be present (Kaplan, 1979; Masters & Johnson, 1970). A second factor is neurological or vascular impairment, since sexual response is dependent on these systems. Thus, diseases such as multiple sclerosis, temporal lobe epilepsy, and diabetes mellitus or traumas such as spinal-cord lesions can impair arousal or orgasmic response (Cooper, 1972; Ellenberg, 1980; Higgins, 1978; Lundberg, 1977). A third factor, endocrinologic imbalance, can impair desire as well as the sexual response cycle, and sexual problems may be an early symptom of some endocrine abnormalities such as pituitary tumors and hyperthyroidism (Spark, White, & Connolly, 1980). Fourth, a wide variety of drugs can influence sexual function.

Organic sources of sexual dysfunction are discussed in greater detail in Chapter Nine. In some cases, psychological factors may override organic factors, and, in most cases of organic impairment, a variety of psychological influences must be considered.

Individual Psychological Influences

☐ *Clinical Data* The following psychological variables have been identified as being important influences in sexual dysfunction: guilt (Kaufman, 1967; Masters & Johnson, 1970); low self-esteem (Barbach, 1975; LoPiccolo, 1977); anger or hostility (Cooper, 1968; Kaplan, 1974); unrealistic or irrational expectations (Ellis, 1971); negative attitudes toward sex, past traumatic experiences, and extreme religious orthodoxy (Masters & Johnson, 1970); and depressive symptoms and anxiety (Kaplan, 1974, 1979).

The basis for the development of these factors is believed, depending on one's theory, to be the result of either the individual's history (including family relationships and prior sociosexual experiences) or the individual's immediate situation (including general life and relationship characteristics). Also, historical factors are thought to influence the development of ideals and expectations about sexual relationships. Some theorists believe that historical influences cause unconscious psychological conflicts (e.g., Kaplan, 1974), and others conceptualize early experiences in terms of learning and conditioning (e.g., Masters & Johnson, 1970).

While no one is certain about all the psychological causes of sexual dysfunction, addressing several of those commonly agreed upon has been found useful in treating such problems. Anxiety is one such factor that has been linked to most sexual dysfunctions. Whether anxiety occurs before or after the dysfunction is present is less critical from a clinical perspective than knowing that a reduction in anxiety is usually necessary for better sexual functioning.

One theory that deals with the origin of anxiety is a Freudian psychoanalytic model. The important features of that model, as outlined by Kaplan (1974), a major clinician in the sex therapy field, are (1) the concept of the unconscious, (2) the importance of childhood experience in shaping adult sexuality, and (3) the role of the Oedipal conflict. Unconscious conflicts refer to irrational and contradictory forces, primitive impulses, and wishes that govern a person's behavior and feelings. A person is not aware of unconscious psychic processes; they are not available to reason and will. The major unconscious conflict in human sexuality is centered on enjoyment of sexuality, particularly with a loved partner, and, at the same time, fear of punishment for the enjoyment. The core of this conflict is believed to occur in the child's Oedipal period, generally between ages four and six. According to this model, all children naturally go through a phase in which they have incestuous desires for their opposite-sexed parent. These desires cannot be realized and are surrounded with frustration, guilt, and anxiety, particularly castration anxiety. The successful resolution of the Oedipal phase depends on the repression of incestuous wishes and identification with the same-sexed parent.

The unsuccessful resolution may result in many problems later on, including the inability to enjoy sex in adulthood.

The social learning model is more concerned with conscious rather than unconscious past experiences as clues to why certain current values and ideals about sexual functioning have been adopted. For example, some men have difficulty in responding to their loved partner, but no difficulty in responding to women who are strangers. A psychoanalyst would probably judge this behavior as being an incomplete resolution of the Oedipal period. A social-learning therapist, on the other hand, would more likely focus on the love-sex split as being a product of the man's experience with prior partners, the impact of sociocultural stereotypes of male and female sexuality, the current interpersonal factors in the man's dysfunctional relationship, and the values and behaviors to which he was exposed in his own family (Leiblum & Pervin, 1980a). Thus, the psychoanalytic and social-learning models are not mutually exclusive in their attempts to explain the anxiety and conflicts present in sexual dysfunction; the emphasis, however, differs in each approach. Clinical evidence has supported both theories; research has confirmed neither.

People reporting sexual problems most often suffer from *performance anxiety* (Masters & Johnson, 1970). During a sexual interaction, if a person is worried or afraid of not becoming aroused, not staying aroused, not having an orgasm, or having an orgasm too quickly, anxious feelings are likely to re-place sexual feelings. Arousal then diminishes, or orgasm may be triggered too early. Sexual encounters become a test rather than an enjoyable experience. Some people may begin to continually "watch" or think about their physical response. They are also likely to realize their worst fears, and the more pressure they put on themselves, the more likely they are not to have an erection or orgasm. Anxiety in this context is influenced by both psychological and physiological factors. Some years ago, Wolpe (1958) claimed that anxiety and sexual arousal were neurophysiologically mutually inhibiting responses—sex inhibits anxiety and vice versa. There is some support for this view since sexual arousal requires predominantly parasympathetic activity, while anxiety is more sympathetically dominated (Heiman & Hatch, 1981).

The major influences on the degree of anxiety experienced are the cognitive factors: People put demands on themselves to "perform" sexually. People with sexual problems that center on performance tend to be thinking thoughts such as, "I must get an erection" or "I have to have an orgasm." Often, the accompanying fears of performance anxiety are the fear of failure and a pressure to please one's partner (Kaplan, 1974). In other words, people may tell themselves, "If I don't have an orgasm, I'm not a good sexual partner"; "If I can't keep an erection, I am not a real man"; "I must perform perfectly every time or else my partner will think I'm inadequate and find someone else"; or "My partner will criticize and make fun of me if I don't please him/

her." When a person's mind is preoccupied with these thoughts, little attention is being focused on the sexual quality of the interaction (Verhulst & Heiman, 1979).

All of the antisexual statements above are frequently expressed by people with sexual problems (e.g., LoPiccolo, 1978; Masters & Johnson, 1970; Zilbergeld, 1978). Sev-

eral therapists have discussed these sexual performance demands in terms of people's self-expectations, which are derived from social, personal, and interpersonal experiences (Barbach, 1975; Ellis, 1975; Heiman, LoPiccolo, & LoPiccolo, 1976; Zilbergeld, 1978). In Box 8–1 we highlight some of the myths that are products of unrealistic ex-

Box 8–1

COMMON MYTHS ABOUT MALE...

If expectations become rigid rules that must always be applied, they become myths. Common myths about male performance include the following:

1. Men always want and are ready for sex.
2. Men should become aroused whenever they are in a sexual situation.
3. Men should always orchestrate sex (initiate it, direct its course, decide on what to engage in).
4. Women expect men to provide them with an orgasm every time sex occurs.
5. Real sex is intercourse, and intercourse should occur every time one has sex.
6. All physical contact must lead to intercourse.
7. Sex requires an erection (the bigger the better).
8. Good sex requires an orgasm.
9. Sex should always be natural and spontaneous.
10. If sex is good, then the relationship will be good.

(Source: Ellis, 1958, 1969; Zilbergeld, 1978.)

pectations that people commonly set for themselves.

None of these myths is either good or bad except to the extent that it dictates what a good or bad sexual experience *must* be at all times, regardless of the individual desires of the people involved. When the expectations become demands, performance anxiety and sexual dysfunctioning are likely results (Ellis, 1962; LoPiccolo, 1978).

☐ *Research Data*   The role of performance anxiety in sexual dysfunctions has not been objectively documented. Only three research studies have attempted to investigate performance anxiety directly (Far-

...AND FEMALE SEXUALITY

The myths surrounding sexual performance anxiety for women are more contradictory and reflect the shifting sociocultural expectations of women. The more traditional sexual beliefs held about women include the following:

1. A woman should be responsive to her partner's sexual advances rather than initiate them.
2. Women should have orgasms during intercourse without any additional stimulation.
3. All women must have a lot of foreplay in order to enjoy sex.
4. Women must be in love with their partners in order to be sexually responsive.
5. Real sex is intercourse which should occur on each sexual contact.
6. Sex is more for the man's pleasure than for the woman's pleasure.

Added to the traditional concepts are these new expectations:

7. Women should have at least one orgasm, preferably several, during each sexual encounter.
8. Women should be aggressive in sexual activities.
9. A lack of arousal means that there is something wrong with a woman's sexuality and her relationship.
10. If the relationship is good, then sex will be good.

(Source: Barbach, 1975; Heiman et al., 1976.)

kas, Sine, & Evans, 1979; Heiman & Rowland, in press; Lange et al., 1981). Instead, studies have examined broader issues such as (1) the kinds of psychological and relationship problems present in sexually dysfunctional individuals and couples and (2) the effect of general anxiety on sexual response.

The relationship between sexual dysfunctions and psychological factors was closely observed in a study of 92 couples who had various sexual problems (Clement & Pfafflin, 1980). One year after therapy, women who had benefited from treatment of orgasmic dysfunction and vaginismus were found to be less nervous, less depressed, less irritable, less psychosomatic, and more self-confident than they were prior to therapy. Similarly, men who were having erectile problems and were experiencing premature ejaculation were reported to be less depressed, less aggressive, and less inhibited at the one-year follow-up than they had been prior to therapy. This study clearly points out that changes in sexual functioning are intimately related to more general psychological functioning.

Several researchers have also examined the effect of anxiety and other emotional states on sexual arousal in a laboratory setting where genital vasocongestion can be measured. For example, in a study measuring the arousal of sexually functional women and men under varied conditions, genital arousal was greater when an erotic videotape was preceded by an anxiety-and-anger-inducing videotape (graphic scenes of car accidents) than by a neutral videotape (Hoon, Wincze, & Hoon, 1977; Wolchik et al., 1980).

Other laboratory studies have concentrated on performance demands. One such study has examined this concept by comparing sexually functional and dysfunctional males (Heiman & Rowland, in press). The functional group showed more penile response to an erotic audiotape that was preceded by performance demand instructions (telling the men that it was very important to try to achieve and maintain an erection continuously during the erotic tape) than when preceded by relaxing, nondemand instructions (informing them that arousal was not important). In other words, functional men followed the instructions. Dysfunctional men showed the opposite pattern: In support of clinical theory, dysfunctional men were more genitally aroused by hearing the erotic tape preceded by the nondemand instructions than to the tape preceded by the demand instructions. When these men rated their subjective feelings of sexual arousal, however, there was no evidence that performance demand had influenced their experience of arousal; instead, the dysfunctional group reported being significantly less aroused by the erotic materials than did the functional group.

What can be concluded from the laboratory studies of sexual arousal patterns and psychological functioning? First, sexually dysfunctional individuals may not be influenced by the same psychological "threats" as sexually functional people. Performance anxiety is one such threat. Second, general anxiety may be very different from anxiety experienced in a sexual context. For example, in the studies of the relationship between anxiety and other emotional states, on the one hand, and sexual arousal, on the other, it is possible that the anxiety-anger tape that preceded the erotic tape provided a physiological and psychological general response "warm-up" (Hoon et al., 1977; Wolchik et al., 1980). This situation is quite different from that existing when a person becomes anxious *during* sexual arousal. It is also quite different from feeling anxious about whether one can function adequately in a sexual situation.

The third conclusion that can be drawn from the laboratory studies reiterates a central theme in sexual problems — that there is often a split between what a person experiences physically and what that person experiences psychologically. A person may experience feelings of sexual arousal, and yet his or her body may not be responding with erections or orgasms. Conversely, a person may find it easy to respond physically, but neither enjoys nor desires sexual activity. Therapy often focuses on healing the split among thoughts, feelings, and physical responses.

Relationship Influences

Couples can sometimes improve the conditions of their sexual relationship without professional assistance. For example,

Janet and Paul are in their mid-twenties. They are sexually involved, neither of them for the first time. Janet feels very uncomfortable about her body and genitals. She enjoys the closeness of sex, but feels too tense to let go. She does not experience orgasm, although she thinks she would like to. Paul enjoys sex, espe-

Many couples have an occasional sexual difficulty that they will solve without seeking a therapist.

cially cunnilingus, which embarrasses Janet. Paul does not criticize or pressure Janet; instead their love-making is very slow and gentle, which is Paul's way of directly expressing appreciation and respect for Janet and her body. Janet begins to relax, and as the months go by, gradually develops an appreciation of her own sexual feelings, allowing herself to respond with increasing abandon.

Similarly, a man with extensive fears about his sexual performance can gradually regain his confidence with a partner who clearly signals her acceptance of his sensitivity and her interest in physical contact apart from intercourse and his erections.

Alternatively, two people who function well sexually on their own or have had satisfying sexual relationships with others may find that certain relationship factors interfere with their degree of arousal.

317

Susan was divorced one year ago. Sex was not a problem in her marriage, but the divorce was very upsetting. John has had several prior sexual relationships, both satisfying and enjoyable. Susan and John met at a party six months ago, had similar interests, and started dating one another exclusively. Initially, sex was mutually satisfying, but recently there has been a change in their relationship. John is interested in increased commitment and has been suggesting marriage. Susan does not want to lose John, but at the same time is frightened of making a commitment so soon after a difficult divorce. She has been avoiding sex with John, and when sex does occur, she does not experience much arousal or enjoyment. Gradually, her sexual desire for John is decreasing.

The main point here is that in addition to individual psychological and physiological factors, the relationship between two people takes on a power and character of its own. What common factors, then, have clinicians identified as destructive to sexual relationships?

☐ *Fear of Rejection* Intimacy between people involves increased sensitivity and vulnerability to one another's actions. One of the frightening possibilities in any intimate relationship is the thought that the other person will withdraw his or her care and attention. Thus, not surprisingly, strong fears of rejection can interfere with sexual feelings (Kaplan, 1974, 1979; LoPiccolo, 1978). Often, rejection fears have little to do with a current relationship but instead have been developed in the past, due to traumatic breakups of old relationships or even because of childhood experiences (Fisher, 1973). For example, Fisher found that the major factor determining orgasmic

ability in women was the degree of trust a daughter had in her father as she was growing up.

☐ *Anger and Hostility between Partners* Most couples have periodic arguments that may or may not have an impact on their sexual relationships. The types of antagonisms that are more likely to diminish the sexual functioning of couples have to do with built-up resentments, disappointments, unfulfilled desires, and power struggles (Kaplan, 1974). Often, people who hold extensive hostility for one another end up in marital therapy or, at the very least, in sex therapy aimed primarily at relationship factors. Two individuals may not begin their relationships being hostile, but the development of a particular relationship may lead to hostile and angry interactions.

☐ *Communication Problems* Most couples can solve routine, daily problems together, including minor complaints that they may have about each other. However, most people never learn to talk about sex, especially when sex is a problem (LoPiccolo, 1978). The great misconception is that sex is supposed to work out naturally and spontaneously, and a couple who cares should automatically be a couple for whom sex is right.

The following are common ways in which couples try to deal with a sexual problem:

1. Ignore it and hope it will get better.
2. Hope and expect that the other person will bring it up first.
3. Try harder to enjoy sex, thus making it more like work than enjoyment.

4. Tease or make jokes about it.
5. Blame someone, either the other person or oneself, meanwhile worrying that one's partner has lost interest or is having an affair, or questioning one's own desirability or sexual role in the marriage.

Sometimes these strategies work, but they can also be responsible for severe marital or personal distress.

☐ *Sex-Role Pressures* One partner may go through a period during which sex is less important to him or her, perhaps due to a recent baby, a new job, or the loss of employment. If these changes are unrecognized or underestimated by the partner, conflict may result. Similarly, sex-role expectations may cause a strain on the sexual or marital relationship (Frank et al., 1979).

The data on sex roles and sexual dysfunction are not entirely clear. Traditional sex roles center on the male being the active, aggressive initiator and the female the passive, receptive responder. Derogatis and Meyer (1979) unexpectedly found that sexually functional men were more traditionally "masculine" (as measured by gender-role scales) than dysfunctional males. On the other hand, functional females scored higher on both femininity and masculinity scales than did dysfunctional women. Clement and Pfafflin (1980) reported still another finding, namely that successful treatment of sexual disorders was accompanied by a decrease in sex-role-stereotypic attitudes toward sexuality in both male and female patients. From the above studies, we can speculate that sex-role issues have a complex bearing on sexual functioning and satisfaction. For example:

1. Changes in sex roles in an ongoing relationship may be the most difficult to adjust to—for example, if a woman suddenly becomes more independent, or if a man stops initiating contact and instead expects his wife to do so.
2. Sex-role stereotypes may be more accepted by sexually functional men because they have never had to question their values.
3. To be sexually functional, women may have to adopt some of the traditionally masculine behaviors—for example, assertiveness.

INTRODUCTION TO SEX THERAPY AND ITS EFFECTIVENESS

General Components of Sex Therapy

The now classic form of therapy designed by Masters and Johnson (1970) began with daily sessions for two weeks at their St. Louis clinic. The treatment, involving both partners, was carried out by a co-therapist team, one male and one female. Treatment began with the recording of a detailed history and a physical examination. Initially, if a male did not have a partner, a surrogate was hired to serve as the male's therapeutic companion. Because of negative publicity and other difficulties involved, however, the use of female surrogates was eventually discontinued, and male surrogates were never used for females.

A few therapists have adopted Masters and Johnson's use of surrogates, and some have even hired prostitutes to serve as surrogates, in the belief that surrogates as therapy partners may be beneficial for men who find sex extremely frightening or even find interacting with a woman who could be a potential sex partner uncomfortable (Apfelbaum, 1977). Whether or not most men improve beyond the specific contact with the surrogate has not been adequately documented. Surrogates are not recommended for men who are in committed relationships.

Following the publication of *Human Sexual Inadequacy* (Masters & Johnson, 1970), other clinicians developed programs to treat individuals as well as couples (LoPiccolo & LoPiccolo, 1978; Marks, 1981). They used one or two therapists and varied the length of treatment, finding that adequate therapy can be provided with alternative treatment arrangements.

Many of the basic ingredients of the original Masters and Johnson program continue to be used. Vital to the program is a graded series of tasks that the couple is to do at home after their sessions with the therapist. The **sensate focus** exercises are designed to decrease performance anxiety and build better communication and sexual enjoyment. The first step involves only a sensual exchange between the couple; the partners touch one another, usually while nude and in bed, but they do not initially touch one another's genitals. The purpose of this step is to reduce anxiety and also to increase communication about each partner's likes and dislikes. As the sessions progress and anxiety diminishes, the contact becomes gradually more sexual, proceeding to mutual manual arousal and eventually to intercourse.

A second and related feature of sex therapy is the **anxiety reduction.** Anxiety is a frequent consequence experienced by people who tell themselves that they must or should be sexually responsive. Some therapists teach clients to go only as far as they can without feeling anxious in a home assignment (e.g., Masters & Johnson, 1970); other therapists teach people to think more rationally about what their problem means to them (Ellis, 1975) or to use hypnosis to replace the negative mental images with positive ones (Aroaz, 1982).

A third major component of sex therapy is **information and education** aimed at providing couples with knowledge of the similarities and differences between male and female sexual functioning. Information and education are also used to correct myths concerning who is supposed to initiate sex, how fast orgasm is supposed to occur, and why females may find coital orgasm difficult. And finally, the fourth cornerstone of therapy stresses open **communication.** Even couples who are at ease and effective in talking about other aspects of their relationship can be at a loss when a sexual problem occurs. Communication skills are necessary if sexual relations are to be improved (Kaplan, 1974; Leiblum & Pervin,

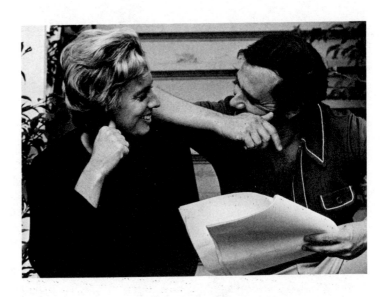

1980b; LoPiccolo & LoPiccolo, 1978; Masters & Johnson, 1970).

Overall Effectiveness of Sex Therapy

Two basic problems block the successful evaluation of sex therapy. First, researchers differ on who is the best source for evaluating change: the people experiencing the problem, the therapist, or a third uninvolved party. Second, people do not agree on what kind of change constitutes an improvement. Let's look briefly at each of these problems.

One is very likely to get a biased view of the degree of change from either the therapist or the client. Although both types of data are useful, they are rarely both reported (Marks, 1981; Wright, Perreault, & Mathieu, 1977). For example, no matter how satisfied and improved a couple in therapy with Masters and Johnson (1970) might have felt, the therapist was the one who made the decision about their success or failure based on the degree of symptom reversal. To some extent, however, improvement is always based on the client's report, since no direct observations are made of a couple's

functioning, nor would direct observation be useful since an observer would most likely influence the sexual interaction.

The measures and criteria for improvement also vary. Most clinicians believe that a change in the initial problem—pain, arousal, or orgasmic response—is important. But how much change? Masters and Johnson (1970) rated treatment failed if a man did not learn to delay ejaculation long enough for his partner to orgasm during 50 percent of their coital experiences. Other researchers look for more gradual changes, such as a change in how frequently orgasm occurs or erections are maintained (Cooper, 1969, 1970; LoPiccolo & Lobitz, 1972). General sexual satisfaction is also considered. For example, some couples change their sexual patterns only slightly, but they report being far more satisfied with their sexual relationship (Heiman & LoPiccolo, 1983). Alternatively, a couple's sex life may improve, but the overall relationship may not.

> In order for sex to be good, they [the couple] had to feign lack of emotional involvement. By remaining distant, they were able to enjoy each other sexually, yet both were emotionally unsatisfied. (Perelman, 1980, p. 221)

So far, Masters and Johnson (1970) have reported the highest overall success rates (80 to 85 percent, although they reported their results in terms of failure rates of 15 to 20 percent) and the largest patient population (790 individuals). They also reported data at a five-year follow-up, noting little reversal in the initial success rates.

Masters and Johnson's results have been challenged because of the lack of a detailed description of their patient population, the probable selectiveness of their screening procedure, and the vague and limited nature of their research measures (Zilbergeld & Evans, 1980). In addition, they had no control sample; nor did they report the extent of their patients' dysfunctions prior to therapy. Nevertheless, their work remains a major reference point.

Since Masters and Johnson's work, other clinicians have reported success rates varying between 40 and 100 percent, depending on the dysfunction (see Marks, 1981; Wright et al., 1977). In reviewing the work of other clinical researchers, one notices that the higher success rates often occurred in the late 1960s and the early 1970s, suggesting that there has since been an increase in the complexity and difficulty of sex therapy cases. Researchers speculate that this change may be due in part to the extensive popular literature that has become available since the early 1970s, offering people the option of solving their difficulties without a therapist (LoPiccolo, 1977). It is possible, although as yet unproven, that people who are successful with "self-help" programs have problems that are less difficult — problems that would definitely be solvable in sex therapy. It is plausible also that people who have not been successful in helping themselves will experience their problem as harder to change.

THE MAJOR SEXUAL PROBLEMS:
DESCRIPTION, THERAPY, AND TREATMENT EFFECTIVENESS

Sexual Desire Problems

☐ *Description and Treatment*   Sexual desire problems generally are reported by people who have *hypoactive* sexual desire, which means they have little desire for sex (Kaplan, 1979). *Hyperactive* sexual desire defines the state of high sexual desire, a condition almost never seen in sex therapy cases. Although a number of therapists claim that low sexual desire is the most prevalent of all sexual dysfunctions (see Kaplan, 1979, p. 57), the definition and treatment of this problem is less clear than for other dysfunctions. The major difference between disorders of desire and other sexual dysfunctions is that problems with arousal, orgasm, and pain have physical

Some people coming to therapy mention that they even feel in competition with the family pets for their partner's attention

points of reference, whereas desire problems usually do not.

Low desire may define sexual interest that is extremely low given the norms for age, sex, occupation, and current life situation. For example, a 25-year-old man or woman who has never been sexually aroused, who does not masturbate, and who has never had any sexual fantasies would probably be diagnosed as having low sexual desire. However, a person under excessive strain either at home or at work or someone being treated for a severe medical problem would be less likely to be viewed as having low sexual desire.

Sometimes a sudden decrease in desire is accompanied by relationship problems or by other sexual problems, such as fewer erections or orgasms, which make the evaluation of which problem came first difficult. Since desire is the fuel for sexual functioning, it should not be surprising that inadequate response is sometimes accompanied by a decrease in desire for sex. Therefore, low sexual desire must be considered carefully in light of the person's more general functioning, the quality of

any current relationships, and the origins of the problem. Physical factors are not to be excluded when someone reports a lifelong or sustained disinterest in sex, and, indeed, the absence of sexual interest may be a sign of other distress or vice versa. For example, Shrom, Leif, and Wein (1979) reported that 80 percent of their patients who had low desire (in this case combined with erectile problems) were also significantly depressed and required psychiatric attention. Whether desire problems or depression came first is not known in this case.

We must remember, too, that low sexual desire is not always a sexual dysfunction. A couple, both in their early thirties, who do not masturbate or fantasize and who agree that sex three times a year is sufficient may be described as statistically low in their frequency of desire, but not dysfunctional. Similarly, a problem in desire discrepancy exists if a male prefers having sex once a month while his partner desires some form of sexual interaction once a day. This is not a true case of desire disorder, however.

Therapists have suggested a careful evaluation of the meaning of sex in a given couple's relationship (Zilbergeld & Rinkleib, 1980). If one person seeks sex primarily for fun and relaxation while the other seeks it for proof of love and commitment, *not* wanting sex may carry very different meanings for each person. Additionally, a clinician reviewed a series of cases of low desire and noted several recurrent themes: a history or current complaint of depression; Catholicism (active or inactive); the presence of a sexual dysfunction; aversion to oral-genital contact; aversion to female genitals (in both men and women with low desire); a history of never masturbating or masturbating at one time and then stopping; and the presence of marital problems apparent to the clinician, but denied by the couple (L. LoPiccolo, 1980).

Most therapists agree that sexual desire problems are difficult to treat (Kaplan, 1979; L. LoPiccolo, 1980). Common strategies include increasing the sensory awareness of sexual stimuli through masturbation or hypnosis, facilitating the couple's erotic responsiveness, dealing with unconscious psychological conflicts, reducing anxiety, improving the relationship in general, and reversing ambivalent attitudes about sex. Sexual desire problems may be difficult to treat because sexual desire is so sensitive to broader aspects of a person's life as well as to one's sexual attitudes and experience, and also because of the quality of the current marital relationship.

☐ *Treatment Effectiveness*   No outcome studies on low sexual desire have been done for the reason that only recently has

this category come to the attention of clinicians. Clinical and case studies of low sexual desire suggest lower success rates than for other sexual problems (Kaplan, 1979; L. LoPiccolo, 1980; Zilbergeld & Rinkleib, 1980).

Sexual Arousal Problems

☐ *Description*   The most often discussed arousal problem is *erectile dysfunction* in men. This does not mean that women do not have sexual arousal difficulties—they do—but it does mean that lack of arousal in men is easier to identify because their psychological arousal usually corresponds to erections. Additionally, many couples are concerned when they are unable to have intercourse. Low lubrication in women may be related to their lack of arousal, but it does not necessarily preclude their enjoyment of or participation in intercourse. Nevertheless, although we talk here about erectile problems, many of the inhibiting arousal features apply to the responses of both men and women.

A large percentage of men, at some time in their lives, are unable to have or maintain erections. Kaplan (1974) estimates that 50 percent of all men have experienced erectile problems. Attempting sex when you really do not want to, when you are very preoccupied with something else, when you are highly stressed or worried, when you are tired, or when you have been drinking heavily are typical examples of situations in which arousal may be inhibited. Such occurrences are a normal part of sexual functioning.

However, when a man does not have an erection in numerous sexual experiences, a problem may exist. Masters and Johnson (1970) have classified erectile problems as either primary impotence or secondary impotence. The term impotence is no longer favored because it conveys an impression of total inadequacy; however, the primary/secondary distinction remains important. **Primary erectile dysfunction** describes men who never have an erection of sufficient firmness to have intercourse. **Secondary erectile dysfunction** describes men who have had at least one intercourse experience that included erection and ejaculation. Kaplan (1979) used *total* erectile dysfunction for those cases in which the man is unable to have an erection under any circumstances, masturbation included, and *partial* erectile dysfunction when it is occasionally a problem.

In the early 1970s, the prevailing opinion about causes of erectile problems was that 95 percent of all cases were due to psychological factors (Kaplan, 1974). That opinion is now disputed. One report has shown that 30 percent of a sample of 95 men with secondary erectile failure had physical problems, including renal disease, cardiovascular disease, diabetes, and hypertension, or were using prescription drugs known to interfere with sexual functioning (Shrom et al., 1979). In another study, a variety of hormonal imbalance factors were found in about 35 percent of the men with erectile dysfunction, the majority of which were classified as secondary (Spark, White, & Connolly, 1980). Appropriate medical treatment for the hormonal problem generally was found to restore adequate erectile functioning.

Psychological factors, however, are almost always present when erectile problems exist, whether or not they are the cause. For example, in one study the psychological profiles of men with erectile problems were compared with a group of men with no erectile problems; significantly greater depression, phobic anxiety, and physical symptoms were found in the sexually dysfunctional group (Derogatis, Meyer, & King, 1981). In another study done in Germany, sexually functional and dysfunctional men with various erectile problems were compared according to their psychological functioning (Kockott et al., 1980). The female partners of all the men were also evaluated. The group most disturbed by their sexual problem, judged by self-evaluations and clinical interviews, was the psychogenic group (men with erectile and premature ejaculation problems of no known organic cause). They rated themselves as having more sexual problems and being more disturbed than did their female partners. Additionally, though the men with diabetes were more anxious than the functional men, they were less anxious than the men with psychogenic erectile problems. The authors concluded that the diabetic men could justify their problem as being out of control: "The diabetic is able to explain his sexual problem as being due to an organic disease that he cannot influence"

(Kockott et al., 1980, p. 472). There was also an indication that men with psychogenic erectile problems overestimated their partners' sexual interest and overidealized them.

This research substantiates clinical evidence that erectile problems are often related to men's and women's expectations about sex. Moreover, erectile problems not only can be destructive for a relationship, but also can be caused by a destructive relationship:

> Some women "castrate" their husbands by behaving destructively in the sexual situation as an expression of their hostility. Others, who are deeply in love and able to express their love freely, may feel rejected and threatened by their husbands' impotence. Frequently, such women attempt to deal with their urgent need for reassurance by demanding that their husbands perform sexually, which creates a pressured milieu and only serves to exacerbate the problem. (Kaplan, 1974, pp. 257–258)

☐ *Assessing Erectile Problems* Marital, psychological, and physiological factors must be thoroughly assessed. Although separating physical and psychological factors is often difficult, if a man reports that he can get normal erections in all situations except with his wife, physiological causation is very unlikely. Similarly, if a male never gets an erection, the likelihood of physical causation is quite high. In the majority of cases, however, the cause is not readily evident and some physiological evaluation is recommended. Several techniques are used for the evaluation of physiological problems. We mention the three most common areas of assessment.

1. Hormonal evaluation is often necessary. Usually testosterone, prolactin, lutenizing hormone, and sometimes the response to lutenizing-hormone-releasing hormone are considered important to test (these hormones are discussed in Chapter Two). Because hormonal examinations are expensive, testosterone is usually tested first and, if low, the other hormonal levels are also evaluated (Spark et al., 1980). However, according to research performed at the Masters and Johnson Institute, men with erectile problems do not necessarily have different hormonal levels (Schwartz, Kolodny, & Masters, 1980).

2. Another means of evaluating the influence of physiological factors on erectile problems is to measure penile blood pressure, which can help to identify vascular disease (Kempczinski, 1979; Velcek et al., 1980). Other researchers have recommended a more detailed assessment of both the venous and arterial systems (Tordjman, Thierrée, & Michel, 1980; Wagner & Ebbehøj, 1978). Arterial erectile failure can be suspected if the man has inadequate erections in all circumstances (semierections), experiences a cold sensation in the penis, and ejaculates with a limp, nonerect penis. Venous-caused erectile problems can be indicated by the fact that a man finds erections easier to attain when standing up (Tordjman et al., 1980).

3. Evaluation of nocturnal penile tumescence, which is done by measuring the presence of erections during rapid-eye-movement (REM) sleep, is a third technique used. Because men usually experience erections during their REM sleep cycles, the

lack of erections during REM could be a sign of physiological erectile problems (Karacan, 1980; Marshall, Surridge, & Delva, 1981). Researchers claim that this procedure can discriminate psychogenic from organic erectile failure with 80 to 95 percent accuracy (Marshall et al., 1981). However, the procedure can be expensive, costing between $500 and $2,000 for a workup that is far from foolproof.

☐ *Treatment*   Although individual therapists differ in their approach to erectile problems, several common treatment strategies exist. One of the major goals is to reduce the anxiety that surrounds sexual interaction. Intercourse is usually banned during the early stages of treatment (Masters & Johnson, 1970). Abstinence allows a reduction in performance anxiety and a chance for the couple to practice sensate focus exercises. (Since the early stages of sensate focus exercises exclude genital contact, there is less need for concern about having "successful" coitus.) During the later stages of these exercises, which include touching the genitals, if one partner feels upset or worried, he or she returns to touching that is nonpressured and enjoyable.

Anxiety reduction is also attempted by discussing with the couple their expectations, thereby helping them to change attitudes that may be anxiety producing. Marital problems are addressed, particularly by helping the couple in achieving more intimate and clear communication, reducing hostility, and managing practical issues. Therapists will sometimes instruct patients

not to have erections in order to decrease anxiety. The **teasing technique,** whereby stimulation is stopped once an erection occurs, also is a frequently used strategy (Masters & Johnson, 1970). By intentionally losing an erection, the catastrophic interpretations of such loss are allayed. The couple learns that a lost erection is not the "end of the world," and that more often than not it can be regained when stimulation resumes.

Finally, some therapists focus on the cognitive components of sexuality. Ellis (1980), for example, spends a great deal of time attacking the myths and beliefs that men and women have about good sexual functioning. One of the more common, unrealistic expectations that men have for themselves is that they should be able to become aroused with any woman, even if they do not care for her as a person. Learning to accept the fact that this is unrealistic can be beneficial for the dysfunctional man. For example:

> One unmarried man felt he needed to know a woman was interested in him as a person, and would not become angry if he could not get an erection. He decided that he needed time to get to know the woman and felt she enjoyed being with him for more than sex. "I'd also need to talk to her about sex, to tell her that I don't always get an erection, and also tell her that her satisfaction is very important to me. I'd want to know if she would let me take care of her orally if my penis wasn't working." He was able to have this conversation and his sex life improved considerably. (Zilbergeld, 1978, p. 88)

A small percentage of men do not benefit from sex therapy because they have had irreversible damage to their vascular or neurological system (Renshaw, 1978). These men may require the surgical implantation in the penis of a device that would aid in sexual functioning; two types are available. The first device is a silicone implant that makes the penis permanently erect, although the erection is not as rigid as a full, natural erection. The other device allows the man to pump fluid from a reservoir surgically placed in his lower abdomen into a balloon-like cylinder placed in his penis.

☐ *Treatment Effectiveness*   Treatment appears to be more successful with cases of secondary than with primary erectile failure. Masters and Johnson (1970) reported 74 percent and 60 percent success rates, respectively. In another study, men with a significant degree of depression were least likely to improve, and only 27 percent of this group did so (Shrom et al., 1979). Additionally, these researchers noted that men in unstable relationships had a lower success rate (64 percent) than men in stable relationships (80 percent success rate). Finally, in a recent study on the effectiveness of sex therapy in treating a group of men with erection problems, while the men themselves reported no significant increase in erectile functioning, their wives did report significant improvement in their husbands' erectile functioning (Heiman & Lo-Piccolo, 1983). The authors suggested that the men's level of functioning after therapy was psychologically experienced as far from good enough in spite of an improvement. Thus these men, in contrast to their wives, underrated current erectile functioning.

Different types of therapeutic procedures have received sparse evaluation. A *therapy group,* usually bringing together ten to fifteen people who offer mutual support while also discussing problems and possible solutions, meets with a therapist who guides the sessions. Groups for men without partners have been reported to be successful (e.g., Lobitz & Baker, 1979), although in one controlled study, treatment improved attitudes and behavior but not actual erectile functioning (Price et al. 1981). *Biofeedback* procedures have also been tried, but they are generally not effective (Csillag, 1976; Reynolds, 1980). Individuals in a biofeedback program are provided with signals, such as tones, that indicate level of genital arousal. The most likely explanation as to why such programs do not work is that they reinforce what many men with erectile problems already do to themselves—they are made continuously aware of their penis, and their concern blocks sexual feelings with worry.

Penile prostheses have not been evaluated sufficiently, but the data thus far suggest caution. One recent study comparing the two devices reported that significant complications were reported in patients with the silicone implant and also in a group using the inflatable devices (Malloy, Wein, & Carpiniello, 1980). A second operation was necessary for 20 to 33 percent of the patients, and 10 to 35 percent of the inflatable devices suffered mechanical failures. Results of this sort, combined with the irreversible nature of the surgery (all erectile tissue is removed), strongly influence some therapists to try sex therapy with patients before they recommend a penile implant (Renshaw, 1978).

Although the administration of testosterone has been shown to be effective for some erectile problems (Spark et al., 1980), others have found hormonal treatment to be minimally effective (Cooper, 1981). Testosterone seems to be least effective for men who have erectile problems but who do not have low hormonal levels. Testosterone or other hormonal therapy is recommended only after careful evaluation for hormonal deficiency, and even in these cases controlled studies of effectiveness are lacking.

Orgasmic Response Problems

☐ *Description and Treatment of Female Orgasmic Response Problems*   Infrequent or total lack of orgasmic response is a fairly common phenomenon in women. **Secondary** or **situational orgasmic dysfunction** is one of the most prevalent complaints in sex therapy, perhaps because it covers so many different problems: women who can only masturbate to orgasm, women who rarely experience orgasm with their partners, women who are not orgasmic except in one very restricted position, women who were at one time orgasmic but are no longer responsive, and women who are only orgasmic outside of their primary relationship (Kaplan, 1974; Masters & Johnson, 1970). Women who have never had an orgasm through any means of stimulation are usu-

ally labeled **primary anorgasmic** females (Masters & Johnson, 1970), although some therapists prefer **preorgasmic** (Barbach, 1974), to suggest that all women are eventually capable of experiencing orgasm. Previously the term *frigid* was used to describe women's unresponsiveness in sex; however, its inadequacy and negative implications forced it out of clinical usage in the 1960s.

Few factors have been clearly related to orgasmic ease in women. Clinicians typically report that anorgasmic women exhibit patterns of restrictive upbringing and extreme religiosity, experience conflicts about being sexual, dislike their bodies and genitals, and have relationship conflicts and stresses (Barbach, 1975; Heiman et al., 1976; Kaplan, 1974; Masters & Johnson, 1970). Research has been contradictory, especially with respect to historical factors (Fisher, 1973; Terman, 1938, 1951).

In a comparison study of anorgasmic women and sexually functional women, anorgasmic women reported many more symptoms of depression and interpersonal sensitivity (Derogatis et al., 1981). For example, more than 70 percent of the anorgasmic women reported "a loss of sexual interest or pleasure, blaming themselves for things, feeling blue, worrying about things too much" and "feeling critical of others, feeling easily hurt by others." These results do not imply causality, nor do they imply that women with sexual problems are usually seriously psychologically distressed. They do suggest, however, that for some women, sexual dysfunction may be related to a set of broader life problems.

The partners of women with orgasmic

Box 8–2

ORGASMIC RESPONSE PROBLEMS IN WOMEN

Mr. and Mrs. E, married twenty-three years with two children, complained of Mrs. E's orgasmic problem, which began in the twelfth year of their marriage.

Both partners had successful sexual experiences before marriage. During the first twelve years of marriage, sex regularly occurred two to three times per week, with frequent orgasms for Mrs. E.

During the twelfth year of marriage, Mr. E was fired from his job and was unsuccessful in finding permanent employment for eighteen months. He became chronically depressed and drank excessively. Sex was either absent or excessive. Then Mrs. E discovered her husband was having an extramarital affair. She refused to sleep with him or to have sex with him for six months while he gradually began working, terminated his affair, and controlled his drinking.

dysfunction have also been studied. Years ago Terman (1938, 1951) found that husbands of these women were less self-sufficient and socially competent as well as more conformist than partners of sexually functional women. More recently, Clement and Pfafflin (1980) found that the partners of anorgasmic women, in comparison with partners of sexually functional women, were significantly more depressed, less self-confident and relaxed, less dominant and assured, and less socially at ease. In short, the psychological profile for the dysfunctional woman was extremely similar to the psychological profile of her partner, emphasizing the importance of dealing with

both partners even if it appears that only one is suffering from any type of sexual problem. Box 8–2 highlights two case histories that illustrate the importance of relationship factors in the backgrounds of anorgasmic women.

Treatment for orgasmic problems is based on a number of factors believed to be important for adequate sexual functioning. Masters and Johnson (1970) conceptualize female orgasmic response "as an *acceptance* of naturally occurring stimuli that have been given erotic significance by an individual sexual value system" (p. 297) rather than as a learned response. Their therapeutic orientation, much like that for

When they began to have sex again, Mrs. E never had an orgasm, and sex eventually decreased to once a week or once every two weeks.

Mr. and Mrs. F, ages 35 and 30, had been married six years. They had one 3-year-old child.

Mrs. F came from a family of seven children, while Mr. F was an overindulged only child. Throughout their relationship, he had made all the decisions, insisting on his way and rarely taking his wife's interests into account. A constant marital friction developed.

Prior to marriage, Mrs. F had not been orgasmic. In marriage, she was occasionally orgasmic with manual stimulation, but not during intercourse. With increased marital tension, she became less responsive. About a year after their child was born, the lack of coital enjoyment became distressing to her and embarrassing to her husband's male image of himself. He seemed more concerned about his self-image than about her satisfaction.

Not surprisingly, Mr. F sent his wife to various professionals for what he saw as "her problem." He took no responsibility for the problem.

(Adapted from Masters and Johnson, 1970, pp. 241–244.)

men with erectile problems, concentrates on reducing performance demand while giving the woman permission to express sexual feelings, instructing the woman not to focus initially on her partner's needs, and enhancing and encouraging sexual communication (especially the woman's expression of sexual stimulation needs). Sensate focus provides the vehicle for reaching these goals in the beginning. Eventually, manual stimulation to orgasm is encouraged, and different coital positions that offer greater stimulation for and control by the female, such as the female-on-top or the side-by-side positions, are tried.

Masters and Johnson (1970) did not use different therapy procedures for primary and secondary anorgasmia, as have other therapists. For example, one effective program for women who have never or very rarely experienced orgasm is a masturbation program developed by LoPiccolo and Lobitz (1972); other therapists have since expanded on the original plan (Barbach, 1974, 1980, Heiman et al., 1976). The program stresses self-acceptance, taking responsibility for one's own sexual responsiveness, and communicating sexual needs to one's partner. The masturbation program includes a graduated series of steps, the first of which the woman completes on her own (see Table 8–1).

TABLE 8-1   BASIC STEPS IN THE SELF-HELP PROGRAM DESIGNED FOR THE TREATMENT OF ORGASMIC PROBLEMS IN FEMALES

1. Body awareness, where the woman looks at and becomes comfortable with the appearance of her own body and genitals, is the first step. She practices Kegel exercises, which involve the contraction of the pubococcygeous muscles in the vagina (Kegel, 1952). These exercises are thought to improve the woman's awareness of sensation in her genital area, increasing the tone and strength of the muscles, as well as giving her a sense of control.

2. Exploring body textures, including genitals, by touch is advised after the initial body awareness exercises have been satisfactorily completed.

3. Touching areas of the body that feel sensitive and/or pleasurable when manually explored follows after a woman learns to feel at ease while exploring her own body.

4. Learning to relax, physically and mentally, and learning to allow oneself to think in more sexual ways, by either fantasizing or reading erotic literature, allow a woman to be freer sexually.

5. Dealing with attitudes about sexual response, masturbation, and fears of letting go is necessary; the patient is also instructed on masturbation techniques and orgasm enhancers.

6. Using a vibrator, if orgasm has not occurred through manual stimulation, is recommended at this time.

7. The patient's partner becomes involved in the program at this point: Sensate focus exercises and sensual stimulation with the woman's partner with an emphasis on initiating and refusing sex, communicating about types of touching (desired or not), and enjoying rather than forcing sexual feelings are attempted. After the woman becomes orgasmic in masturbation, she does so with her partner present.

8. The partner stimulates the woman to orgasm, with her guidance.

9. Intercourse, with additional manual or vibrator stimulation, as another form of sexual stimulation to orgasm, is the final step.

(Adapted from Heiman et al., 1976; LoPiccolo & Lobitz, 1972.)

Although LoPiccolo and Lobitz (1972) designed their program for couples, others have adapted it for women seen individually and also for therapy programs designed for small groups of women (Barbach, 1975, 1980). The latter approach can be less expensive and does not require a woman to have a partner. What may be even more important about this type of program is that being in a group of women "eliminates the feelings of isolation and abnormality as each woman works with and learns from others like herself" (Barbach, 1980, p. 116). Nevertheless, the masturbation program can be quite difficult for a woman's sexual partner because initially the woman's goal is to become orgasmic on her own. The partner's feelings of alienation and uncertainty may have to be dealt with in the therapeutic process, regardless of the format used (Heiman et al., 1976).

Another program has been developed

that is sometimes successful in dealing with a difficult but common complaint: the lack of arousal and orgasm during coital stimulation (Zeiss, Rosen, & Zeiss, 1978). In this program, the woman uses fantasy and masturbation in the early stages and must later use a dildo or similar object to get accustomed to vaginal containment during self-stimulation. The woman also uses the dildo while masturbating and fantasizing about intercourse. The woman's partner only observes during the early stages. The gradual transition to intercourse occurs in the final stage. Each of these steps can take several weeks. Therapists recommend that sensate focus exercises be used in the program as well.

Before we end our discussion of orgasmic problems in women, two other issues deserve mention. One is that women can pretend to be orgasmic. No one knows how many women fake orgasms on a regular basis, although therapists have reported that this is not unusual in women who find it difficult to become aroused or experience an orgasm (Barbach, 1974). Usually women who frequently fake orgasms have felt pressure to be sexually responsive, to please their partners sexually, or to "get sex over with."

The second issue of interest is that occasionally women report that they reach orgasm too quickly, meaning that before they have an opportunity to enjoy being aroused, they have an orgasm. This problem is so infrequent that most therapists do not write about it. Some of the procedures used for men who experience premature ejaculation are undoubtedly relevant. In particular, learning to tolerate higher levels of arousal in a low-tension atmosphere would appear to be useful for these women. (Premature ejaculation is discussed in the following section.)

□ *Description and Treatment of Male Ejaculatory Problems* When men ejaculate too quickly, the condition is called **premature ejaculation.** How fast is too fast? There are no absolute rules that determine the right amount of time between initial arousal and orgasm. Masters and Johnson (1970) have defined "premature" relative to the couple; that is, it is dependent on the inability of the male to delay ejaculation until his female partner reaches orgasm 50 percent of the time in intercourse. This time period will vary. Recall that Gebhard (1965) found that almost 28 percent of the women he studied were orgasmic during 90 to 100 percent of their coital contacts that lasted less than one minute. Also, approximately 10 percent of the women studied were never orgasmic during coitus, regardless of its duration. Thus premature ejaculation is a relative term, dependent on the individual male and his partner.

A variety of explanations have been offered to account for premature ejaculation. Years ago the Kinsey group (1948) suggested that there was an evolutionary value for rapid (though not "too" rapid) ejaculation. Rapid ejaculation, according to this hypothesis, was a biologically adaptive mechanism for avoiding attack from predators while in a defenseless position. Another hypothesis is that early conditioning of rushed and secretive coitus results in a later pattern of rapid ejaculation (Masters and Johnson, 1970). For example, early sexual experiences in a parked car might lead to this pattern. Also possible is that a man may not be aware of the level of his arousal, and may, in fact, not realize that he is ready to ejaculate because of the stresses of anxiety or because he is concentrating on nonerotic thoughts to slow down arousal (Perelman, 1980). Another study suggests that for unknown physiological reasons some men may ejaculate at a lower level of arousal (Spiess, 1977). Relationship factors, such as the need for power and control over one's partner, may also influence ejaculatory control problems (Kaplan, 1974).

Typically, a premature ejaculator tries to solve his problem in three ways: He avoids direct stimulation, he uses distraction techniques, and/or he employs anesthetizing procedures such as using several condoms at one time or applying anesthetic creams (Perelman, 1980). Although these self-help procedures may work for some men, generally they do not adequately deaden sensations. Therefore, the major aim of treatment for premature ejaculation is to teach the man to recognize the sensations he feels immediately prior to orgasm, and to do so in a relaxed manner, concentrating on the sensual pleasures of the experience.

Gaining ejaculatory control is significantly helped by the practice of two techniques: the Semans (or pause) technique and the squeeze technique. Developed by James Semans (1956), the **Semans technique** requires manual stimulation of the penis by the male's partner until he feels that he is about to ejaculate. The couple pauses, allowing the sensation of impending orgasm to subside. Stimulation of the penis is then resumed and again discontinued just prior to the feeling of inevitability. This procedure is repeated three or four times before the man allows himself to ejaculate. The purpose of the exercise is to teach the premature ejaculator his point of inevitability (usually learned after a few occasions of not stopping soon enough). With practice, usually several times per week for several weeks, fewer and shorter pauses are necessary, and the man is able to continue stimulation with only an occasional pause.

The **squeeze technique** is basically the same as the Semans procedure, with one exception: When the couple pauses at the point when the man feels close to orgasm, he or his partner squeezes just below the coronal ridge of the penis for about 20 seconds, or until the feeling of the urge to ejaculate subsides (Masters & Johnson, 1970). This procedure is illustrated in Figure 8–1. Squeezing usually causes a partial loss of erection and does not hurt the man as long as his penis is fully erect. The squeezing must not be done too late, however, as the action will force the ejaculate back into the urethra and could in rare cases cause damage to the urethra, bladder, or seminal vesicles (LoPiccolo, 1978). The process of stimulating and squeezing is done three or four times before the man ejaculates.

A number of therapists suggest that the premature ejaculator should first practice one of the techniques just described during masturbation, allowing him to decrease his anxiety and build self-confidence without the added stimulation of a partner. Then

Figure 8-1. There are many ways to integrate the squeeze technique into lovemaking.

with his partner, after doing sensate focus exercises, manual or oral stimulation is tried, using the Semans or squeeze method. Eventually, vaginal containment without pelvic thrusting is introduced. The couple gradually progresses to slow movements and then finally to vigorous thrusting, while still using the ejaculation avoidance techniques when necessary. The female's cooperation and the couple's open communication are vital to the success of ejaculatory control. The female partner may go through a period during which she is not very enthusiastic about the technique. With patience and mutual cooperation, however, this phase passes, and the male usually sees improvement in his ability to control ejaculation.

Although ejaculating too quickly is a fairly common problem, a few men, approximately 1 to 2 percent of an average clinical population, experience **retarded ejacula-**

tion, also called ejaculatory incompetence (Apfelbaum, 1980). Men with this problem may be unable to ejaculate under any circumstances. Most of the clinical cases, however, consist of men who can easily ejaculate during masturbation or foreplay, but find they cannot experience orgasm during coitus. Many of these men can maintain an erection without ejaculating for 30 to 60 minutes of intercourse (Masters & Johnson, 1970). Usually the retarded ejaculator's wife is multiply orgasmic (Apfelbaum, 1980; Masters and Johnson, 1970).

Although there are no consistent historical factors that seem to cause retarded ejaculation, Masters and Johnson (1970) have stressed the frequent themes of religious orthodoxy, fear of impregnating a woman, and lack of interest or active dislike of one's female partner. Occasionally, a sudden psychological trauma, such as a discovered affair or being surprised by someone while engaged in intercourse, can produce ejaculatory incompetence (Kaplan, 1974; Munjack, 1975).

Personality factors associated with retarded ejaculation have included self-criticism and guilt (Cooper, 1968) and passivity (Kaplan & Abrams, 1958; Razani, 1972). Apfelbaum (1980) offers a different explanation. He describes the retarded ejaculator as someone whose psychological arousal and physical arousal are not in tune—thus he remains erect although he feels little erotic desire.

Sensate focus exercises, education about the dysfunction, and home assignments geared toward minimizing anxiety are typical treatment strategies for retarded ejaculation (Masters & Johnson, 1970). Other therapists have included masturbatory practice, desensitization for performance anxiety, fantasy during coitus, and having the man rapidly switch from masturbation to coitus near the point of ejaculation (Heiman et al., 1981; Kaplan, 1974).

Two additional procedures have been noted as useful in the treatment of retarded ejaculation. The **male bridge maneuver** has the female partner manipulate the male's penis close to the point of ejaculation and then rapidly insert it into her vagina (Kaplan, 1974). In **counterbypassing,** the male expresses during the sexual interaction his complaints and negative feelings about sex, such as feeling that coitus is drudgery and not enjoyable or that he is afraid his partner will criticize him (Apfelbaum, 1980). Apfelbaum provides evidence that with a therapist's guidance, the expression of all of these antisexual feelings relieves the male partner, helps clear the air for sexual feelings to surface, and permits his mate to better understand his conflicts. Again, the female's cooperation is critical to this strategy, and her role is difficult. The therapist helps her to understand that the interaction is a way of opening communication channels and reducing the fears of the male, and is not a criticism of her.

☐ *Treatment Effectiveness: Women* Many studies do not distinguish between primary and secondary categories for problems of orgasm in women, making statements about therapeutic success difficult to interpret (Wright et al., 1977). However, what generally seems to be happening is that women in therapy who are totally inorgasmic have an 85 to 95 percent chance of becoming orgasmic during masturbation, but only a 35 to 50 percent chance of becoming orgasmic during intercourse (Heiman et al., 1981). Women with secondary orgasmic dysfunctions have success rates varying between 45 and 77 percent (Cooper, 1970; Masters & Johnson, 1970). Group treatment for nonorgasmic women seems to be effective, although it is somewhat more effective for younger women (Schneidman & McGuire, 1976).

The effectiveness of biofeedback treatment for arousal problems has not been evaluated in sexually dysfunctional women. However, two studies on the value of this type of procedure to increase or decrease sexual arousal have suggested that feedback is not particularly effective and may even interfere with arousal (Cerney, 1978). These results, when combined with the similar results on erectile failure, indicate quite clearly that biofeedback is not a particularly effective procedure for correcting sexual problems. Perhaps the procedure teaches the person to watch and focus on his or her performance—the opposite message from the one sex therapy tries to teach (Heiman & Hatch, 1981).

☐ *Treatment Effectiveness: Men* Some of the highest success rates in the outcome literature, between 85 and 95 percent, are reported for premature ejaculation. An exception is Cooper's (1969) study, where 43 percent of the men were rated as improved and 7 percent became "worse." Cooper, however, used very strict criteria for improvement: the consistent delay of ejaculation for twice as long as had been common before treatment, along with psychological satisfaction.

The success of treatment for retarded ejaculation is difficult to evaluate since so few cases are reported. Masters and Johnson (1970) reported success in fourteen of seventeen cases; Cooper (1968) reported improvement in six out of thirteen cases, using a combination of deep muscle relaxing exercises and other behavioral techniques; and Ovesey and Myers (1968) used psychoanalysis successfully with five of ten males. Other studies have reported limited success with a smaller number of cases (see Munjack & Kanno, 1979, for a review).

Sex with Pain: Dyspareunia and Vaginismus

☐ *Description and Treatment* Painful sex is called **dyspareunia,** which means "badly mated." Pain is experienced as tearing, burning, aching, or feelings of pressure, and it typically occurs during or just after intercourse. For the individual experiencing pain, and for his or her sexual partner as well, sexual interactions often become extremely stressed. In such cases, sex generally is not pleasurable and often is avoided.

A variety of physical factors can cause dyspareunia—factors that must be carefully explored prior to looking for psychological origins. Sometimes physical factors are obvious. For example, in women, postsurgical damage to the vaginal or abdominal area, childbearing damage to the uterine or vaginal structures, endometriosis (fibrous tissue attached to the internal genital tract causing pain when irritated during intercourse), recurrent urinary tract infections, tumors, and insufficient lubrication are all sources of discomfort during intercourse (Kaplan, 1974; Masters & Johnson, 1970). Other physical signs are not so obvious and may include small scars or abrasions in the vaginal or vulva area, which can easily be overlooked (Abarbanel, 1978).

Although dyspareunia is less common in men than in women, male dyspareunia can also be caused by physical problems. Among the more frequently mentioned causes of painful sex in men are **Peyronie's**

disease, where fibrosis of the corpora cavernosa tissue may cause the penis to erect at an angle uncomfortable for intercourse; **penile chordee,** the excessive downward bowing of the penis; hypersensitivity of the glans of the penis, causing pain when touched or when subjected to the vaginal environment; foreskin irritation in the uncircumcised male, often due to unhygienic habits or to **phimosis,** where the foreskin is too tight to be fully retracted over the penis; prostate problems; gonorrhea scars; **priapism,** the excessive duration of erection without desire, stimulation, or ejaculation; or bladder infections (Masters & Johnson, 1970). Additionally, men may find the use of a contraceptive diaphragm by female partners to be irritating, and both men and women may be sensitive to certain spermicidal creams or jellies.

For a number of the physical problems associated with dyspareunia, surgery or the use of medications may be very helpful. However, if the pain has been part of a person's sexual pattern for a long time, eliminating the pain is only the first step toward normalizing a couple's sexual interactions — it takes some time and experience to relax and enjoy sex if it has always been painful (Heiman et al., 1981).

Most of the psychological factors associated with dyspareunia have focused on women, perhaps because male dyspareunia is much less commonly reported. Major psychological factors associated with female dyspareunia include histories of traumatic sexual experience (incest, rape, or an extremely painful first sexual experience); severe conflicts about being sexual and

having intercourse; and a poor relationship with one's male partner (Lazarus, 1980; Masters and Johnson, 1970). Treatment, therefore, centers on these issues, with emphasis placed on increasing relaxation for both partners during physical contact, since tension may make pain more noticeable. Desensitization to sexual contact and hypnosis have been used with some success for women who have had traumatic past experiences. The very gradual inclusion of genital stimulation, with the woman controlling the type of approach to be used, has been attempted in the context of sensate focus exercises (Masters & Johnson, 1970). Vaginal dilators may also be used if vaginal muscle contractions make intercourse difficult.

Lazarus (1980) stresses the need for what he calls multimodal history taking when treating dyspareunia, which includes fact finding about a person's behavior, emotional state, sensations, imagery, cognition, interpersonal factors, and other organic factors, including drug use. He abbreviates this list as BASIC-ID. In Box 8–3, we offer a condensed version of one case he treated successfully using his history-recording method. This case illustrates the importance of the partner's role, as well as the importance of the individual's beliefs about sexual intimacy, in spite of the fact that only one person may appear to have the sexual problem.

Another coital problem is **vaginismus.** A vaginismic woman experiences spasmodic involuntary contractions of the vaginal muscles. This condition can make intercourse painful or even impossible. Severe

Box 8–3

FEMALE DYSPAREUNIA: CASE STUDY

C.S. was a 29-year-old computer programmer, married for two years. She and her husband had enjoyed mutual manual stimulation to orgasm prior to marriage, but they had not attempted intercourse premaritally due to the husband's religious reservations. C.S. had had satisfactory intercourse with a former fiancé. Since marriage, her pain during and after intercourse increased in intensity and eventually she and her husband only had oral-genital sex. The couple had unsuccessfully tried sex therapy before.

C.S's behavior was to avoid sex, though she felt guilty, anxious and frustrated. She experienced sharp pains throughout intromission. But the most outstanding feature was her imagery: she could, in fantasy, imagine having pleasurable sex *before* but not after marriage, "as long as we're not married, it's alright." Basically, C.S. had been taught that keeping a man was possible if she did not give in sexually so that all images of coital activity with her husband resulted in feelings of rejection and abandonment.

Much of the therapy centered on *coping and mastery imagery*. C.S. would imagine that her husband left her and how she coped with the loneliness and humiliation. Along with developing her ability to imagine this scene without feeling devastated, she was asked to imagine doing things to offset the loneliness and abandonment. The rationale for this imagery was that believing in one's personal survival after a loss mitigates the terror of becoming deeply attached and intimate. Other "irrational" cognitions such as excessive need for approval and the stigma of divorce were also addressed.

The husband of C.S. refused to come into therapy until three and a half months into treatment when C.S. had suggested that they try intercourse and her husband experienced erectile failure. From this, it was learned that he had strong performance anxieties due to an experience with a prostitute a year before meeting C.S. He gradually became more comfortable and had no difficulty on the honeymoon, but again lost his ardor when he felt her lack of sexual pleasure and his guilt for causing her pain. His erectile problem was treated and the couple was told to try a sensate focus regimen at their own pace. In spite of some setbacks and relapses, eighteen months later the couple was functioning well.

(Adapted from Lazarus, 1980, pp. 151–154)

cases include women who cannot be examined in a routine gynecological exam, as their muscles are too contracted to allow any penetration. Sometimes, however, these women are able to become aroused and experience orgasm through nonvaginal stimulation. There is evidence that women who are orgasmic are more likely than nonorgasmic women to benefit from treatment for vaginismus (Ellison, 1972).

Common descriptive features of these women include a fear of pregnancy, prior sexual trauma, severe sexual conflicts, religious orthodoxy, a fear of intercourse, a homosexual orientation, and prior dyspareunia (Ellison, 1972; Fuchs et al., 1973; Masters & Johnson, 1970). The attitudes and beliefs of a woman's partner also contribute to vaginismus. In fact, Ellison (1972) has reported that therapy is not generally successful for couples who find sex dirty and revolting.

The treatment of choice for vaginismus is the use of graduated Hegar dilators (Masters & Johnson, 1970), beginning with a very small size and gradually increasing to the approximate size and shape of the erect penis. Sometimes the woman's fingers or her partner's are used instead of dilators. The insertion may initially be done under the direction of a gynecologist, but eventually it is done in private. The woman must be relaxed, and must be in control of the speed and timing of the procedure. To encourage relaxation, systematic desensitization and hypnosis have proven helpful (Fuchs et al., 1973). The dilator procedure is a highly effective way to remove the vaginismic symptoms and to prepare the couple for the communication and control issues that are important during intercourse (Leiblum, Pervin, & Campbell, 1980).

□ *Treatment Effectiveness* Dyspareunia is reportedly difficult to treat, and there are no reported statistics on its degree of success in therapy (Abarbanel, 1978; Masters and Johnson, 1970). In contrast, the outcome for vaginismus is extremely good—in fact, close to 100 percent (Kaplan, 1974; Masters & Johnson, 1970). This figure has been questioned, however, because failures may not be reported; for example, the success or failure rate of therapy "dropouts" may not be included.

Factors Influencing Sex Therapy Outcome: Who Improves?

We know that currently some sexual dysfunctions seem easier to treat than others. For example, people in therapy for vaginismus and premature ejaculation tend to have the highest success rate; those being treated for primary inorgasmic dysfunctions are next, with erectile problems and secondary inorgasmic dysfunctions the least successfully treated of this group. Little data or too few cases on retarded ejaculation, dyspareunia, and sexual desire disorders are available at the present time to be able to rank the success of therapy in these areas. In any case, indications are that sex therapy—with its combination of sex education, communication, specific training exercises, and anxiety-reduction tech-

TABLE 8-2 SOME FACTORS THAT INFLUENCE TREATMENT RESPONSE FOR SEXUAL DYSFUNCTIONS

VARIABLE	*RELATIONSHIP TO TREATMENT RESPONSE*
Duration of sexual inadequacy	Disorders of longer duration generally are more difficult to treat successfully. Duration is less important in females.
Time of onset	Primary sexual inadequacy (especially impotence) is much more difficult to treat successfully than secondary dysfunctions. Time of onset is less important in females.
Developmental characteristics of sexual inadequacy	A problem arising acutely in response to a specific psychophysical stress (i.e., bereavement, marriage, or pregnancy) is a better treatment prospect than a disorder of uncertain origin. A better outcome is associated with an intermittent rather than a persistent dysfunction.
Age	The older the patient the less "complete" the response to treatment. Age is relatively less important in females.
Strength of sex drive	Subjects with very low sex drives are more difficult to treat. This is relatively less important in females.
Premarital experience	Physically and emotionally rewarding premarital sexual experience (masturbation and coitus) is a good prognostic indicator; it is of much greater significance in the male.
Emotional feelings during sexual activity	In both sexes disgust or revulsion is not a good sign. Anxiety, unless disproportionately great, is not so important.
Personality of partners	An integrated personality is associated with a better outcome. Abnormal personality and relationship problems, and especially high levels of hostility, may compromise treatment.
Emotional relationship between partners	Positive emotional feelings are associated with a better outcome. This is proportionately more important in females.
Motivation for treatment	Assessed by regularity of clinic attendance and level of commitment to home assignments: A high level of positive motivation correlates with a good treatment response.
Initial treatment response	Early improvement, within two to five sessions, indicates a favorable outcome.

(Adapted from Cooper, 1981)

niques—is relatively efficient in dealing with sexual problems.

Across a number of studies, several factors have emerged as generally predictive of better or worse outcomes in sex therapy. The items listed in Table 8-2 are selected from a list gathered by Cooper (1981); they are based on his work and that of other clinicians and researchers. The list shows that the degree of positive feelings about one's partner is more important for females than for males, while age, premarital sexual sat- isfaction, sex drive, the length of time the problem exists, and whether the problem is diagnosed as primary or secondary are more important for males.

CHOOSING A THERAPIST

When looking for a therapist, the following considerations should be kept in mind (see Heiman et al., 1976, for further details):

1. A personal recommendation of a friend or professional whose opinion you respect (and who has some knowledge of the competence and type of practice of that individual) is one of the better sources for locating a therapist.
2. Ask about the therapist's qualifications: Experience, licensure, and board certification are clues, though not guarantees. You cannot be assured of good treatment just because a professional is licensed, but such credentials do provide the consumer with more legal protection than if the therapist is *not* licensed.
3. When you visit a therapist, decide for yourself whether the person is someone you can trust. If you are concerned about what might go on during therapy, or whether the information you give to that person will remain confidential, ask. Most therapists are willing to explain their general orientation concerning therapeutic problems.
4. Be wary of paid advertisements. Advertising is not ethically accepted by any of the professional organizations. However, this does not apply to public announcements or public-interest stories prepared by news agencies or community services. For example, a college may announce the beginning of a new program, or an article may appear in the newspaper about a new service.
5. No sex therapy program legitimately includes any sexual activity between client and therapist, or for that matter any observed sexual activity.

SUMMARY

1. Defining a sexual problem is not an easy task. A definition is determined by whatever is currently classified as "good" functioning by the individual, the couple, and the sociocultural climate.
2. Estimating the incidence of sexual problems is difficult. One reason

is that there is a difference between sexual *functioning* and sexual *satisfaction,* and yet the distinction is not always made. Thus we are sometimes unsure about what is being reported.

3. Sexual dysfunctions are classified according to *desire, arousal, orgasm,* and the presence of *pain* or *discomfort.* Problems are evaluated according to how frequently they occur (*temporal dimension*) and whether they are present in all situations or only occur under certain conditions (*situational dimension*). There are degrees of sexual functioning/dysfunctioning, and most people experience some type of problem in their lifetime without being considered dysfunctional. Sexual problems often overlap as well, meaning that a person will experience trouble in more than one category.

4. Most sexual problems incorporate both physical and psychological factors. Illness has psychological consequences for the individual and can very well affect one's sexual response. On the other hand, stress can contribute to erectile problems as well as to vaginal infections (Chapter 9). We must not lose sight of the body-mind connection in both sexually functional and sexually dysfunctional circumstances.

5. *Performance anxiety* is common among people who are experiencing sexual difficulties. Such anxiety is often the crucial factor in determining whether or not someone is able to function sexually: The more one concentrates on the performance, the more trouble he or she may have in functioning, and certainly a good deal of satisfaction will be lost. An important aspect of therapy is teaching people to relax.

6. Sexual desire problems are not easy to define, nor are they easy to treat. Sexually *hypoactive* people have little desire for sex, while those who are *hyperactive* have high sex drives. Problems of this nature are different from arousal, orgasmic, or pain-causing dysfunctions because these other types of dysfunctions have physical points of reference.

7. *Erectile dysfunction* is a common arousal problem in males. Those with **primary erectile dysfunction** have never had an erection firm enough for intercourse, whereas men who have had at least one erection that has led to intercourse are said to have a secondary dysfunction. Physical as well as psychological problems are associated with erectile dysfunctions.

8. **Sensate focus** exercises are used in the early stages of treatment for erectile problems. These tasks are designed to decrease performance anxiety and to improve basic communication skills and sexual enjoyment. The first step involves only sensual touching, with the genitals being off limits. Eventually, the couple moves on to genital touching and intercourse. The **teasing technique** is also used in treating erectile problems. Couples employing this method are instructed to stop stimulation of the penis once it has become erect. The procedure is then repeated.

9. A **primary anorgasmic,** or **preorgasmic,** woman is one who has never had an orgasm through any means of stimulation. A woman who is only orgasmic under certain conditions is suffering from the secondary form of this dysfunction. A masturbation program was developed to treat women who never or rarely experience orgasm.

10. **Premature ejaculation** is the condition that exists when a man ejaculates too quickly. Whether or not a man is suffering from premature ejaculation is generally defined relative to the individual and his sexual partners, because what is considered sexually satisfying varies from person to person, and from couple to couple. The **Semans technique** was developed to help men learn to control ejaculation. The **squeeze technique** is similar to the one developed by Semans, with the exception being that when the man feels he is close to ejaculating, he or his partner must squeeze the penis just below the coronal ridge until the feeling subsides.

11. **Retarded ejaculation** is sometimes called *ejaculatory incompetence.* The basic problem here is that a man is able to ejaculate only under certain conditions. The **male bridge maneuver** is one method of treating this dysfunction: The female partner manipulates the man's penis until he is close to orgasm, at which point she inserts the penis into her vagina. **Counterbypassing** is when a man expresses his complaints and inhibiting feelings about intercourse while interacting sexually with a partner.

12. **Dyspareunia** is the experiencing of pain during or just after intercourse. Although it is most common among women, some men also suffer from it. Dyspareunia has a number of physical causes; for example, in women, postsurgical damage to the vaginal or abdominal area or recurrent urinary tract infections can be sources of discomfort. Psychological factors are also associated with dyspareunia.

13. **Vaginismus** is involuntary contractions of the vaginal muscles that can make intercourse painful, and sometimes impossible. The use of dilators is a common method of treatment.

14. A number of guidelines are suggested for choosing a therapist. Personal recommendations are valuable, and it is wise to ask about the therapist's qualifications. When you first visit a therapist, evaluate your feelings about this person and ask about anything that concerns you.

SUGGESTED READINGS

Barbach, L. *Women discover orgasm: A therapist's guide to a new treatment approach.* Riverside, N.J.: Free Press, 1980. A book to find out how other women have dealt with orgasmic response problems.

Heiman, J., LoPiccolo, L., & LoPiccolo, J. *Becoming orgasmic: A sexual growth program for women.* Englewood Cliffs, N.J.: Prentice-Hall, 1976. A self-help book for women with or without partners that deals with orgasm and other aspects of female sexuality.

Robinson, P. *The modernization of sex.* N.Y.: Harper & Row, 1976. An excellent critique of intellectual ideas surrounding the leaders in sex research from Havelock Ellis through Masters and Johnson.

Zilbergeld, B. *Male sexuality.* N.Y.: Bantam, 1978. An informational and sensitive guide on male sexual functioning and problems.

CHAPTER NINE

MEDICAL ASPECTS OF HUMAN SEXUALITY
Drugs, Illness, and Disease

. . . there are times in the life of everyone when the secure possession of his [/her] body (as an unchanging entity) is by no means certain: childhood, puberty, pregnancy, the menopause, old age, illness and injury constitute some of the most important situations in which effects are experienced in connection with the body.
Szasz, *Pain and Pleasure*

We have discussed the importance of health to sexual functioning without mentioning specific relationships among drugs, illnesses, and sexual problems. Some of the information that follows applies to many people, mainly because the use of alcohol is common and because sexually transmitted diseases are occurring in epidemic proportions. Other conditions, such as depression, epilepsy, and spinal cord injury, are restricted to a smaller percentage of the population. Nevertheless, these disabilities and many others af-fect people's behavior, physiology, and not surprisingly, their sexual functioning.

In this chapter, we describe some of the more commonly used drugs and explain how they influence the way people behave sexually and the problems that can develop from their use. Certain illnesses and diseases also influence sexual functioning, and we review the illnesses that are most problematic. Finally, we concentrate on the sexually transmitted diseases (STDs) and offer information on symptoms, causes, and available treatments.

DRUGS AND SEX

Most common drugs are taken with the intent of making a person feel better by giving relief from pain, providing increased stamina, increasing relaxation, or controlling unpleasant mood states. Drugs do indeed have a physiological effect, but that physiological effect may be modified by factors such as the duration of use of the drug, its dosage, the setting in which it is taken, and the expectations one has about the drug. A good example of how these factors interact is seen in the relationship between alcohol and sexual functioning.

Alcohol

One of the beliefs about alcohol is that it is a socially disinhibiting drug. Alcohol is supposed to alter conventional behavior by making people more relaxed and by allowing them to lose some control of their emotions. Many people think that alcohol also enhances sexual functioning. For example, 45 percent of the males and 68 percent of the females in a *Psychology Today* survey believed that alcohol increased their enjoyment of sex (Athanasiou, Shaver, & Tavris, 1970).

Alcohol appears, in fact, to diminish sexual responsiveness, at least physically. For example, one laboratory study done on males measured the physiological changes that occurred while they watched an erotic film (Farkas & Rosen, 1976). It demonstrated that increasing doses of alcohol resulted in slower penile response and the suppression of erection. The men also showed increased heart rates and reported greater discomfort with higher alcohol doses.

Two other laboratory studies that examined the effects of people's expectations on their sexual responses to erotic stimuli while under the influence of alcohol confirm the results of the Farkas and Rosen study (Bridell & Wilson, 1976; Wilson, Lawson, & Abrams, 1978). Greater penile tumescence was found in men who expected alcohol to enhance their sexual functioning, whether or not they had actually received alcohol in their drinks (Bridell & Wilson, 1976). Comparable results were found for a sample of alcoholic men (Wilson, Lawson, & Abrams, 1978).

A similar study of women showed that vaginal vasocongestion decreased as the alcohol doses increased (Wilson & Lawson, 1976). However, increased alcohol doses resulted in reports that subjectively, the women felt more sexually aroused. For women, alcohol was a psychological enhancer and a physical inhibitor.

Two major problems develop because of the effects of alcohol on sexual functioning. First, a lack of sexual functioning that is experienced on one or two occasions may be the start of a vicious performance-anxiety cycle: On subsequent sexual contacts the individual may worry about having the same difficulty or about the partner's possible negative reactions. Second, long-term heavy use of alcohol may result in irreversible endocrinological, neurological, and vascular damage and permanently reduced sexual responsiveness.

Marijuana

The effect of marijuana on sexual response is difficult to assess since almost all of the studies have a "positive" bias in that they ask whether the drug enhances sexual enjoyment and not whether it interferes with sexual response. Among college students, for example, one study demonstrated that over half of the sample reported increased sexual feelings while the rest reported no change (Halikas, Goodwin, & Guze, 1971). Another researcher found that 39 percent of the males and 50 percent of the females reported increased sexual desire and pleasure when they were high (Goode, 1969).

Marijuana has been claimed to be associated with lower testosterone levels in males (Kolodny et al., 1974), although a more carefully controlled study found no evidence of such a relationship (Mendelson et al., 1974). It would be interesting to know if marijuana, like alcohol, has a positive effect on the subjective experience of arousal and sensory experience, but a neutral or negative effect on physical response. Only one questionnaire study thus far has shown that higher doses of marijuana tend to be related to reduced sexual pleasure and desire (Koff, 1974).

Narcotics and "Recreational" Drugs

Although there are no controlled studies on the effects of heroin on sexual functioning, addicts and clinicians have reported clear evidence that this drug interferes with sexual response. The evidence is less clear for methadone, the maintenance drug used to treat heroin addicts. Both drugs are known to relax users and to deaden their awareness of immediate surroundings. Delayed ejaculation, which may initially be seen as a positive side effect, has been reported. In one study, ejaculation was delayed an average of forty-four minutes for a group of heroin addicts (DeLeon & Wexler, 1973). More commonly, erectile problems are noted (Cicero et al., 1975; Mintz et al., 1974). These studies did not show a consistent pattern of erectile problems among those on methadone. Apparently, the effect of methadone is unpredictable, for another study showed that 65 percent of methadone patients described themselves as having average enjoyment, activity, and libido, although some subjects reported worse effects than those arising from heroin use (Wieland & Yunger, 1971).

Several street drugs have been reported to either heighten or decrease sexual performance (see Kaplan, 1974). Cocaine and amphetamines ("speed") tend to increase erectile ability but delay ejaculation, while giving the user a psychological rush. Barbiturates fairly consistently decrease sexual and social behavior. Quaaludes, in low doses, can inhibit sexual performance but increase desire, thus giving the drug a street reputation as an aphrodisiac. Long-term usage of all of these drugs may decrease sexual activity and interest.

Amyl nitrate, actually a prescription drug used for the relief of chest pains in heart patients, causes the blood vessels to expand rapidly. It has been used primarily among the gay subculture as an orgasm intensifier. The drug, however, can be dangerous because of its rapid and intense physiological impact; its effect is usually limited to one to three minutes.

Prescription Drugs

Because of the small number of adequately controlled studies on a reasonably large number of subjects, few conclusions can be drawn about the effects of medications on human sexual response. We shall therefore rely on Kaplan (1979) and Segraves (1977) for their comprehensive reviews of the more common drugs and their effects.

☐ *Antipsychotic Medication* Although reports of the effects of major tranquilizers on ejaculatory functioning are scattered, the most data are available on thioridazine (Mellaril), a drug prescribed for certain types of psychoses. The results are contradictory. Use of this drug usually inhibits ejaculation, although erection and orgasm do occur (Segraves, 1977). There is also a report of four cases of priapism (constant erection) associated with thioridazine use (Dorman & Schmidt, 1976). In contrast, erectile problems have been reported in several studies of this drug; for example, 44 percent of a sample of fifty-seven men had experienced erectile difficulties (Kotin et al., 1976). Another study revealed no erectile problems among fifteen men (Tennent, Bancroft, & Cass, 1974).

☐ *Antidepressant Drugs* In the studies on antidepressants and their effects, the number of individuals evaluated is so small that any conclusions are not dependable. Basically, all we can conclude from the current data is that these drugs *may* have sexual side effects (Segraves, 1977).

☐ *Antihypertensive Drugs* Antihypertensive drugs are prescribed for people who have high blood pressure and/or a history of serious cardiovascular problems, such as those who have suffered a stroke or a heart attack. On theoretical grounds, one might expect these drugs to interfere with ejaculation since many act on neurological and vascular systems. There is evidence indicating ejaculatory problems, although more with some drugs, such as quanethidine (Ismelin), than with others, such as alpha-methyldopa (Aldomet) (Bauer et al., 1961; Bulpitt & Dollery, 1973; Carver & Oaks, 1976). Erectile problems are also reported with many antihypertensives, but, again, some drugs are more problematic than others (Bulpitt & Dollery, 1973). Of special interest is that diuretics—drugs taken to reduce fluid retention in hypertensive patients—have been reported to interfere with ejaculation and erectile functioning (Bulpitt & Dollery, 1973).

The above results need to be carefully reviewed because control groups of nontreated individuals or those unaffected by the problem have almost never been studied. Hypertensive patients, in addition to having this serious disease, are often older and less active sexually; these factors may influence sexual functioning. However, since there is some indication that certain drugs may have a greater impact on sexual functioning, and reactions are often idiosyncratic, individuals who complain of sexual problems may benefit from switching medications. Also, individuals are often relieved to learn that their medications are the reason for their sexual problems.

DISEASE, ILLNESS, AND DISABILITY: HOW THESE CONDITIONS RELATE TO SEXUAL FUNCTIONING

A variety of health problems can affect sexual functioning (see Kaplan, 1974, 1979, for example). Since sexual response is based on adequate hormonal, neurological, and vascular functioning, any disturbance to these systems can impair sexual response or desire. Thus temporal lobe epilepsy, multiple sclerosis, and Parkinson's disease have been reported to produce a variety of arousal and orgasm difficulties in men and women (Lundberg, 1977). Men with diabetes mellitus are 30 to 60 percent more likely than nondiabetic men to have erectile problems (Cooper, 1972; Ellenberg, 1980). Contradictory results have been found for diabetic women. In one study, problems in achieving orgasm were found in 35 percent of the diabetic women (Kolodny, 1971), while another study reported that desire and orgasm levels did not differ between diabetic and nondiabetic women (Ellenberg, 1977; Jensen, 1981). In addition, a number of diabetics complain of reduced sensations during sexual experiences (Heiman & Hatch, 1981). The progression of diabetes differs in each person, so the relative influence of neurological, vascular, and hormonal factors is unclear.

Spinal cord lesions have variable and unpredictable effects on sexual functioning. The research in this area is difficult to evaluate because it is restricted to collection *after* an accident, when the diagnosis of damage is inferred from what the person is able to do rather than being based on a precise physical examination (Higgins, 1978). Thus we really do not know exactly what level of physical damage, and what level of sexual capability, a particular spinal cord patient has. In the existing data of the evaluated males, erectile capacity is retained by between 48.2 percent (Joccheim & Wahle, 1970) and 91.7 percent (Fitzpatrick, 1974). Ejaculatory ability remains for 2 percent (Joccheim & Wahle, 1970) to 16 percent (Hohmann, 1966) of patients studied. Little research exists on cord-injured women, although the data suggest that they retain their ability to experience orgasm (Higgins, 1978).

Coronary heart disease can interfere with a person's desire and performance during sex. However, whether the problem is physiologically or psychologically based is not clear. Stein (1980) notes that only 25 percent of couples who were sexually active prior to the heart attack resume sexual activity afterward, a reduction he views as "by and large unnecessary in terms of medical or physiological limitations" (Stein, 1980, p. 302). Support for this position comes from earlier work by Hellerstein and Friedman (1970); they had patients use portable EKG machines to record their cardiac patterns throughout the day. The average maximum heart rate during orgasm was 117 beats per minute, a level exceeded during the day by occupational or recreational activities.

Stein instructs his patients to routinely evaluate their cardiac work capacity with a bicycle ergometer, which measures the amount of work done by the heart over a period of time. He also prescribes a mild exercise program. In addition to evaluating the relative safety of physical activity, he reassures patients and their partners that death due to heart failure during intercourse is highly unlikely. The most frequently cited study on this topic comes from Japan, where researchers found only 0.6 percent of sudden death cases resulted from heart failure during sexual contact. The majority of coital deaths occurred when a person was with an unfamiliar, non-marital partner, and usually in new surroundings, such as a motel (Ueno, 1963). These data suggest that emotions, whether anxiety or general excitement, associated with clandestine sexual activity may be taxing for the coronary-prone individual. More recently, Myers and Hewar (1975) found that in one hundred coronary patients no cases of sudden death were related to coital activity. Other researchers, however, have suggested further evaluation of cardiac patients (Derogatis & King, 1981; Fletcher, 1979).

In the case of a chronic or life-threatening illness, the patient's partner is often as fearful and uncertain as the patient about initiating sex. The following excerpt is from *Heartsounds,* a book written by the wife of a person who had recently suffered a massive heart attack.

> It seemed crucial that he not know how scared I was. Lying there silently as though my mind were on my pleasure. . . .
>
> I felt poised at the edge of an irredeemable mistake. It would be dreadful to make him feel like an invalid here, of all places, in the bed. One wrong word and I might ruin it, erection gone, impulse gone, confidence gone, goodbye and maybe for good.
>
> And yet it might be even more dangerous to say nothing. For his body was in motion again now, and what if he was feeling pain, denying it, pushing himself to perform?

> "Do you want to rest a moment?" I whispered. Wrong. He made a sound like a sob and fell away from me, and we lay silent, not touching in any way. (Lear, 1980, p. 64)

All serious diseases or disabilities have a psychological impact that may substantially influence sexual functioning. Heart problems, kidney disease or transplants, cancer, multiple sclerosis, and spinal cord injury are only a few of the medical problems that affect people's lives and how they feel about themselves. There is no denying that illness, surgery, and physical disability can be major sources of psychological stress.

HEALTH AND DISEASE: THE REPRODUCTIVE ORGANS

Several serious diseases and pathological conditions occur in the reproductive organs. Some of them can be corrected with early identification and treatment; others cannot. The following discussion is focused on a description of the more common and/or more curable of these problems and their treatment.

Cancer

Cancer is the number two cause of death in the United States, outranked only by heart disease. Twenty-five percent of those who reach the age of 70 will develop some form of cancer, although not all will die from it. No one knows the cause of cancer—possibly different cancers have different origins. Apparently cancer begins by a change in a few cells, which are unable to limit their own growth. A **tumor**, or mass of cells, results. The tumor is *benign* if it does not spread to other parts of the body. Benign tumors are usually harmless. *Malignant* tumors do spread to other parts of the body in a process called **metastasis.**

Breast cancer is the most common type of cancer in women; it is the leading cause of death of women in their forties, and the

Box 9–1

THE BASIC BREAST SELF-EXAMINATION

Current recommendations are that all women examine their own breasts, monthly, preferably right after their menstrual flow is finished. If a woman checks herself regularly, she will become familiar with how her own breasts look and feel and be more able to recognize anything unusual. Self-examination also provides an early detection system in case there is a problem. Early detection can save a woman's life and often her breast. However, many women feel more comfortable if they first go through a BSE in the presence of their physician so as to identify various tissues and clarify what is normal. The following is a guideline for the monthly self-examination (from Budoff, 1980, and the Boston Women's Health Collective, 1976):

1. Look at your breasts in the mirror; note their shape and outline and look for any bumps or thickening. Look also at the nipples and see if one is pushed to the side or if it has recently inverted.
2. While checking your breasts, raise your arms over your head and push your hands together. Then put your hands at your hips and press down, all the while looking for the features noted in item 1.
3. Lie down on a bed. Place a small pillow under your left shoulder and let your left arm rest back above your head. With the fleshy part of the fingertips on your right hand, begin making small circular motions at

second leading killer of women of all other ages. Even so, only 7 percent of women ever get breast cancer, and if detected early, the survival rate can reach 95 percent (Budoff, 1980).

The most common first sign of breast cancer is a lump in the breast. However, not all lumps are tumors. Breast glands, most of which are located near the underarm side of the upper breast, are lumpy and tend to slide over the chest wall when pushed. Fibroadenomas, usually not carcinogenous, are breast tumors that feel rubbery, firm, and smooth, and can be pushed from side to side. The most common lumps are cysts, which occur in 30 percent of all women. Cysts usually increase in size and tenderness before menstrual flow, and they feel like movable pebbles when touched. Less than 1 percent of all cysts are cancerous; however, women with cystic breasts should have their breasts checked more often, as they are three to four times more likely to develop breast cancer (Parsons & Sommers, 1978). Cancerous lumps are usually harder than cysts and resist moving when pushed.

the colored edge of your left nipple and move in a slow clockwise circle until you have felt the entire breast. Normal breast tissue has different consistencies, so do not be alarmed if you feel unevenness—you will gradually learn what your breast feels like if you do this each month. You should feel a firm tissue in the lower portion of your breast, as you feel all the way to the beginning of your armpit. There, you may feel lymph nodes, which are soft, freely moving, but not tender, bumps.

4. Repeat this procedure on the right breast.
5. Squeeze each nipple gently to see if any secretion is present.

If you see or feel any lumps, discharge, or change since your last breast exam, see your physician immediately. Remember that most lumps (over 75 percent) are nonmalignant; but if you do find one, time is essential for avoiding negative consequences!

The more important characteristics associated with an increased chance of breast cancer are increasing age, a mother or sister with breast cancer, other types of cancer in several family members, previous breast or other cancers, and previous multiple exposures to chest X-rays. Less important but related factors are a history of cystic breast disease, childlessness or birth of first child after age 30, first menstruation at 11 years old or less, and being overweight (e.g., Budoff, 1980). Genetic factors, hormonal factors, and environmental factors all appear to be related to breast cancer. Exactly how they operate and the relative importance of each are currently unknown.

Early detection is vital to the cure of breast cancer. Most physicians recommend breast self-examination (BSE), since 90 percent of cancerous tumors are first noted by the patients. (A version of the BSE procedure is described in Box 9–1.) BSE should be done monthly so that a woman becomes familiar with her breasts. However, many women hesitate to examine themselves for fear of what they might find or what they might miss. The truth is that nearly 80 percent of breast lumps and changes are benign, and women are usually better detectors than their doctors, who examine them only once or twice a year.

Some physicians prefer technological detection devices because they can detect the cancer earlier. The most common of these techniques is mammography, a special X-ray technique that correctly identifies 85 to 90 percent of cancerous tumors. Although exposure to radiation from X-rays increases the risk of cancer, newer machines minimize the radiation output. Mammography is particularly recommended by the American Cancer Society when there is a strong clinical indication for breast cancer in women under 35, when a woman under 40 has a personal history of breast cancer, and when a woman under 50 has a personal history or immediate family history of the disease. The American Cancer Society also recommends that every woman over 50 should have mammography every one to two years, regardless of her history. Other nonradiation detection techniques are being developed, including thermography, which photographs heat patterns, and ultrasound or sonography, which uses high-frequency sound waves to detect masses. Thus, in the near future, early stages of breast cancer may be detected without the use of radiation techniques.

Once cancer is diagnosed, surgery is usually recommended for cancer localized to the breast area. The surgery of choice for many years has been a **radical mastectomy,** or the **Halsted procedure,** which includes removal of the breast as well as the underlying muscle, fat, and lymph nodes. Developed in the 1890s, this procedure saves many lives. While it is often the only available alternative, it can be psychologically devastating because it is extremely disfiguring, as is any massive amputation, and the surgery itself leaves a woman physically exhausted and subject to feeling chilled. Other techniques have since been developed, including **lumpectomy,** in which the lump and a small amount of surrounding tissue are removed. Following lumpectomy, radiation treatments are given for a two-month period to protect the remaining breast tissue. Success with radiation therapy used without surgery has also been reported (Rotman et al., 1979). Although still being evaluated, this procedure appears to be as effective as mastectomy; it tends to make the breast harder but is far less mutilating (Rotman et al., 1979).

The psychological impact of breast cancer and breast removal is significant in several respects. First, it forces the woman, and her partner, if she has one, to face the possibility of her death. Second, the loss of a body part is always traumatic. Third, because the female breast is so important in our culture as a symbol of femininity and sexual desirability, breast removal can be far more psychologically traumatic than loss of another body part. A woman does not know how her partner will respond and, indeed, some men have considerable difficulty adjusting to their partner's mastectomy (see Box 9–2). Marriages in trouble before surgery may end in divorce. Approximately one-third of women in this group

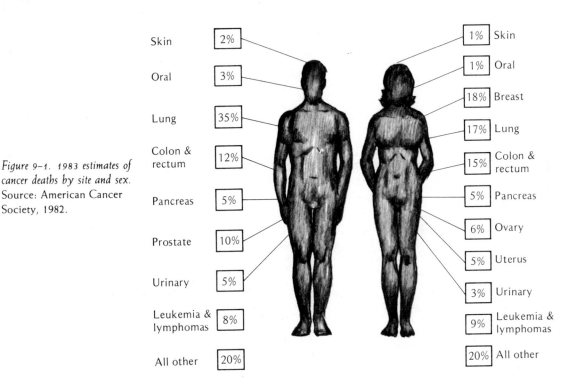

Figure 9–1. 1983 estimates of cancer deaths by site and sex. Source: American Cancer Society, 1982.

	Male				Female	
Skin	2%			1%	Skin	
Oral	3%			1%	Oral	
Lung	35%			18%	Breast	
Colon & rectum	12%			17%	Lung	
Pancreas	5%			15%	Colon & rectum	
Prostate	10%			5%	Pancreas	
Urinary	5%			6%	Ovary	
Leukemia & lymphomas	8%			5%	Uterus	
All other	20%			3%	Urinary	
				9%	Leukemia & lymphomas	
				20%	All other	

give up sexual activity with a partner (Budoff, 1980). For those women and couples who do eventually adjust to the mastectomy, many go through a difficult period around the time of the surgery and a few months afterward. These psychological factors are important to keep in mind, since often the fear of a possible mastectomy keeps women from seeking consultation and frequent breast exams.

Cancers of the female pelvic region occur about as frequently as prostatic cancer in men (see Figure 9-1), but, excluding ovarian cancer, they are easier to detect (American Cancer Society, 1982). Pelvic cancers in women are more likely to occur as a woman matures. Regular examinations become increasingly important over a woman's lifetime because many forms of pelvic cancer occur without accompanying painful or visible symptoms. Unusual vaginal bleeding or discharge can sometimes be a symptom of pelvic cancer, but it is also a

signal for many other less serious problems.

Cervical cancer is thought to be a sexually transmitted disease, as it is almost never found in virgins or nuns. It is most frequently found in women who began having coitus at an early age or who have had many sex partners. Furthermore, there is evidence that some men are more likely than others to transmit cervical cancer (Singer & Reid, 1979). For example, in one study the wives of men who had been previously married to women with cervical cancer were found to have a higher than expected incidence of this cancer (Kessler, 1976). Cervical cancer is the easiest to detect, thanks to the Pap test developed in the 1940s by George Papanicolaou. A sample of cells is painlessly removed from the cervix and examined. The test, recommended every one to three years for women who do not have any symptoms that put them in a higher risk category, is 90 to 95 percent accurate.

Box 9–2

ONE WOMAN'S STORY

Illness has an impact on the physiological and psychological well-being of the individual, and that impact can often be sharpened or eased by the reactions of people close to the patient, as the following sketch illustrates.

A woman, whom we shall call Jeanette, came to the office of one of the authors and wished to discuss her difficulty in making a decision to marry. She was then in her late fifties and had been seeing a particular man for about two years. They had become sexually intimate, which was satisfying to both. Jeanette, however, was almost panicked about marrying this man, even though she cared very much for him and wanted to continue seeing him. She felt she had to make a decision because each of them lived with other people—she with a female boarder and he with his adolescent children—and her value system did not easily accommodate their living together. In addition, she was beginning to tire of their limitations—the only privacy they enjoyed was in his station wagon or during an occasional hotel visit—and she felt it was time that their relationship progressed beyond its current stage.

When Jeanette offered some background information, her anxiety became more understandable. She had been married before, quite happily, for eighteen years. When she was in her early forties, she had a radical mastectomy due to breast cancer. On the day of her return from the hospital, her husband left, saying he simply could not bear her being "deformed." Her worst fear had come true. She gradually recovered, raised her daughter, returned to school, gained a Ph.D. in German, and eventually assumed a teaching position at a university. In spite of her professional accomplishments, Jeanette did not begin to heal, emotionally, from this experience for a long time, and she did not date any men for twelve years; the shock of being abandoned when she "most needed someone" had never really subsided. Now, when faced with the possibility of a commitment, she was fearful of letting herself trust someone again, despite his tender appreciation of her body and his affection for her.

Uterine cancers are most common in women who have not borne children, are obese, or are diabetic. A dilation and curettage (D and C) procedure or an intrauterine aspiration procedure is required to diagnose this type of cancer. The D and C requires general anesthetic, but the aspiration procedure does not; both involve taking sample cells from the uterine wall. Ovarian cancers are difficult to detect and are usually found during a pelvic examination performed by a physician, or sometimes in a sonogram. Currently, ovarian "tumor markers"—substances in the body chemistry that may increase or decrease with the tumor's growth—are being sought to detect the cancer in its earlier stages (Budoff, 1980).

A **hysterectomy,** the removal of the uterus, is the most common treatment for cancer of the uterus or nearby tissues. **Ovarectomy** is often done as well, although this procedure is primarily used when the cancer is actually in the ovaries, when the woman is postmenopausal, or when a woman has a history of breast cancer. Both procedures involve major surgery. The removal of both ovaries in young women, especially those under 35, has been associated with a sevenfold increased risk of heart attacks (Rosenberg et al., 1981). The removal of the uterus alone has been associated with a threefold increase in coronary heart disease in premenopausal women (Centerwall, 1981).

Researchers do not know why the removal of the ovaries or uterus should be related to an increased risk of cardiovascular disease. Some researchers have hypothesized that these organs may provide a hormonally mediated "protection." There may be other important and yet undiscovered differences between women who do and do not have early hysterectomies, especially in terms of general health, number of pregnancies, and life-style stress. The hysterectomy itself is major surgery, with a .05 percent operative death risk for premenopausal women (Centerwall, 1981). In addition, 30 percent of women suffer nonfatal complications, and 15 percent require blood transfusions (Cole & Berlin, 1977).

Not surprisingly, a great deal of controversy has arisen over "unnecessary" hysterectomies. Most physicians agree that cancer, uterine prolapse (a condition in which the uterus drops down into the vagina due to loss of muscular support), and uncontrollable uterine bleeding require the removal of the uterus. However, no one can agree on what is an unnecessary hysterectomy. One example of this "gray area" is the use of hysterectomies to prevent uterine and cervical cancer. Although the hysterectomy is 100 percent effective in preventing such cancers, these cancers are relatively rare and easy to detect early. Nevertheless, hysterectomies are one of the more frequent major surgeries, performed, as of the mid-1970s, on 800,000 women per year (Bunker, McPherson, & Henneman, 1977).

The psychological impact of hysterectomies is an important consideration. Many women feel neutered and sexless, and the likelihood of severe depression following surgery increases (Cole & Berlin, 1977), although women for whom surgery is a life-saving procedure usually deal with the psychological aspects of it more easily. Younger women often experience more difficulty adjusting psychologically. As with mastectomies, the support of one's male partner and/or family seems to facilitate convalescence (Gizynski, 1978).

Cancer of the prostate is the third most common cause of death in men and the leading cause of death in men over 70 (Kaufman, 1981). Prostatic cancer is a separate condition from benign prostatic enlargement, which is a condition that affects, to various degrees, most men over 50. In some men the prostate increases to such an extent that it constricts the bladder-urethral junction it surrounds; the result is urinary frequency, a sense of urgency to urinate, and incomplete emptying of the bladder. If the prostate enlargement is too great, or if the organ becomes infected, surgical removal of the prostate may be the only option.

Cancer of the prostate is not easily detected; therefore men over 40 should have annual checkups for prostate enlargement and tumors. A physician examines the prostate by feeling it through the rectal wall. If prostate cancer is suspected, a biopsy may be performed. Treatment consists of radiation, hormonal therapy, or surgery. Erectile problems are common side effects of radiation and hormonal treatments. **Prostatectomy,** the surgical removal of the organ, results in a variety of sexual problems, depending on how much of the tissue is removed. In some cases retrograde ejaculation (when ejaculate goes back into

the bladder rather than out the urethra) results and can either be a temporary or permanent condition. For men who are uninformed about this possibility, the lack of ejaculate can be frightening. Men may also experience different sensations during sex because the urethra is less involved in the orgasm. Occasionally, a less frequent type of prostatectomy results in total lack of erection because the nerves that affect erections are no longer intact. More often, surgery on the prostate does not affect the ability of the penis to become erect, but it psychologically troubles the male, which interferes with his sexual functioning. Psychological factors may be related to misinformation, fear of genital surgery, or a general lack of interest in sex prior to surgery.

Cancer of the testes and penis are very rare in the United States. Penile cancer is almost unknown in circumcised males; thus, researchers suspect that retained smegma, a penile secretion that can accumulate under the foreskin, or infection fostered by the prepuce covering may be partially responsible for penile cancer (Kaufman, 1981). Testicular cancer causes less than 1 percent of all cancer deaths in men, but its highest incidence is in men between the ages of 20 and 35 (American Cancer Society, 1982). Early detection is the key to ridding a person of the cancer. Thus, men are encouraged to examine their testes every two to three months (i.e., following a shower when the skin is relaxed). If any abnormality is present, such as an unusual lump that was not previously detected, it must be brought to the attention of a physician at once. In rare cases, when the testes have to be removed, the results are usually traumatic for the patient: He is no longer fertile, and he loses his source of androgen, which affects his sex drive and erectile functioning. Testosterones may be given to replace hormonal loss, and artificial testes are available. Nevertheless, testes removal has a strong psychological impact on the male because the testes are visual signs of his maleness; he may feel very uncomfortable in sexual encounters, even with artificial equivalents.

Other Genital Problems

A variety of different diseases and malfunctions in the reproductive organs are not cancer related and are not sexually transmitted. Some of these conditions cause reproductive problems, which, in extreme cases, can lead to infertility, while others affect sexual functioning and enjoyment. In the following sections, we discuss the more common diseases and malfunctions and how they can be treated.

□ *Female-Specific Problems*   Several conditions are particularly problematic for women: endometriosis, pelvic inflammatory disease, dysmenorrhea, and cystitis. Another set of problems, vaginal infections, is covered in the section on sexually transmitted diseases (STDs) because some vaginal infections appear to behave like STDs. Endometriosis is the displacement of the endometrial tissue lining of the uterus into any abnormal place, such as the ova-

ries or uterine surface. This condition only occurs in premenopausal women, and often among those in higher-income groups who have fewer children. Typical symptoms are extreme pain during menstruation, pain during defecation, and other menstrual irregularities. If the tissue attaches to the ovarian structures or uterine surface, infertility may result. Treatment consists of hormone therapy to suppress ovulation and, in severe cases, surgery to remove the endometrium, ovaries, or uterus (Wilson, Beecham, & Carrington, 1975).

There are two types of dysmenorrhea, or painful menstruation: primary, in which there is no physical abnormality, and secondary, in which pain is caused by some organic problem. Primary dysmenorrhea is of special interest because it historically was considered a natural part of being female and therefore was not taken seriously. In fact, menstrual cramps for many years were considered to be primarily psychologically caused. While a psychological element may be involved, there is now clear evidence that physical factors do play a role.

Budoff (1980) reports that nearly half of all menstruating women experience fairly regular discomfort, and, of these, approximately 10 percent are completely incapacitated for one to two days because of the pain. Research has found that the prostaglandin level in women who experience pain while menstruating differs from the level in women who do not experience pain. Prostaglandins are hormones found in nearly every cell of the body; they regulate the tone of the smooth, involuntary muscles, such as the uterus and intestines. The prostaglandin level rises as menstruation approaches. If the prostaglandins, which cause contractions, are in excess, the uterus squeezes so hard that it cuts off the blood supply and at the same time cuts off the oxygen to the uterine muscles.

Painful cramps were associated with excess prostaglandins as early as the mid-1960s (Pickles et al., 1965), but not until the late 1970s was an adequate medication—drugs that decreased prostaglandin levels—made available to treat this cause of dysmenorrhea (Budoff, 1977). Anti-inflammatory medications, used predominantly for arthritis, had been tried and were apparently successful because they interfered with the production of prostaglandins. Aspirin is also partially effective as a prostaglandin inhibitor, and may provide sufficient relief for some women. Antiprostaglandins have relatively few side effects unless one is allergic to the medication or has gastrointestinal problems.

Cystitis is an inflammation or infection of the urinary bladder caused by bacterial growth. Although it occurs in men, it is far more frequent in women, perhaps because the urethra is much shorter in women and the wall between the vagina and urethra is relatively thin. The major symptoms of cystitis include the urge to urinate frequently and a sharp, burning pain before or during urination. Occasionally, the urine turns cloudy or bloody.

Cystitis can be caused by a variety of factors, one of the most common being vigorous sexual intercourse—thus the term "honeymoon cystitis"—which can bruise the urethra. Occasionally, a diaphragm can press on the bladder and cause discomfort, or an irritation can be caused by the use of feminine hygiene sprays, douches, or harsh soaps. Bacteria can also enter the urethra either during intercourse or if a woman wipes herself from back to front after urinating or defecating. Once bacteria enter the bladder, they multiply rapidly.

Certain preventative measures can be followed to discourage bacterial growth, and they are strongly recommended for women who have recurrent bouts of cystitis. These women are advised to drink at least two quarts of water daily, avoid eating spicy foods, and control caffeine consumption. Some physicians recommend a glass of cranberry juice at bedtime since its acidity may inhibit bacterial growth. Recently, some physicians have suggested that having sex with an empty bladder will help avoid the spreading of bacteria, although other professionals advise that women should urinate soon after intercourse. Additionally, the vagina should be carefully cleansed before intercourse, and adequate vaginal lubrication, either natural or artificial, is recommended. Tight clothing and undergarments should also be avoided as they cause added warmth in the genital area, which promotes bacterial growth.

For women who are constantly bothered by cystitis, preventative antibiotics are sometimes prescribed. When an attack occurs, a woman will often be in so much pain that she must see a physician immediately. Rapid treatment is important because more serious bladder damage can result if the infection is left untreated. Typically, the physician diagnoses the condition with a sample of urine and prescribes both an antibiotic and a drug to decrease the inflammation.

☐ *Male-Specific Problems* Certain conditions that affect the penis may make erection or intercourse painful for males. Phimosis occurs when a man's foreskin is too tight to retract over the glans of the penis. Erection is painful because the foreskin cannot move freely, and infection under the foreskin is a common problem, as was mentioned earlier. Circumcision is the usual remedy.

Peyronie's disease is characterized by the development of dense fibrous tissue that can calcify into bonelike material around the corpora cavernosa. This disease may cause an angular deformity of the penis and make erections and intercourse extremely painful. There is currently no adequate treatment for this disease. Surgery may be performed, but it is likely to result in erectile incapacity due to interference with the blood flow to the penis. Penile chordee, the downward bending of the penis, is a rare condition that is usually the result of damage to the erect penis. This problem also currently has no adequate treatment (Masters & Johnson, 1970).

Some penile irritation or blistering may occur in men who are extremely sensitive to the vaginal secretions of women. The reaction may be due to an abnormal environment caused by a vaginal infection or the use of douches or contraceptive creams. In very unusual cases a man may be sensitive to the natural, healthy physiological makeup of a woman's vagina (Masters & Johnson, 1970).

SEXUALLY TRANSMITTED DISEASES

Some disorders can be directly transmitted through sexual contact. Collectively, these problems are known as **sexually transmitted diseases (STDs)**. Historically, they were known as venereal disease (VD), venereal from the latin *venus,* referring to love or lust. The new category, STDs, allows for the inclusion of diseases that are generally transmitted sexually but also includes diseases that can sometimes be transmitted by other means. This term is also useful because it does not (yet) suggest the negative connotations that people have learned to associate with VD.

Sexually transmitted diseases may be caused by viruses, bacteria, or other organisms that thrive in moist, warm environments such as the mouth, genitals, or rectum. Therefore, transmission of the disease can occur through any type of vaginal, anal, or oral sexual contact. In spite of popular opinion, it is very difficult to get STDs from (dry) doorknobs, toilet seats, or drinking cups, although some of the parasitic varieties can survive for a while on clothing, towels, and other fabrics.

Although some people feel that STDs are reaching epidemic proportions and are becoming more resistant to treatment, the exact prevalence of STDs is difficult to estimate. The figures available are not necessarily accurate because many middle-class patients are privately treated and their diseases may therefore not be reported. Another reason for inaccurate estimates is that the diseases usually occur in several stages: A person in contact with an infected individual may have unknowingly passed the disease on to a third party because the symptoms had not yet appeared. So, at any one time, people may not know that they have contracted the disease, thus making the incidence difficult to estimate.

STDs are not very openly discussed as a health problem, especially among young people, who are the most common target of these diseases. The Department of Health, Education and Welfare (1979) found that men and women between the ages of 17 and 24 experienced the highest rates of syphilis and gonorrhea. The lack of education about STDs has led to a number of myths surrounding their causes and treatment:

1. *You can tell when you have an STD and then treat yourself.* Tests are needed to confirm the presence of venereal disease, and, except for scabies, prescription drugs are required to treat it.

The Middle Ages hospital for the syphilis sufferers.

2. *You cannot get an STD more than once, nor can you have gonorrhea and syphilis at the same time.* Reinfection is very possible, and multiple forms of STDs frequently occur at the same time.
3. *You can only get an STD from someone of the opposite sex.* STDs do not discriminate between genders. The American Health Association found that in 1971, 23.3 percent of the sexual contacts of syphilis patients were same-sex contacts.
4. *STDs are only transmitted by genital-genital contact.* These diseases can be transmitted just as easily by kissing and oral-genital contact.
5. *Only people who are lower class, unclean, and promiscuous get STDs.*

Anyone can get an STD. Experience with a large number of sexual partners, however, can increase the chances of contracting an STD, presumably because of the increased likelihood of exposure to disease.

6. *STDs are incurable and you should never tell someone else if you carry one of these diseases.* With the exception of herpes, all STDs are curable if caught in time. Therefore, it is critical to be treated and to inform one's sexual partner immediately. Some people hesitate to do this because not all sexual contacts with a person who has an STD will lead to the contraction of the disease. However, the consequences of untreated STDs are serious, and thus a partner should be informed.

Syphilis

Syphilis is usually contracted through intercourse and is caused by a corkscrew-shaped (spirochete) bacterium called *treponema pallidum.* Identification of the disease is made with a blood sample. If detected early, it is easily treated with penicillin; if ignored, heart damage, brain damage, or other organ diseases may result. A blood test is routinely done for pregnant women to determine whether or not they have syphilis because the fetus can contract the disease and be severely affected at birth or afterward with a variety of difficulties, including kidney problems, bone deformities, and anemia. Fortunately,

syphilis is relatively infrequent—in 1977 new cases in the United States numbered 20,000 (Holmes, 1980).

Syphilis is usually described as occurring in three stages. During the first stage, which begins at infection and lasts for ten to ninety days after sexual contact, an open sore called a chancre develops on the skin where the germs have invaded the body. The chancre is often not noticeable, especially when the sore surfaces inside the vagina. As the disease spreads throughout the body, a rash may develop, along with swelling in the lymph nodes of the groin. These symptoms last about two to five weeks and then disappear, marking the end of stage 1. Even though the symptoms may vanish, the person still has the disease.

The second stage is marked by moist and highly infectious flat warts that appear around the genitals; they are accompanied by slight fever, sore throat, and headache. The symptoms, except for the warts, resemble those of the common cold. During this phase, the body produces antibodies, and a spontaneous cure is possible. Stage 2 usually begins anywhere from a few days to six months following the end of Stage 1, and lasts from three to six months. This stage may persist, on and off, for several years. Usually, however, untreated syphilis will either stay in this stage or move into its third stage after many years of lying dormant (sometimes called the latent stage). The third stage of syphilis is dangerous. The germs frequently affect the spinal cord and the brain, and over twenty or thirty years a person may develop sores in the heart or other organs. Individuals can eventually die

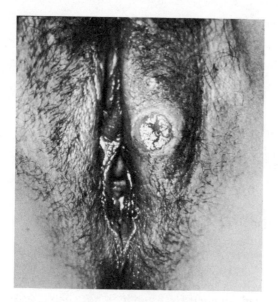

Syphilis Stage 1.

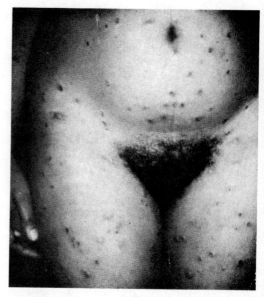

Secondary syphilis.

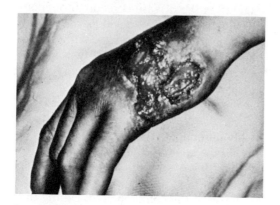

Late Syphilis.

or become mentally and physically in-competent from the disease.

Gonorrhea

Gonorrhea is caused by a coffee-bean-shaped bacterium called *neisseria gonor-rhea*. Gonorrhea, from the Greek word meaning flow of seed, is extremely con-tagious and is ranked by the World Health Organization second only to the common cold among the most infectious diseases. In 1960 approximately 250,000 cases were re-ported; in 1979, over one million cases were reported (Center for Disease Control, 1979). Unlike syphilis, gonorrhea can only enter the body through moist, warm surfaces, and it tends to be focused in the genital area, although it can infect the throat or rectum.

The symptoms of gonorrhea include a yellow or white discharge from the genitals; unfortunately, between 60 and 80 percent of the women with this disease experience no symptoms. Signs of gonorrhea occur five days to two weeks after exposure. Diagno-

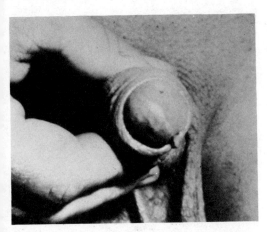

Gonorrhea drip.

sis is made by analyzing a sample of genital or rectal secretions or saliva taken from the throat area to determine if the bacterium is present. Penicillin is the best treatment, and usually several follow-up visits to a physician are needed to make sure that the disease is cured. If untreated, the disease can spread to other pelvic areas and, in rare cases, to the heart, nervous system, or bone joints. Women need to be especially cautious, for if the disease spreads to their reproductive organs, pelvic inflammatory disease may result, causing pain, fever, menstrual irregularities, and vomiting. Ultimately, because of scar tissue blocking the oviducts, sterility may result. In fact, gonorrhea is one of the most common causes of sterility in women. Sometimes this sterility can be reversed through microsurgery on the oviducts (Scofield, 1979).

Herpes

A virus, herpes simplex type II, causes infections in the genitals, which are commonly known as herpes. This virus is different from herpes simplex type I, which causes cold sores in the mouth. To complicate matters, however, in over 10 percent of the cases, type I virus is found or can be transferred to the genitals. Genital herpes has been around for centuries and probably longer, although exact definitions are hard to retrieve from history. However, its epidemic proportions are apparently new; in 1980 it was estimated that over 400,000 new cases and several million recurrent episodes were occurring annually (U.S. Dept. of Health, Education & Welfare, 1980).

The symptoms of herpes are usually strongest during the first attack. In men, small blisters may appear on the genitals, thighs, buttocks, or in the urethra, causing burning and itching sensations and tenderness. In women, blisters may show up on the vulva, cervix, thighs, or buttocks. In extreme cases, general flulike symptoms, including swollen glands and fever, may occur. Pain may be severe enough to require hospitalization. Although the symptoms may disappear in one to three weeks, the virus does not; most people will have recurrences throughout their lives, often during times of physical or emotional stress or, in women, during their menstrual cycle. People who have type II herpes may have a greater risk than noninfected individuals of cervical or prostate cancer (e.g., Nahmias & Sawanabori, 1978).

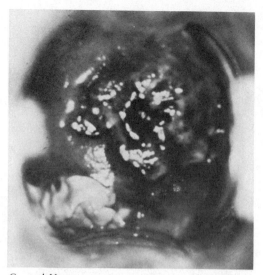

Cervical Herpes.

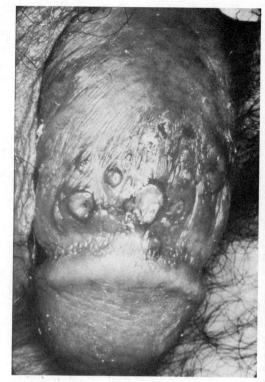

Herpes Corona.

Another alarming problem is the possibility of passing herpes on to a child during birth. A mother in whom the type II virus is active during delivery can transmit the disease to the newborn, causing severe illness or irreversible brain damage, or in 50 to 70 percent of the cases, death to the child (Nahmias, 1975). For women suspected of having herpes at the time of delivery, a Caesarean section is recommended. For women with a genital herpes infection during pregnancy but not active at delivery, vaginal delivery may be safe, as the virus is rarely transmitted through the placenta. Amniocentesis, a procedure that samples the amniotic fluids, may be useful close to labor (Nahmias et al., 1969).

Currently, there is no known cure for herpes. Painkillers or antibacterial medications help decrease the discomfort of the symptoms. An antiviral agent known as a cyclovir has been reported to decrease the length and severity of the first herpes attack (Mindel et al., 1982). Abstinence from sex for at least two weeks after the sores disappear is important so that others are not infected. Unfortunately, the small sores may be present before the individual is aware of them.

Other STDs

Other, less common, STDs can be equally as uncomfortable and dangerous as syphilis, gonorrhea, and herpes. Chancroids are smooth, round ulcers, similar in appearance to syphilitic sores, but they are usually painful and are located only in the genital area. The disease can spread to the lymph nodes and cause abscesses in the groin. Sulpha drugs are used to treat this disease and are effective within three weeks.

Venereal warts are similar to warts in other parts of the body and thus are usually painless and go unnoticed. They may cause itching, but often if left alone they disappear on their own. If not, the warts can be chemically or electrically removed. Warts are caused by a virus and can be passed on to a sexual partner.

A frequent problem in men that mimics some of the symptoms of gonorrhea is called nongonococcal urethritis (NGU). NGU generally causes a burning sensation during urination and/or a genital pus discharge; it is treated with tetracycline, an antibiotic. This disease may be a chronic condition that requires repeated treatments. Its origins are unclear, but it has been associated with chlamydia, as well as other organisms and with chemical and allergic reactions (e.g., Barlow, 1979). NGU may be twice as common as gonorrhea (Felman & Nikitas, 1981).

Pelvic inflammatory disease (PID) is a general infection of the pelvic organs. It can be signaled by abdominal or pelvic pain, dyspareunia (see Chapter Eight), fever, and abnormal vaginal discharge or prolonged and heavy menstrual bleeding; severe infections can lead to sterility. Since there appears to be a higher incidence of PID in women using intrauterine devices for birth control, young women who eventually intend to have children are sometimes counseled to use another form of contraception. The organism chlamydia is thought to result in 200,000 cases of PID each year, as well as about 50 percent of the cases of neonatal pneumonia in babies who are infected by their mothers (e.g., Holmes & Stamm, 1979). An antibiotic is usually effective against PID.

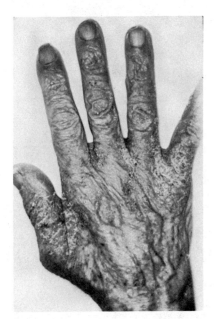

Scabies infection.

Lymphogranuloma venereum is caused by chlamydia. The first and often only symptom is a small and easily overlooked blister. The blister often disappears on its own, but in the next stages the lymph nodes swell and become painful, eventually causing extreme swelling in the genitals. In 1981, chlamydia was reported to be twice as common as gonorrhea, with one to three million cases reported each year.

Pubic lice, also known as crabs, are parasites that appear where there is body hair, but they generally cling to pubic hair. They bite the skin to suck the blood needed for their survival; these bites cause severe itching. Crabs can be passed from person to person through sexual contact. They can also be picked up from contaminated clothes and bedding. Treatment includes an external cream or lotion. In addition, infected people should bathe frequently, wash their sheets and towels, and wear clean clothes.

Scabies are parasites that penetrate the skin and breed; they cause intense itching

369

Box 9–3

AIDS: A NEW SCARE

A mysterious disease, attacking specific populations with voracious lethality and no known cure or vaccination in sight, AIDS — Acquired Immune Deficiency Syndrome — is currently one of the most feared diseases in the United States.

AIDS was first reported in 1981 by physicians who noted that a few of their patients, all homosexual men, had extremely weak immune systems. The immune system protects the body from the takeover of infection. By June 30, 1983, the Center for Disease Control (CDC) in Atlanta had reported over 1,600 cases of the disease, with at least 150 new cases being reported each month. Over 75 percent of the victims are male homosexuals, and about 22 percent are intravenous drug users, Haitian refugees, and hemophiliacs (Fisher, 1983). Thus far, only 3 percent of the victims do not fall in any of the above categories.

There is no proof at the moment that AIDS is a sexually transmitted disease; we mention it here because the disease appears to be partially related to sexual contact and is certainly relevant to the practice of a particular sexual lifestyle. The social result is that gay men, as well as Haitians, are being physically attacked, refused service in restaurants, and are suffering job discrimination.

Why the panic? First, AIDS is a lethal disease. So far, 40 percent of the victims have died within 1 year, 80 percent within 2 years. Second, no one knows what causes AIDS. An infectious agent of some sort, probably transmitted directly by sexual contact or dirty needles, is the leading clue. It is unlikely to be an airborn disease like a cold. The incubation period for AIDS may be between 6 months and 3 years and thus many people may have the disease and not know it. More worrisome, some people may receive blood transfusions with infected blood.

There are no definitive first symptoms of the disease. Fatigue, long-lasting infections, and swollen glands are common to AIDS but also to other diseases. Some people, especially gay men, may suffer from Kaposi's sarcoma, a rare cancer that produces skin lesions, or from pneumocystis carinii, also rare in people with normal immune systems. It may be more common in men with a high number of sexual partners. In one study of 21 patients, 10 had had over 1,000 sexual partners (see Fisher, 1983).

As a result, the current recommendation is for gay men not to give

New York City, 1983: A gay rights march to increase public awareness of AIDS.

blood, to reduce the number of sexual partners, and to avoid using needles with drugs. Additionally, there may be some effort to keep stress levels at a minimum to keep the immune system healthy.

However, this advice may change as new facts about the disease are discovered. Indeed, the wits of scientists and nerves of the general population may be tested for their acuity, fairness, and humanity. Fisher, 1983, pp. 1, 20–21.

and general irritation. Repeated scratching may cause bleeding and a secondary bacterial infection. They typically appear and easily multiply in the genital region, armpits, knees, wrists, between fingers, and under female breasts. They are transmitted through sexual contact or from the clothes and bedding of an infected person. Thorough washing and an ointment such as sulfur are recommended to treat scabies.

Granuloma inguinale is caused by a bacterium that causes a continuous growth of scar tissue around the genitals. Early symptoms are painless ulcers that begin on the genitals and move to the thighs or buttocks. It can be treated with antibiotics.

Vaginal Infections

Estimates are that one out of four women will experience vaginal infections at some time in their lives. Some women are more susceptible than others, and some infections are more likely to occur during times of stress. Unlike other STDs, most of the vaginal infections are not life or health threatening. However, they can be unpleasant, irritating, and painful, and they can interfere with the enjoyment of sexual activity. Although men rarely show the symptoms, they are frequently carriers and can reinfect women who are in the process of treating themselves for a vaginal infection. Thus, at least for monogamous partners, men are often treated along with their female partners. Because a number of vaginal infections can be passed back and forth between partners, we have included them in our discussion of STDs.

Most of the organisms involved in vaginal infections are present, but not a problem, all of the time. It is when they suddenly multiply that they become an unpleasant infection. Such an increase can be spurred for a variety of reasons, resulting in an imbalance of the chemical environment of the vagina. Birth control pills, antibiotics, commercial female douches, menstruation, and pregnancy can all contribute to this imbalance.

In order to prevent vaginal infections, physicians advise, in addition to daily bathing of the genitals (for both females and their partners) avoidance of artificial chemical douches or other products that might irritate the vagina; nylon underwear and tight clothing, which increase the amount of heat and moisture in the genital area; antibiotics, unless absolutely necessary, since they reduce the body's natural defenses; and excessive sugar intake, since sugar encourages the growth of many infections.

Trichomonas is a one-celled parasite found in over 50 percent of all women. It becomes a problem when it increases in number and produces a yellow or gray, slightly foamy discharge that usually has a strong and unpleasant odor. Irritation and inflammation may result, and the disease can be passed back and forth between male and female sexual partners. A medication, Flagyl, is usually taken by both partners for about one week. Flagyl has some adverse side effects, however, including some carcinogenic implications, so it must be used with caution. This infection is difficult to cure permanently.

Yeast infections, also called thrush (*candida* or *monila albicans*), are difficult to cure without a chance of reinfection. A thick white discharge that irritates the vulva and causes intense itching, especially during the night, or burning sensations during intercourse are symptoms of a yeast infection. The condition is usually treated with Nystatin, given in vaginal suppository form.

Hemophilus, like trichomonas, produces a gray vaginal discharge that has a strong odor, although it is often less irritating to the woman. It can be treated with antibiotics or Flagyl given to both partners, although vaginal creams and local antibiotics are also effective.

Prevention of STDs

Although there is no absolute method for prevention of STDs, taking certain precautions can reduce the risk of contracting one of these diseases (Brecher, 1975). Educating oneself is a start. The incidence and prevalence of STDs have increased markedly in the last twenty years, and there are no signs to indicate that this trend is reversing.

Thus, if you have sexual relations, you are at risk for an STD. Knowing possible symptoms and watching for them are important. This advice may not be easy with a new sexual partner, but the risk could mean a lifelong complaint. Thus, a second important factor is consideration. For yourself and the other person, inform him or her if you have symptoms of an STD. If you don't know the person well enough to trust his or her response, the safest action is to avoid sexual contact. If you decide to have sex, take mechanical precautions, such as the use of a condom. Condoms, as well as contraceptive foams and jellies, provide some protection, but they are not foolproof. Additionally, rapid assessment and treatment after a questionable encounter are important. Meanwhile, do not engage in further sexual activity until your condition has been evaluated. Should you have unknowingly exposed others whose identity you know, they must be contacted so they can be treated. Prophylactic measures that are effective on only a portion of the population will still help to reduce the high incidence of new cases reported each year (Lee et al., 1972).

SUMMARY

1. *Alcohol* decreases physical sexual responsiveness, especially if taken in high doses and/or over a considerable period of time. Nevertheless, because many believe that alcohol is a disinhibitor, psychological sexual arousal and even mild physical enhancement of arousal can occur.

2. More research is needed concerning the effects of *marijuana* and *heroin* use on human sexual response. Addicts and clinicians, for example, have reported that heroin interferes with the ability to respond sexually, but only limited clinical studies have been conducted to verify this claim. *Cocaine* and *amphetamines* tend to increase erectile ability but delay ejaculation. *Barbiturates* decrease sexual and social behavior; it has been suggested that *Quaaludes* can inhibit sexual performance but increase sexual desire. Long-term use of these drugs may decrease sexual activity and interest. Finally, *amyl nitrate* is used as an orgasmic intensifier, primarily by members of the gay subculture.

3. Most *antipsychotic drugs* and several *antihypertensive drugs* have been found to affect sexual arousal or desire. The information on *antidepressants* is inconclusive.

4. Illness in general often upsets a person's sexual desire, and specific diseases may impair physiological functioning. Illnesses that involve neural, hormonal, and vascular pathways are particularly likely to impair sexual functioning. Diabetic men, for example, are more likely to have erectile problems. With most of these diseases, however, predicting the likelihood that a sexual problem will develop is almost impossible.

5. Other illnesses, such as heart attacks and disease, need not interfere with the physiology of sexual response, but they often do reduce sexual activity and limit sexual behavior. Whether these problems are physiologically or psychologically based is not clear. In some cases erectile ability may be reduced because of the medications.

6. The reproductive organs are also subject to a variety of pathological conditions. Women are more likely to get *breast cancer* than any other type of cancer. Early detection is critical, and newer methods of detection are being developed. All women are advised to perform *breast self-examinations* on a monthly basis, and some high-risk women are counseled to have regular laboratory tests for early detection. Stopping breast cancer may involve a **mastectomy,** which is the removal of the breast and its underlying tissue, fat, and lymph nodes. Other methods can be as effective for many cancers.

7. *Prostatic cancer* is the third most common cause of death in men. Additionally, most men experience prostatic enlargement as they age, which may affect their bladder-urethral functioning.

8. *Pelvic cancers,* with the exception of ovarian cancer, are easier to detect in women than *testicular cancer* in men. The highest incidence of cancer of the testes is in men between the ages of 25 and 35. Early detection is vital, and self-examination is strongly recommended. Fortunately, testicular cancer is rare.

9. Surgery for removal of any reproductive organ is psychologically difficult for most people and as a result may lessen sexual desire and arousal. Additionally, the removal of certain tissues, such as the ovaries or testes, will upset hormone levels and thus influence sexual interest or responsiveness.

10. The more common noncancerous genital problems in women include endometriosis, pelvic inflammatory disease, cystitis, and dysmenorrhea. *Endometriosis,* the displacement of the endometrial tissue lining of the uterus into any abnormal place, and *pelvic inflammatory disease* (PID), a general infection of the pelvic organs, are usually accompanied by considerable pain and, if not treated, may result in sterility. *Dysmenorrhea,* painful menstruation, incapacitates approximately 10 percent of women once a month, but currently can be well controlled with drugs that inhibit prostaglandin production. *Cystitis,* an inflammation or infection of the bladder, occurs in both sexes, but is far more frequent in women.

11. Noncancerous genital problems in men include *phimosis,* which occurs when a man's foreskin is so tight that it does not retract over the penis, and *Peyronie's disease,* in which fibrous tissues calcify around the corpora cavernosa. Both of these conditions cause pain during intercourse. *Penile chordee,* the downward bending of the penis, is usually the result of penile damage and is very rare.

12. A variety of problems are passed on through sexual contact (including kissing) and are called **sexually transmitted diseases (STDs).** Most STDs are easily treated, but if left untreated they can be very harmful. *Syphilis,* a disease caused by bacteria, may lead to death or mental impairment if not treated. *Gonorrhea* is an extremely contagious disease caused by bacterial growth and is the most frequent infectious disease except for the common cold. *Herpes* is a painful and potentially dangerous disease for pregnant women that develops due to the transmission of a specific virus. It is the only major STD for which there is currently no treatment. Chlamydia is easily treated, is becoming increasingly common, and is thought to be one cause of pelvic inflammatory disease in women. Other STDs include *granuloma inguinale, lymphogranuloma venereum, pubic lice, scabies,* and the growth of *chancroids* and *venereal warts.*

13. A variety of vaginal infections can cause irritation, itching, or unpleasant odor, and they can be painful. Some of these problems can be passed back and forth between partners, so it may be necessary to treat the male and female partners to stop the infection. *Trichomonas* and *yeast infections* (*candida* or *monila albicans*) are common vaginal infections.

14. Precautionary measures should be taken to prevent the

transmission of STDs. Self-education and awareness are important. Consideration for others can help curb the spread of various infections. Consideration for one's self may require saying "no" to a sexual interaction. Condoms and spermicides offer some mechanical protection, and, of course, rapid assessment and treatment are necessary for one's own health.

SUGGESTED READINGS

Barlow, D. *Sexually transmitted diseases — the facts*. New York. Oxford University Press, 1979.
    A short but very informative and entertaining description of STDs.
Budoff, P. W. *No more menstrual cramps and other good news*. New York: Penguin, 1980.
    A provocative, interesting critique of women's health care written by a physician.
Kolodny, R., Masters, W., & Johnson, V. *Textbook of sexual medicine*. Boston: Little, Brown, 1979.
    Comprehensive, broad, and authoritative text on illness, drugs, and surgery as they impact sexuality.
Lear, M. W. *Heartsounds*. New York: Simon & Schuster, 1980.
    This sensitively written, true story gives a personal portrayal of the effect of a heart attack on a physician and his wife. Only minor mention is made of sex, but the role of intimacy in this crisis is very well described.

CHAPTER TEN

SEXUAL DEVIATIONS
Atypical Sexual Behavior

That which promotes love, caring, and affection between people is normal; that which divides them is abnormal.
Gosselin & Wilson 1980

*T*erms such as "atypical sexual behavior" or "sexual variations" are often used by contemporary researchers to describe those sexual behaviors that in the past would have been called **sexual perversions** or **sexual deviations.** The emotional impact of each set of terms is quite different. Think of the contrasting images brought to mind by labels such as "sex pervert" or "sex deviate" as compared with "a person who engages in atypical sexual behavior."

What is a good way to define sexual deviations? Should a definition be based on moral, medical, legal, or statistical grounds? When should a mild sexual variation be considered a full-blown deviation? Ultimately, whether or not a pattern of behavior is considered deviant is based on other people's reactions. If the behavior repulses or threatens other people, it is considered deviant. Standards will therefore vary among cultures and subcultures and over time in the same culture.

In a very general way, sexual practices likely to be considered deviant in our society are those that habitually and preferentially do not involve sexual intercourse. As Marmor (1971) points out, the key terms here are "habitually" and "preferentially," since many couples will on occasion substitute such variations for penile-vaginal inter-course. However, when a variant activity becomes an exclusive end, when sexual gratification cannot be obtained in any other way, and when such practices are characterized by a compulsive and driven quality, then they are likely to be labeled "deviant." Finally, sexual practices that do not involve mutual consent or that are presumed to be psychological or physically harmful to those involved are usually considered sexual deviations (or sex offenses).

What we are talking about is strictly overt behavior. Sexual fantasies are sometimes of a "way out" nature, but unless they are acted upon in a repetitive manner, they are not considered sexual deviations. A person who feels that certain personal sexual fantasies are unusual should *not* think that he or she is suffering from a sexual deviation. (See Chapters Four and Six for more detailed discussions of sexual fantasies.)

Classical sexual deviations are sometimes categorized in terms of either (1) unusual activities pursued (exhibitionism, voyeurism, and sadomasochism) or (2) unusual objects desired (pedophilia, incest, and fetishism). Transvestism and transsexuality seem to overlap both categories. Since pedophilia and incest involve the very serious societal problem of sexual abuse of children, they are discussed elsewhere (see Chapter Eleven).

EXHIBITIONISM

Exhibitionism can be defined as the deliberate exposure of male genitals to unsuspecting females without any serious intention of further sexual contact or activity; exhibitionism is rare in females. The most notable feature is the compulsion to exhibit in public situations; sexual gratification or other forms of gratification, such as feelings of power or hostility, are primarily derived from the victim's reaction. This definition of exhibitionism distinguishes it from public genital exposure, which can occur in other contexts. Examples are the person who urinates publicly while intoxicated, nude sunbathers, and strippers or employees in "topless" or "bottomless" bars. Youthful escapades of "mooning" and "streaking" are also excluded from this definition. Although we will confine our discussion to the classical description of exhibitionism, it might be pointed out that in modern times obscene telephone calls could be considered a subvariety of exhibitionism. Like exhibitionism, the obscene telephone call is aimed at shocking women and involves sexual gratification without any physical contact with the victim.

In the United States, Canada, and England, exhibitionism is the most common sexual offense and accounts for one-third of all convicted sexual offenders (Rooth, 1976). That is not to say exhibitionists necessarily outnumber other sexual offenders—only that these people are most often caught. The rate of exhibitionism can also be judged by examining the number of female victims. For instance, in one sample of women, 44 percent had been victims of exhibitionism at least once in their lives (Gittleson, Eacott, & Mehta, 1978).

Place, Time, Type of Activity, and Effect on Victims

Over 70 percent of exposure incidents occur in public areas such as streets, parks, automobiles, and public buildings (Mac-

Stripteasing is not considered exhibitionism in the strict clinical or legal sense. Read the section on exhibitionism and list the critical features distinguishing stripteasing from exhibitionism.

Donald, 1973). Furthermore, unlike rape, which tends to occur more often at night, exhibitionists are most active during the day (Arieff & Rotman, 1942). As might be expected, there is some seasonal variation in favor of warmer weather.

Some exhibitionists will have erections and will masturbate as they expose themselves, and others will not; data on the exact percentages in each group are inconsistent. Of those who do not masturbate on the scene, many will do so afterward in privacy (Hackett, 1971).

Whether adult women are subjected to exposure more often than children and adolescents is unclear. When convicted exhibitionists have been interviewed, about two-thirds report exposing to adults as compared with one-third to children or adolescents (Radzinowicz, 1957). However, studies based on samples of victims rather than on samples of offenders found that the highest percentage of victims were between the ages of 10 and 16 at the time of the incident (Cox & Maletzky, 1980; Gittelson et al., 1978).

Victims' reactions to exhibitionists vary. The most common immediate reaction in a study conducted by Gittelson and associates was to either run or walk away. Others reported screaming, doing nothing, being stunned, and verbally attacking the offender. More than half (64 percent) said they were upset, but for most such feelings were very transient; a large majority (91 percent) reported they were no longer bothered by the incident two months after it happened (Gittelson et al., 1978).

Most researchers agree that the typical, chronic exhibitionist simply wishes to be seen exposing without engaging in any other sexual activity with the victim. Therefore, any verbal behavior that accompanies exposure is mainly designed to attract the observer's attention. In a minority of cases, such verbal statements can sometimes include an invitation to touch the genitals. Some people are frightened that the act of exposure may be a prelude to some other more violent sexual offense such as rape, but such cases are very rare (Rooth, 1973).

Motivation

Why men expose themselves is far more intriguing than what actually happens; three major explanations predominate in the current literature. The first hypothesis is that exhibitionists use the act of exposure to assert their masculinity. A shocked-looking victim confirms to the exhibitionist that he has some power—that he has a penis that is still effective in evoking a response from a female (Hirning, 1947; Witzig, 1968). By limiting the act to exposure he does not run the risk of rejection. In fact, contrary to what one may expect, a majority of exhibitionists unrealistically hope for a positive response from their victims (Jones & Frei, 1977). One group of investigators found that "a substantial number of the men wanted the females to whom they expose to be impressed by the size of their penis and to receive enjoyment from the exposing" (Langevin et al., 1979). The reaction the exhibitionist most dislikes is indifference. He needs some indication that the female has noticed his exposed penis.

The second hypothesis is that exposure is an indirect expression of hostility and aggression. Although closely related to the first hypothesis, this second one puts more emphasis on anger than on masculine assertion. The argument is that the act of exposure is an attempt to strike back at those who have injured the exhibitionist's self-esteem, both in the past and the present. Because he may find it too dangerous to express his anger directly, the exhibitionist attempts instead to impose his will on and humiliate a defenseless stranger. Support for this hypothesis is obtained primarily from clinical studies that have noted that the impulse to exhibit almost always followed some conflict or situation perceived by the exhibitionist as an insult to his masculine image (Mathis & Collins, 1970). Others have suggested that this anger may be a carryover from early childhood experiences and particularly a defiant gesture of rebellion against possessive, domineering, and seductive mothers (Rickles, 1950).

The third hypothesis places more emphasis on the sexuality of the behavior than on its aggressive intent. According to this theory, early exposure experiences become fixated through the repeated use of exposure fantasies during masturbation. McGuire, Carlisle, and Young (1965) believe that the initial deviant act is only important in so far as it supplies the fantasy that is later used during masturbation. With each masturbation, the deviant fantasy and the deviant behavior are strengthened by their association with arousal and orgasm.

Keep in mind that these three hypotheses are not mutually exclusive, that supporting evidence is far from convincing, and that all exhibitionists do not have the same motivations.

Characteristics of the Exhibitionist

Clinical descriptions suggest that the typical exhibitionist is a shy, withdrawn, unassertive, passive, individual who is sexually inhibited and unusually uncomfortable in interactions with members of the opposite sex. Standardized psychological tests of personality and psychopathology such as the MMPI (Minnesota Multiphasic Personality Inventory), however, have shown that exhibitionists fall entirely within the normal range (Langevin et al., 1978; McGreary, 1975; Rader, 1977; Smukler & Schiebel, 1975).

Another interesting discovery is that males often begin exposing in their mid-teens or mid-twenties, a far cry from the cartoon stereotype of the "dirty old man" dressed in sneakers and raincoat. Convicted exhibitionists are most commonly between 20 and 30 years of age (Gebhard et al., 1965; MacDonald, 1973; Mohr et al., 1964).

Studies that have examined sociodemographic characteristics of exhibitionists also fail to reveal any striking differences from the norm. Work histories tend to be good, and intelligence is average or slightly above when compared with other sex offenders. On the other hand, some observers have suggested that in light of their intelligence, exhibitionists often seem to be "underachievers" in school (Mohr et al., 1964).

A number of studies have found that the majority of men over age 20 who have been convicted of indecent exposure were married at the time of the incident (see Table 10–1). Clearly, marriage in itself does not remove the compulsive urge to expose. In fact, one study found that married exhibitionists actually expose *more* frequently than did single exhibitionists (Langevin et al., 1979). Some researchers believe, however, that many of these marriages are fraught with conflict and sexual difficulties (Hackett, 1971; Rooth & Marks, 1974).

Rooth and Marks (1974) also reported that the masturbation frequency of their subjects was nearly three times per week, occurring twice as often as intercourse, even among those who were married or living with a woman. In another study, reliance on masturbation as a sexual outlet

TABLE 10-1 MARITAL STATUS OF EXHIBITIONISTS

SOURCE	PERCENTAGE MARRIED	PERCENTAGE SINGLE
Arieff & Rotman, 1942	52	48
Radzinowicz, 1957	62	38
Mohr et al., 1964	63	37
Gebhard et al., 1965	64	36
Hackett, 1971	56	44

was reported to be higher for exhibitionists both before and after marriage than was the case for other sex-offender groups, prison controls, and normal controls (Gebhard et al., 1965).

To date there are no controlled studies of family backgrounds of exhibitionists involving comparisons with matched groups. Clinical accounts, however, suggest a distant relationship with fathers and a much closer and intense relationship with mothers, involving unusually strong attachment, resentment, or both (Gebhard et al., 1965; Mohr et al., 1965; Rooth, 1976). Other clinical studies also consider puritanical attitudes toward sex and inhibition of anger to be important characteristics in the family history of exhibitionists (Hackett, 1971). Whether or not these factors are unique to exhibitionists, however, still awaits more objective and systematic investigation.

Legal Controls and Recidivism

In most states "indecent exposure," the legal term for exhibitionism, is considered a misdemeanor; thus it is usually treated as a minor offense. Penalties, however, still can vary widely, and they often vary according to whether the victim is an adult or a child. In Texas, for example, exposure to adults may result in a $200 fine, but exposure to children can lead to a fifteen-year prison sentence (MacDonald, 1973).

Recidivism rates, or reconviction rates, are higher for exhibitionism than for some other types of sexual offenses, such as child molesting or rape. (Of importance to remember is that recidivism means reconviction; a person may repeat an act and not get caught, charged, or convicted and therefore not be counted in recidivism rates.) Three follow-up studies of at least several years duration have reported recidivism rates of 18.6 percent, 20 percent, and 40.7 percent, respectively (Frisbie, 1965; Mohr et al., 1964; Radzinowicz, 1957). Recidivism varies, however, as a function of the number of prior convictions, and for those with a record of both prior sexual and nonsexual offenses, a Toronto study reported a dismal reconviction rate of 71 percent (Mohr et al., 1964). Chronic exhibitionists obviously represent a population at high risk of repeating their offense. These men are in special need of help from agencies other than the legal system.

Treatment

The three most commonly used approaches to treatment of exhibitionism are individual psychotherapy, group therapy, and various forms of behavior therapy. Hackett (1971) has provided the most detailed description of individual psychotherapy with the largest number of exhibitionists. He believes that anger is the underlying cause of exhibitionism, and that the major focus of therapy should be on helping the client become aware of the connection between the feelings of anger and the events that bring on the anger, and the ensuing urge to expose (Hackett, 1971). While his method of selecting offenders for therapy is unclear, Hackett's results do suggest that short-term individual therapy designed to provide insight into situations provoking anger and to offer alternative methods for dealing with this anger can be useful. Especially encouraging is the fact that nearly half of Hackett's sample were repeat offenders. Hackett argues that therapy should be required since few exhibitionists will initially seek out assistance on their own.

Mathis and Collins (1970) prefer a group therapy format and advocate that treatment should be mandatory for a minimum of 6 months. Of 45 men who attended their group sessions over a three-year period, 32

voluntarily continued past the mandatory time, and not one of these men was re-arrested. All of these exhibitionists were court referred, and a majority were multiple offenders.

Although the outcomes of these studies of individual psychotherapy and group therapy are encouraging, what must be stressed is that these are not controlled outcome studies in which comparable groups of exhibitionists are assigned to therapy and nontherapy conditions and then subsequently compared during a follow-up period of at least one year. No such study has ever been conducted. In a retrospective analysis of case records, however, Mohr and his associates failed to find any significant difference in recidivism rates between those who received some form of therapy and those who did not (Mohr et al., 1964). Unfortunately, no attempt was made initially to match these groups, and the authors suggest that the treated group may have consisted of the more difficult cases.

Behavior therapy approaches have historically, although mistakenly, often been perceived as "last resort" efforts, best-suited for those individuals least likely to benefit from other more "insight-oriented" forms of psychotherapy. The basic premise of the behavioral approach is that specific behaviors, cognitions, and feelings can be either increased or decreased by the application of precise educational (training or learning) procedures. Since any individual exhibitionist may have a host of different problems in addition to exhibitionism (e.g., marital discord, sexual dysfunctions, and social skills deficits), different sets of behavior therapy procedures have to be used with each set of problems presented. Most of the published research on behavior therapy and exhibitionism, however, has concentrated on *suppressing* exhibitionism with different aversive conditioning techniques. Far less attention has been paid to alternative procedures that *promote more adaptive social and sexual behaviors* in place of exposure (Barlow, 1973). For example, given the association between sexual dysfunction and exhibitionism, surprisingly no controlled study has ever been conducted to determine if exhibitionism would decline if sexual dysfunction problems were relieved.

In regards to suppression, a number of different aversive conditioning techniques have been reported to have had some beneficial impact. The two most common techniques are electric shock aversion and shame aversion. Patients who undergo electric shock therapy all do so voluntarily. The intensity of the shock employed is usually selected by the patient and is only moderately painful. The treatment causes no physical damage whatsoever and is less painful than injections received in a dentist's chair. In fact, most therapists check out the intensity on themselves before beginning the conditioning trials with the patient. The conditioning trials can be arranged in various ways, but the basic format for exhibitionism is to have the individual imagine exposing himself; when he signals arousal, he receives a brief shock. This sequence is repeated a number of times over succeeding sessions. According to theory, the repeated pairing of the erotic stimulus with a painful shock is supposed to lead to a conditioned response so that imagery of exposure will now provoke an aversive reaction rather than an erotic reaction. Results have been both positive (Fookes, 1969; Roth and Marks, 1974) and negative (Evans, 1970). One researcher substituted a noxious odor for electric shock and reported exceptionally good results (Maletzky, 1974).

The most innovative and possibly the most effective behavioral procedure so far used with exhibitionists is shame aversion therapy, first described by Serber (1970). This procedure has since been further developed and partially evaluated in other studies (e.g., Jones & Frei, 1977, and Wickramaskera, 1972, 1976). In each session the exhibitionist is required to expose himself several times in front of a mixed-sex audience, typically a group of mental health professionals. If he normally masturbates while exposing, he does this as well. The observers maintain an atmosphere of studied objectivity, without any sign of being judgmental. They do, however, engage the patient in conversation and ask probing questions regarding current and past feelings, fantasy, and exhibitionist behavior. The procedure is quite an ordeal, with a patient enduring between one and four live sessions. Additional sessions in which the patient views videotape playbacks are sometimes arranged. Both Serber (1970) and Wickramaskera (1976) warn that this method should be used only with those exhibitionists who are likely to be embarrassed and upset. Although Wickramaskera (1976) and Jones and Frei (1977) report relatively good results, further research is

certainly warranted before aversion therapy can be recommended for standard use mainly because this procedure is so degrading.

VOYEURISM

Voyeurism, or *scoptophilia,* can be defined as a compulsive desire to observe women partially or completely nude without the consent of the females. (As in the case of exhibitionism, voyeurism is primarily associated with males; women are seldom brought to the attention of therapists or the legal system.) To a large extent, of course, everybody is sexually stimulated by looking at someone who is partially or completely nude. Men looking at women and women looking at men is a normal part of sexual behavior. Enjoying and being aroused by looking at people on a beach, going to striptease shows and topless and bottomless bars, viewing nude pictures in magazines, and attending X-rated films are *not* considered examples of deviant voyeurism. What distinguishes stereotypic "peeping" from the norm is that voyeurism is engaged in secretly and often in place of other sexual activity.

The most striking aspect of the voyeurism literature is that very little has been written about the subject (Smith, 1976). The only source of statistical data concentrates on 56 imprisoned voyeurs (Gebhard et al., 1965). The lack of information probably reflects most people's opinion that voyeur-

ism is a minor nuisance unless the "peeper" becomes too intrusive and persistent in invading the privacy of a given individual. Furthermore, voyeuristic tendencies can be satisfied in so many socially acceptable ways in contemporary society, that no longer does the "peeper" need to lurk outside bedroom windows or bore holes in the walls of public bathrooms in the hope of observing a woman disrobe. The study by Gebhard and his colleagues can be summarized as follows:

1. The convicted voyeur almost never watches females he knows well.
2. Voyeurs are almost always on the outside looking in. Only 6 percent of the offenses took place while the offender was within a building.
3. Voyeurs tend to be much younger, as compared with other imprisoned sex offenders. The median age at first conviction for men in this study was 24.
4. Perhaps because of their younger age, only 45 percent had ever been married.
5. Twenty-nine percent of the voyeurs had a record of juvenile conviction of some sort—statistically higher than the general prison control group.
6. As was true for exhibitionists, persistent

voyeurs seem to be lacking in social skills and suffer from considerable interpersonal anxiety and fears of rejec-

tion. The most common clinical impression is of a timid, shy, and "sociosexually underdeveloped" man.

FETISHISM

Fetishism is characterized by intense preoccupation with certain objects as additional means of sexual arousal or as substitutes for normal sexual activity. Usually fetishism has been divided into two major types. The first type of fetish involves a limited portion of the body, such as the breasts, buttocks, feet, or hair; this preoccupation is sometimes called **partialism.** The second type of fetish is characterized by an obsession for an inanimate object, usually some article of clothing such as shoes, boots, lingerie, gloves, or clothing made of a particular material such as rubber, leather, or fur (Gebhard, 1969). Partialism need not concern us further, since to some degree everyone is especially attracted to particular physical attributes. Fetishism in the extreme clinical form is almost always associated with inanimate objects and is distinguished from normal arousal in that a person is compulsively attracted to the object.

The fetishist usually comes to the attention of clinicians when the attraction to the fetish has become so overwhelming that it serves as the primary focus of sexual arousal and gratification. As far as can be determined from existing clinical literature, pathological fetishism is exclusively a male phenomenon. Published case histories also

reveal that the compulsive urge to possess and touch the inanimate object can lead to bizarre behaviors, including the repetitive theft of articles of clothing and the chasing of women wearing certain clothes (Bethell, 1974; Grant, 1953; Malitz, 1966). Epstein, (1960) claims that the threshold for sexual arousal is so easily reached that some fetishists can ejaculate simply by seeing or touching the object without engaging in any masturbatory activity. Most fetishists, however, will caress, fondle, smell, or put on the article of clothing and then masturbate.

Etiology

Various theories have been proposed about the cause of fetishism. Freud believed that castration anxiety was the source of the problem. This hypothesis is somewhat complicated. The fetish supposedly serves as a penis substitute or symbol, and its function is to alleviate the fear of castration. This theory has absolutely no empirical support.

An explanation that seems to be more direct and has the most experimental and clinical support was first proposed by Alfred Binet in 1877 (Hoenig, 1976). According to Binet, the fetishistic object assumed

A police official examines some of the shoes collected by the Seattle "shoe bandit." He accosted women on the street and stole a single shoe from each.

a sexual symbolic value through association with a sexual experience in childhood or adolescence. More recently, Rachman and Hodgson (1968) conducted an experimental study to demonstrate that people can be conditioned to respond sexually to inanimate objects.

In real life, as distinguished from the laboratory study conducted by Rachman and Hodgson, early sexual experiences associated with fetishistic stimuli are probably unexpected and much more intense (e.g., a young boy observing an attractive woman putting on provocative undergarments). Once the association to sexual excitement has occurred, the value of the fetishistic stimuli can become fixated through repeated association in fantasy, and subsequently in reality, with masturbation. This theory goes along with the idea that the fetishist has never progressed beyond **autoeroticism;** without masturbating, fetishism could not be maintained (Stekel, 1952).

Fetishism may also develop because of fears or uncertainties about women and sex, thus interfering with normal sexual development. Nagler (1957) argues that fetishism represents a fear of the male social role in its entirety. According to both Nagler (1957) and Epstein (1960), fetishism predominates in socially inadequate men with low self-esteem. As a result, the extreme fetishist may not have had much success or exposure to alternative forms of sexual activity. This personality deficit may

---

Box 10-1

A BRIEF CASE DESCRIPTION OF A FETISHIST

The patient was a 24-year-old salesman referred for treatment of a fetish for women's underwear. The patient reported his usual sexual behavior consisted of dressing in women's panties and masturbating to orgasm. He estimated his frequency of heterosexual dating to be six or seven times per month, primarily with the same woman. Intercourse with this woman was estimated to occur approximately one or two times per week. The patient reported being impotent during sexual activities unless he wore women's undergarments. He complained that while he did not really enjoy regularly dating the same woman, she appeared to understand and accept his unusual sexual behavior. The patient reported no desire to dress in women's underwear at any time other than during masturbation or intercourse.

A sexual history revealed that the patient first remembered masturbating as a youth by rubbing his penis to orgasm with a pair of his mother's silk underwear. This activity was repeatedly engaged in whenever he was alone in the house. After a while the patient stole a pair of underwear from a neighbor's clothesline, hiding it in his room where he would employ the garment in masturbation almost nightly.

When the patient was approximately 14 years old, he began regularly dating a girl from his school. During the first several months of his relationship the patient continued masturbating with the aid of women's underwear while fantasizing about the young girl. Sexual activities between the two gradually progressed to the point where the girl would allow the patient to unbutton her blouse, pull up her skirt, lie between her legs, and masturbate himself to orgasm by rubbing his penis against her panties and mons pubis. During this time he confiscated a piece of his partner's underwear which he would enjoy in masturbation.

also explain why the fetishist often steals rather than purchases the inanimate object of desire. Perhaps the theft (like exposure in an exhibitionist) is a way of asserting masculinity.

Treatment

The literature has reported several successful case studies using shock aversion therapy in the treatment of fetishists (Marks

---

During the patient's teenage years he continued masturbating to fantasies and photographs of women in underwear, collecting a scrapbook of pictures of women's underwear advertisements from catalogs and magazines. During this time the patient also began regularly stealing undergarments from laundry rooms and clotheslines. This unusual behavior later generalized to stealing from a number of women, most of whom he knew, until he was stealing approximately once a week. Each pair of panties stolen was carefully labeled to note the name of the owner and the date taken. Masturbation activities during this period involved carefully choosing a pair of panties from his collection, fantasizing about the owner dressed in the underwear, and rubbing his penis to orgasm.

The patient reported one episode of sneaking into the girls' locker room and stealing several pairs of panties while the girls' swimming team was practicing in the gymnasium pool, and using these garments as both olfactory and tactile masturbatory aids. He later found an underground newspaper offering to sell soiled panties by mail. He purchased several pairs of panties by mail which aroused him because of their odor and texture.

The patient had never been discovered stealing, although in one adventure he was chased by a dog, collided with a lawn mower in the dark, and suffered a leg wound that required 15 stitches. He told us he had revealed his sexual orientation to three different women with no immediate adverse reaction from any of them. Two of the three women allowed him to wear feminine undergarments during intercourse but later refused further dates with him. The third woman was his regular sexual partner. At the time of referral the patient reported that he frequently wore women's underwear under his usual clothing, especially on weekends. He claimed he found the thought and texture of the garments so extremely arousing that he would feel the desire to masturbate repeatedly.

Tollison & Adams, 1979, pp. 268–269.

& Gelder, 1967; Marks, Gelder, & Bancroft, 1970; Marks, Rachman, & Gelder, 1965; Marshall, 1974). However, in many cases individuals also were masochists or transvestites, and different behavioral tech- niques were sometimes combined with the aversion procedure. Because of the absence of more controlled research with larger samples, concluding that aversion therapy is the best treatment available is premature.

SADOMASOCHISM

Sadomasochism is the term used to describe sexual arousal that is produced by giving or receiving physical pain, usually in the form of spanking or whipping. The term **sadism** was coined in reference to the French writer Marquis de Sade (1740–1814), who both practiced and wrote about various sexual deviations, especially those involving pain. The term **masochism** is based on the name of an Austrian novelist, Leopold Von Sacher-Masoch (1836–1895), who indulged in his compulsion to be beaten and humiliated by domineering women and who also wrote about it. However, few sadomasochists are exclusively sadists or masochists; although one role might be preferred for the other, roles are often exchanged (Gebhard, 1969). **Bondage,** which involves tying up a partner with ropes, chains, or leather straps, is considered a subvariety of sadomasochism. At the most general level, bondage and sadomasochist scenarios share common elements of sexual dominance, submission, and humiliation. Note that we will not consider here extreme forms of sadism such as sexual mutilation as part of murderous attacks or rapes of a sadistic nature (see Chapter Twelve).

Only a small percentage of the general population report engaging in any sadomasochistic activity; many more report being aroused by sadomasochistic fantasies or stories. A survey conducted by Hunt (1974) indicates that less than 5 percent of males and females in the United States report ever having experienced sexual pleasure from inflicting or receiving pain. Of those, more males reported pleasure from administering than receiving pain; the reverse was true for females. Hunt also found that the percentages were slightly higher among people under age 35, suggesting that there may be a trend toward greater acceptance of this sort of sexual behavior in recent times.

Cross-species and Cross-cultural Perspectives

The connection between sexual excitement, aggression, and pain is evident in the mating behavior of many species lower than humans on the evolutionary scale. Mock combat is a frequent component of courtship rituals, and during copulation many mammals bite their partner's neck.

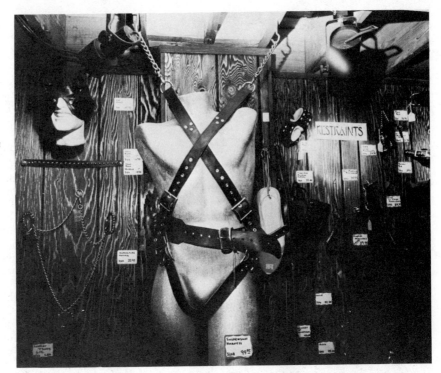

Sadomasochistic paraphernalia for sale.

Among nonhuman primates, such as baboons or macaque monkeys, when a male is sexually aroused by his partner, he "often chases her about, alternately biting and copulating with her" (Ford & Beach, 1951, p. 60).

In our own society, mild forms of painful stimulation may accompany normal sexual activity, especially biting and scratching. Ford and Beach (1951) believe that all men and women are physiologically predisposed to sexual excitement in response to mild degrees of pain, but this underlying capacity is shaped in one direction or another by the particular culture in which one is reared. It could be argued that at some level sadomasochism is an integral part of our own culture. Explicit links between violence and sexuality are commonly found in novels, rock music, movies, and commercial advertisements. It is also probably no coincidence that slang expressions for sexual behavior and genitals are also used as expressions of hostility and degradation—"fuck you," "screw her," "you suck," and "stupid prick" are prime examples.

Description of Sadomasochistic Activities

Sadomasochism follows an intricate behavioral pattern. In some cases it is indulged in only on occasion and as a prelude to sexual intercourse. In other instances it is the sole form of sexual outlet, heavily reliant on fantasy, pornography, prostitution, or masturbation. Gebhard (1969) points out that ritualized features of sadomasochism resemble fetishism. The paraphernalia collected and worn by bondage and discipline devotees, such as boots, leather clothing, masks, collars, paddles, canes, and whips, are sexually stimulating even when not used.

A leather outfit often symbolizes the sexually arousing theme of dominance-submission.

Clinical case descriptions and impressions obtained from advertisements for partners and from letters published in sex magazines and papers suggest that sadomasochistic activity is very ceremonial and controlled.

Submissive male, 30, 5'6", shy and inexperienced. Needs dominant women to teach proper respect for females through humiliation... Male slave, 31, obedient but untrained, seeks goddess to train, discipline, and humiliate me. Let me live under your feet....

Tall (6'), beautiful, blue-eyed, blonde Goddess seeks correspondence and meeting with submissive men who enjoy being dominated, bound, and humiliated. I enjoy wearing leather and latex, and forcing a man (you) into total submission. I can be mildly sadistic and cruel, and thoroughly enjoy it, as long as you can enjoy it too. Come to me, come to my private dungeon for a fantasy scenario that you will treasure for a lifetime. Come to my exotic power. Write now, worm!

Submissive Cindy. Use me, abuse me, my body is yours to command. Anything that gives you pleasure. I love a masterful man. I believe a girl was born only to give pleasure and to be a devoted slave. I would love to watch you get hot by calling me dirty names and spanking my beautiful, round ass. Give me a call and let me serve you. My number:

Scenarios are usually carefully scripted and fantasy laden. They include the misbehaving student and the dominant schoolmaster or mistress, the strict governess and her ward, the misbehaving spouse and his or her disciplining partner, and the master and the submissive slave. In one of the typical scripts, the individual in the role of masochist makes believe he or she did something wrong, deserving of punishment. Submission and humiliation are desired, and the person playing the sadistic role caters carefully to the wishes of the masochistic partner. Both must pretend or show sexual arousal at the moment of punishment, or neither party will be satisfied. Greene and Greene (1974) claim that outright enjoyment of cruelty and torture does not characterize the typical sadomasochist. In fact, delivery or receipt of pain per se is not enjoyable except as it occurs within the confines of the agreed-upon and prearranged script. Often the theatrics seem more important than the actual pain:

> My wife and I do play dominance and submission games, and maybe we have the marks to prove it on occasion. But the one playing top dog watches like a hawk to make sure we stop when the other one doesn't like it any more (Gosselin and Wilson, 1980, p. 54).

Etiology

We can only speculate as to why some people find sadomasochistic activities so exciting. Some people may find painful stimulation of the buttocks and anal area to be more highly erotic than other people. In general, pain increases physiological arousal, and up to some level may thus enhance sexual arousal.

Biographies and autobiographies of famous masochists, such as Von Sacher-Masoch, Rousseau, and Swinburne, suggest that early childhood experiences may sometimes be responsible for establishing an association between sexual pleasure and corporal punishment. A recent study, however, did not find any difference in experience with corporal punishment during childhood between a group of sadomasochists and a control group (Gosselin & Wilson, 1980). Early experience alone, therefore, cannot entirely account for the development of sadomasochistic behavior. Another prevalent explanation of sexual masochism is that it relieves guilt associated with sexual pleasure. For example, the bondage enthusiast may enjoy the sense of helplessness caused by restraint because if anything sexual transpires it is not his or her fault. For the sadist, the feeling that the masochist is helpless and at his or her mercy may also be a sexually liberating experience. The resulting sense of dominance, power, and control could counter underlying fears of inadequacy and rejection. Also, since traditional male and female roles are often reversed or exaggerated in scenarios of dominance-submission, acting out different scripts may be a way for people to *play* with these roles.

Some interesting conclusions were drawn by Spengler (1977) after analyzing the results of his survey study. First, sadomasochism is more prevalent among male homosexuals than among heterosexuals. Second, males, whether heterosexually or homosexually inclined, are more likely than females to want to engage in sadomasochism, thus accounting for the greater frequency of this activity among male homosexuals. Aggression and the desire to subdue one's partner seem to be more acceptable in overt male sexuality than in female sexuality in most cultures. When two males get together for sexual activity, sadomasochism is simply more likely than is the case when two females or a male and a female engage in sex together. Even among male homosexuals, however, sadomasochism is a very infrequent phenomenon.

Treatment

As noted, pain in itself is not pleasurable to sadomasochists unless it occurs as part of a prearranged sexual script. Thus, not surprisingly, a number of sadomasochists have been effectively treated with aversion therapy (Marks, Gelder, & Bancroft, 1970). Of course, most males who engage in sado-masochism do not believe that therapy is necessary if they are able to find consenting partners. Furthermore, since mutual consent between two adults is the typical pattern, most sadomasochists are unlikely to come in contact with legal authorities. Thus, they are not forced into therapy as part of sentencing, as is the case with exhibitionism, voyeurism, and even fetishism.

TRANSVESTISM

The most obvious feature of **transvestism** is *cross-dressing*, the wearing of clothes customarily worn by persons of the opposite sex. Cross-dressing alone, however, is an insufficient definition of transvestism: Not all people who cross-dress are transvestites. Attempts have been made to distinguish cross-dressing as it occurs in male transvestites from this behavior in transsexuals and homosexuals. Table 10-2 highlights the differences among trans-vestites, transsexuals, and homosexuals.

There are supposedly two major types of the male transvestite. The first has a fetish for wearing certain selected female garments from time to time. Touching and putting on these clothes is associated with sexual excitement. The second type of transvestite is the man who occasionally dresses entirely in stereotypic female clothing and who adds such items as makeup and a wig to transform his ap-

TABLE 10-2 DISTINCTIONS AMONG MALE TRANSVESTITES, TRANSSEXUALS, AND HOMOSEXUALS

	DESIRED GENDER IDENTITY	DESIRED CROSS-DRESSING FREQUENCY	SEXUAL PARTNER	FETISHISTIC COMPONENT TO CROSS-DRESSING	DESIRE FOR SEX-CHANGE SURGERY
Transvestite	Male	Occasional	Female	Sometimes Present	No
Transsexual	Female	Permanent	Male	Seldom Present	Yes
Homosexual	Male	Rarely	Male	Seldom Present	No

pearance so that he can "pass" as a female. For him, sexual excitement while dressed as a woman may be absent (Benjamin, 1966; Brierly, 1979; Feinbloom, 1976). Rather, he reports that he has a feminine side that needs to be expressed and that wearing female clothes is satisfying and relaxing without any overt sexual stimulation. Neither type of transvestite experiences gender identity confusion. They both believe they are primarily male. Even while dressed as a woman they enjoy knowing they have a penis. In fantasy and in reality both are only interested in sexual activity with females, and there is no evidence of any heterosexual inadequacy or dysfunction.

Transvestism appears to be unique to males. Stoller (1968) argues that female transvestites are for all practical purposes nonexistent in our culture. Women, of course, often wear "men's" clothes, but they are usually not striving to pass as males when they do so. Our society permits a much greater range of fashion for women than for men. For example, no one looks twice at a female in slacks, but the same cannot be said of males who wear dresses. Perhaps if the same flexibility in fashion were available to men, there would be no such thing as male transvestism.

Etiology

No one really knows what causes some men to become transvestites. Certainly there is no evidence of any hormonal, genetic, or anatomic abnormality (Buhrich, Theile,

Yaw, & Crawford, 1979; Housden, 1965). The more usual hypothesis has to do with early childhood experience, which could take various forms. For example, mothers may have wanted a girl instead of a boy and initially dressed and reinforced the child accordingly. Another possibility is that early childhood experience with cross-dressing may have been accidentally associated with sexual play, pleasure, and arousal. Thus, initially, cross-dressing developed in the same manner as any other sexual fetish.

Stoller (1975) suggests still another hypothesis. He believes that transvestism is a way of gaining revenge for the humiliation suffered as a boy at the hands of powerful women who threatened his masculinity. By having an erection and engaging in sexual intercourse, despite being garbed in female clothing, he converts the original humiliation into one of mastery.

Cross-cultural and Historical Perspective

Anthropological descriptions unfortunately often confuse transvestism, transsexuality, and homosexuality. Nevertheless, many examples in other cultures of cross-dressing behavior and exchanging of roles between genders resemble transvestism. For instance, cross-gender behavior was commonly noted during the early decades of this century among various North American Indian tribes (Green, 1974). In paleo-Siberian, Mediterranean, Indian, Oceanic, and African tribes, men who assumed the feminine role were often thought to have supernatural or magical powers, including the ability to promote good or evil, and health or sickness (Ford & Beach, 1951; Green, 1969). Apparently, a widespread cross-cultural belief was that being dual-sexed resulted from mystical knowledge and abilities, giving these men special powers.

Instances of cross-dressing have been recorded throughout history. The last king of the Assyrian Empire, as well as some later Roman Emperors, was said to enjoy appearing as a woman. In the sixteenth century, King Henry III of France wished to be considered a woman and was addressed as "her Majesty" (Green, 1969).

Demographic and Personality Characteristics

Although transvestites come from all "walks of life," the higher socioeconomic and educational brackets may be over-

represented (Prince & Bentler, 1972). In a series of separate studies, these researchers have also shown that neuroses and psychoses or any other psychiatric disturbances are no more common in a transvestite population than in control groups of nontransvestite men (Bentler & Prince, 1969, 1970; Bentler, Sherman, & Prince, 1970).

The majority of transvestites are currently married or have been at one time. In the Prince and Bentler (1972) sample, 78 percent were either currently married or had previously been married, and 74 percent reported having one or more children. Little is known, however, about the wives of transvestites. In the Prince and Bentler (1972) sample, 20 percent of the men reported that their wives were unaware of their transvestism. Of those who knew, only 23 percent were reported as accepting and cooperative, and 20 percent were completely antagonistic. Clearly, transvestism is often a source of friction in marriage, and worked until early evening and the patient arrived home in the afternoon, he would engage in this behavior during his wife's absence. The patient had concealed his sexual preference from his wife for the first four years of the five-year marriage. During this time the couple would frequently argue and disagree over the frequency of sexual intercourse, the wife claiming that she could not understand why the patient did not desire sexual relations more often. It was only after being accidentally discovered by the wife that the patient admitted his cross-dressing. Both partners agreed that the wife initially accepted the patient's behavior and, in fact, claimed that the marriage improved for a short while afterward. During this period of marital improvement the couple would engage in intercourse approximately three to four times weekly with the patient dressed in his wife's clothing and the wife nude. The wife claimed that she had originally accepted the idea because of the novelty and the pleasure of increased coital frequency. However, she soon tired of the patient's transvestism and claimed to be disgusted at the sight of her husband dressed in her clothing. During the year prior to seeking therapy, the frequency of intercourse had again decreased to approximately once every three weeks, and arguments and discord had increased.

From Tollison & Adams, 1979, pp. 283–284.

it is probably the one reason over all others that would cause the transvestite to seek therapeutic counseling.

Treatment

Most transvestites feel that therapy designed to eliminate cross-dressing behavior is unwarranted because they do not believe that it is a problem, despite society's disapproval (Prince & Bentler, 1972). In fact, many organized transvestite groups feel that the mental health profession should be more concerned with changing society's attitudes than with changing the behavior of transvestites.

For those transvestites who do want to discontinue cross-dressing, however, behavior therapy approaches appear to offer some promise of success, particularly if there is a clear fetishistic component present. An electric aversion conditioning model has been used, and positive results have been reported (Marks, Gelder, & Bancroft, 1970). Moss, Rada, and Appel (1970) described the successful use of a different behavior therapy procedure, which focused on strengthening alternative sexual behaviors between the man and his wife.

TRANSSEXUALITY

Transsexuals are biologically normal males and females who question their gender identity and wish it changed. Thus, a male transsexual is a person who rejects his male body and the "male role" because he thinks of himself as a female. A female transsexual has the same feelings regarding her "femaleness"; she rejects her female body and the "female role" because she thinks of herself as a male. This "gender dysphoria" that transsexuals suffer from, which is typically longstanding, has its origins in early childhood. As adults they seek hormonal and surgical treatment so that they can live as members of the opposite sex.

A request for sex reassignment surgery is not automatically granted. A trial period of one to two years duration is usually imposed before surgery is seriously considered. During this period the candidate for surgery must prove that he or she can live as a member of the opposite sex. A hormonal therapy program may be started; presurgical counseling on the limitations of surgery will be provided; the motivation for seeking surgery can be fully explored; speech therapy can be provided to alter the voice in a more appropriate direction; and other difficulties in mannerisms, physical characteristics, and family and social adjustment can be addressed.

Transsexuality and sex reassignment surgery have received a good deal of media attention and seem to have gained social acceptance. Within the medical and mental health community, however, the topic continues to provoke considerable controversy. The modern history of transsexuality and **sex-change** surgery is actually quite short and volatile. Although autobiographical accounts and instances of sporadic surgery were reported earlier in Germany, Casablanca, and Switzerland, the first case to draw a great deal of attention in the United States occurred in 1952 when Christine Jorgensen (formerly George Jorgensen) went to Denmark for sex-change surgery (Jorgensen, 1968). In the 1950s and 1960s, acceptance of transsexuality continued to grow (Benjamin, 1966). However, the stamp of ultimate legitimacy in the United States did not occur until 1966 when the **gender-identity** clinic that performed sex reassignment surgery was established at the Johns Hopkins Medical Center. In the first two and a half years of the clinic's existence, more than 1,500 people requested sex reassignment surgery. Presently, a number of other highly reputable university-affiliated hospitals offer such surgery.

Approximately 3,000 to 4,000 transsexuals have undergone sex-change operations in the United States since 1966. However, as with many other forms of surgery that were once faddish and are no longer so, such as tonsillectomies and hysterectomies, there is reason to believe that sex reassignment surgery is becoming less popular. In 1979, Johns Hopkins closed its clinic, and sex reassignment surgery is no longer being offered there. Other hospitals may follow suit. The explanation for this shift in professional practice is not simple: It may have to do with practicality and cost (no surgeons available in a particular setting) or no insurance coverage, or it may have to do with a growing suspicion that the entire transsexual phenomenon is based on a corrosive sexist and homophobic foundation. The latter point will be discussed in the sections that follow.

Incidence and Prevalence

Studies performed in Sweden, the United States, England, and Canada suggest that approximately one out of every 35,000 males over age 15, and one out of every 100,000 females over age 15 are transsexuals (Hoenig & Kenna, 1974; Walinder, 1968). Why should so many more males than females be seeking sex reassignment surgery? A number of explanations have been suggested. One is that greater publicity of male transsexuals—the three most well known being Christine Jorgensen, Jan Morris, and Renee Richards—has encouraged more males than females to come forward. Another is that surgery for males is more advanced; constructing a functional vagina for a male is far easier than constructing a functional penis for a female. These explanations are based on the assumption that the number of male transsexuals equals female transsexuals, but that circumstances have caused more males to be counted because they come to sex-change clinics. Another set of explanations, however, suggests that social, or sexist, forces have led to a real difference in the number of male and female transsexuals. In the case of children, "tomboys" are more acceptable than are "sissies." Society is also somewhat more tolerant of adult females who dress and act "like a male" than vice versa. Why? One possible answer is that it places a higher value on stereotyped masculine characteristics than on female characteristics, on males than on females. In any case, if society is more

Christine Jorgensen before (top) and after hormonal treatment and surgery (bottom).

hostile to males than to females who deviate from stereotyped sex-role norms, then one can hypothesize that male transsexuals have greater motivation to take the drastic step of genital surgery than do females.

In addition, Morgan (1978) estimates that about 30 percent of the males who request sex-reassignment surgery can be considered "homophobics." They are repulsed by homosexuality and strongly deny any such tendency in themselves. Thus male transsexuals may outnumber female transsexuals because males have greater fears of being considered homosexual than do females (see Chapter Seven). Also, contrary to what might be expected, transsexuality carries less of a stigma than does homosexuality (Leitenberg & Slavin, in press). Transsexuality implies a greater biological basis and is apparently more easily excused than "perverse homosexuality."

Etiology

Most transsexuals report that they always believed they were of the opposite sex (Green, 1974). What is the basis for this belief? There is no solid evidence of any history of chromosomal abnormality, anatomic abnormality, or hormonal abnormality in transsexuals. These people are apparently judging their behavior and feelings according to stereotyped conceptions of masculine and feminine role behavior. The adult male transsexual will report that as a child he preferred female toys, did not like rough-and-tumble games, preferred to play with girls rather than boys, and preferred frilly clothes. The way transsexuals speak about themselves (as well as the way professionals speak about them) reflects these stereotypes, as can be seen in the following examples:

> Self-reliance, a certain aggressiveness, and dominance are expected of a man. This is against my nature. It is not expected of a woman. Therefore as a woman, I feel at ease, more secure and my true self (Benjamin, 1966, p. 43).

> Finally, but highly important, how do you know you can make a living as a woman? Have you ever worked as a woman before? I assume that so far, you have only held a man's job and have drawn a man's salary. Now you may have to learn something entirely new. Could you do that? Could you get along with smaller earnings? (Benjamin, 1966, p. 109)

Raymond (1979) convincingly argues that if the culture were more tolerant of nonstereotyped sex-role behavior and homosexuality, there would probably be no gender-identity confusion and little desire for a change in genitals. She believes that dominant mothers, poor male role models, and other inappropriate rearing practices are not the real cause of transsexuality. If culturally engrained sex-role stereotyping didn't exist, then there would be no social sanctions against cross-gender behavior, nor anguish because of it—and no transsexuality.

Sex Reassignment Surgery

□ *Description* Surgery does not really change a biological male into a biological female, or vice versa. Raymond quotes George Burou, a Casablancan physician who has operated on over 700 American men: "I transform male genitals into genitals that have a female aspect. All the rest is in the patient's mind" (1979, p. 10). Hormonal treatment and sex-change surgery does not alter chromosomal makeup or reproductive capacity. Following surgery a male transsexual cannot ovulate and become pregnant, and a female transsexual cannot produce sperm or ejaculate. Hormonal treatment and sex-change surgery can, however, dramatically alter external genitals and physical appearance.

Since men have more facial hair than women, a male considering sex reassignment will first embark on a slow and costly process of hair removal. Next he will receive estrogen therapy. After surgery, the transsexual will have to continue with hormonal treatment indefinitely. The third step in the male-to-female conversion process is genital surgery. Three phases are involved: (1) testicular castration, (2) penile amputation and shortening and redirection of the urethra, and (3) construction of a vaginal channel, vaginal lining, and labia majora and minora. Scrotal and penile tissues are used to construct the vagina. Since these tissues contain erogenous sensory nerve endings, sexual stimulation and orgasm are possible following surgery. Aside from further surgery to correct complications, some male transsexuals seek additional cosmetic surgery for the nose, the Adam's apple, or to change eye shape, for example, in an attempt to achieve their idealized physical image of a woman.

The female transsexual who wishes to undergo sexual reconstruction also receives hormonal treatment prior to surgery. As with male transsexuals, hormonal treatment has to be maintained indefinitely. The most frequent surgical operation for female transsexuals is breast removal. Hysterectomies are also common. However, surgical procedures for constructing a penis and scrotum are still experimental. Furthermore, even if a penis is constructed in a cosmetically satisfactory manner, it will not be capable of a normal erection. The clitoris is usually maintained to provide sensory sexual stimulation.

☐ *Outcome* Hormonal treatment and sex change surgery do not guarantee happiness for the transsexual. Most reports, however, are quite favorable (Pauly, 1968; Randall, 1969; Money, 1971). Understandably, transsexuals who have undergone surgery do not have to worry about being detected, and they may feel more at peace with themselves. Unfortunately, these are not rigorous outcome studies.

In the only comparison study of transsexuals who had been operated on and those who had not, researchers found that although a positive shift in adjustment had occurred, *no significant difference existed between the operated and unoperated* transsexuals on any of the measures (Meyer & Reter, 1979). They conclude: "Sex reassignment surgery confers no objective advantage in terms of social rehabilitation, although it remains subjectively satisfying to those who have rigorously pursued a trial period and who have undergone it" (Meyer & Reter, 1979, p. 1015). This opinion may not be the final verdict on sex reassignment

Box 10–3

THE CASE OF JAN MORRIS

Jan Morris is a famous English male-to-female transsexual who wrote an eloquent autobiography about her experiences entitled *Conundrum* (Morris, 1975). Prior to going through hormonal and surgical treatment at age 46, she was known as James Morris. Both as James Morris and since as Jan Morris, she has authored many well-received books on travel and history. Jan Morris fathered four children, served for four years in the 9th Lancers Brigade, and was a journalist. In addition, she climbed a good part of Mount Everest as the reporter assigned to the first British expedition to successfully climb this mountain. Yet even during these "manly" exploits, she always felt female and detested being a male. Why?

From her autobiography, Jan Morris seemingly aspired to be a woman primarily because she developed an idealized image of a female during childhood. Despite her complaint about the way society downgrades women, her autobiography is filled with conventional stereotypes about both women and men. She believed that women were more gentle, less interested in material accomplishment, less deceitful, more nurturing, yielding, passive, real, and so on, characteristics that she valued and felt could only be completely realized through a sex transformation.

surgery, but the negative results, combined with the fact that the study was performed at Johns Hopkins, the institution associated with introducing sex reassignment surgery to the United States, may have a chilling effect on the prevailing positive attitude toward such surgery.

☐ *New Alternatives to Surgery*   Sex reassignment surgery was originally made available to transsexuals not only because they demanded it, but also because there

was considerable pessimism about the effectiveness of any alternative intervention. Traditional psychotherapy had not succeeded in persuading transsexuals to accept their biological sexual identity. However, more recent research suggests that overvalued ideas about cross-gender identity and sex-role behaviors can, in fact, be modified. Therapists using a mixture of different behavioral therapy techniques reported successful outcomes in three male transsexuals (Barlow, Reynolds, & Agras,

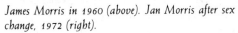

James Morris in 1960 (above). Jan Morris after sex change, 1972 (right).

1973; Barlow, Abel, & Blanchard, 1979). The therapeutic procedure involved rather painstaking and detailed training in how to sit, stand, walk, and talk in a more masculine manner. It also involved other social skills training and modification of sexual fantasies and arousal patterns. Although these cases are very few, they are striking because they counter the belief that such changes in gender identity are *not* ever possible in adult transsexuals. However, their applicability to a large number of transsexuals remains questionable.

Still another approach to surgery should be considered. Rather than training a male transsexual to engage in more masculine motor, social, and sexual behaviors (and the reverse for female transsexuals), perhaps "consciousness raising" groups would be even more appropriate. In this way, individuals seeking sex-change surgery might instead learn to accept their atypical gender-role behaviors and their homosexual desires without having to resort to surgery. In general, if more flexible masculine and feminine role behaviors were supported, people who formerly would be transsexuals may be able to achieve their goals of living and acting the way they want to without having to disguise and disfigure their bodies to avoid social censure.

Transsexuals' Childhood and Early Intervention

Can early signs of transsexualism be detected and corrected during childhood? Because adult transsexuals characteristically report that they did not act like or have the same interests as other children of their sex when they were young does not mean that all or even most children who fail to show stereotypic "masculine" or "feminine" patterns of behavior develop into transsexuals as adults.

Studies of atypical sexual identity in children have focused almost exclusively on boys (Green, 1974). One reason is that young girls who exhibit so-called "masculine" behavioral traits are not typically considered abnormal, and, therefore, are not referred for treatment. There is sufficient evidence to conclude that stereotypic feminine role behaviors in young boys can indeed be changed via systematic behavioral retraining, the provision of appropriate male role models, and changes in parental reinforcement patterns (Green, Newman, & Stoller, 1972; Rekars, 1977; Rekars and Lovaas, 1974). The question is what is the justification for such treatment (Wolfe, 1979). If it is to prevent these young boys from experiencing alienation and ridicule during childhood, perhaps such treatment might be defensible. However, if the purpose is to prevent adult transsexuality, the treatment is very questionable. There is little evidence that even very feminine boys are likely to grow up to be transsexuals. For example, out of a total of 27 extremely feminine boys who were followed to adulthood, only three developed into transsexuals; the rest were either heterosexual or homosexual (Green, 1974; Lebovitz, 1972; Zuger, 1966). This topic is controversial to be sure and will most likely remain unresolved until a comparison is made of the long-term adjustment of treated and untreated cross-gender-oriented boys, which to date has not been done.

MISCELLANEOUS DEVIATIONS

A number of other sexual deviations exist, but beyond listing and defining them, further discussion would serve little purpose. They are poorly researched, relatively rare, pose few serious problems for society, and would add little more to our understanding of the origins of sexual deviations, the makeup of individuals engaged in them, or the clinical management of the deviations.

Coprophilia refers to an erotic interest in human excrement. A related preoccupation with observing others urinating and being urinated on is labeled **urolognia.** Two unusual fetishes not previously mentioned are **monopedia,** a compulsive attraction to a person of the opposite sex who has had a leg amputated and **klismaphilia,** in which enemas serve as the primary source of sexual gratification. **Frottage** describes the behavior of men who press and rub against women in crowded places such as subways. Any sexual activity between people and animals is known as **bestiality.** Finally, **necrophilia** involves the use of dead bodies as sexual objects.

SUMMARY

1. A pattern of sexual behavior ultimately will be considered deviant based on other people's reactions. Standards, therefore, will vary between cultures, and over time within one culture. Other qualifiers include whether or not an activity is the only means by which one can achieve sexual gratification, and if mutual consent has been established. Another determinant of deviancy is whether or not someone may be physically or psychologically harmed by the activity.

2. **Exhibitionism** can be defined as the deliberate exposure of male genitals to unsuspecting females without any serious intention of further sexual contact. Most incidents of exhibitionism occur in public areas such as streets, parks, autos, and public buildings, and usually during daylight hours. This type of atypical behavior can be treated with individual psychotherapy, group therapy, and various forms of behavior therapy, including aversion therapy.

3. **Fetishism** is characterized by intense preccupation with certain objects as additional means of sexual arousal or as substitutes for normal sexual activity. The inanimate object of desire is usually an article of clothing, such as shoes or lingerie. Sometimes the material that the article is made of is the turn on—for example, rubber, leather, or fur.

4. The compulsive desire to observe women partially or completely nude without the consent or knowledge of the females is known as **voyeurism.**

5. Sexual arousal that is produced by giving or receiving physical pain is **sadomasochism.** There are few exclusive sadists or masochists; while people may prefer one role over the other, these roles are often

exchanged. Sadomasochistic activity usually follows specific scripts and is heavily dependent on fantasies.

6. **Transvestites** are characterized by their desire to cross-dress, which means wearing clothes typically worn by the opposite sex. Some transvestites exhibit a fetish for wearing certain female garments, such as a bra, while others wear complete outfits, including makeup and wigs. Transvestites are sexually excited by the articles, or at least find cross-dressing to be a very satisfying experience. It is important to carefully differentiate between transvestites, transsexuals, and homosexuals.

7. A biologically normal male or female who questions his or her gender identity and seeks to change that identity is a **transsexual.** Sex reassignment is a long process. Hormonal therapy and presurgical counseling precede the actual surgery. A person has to evaluate carefully his or her motivation before making a final decision. Male-to-female surgery is more complete than female-to-male surgery, and is performed more frequently.

8. Many more men than women are engaged in deviant sexual activity in our society. In fact, most classic sexual deviations, including exhibitionism, voyeurism, fetishism, and transvestism, seem to be exclusively male phenomena. A number of explanations are possible. For example, variations in sexual behavior are simply less frowned upon in women and are less likely to be *labeled* deviant. Also, the difference in frequency of sexual deviations between men and women appears to be intricately tied to sex-role stereotypes and pressures.

9. The sexually deviant man is typically characterized as being shy, passive, timid, and unassertive. Interpersonal relationships with peers, spouse, and authority figures tend to be troubled, and limited or dysfunctional sexual histories are common.

10. Exhibitionists, voyeurs, fetishists, transvestites, and most sadomasochists rarely engage in violent acts, and not all sexual deviations involve innocent victims. Some may involve no partners at all (fetishism), while in others mutual consent is the norm (sadomasochism).

11. Questions regarding whether or not to treat sexual deviations and how to treat them are largely unresolved. In cases in which the activity usually involves no one else or a consenting partner, as is generally the case with those deviant activities covered in this chapter, the need for therapy is somewhat questionable. Therapy, however, should be available for those who wish to alter their deviant patterns.

SUGGESTED READINGS

Cox, D. J., & Daitzman, R. J. (Eds.). *Exhibitionism: Description, assessment and treatment.* New York: Garland STPM Press, 1980. A review of the most recent research on treatment of exhibitionism.

Gosselin, C., & Wilson, G. *Sexual variations.* New York: Simon & Schuster, 1980. A descriptive study of fetishism, sadomasochism, and transvestism.

Green, R. *Sexual identity conflict in children and adults.* Baltimore: Penguin Books, 1974. A description of transsexuality in adults and gender identity disorders in children.

Morris, J. *Conundrum.* New York: New American Library, 1975. A fascinating autobiography of a male-to-female transsexual.

CHAPTER ELEVEN

PEDOPHILIA AND INCEST
Sexual Victimization of Children

I certainly didn't think it had happened to anyone else. This was the strange feeling I had when it was going on. I think maybe most women do. I thought I was the only person in the world this was happening to. And I must be a terrible person otherwise this wouldn't be happening to me, see?
Armstrong, 1979

We have intentionally used as part of the chapter title the phrase, "Sexual Victimization of Children." More neutral terminology would have been, "Sexual Contact or Interaction between Adults and Children," or even, "Sexual Misuse of Children." In our society, however, children are protected by and taught to obey adults; thus, regardless of how it is initiated or what the consequences are, sex between an adult and a young girl or boy is abusive. Such a relationship abuses the trust the child has in an adult to know better, to act in the best interests of the child, and to not take advantage of the child's helpless position. No other sexual behavior is more universally condemned in contemporary culture than the sexual abuse of young children.

This chapter considers only two specific subcategories of sexual victimization of children—namely pedophilia, or child molestation, and incest. We should emphasize that sexual exploitation or victimization of children encompasses much more than pedophilia and incest alone. For example, it includes the use of children in the production of pornographic films and magazines and child prostitution; these topics, while related to the sexual abuse of children, are reviewed in Chapter 13.

EXTENT OF THE PROBLEM

The true incidence of sexual abuse of children is unknown, the major reason being that sexual acts between adults and children are seldom reported to either police or social agencies. This lack of disclosure is clearly revealed in two general population studies in which adults were asked to recall their childhood sexual experiences. Of those who noted sexual contact with adults when they were preadolescents, only 6 to 10 percent indicated that any outside authority such as the police had been informed (Gagnon, 1965; Landis, 1956). Hesitancy about disclosure is especially understandable when one considers that with the exception of exhibitionism, approximately 80 percent of the sexual interactions between children and adults involve acquaintances or relatives. Fear, embarrassment, a desire on the part of parents not to compound the problem, and concern about the possible response of social, medical, and legal agencies further contribute to underreporting. It is generally acknowledged that for every reported case, approximately five to ten cases are not reported.

The number of reported cases of sexual abuse of children has increased dramatically in the past few years, an indication perhaps that such abuse is becoming more common. Childrens Hospital in Washington, D.C., for example, noted a threefold increase in complaints when they publicized a program in 1978 aimed at dealing with sexual abuse (Makstein, McLaughlin, & Rogers, 1979). Passage of more effective legislation for general child abuse, better recording systems, and greater community sensitivity to the problem may account for this increase in cases being reported rather than a change in actual incidence.

Perhaps the most accurate and revealing statistics are contained in surveys of the general female population. The percentage of women who report having had this type of childhood encounter is both remarkably high and remarkably consistent across a series of five different studies conducted during the past twenty-five years. Excluding instances of exhibitionism and/or verbal abuse, the range is from 11 percent to 16 percent (Finkelhor, 1979a; Gagnon, 1965; Kinsey et al. 1953; Landis, 1956; Walters, 1975). These percentages indicate that several million female children in the United States will be victims of some form of sexual abuse prior to reaching mid-adolescence. Another way to look at this question is to consider the number of children affected in a given year. The U.S. National Center on Child Abuse estimated that in 1976 there were over 100,000 new cases of sexual abuse against children (Geiser, 1979).

PEDOPHILIA

Pedophilia can be defined as sexual contact between an adult and a child who are *not* legal or blood relatives. Clinical research, and criminal statistics suggest that pedophiles are almost uniformly male; therefore, if the child is female, we speak of *heterosexual pedophilia,* and if the child is male, we speak of *homosexual pedophilia.* These terms apply only to the sex of the child. Thus, later in the chapter when we refer to a homosexual pedophile, all that is meant is that the victim is a young boy; the adult need not have a homosexual orientation.

Both the age of the child and the nature of the sexual activity contribute further to the confusion about the way to define pedophilia. First, consider age. Some investigators feel that pedophilia should refer only to acts involving children who have not yet reached puberty, while others suggest that the age limit should be 12, 14, or even 16 years. Research indicates that the typical adult male offender is primarily attracted to the child who is physically and socially immature, and therefore an argument could be made that pedophilia should be used only in reference to sexual contacts between an adult and a prepubescent child.

The nature of the sexual activity engaged in by the adult is the second major area of confusion when trying to define pedophilia. Typically, the behavior does not involve intercourse but rather fondling of the genitals, masturbation, and exposure. Thus, the distinction between pedophilia and exhibitionism may be blurred unless the intention behind the act is taken into account. If

Perhaps all children need to be gently told that no adult has the right to touch their bodies in ways they do not like, and that if that happens, they should tell their mothers.

exposure occurs at a distance and is the ultimate goal and the primary source of gratification, then it probably should be considered an example of exhibitionism rather than pedophilia, even if the adult is exposing his genitals to a child (Mohr, Turner, & Jerry, 1964).

Who are the Victims?

Children who become the sexual targets of adults share no common characteristics. No one racial, ethnic, or socioeconomic group is more frequently represented, nor are specific environments (rural vs. urban), intellectual abilities, or personality characteristics more prevalent among these children (Landis, 1956).

□ *Girls versus Boys*   Many more preadolescent girls than boys are sexually molested. For example, based on police records in New York City, DeFrancis (1971) estimates that there are approximately nine

female victims to every male victim. Similar findings were revealed in a review of Minneapolis police statistics; there was a ratio of 88 percent female victims to 12 percent male victims (Jaffe, Dynaeson, & Tenbensel, 1975). Surveys of the general population also suggest that preadolescent girls are much more likely than boys to have had sexual contact with adult males. For example, in a study of college students, 19.2 percent of the females versus only 8.6 percent of the males surveyed by Finkelhor (1979a) reported childhood incidents of sexual activity with adult or adolescent males who were at least five years older than themselves.

□ *Age and Age-Sex Interactions*   The age of the children involved in episodes of pedophilia varies as a function of their sex. Female victims tend to be somewhat younger than male victims. In one study of offenders, the mean age for male victims was 12.2, whereas the mean age for females was 9.4 (Mohr et al., 1964). The highest percentage of male victims fell in the upper age range of 12 to 15 years, but for females the percentage dropped off sharply past age 11.

The Pedophile: Who is He?

Most of what we know about demographic and personality characteristics of the adult pedophile comes from studies of convicted and usually imprisoned offenders. (Keep in mind that data derived from such samples may not be an accurate reflection of all pedophiles.) An examination of a number of characteristics shows that pedophiles may not be very different from nonpedophiles, at least insofar as certain basic demographic factors are concerned. For example, several studies have found a normal intelligence distribution in groups of pedophiles (Hammer & Glueck, 1957; Mohr et al., 1964; Shoor, Speed, & Bartelt, 1966), and marital status also appears remarkably similar to the general population.

Age of offenders varies depending on the population studied. In adult prison samples, researchers have found that the typical age of pedophile offenders is between 30 and 40 (Fisher, 1969; Gebhard et al., 1965; Toobert, Bartelme, & Jones, 1953; McCaghy, 1968). However, in studies conducted in nonprison settings, the mean age of the adult is much younger (Makstein et al., 1979; Mohr et al., 1964).

A prevailing myth about child molesters is clearly contradicted by these age statistics. Most pedophiles are not "degenerate old men." Nor, as we shall see, are they usually retarded, illiterate hillbillies, or strangers. In fact, study after study clearly demonstrates that strangers represent a small percentage of offenders and that most pedophiles are either friends or acquaintances of the family. These myths are based less on reality than they are on wishful thinking. Perhaps people feel safer if the picture painted of the pedophile is as different from the general male population as is possible.

Although mental disorders among pedophiles are no more frequent than for other criminal offenders (Mohr et al., 1964), a high percentage of alcoholics have been reported in pedophile samples (Rada, 1976; Swanson, 1968). However, claims of drunkenness may be a way of trying to evade responsibility for deviant behavior, and researchers have found no greater percentage of alcoholics among either heterosexual or homosexual pedophile offenders than among nonpedophile prisoners (Gebhard et al., 1965).

Subcategories of Pedophile Offenders

In general, then, we can conclude that simple demographic factors fail to differentiate the pedophile from comparable populations of nonpedophiles. Why, then, do certain adult males engage in sexual activity with prepubescent children while others do not? There is no one reason or even a common set of reasons on which to base an explanation, mainly because not all pedophile offenders are alike.

The broad distinctions between pedophile offenders based on age of the child and sex of the child have already been mentioned. Other investigators have attempted to refine these categories still further. The major categories of pedophiles proposed are as follows (Fitch, 1962; Cohen, Seghorn, & Calmas, 1969; Groth & Birnbaum, 1978).

Fixated type: Since adolescence, these men have been exclusively interested in children as sex objects. They cannot identify with an adult sexual role, and have never been able to establish mature sexual relationships with peers during their adolescent, young adult, or adult years. Their sexual behavior is primarily directed at fondling, exposure, and masturbation rather than intercourse.

Regressed type: These are men who turn to children in reaction to sexual and psychological stress in their adult relationships. Mature relationships begin to overwhelm them, and they turn to children out of a sense of sexual and social inadequacy with adults. Frequently, they seek out children for both emotional and physical gratification in response to feeling rejected by their wives or in response to some other interpersonal stress or anxiety.

Aggressive or sociopathic type: According to Fitch (1962), aggressive or sociopathic offenders have records of instability and marginal adjustment to society throughout their lives, and their sexual offenses against children are generally committed in an impulsive acting-out manner in response to a temporary aggressive mood. Although this category was not used by Groth and Birnbaum

(1978), the other two studies found that the majority of men in this group will select boys as victims (Cohen et al., 1969; Fitch, 1962).

Organic type: Only Fitch (1962) included this category of pedophiles. He is referring to the small minority of cases in which psychoses, brain damage, mental deterioration due to age, and mental retardation are evident.

Even in institutional settings, fixated and regressed types account for the great majority of pedophiles (at least 75 percent). Both the fixated and regressed pedophiles lack social skills and greatly fear rejection by adult women. A history of sexual failure and frustration is quite common to these men, and they tend to be passive, unassertive, dependent, and guilt-ridden. Such offenders also tend to identify with children and perceive themselves at the same immature sexual level as the child. The need for emotional gratification (to feel close to the child) may sometimes be more powerful than the need for sexual gratification.

One striking early childhood sexual experience seems to have been reliably documented in the case of homosexual pedophilia. Compared with other prison populations, normal controls, and even with other sex offenders, many more homosexual pedophiles were themselves the objects of homosexual abuse when children (e.g., Gebhard et al., 1965). This means that childhood homosexual experiences with adults may be a risk factor for the later development of similar preferences for young boys.

BRIEF CASE DESCRIPTION OF A PEDOPHILE

The patient was a 37-year-old white, single male who referred himself for treatment of pedophilia, both in actual practice and obsessive imagery, plus excessive masturbation and clinical depression. He had entered into treatment for this condition on several previous occasions with no measurable change in his deviant functioning. He had no legal record as a sexual offender.

The patient came from an Irish Catholic family of lower socioeconomic class, and remembers his parents as having few parenting skills. At the age of 14, the client had his first pedophilic experience. During the next years, he actively solicited fellatio and anal intercourse with younger boys. He stated that he pursued doctoral training in clinical psychology at an accredited university to "help understand this pathology."

While in graduate training on full academic scholarship, he married a woman who was pregnant with another man's child. He and his wife had sexual intercourse infrequently, and he stated that during coitus he fantasized about earlier pedophilic experiences to maintain his erection. The marriage was dissolved after one year, and the client retained custody of the baby.

Following the divorce, he withdrew from doctoral training one year short of completion and was employed as a prison psychologist and probation officer. During the next ten years he began to drink heavily, his work record deteriorated, and he began to act on his pedophilic impulses with individuals from his caseload. He became seriously depressed, quit his job, and was hospitalized on two occasions for attempted suicide.

Adapted from Josiassen, Fantuzzo, & Rosen, 1980, p. 56.

☐ *Homosexual versus Heterosexual Adults*
We stress that homosexual pedophilia and adult homosexuality are not synonymous. Groth and Birnbaum (1978) found that individuals attracted to prepubescent boys are typically uninterested in adult males. In fact, many of these fixated pedophile offenders expressed considerable aversion to adult homosexual activity. In other words, the adult heterosexual male rather than the adult homosexual male is potentially more threatening to prepubescent children, regardless of the sex of the child. Even in the case of involvement with postpubescent boys, Rossman (1976) has found that the majority of these adult males are otherwise heterosexually oriented.

Clinical experience with men who are attracted to young boys but express an aversion to adult homosexuality suggests that this is sometimes a way of denying homosexual interests. Their fear of homosexuality is overwhelming, and somehow they are able to rationalize their interaction with young boys as not being "real homosexuality." Also, they are less threatened by young boys than they are by adult males. As a result, several investigators have advocated that therapy for these pedophiles should be aimed at increasing their acceptance of adult homosexuality (Serber & Keith, 1974).

☐ *The Fixated and Regressed Pedophile versus the Rapist* Groth (1979) argues that although adult sexuality is threatening for a variety of reasons to both the pedophile and the rapist, they both react to this threat differently. The pedophile retreats and avoids the threat by turning to a safer substitute. A child is less likely to reject the man, and even if rejection occurs, it is less of a psychological blow to the adult. Also, a child does not know what to expect, and thus the pedophile does not suffer as much from performance anxiety. The rapist, on the other hand, denies his fears by counterattacking, by striking out in hostility at the adult female. Another difference is that the regressed pedophile often has an emotional regard for his victim unlike the rapist. The pedophile will frequently be interested in maintaining an ongoing mentor or parent-child relationship with his victim. Most rapists, on the other hand, treat the victim as an object of contempt, someone to be conquered. They are not interested in establishing affectional bonds with their victims. Rapists also tend to be much younger than regressed pedophiles. (For a full discussion of rape, see Chapter 12.)

Use of Force

Most adults who try to engage young children in sexual activity do not typically use excessive overt physical force as a means to induce children to participate. As we mentioned earlier, deception and enticement, as well as the occasional threat of force or other "milder" forms of coercion and intimidation, are the most common means used. Violent assaults are estimated to occur in no more than 5 to 10 percent of such incidents (Geiser, 1979). This does not mean, however, that children are never victims of rape. Statistics reported by different rape centers in the United States indicate that anywhere from 6 percent to 40 percent of all rape cases involve children under age 16 (Geiser, 1979; James & Meyerding, 1977). Nevertheless, rape of children is not typically a part of pedophilia. Widespread media publicity of sexual murders of children also can convey a misleading picture that brutal assaults may be the norm rather than the rare exception in cases of child molestation (Groth, 1979; Mohr et al., 1964).

Perhaps the issue of how the adult gets the child to agree to sexual activity is, in a sense, beside the point. Regardless of whether or not seduction or coercion is involved, and regardless of whether or not the child participates because of curiosity, a need for affection, bribery, general obedience to adults, or plain fear of being abused because of resisting, the point must be stressed that *prepubescent children are, by definition, unable to provide informed consent to sexual activity with adults.* They clearly do not know all that is involved. They may not be aware of society's disapproval, and they do not generally know of the potentially harmful consequences. A very important factor is that they are completely powerless and dependent on adults (Finkelhor, 1979b).

Location and Type of Sexual Activity

Most sexual acts with children do not take place as is sometimes supposed in dark alleys, parks, public bathrooms, schoolyards, movie theaters, or automobiles. Instead, the home of the offender ranks first, and the home of the child, second (Gebhard et al., 1965; Mohr et al., 1964). These statistics are especially true in the case of females. Peters (1976) found that 55 percent of female children, as compared with 21 percent of male children, were sexually victimized in their own homes.

Information about the specific nature of sexual acts with prepubescent children is usually obtained from reports by convicted offenders and, less frequently, from children themselves. Neither of these sources are completely reliable. The adult offender has obvious incentives to conceal and distort events in the hope of reducing social condemnation and legal penalties. On the other hand, the testimony of children, and especially those under age 6, may simply be inaccurate. Despite these methodological shortcomings, the consistency of findings across several studies inspires some confidence in the reports. Excluding exhibitionism, clearly the great majority of sexual acts with prepubescent female children involve fondling and caressing of both nongenital and genital areas. Intravaginal pene-

tration occurs infrequently, probably in less than 20 percent of the incidents (Peters, 1976; Mohr et al., 1964; Swanson, 1968); an increase in coitus can be expected, however, if the child is older and if some force is involved (Gebhard et al., 1965). Oral-genital sex also occurs in only a small minority of cases, around 10 percent (Gagnon, 1965; Gebhard et al., 1965; Kinsey et al., 1953; Mohr et al., 1964).

On the basis of such data, researchers have argued that at least in the case of heterosexual pedophilia, the nature of the sexual act corresponds more to the age of the child rather than to the age of the offender (Mohr et al., 1964). Although sexual gratification is desired, genital touching, fondling, and rubbing rather than intercourse are what typically take place—somewhat more in line with the type of sexual exploration one might expect to see between children of the same age.

Effects on the Victim

One almost automatically assumes that sexual molestation of a child will have harmful, long-term psychological consequences. Such an assumption, however, is apparently not always true. For example, researchers who did a follow-up study on sixteen victims of child molestation reported that the great majority adjusted satisfactorily as adults (Bender & Blau, 1937). On the other hand, retrospective studies of female drug abusers, prostitutes, and delinquents all report unusually high incidences of childhood sexual abuse, and Peters (1956) found frequent short-term eating, sleeping, and academic problems, as well as fears of safety and nightmares.

Recent research has taken a more sophisticated direction, namely to determine what factors contribute to or protect against harmful effects. A major drawback of these studies, however, is that incest cases have not been distinguished from pedophilia cases. Unfortunately, no one has ever examined this question for a sample exclusively restricted to pedophilia victims. There seems to be general agreement among investigators that if the adult is known to the child, the effects are likely to be more traumatic and longer lasting than if the adult is a stranger. The relationship factor is strikingly illustrated in a study performed by Tsai and Wagner (1978). They advertised the availability of therapy groups for women molested as children. Over 80 percent of those who responded to the advertisement had been molested by relatives, strongly suggesting that these were the women who felt most harmed by the experience and in need of therapeutic assistance. We will explore this tendency further in our discussion of the effects of incest later in this chapter.

As might be expected, the amount of subsequent psychological trauma is also very much influenced by the degree of physical force used. Finkelhor (1979a) conducted a large-scale survey of college students' sexual experiences as children. Students who responded to being asked how negative they felt the experience was indicated that

a major factor was whether or not force was used or whether the offender threatened to use it. Not being able to resist and to say no may be much more destructive than the act itself.

A third factor that has been demonstrated to be important is the age of the child at the time of the experience. Contrary to what might be expected, the long-term effects are apparently more harmful for older children than for younger children (Finkelhor, 1979a; Tsai, Feldman-Summers, & Edgar, 1979). Presumably, older children are more aware at the time of what is going on and realize that society condemns such behavior; they might also be more likely to blame themselves for what happened. Lingering feelings of guilt and shame are often associated with anxiety and depression in later life.

Although multiple incidents are known to be more harmful than single incidents, the research literature is unclear as to whether or not the type of sexual activity influences long-term effects. For example, Finkelhor (1979a) did not find more negative ratings if sexual intercourse took place as compared with genital fondling. In another study, however, this factor separated those who sought therapy as adults and those who did not (Tsai et al., 1979).

A number of professionals have suggested that parental overreaction may also be harmful, especially if any hint of blame for the event is attached to the child. Peters (1976) recommends that parents be sensitive to the child's feelings of confusion and be careful that their concern and anger over the event is not inappropriately displaced onto the child. Actually, there is no empirical evidence suggesting that being molested is only traumatic if parents make it so. For example, Finkelhor (1979a) found that men and women who had been sexually victimized as children and who had told their parents did not have more negative long-term consequences than those who had not informed their parents.

Legal Controls and Recidivism

If excessive physical force is involved, or if vaginal or anal penetration has taken place, the adult would typically be charged with rape. In the more typical incident involving genital fondling, the individual generally is charged with lewd and lascivious conduct or sometimes indecent assault of a minor.

Many individuals in our society believe that child molesters should be imprisoned for a long time, not only because people are terribly offended and frightened by the nature of the crime but also because they feel that child molesters are incorrigible. The rationale for longer imprisonment for pedophiles, however, cannot be justified on the basis of higher recidivism rates. The probability of a convicted pedophile being reconvicted for another sexual offense actually is surprisingly low (Frisbie, 1965; Mohr et al., 1964), especially for heterosexual pedophiles who are convicted for the first time. In one study the reconviction rate for first offenders was only between 5 and 8 percent (Mohr et al., 1964). (For those with more

than one conviction prior to referral, the recidivism rate increased to 22 percent, and for offenders with both previous sexual and nonsexual convictions, the recidivism rate went up to 33 percent). The rate of reconviction for homosexual pedophiles, however, is approximately twice that of heterosexual pedophiles (Fitch, 1962; Frisbie, 1965). Recidivism rates in prison populations might be expected to be somewhat higher because proportionally more repeat offenders are likely to be in prison than are outpatients and individuals on probation. But even these samples show relatively low recidivism rates. Frisbie (1965) did follow-up studies on over 1,500 child molesters released from Atascadero State Hospital between 1954 and 1960. For heterosexual pedophiles, the cumulative recidivism rate over a five-year period was 18.2 percent.

In summary, then, we can conclude that heterosexual pedophiles convicted for the first time have a very low rate of subsequent reconvictions, especially the regressed type of offender, who has sometime in the past been able to establish mature sexual relations with adult women. There is no question, however, that a record of multiple convictions for sexual offenses against children, especially when combined with a record of other criminal offenses, is a very poor sign, with recidivism rates in some instances close to 50 percent. Also, some may take issue with the validity of any of these recidivism figures. Perhaps they do not reflect the likelihood of repeating an offense as much as they do the likelihood of being caught. Being arrested and convicted once may make 90 percent of the first offenders *more careful* in the future.

Therapy for the Pedophile Offender

Before mentioning some of the specifics of different therapeutic approaches, the context in which therapy occurs must be considered. At the present time, pedophiles generally do not enter therapy programs voluntarily; instead, the judicial system makes the decision. An individual who is sentenced to prison realizes that satisfactory participation in therapy is frequently a determining factor when the decision regarding parole is made. Also, if instead of being imprisoned an individual is lucky enough to be put on probation, therapy is almost always a required condition of probation.

Some pedophiles, of course, defy the system and refuse therapy. Of these individuals, a few see no harm in engaging in sexual activity with children; others deny having any sexual attraction to children, and claim that what took place happened by accident because they were drunk. They insist that it will never happen again and that they thus do not need therapy. Some individuals will agree to therapy but then try to deceive the therapist into believing that the treatment has been successful. It is important to keep these problems in mind as we turn now to an examination of some of the therapeutic procedures.

☐ *Group Therapy* Group therapy has long been considered the treatment of choice for offenders in institutional settings (Costello and Yalom, 1972). One advantage of the group therapy approach is that peer pressure presumably will help break down defensiveness, evasiveness, and denial of responsibility so often encountered in convicted pedophiles. Most groups include about eight to twelve patients who usually meet several times a week. Some groups are homogeneous (contain only pedophiles), while others are made up of different kinds of sex offenders. The prevailing opinion is in favor of homogeneous groups whenever possible. Group cohesiveness, interpersonal relations within the group, and expressions of current feelings are the therapeutic ingredients assumed to exert the most powerful effects once the therapy process is underway. The hope, of course, is that such themes as poor impulse control, fear of masculine competition, fear of rejection, the inability to be assertive, and other relevant interpersonal problems will be provoked and addressed in the context of the relationships developed within the group. Unfortunately, group therapy for pedophile samples has never been evaluated adequately (Quinsey, 1977). No study has ever compared the long-term outcome of pedophiles who underwent group therapy with those who did not.

☐ *Behavior Therapy* Behavior therapy has only recently been employed to treat pedophiles. As is the case with exhibitionists (see Chapter 10), individual pedophiles may have a host of different problems (e.g., marital discord, fear of rejection, sexual dysfunctions, anger and poor impulse control in response to interpersonal stress, and alcohol abuse) in addition to their primary problem of sexual activity with prepubescent children. Treatment, then, can become quite involved because different behavior therapy procedures have to be used with each set of problems. Unfortunately, reviewing all of the possible combinations of behavioral interventions that can be used to treat these problems is beyond the scope of this chapter.

Let us, however, focus solely on the sexual problem, which for pedophiles is usually a two-sided problem. A man's sexual attraction and activity with young children is one aspect of the problem, and the other is low sexual arousal and/or sexual problems with adults. Should the behavior therapist try to use procedures to suppress a person's sexual attraction to children and hope that sexual behavior with adults will automatically develop or improve on its own? Or, should the behavior therapist concentrate on the patient's social and sexual difficulties with adults in the hope that once these problems are resolved, sexual interest in children will automatically diminish? A third possibility is for the therapist to work with both problems simultaneously. Currently, there is no definitive answer to this question, as case reports provide support for each strategy (Callahan & Leitenberg, 1973; Quinsey, 1977; VanDevanter & Laws, 1978).

☐ *Surgical and Hormonal Treatment* Various medical procedures have also been employed in the treatment of pedophilia. These range from extreme methods, such as **castration,** which is the surgical removal of the testes from the scrotum, and brain surgery (Diekman & Hassler, 1977) to the less

radical procedure of hormonal treatment. The purpose of each of these interventions is the same: to eliminate or reduce the offender's overall sex drive. Arguments against castration and brain surgery are numerous. Obviously both procedures are irreversible and can have serious negative medical side effects. In the case of castration, arousal is not immediately eliminated; therefore, castration will not necessarily affect the pedophile's attraction for children. Also, since sexual intercourse is not a common act in cases of pedophilia, erection capacity generally is irrelevant. Moreover, irreversible procedures that eliminate the possibility of normal sexual activity may ultimately lead to further psychological problems and antisocial acts (Gaensbauer, 1973; Heim and Hursch, 1979). These procedures also may be considered unethical because true voluntary consent is impossible; the sexual offender may feel he has no choice if the alternative to surgery is prolonged imprisonment.

Hormonal and other pharmacological interventions have been used for the past twenty years in an attempt to alter deviant sexual behavior through "chemical castration" (Bancroft et al., 1974). Unfortunately, none of these methods is problem-free. Estrogens were first tried, but negative side effects such as nausea, vomiting, and breast enlargement, and more rarely, breast cancer and thrombosis, virtually ruled out their use. More recently, the use of antiandrogenic drugs has been explored. These hormonal procedures work on the premise that sexual drive and behavior can be altered by lowering the levels of plasma testosterone produced by the testes. Although several studies have reported reductions in sexual fantasy and activity as a result of such hormonal treatment, their ultimate value remains questionable (Bancroft et al., 1974; Money, 1972; Spodak, Falck, & Rappaport, 1978). One reason is that antiandrogens cannot selectively affect only one form of sexual behavior. Moreover, if the drugs indiscriminately suppress sexual arousal and response to adult as well as child stimuli, men may eventually refuse to continue medication. A further problem is that the use of antiandrogens can, in time, lead to testicular atrophy; it is not yet known whether this condition is reversible (Rooth, 1976).

Prevention of Pedophilia

Who would disagree with the premise that it would be far better to promote healthy sexuality than to treat the offender after the fact? The problem is that no one can identify with certainty who is likely to molest children before it happens. Thus prevention programs, if they were to be mounted, would have to be addressed to the entire population rather than to more limited at-risk groups. We do know that most regressed and fixated pedophiles suffer from fears of sexual rejection and failure in interactions with adults. It follows then, that if fear can be reduced in the general population of males, incidents of pedophilia could also be reduced. If they were made widely available, marital and sexual enhancement groups might also have a preventative effect.

Social attitudes about "appropriate" masculine behavior also seem central to the prevention of pedophilia. If the adult pedophile were not so obsessed with proving himself, with not making a "fool of himself" in encounters with other adults, he would not need to seek what he thinks of as "safer" encounters with children. Also, in our society males are supposed to be powerful and able to dominate others and, in a sense, own their wives and children. These attitudes need to be changed.

The topic of prevention touches upon a controversial topic, namely the relationship between exposure to pornography and sexual abuse of children. Does pornography induce adults to make sexual attacks on children? Research cannot completely answer this sort of question for any given individual. However, statistical evidence of a correlational nature provides no hint that availability of pornographic material causes men to abuse children sexually. In fact, contrary to expectation, the data point in just the opposite direction. Goldstein (1973) found that when compared with a control group of men drawn from the community who were matched for age and educational level to the pedophile sample, the sex offenders surveyed reported having less exposure than the control group to such pornographic material. Apparently, sex offenders have less experience with pornography than do nonoffenders—or at least they admit to less. It has even been suggested that accessibility of pornographic materials might actually serve to reduce the likelihood of sexual offenses such as pedophilia (Kutchinsky, 1973; Wilson, 1978).

INCEST

Incest can be defined as any sexual activity between family members, including not only intercourse but also such sexual activities as genital fondling, mutual masturbation, and oral-genital sex. The two major types of incestuous relationships are father-daughter and brother-sister, with the latter being more common. Although sexual activity between other relatives does take place, these episodes are relatively less frequent and often less disturbing, as in the case of relations between first cousins. Because the consequences are probably more serious, we will focus almost exclusively on father-daughter incestuous relationships.

Cross-Cultural and Historical Perspective: The Incest Taboo

Incest is a central theme in some of the earliest creation myths and folktales of many cultures. For example, in Greek mythology, Zeus was said to have raped his mother Rhea and married his sister Hera. He later also slept with his daughter Persephone. Zeus himself was the child of Cronus and Rhea, who were siblings. The Old Testament also contains stories of several incestuous liaisons, the most famous involving Lot and his two daughters. The point is that incest has been a central theme in literature and mythology, and that the outcome of incest, even in mythology, is often negative and sometimes disastrous. It should be noted that as with the story of Adam and Eve, many of these myths are creation myths that emphasize not incest itself, but the "sharing of all human blood," or the relatedness among all humans.

Incest is strictly prohibited in most current and past cultures. Murdock (1949) found evidence of an incest taboo in 250 different primitive societies. **Taboo** implies that the behavior in question is absolutely forbidden. There was not a single exception, and more than half extended incest prohibitions beyond the nuclear family unit. In many preindustrial cultures, incest was considered the most terrible of all crimes and one that might bring down the wrath of supernatural powers. For example, inhabitants of the Northern Gilbert Islands believed that the sun would fall from the sky if cases of incest were not severely punished. Some primitive cultures believed that incest caused droughts, earthquakes, and other natural disasters.

The question of why there is such a universal and strong taboo against incest has preoccupied scholars in fields such as anthropology, sociology, and psychology for at least the past century. The major suggested hypotheses include the genetic theory, the role and family cohesiveness theory, the exogamy theory, and the indifference and natural aversion theory.

□ *Genetic Theory* Because blood relatives share a common gene pool and because recessive genes often have more damaging rather than beneficial effects, offspring of incestuous matings are more likely to die or suffer from birth defects than offspring resulting from nonincestuous relations. Seemanova (1971), in a very elegant piece of research carried out in Czechoslovakia, compared 161 offspring of incest (88 father-daughter pairs, 72 brother-sister pairs, and one mother-son pair) with 95 control children from the *same* mothers but unrelated fathers. Among the incestuous group, 21 children died, and there were 40 additional cases of congenital malformation. Among the control children, only 5 died, and there were no obvious congenital defects.

Even though members of primitive societies were unaware of the genetic implications or the long-term evolutionary disadvantages of incest, they probably were aware of the increased number of deaths and birth defects among infants born to parents who were related (Meiselman, 1978). Furthermore, if human inbreeding is harmful to offspring, natural selection pressures over time would simply favor the survival of groups that prohibited incest. The evolutionary model would also argue against incest on the grounds that genetic variability is reduced. A moderate degree of variability increases an individual's (and ultimately a species') chances for adapting to a changing environment.

☐ *Role and Family Cohesiveness Theory* Bans against sexual relations between members of a nuclear family protect against jealousy and competition that would otherwise be terribly disruptive.

Thus, one function of incest taboos is to promote more harmony and cooperation within the family unit. In this way, the roles of parent and child do not become distorted or confused.

☐ *Exogamy Theory* This theory is essentially a socioeconomic hypothesis based on the premise that survival depends on cooperation between families and tribes. The incest taboo guarantees marriages between different families and groups, thus forging stronger networks of economic, political, and military alliances.

☐ *Indifference and Natural Aversion Theory* According to this hypothesis, children and parents, along with brothers and sisters, never develop any sexual attraction to each other because they live in such close proximity during a critical period of development. However, if a natural aversion between family members does exist, why would there be a need for such strict prohibitions against incest in the first place? This hypothesis is also in direct contradiction to all known cases of actual incest, and to incestuous desires kept in check because of social pressure. On the other hand, a recent report on sexual behavior and marriage of children reared in kibbutz environments in Israel suggests that there may be some validity to this hypothesis. In a traditional kibbutz, children from different families are brought up and educated together from infancy to adulthood; they do not sleep in the homes of their parents except on some weekends. In his studies, Shepher (1971) did not find one incident of intragroup marriage or of heterosexual activity between any members of the same peer group. Shepher suggests that constant exposure and intimate contact with peers from the first days of life automatically results in sexual disinterest and avoidance.

Despite these almost universal prohibitions against incest, however, it does, of course, occur. In fact, in history it has, in a few rare exceptions, been condoned, especially in the case of brother-sister liaisons among privileged groups such as royalty. For example, during some periods in Egypt, a brother could only assume his throne through marrying his sister. Instances of accepted father-daughter incest, although even rarer, have also been noted in historic times (Masters, 1963; Santiago, 1973). Commoners, however, have always been bound by incest rules.

Incidence of Incest

How common is incest today? As with pedophilia, reported or detected cases represent only a fraction of the actual cases. Meiselman (1978) found that less than 30 percent of her sample of incest victims ever reported the event to law enforcement or social agencies. However, these statistics come as no surprise. Incest is socially unacceptable, and many victims are ashamed to admit to it. Also, they are often fearful of the effect such a disclosure will have on the family. Thus, the numbers that follow are approximations.

Tutankhamun

Akhnaton

Akhnaton, king of Egypt married his daughter Ankhesenpaton. When he died, his son Tutankhamun became king. He in turn also married Ankhesenpaton (new name Ankhesenamun), his sister and stepmother. When Tutankhamun died, his mother married Ay, her grandfather. Complicated, isn't it!

425

In three survey studies, the percentages of females who reported any form of incestuous activity with *any* relative were 6, 9, and 28 percent, respectively (Kinsey et al., 1953; Hunt, 1974; and Finkelhor, 1979a). Kinsey did not report statistics for males, but the Hunt and Finkelhor surveys revealed surprisingly high figures, 14 and 23 percent, respectively. The Finkelhor and Hunt surveys indicate that most incestuous experiences for both girls and boys are either with marginally related relatives, such as cousins, or with siblings of the same generation. According to these statistics, father-son incest is very rare, and even father-daughter incest is relatively infrequent, occurring in only approximately 0.5 to 2 percent of the general female population. While this figure is low, it is possible that parent-child incest is the most difficult to admit, and as Finkelhor (1979a) points out, although a figure such as 1 percent may seem very small, "it means that approximately three-quarters of a million women 18 and over in the general population have had such an experience, and that another 16,000 cases are added each year from among the group of girls aged 5 to 17" (p. 88).

In parent-child incest, there is a vast difference in the frequency of reported cases in which the mother is involved as compared with those in which the father is involved. This discrepancy may be due to a double standard in reporting, or it may reflect a real and striking difference in actual occurrence. The latter seems more likely. Herman and Hirshman (1977) argue that in a patriarchal society such as ours, incest is much more likely to occur between fathers and daughters than between mothers and sons.

In reporting the incidence of father-daughter incest, one should distinguish between stepfathers and biological fathers. Three studies show an almost equal involvement of stepfathers and biological fathers (Frisbie, 1959; Kroth, 1979; and Maisch, 1975). However, since the percentage of households containing stepfathers and stepdaughters is so much lower than the percentage containing biological fathers and biological daughters, these figures indicate a higher rate of incest between nonblood relatives than between blood relatives. Finkelhor (1979a) estimates that a stepfather is five times more likely than a biological father to sexually approach a child. Whether or not the lower rate for biological fathers is a function of a greater caring for the child, a greater taboo, or a greater familiarity with the child during development is unknown.

Some Differences Between Father-Daughter Incest and Pedophilia

☐ *Age of the Child*   The age of the female child at the time of the sexual offense is particularly interesting because it points out an important distinction between pedophilia and incest: The female incest victim tends to be older than the pedophilia victim. The mean ages at which children first become victims of incest, according to a series of different studies gathered

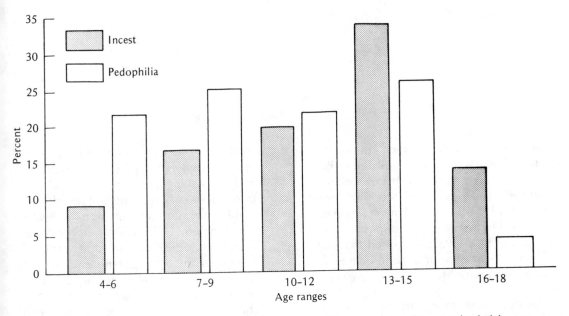

Percent

Age ranges

Figure 11-1. Age of incest and pedophilia victims in a California study. (Adapted from Kroth, 1979.)

by Maisch (1975), is between 12 and 15, whereas in the pedophilia studies, the usual age is around 8 to 10. Apparently, in cases of incest, unlike pedophilia, the sexual maturity of the child is arousing for the relative. As the daughter develops, sexual activity increases, whereas in the case of heterosexual pedophilia, sexual interest declines as the child matures. Nevertheless, not all female incest victims are postpubescent. The range varies considerably. Children as young as 2 years of age can be victims of incest (see Herman & Hirshman, 1977; Lukianowicz, 1972; Molnar & Cameron, 1975).

☐ *Type and Duration of Sexual Activity* Another distinction that can be drawn between father-daughter incest and heterosexual pedophilia is that intercourse is more likely to occur in incestuous relationships. Studies of incest offenders revealed that coitus occurred in approximately half of the cases (Gebhard et al., 1965; Maisch, 1975). The type of sexual activity seems to vary directly with the age of the daughter. Gebhard and his colleagues found that when the child was under 12 years of age,

intercourse took place in only 9 percent of the cases, whereas when the child was between 12 and 16, intercourse took place in 72 percent of the cases.

An incestuous relationship also tends to last much longer than a pedophilic relationship. Kroth (1979) made a direct comparison of the duration of relationships between the two groups seen at the California Sexual Abuse Treatment Program and found that close to 25 percent of the incest cases had lasted for over three years, whereas not a single case of pedophilia had continued for so long. These findings are supported by other studies as well.

Is It the Daughter's Fault?

Fathers, like unrelated adult males, primarily rely on seduction, deception, their position of authority, and various forms of emotional blackmail rather than excessive

427

physical force to persuade their children to engage in sexual activities with them. Because extreme physical force is seldom employed, the question of the child's responsibility in initiating and maintaining incestuous relations is sometimes raised. Bender and Blau (1937) suggested that the "seductive" behavior of daughters may instigate such relationships:

> This study seems to indicate that these children do not deserve completely the cloak of innocence with which they have been adorned by moralists, social reformers, and legislators. The history of the relationship in our cases usually suggested at least some cooperation of the child in the activity and in some cases the child assumed an active role in initiating the relationship. (p. 514)

This statement is both controversial and misleading. Of course children have sexual feelings and can act in a sexual manner. In the course of growing up and observing adult models, a child will undoubtedly experiment with "seductive," appealing, and pseudosexual mannerisms. But the suggestion that children purposefully "seduce" their fathers is very objectionable:

> When we say an adult woman is *seductive,* the term implies that her behavior is willful and that she can foresee the consequences of it. If an 18-year-old daughter is observed to sit in her father's lap while dressed in a bikini, we may be justified in assigning the seductive label to her. But what if an 8-year-old daughter does exactly the same thing? Is it really accurate to describe her behavior as seductive, or are we . . . ascribing adult motives to a child's behavior in doing so? (Meiselman, 1978, p. 165)

In all likelihood, the child (and even the 18 year old) may simply be seeking affection without having any explicit sexual intentions. Blame should not be placed on the child who is exhibiting normal, healthy, developmental behaviors; rather, blame should be placed on the adult father who interprets and *acts* upon his daughter's behavior according to his own needs. Indeed, many fathers may be sexually attracted to their daughters, but they are sufficiently capable of containing this impulse and have the responsibility to do so.

In actuality, most evidence indicates that few daughters actively encourage their fathers to engage in sex with them (Gligor, 1966; Maisch, 1975; Meiselman, 1978). Also, recent data suggest that incest victims do not have unusually strong needs for affection, are not more sexually precocious, and are not in any other way different from girls their age who are not victimized by their fathers (Maisch, 1975; Meiselman, 1978).

The long duration of the incestuous affair and the fact that the daughter seldom reports what her father is doing has also been interpreted by some as evidence that the child is not a helpless victim but is instead often an active and willing participant who is gratified by the relationship with her father (Friedlander, 1947; Sloane & Karpinski, 1942; Weiner, 1962). Such a conclusion ignores the child's fears, which can, indeed, inhibit disclosure. She is often terrified of a negative response from her mother, of her father's threats, of the family breaking up, of being sent away, or of not being believed. Statements obtained from incest victims illustrate the dilemma the

WHY DAUGHTERS KEEP SILENT

My father told me if I ever let anyone know what he had been doing with me, that the police would send him to jail. Living in my neighborhood, all of us kids knew what kind of place jail was, and I knew that if Daddy went there we would have to go on welfare and Mom just wouldn't have been able to keep things together. (Butler, 1979, p. 28)

Nobody would have believed me. Daddy was a big executive. He was a member of the Community Chest, the Rotary Club and always had his picture in the newspaper. I never felt anyone would believe a kid saying anything like that. (Butler, 1979, p. 28)

Little kids still need the idea of a family, even if they never really had one. If you tell, you'll be left with no family at all. (Butler, 1979, p. 34)

When I was younger, I used to feel sorry for him because my mother was so cold. Not only to him but to us kids, too. She spent all her time alone in the back of the house watching television or sewing funny little costumes for dolls she collected from different parts of the world. I never felt I could tell her about what Daddy was doing to me because I knew she hated him for being with other women. I was afraid if I told, she might hate me too. (Butler, 1979, p. 41)

She wouldn't have believed me. Not only that, I think in my mind I knew she would do nothing about it and that would hurt me even more. Do you follow what I mean? If I told her and she did nothing, it would kill me. (Armstrong, 1979, p. 35)

I felt it was more like a secret that I really had to guard because I knew that it would just kill my mother to find out. I wasn't glad to have the secret I had. I was very much concerned about protecting her. (Armstrong, 1979, p. 67)

But he used to say to me. "You have to let me do what I want to you because I made you and you belong to me." And I got very trapped. Because somehow even when I was thirteen, I had a feeling that if I told my mother she would see me as the other woman. Or maybe nobody would believe me and maybe he would beat up on me. And I couldn't risk either of those things, so I didn't say anything to her — and there wasn't anybody else I could talk to. (Armstrong, 1979, p. 245)

child faces in a most poignant manner (see Box 11-2). Disclosure is hardly an easy alternative.

Cormier, Kennedy, and Sanjowicz (1962), as well as other investigators, have found that the daughter often only rebels in her late teens when her father becomes more and more possessive and attempts to restrict her new relationships with boys her own age. The daughter is then old enough to seek freedom either by running away or by revealing the incestuous relationship to other people (e.g., friends, counselors, and less often, mothers).

Family Dynamics:
Is It the Mother's Fault?

Professionals who have studied incest agree that the role of either the father, daughter, or mother cannot be considered apart from the others. Incest typically reflects a complex interaction in the family system (Lustig et al., 1966). Recurrent family features include the following:

1. Marital and sexual conflict between husband and wife.
2. Combination of a dominant and tyrannical husband/father and a passive, helpless, and rejecting wife/mother.
3. Estrangement between mother and daughter, usually preceding onset of incest.
4. Role reversal between mother and daughter, or absence of mother from household.
5. Often a history of both father and mother having been physically or psychologically deserted by their own parents. As a result, fear of family dissolution and abandonment is considered both a cause of incest and of the subsequent "conspiracy of silence" that serves to maintain the incestuous relationship.
6. Unwillingness or inability of the father to seek a partner outside of the nuclear family either because he fears rejection or because he wishes to maintain a public facade of being a stable and competent "patriarch."
7. History of sexual abuse in one or both parents.

According to this model of family dynamics, the mother indirectly plays both a causal and a collusive role. The father complains that his wife is rejecting and that sexual relations are unpleasant and/or nonexistent. The child may take on the role of "wife," including housekeeping and childcare responsibilities, because the mother is unable or unwilling to fulfull this function. The child also feels betrayed because the mother fails to protect her and deprives her of needed affection.

Lest too much blame be attached to the mother, however, it should be understood that the husband's behavior (e.g., alcoholism) may be responsible for the wife's rejection. Also, the often-reported depression on the part of the mother obviously does not occur in a vacuum. Clinical studies of these families that note high rates of chronic depression and physical illness in mothers or that characterize mothers as being cold and rejecting to both husbands and daughters are difficult to interpret because they do not compare such findings with the incidence of these behaviors in families in which incest does not occur.

Also contrary to myth, most mothers don't know what is going on, to a large extent, because the daughter and the father try to keep her from finding out and, to a lesser extent, because she simply doesn't want to know.

The tendency to blame the mother for provoking incest and/or for not putting a stop to it is probably as wrong as blaming the daughter. Once an incestuous relationship has been established, fears of abandonment on the part of all concerned become very strong. These fears are to some extent realistic. Authorities frequently do

TABLE 11-1   CLASSIFICATION OF INCESTUOUS FATHERS

Endogamic
- Heavily dependent on family for emotional and sexual needs.
- Unwilling or unable to satisfy sexual needs outside of the family.

    Personality disorder
- Shy and ineffectual in social relations.
- Intellectual defense structure and tendency to paranoid thinking.
- Intensely involved with daughter, overcontrolling of her.
- Sometimes preoccupied with sex.
- Often involved with prepubescent daughter.

    Subcultural variety
- Lives in isolated, rural area.
- Moralistic, periodically atoning for sins.
- Social milieu semitolerant of incest.
- Usually involved with postpubertal daughter.

Psychopathic
- Criminal history.
- Sexually promiscuous, unrestrained by marital bonds.
- Little emotional attachment to daughter.

Psychotic
- Severe ego disorganization of organic or functional origin.

Drunken
- Incest occurs only when father is extremely intoxicated.

Pedophilic
- Generally attracted to young children as sex partners.

Mental Defective
- Low intelligence a factor in reduced ego controls.

Situational
- Incest occurring only during high-stress period for father.

From Meiselman, 1978, p. 111.

remove children from the home, and if the husband is also jailed, there is, in fact, no longer a family. In view of these possible consequences, no wonder incest often is sustained for long periods of time.

Who Are the Fathers and Why Do They Do It?

Several investigators have tried to develop a classification system to describe different types of fathers involved in incest, but Meiselman (1978) provides the most comprehensive description (see Table 11-1). A classification system such as Meiselman's does not mean that each category is necessarily mutually exclusive of the other. Most incestuous fathers fall into what has been called the "endogamic personality" category. It is also known as the "symbiotic" or "dependent personality" category. Very few are interested in extrafamilial pedophilia, either in fantasy or in reality (Quinsey, Chaplin, & Carrigan, 1979).

Perhaps the most salient characteristic of the incestuous father is his attitude about his child and spouse: He feels they belong to him — that they are his property. He is the epitome of the authoritarian head of the family, or at least that is the role he wants to assume, because often enough, in fact, he is a weak and insecure man. As Armstrong puts it "he must see his children as there to meet his needs — rather than the other way around" (1979, p. 268).

Alcoholism often has been suggested to be an important factor in father-daughter incest, and, indeed, incestuous fathers often have a history of alcohol abuse (Lukianowicz, 1972; Browning & Boatman, 1977). However, although alcohol often is used as a rationalization by the incest offender, available statistics indicate that serious intoxication at the time of incest occurs in less than 10 percent of the cases (Gebhard et al., 1965; Maisch, 1975).

Other factors describing the father have been examined, including intelligence, education level, socioeconomic status, and occupational history. Biased sampling procedures, however, make findings in these areas largely meaningless (Hunt, 1974; Weiner, 1964). The safest conclusion to draw at this point is that no great differences exist between the demographic characteristics of incestuous parents and those of nonincestuous parents — or for that matter between incest victims and nonincest victims (Meiselman, 1978). Similarly, such variables as rural versus urban environments and overcrowded versus uncrowded home conditions fail to reveal any significant difference between incest samples and nonincest controls (Cavallin, 1966; Maisch, 1975; Weinberg, 1955; Weiner, 1964).

The father's age at the onset of incest episodes has consistently been shown to be close to 40. This is often a time of family transition, with family members reevaluating their current roles and/or assuming new ones, as well as being a time when many daughters are in their early teens and becoming more sexually attractive.

Effects of Incest

It is generally assumed that father-daughter incest invariably has a strong negative impact upon the psychological development and subsequent adult behavior of the incest victim. Although some studies indicate that incest may have minimal long-term negative effects (Rasmussen, 1934), adverse effects have been reported far more frequently (Herman & Hirshman, 1977; Kaufman, Peck, & Tagiuri, 1954; Lukianowicz, 1972; Molnar & Cameron, 1975). Also, studies of special populations, such as prostitutes and female residents of drug-abuse centers, reveal that high percentages — between 40 and 75 percent — had been victims of incest (Geiser, 1979). Finally, in an important study that compared incest victims who were in therapy with a randomly selected group of patients who did not have incest histories, the incest group averaged more problems overall than the control group (Meiselman, 1978). The most striking difference between the two groups, however, was in the area of sexual function: 62

percent of the incest patients reported sexual problems, as compared with only 20 percent of the control patients.

Not surprisingly, therefore, sexual problems resulting from incest—including **promiscuity** in adolescence and sexual dysfunction in adulthood—have been the most frequent focus of research. One hypothesis about promiscuity motivated by incest is that it grows from a distorted self-image. The girl blames herself for what has taken place and may believe she is either "bad" or has unusual seductive powers. Sex with a large number of partners then becomes a self-fulfilling prophecy. Another possibility, also related to prostitution, is that promiscuity is a way of detaching one's personal self from the sexual interaction—treating one's body as an object for someone else's enjoyment rather than taking the risk of becoming personally attached and involved. This attitude is a defensive, protective style—one that the girl may have learned in the past as a way of coping with her father's behavior. Finally, as a result of having had incestuous experiences with her father, the girl may also develop the belief that the only way to have relationships with men is on a sexual basis. "That was the only way I could be accepted—if I put out. That was the only tool I had. Nothing else" (Armstrong, 1979, p. 106).

As Meiselman points out, sexual problems in adulthood represent the largest area of concern. Tsai, Feldman-Summers, and Edgar (1979) found that incest victims who sought therapy as adults were significantly less responsive, less orgasmic, and less satisfied with sexual activity than were control women who had also been sexually molested as children but who did not feel in need of therapeutic assistance. The incest victims who had sought therapy also reported more pressure to participate, more guilt, and stronger negative emotional responses at the time than did the control group. The investigators suggest that these negative qualities are generalized to all sexual activity with men, thus accounting for their greater sexual difficulties in adulthood.

Up to this point, we have only discussed the short- and long-term effects of incest on the daughter. The research literature has seriously neglected similar studies of either the mother or the father. Some personal accounts have been recorded regarding the immediate reaction of fathers (and to a lesser extent, mothers) following disclosure of incest, but no long-term, follow-up studies have ever been performed. Cormier, Kennedy, and Sanjowicz (1962) reported strong feelings of guilt, anxiety, and depression in fathers after incestuous activities were revealed. The father also often tried to reduce his guilt feelings by either denying his offense or by providing a variety of rationalizations for its occurrence. Here is a sampling of the many excuses offered: "I was drunk"; "My wife was gone, or frigid, or rejecting"; or "It was a form of sex education." Sometimes guilt feelings are also relieved by a revived or newly formed interest in religion (Gebhard et al., 1965).

Clinical impressions of the mother following revelation of incest indicate a myriad of possible reactions, including denial, anger at the husband, anger at the daughter, fear of legal consequences, fear of social scandal, self-blame, depression, and anxiety. We do not know which reaction or combination of reactions is most frequent or what the long-term course is for the mother. Obviously, the family is usually shattered, and one would expect, at the least, the normal anxiety and depression associated with more routine family break-ups.

Family Intervention and Treatment

The customary procedure in the United States following disclosure of incest is to remove the father, and sometimes the child as well, from the home. Because family breakup is such a drastic and traumatic event, many professionals question whether or not this sort of practice does more harm than good. Regretfully, no method has yet been developed that can be used to decide whether any one approach is better than any other in dealing with incest victims, offenders, or other family members. No controlled studies have ever been conducted to determine if the removal of fathers and/or children from their homes is more beneficial than using some alternative means of intervention. This decision will probably always have to be a clinical one, determined on a case-by-case basis in accordance with what appears to be in the best interest of the child. Similarly, we do not know if recidivism of offenders is any different if they are or are not imprisoned (Kroth, 1979). Most existing evidence suggests that once incest has come to the at-

tention of people outside of the family, recidivism rates tend to be exceptionally low, ranging anywhere from 0.6 to 2 percent (Kroth, 1979).

McGuire and Wagner (1978) described a treatment program for women who were molested as children and who currently do not experience arousal or enjoy sexual contact. Four special features considered particularly relevant to incest victims were incorporated into a 3- to 5-week "sensate focus" program (see Chapter 8). These features were (1) getting the woman to identify and experience her repressed anger; (2) making the woman aware of the association she is making between the molesting adult and her current partner; (3) getting her to be aware of guilt feelings associated with the experience of sexual pleasure; and (4) teaching her how to have exclusive control over initiating sensual or sexual contact.

Prevention of Parent-Child Incest

Most of the comments directed toward prevention of pedophilia apply equally well to parent-child incest. In addition, we would emphasize that father-daughter incest is in large part a reflection of long-standing sexist cultural values, which now, hopefully, are in the process of changing. Women do not belong to men, they should not be forced to submit to male domination, and they have no greater responsibility to please men than men have to please women. Once these new attitudes truly take hold, we may see a reduction in sexual abuse of female children by their fathers. Until this time, however, improved parent education both in general parenting skills and in human sexuality might be useful. Also, if schools had counselors with which a child could feel comfortable discussing *any* sexual concerns, the incidence of sexual exploitation in the home might decline. One major problem with this approach is that it violates the notion of family privacy. Many people object to society's inquiring into what goes on in the family. They also object to sex education of any kind outside the home (see Chapter 14).

SUMMARY

1. Only in the last five years or so have people begun to realize that sexual abuse of children is a widespread and serious problem. Literally millions of women (and a somewhat lesser number of men) in the United States have been sexually abused by adults during their childhood. Each year there are over 100,000 newly reported cases of sexual child abuse.

2. **Pedophilia** is the sexual abuse of a child by an adult who is not a legal or blood relative. Pedophilia usually refers to the sexual contact between an adult and a prepubescent child; genital fondling, rather than intercourse, is the most typical act.

3. There are many more female than male victims of pedophilia, and females tend to be younger than males at the time of the incident.

4. The pedophile is almost always male. Prison studies have determined that he is typically between 30 and 40 years of age; however nonprison samples suggest that another large group of these sex offenders may often be in their late teens.

5. Pedophiles are usually not complete strangers to their victims. Friends and acquaintances of the family are the people who most frequently commit the acts.

6. Adult homosexuals are *not* more likely than adult heterosexuals to sexually molest children. Not only are girls more often than boys the targets of sexual abuse by adult males, but even the pedophile who molests boys usually has a heterosexual orientation to other adults.

7. The child molester seldom uses excessive physical force, and there is no evidence of a progression toward greater violence over time. Instead, deception and enticement, and sometimes mild forms of intimidation, are used to induce the child to participate.

8. There is no single reason yet discovered as to why some adult males sexually abuse children. One characteristic, however, does seem to come up frequently. Adult sexuality is often problematic to these men, and they seek out young children because they feel safer with them. They are less likely to be rejected than if they approached another adult, and in any case, rejection from a child is less threatening to their self-esteem than is rejection from another adult.

9. If the child knows the adult offender, the effects are apt to be more traumatic and longer lasting for the child than if the adult is a stranger. Other factors influence the extent to which the child is psychologically harmed, including the amount of physical force used and the age of the child at the time of the incident, with older children being more at risk.

10. As part of their sentence, convicted pedophiles are often obligated to participate in therapy. A number of procedures have been used to treat pedophilia, including group therapy, behavior therapy, and surgical or hormonal treatment. Group therapy has long been considered the treatment of choice for offenders in institutional settings, although there is no solid evidence of its effectiveness. Surgical procedures, namely brain surgery and **castration,** are extreme methods of dealing with pedophilia that are not used in the United States. Although various hormonal treatments have been used over the past twenty years, they all have led to various side effects or problems.

11. **Incest** is any sexual activity between family members. There are two major types of incestuous relationships: Father-daughter incest, although the most psychologically damaging, is *not* the most frequent kind of incest; sex between same-generation brothers and sisters is far more common. Also, the likelihood of incest between stepfathers and stepdaughters is much greater than between biological fathers and daughters.

12. Several differences between pedophilia and incest can be highlighted. In father-daughter involvements the child tends to be older, the incestuous relationship tends to last longer, and intercourse is more likely to occur eventually especially as the relationship continues and the daughter matures.

13. Although family dynamics are often complex in cases of father-daughter incest, the tendency to assign fault to the child and/or to the mother for what the father does is wrong. The child, by definition, cannot give voluntary consent and does not, in fact, encourage the father. She gives in to his demands because she does not understand what he is doing or because she feels she has no other choice. The mother does not always or even usually know what is going on. What all members of the family

share in common is a terror of abandonment and family disintegration — a likely outcome once an incestuous relationship is reported.

14. There is no clearcut explanation for why fathers engage their children in sexual activity. However, one characteristic of the incestuous father does stand out: These men often believe that their families are their private property, to do with as they see fit. Inside the home they act out the dominant and patriarchal role, more often than not to compensate for their insecurity and weakness outside of the home.

15. Two of the most frequently suffered problems of incest seem to be sexual in nature: **promiscuity** in adolescence and sexual dysfunction in adulthood.

16. Although no easy solution awaits the problems of child molestation and incest, a number of preventative measures have been suggested, including increased sex education, decreased sexism, free marital- and sexual-enhancement counseling, and free training in parenting skills.

SUGGESTED READINGS

Armstrong, L. *Kiss Daddy Goodnight.* New York: Pocket Books, 1979. An illuminating personal account of incest.

Cook, M., & Howells, K. (Eds.) *Adult Sexual Interest in Children.* New York: Academic Press, 1981. A collection of chapters on current research written by different experts.

Finkelhor, D., *Sexually Victimized Children.* New York: The Free Press, 1979. Results of a large-scale survey study addressing this topic.

Mrazek, P. B., & Kempe, C. H. (Eds.) *Sexually Abused Children and their Families.* New York: Pergamon Press, 1981. A relatively comprehensive review of recent research on incest written by different investigators.

CHAPTER TWELVE

RAPE
Sexual Victimization of Adults

"I keep wondering maybe if I had done something different when I first saw him, it
wouldn't have happened—neither he nor I would be in trouble. Maybe it was my fault.
See that's where I get when I think about it. My father always said whatever a man did
to a woman she provoked it."—A woman's comments after a man assaulted her in the
hallway outside of her apartment, forced his way inside, and severely bruised, beat and
raped her as she fought against him to the point of taking his knife and using it on him.
Burgess & Holmstrom, 1974a

Rape is the fastest-rising violent crime among the FBI's major crime categories, which include assault, robbery, and murder (FBI Uniform Crime Report, 1973, 1979). In 1973, there was a 62 percent increase in reported rapes over the previous five years, and by 1979 there was an additional 13.7 percent increase. Estimates are that in the United States a rape is committed on an average of every seven minutes (FBI, 1979). The figures are both alarming and complex to interpret: While more women are reporting rapes than in past decades, many rapes still go unreported. In the great majority of cases, women are the victims of this violent crime and men the offenders.

Rape is usually defined as a sexually aggressive crime; its legal definition is typically restricted to forced sexual intercourse. A number of other related legal terms are often used. **Statutory rape** is sexual intercourse with a female below the age of consent; the term is used even if both parties agree to the act and no force is involved. **Indecent assault, sexual abuse,** or **attempted rape** are terms used if penetration does not occur due to the aggressor's impotence or because the assault is interrupted. Touching a woman's breasts or genitals without her consent is also classified as sexual assault or abuse.

The current conceptualization of rape stresses its overriding aggressive features (e.g., Brownmiller, 1975; Burgess & Holmstrom, 1974, 1979a, b; Groth & Birnbaum, 1979). Brownmiller (1975) has taken a particularly outspoken stand on this issue:

From prehistoric times to the present, I believe, rape has played a critical function. It is nothing more or less than a conscious process of intimidation by which *all men* keep *all women* in a state of fear. (p. 15)

Other researchers have offered a classification of *patterns of rape* in which the nonsexual psychological motivation is stressed, although the sexual component is not ignored (Groth & Birnbaum, 1979; Groth, Burgess, & Holmstrom, 1977; Holmstrom & Burgess, 1980). Table 12–1 lists these classifications, which are based on interviews with both rapists and victims. What we learn from this classification system is that there are many types of rape assaults and rapists, and that at least some patterns of activities and moods seem to fall together. The consequences suffered by the victim are usually degrading and sometimes life threatening.

Some authors have expressed concern that the sexual aspect of rape has been minimized (Groth et al., 1977). One study examined the types of sexual behavior that occur during rapes, based on in-depth interviews with 115 victims admitted to a hospital emergency ward (Holmstrom & Burgess, 1980). The sample included women between 5 and 73 years of age, though most were in their late teens or early twenties. The most frequently reported sexual activities were those the rapists performed on the victim; other activities were those demanded of the victim (see Table 12–2).

Ultimately, the two components of rape

TABLE 12-1 MAJOR PATTERNS OF RAPE			
	ANGER RAPE	*POWER RAPE*	*SADISTIC RAPE*
1. Assault plans and length	Impulsive and of relatively short duration.	Premeditated and preceded by persistent rape fantasies. Assault may continue for an extended time period during which victim is held captive.	Calculated, preplanned, and of extended duration. Victim is kidnapped, assaulted, and disposed of.
2. Offense pattern	Episodic.	Repetitive and may show increased aggression over time.	Ritualistic, usually involving torture, bondage, and bizarre acts, which are interspersed with nonsadistic assault.
3. Offender's mood	Anger and depression.	Anxiety.	One of intense excitement.
4. Offender's language	Abusive.	Unstructured and manipulative—offender gives orders, asks personal questions, tells the victim to say things, asks about the victim's responses.	Commanding and degrading.
5. Dynamics, motivating factors	Retribution for perceived wrongs or injustices against the offender; he feels "put down."	Compensation for offender's depreciated feelings of inadequacy and insecurity.	Symbolic destruction and elimination.
6. Aggression	More physical force than necessary is used to overpower the victim; she is battered.	Offender uses whatever force or threat is necessary to control victim.	Physical force (anger and power) is eroticized.
7. Victim's injury	Physical trauma to all areas of her body.	May be physically unharmed; bodily injury usually not intentional.	Physical trauma to sexual areas of victim's body; in extreme cases victim is mutilated and murdered.

(Adapted from Groth & Birnbaum, *Men Who Rape: The Psychology of the Offender*, N.Y.: Plenum Press, 1979.)

—aggression *and* sex—cannot be separated. To call rape purely sexual or purely aggressive will prevent us from understanding, even minimally, the nature of the act and its immediate and long-term impact on the victim.

TABLE 12–2   FORCED SEXUAL-EXCRETORY-SADISTIC ACTS[a] DURING
REPORTED RAPES AND NUMBER OF SEXUAL ASSAILANTS[b] IN 112[c] CASES

FORCED SEXUAL-EXCRETORY-SADISTIC ACT	NUMBER OF SEXUAL ASSAILANTS					
	SINGLE ASSAILANT (N = 78)		MULTIPLE ASSAILANTS (N = 34)		TOTAL (N = 112)	
Vaginal intercourse	73	94%	34	100%	107	96%
Fellatio	13	17%	12	35%	25	22%
Breasts pulled, bitten, touched, or burned	7	9%	6	18%	13	12%
Cunnilingus	6	8%	0	0%	6	5%
Manual touching of victim's genitals	5	6%	1	3%	6	5%
Anal intercourse	3	4%	3	9%	6	5%
Urinating on victim or on victim's under-wear	2	3%	2	6%	4	4%
Victim manually touching rapist's penis	1	1%	2	6%	3	3%
Rapist kissing victim	2	3%	0	0%	2	2%
Victim kissing rapist	2	3%	0	0%	2	2%
Object inserted into victim's vagina (e.g., knife handle)	1	1%	0	0%	1	1%
Victim licking rapist's body and anus	1	1%	0	0%	1	1%
Victim inserting finger in rapist	1	1%	0	0%	1	1%
Victim required to "have an orgasm"	1	1%	0	0%	1	1%
Victim required to dance nude	1	1%	0	0%	1	1%
Victim required to perform sexual acts with another female for rapist to watch	0	0%	1	3%	1	1%
Rapist masturbating	0	0%	2	6%	2	2%
Semen placed on victim's body	0	0%	2	6%	2	2%

[a] Table based on answers to open-ended questions about what happened sexually plus specific follow-up questions on oral and anal sex. Beating, knifing, etc.—although they would be considered sadistic acts—are not included in this table.

[b] Number of assailants who committed a sexual act. Total number in incident may be greater (e.g., two for robbery, one for rape). In nine cases (six cases of single sexual assailant and three cases of multiple sexual assailants) there was an additional male(s) who observed the rape but did not perform a sexual act.

[c] Excluded are one female victim who was immediately strangled to unconsciousness (and thus unable to report sexual details or number of assailants) and two male victims.

(*Source:* Holmstrom & Burgess, 1980.)

CONDITIONS FOR RAPE

About half of all victims are raped by strangers. The 1969 report of the National Commission on the Causes and Prevention of Violence (NCCPV) found that 53 percent of the rapes committed were between total strangers, 30 percent involved people who were slightly acquainted, 7 percent involved family members, 3 percent occurred between people who were not currently related but had been in the past, and the relationship between the remaining 7 percent was undetermined. Nevertheless, these figures probably underestimate the number of nonstranger rapes. The data are based on records of "founded" rapes—rapes believed *by the authorities* to have occurred. When the victim knows her assailant, the rape is frequently designated as unfounded (Brown, 1974).

Even more striking, a study of 930 women revealed that 14 percent of the women who had been married were raped by their husbands or exhusbands (Russell, 1982). In comparing wife rape to other categories of rape, Russell (1982) remarks, "wife rape is clearly one of the most prevalent types of rape and by some measures it is the most prevalent form" (p. 68). For further discussion of this topic, see Box 12-1.

In the Amir (1971) study, more than half of the rape incidents were planned, and more rapes occurred on the weekends between 8:00 P.M. and 2:00 A.M. than at any other time. The most common location for the rape was the victim's home (56 percent), while the remaining assaults took place in an automobile, an indoor location, or an open space.

MEN WHO RAPE

To present a single profile describing the typical rapist would be dangerously misleading. The major problem is that few rapes are reported—the FBI estimates that between one in five and one in twenty cases are brought to the attention of the authorities. Of reported rapes, approximately half of the men are apprehended, and approximately thirteen out of one hundred of these men are convicted (Horos, 1974). The most likely rapists to be studied are those who

are apprehended and/or convicted—a very select sample indeed.

Statistics from the group of arrested and convicted rapists have been surprising in certain respects. According to the *FBI Uniform Crime Reports* (1973), the majority of arrested rapists were 16 to 25 years old, with 61 percent under 25 years of age. The majority were of the lower socioeconomic classes; 47 percent were black, while 51 percent were white. Of convicted rapists, approximately 40 percent were married, and approximately 50 percent had previously been convicted for rape or other offenses.

A somewhat older study, important for its in-depth analysis of rape, was based on Philadelphia Police Department files of 1,292 offenders involved in 646 cases during 1958 and 1960 (Amir, 1971). This study was not limited to convicted or arrested rapists, but included all reported rapes that the police believed actually occurred.

The profile of the Philadelphia rapist differed slightly from the FBI's convicted rapist profile. Amir reported the following findings:

1. Men between 15 and 19 years of age were most likely to commit rape (the median age was 23).
2. Most were not married, and 90 percent came from lower occupational ranks or were unemployed.
3. Most of the rapists were black (Philadelphia had a larger black ghetto than many cities), and the vast majority of rapes occurred between a black male and a black female.
4. A large number of rape cases, 43 percent, involved more than one rapist and a single victim. Of the total number of rapists, 55 percent raped in gangs and 15 percent raped in pairs.
5. In 85 percent of the cases, physical force or a weapon was used.

Similar statistics have been reported in other studies that have examined arrested or convicted rapists. What we can conclude from all of these studies is that there is at least one subgroup of rapists—those who

are reported and those more likely to be arrested. They are young, likely to have been previously arrested for nonsexual offenses, likely to use force, from lower socioeconomic groups, and far more prone to rape women of their own race. Furthermore, a surprisingly high percentage of this group is likely to be in the company of at least one co-rapist when assaulting a single victim. Blacks are usually overrepresented in rape statistics—a finding that must be tempered by the fact that more blacks than whites occupy the lower socioeconomic strata, where violence is a far more predominant means of getting what one wants:

> . . . there is no getting around the fact that most of those who engage in antisocial criminal violence (murder, assault, rape and robbery) come from the lower socioeconomic classes; and that because of their historic oppression the majority of black people are contained within the lower socioeconomic classes and contribute to crimes of violence in numbers disproportionate to their population *but not disproportionate* to their position on the economic ladder. (Brownmiller, 1975, p. 181)

In addition, reports have shown that a large number of rapists may be alcoholics, that testosterone levels are higher among the most violent offenders, and that rapists often score highly on measures of hostility (Rada, Laws, & Kellner, 1976).

To learn more about rapists, researchers have developed various laboratory methods. One such method involves exposing rapists to video or audiotapes that vary in content (e.g., mutually enjoyable intercourse, aggressive assaults, or rape descriptions) and recording their responses by measuring erections and evaluating self-reports about arousal (Abel et al., 1977). The work of Abel and his colleagues is important for its use of objective measures to evaluate components of rape and the distinctions that can be made among the different types of rapists. However, it is restricted to individuals who are relatively cooperative, and it is not a foolproof technique if a rapist chooses to conceal his arousal. Furthermore, it is not intended to reveal the causal factors that distinguish different categories of rapists.

Another group of researchers used such a technique to compare the sexual responses of ten incarcerated rapists and ten graduate students (Barbaree, Marshall, & Lanthier, 1979). The graduate students' sexual histories involved only mutually consenting sex with postpubescent females. Erections were measured while subjects viewed three types of audiotapes: mutually consenting sex, rape, and nonsexual assault. In this study, the rapists were similarly aroused when watching both the consenting and nonconsenting sexual stimuli, while graduate students showed less arousal to the forced-sex stimulus. These researchers propose that force and violence inhibit sexual response in nonrapists, while, for rapists, the presence of force or violence neither inhibits nor enhances sexual arousal. This study, as well as the study conducted by Abel and his colleagues (1977), suggest that for some rapists, the major problem may have to do with their tolerance for coercive sex rather than their intolerance for consenting sex.

THE VICTIMS OF RAPE

As can be gathered from the description of the rapist, the victims of rape are most likely to be females from lower socioeconomic classes, from urban settings, and between the ages of 15 and 25. However, women and children of all ages and all economic strata are vulnerable to sexual violence and rape.

Behavior during Rape

The implication is often made that the victim encouraged the rapist's behavior, especially when she knows the assailant. Yet what may be perceived as an open invitation to one male is not to another. One study found that rape was the least likely crime to be caused by the victim, especially in comparison with homicide and other violent crimes (NCCPV, 1969).

A more important question concerns the reactions of victims during rape incidents. Amir (1971) found that of completed rapes (rapes with at least one inch of vaginal penetration), 55 percent of the victims were submissive, 27 percent screamed or tried to escape, and 18 percent fought back. Of the

A rape or an attempted rape makes many women fear for their lives—even for months after the assault.

cases in which the men carried a weapon, most of the women were submissive. The least submissive women were the most likely to be physically harmed. However, being submissive does not guarantee a less traumatic rape. The infamous "Boston Strangler" sexually mutilated and killed eleven women between 1962 and 1964. According to his confession, several of his victims did not resist, but he killed them anyway.

Short-term and Long-term Effects on the Victim

The effects of rape vary, depending on the victim's individual situation and the type of rape she experiences. One of the few studies to examine the immediate as well as the long-term impact of rape was done by Burgess and Holmstrom (1974a). They interviewed ninety-two adult victims within thirty minutes of their entrance to the Boston City Hospital, with a follow-up of 85

percent of the women. Most of the women were under 29 years of age, although the age range was 17 to 73.

These researchers identified the **rape trauma syndrome,** which refers to the behavioral, physical, and psychological acute stress reaction to rape or attempted rape. Burgess and Holmstrom divide the rape trauma syndrome into two phases: disorganization, or the acute phase, and reorganization, or the long-term process. During the *acute phase,* which immediately follows the rape, the victims they interviewed showed one of two emotional styles, either expressed or controlled. Women experiencing the expressed style showed anger, fear, and anxiety by crying, sobbing, being restless, or smiling, while controlled women appeared subdued and calm. During the first few weeks, all the women had various physical problems, including pain and soreness from the attack, skeletal muscle tension, gastrointestinal reactions, and genitourinary disturbance. The major emotional reaction was fear of physical violence and death—many victims were more traumatized about the fact that they could have been killed during the assault than they were about being raped. Additional common reactions were humiliation, embarrassment, anger, desire for revenge, and self-blame.

The *long-term* reactions, reported by all but nine victims, included a variety of lifestyle and emotional changes. Forty-four women changed their residences, and many changed their phone numbers, out of fear that their assailants would return or find them. Many women turned to friends or family for support. Nightmares were frequent, as were a variety of phobic reactions. The most common phobias involved situations that reminded the women of the rape: fears of the indoors, outdoors, being alone, crowds, being followed, and sex. Burgess and Holmstrom (1974a) note that the patterns seen in rape victims' reactions are akin to poststress reactions seen in individuals who have experienced other life-threatening crises. As one raped woman stated, "This wasn't an act of sex I was going through—I felt I was being murdered" (Brownmiller, 1975, p. 358).

Long-term reactions to rape have been reported in other studies. For example, 179 women, 95 percent of whom were Caucasian and none of whom had reported their rapes to any public agency, were asked retrospectively about changes in their lives since they had been raped (Norris & Feldman-Summers, 1981). A means of 3.4 years had passed since the assaults. Table 12-3 describes the changes women reported. Similarly, raped women interviewed one year after being assaulted reported significantly greater depression and less vigor and pleasure from daily activities than did matched controls (Ellis, Atkeson, & Calhoun, 1981). The victims of assault by strangers, who were also more violent, seemed to be the most severely affected; they showed greater depression, fear, and lower frequency of dating one year after the rape than did victims of nonstrangers (Ellis et al., 1981). These reactions are common. In the words of a woman interviewed:

> I was black and he was black. The encounter caused a tremendous change in my overall attitude toward men and especially toward black men. For three months, I was afraid to go out with a black man. I was afraid to be out on the streets alone at night. Until I met the man in the alley I thought I was really in control of my life. It taught me I wasn't. (Brownmiller, 1975, p. 362)

Rape seems to have a pervasive effect on sexual behavior (e.g., Burgess & Holmstrom, 1974a; Feldman-Summers, Gordon, & Meagher, 1979; Kilpatrick, Veronen, & Resick, 1979). In a study of sixty-three women who were sexually active prior to being raped, 19 percent reported no change in sexual frequency, 10 percent reported an increase in frequency, and 71 percent were less sexually active for the first six months (Kilpatrick et al., 1979). Of those who reported a decrease in frequency, 38 percent gave up sex completely. At a later follow-up, the majority of women still found sex to be aversive, and some reported arousal problems, pain, and discomfort.

According to other researchers, the effect of rape on sexual functioning may be

TABLE 12-3 PERCENTAGE OF VICTIMS REPORTING PSYCHOSOMATIC SYMPTOMS, CHANGES IN RECLUSIVENESS, AND CHANGE IN SEXUAL FREQUENCY AND SATISFACTION

IMPACT	% BEFORE RAPE	% AFTER RAPE[a]
Symptom		
Difficulty sleeping	13.5	83.7
Appetite/eating problems	19.2	63.8
Cystitis	7.4	18.0
Menstrual irregularity	20.2	28.6
Headaches	23.2	40.0
Rapid mood changes	29.4	63.6
Depression	30.4	79.6
Excitability	24.1	42.9
Frequent crying	13.2	59.1
Loss of temper	18.6	42.7
Reclusiveness (never going out alone)		
Movies/concerts	65.7	91.9
Restaurants	41.1	75.4
Bars	71.3	89.5
Public places such as parks	28.6	64.7
Sexual Behavior	No decrease after rape	Decrease after rape
Frequency of oral sex	74.5	25.5
Frequency of intercourse	71.1	29.9
Frequency of orgasms	79.3	21.7
Overall sexual satisfaction	67.3	32.7

[a]Where items asked the participant to indicate whether an event or state of affairs occurred or existed immediately after or one to six months after the rape, an affirmative response to either query was treated as after the rape.

(*Source:* Norris & Feldman-Summers, 1981)

restricted to specific kinds of sexual interactions. Even though one group of women reported sexual problems after being raped, their satisfaction with masturbation or *non-sexual* affectionate behavior with men did not change (Feldman-Summers et al., 1979).

And yet a few women have reported an increase in the frequency of sexual activity. Why? The 10 percent in the Kilpatrick et al. (1979) study did so for a number of reasons: Some wished to counter the negative experience of the rape, others became indiscriminately sexual in an attempt to "take con-

trol," and a few went into prostitution (see Chapter 13 for more information about the influence of rape on prostitution). The women who became prostitutes seemed to experience extreme difficulty in developing any type of emotional bond with men, and they treated sex mechanically in order to cope with the aftereffects of rape.

Not all women are extremely traumatized by rape. As illustrated in Figure 12-1, based on 930 interviews with women in San Francisco (Russell, 1982), how upset a woman feels depends somewhat on her re-

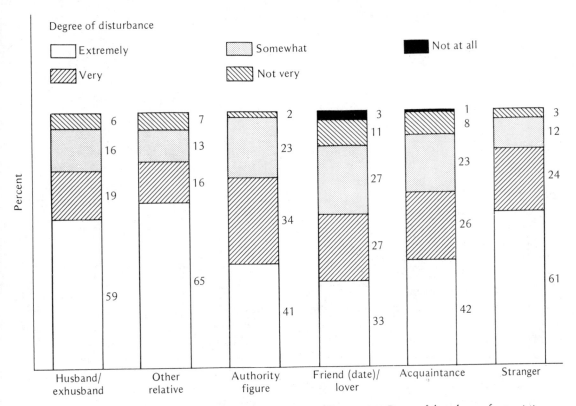

Degree of disturbance

☐ Extremely   ▦ Somewhat   ■ Not at all

▨ Very   ▧ Not very

Percent

Husband/ exhusband	Other relative	Authority figure	Friend (date)/ lover	Acquaintance	Stranger
6	7	2	3	1	3
16	13	23	11	8	12
19	16	34	27	23	24
59	65	41	27	26	61
			33	42	

Figure 12-1. Degree of disturbance of rape victim according to relationship with assailant. Source: Adapted from Russell, 1982, p. 192.

lationship to the rapist. Also, some women are better able to cope with the experience by minimizing whatever negative effects might have occurred:

I was raped in an elevator after he took my wallet. He had a knife. He told me to lie down and I lay down. It was over in two seconds, just like that. The sex was nothing at all. What do you want me to do? Be angry and hate all men? I just want to forget it. It's New York City life and I'm not going to let it destroy me. (Brownmiller, 1975, p. 361)

SOCIAL ATTITUDES TOWARD RAPE

Although the majority of people today are likely to view rape as an unforgivable crime, there is still, as there has been historically, a strong tendency to blame the female victim or at least to hold her somewhat responsible for the rape. This view is slowly changing, but many people, including professionals, physicians, police, jury members, and judges, traditionally have leaned toward assuming that the female victim is lying or is a co-conspirator until proven otherwise (Brownmiller, 1975; Burgess & Holmstrom, 1974b). What is the basis for this attitude?

449

Historical Factors: Real and Mythical

Historically, rape often has been a punishable crime having more to do with the violation of property rights among men than with the violation of a woman's right to protect her own body (Brownmiller, 1975). In early Babylonia and Assyria, the punishment of rape depended on the chastity of the victim. If the woman was a virgin, a married rapist would be killed, but an unmarried rapist would be forced to marry the victim and pay her father three times the going price of a bride. Also, the victim's father had the right to rape the wife or sisters of the rapist (Epstein, 1948).

Later, according to the code of Hammurabi (c. 2000 B.C.), the rape of a Babylonian virgin resulted in the slaying of the rapist and no blame assigned to the victim. The married woman, however, had the most to lose if she were raped under Hammurabi's laws. She shared the blame of adultery with her offender, and both were bound and thrown into the river. Lucky victims were permitted to have their husbands save them, and lucky rapists might be set free by the king.

Similarly, ancient Hebrews considered married women who were raped to be as blameworthy as their attackers, and both faced being stoned to death. The punishment of a raped virgin varied according to where the offense occurred, her betrothal status, whether she clearly resisted, and the rapist's social class. For example, if the rape took place in the city, both parties were stoned because the victim should have screamed for assistance. Rape in a secluded spot outside of earshot, however, meant that the rapist had to pay his victim's bride price and marry her. Many centuries later (A.D. 900 to 1400), the Talmudic interpretation permitted a young virgin (between 3 and 12½ years of age) to keep the fine money, which in earlier times had been given to her father; she also was excused from marrying the rapist. This step was an important one in shifting the subject of the crime, as the victim was paid for bodily injury and the rapist was fined for having sex with a virgin (Epstein, 1948).

In medieval Europe, however, women were considered sexual property. *Jus primae noctis,* the right of the first (wedding) night, or of the *droit de seigneur,* the right of the manor lord to take the virginity of any bride of his vassals or serfs existed and was enforced, unless the bridegroom could pay a certain price. In England, before the tenth century, the rapist of a well-born virgin with property and a powerful lord faced death and dismemberment; the fate of unpropertied virgins is not clear. During the tenth century, the rapist lost his life, and his horse and dog lost their scrotums and tails. Meanwhile, the rapist's property was given to the raped virgin. However, his victim was allowed to save his life by marrying him. By the thirteenth century, punishment was based on an eye-for-an-eye (*lex talonis*) guideline: castration for his lust and the loss of both eyes for his enjoyment of the sight of the virgin (Coulton, 1938).

By the end of the thirteenth century, all classes of women in England came under formal law with respect to rape. Originally, whether the victim was virginal or married, a rapist was sentenced to two years in jail plus a fine, but some years later the sentence was changed to death. Eventually, the death penalty was replaced with life imprisonment, which is the current law in England. This new legal arrangement was a tremendous gain for married women, with two exceptions: (1) if it was shown that a married woman did not resist enough, the wife lost her dowry, and (2) rape between husband and wife was not legally possible because the marriage vows included automatic consent to intercourse.

In Asia, too, there were different considerations for virgins, married women, and social class. One interesting example comes from thirteenth-century China. At this time a table of merits and demerits was circulated. The Chinese could work out the relative value of their sins and good deeds as a quick check on the running total of their moral stature. Sex with a nun was the worst offense. Sex with widows and virgins was treated as equally abominable, reflecting the Chinese reverence for age. Sex with married women was less sinful. Interestingly, the rape of a prostitute incurred demerits, an unlikely state of affairs in the Western world of the same time period.

Current Attitudes Toward Rape

Little if any research directly investigates general social attitudes toward rape, rapists, and victims. The major social spheres in which one can indirectly evaluate such attitudes are (1) the laws and legal proce-

Hotlines have increased the likelihood of women reporting violence when it occurs.

dures involved in a rape charge, (2) evidence of the social treatment of rapists as compared with the treatment of victims, and (3) evidence from the various media as to the degree of violent and coercive sexual themes. We will consider here several aspects of points 2 and 3; legal issues are discussed in a later section.

Although casual observations in the popular press have noted the consistent and allegedly increasing portrayal of violent sex in various popular and specialized media (*Time*, 1977), there is little documentation of the degree to which rape or even sexual coercion is a recurrent theme. One study examined the frequency and proportion of violent sexual themes in two popular men's magazines, *Penthouse* and *Playboy* (Mala-

Box 12-1

RAPE IN THE MARITAL RELATIONSHIP:
UNSEEN AND UNNAMED CRIMES

In a number of states, a man cannot be charged with raping his wife—marriage in these states essentially provides a license to rape. As of July 1980, only New Jersey, Nebraska, and Oregon had completely outlawed spousal rape. Legislation on this issue is slow to change.

Behavior is, too. In a San Francisco study, which defined rape as forced coital, anal, oral or digital penetration, and which was based on a random sample, a surprisingly large percentage of women—about one in seven—reported at least one instance of rape by a husband or exhusband (Russell, 1982). In spite of the legality of marital rape, this number should be rather shocking. What also disturbs many people is why some wives stay with their husbands even though their husbands rape them. Russell's (1982) analysis of the San Francisco women, in which 22 percent of the raped wives stayed with their husbands, offers several factors that are important.

- *Low level of trauma* was experienced in reaction to the rape. Some of these women may minimize the effect in order to remain in the marriage, and others may simply not view it as important because they never really enjoyed sex, had low expectations for sexual happiness, or because their husbands were very apologetic afterward.
- *Some husbands stop.* Thirty-one percent of the rapes were one-time events.
- *Few resources.* Women who have never worked outside the home, who have young children, and who are solely dependent on their husband's

muth & Spinner, 1980). Examining the issues between 1973 and 1977, two raters, one male and one female, identified sexually violent pictures and cartoons, including illustrations of rape, sadomasochism, and exploitive/coercive sexual relations. Pictorial material was found to be increasing over the five-year period, although only 5 percent of the 1977 pictorial material included violent themes. The same pattern was not found for cartoons, with *Penthouse* containing a greater percentage (13 percent) of sexually violent cartoons than *Playboy* (6 percent).

Although this study examined only a limited number of sources of violent materials, Malamuth and Spinner suggest that sexual arousal to mass media violent stimuli such as these are correlated with callous attitudes toward rape, as well as with a self-reported possibility of committing rape (Malamuth, Haber, & Feshbach, 1980; Malamuth, Reisin, & Spinner, 1979). These materials may also reduce perceptions about the degree of suffering experienced by the victim (Malamuth et al., 1980). The major issue is that *Playboy* and *Penthouse* magazines presumably reach a much larger audience incomes are more likely to stay. *All* of the women who were sole providers of their household at the time of the first spouse-rape divorced their husbands.

- *Self-blame.* As in many rapes, wives often blame themselves for the rape because, for example, they are not good enough sexual partners, or they do not enjoy certain types of sexual interactions. Wives who blame themselves are also more likely to excuse their husband's behavior.
- *Fear of sexual assault outside the home.* Women who stay are far more worried than women who leave about being sexually assaulted or violated outside of the home. These women may feel that they have the best of a bad lot.
- *Alienation or isolation.* To leave, wives need some family or funds for support. With continued violence in the home, these women often become isolated from their friends and family. Similarly, Russell found that nonwhite wives (e.g., Asians, Blacks, Hispanics) tended to stay with their husbands. Although the numbers are too small to make any conclusive statements, one factor in these cultural differences may be the lack of support networks. Indeed, many of these wives had no place to go.

Which of these factors best explains why some wives stay? According to Russell's statistical results, these are the top eight factors influencing wives to stay: (1) self-blame; (2) coming from a third-world background; (3) less violence during or before the rape; (4) the husband was the main provider at the time of the first rape; (5) the wife perceives a high likelihood of being raped outside of the marriage; (6) less upset and effect reported around the rape; (7) the wife is foreign-born; (8) the wife is more "traditional," less likely to have worked outside the home as an adult, has children, and her husband is the main provider.

than specialized pornographic materials do, and the effect of the former media on people's values and behavior is of concern.

The violent theme in pornography has been denounced not only because it suggests that women need excessive and even brutal male domination (Griffin, 1981; Smith, 1976), but also because it reinforces the belief that women—especially "cool or resistant" women—will enjoy the forceful, overpowering male assailants (Brownmiller, 1975). Behind these themes lurk two common social myths about rape (Brownmiller, 1975): All women secretly want to be raped, and women are "asking for it." There is no evidence to support either of these ideas, and yet they have remained a part of the collective beliefs about women.

In the *Psychology of Women*, Deutsch (1944) claimed that coitus, loss of virginity, painful penetration, and rape were all closely associated with women's feelings about their own sexuality. Some studies have shown that rape or being dominated during sex is a fairly frequent fantasy theme of women (e.g., Hariton, 1972). However, fantasies must be distinguished from the actual act. Fantasy is not reality, and most people have a variety of fantasies that they would never act out. A woman's fantasy is very much within her own control; a rape is not. Also, rape fantasies do not usually include pain, mutilation, and the fear of being killed. In fact, rape or domination fantasies include a variety of subthemes — being irresistibly desirable, enjoying passionate sex with wild abandon, and not being responsible (or making men responsible) for one's own sexual responses and desires. Since women in our culture are traditionally expected to resist men's advances and to inhibit and control their own sexuality, the imagined domineering male is a predictable solution that permits women to be sexual (LoPiccolo & Heiman, 1978).

The differential attitudes toward rape victims and rapists are expressed in a variety of other subtle ways. One of the more startling examples was a rape of a Boston nurse by three physicians in September 1980, all of whom worked in the same hospital. The three men were found guilty. The nurse was given a leave of absence from the hospital, which she requested, but it was granted without pay. The physicians were forced to accept leaves, but at full salary, and only after they had been indicted and the hospital had been criticized by many for not acting sooner. The nurse eventually took a lower-paying job at another hospital and received no moral support from her former hospital. However, one of the physicians, *after* his conviction, was given a letter of recommendation from the hospital chief for a position in a hospital in another state. Shortly after this, the same physician was later arraigned on charges of rape, attempted rape, and assault and battery of two female patients at a hospital in which he had worked in 1978 (Wechsler, 1982).

TREATMENT FOR RAPISTS

Most convicted rapists in the United States are imprisoned for varying lengths of time. Unfortunately, serving time in jail does not guarantee that when released the individual will not rape again. Convicted rapists repeat the same crime approximately 35 percent of the time (Feisbie & Dondis, 1965; Kozol, Boucher, & Garofalo, 1972). Since conviction records underestimate the true incidence of rape, and since rapists may commit a hundred rapes even though they are only convicted for one, imprisonment alone is not the treatment of choice.

Treatment for rapists depends first on careful diagnostic assessment of the offender. Individuals who are found to be psychotic, sociopathic, or retarded require special and extended treatment, and in some cases confinement away from society may be the only alternative. The more typical repetitive and/or compulsive offender is the one toward whom society and therapists have directed much of their attention. Since treatment for rapists is similar to treatment described for other sexual offenders (see Chapters 10 and 11), we will highlight only the major features. It should be noted that most of the clinical research published has focused on offenders other than rapists.

In some cases, surgical and chemical castration has been used to control rapists and other sexual aggressors; these procedures were previously discussed in Chapter 11. Castration is obviously a drastic measure in that it severely affects a man's ability to respond sexually. Castration may help curtail rape but it also may greatly discourage the development of socially appropriate relationships, contrary to the goals of most typical therapeutic interventions. Also, keep in mind that sexual assault does not require erectile capacity.

Therapy for rapists generally aims at reducing their arousal to deviant cues and increasing their interest in arousal that is socially appropriate. Today's therapists agree that more than one therapeutic approach in treating rapists is necessary, and that therapy often takes a long time (Rosen & Kopel, 1977). Usually, some combination of the following interventions are used (see Abel, Blanchard, & Becker, 1978; VanDeventer & Laws, 1978; Witt, 1981):

1. *Individual therapy:* is used to explore and correct attitudes dealing with sexual urges and peculiar characteristics uncovered in the individual's particular history.
2. *Group therapy:* involves attitude and behavior change also, but with the added advantage of group discussion and social pressure to challenge assumptions rapists have about violent sex. Sometimes educational and behavioral suggestions are used.
3. *Marital/couples therapy:* includes the rapist's wife or partner in the therapy sessions. Communication skills, conflict resolution, and strengthening of the marital unit can make the rapist's reentry into society (if he is imprisoned) less tense and may also lower the potential for recidivism.
4. *Sex education:* examines the rapist's sexual fantasies, sexual skills, and misconceptions about males and females.
5. *Social skills training:* teaches the rapist alternatives to aggression as ways to get what he wants: learning more appropriate means of assertion, expressing negative and positive emotions, accepting criticism, expressing tenderness, improving daily interactions and conversations, and clarifying fears and misconceptions about women.
6. *Orgasmic reconditioning:* attempts to change fantasy content during masturbation and orgasm, pairing orgasm with appropriate sexual activities. Two methods of reconditioning are *covert sensitization,* the decreasing of arousal to the inappropriate sexual activity by pairing an extremely negative thought or image with the rape, and *masturbatory satiation,* in which the offender is asked to masturbate to orgasm and then continue to masturbate while looking at a rape scene after he has ejaculated.
7. *Preparation for reentry into the community for hospitalized or jailed individuals:* involves planning for jobs, living ar-

rangements, and dating. Such preparation helps the individuals deal with expected stresses and offers some guidelines about what to do if a deviant sexual urge or fantasy occurs.

Success rates for these methods are not available, and there are no data on which procedures work for particular types of rapists. Evaluating the success of any of these therapies is a major challenge. Recidivism is not the best measure because so many rapes go unreported and rapists often are not arrested. Evaluating a decrease in a man's desire to commit sexual assault—whether by self-report or by penile tumescence measures—is dependent on individual motivations to rape at particular times and the rapist's cooperation and honesty when being evaluated. No test is really foolproof (Laws & Holmen, 1978). Similarly, although the treatment procedures require a certain level of motivation to change, the major motivation for many of these men is freedom from jail rather than a true desire to change.

THERAPY FOR THE VICTIM

In response to the two phases of the rape syndrome, the rape victim requires two levels of care. In the acute phase, medical attention and immediate psychological evaluation are necessary. In the long-term recovery phase, additional psychological and social assistance may be needed.

If a woman, immediately following a rape, goes to a treatment center, she will be given a physical and gynecological examination. In severe cases of brutality, she will be hospitalized. To protect against pregnancy, high doses of estrogen may be given for several days; to protect against venereal disease, penicillin may be administered.

Management of the psychological reactions of the woman usually involves some type of crisis counseling—helping her deal with the rape, giving her support, and mobilizing her social resources (Burgess & Holmstrom, 1974b). This style of intervention may be all that is necessary for the woman who did not have other significant psychological and social problems prior to the rape. Of course, handling the rape as a crisis assumes that the rape was, in fact, a crisis disrupting the woman's life.

Burgess and Holmstrom (1974b) have mentioned the importance of being aware of what they term the **silent rape reaction.** Women who do not tell anyone of the rape, who have feelings about the rape that remain unsettled, and who may be carrying a psychological burden as a result are suffering from this reaction. Some of the specific signs include the following:

1. Increasing signs of anxiety involving long silences, physical distress, and minor stuttering during conversations.
2. Sudden marked irritability or avoidance in relationships with men or marked sudden changes in sexual behavior.
3. The sudden appearance of phobias, such as fears of being alone, going outside, or being alone at home.
4. Persistent loss of self-confidence, an attitude of self-blame, paranoid feelings, and/or violent dreams.

PREVENTION AND AVOIDANCE OF RAPE VICTIMIZATION

No strategy can guarantee protection from rape. Some general precautions that women can take, however, will help to reduce the chances of a rape occurring. Similarly, while specific behaviors may reduce the likelihood of being raped even after a male has approached, there is no formula that will work with all situations and with all rapists.

Setting

As we have previously mentioned, a high percentage of rapes occur in the woman's home. The conservative strategy is to keep the doors locked at all times, especially when alone, avoid admitting strangers, and list only last names with first initials on mailboxes and telephone directories. Requesting identification from delivery or repair people has also been recommended. If a woman lives alone, she should become acquainted with her neighbors and arrange for mutual house watching. Any enclosed or deserted areas, such as dimly lit streets

and cars, are high risk sites for rape. Hitchhiking is not safe for a woman, and it is advisable for a woman to check her own car before getting in and locking it once inside. Being accompanied by a male is often a deterrent, except in some cases of gang rape when the male may also be vulnerable to attack.

Most women are forced to take some chances either because of special circumstances or due to economic necessity. For example, a woman may experience car trouble late at night, or a job may demand working an 8:00 P.M. to 4:00 A.M. shift. The important issue is for women to be aware of settings of higher risk and to be more careful, adjusting their behavior to suit the circumstances.

Behavior

Strategies for dealing with a person who is attempting sexual assault vary between two extremes, from being passive to actively resisting the attacker. The passive approach (e.g., Storaska, 1975) stresses behaving in a way that will minimize the rapist's anger and potentially decrease his assaultiveness and intent to rape. The active strategy suggests that making the assault more difficult for the rapist may minimize the damage done.

One researcher (Abel, 1981) advises the use of several different strategies where possible, including, in order, (1) escape, (2) acting assertively rather than fearfully, and (3) trying to talk about oneself in order to establish individuality, as many rapists concentrate on the victim as an object rather than as a person.

Strategies from the victim's perspective have been studied more carefully than those determined by information from offenders. Of particular interest is a comparison between women who were raped and women who were approached but not raped. One study of 320 women (McIntyre, 1979) found that aggressive behavior (fighting, screaming, running, or verbal aggression) on the part of the victim reduced the likelihood of rape, and aggressive behavior early in the interaction was more effective in reducing the odds of being raped than when it was attempted at some later point. Contrary to Abel's (1981) observation, non-aggressive talking to gain sympathy or consideration was not a successful strategy. Neither was crying. However, a woman who was consistently aggressive was more likely to be "nonseriously" injured—bruises, sore muscles, black eyes, and abrasions—while avoiding rape. Rape plus injury tended to be associated with a complete lack of aggression, or aggression used only when the assailant attempted sex. Serious injury was usually not a consequence of victim resistance.

Bart (1979) also studied the effectiveness of various strategies, which she discovered in interviews with forty-three women who were raped and with fifty-one women who were attacked but avoided rape. She found that (1) fleeing was more effective than all other strategies, with 81 percent of the twenty-one women who tried to escape avoiding rape; (2) physical resistance was the second most effective strategy, with 68 percent of the forty-four women who tried this tactic being successful; (3) screaming was effective for 63 percent of the twenty women who tried this strategy; (4) the cognitive verbal strategy, which includes reasoning, conning, or personalizing oneself to the attacker, worked for 54 percent of the sixty-seven women who tried this strategy; and (5) the least effective strategy was pleading—44 percent of the twenty-five women who pleaded avoided rape. Bart (1979) also found that there was a slightly greater likelihood of being beaten up if physical resistance occurred, but the sooner women used force, the more likely they were to avoid rape.

Bart (1979) suggests two other factors that may have a bearing on a woman's successful avoidance of rape. One factor is competency in managing emergency situations independently. In comparison with those raped, more of the avoiders knew first aid and twice as many had learned self-defense. A second factor was physical condition: Twice as many avoiders as victims were regularly active in sports. A physically

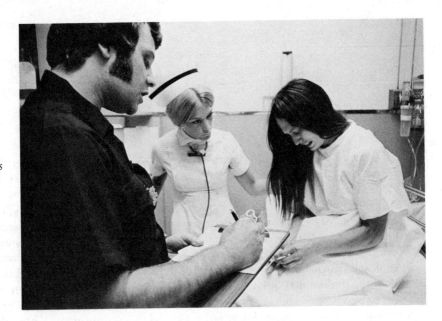

Fewer than 20 percent of rapes are reported. For some women, the process of reporting is an additional trauma.

fit person may be more self-confident about facing an attacker, which may, indeed, give her a psychological edge.

Interestingly, few studies mention the use of weapons. Typically, weapons such as hatpins, corkscrews, keys, umbrellas, or mace have been recommended. Apparently, they are too infrequently used to record their effectiveness.

The above data describe more effective and less effective strategies for avoiding rape, and all have success and failure rates.

Furthermore, with some rapists, no strategy will be successful. The most a woman can do is take reasonable precautions and, if faced with an assailant, quickly assess the risks and use the best possible strategy. Ultimately, even if a woman freezes in fear and totally cooperates with the rapist, that may be the best strategy and she does not deserve to be blamed for cooperating. In fear of her life, she most likely will do whatever she can to protect herself.

RAPE AND THE LAW

Less than 20 percent of all rapes are ever reported. Approximately 51 percent of reported rapists, in cases in which the victim is believed by the police, are apprehended; about 75 percent of the apprehended cases are brought to trial. Overall, less than 13 percent of rapists are convicted (Brownmiller, 1975).

Why are so few rapes reported? The FBI claims underreporting is due to fear and embarrassment on the part of the victim (FBI Uniform Crime Reports, 1973), but no one has studied this question in depth. Although a number of police departments are becoming more sensitive in their dealings with rape victims, simply reporting the rape can be difficult for the victim because her word and her character are likely to be doubted. If a victim knows the assailant, waits before going to the police, has consumed some alcohol, does not struggle during the rape, or is a black woman raped by a black man, her case is less likely than others to be believed (Brownmiller, 1975; Kalven & Zeisel, 1966). Police may joke or they may interpret the victim's lack of reaction (the unexpressed stress reaction described earlier) to mean that she is lying. The following victims' statements from Brownmiller's (1975) files are typical:

> I went to the police station and said, "I want to report a rape." They said, "Whose?" and I said, "Mine." The cop looked at me and said, "Aw, who'd want to rape you?" (p. 364)

> They finally told me they thought I was lying. They said I'd probably been having sex with my boyfriend and was afraid I was pregnant. They also theorized that my boyfriend had set me up for it. They wanted to know if he'd ever asked me to have sexual relations with his friends. (p. 366)

In fact, few rapes are false reports—one study found that only 2 percent of rape complaints were false (1974 data cited by Brownmiller, 1975).

Judges and juries are no easier to convince. Many courts are hesitant to convict without extensive proof because the rape penalty may mean life imprisonment or even a death sentence for the rapist. Some states (Massachusetts, for example) apply lighter sentences in hopes of getting more convictions. The most convincing evidence is injury, the use of weapons, lack of con-

sent and cooperation, the presence of sperm, and the lack of relationship between rapist and victim. Traditionally, and in many states today, courts have admitted as evidence the woman's prior sexual history—if she was single and had had a number of sexual partners, her account of the rape was doubted. In some states, the woman's sexual character is *not* considered permissible testimony, with the frequent exception of a prior sexual relationship between a specific victim and her accused offender.

The legal process surrounding rape repeats themes that are mentioned in the discussion of prostitution (see Chapter 13). Women who are identified as sexual, particularly outside of the marital context, are seen as bad or guilty. In the case of rape, a woman must prove her goodness and honesty— she must defend her right not to be raped— while the rapist often finds it quite plausible to argue that she forced him to rape her. Certainly, forcible intercourse is sometimes difficult to prove. With no witnesses, assault marks, or semen, the case is one person's word against another. Nevertheless, it is almost impossible to ignore the sex bias in the legal handling of rape.

Ultimately, a major legal question is whether individuals have bodily self-determination, meaning that a person controls what is done with his or her own body. The most clear-cut evidence against "body rights" is in the legal view of marriage. In many states, husbands cannot be accused of rape (the legal solution is to charge assault). In the legal institution of marriage, one's body can become the right of one's marital partner. Broader than that, the differential arrests and conviction rates for strangers versus nonstrangers suggest that once a woman has allowed a man access to her body, he forever more has certain inalienable rights.

There is no easy solution to these problems. Proof is difficult, and the social framework is predisposed against the victim. Holmstrom and Burgess (1980) note that even the victim's report of the rapist's behavior may be held against her. One woman in their case files testified that the rapist forced her to have intercourse and then masturbated. The defense counsel discounted the validity of her testimony by saying that the man would not have driven fifty-two miles to masturbate. The defendant was found not guilty.

The current status of rape and the law is discouraging. The low report, arrest, and conviction rates do little to slow the increasing number of rapes in the United States. Many rapists commit hundreds of assaults (Abel et al., 1977), and even if convicted they are often back on the streets raping again. Reforms in the legal system are needed to enable the victim to defend her rights.

SUMMARY

1. **Rape** is a sexually aggressive crime. Its two basic components — sex and aggression — cannot be separated.

2. The rapist is typically young, likely to have been arrested previously for nonsexual offenses, belongs to the lower socioeconomic group, in most cases will rape a woman of his own race, will probably use force, and often is accompanied by a co-rapist. Alcoholism is a problem with some rapists, testosterone levels are higher among violent sex offenders, and rapists are often very hostile.

3. The victim of rape is most frequently a female from the low socioeconomic class, lives in an urban environment, and is between the ages of 15 and 25. However, women of any age, race, and socioeconomic class are vulnerable to being raped.

4. There are both short- and long-term effects of rape. The **rape trauma syndrome** occurs in two phases. The *acute phase,* which the victim experiences immediately following the rape, is expressed in two ways — either the woman is extremely controlled or very emotional. The *long-term phase* is noted by a number of changes in life-style and emotional behavior. In short, the victim suffers significant psychological, physical, and social aftereffects from rape, which may last for years.

5. The most common "treatment" for rapists is imprisonment, which has not been very successful, as indicated by high recidivism rates. Surgical and chemical castration have been used for some rapists, but castration is not an effective means of treating these sex offenders. Therapy aimed at reducing deviant arousal and improving socially appropriate arousal is currently preferred. However, male cooperation is required for therapy to be successful.

6. The rape victim requires two types of therapy, the first dealing with the immediate effects of the rape, and the second with helping the victim resolve long-term problems resulting from the sexual offense.

7. A number of suggestions are made regarding ways to prevent rape victimization. Some commonsense measures include living in secure housing and avoiding deserted areas. It must be stressed that a woman needs to evaluate a particular situation to determine the best strategy for avoiding rape and for survival. While some studies of victims have shown that aggressive behavior on the part of the victim can interfere with the successful completion of the rape attempt, in some situations not resisting may be best.

8. There is a tendency in society, especially among the police and the courts, to at least partially blame the victim for the rape. Traditionally, the victim's previous sexual activities have been used as evidence against her, and this practice is still permissible in many states. Unfortunately, forcible intercourse is sometimes difficult to prove because there is often little evidence beyond the testimony of each party.

SUGGESTED READINGS

Brownmiller, S. *Against our will: Men, women, and rape.* New York: Simon & Schuster, 1975. A review of rape from historical, legal, and social perspectives; also summarizes data from a variety of sources.

Groth, A. N. *Men who rape: The psychology of the offender.* New York: Plenum, 1979. A careful analysis of over 500 men who committed and were convicted of rape.

Russell, D. E. H. *Rape in marriage.* New York: Macmillan, 1982. A study of over 500 women, randomly sampled, who were asked questions about rape and nonsexual assault, in particular with husbands or former husbands.

CHAPTER THIRTEEN

PORNOGRAPHY AND PROSTITUTION
Questions of Relationships and Values

Later they made me go back to Clara's room to lie down. . . . She said she started it with a bunch of boys in an old shed. She said nobody had paid any attention to her and she became very popular. . . . They like it so much, she said, why shouldn't you give it to them and get presents and attention? I never cared anything for it and neither did my mama. But it's the only thing you got that's valuable.
Le Sueur, *The Girl*.

Socially and legally, sex in the context of pornographic materials and prostitution has been cause for conflict and outrage. Three basic values appear to be affronted by these activities:

1. *Sex is a private activity,* and both pornography and prostitution publicize sex. Pornography portrays sexual activity to an audience of readers, listeners, or viewers. Prostitution puts sexual favors into public access.

2. *Human sexual relationships are based on mutual consent and mutual personal interest.* Within pornography, relationships are based on sexual interests that are often of an impersonal nature, highlighting nonmutual concerns. When people use pornography material, they engage in a nonmutual, autoerotic activity. In prostitution, there is mutual consent, but the basis of the sexual exchange is money rather than interpersonal interest.

3. *Sex is more than a purely physical act.* It is connected to certain emotional reactions including love, play, respect, trust, pleasure, intimacy, and joy. In both prostitution and pornography, the physical component of sex is the primary focus of the relationship. Different emotional contexts may play a part, but certainly love and respect are extremely unlikely.

Pornography and prostitution challenge a variety of other values and beliefs about proper sexual conduct. Each has a long history, although pornography and prostitution have not always been illegal or viewed as negative. In considering each topic, therefore, the current legal and social context surrounding the people involved, the degree of victimization, and the types of sex-role relationships portrayed must be examined.

PORNOGRAPHY

What is meant by **pornography?** The word is derived from the Greek adjective *pornographos,* meaning the writing about harlots. The actual definition of pornography has shifted over the years, sometimes being connected with obscenity and other times with erotica. These meanings are quite different from each other, one bearing positive connotations while the other carries negative ones. *Erotica* comes from the Greek name *Eros,* the god of love and the symbol of pleasurable life instincts derived from the libido. *Obscenity,* on the other hand, is derived from the Latin word *obscenus,* meaning dirt or filth. In common usage, erotica and pornography connote the intention to increase sexual desire and arousal, while obscenity has come to mean offensive and depraved sexuality. As we discuss it here, pornography refers to the specific depiction of sexuality that has the potential to be sexually arousing, with the implication that it may include portrayals of sexual acts that are generally "offen-

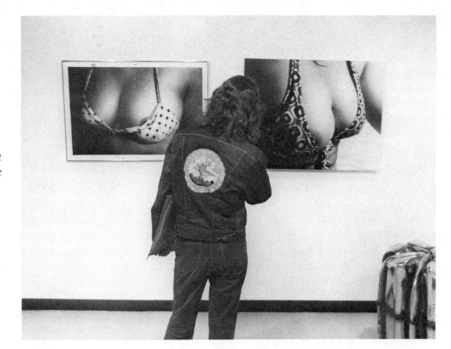

One definition of erotic art is that it leaves more to the imagination than pornography.

sive." Erotica is similar in intent but with less offensive implications. In some cultures and at certain times, erotica can be categorized as pornography or even obscenity.

Historical Perspective

Explicit and detailed sex manuals first appeared in China, sometime between 206 B.C. and A.D. 24. The official biography of the Han dynasty included eight such manuals. None of these manuals remain, and only fragments of the Sui dynasty manuals (A.D. 600) have been compiled and preserved in a Japanese book, *I-shin-po.* The Chinese handbooks were apparently divided into six sections: (1) the cosmic significance of the sexual encounter, (2) advice on foreplay, (3) a description of sexual intercourse techniques and positions, (4) the therapeutic value of sex and how to choose the right woman, (5) how women should act during

pregnancy, and (6) health recipes and prescriptions (Tannahill, 1980).

Although these ancient manuals were used as serious educational texts by both men and women, most Westerners would consider them pornographic. In fact, the Indian *Kama Sutra* — a combination of sexual, religious, and spiritual writings from the fourth and fifth centuries A.D. — was denounced as obscene when it was introduced into Western cultures in the 1960s. The *Kama Sutra* contains a variety of practical advice about passion, marriage, possessiveness, and love.

These works, then, were not considered pornographic in their time, though they have been in ours. Pornography first became a social problem in Western societies in the 1700s. Early pornography in England tended to focus on suggested lewd and lustful activities of the clergy, thus making a mockery of religious leaders who were directly connected with the ruling government. Needless to say, the government did not approve of such publications and, in fact, declared them to be *obscene libel* if religious values were disrespected. *Venus in the Cloister* and *The Nun in the Smock* are examples of libelous works. A number of other sexually explicit books were written in the 1700s, but these were not illegal because they omitted religious themes. In 1857 Parliament passed a law that allowed police to seize and destroy those publications that were written for the "single purpose of corrupting the morals of youth and of a nature to shock the feeling of decency in a well-regulated mind" (Taylor, 1956, p. 216). Obscenity was later defined in 1868 as material that corrupts and depraves the minds of consumers (*Queen* v. *Hicklin*). This decision caused great uncertainty concerning how one proves corruption, depravity, and indecency in the courts; this uncertainty is still a problem today.

In the United States, early antiobscenity statutes were also restricted to *blasphemy*—words written or spoken against the established religion. In seventeenth-and eighteenth-century Massachusetts, for example, the Puritans viewed blasphemy as a serious crime, punishable by death or by torture with a hot iron used to bore a hole through the tongue. Sexual obscenities were prosecuted for the first time in 1815 in Pennsylvania. The first erotic book to be banned in Massachusetts in 1821 was an illustrated edition of John Cleland's *Memoirs of a Woman of Pleasure,* sometimes called *Fanny Hill* (a book owned by many prominent early Americans, including Benjamin Franklin).

Anthony Comstock, a zealous campaigner against immorality, persuaded Congress in 1873 to pass a federal bill banning "obscene, lewd, lascivious or filthy" publications from the mails. Comstock was appointed anti-obscenity agent of the Post Office Department, and his organization, the New York Society for the Suppression of Vice, was given police powers. Comstock devoted himself to arresting hundreds of people and relentlessly tracking down offensive books and pamphlets.

A new definition for obscenity emerged from the landmark case of *Roth* v. *U.S.* in 1957, although it was no more precise than any that had come before. According to this decision, something was obscene if (1) the dominant theme of the work appealed to "prurient" (depraved and improper) interests, according to the average person applying contemporary community standards; and (2) the work was utterly without redeeming social importance. Samuel Roth was already serving a five-year prison term for publishing Aubrey Beardsley's illustrated *Venus and Tannhauser* and for mailing sexually suggestive advertising. In fact, Roth was a longtime target of the police and FBI for repeatedly publishing or distributing censored books, including James Joyce's *Ulysses,* an Arabian volume called *The Perfumed Garden* that illustrated 237 positions for sexual activities, D. H. Lawrence's *Lady Chatterley's Lover,* and the *Kama Sutra*. Although the Supreme Court upheld the decision against Roth, the redefinition of obscenity allowed many later works to avoid obscenity charges. For example, Hugh Hefner's *Playboy* magazine, which contains alluring, mostly nude models, has been very successful, even in 1957.

In 1969, adults were given the right to possess but not distribute pornographic materials (*Stanley* v. *Georgia*). However, a 1973 decision (*Miller* v. *California*) ruled that obscenity prosecution was a local issue. Local courts could assume that pornographic material had negative effects rather than having to prove it. The latter decision is especially surprising in view of the federally conducted *Report of the Commission on Obscenity and Pornography* (1970), which concluded that no harmful effects developed from exposure to pornographic materials.

The potential danger in having obscenity so vaguely defined is that the likelihood of subjective judgment is increased. An often-quoted phrase of Chief Justice Potter Steward regarding a 1964 case (*Jacobellis* v. *Ohio*) clearly illustrates how personal bias can influence decisions because there is no concrete definition: Though obscenity is difficult to define, "I know it when I see it." Furthermore, legal judgments about obscenity must consider protection of the First Amendment, which essentially guarantees individuals the right to free speech. Liberals on the Supreme Court have often permitted pornography to be available based on the existence of the First Amendment. The reasoning for this position centers on the concern for censorship in general—including the censorship of political and religious beliefs. Other Court opinions, however, have often claimed that the First Amendment excludes obscenity.

The problem remains complicated. Pornography and obscenity are areas in which morals and legal issues clash. We are likely

Sexual horoscopes: A pornographic fortune telling.

to continue to see shifts in the availability and regulation of pornography and obscenity, depending on the shifts in their cultural definitions.

Effects of Pornography on Behavior in the General Population

One major concern about pornographic materials is the possibility that they may encourage behaviors that are portrayed in the content—for example, rape, pedophilia, group sex, and sadomasochism. One theory holds that pornography has no effect on behavior, that exposure to pornographic materials is no more or less likely to encourage the illustrated activity than is watching a film on becoming a priest or a TV program that includes realistic methods of burglarizing a house.

A second theory, based on modeling, suggests that some people will be stimulated to act out the images to which they are exposed. In fact, some people have reported being "motivated" by a book or film to commit antisocial acts. Musician John Lennon's self-confessed killer quoted J. D. Salinger's *Catcher in the Rye* during one courtroom appearance, indicating that he had found a message in the book instructing him to carry out the act in spite of the fact that millions of people who have read this book have not been driven to violence.

A third theory about the effects of pornography on behavior holds that the pornographic materials permit outlets for discharging sexual desires. According to this theory, pornography is a safety valve that helps prevent people from carrying out their aggressive sexual desires against other people.

Each theory is supported by some evidence, but not one has been proved. Research in this area is difficult for a number of reasons. Sexual response to erotic materials depends on the specific materials used, a person's experience with pornography in the past, a person's desire to be seen in a certain way (for instance, as very sexy or as very proper), the type of stimuli used (written, auditory, or visual), and the person's nonsexual feelings about the material (for instance, it is difficult for individuals to admit, acknowledge, or even be aware of their ability to be aroused by materials they find personally disgusting or

degrading). Because of these factors, dependable information is difficult to obtain.

One of the most comprehensive studies of the effects of pornography is contained in the *Report of the Commission on Obscenity and Pornography* (1970), a two-year governmental project undertaken during the Johnson administration. Contributors to the report included researchers, teachers, legal authorities, clergy, and health-care professionals. The following are some of the most prominent findings of the report:

1. In the United States, approximately 85 percent of adult men and 70 percent of adult women have at some time been exposed to explicitly sexual material. Men usually have earlier and more extensive exposure.
2. "Conventional" sexual practices are more arousing than "less conventional" sex, and repeated exposure leads to satiation and lack of interest in erotic materials.
3. A person's sexual patterns are seldom altered. Instead, there tends to be a temporary twenty-four- to forty-eight-hour increase in the number of fantasies and conversations one has about sex as well as increases in a person's customary sexual activities (Kutchinsky, 1970). For example, masturbation tended to increase in some single males (Ambroso et al., 1970; Schmidt et al., 1973; Sigusch et al., 1970) and single females (Schmidt & Sigusch, 1970), but not in men and women with sexual partners (Byrne & Lamberth, 1970; Mann, Sidman & Starr, 1970). For these people, coital frequency increased in the twenty-four hours fol-

lowing exposure to sexually explicit materials.

Additionally, the report noted that the typical pornographic film viewer was a white, married, 26- to 45-year-old male, college educated, white-collar or professional worker, whose income was above the national average at the time of the study.

The question remains whether long-term exposure to pornography might have harmful effects. Two separate studies suggest otherwise. One group of researchers exposed a group of young adult males to sexually explicit films for ninety minutes a day, five days a week, over a three-week period (Howard, Liptzin & Reifler, 1973). Initially, these men's thoughts about sex increased, but they soon decreased below the level at which they were when the men entered the study. The men also found that they had been exposed to more pornography than they cared to be, and many reported that without the payment offered in the study they never would have completed the three-week program.

Another study, this one based on experiments with married couples (Mann et al., 1973), supported the findings of the *Report of the Commission on Obscenity and Pornography* (1970). Unusual sexual behaviors did not increase in frequency. What was more surprising was that these couples increased their sexual behaviors more during the weeks before exposure to pornographic films than during the exposure weeks. One could perhaps conclude that the anticipation of sexual materials, maybe due to the fantasies people create, is far more

stimulating than the actual witnessing of the contents.

Pornography and Aggression

Does exposure to pornography increase aggressiveness? This question is important not only because pornography often contains a great deal of aggression combined with sexual activities, but also because aggression and sexuality are often seen as linked behaviors and emotions (Barclay, 1971; Freud, 1933). We find that the data available on this issue are mixed. Some studies have found that exposure to sexually explicit materials has facilitated later aggression (Jaffe et al., 1974; Meyer, 1972). Other studies have found that increased sexual arousal may inhibit later aggression (Baron, 1974a,b). Researching this topic is difficult, primarily because aggression and sexual response must be provoked and measured in a laboratory. These data depend on how believable the circumstances presented in the particular study are to the participants.

Donnerstein, Donnerstein, and Evans (1975) discovered several important factors about the relationship between aggression and arousal. These researchers worked with a large group of men in a complex experimental situation. One important aspect was the use of different types of pictures: highly erotic, mildly erotic, and neutral. The men were also subjected to different "insult" conditions at different times during the presentation of the erotic pictures. Aggression was measured by the amount of "shock" (which the subject falsely assumed was a real shock) delivered to the person who had been insulting. The results show that for the subjects who were insulted before being sexually aroused, the exposure to mildly erotic material reduced their aggression, while exposure to highly erotic materials brought their aggression back up to the same level as a neutral stimulus. However, if subjects . viewed highly erotic materials prior to being insulted, they were more aggressive than if they saw mildly erotic or neutral stimuli. Thus aggression may be increased by just being angry, or by seeing highly erotic material immediately before being angered. But aggression may be decreased by seeing mildly erotic material after having been angered.

The above study looked at aggression between males. What about male aggression toward females? Donnerstein and Barrett (1978) found that highly arousing sexual material increased aggression in angered males, but that there was no substantial difference in the degree of aggression they directed toward males or females. In fact, even though higher levels of physiological arousal, in this case blood pressures, were recorded when the males directed their attention toward females, there was a tendency to show less aggression toward them. This result was thought to be related to the fact that aggression toward females is generally not approved of, and that fear of disapproval could act to inhibit aggression (Donnerstein & Hallan, 1978).

In a study that was designed to reduce the inhibitions about aggression (by giving subjects two opportunities to be aggressive), Donnerstein and Hallan (1978) found that sexually aroused males would be more aggressive toward females than males if they were given a second opportunity (ten minutes after the first) to be aggressive. One presumes that allowing a subject a second chance to respond tends to "give permission" to aggress.

For men and women, there is evidence that greater sexual arousal corresponds with more uninhibited aggressive responses (Malamuth, Feshbach, & Jaffe, 1977). These studies, however, are all based on self-report of sexual arousal and different measures of aggression and provocation. Thus, the relationship among sexual arousal, aggression, and anger is not well understood, and no firm social recommendation can be made based on the research done to date.

Pornography and Sex Crimes

The information we have presented on pornography and its effects on behavior would indicate that pornography is not generally harmful. However, when the same conditions exist for individuals with a history of sex crimes, there are several disturbing implications. For example, for men who have a history of rape or assault, exposure to pornography may stimulate their fantasies to the point of acting on them, particularly in the twenty-four hours after exposure to pornography (Malamuth, 1981). Furthermore, a man in this group may be more apt to attack a person he meets after seeing a por-

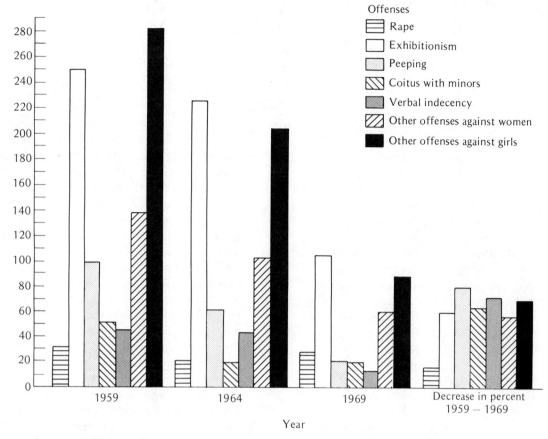

Offenses
- ⊟ Rape
- ☐ Exhibitionism
- ▨ Peeping
- ◩ Coitus with minors
- ▨ Verbal indecency
- ▨ Other offenses against women
- ■ Other offenses against girls

Figure 13-1. Sex offenses against females in Copenhagen. Source: Kutchinsky, 1973

nographic film if the person frustrates or angers him.

Although there is no conclusive evidence either to support or to negate these effects of pornography, recent experience in Denmark and studies of sex offenders can clarify several facts. In 1967, Denmark abolished all legal restrictions on pornographic writings sold to or in the possession of individuals over sixteen years of age. In 1969, other media, including photos and films, were included in the legalization. Prior to that time, in the early 1960s, the use of pornographic materials was steadily increasing. Studies showed that incidence of sex crimes remained stable until about 1966 and then dramatically declined (see Figure 12-1). Some crimes decreased more than others. For example, Kutchinsky (1973) found that voyeurism decreased the most (80 percent), and rape decreased the least (16 percent).

These Danish results must be regarded with caution (Bachy, 1976). All of the data are based on police reports, and perhaps these offenses did not really decrease but instead tolerance for some of the offensive activities may have increased. Furthermore, we cannot assume that the impact of more easily available pornography would be the same in the United States as it is in Denmark. Nevertheless, Denmark's statistics suggest that pornography may serve as an important alternative to committing sexual crimes. The results of the study also suggest that pornography may have a different impact on, or be used differently by, certain types of sex criminals.

As to the use of pornography by sex offenders, research has shown that convicted sex offenders report that they were less likely to have been exposed to pornography (Goldstein & Kant, 1973) and were less aroused by it (Gebhard et al., 1965) than non–sex offenders. Of course, one can never eliminate the possibility that convicted sex offenders may be less likely to admit to these experiences. Goldstein and Kant (1973) suggested "a reasonable exposure to erotica, particularly during adolescence, reflects a high degree of interest and curiosity that coincides with adult patterns of acceptable heterosexual interest and practice" (p. 70). Less than average exposure during adolescence may reflect either an active avoidance of heterosexual stimuli or some kind of restrictive environment in which such materials are unavailable. A male may be socially atypical if he has not gone through the basic socialization process that includes, for better or worse, a certain amount of exposure to pornography. Thus, in spite of what one might assume about pornography's stimulating the likelihood of sex crimes, research to date does not support this assumption. However, data in the United States are sparse, and too little is known about the interaction of violence and sexual response to conclude that pornography has an insignificant impact on the behavior of sex offenders.

In fact, some researchers have examined whether the idea of sexual force or coercion is appealing to young males who are not criminals (Briddell et al., 1978; Malamuth et al., 1980). For example, Malamuth (1981) asked Canadian undergraduate volunteers to fill out a questionnaire that included several questions on sexual activities. Twenty-three of the sixty-seven men who completed the questionnaire reported that they found the idea of force somewhat or very attractive. Thirteen men from this group, labeled the "force-oriented" group, were compared with sixteen "nonforce-oriented" men. Half of the men were then exposed to an audio slide series depicting a rape, and the other half to a series with a mutual consent theme. All the men then heard a description of a rape read by a female. Afterward, subjects were asked to create a fantasy that would maximize their sexual arousal. Penile erection and self-reports of sexual arousal were similar for both groups across the various rape and mutual consent stimuli. The female's consent made little difference in the men's levels of arousal. However, men who had been previously classified as force-oriented created more arousing fantasies after exposure to the rape slide show, while the nonforce-oriented men created more arousing fantasies after the slide show depicting sexual activity where both parties consent. More importantly, men in both groups, when exposed to the rape slides, created fantasies with more violent sexual themes than those exposed to the slides of mutual consent situations.

We must interpret these results with cau-

tion. They demonstrate that men who find force attractive are more sexually aroused by a subsequent fantasy, and that exposure to a stimulus representing a situation of force increases the frequency of violent fantasy themes in men (or at least the admission of such themes) regardless of their force orientation. What we do not know is where fantasy stops and reality begins: How many of these men would be prone to rape?

Social Significance of Pornography

Whatever the effects of pornography on behavior, many objections and much rage is directed toward the way females and males are portrayed in pornographic literature. Female writers, and feminists in particular, have been the most outspoken on this topic. In fact, certain organizations, the major one called Women Against Pornography, are attempting to limit public access to pornographic materials.

The problem is that hard-core por-nography, the type one finds in adult bookstores or presented in X-rated films, depicts women, and sometimes children, as sexual objects who are forced, used, bound, raped, and mutilated. "Soft porn," as seen in advertisements luring customers with subtle sexual promises or nude sensual displays in the more popular magazines, also conveys the image of women as sexual playthings, convenient and always-available pieces of entertainment to accompany one's vacation, whiskey, and stereo receiver. The frequently repeated message is that women are sexual objects whose only desire and enjoyment come from male domination. Thus two major arguments are cited against the use of pornography: the objection to the public display or discussion of any form of sexual activity or nudity, and the objection to the portrayal of certain types of sexual relationships, particularly those that are demeaning toward women.

473

Many writers view the major theme in pornography as power, especially male power over women (De Beauvior, 1970; Dworkin, 1981). Dworkin (1981) notes that male power takes many forms, including physical power, power to terrorize, power to own possessions, power of money, and power of sex. Susan Griffin (1981) approaches the subject differently, by describing the pornographic versus the erotic. She sees the erotic as a unity of pleasure and beauty, nature and women, physical and psychic love. She describes pornography, however, as a type of sexual response that is isolated from most "natural" feelings and associated instead with degradation and fear.

The solutions to the social issues surrounding pornography are not easy. Although hard-core pornography probably is not widely or repeatedly experienced by individuals, much of it is offensive to the average person. Would pornography's removal or, alternatively, its widespread legal availability change the values that support its sales, such as a taste for cruelty and violence toward women and children?

PROSTITUTION

Prostitution is defined as the exchange of sexual services for money. Sex within this arrangement is a business deal, and from the prostitute's perspective, the exchange typically omits sexual pleasure and interpersonal affection. Although health factors such as venereal disease are often cited as the cause of social concern, morality is the primary reason that certain countries call prostitution a crime. Prostitution is illegal in the United States, with the exception of a small number of rural counties in Nevada.

We concentrate our discussion on female prostitution because prostitutes are most often females. Male prostitution has apparently always been rare; in fact, only among male homosexuals does it occur with any noteworthy frequency. Prostitutes vary in status from *streetwalkers,* who wait to be picked up on the street, to upper-class *call girls,* who make appointments by phone.

Historical Perspective

While perhaps not the oldest profession (shamans and witch doctors were probably in practice first), some form of what twentieth-century Western societies would call prostitution has existed for several thousand years. For example, priests, priestesses, servants, artisans, and sacred prostitutes lived in the Babylonian temples during the period of Hammurabi (c. 1750 B.C.). Worshipers made contact with a deity through sexual liaisons with these prostitutes, whose earnings provided substantial contributions to the income of the temples. There were different status levels of prostitutes. The higher-ranking sacred prostitutes seem to have been secluded within the temple, but other prostitutes lived outside of the temple and picked up clients in public places such as the taverns and on the streets. Street prostitutes were forbidden to wear the veils worn by other women, which served both to "advertise" the harlots and to protect the other women in the society from sexual harassment (Saggs, 1965).

In ancient Greece, a well-respected group of prostitutes emerged, the *hetaerae* (from the Greek word meaning "female companion"). These women were well educated, socially adept, talented, and often influential in political affairs. They called themselves servants of Aphrodite, the goddess of marriage and fertility. In many parts of western Asia (Cyprus, Babylon, Phoenicia, and Syria), similar customs were practiced whereby, prior to marriage, all women were obliged to prostitute themselves to strangers at Aphrodite's temple. They did not keep their earnings but instead turned them over to the temple. However, the higher status assigned to the hetaerae was probably related to its semisacred heritage. The sacred and secular may have blended at some levels to retain the elevation of certain prostitutes above others.

The hetaerae were unusual because they were successful women living in a male-dominated society, they were appreciated for their minds as well as their bodies, and they stood in sharp contrast to the rest of the women in Greece, particularly the wives of their patrons. "Respectable" women, at least until the fourth century B.C., had no formal education, had limited legal rights, bore children, tended the house, and were considered the property of their husbands.

Below the hetaerae on the social scale of prostitutes was the *concubine,* a woman who served as the mistress of one man but without the legal rights of a wife. Below the concubine was the common prostitute or *pornē* (from which comes the definition of pornography); she could be purchased for almost any price.

In Rome, particularly after the conquest of the Greeks, prostitutes claimed a patron goddess, Venus. However, prostitution in Rome seems to have been limited, and there is no evidence of a high-status prostitute class. Women served as prostitutes in brothels, some "served" the military, and others catered to the patrons of the Circus Maximus games. However, the rest of the women of Rome, though not equal in rank to men socially, had far more power in the family and eventually more rights in marriage and divorce than the average Greek woman. The status of these women, combined with the fact that adultery was very common, may partially explain why there was no need for high-class prostitution in this society.

The historical relationship of prostitutes to family life was somewhat different in China. Beginning in the last two centuries B.C. and lasting for quite a long time, polygamy was a part of middle-class life. It was common for men to have four to twelve wives and concubines. All female household members were expected to be uneducated, and contact between wives and husbands was restricted to meals and bedtime. All wives and concubines had guaranteed rights, economically and sexually, and it was the man's responsibility to provide for the women fairly, as favoritism could make his home life miserable. The Confucian Book of Rites, the *Li-chi,* for example, stressed that concubines should have intercourse once every five days until the age of 50 (Van Gulik, 1961). Essentially, a calendar of sexual activities had to be adhered to, and perhaps for that reason, casual physical contact was prohibited as it might arouse desire.

Prostitutes in China during this time, then, offered different services than did their European counterparts. The Chinese men sought a chance to relax in a luxurious atmosphere with good wine, music, hospitality, and sexual activities were of less importance (sex-only brothels were rare in China until the 1800s). Prostitutes were of several classes, including high-class courtesans who could select their suitors and, like the Greek hetaerae, were skilled in business, politics, literature, and the arts. Although the classier brothels, the *tea houses,* did not stress the sexual favors available, sex very likely occurred, as it was far less of a burden to men in this setting than at home. It was the *wine houses,* which provided top wines, excellent appetizers, and a cheerful atmosphere, as well as female companions, that would hang out red silk bamboo lamps to advertise their services. Perhaps this tradition was the origin of the "red-light district" (Tannahill, 1980).

In Europe, between 1100 and 1600, there

A New Orleans Prostitute, 1912

were contradictory attitudes toward prostitution. Although prostitution was seen as immoral and shameful, the teachings of Saint Augustine and Saint Aquinas warned that the abolition of prostitution would pollute the more righteous women in society and place undue sexual demands on them. Church brothels were thus made available, and the women living in them were responsible for religious duties as well as sexual ones (Taylor, 1956). Yet during the same period, Magdalene homes (named for Mary Magdalene, a repentant follower of Jesus and an alleged prostitute) were built to help prostitutes give up their sinful ways. Meanwhile the more secular brothels flourished, and high-status prostitutes emerged during the Renaissance. Syphilis cases reached epidemic proportions during this period, and in the early part of the sixteenth century, men generally avoided lower-status prostitutes.

Prostitution was very common in

In the late 1800s, young New Orleans women are recruited as whores for Texas brothels, though they expected reputable jobs.

Working the Elevated: Man-Fishers on Sixth Avenue, New York City—Siren Games they play to rope in their trade. The Illustrated Police News, late 1800s

nineteenth-century Europe, England, and America. Three factors seemed to be responsible: religious attitudes, cultural views of women and sexuality, and economic conditions. Christians, and especially Protestants, of the 1800s took Saint Augustine to heart: Animalistic desires were not to be directed at one's wife more than once a month, and marital coitus was acceptable only if it was carried out without excessive emotion. Therefore, prostitutes became a very popular solution to men's sexual needs. The line between good women (nonsexual) and bad women (sexual) was thin: One sexual experience outside of marriage was all it took for a woman to fall into the category of prostitute (Taylor, 1956; Heiman, in press). Women were sometimes drawn to prostitution out of financial necessity, as not many jobs were available to women and those that were available often did not pay well.

Historically, then, prostitution has been available in most cultures, and more available during certain periods than others. Prostitution apparently was usually neither totally embraced nor totally dismissed by the rest of society. It flourished in periods when the rest of the women in a given society (and wives, in particular) were extremely restricted socially and legally.

Becoming a Prostitute

What draws a female into prostitution? The most commonly cited factor is the need for money (James, 1977). In one study of 175 prostitutes, 85 to 95 percent were motivated by economic factors (Pomeroy, 1965). In the late 1970s, prostitutes at the upper end of the economic ladder could make $40,000 to $75,000 per year—a financial level unavailable to most women. Furthermore, prostitutes are usually in heavy demand, and little or no training is needed.

Another factor drawing females into

prostitution is what several authors have called *drift:* Women may drift into prostitution due to early life experiences. James and Meyerding (1977) examined the early sexual experiences of 328 prostitutes. They found that as adolescents these women were more likely than other adolescents to be sexually active and less likely to continue to have intercourse with their first coital partner. When asked if they had had early experience with an older person attempting sexplay or intercourse, 45 percent of the prostitute sample, compared with 24 to 28 percent of nonprostitute samples studied by other researchers (Gagnon, 1965; Kinsey et al., 1948), said "yes." Of a subsample of 136 prostitutes, 57 percent reported that they had been raped at least once in their lives, and of these, 36 percent reported multiple rapes. In summarizing their data, James and Meyerding (1977) concluded that sexual experiences may influence the drift of some women into prostitution by (1) the lack of parental guidance, which leads to early and casual sexual intercourse; (2) using sex as a short-term status symbol only to discover that others perceive this status in a way that makes the adolescent socially unacceptable; and (3) early experiences with incest and rape, which might teach a woman to use her sexuality as a commodity—to put a price on sex.

Other early experiences found to influence the development of prostitution include having a relative who is a prostitute, being institutionalized in a girls' home or youth center, early deviance (a broken home or premature withdrawal from high school), a juvenile record, early drug use, and a greater percentage of pregnancies lost in stillbirth, abortion, and miscarriage (James, 1977; James & Vitaliano, unpublished paper, 1981; Vitaliano, Boyer & James, 1981). Although many people believe that most prostitutes begin selling their sexual services because they need to support a drug habit, this, in fact, is not that frequently the case.

The idea of drifting from promiscuity to prostitution, or from mild deviance to greater deviance, is a process that eventually closes off other career avenues (Davis, 1971; Jackman, O'Toole, & Geis, 1963; Rosenblum, 1975). The drift may begin when a woman gets a reputation for being "fast" or "promiscuous," but once she is labeled as "that kind of woman," she begins to see herself as deviant. Since others do not accept her as nondeviant, she finds it difficult to alter her pattern.

Promiscuous is a label that is applied to juvenile females, but not males. Strouse (1972) reported numerous cases in which families referred their daughters to the police because the girls were suspected of being sexually active. Similarly, girls who are referred to juvenile authorities for acts of minor delinquency such as running away or petty larceny have routinely been given gynecological examinations to determine virginity, the possibility of pregnancy, or the presence of venereal disease (Chesney-Lind, 1973). On the other hand, boys are rarely condemned for being sexually active. In fact, males are usually indirectly or directly encouraged to be sexual. The result is that the *double standard*—one set of rules for men and another for women— which supposedly is used to protect females, may in reality do more to harm them. The restrictions are stronger, the range of acceptable sexual behavior far narrower, and the degree of punishment far more severe for girls than for boys.

Although many females become prostitutes because of unfortunate beginnings, not all are victims of a traumatic past. Some women choose prostitution because of the advantages it offers. For example, call girls often enjoy glamorous life-styles that would be unattainable for them under other circumstances (James, 1977). Prostitution also affords a level of control and self-sufficiency. The woman is in a position of power: She does not give anything away for free, and she may derive some satisfaction from the knowledge that a male will pay for access to her body.

Characteristics of Female Prostitutes

Most studies done on prostitutes draw subjects from small, select samples such as mental health patients or women who are in prison. The types of characteristics psychotherapists identify in prostitutes are low self-esteem, anxiety, "frigidity," hostility toward males, poor impulse control, subconscious homosexuality, mental defectiveness, and anger and rebellion toward fathers (e.g., Caprio, 1963; Segal, 1963; Rubin, 1961). However, in examining a larger random sample of women, research has shown that prostitutes do *not* differ

very much from normal controls (James, 1971, 1976, 1977). Most psychological and intellectual functioning in prostitutes has been reported to be within the normal range of the general population (Townes, James, & Martin, 1981).

From what little research is available, prostitutes as a group appear to be neither psychologically unique nor pathologically disturbed as measured by the results of standardized tests. What does separate prostitutes from most other women are personality patterns that are classified as antisocial and impulsive, with overexcitable, excessively active, and slightly more "masculine" (active, energetic) and less "feminine" (passive, receptive) social role qualities. Several conclusions can be drawn by combining this information with the greater frequency of abuse and neglect suffered during childhood, early introduction into sexual activity but not continuity with the first partner, and a greater incidence of lesbian relationships without adopting a lesbian identity or life-style. Although there is no single kind of person who becomes a prostitute, the life-style of a prostitute, whether she chooses it or accepts it only out of desperation, requires behaviors and attitudes that are atypical or deviant for women. Thus the women who become prostitutes may have experienced apparent promiscuity at an early age, while other women may be more generally antisocial, impulsive, and active/aggressive. And still other women may become more antisocial and deviant after they have been prostitutes since being a prostitute is by definition deviant in our society.

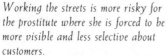
Working the streets is more risky for the prostitute where she is forced to be more visible and less selective about customers.

Selecting the purchase.

The Subculture of the Prostitute

The prostitute lives in an environment that is quite different from the norm. The people she is most involved with are pimps, bell-boys, bartenders, hotel clerks, other prostitutes, and, of course, her clients (Gagnon & Simon, 1973). Her contact with the larger society is often limited to the police, the courts, and those working in correctional facilities. That this subculture is very separate from the conventional world must be considered when the characteristics and life-style of the prostitute are evaluated.

> By this act of exclusion from the larger society, she is included in a set of relationships with the criminal world that complicate her life through contacts with narcotics, petty and major crime, and the corruptions of agencies of criminal justice. . . . At the same time, the existence of this [the prostitute's] culture means that the prostitute's capacity to return to the conventional society is reduced. (Gagnon & Simon, 1973, pp. 232–233)

☐ *The Role of the Pimp* Many prostitutes, especially streetwalkers, operate under the guidance of a pimp. Traditionally, **pimps** would find customers for prostitutes; more recently, the pimps, called *fast-steppers* or *players* (James, 1972), hire others to do this direct service while they collect, manage, and control the profits. They take care of bills, investments, clothes, entertainment, bribes, medical care, bail money, and lawyers' fees. Usually, the pimp is a man, but some lesbian prostitutes prefer to work for a female pimp.

In addition to acting as business manager, the pimp may provide support and protection for the prostitute. The ethic in the world of prostitution, much like the conventional world, is that a woman needs a man. Without a man, the prostitute may be in danger of being robbed and assaulted, and may not be respected by the rest of her subculture. In fact, the more successful a pimp (wealthy, good-looking, well-dressed), the more a prostitute's reputation will be enhanced. Thus, although society considers the prostitute's behavior to be deviant from that of the typical female model, the prostitute often takes on a very conventional role while interacting with her pimp. The prostitute-pimp relationship is all the more surprising because the prostitute financially supports her pimp. In the words of one prostitute interviewed by James (1977):

> I gave him all the money and, like I say, all my business was taken care of. If I went to jail I'd be right out, if I needed an attorney he'd pay for it, and he sent money to my kids, and he was always bringing me something. We had our little misunderstandings but nothing really serious. We did a lot of things together. . . . We traveled together, we even bought a house, but after the Feds were bothering me so we had to give it up. (p. 198)

The relationship with the pimp is also one of the few possible sources of emotional stability in the prostitute's life. Pimps and prostitutes rarely marry, although marriage is not an uncommon hope for a prostitute. Usually, prostitutes drift out of prostitution as they age; they tend to take legitimate jobs, go on welfare, or marry. Pimps, on the other hand, seldom exit from the "fast life" before they have become drug addicts,

Prostitutes are more likely to survive the fast life than are their pimps.

been imprisoned, or suffered some form of violence (Milner & Milner, 1972).

☐ *The Clients* In 1948, Kinsey and his associates reported that 69 percent of the men they surveyed had had some experience with prostitutes. Less than 20 percent of these men had more than a few contacts with prostitutes per year, with lower-socioeconomic status men and single men having more frequent contacts than married, higher-status men. Hunt's (1974) data suggest that the frequency of sexual contacts with prostitutes has decreased.

Not much research has focused on the client served by the prostitute. One researcher who studied a group of men who visited call girls identified nine classifications of male clients (Stein, 1974, 1977). For example, *opportunists* wanted sex without emotional demands or risks, whereas *guardians* preferred younger prostitutes with whom they could behave in a fatherly manner. This researcher found that prostitutes mostly provided a variety of services, sexual and nonsexual, to middle-aged professionals or businessmen who had no alternative sexual outlet.

Whether Stein's categorization can be applied to men who frequent other classes of prostitutes is not known. James (1977) has suggested a variety of other circumstances that may draw men to prostitutes. For example, men may seek the services of prostitutes in order to deal with sexual deprivation, as when they are in the armed forces or traveling; they may wish to avoid the risk of rejection because of physical handicaps; some men may have the desire to perform unusual sexual acts that regular partners won't perform or the men may not wish to suggest; prostitutes can satisfy the need for companionship or provide variety; some men may wish to avoid involvement; and for men experiencing erection problems, prostitutes can provide sexual involvement without any demands for performance. Some of the services provided by prostitutes and attitudes prostitutes have toward their clients are described in the following accounts offered by prostitutes (from Young, 1967):

And another thing; when I'm with a client I always put the rubber on him very gently, you know, stroking him and spinning it out as long as I can. "You ought to have been a nurse," they say. That's always what it makes them think of. And then with a bit of luck they come before they even get into me. When they do I look ever so loving and gentle and say: "Traitor!" Well, I'm not paid just to be a bag, am I? I'm paid to make them feel good. It's easy for me, so why not? That's how I see it. (p. 109)

I get my kicks from dancing, Latin American dancing mostly. I don't know, there's something about the movements. My first man was after a dance; I didn't know where I was. And the father of my child was after a dance too. It's always dancing with me. (p. 111)

Sandra would be no good on the game. She likes men and enjoys fucking. (p. 112)

You know, half my work's what we call social work. That is, say some friend of mine has someone come to London to visit his firm, and he gives him my number. I have connections with a lot of good firms. All right, he takes me out; dinner, a show, perhaps a party. I go down on his expense account, or something. It may lead to sex, it may not. Often it doesn't. I don't mind. In fact, I'm pleased. (p. 121)

Male Prostitution

The exact counterpart of female prostitution—a male paid for his sexual services by a female customer—is apparently very rare in almost all known cultures. The reasons for the infrequency of this activity are not certain, but speculations include the following:

Money—and who has it—
can determine the type of
sexualized entertainment
available.

1. Women can almost always find sexually cooperative males.
2. Women are not raised to believe that they "need" sexual release or that they are not biologically predisposed to need it.
3. Women are raised to view their self-worth in terms of their sexual desirability and having to pay for sex is demeaning, extremely socially deviant, and contrary to all traditional sex-role stereotypes about sexual assertiveness and initiation.
4. Most women do not have the financial resources to pay for sexual services.
5. Women simply do not have the desire for sexual exploration or unusual tastes in sexual practices.

Indeed, male prostitutes more commonly serve male homosexuals. Male prostitutes, or "hustlers," are classified much like female prostitutes; there are *street hustlers, bar hustlers,* and *call boys* (Ross, 1959). Street hustlers have the lowest social status, primarily because their work is more dangerous and less profitable. The self-concept of these men, or boys in certain cases, seems to vary. A study in the 1950s found that these males defined themselves as homosexual hustlers. In the 1960s and early 1970s the male prostitutes considered themselves neither homosexuals nor gay (Gagnon & Simon, 1973; Hoffman, 1972; Reiss, 1961). In fact, the male prostitute's success reportedly depends on his ability to present himself as exclusively heterosexual (Gagnon & Simon, 1973; Hoffman, 1974). More research is needed on male prostitutes who serve male clients because attitudes within and about the gay community and its members have changed within the last decade.

Several similarities surface when male and female prostitution are compared: Money is exchanged for sexual services, there are stratified ranks of prostitution, and youthful appearance is important. However, there are also some important differences between male and female prostitutes (see Gagnon & Simon, 1973, for more details). One difference is that the degree of anonymity can be far more important in the homosexual encounter. For example, the social repercussions are likely to be far less damaging if it becomes public knowledge

PROSTITUTION: TO CRIMINALIZE OR NOT?

In 1959, the United Nations Commission considered the pros and cons of whether prostitution should be a criminal offense. The commission presented the following arguments in favor of the criminalization of prostitution:

1. The question of public morals for public good is the responsibility of a government.
2. If prostitution is not made punishable, then abolishing the regulation of prostitution simply results in deregulated, clandestine prostitution replacing controlled prostitution.
3. If prostitution is not a punishable crime, it will be difficult to enforce legal protection of the prostitution of others.
4. If prostitution is legal, many females who might otherwise hesitate will be encouraged to become prostitutes.
5. Without prohibitions against prostitution, the public may assume that the government tolerates commercialized vice because it is necessary.

The commission's arguments against criminalization of prostitution include the following:

1. Prohibiting prostitution requires a definition of the term *prostitution*. A narrow definition would make it difficult to bring charges. A broad

that a well-known politician or businessman pays for heterosexual rather than for homosexual services (Lenzoff & Westley, 1956). Females who service men usually become prostitutes after a number of heterosexual experiences that do not involve payment. Many males prostitute themselves only under certain circumstances—perhaps when in need of money, or when traveling alone. Outside of these confined situations, a subgroup of these men will not engage in homosexual activities (Gagnon & Simon, 1973). Additionally, while the female prostitute is paid for giving her client an orgasm, the male prostitute serving a male is more likely to be paid for his own orgasm. Thus the number of contacts a male prostitute can have in one day is limited, as he is expected to

become aroused and ejaculate with each partner—a requirement that the female prostitute does not have to meet. Finally, a factor distinguishing prostitutes of each sex is that women are degraded for accepting payment for sex and also for paying for sex. Male prostitutes are less often degraded for the same activities.

Legal Issues and Prostitution

Legally, in the United States, anyone engaging in sex for money or anyone loitering and soliciting for that purpose is a prostitute and subject to arrest. Although arrests of male homosexual prostitutes are on the rise, they are still remarkably low, and in some states *only* women can be found definition could constitute an interference in private life, thus contradicting Article 12 of the Universal Declaration of Human Rights. Article 12 states that everyone has the right to lawful protection against interference with privacy, family, home, correspondence, and attacks upon one's honor and reputation.

2. Prostitution acts involve equal responsibility of client and prostitute. A law must not discriminate against women. In actual practice, only the prostitute receives the penalties.

3. There is a thin line between sex in prostitution and sex in other nonmarital contexts. Thus, to limit the penalty to individuals who meet the arbitrary criteria of legally defined prostitution would be unjust.

4. Penal law should not recognize every immoral act. Prostitution of minors, to protect them and maximize public order, along with soliciting for prostitution, may be prosecuted. However, adult prostitution should not be singled out from all other moral sins by bringing it under the jurisdiction of the law.

5. Past experience clearly proves that the criminalization of prostitution does not eliminate it. Instead, illegal prostitution becomes regulated by a criminal underground. As long as men provide the demand for prostitution, women will supply it.

6. Prohibiting prostitution requires police espionage and entrapment—activities detrimental to the common good—for enforcement.

7. Making prostitution illegal creates an antagonistic attitude between prostitutes and society, which hampers the chances for rehabilitation.

(Based on U.N. Study on Traffic in Persons and Prostitutes, ST/SDA/50/8, 1959, pp. 10–11.)

guilty of prostitution (James, 1977). Proof must be furnished that the prostitute, not the customer, proposed the sexual invitation. Sometimes this is done by having a plainclothes police officer pose as a potential client. Such circumstances, however, can sometimes be cited as entrapment— that is, tricking a person into doing something that he or she might otherwise not do. If entrapment is proven, conviction of the prostitute is impossible.

In 1973, 34,226 women were arrested for prostitution (FBI Crime Reports, 1974). Additionally, approximately 70 percent of women in prison were initially arrested for prostitution (James, 1977). The police generally arrest streetwalkers but rarely pursue call girls or women in prostitution houses. Within recent years, some people have objected to the fact that prostitutes are arrested but not their customers. A number of feminist writers and other researchers have pointed out that women are far more likely to be condemned for being sexually active than are men (Gagnon & Simon, 1973). In fact, the traditional view is that men are naturally promiscuous. In other words, "The prostitute is a *deviant* woman; her customer is a *normal* man" (James, 1977, p. 201).

Solutions: Revisions of the Law, Challenges to the Roles

The conclusions from the arguments of a 1959 United Nations Commission considering the criminalization of prostitution (see

Box 12–1) were that education and retraining for women would be better than prohibition of prostitution (U.N. Study on Traffic in Persons and Prostitutes, ST/SOA/50/8, 1959, pp. 10–11). Indeed, different nations have come up with different solutions. Many countries in South America, the Middle and Far East, and the Caribbean require prostitution houses to be licensed and prostitutes to have medical examinations. Many European countries (e.g., Britain, France, and Italy) and a hundred other U.N. members have long abandoned categorizing prostitution as a crime and have instead tried to discourage pimps and to control public solicitation (United Nations, 1951). On the other hand, in Cuba and Russia, heavy fines are imposed on customers, and prostitutes are sentenced to prison terms.

Some interesting approaches to dealing with prostitution are found in West Germany, Sweden, and Denmark. Sweden and Denmark require prostitutes to hold full-time legitimate jobs in addition to being prostitutes, and the West German government supports pimp-free prostitution hotels where women can work, live, and have mandatory medical examinations. China also has attempted some innovative methods of dealing with prostitution, and although accurate data are scarce, this country appears to be the only nation that has significantly reduced prostitution. In addition to more equal participation of the sexes in domestic and economic areas and an emphasis on discipline and commitment to Communist ideology, China imposes heavy prison sentences on customers, sentences prostitutes to five-year terms of "rehabilitation," and provides women with equal economic opportunities (James, 1977).

The United States clearly has a restrictive and criminalizing view of the prostitute. A case has been made for decriminalization of prostitution, which would mean that it would still be considered a crime, but there would be no victim (see Box 13–1). Decriminalization would permit the regulation of solicitation, age of consent, disease, taxation, and business zoning by a community. Decriminalization would also be restrictive and would not, as legalization might, necessarily give the message that prostitution is socially sanctioned as a respectable and viable business for all women to consider — a fear of many communities.

At the present time, however, the double standard still holds. As the 1959 U.N. report suggested and others have stated more directly (Gagnon & Simon, 1973; James, 1977), until both men's and women's views of sexuality are understood and accepted, and the position of women in the work force improves, prostitution will not be eliminated.

SUMMARY

1. Pornography and prostitution act in opposition to three basic sociosexual values: sex is a private activity; human sexual relationships are based on mutual consent and mutual personal interest; and although sex is a physical act, it has great human value in relation to many emotional reactions.

2. **Pornography** refers to specific depictions of sexuality that have the potential to be sexually arousing. It is not an easy term to define and, in fact, its definition has changed over the years in accordance with changing social attitudes. Pornography is sometimes connected with *obscenity,* which means dirt or filth, and at other times its meaning is based on *erotica,* from Eros, the god of love.

3. Early anti-obscenity rulings in seventeenth- and eighteenth-century England and America sought to restrict *blasphemy*—spoken or written pornographic pieces that mock the established religion—suggesting, for example, that the clergy were involved in illicit sexual activities. Laws have changed often since then, and rulings are often subjective, left to the discretion of the court. The First Amendment's guarantee of free speech is frequently cited in defense of pornography.

4. The behavioral effects of pornography are questionable. While some studies cite negative behavioral reactions (e.g., aggression, sex-related crimes) to exposure to pornographic material, others report no change at all. There is great concern about the way women are portrayed in pornography and how it colors societal attitudes about women. More research is needed to understand the function of pornography in society.

5. **Prostitution** is the exchange of sexual services for money. Prostitutes are most often females. Many people consider prostitution a morally objectionable practice, which is the primary reason why it is illegal in certain countries, including the United States, except for a few rural counties in Nevada.

6. Prostitution is one of the oldest professions, having been in existence for several thousand years. At some points in history prostitutes were respected citizens, such as the *hetaerae* of ancient Greece, who were well-educated, socially prominent, and influential women. Prostitutes have not always been so fortunate, however, During the Victorian period, for example, prostitutes were considered a necessary evil—useful in that they relieved the "good" women of performing sexual services for their husbands.

7. Why do women become prostitutes? The need for money and early life experiences, such as being molested as a child, are important factors

that contribute to many "drifting" into prostitution. Also, some women choose this life-style because it offers them advantages; call girls, for example, are well paid and have the opportunity to lead glamorous lives that might otherwise be out of their reach.

8. Characteristics common among prostitutes are frequency of neglect suffered during childhood, early experience in social deviance, early introduction into sexual activity with multiple partners, and a greater incidence of lesbian relationships, but not of a lesbian identity or life-style. Few personality characteristics or intellectual abilities distinguish prostitutes from nonprostitutes, although they do seem more antisocial, impulsive, overexcitable, excessively active, and less passive and receptive.

9. The **pimp** acts as business manager for the prostitute, as well as sometimes providing support, protection, and emotional stability for her. The prostitute is usually quite dependent on her pimp, although she financially supports him.

10. Men employ prostitutes for many reasons. For example, some men are isolated and are interested only in a sexual outlet; physically handicapped men will go to prostitutes to avoid rejection; a man desiring unusual sexual activities may decide to visit a prostitute; and men experiencing erection problems may find less pressure in a noncommittal sexual relationship with a prostitute.

11. Female prostitutes are most often arrested, as compared with male prostitutes, pimps, and clients. In recent years there has been a movement to decriminalize prostitution, but it has yet to succeed in the United States.

SUGGESTED READINGS

Dworkin, A. *Pornography: Men possessing women.* New York: Perigee (Putnam), 1981.

Griffin, S. *Pornography and silence: Culture's revenge against nature.* New York: Harper & Row, 1981. Two feminist accounts of the meaning and social price of pornography, which try to tie in the issue of pornography to broader cultural and historical trends.

Kronhausen, P., & Kronhausen, E. *Erotic art.* New York: Bell, 1968. A compilation of different types of erotic art, from primitive to modern, presented in an international 1968 exhibit in Sweden.

Stein, M. *Lovers, friends, slaves.* New York: Berkeley/GP Putnam's Sons, 1974. An account of research based on sixty-four New York City call girls and 1,242 upper-middle-class white customers. Stein spoke with prostitutes and observed sexual transactions through a variety of means.

CHAPTER FOURTEEN

SEX EDUCATION
Then and Now

The traditional course with children was to keep them in as great a degree of ignorance as parents and teachers could achieve.
Bertrand Russell: *The Taboo on Sex Knowledge*

Children's curiosity about sex and sex differences is natural.

*E*ducation about sex can and does take place in a variety of settings, from the lectures by trained professionals to the whispered conversations behind closed doors of 11 year olds. In fact, unquestionably, everyone who is reading this text has learned more about sexuality outside rather than inside the classroom. This statement is particularly true in regard to the values and ethics of sexuality. In this chapter, we examine how people learn about sex. We will look at both formal and informal methods of sex education.

We are all confronted, sometimes at a bewildering rate, with choices concerning sexuality. Being informed about sexuality has a much broader meaning than just knowing the mechanics of sex. The choice of a partner and the pattern and progression of sexual activity are shaped much less by knowledge of anatomy and physiology than by the emotional tone that surrounds sexual matters. The choice of whether or not to enter into a sexual relationship has powerful implications for both males and females. The personal consequences of a

Margaret Sanger: A pioneer in advocating birth control and family planning.

sexual relationship can be greatly rewarding or powerfully disappointing. On the practical side, pregnancy, sexually transmitted diseases, and abortion are serious realities. On the emotional side, love, security, and a fulfilling relationship are important potential rewards. The choice, therefore, should not be based on naive guesswork. Unfortunately, we do not know how much information is needed to make appropriate choices and intelligent, informed decisions.

For the most part, formal sex education in the first half of the twentieth century consisted of repression, suppression, and denial of sexuality. Parents, the educational system, and society tended to ignore the need for educating our youth about sex. Warnings and lessons in anatomy and phys-

iology have often been considered the only concerns of sex education. As Gagnon and Simon (1973) note, "the concept of sex education classes was that the teacher was imparting safety precautions such as those used in handling highly explosive materials" (p. 113). Educators and parents alike were terrified that discussing sex would tempt youngsters, and they would be more apt to become sexually active. The available books were not only heavily moralistic but also often full of misinformation.

Population growth provided the first incentive to establish formal sex education programs. In the United States, the cause of sex education was championed by Margaret Sanger, who wanted to promote "birth control," a term that she and her associates coined. Sanger became the focus of great controversy surrounding the distribution of information on contraceptives. In fact, in 1916 she was jailed for opening a birth control clinic and making contraceptive information available. Many assumed that advocacy of birth control was advocacy of promiscuity. Actually, Sanger was quite traditional in her views on sexuality. She wrote a marriage manual that contained very little startling or controversial material. Regardless of the actual nature of her beliefs on sexuality, however, Sanger and the family planning movement were responsible for much of the early interest in sex education.

Today the Sex Information and Education Council of the United States (SIECUS) is the most influential nongovernmental organization; its primary goal is the advancement of sex education. SIECUS has been attacked by groups and individuals who oppose sex education, and controversy still surrounds the organization and its leaders.

ISSUES IN THE SEX EDUCATION CONTROVERSY

Sex education generates a great deal of tension and high levels of emotion in many people. Some specific concerns of anti-sex education groups include information content, qualifications of teachers, and the removal of sex education from the home. Lentz (1972) cites the parent who was concerned over a "pilot class (co-ed, I might add) where the rawest facts on dating, necking, petting, emotions, pregnancy, the pill and contraception were discussed."

Many people are concerned that teachers of sex education may not only be unqualified but also a threat to children. The worry is that teacher's personal problems with sexuality will be reflected in the quality and content of sex education courses. Further, there is a concern that some teachers will pose a direct threat to students (Lentz, 1972). Teacher qualification is an issue that cannot be disregarded: Allowing unqualified and unprepared teachers to conduct sex education courses is unthinkable.

Finally, some parents are concerned that removing sex education from the home gives school authorities the responsibility of making decisions about what children will learn and how, and they worry that the values taught in the classroom will differ from those held at home (Lentz, 1972). Moving sex education into the schools is seen by opponents as a very serious and direct threat to family stability and to society at large. Involving parents in the development of sex education courses should be reassuring for some people.

What are the reasons for advocating formal sex education? A general statement strongly supporting sex education was made by the President's Commission on Pornography and Obscenity (Commission Report, 1970):

> Failure to talk openly and directly about sex has several consequences. It overemphasizes sex, gives it a magical, non-natural quality, making it more attractive and fascinating. It diverts the expression of sexual interest out of more legitimate channels, into less legitimate channels. Such failure makes teaching children and adolescents to become fully and adequately functioning sexual adults a more difficult task. And it clogs legitimate channels for transmitting sexual information and forces people to use clandestine and unreliable sources.

The commission's goal of directing or guiding sexual interests into "legitimate channels" is similar to the goal of the opponents of sex education. There is, of course, great disagreement on how best to accomplish this aim.

A second major reason for supporting sex education is that such programs may help solve some of the social ills that arise either directly or indirectly from sexuality. Many groups interested in dealing with the problems of unwanted pregnancy, sexually transmitted diseases, abortion, population control, and the like turn to sex education as a means of coping with these problems. For example, over 1 million teenagers become pregnant in this country each year and over two-thirds of those pregnancies are unintended (Alan Guttmacher Institute, 1976). Advocates of sex education argue that information on birth control techniques may help to deal with this serious problem. Furthermore, they argue, the family may actually be a poor vehicle for transmitting sex education. As explained by Hottois and Milner (1975):

> Those favoring sex education in the schools are more willing to transfer the responsibility of much of sex education away from the family. They view the family as perhaps ideally the most proper source of sexual information, but insist that, like other subjects, sex and sexuality have become far too complex and technical to leave to the typical parent, who is either uninformed or too bashful to share useful sexual information with his child. Parents simply do not have the qualifications that a correctly trained schoolteacher has. (Hottois & Milner, 1975, p. 6)

If parents are to teach their children about sexuality, they must acknowledge the sexual nature of their children and be willing to expose to their children their own sexuality. Concerns over modesty and the hesitancy of parents to discuss sexual activities are readily understood. Many parents avoid discussion of such topics because they are anxiety producing (Gagnon & Simon, 1973).

The final major argument in support of sex education stresses the importance of teaching and developing the values of the students. As it was put by one program in sex education, the goals are" ... increasing self-awareness, catalyzing individual thought, critical self-assessment, and—through a confrontation with diversity—value clarification" (Morrison & Price, 1974, p. 10).

ATTITUDES TOWARD SEX EDUCATION

Both sides in the sex education battle argue that their view is widely held. In reality, most people are not terribly excited about sex education, unless there is a direct issue facing them, such as a program proposed in a local school; then the likelihood of becoming involved increases. In general, the controversy generates only occasional battles. Some data, however, have been collected about the attitudes and views held by various groups of people surveyed. The clearest finding is that attitudes toward sex education have been relatively stable over a long period of time, with most people supporting the concept of sex education in our schools. Nevertheless, those opposing sex education are often quite effective in blocking or modifying proposed programs.

Box 14-1

RELIGIOUS ORGANIZATIONS IN SEX EDUCATION

Many would assume that much of the resistance to formal sex education comes from the views and teachings of religious organizations. Such is definitely not the case, and what follows is a brief description of some of the better-known church-affiliated efforts in sex education. These examples are clear indicators that sex education is seen as a valuable and worthwhile enterprise by many within the church.

The United Church of Christ has developed the "Neighbors in Need" program. One of the projects in this program deals specifically with teenage pregnancy, offering pregnancy prevention information and supporting services that provide family planning information. The program has given grants of up to $10,000 to agencies that provide support and services to pregnant teens and their families. They also fund organizations that counsel teenagers on contraceptives. The United Church of Christ has been active in contacting affiliated churches to determine the need for direct confrontation of sexuality issues within the Church.

SOURCES AND QUALITY OF SEX INFORMATION

We all learn about sexual concepts and develop attitudes toward sexuality. Where do we get our information? At what age do we get it? Is the information adequate, or is it often incorrect?

Researchers agree that sex information is obtained mainly from same-sex peers. Various investigators have found differing percentages when inquiring how much was learned from what source, but all report that peers are the largest single source of sex information. Others include parents, schools, the mass media, books, and siblings. Table 14–1 summarizes the findings of four representative studies on the source of sex information; after peers, books and printed materials are second, and parents a distant third. According to these studies, school or formal sex education programs contribute little to the sex education of our youth.

"Catholic Alternatives," an organization affiliated with the Roman Catholic Church, first became involved with sex education by opening a counseling center. Eventually, workshops for teenagers were formed; they provide information on pregnancy prevention, sexually transmitted diseases, and other topics generally included in sex education programs. In addition, the National Catholic Education Program claims that about one-half of youngsters in grades 9 through 12 in Roman Catholic parochial schools are involved in sex education programs.

The Unitarian Universalist Association has developed a multimedia program in sex education. This group uses filmstrips, photographs, and recordings to create an open environment in which the discussion of issues and concerns over sexuality can freely take place. Booklets covering topics such as masturbation, birth control, and sexual anatomy are made available. The discussion sessions, often held in church facilities, are usually conducted in small groups, each headed by trained leaders, one male and one female.

The point to be made here is that all people who believe in Christian theology are not automatically sexually repressed, nor opposed to formal sex education programs. Many responsible church groups are advocating the need for sex education. Most of the available programs stress the needs of teenagers and the role of sexuality in the family.

TABLE 14-1   SOURCES OF INFORMATION CONCERNING SEX

| | ATHANSIOU (1970) | | HUNT (1974) | | KINSEY (1953)* | | SCHOFIELD (1973)* | |
	MALES	FEMALES	MALES	FEMALES	MALES	FEMALES	MALES	FEMALES
Peers	64%	51%	59%	46%	61%	39%	74%	81%
Parents	8	17	9	17	5	14	18	31
School	3	3	3	5	1	5	5	8
Books	23	23	20	22			26	20
Mixed & Others	2	6	9	10	33	42		

*Includes "workmates," and respondents could give more than one answer.

Supporters of sex education often assume that the anti-sex education forces are composed primarily of individuals who are politically conservative. Indeed, Hottois and Milner (1975) suggest that the anti-sex education movement reflects values relating to issues beyond sex education. A study by Mahoney (1979) investigated that possibility and found that this stereotype does not hold. In this study, anti-sex education views were associated with "traditional orientation toward the family, the women's place being in the home, and premarital sex. To a much lesser extent, social class indicators, attitudes toward education, and political liberalism-conservatism are important" (Mahoney, 1979, p. 273).

Table 14-1 also shows that young women are told more by their parents than are young men. We do not learn from this table, however, anything about the quantity or quality of parental information; nor does it tell us about differing roles for mothers and fathers.

Several other researchers have reported on the role that parents play in the sex education of their children. One group found that about 80 percent of the individuals surveyed reported either very little or no discussion of sex in their home (Anthansiou, Shaver, & Tavris, 1970). Note, however, that this study and others reported that young adults expressed a wish that their parents had been more open about sex and that they had been a more reliable source of sex information.

Most parents discuss sex with their children only when forced to do so by circumstances (Gagnon & Roberts, 1983; Angelino & Mech, 1955). Believing that their children will have fewer problems, parents tend not to educate them about sexual matters; instead, they usually give information after problems have arisen. Most parental information, moreover, is presented in a negative vein that emphasizes problems and seldom notes the positive aspects of sex (Spanier, 1971). Libby and Nass (1971) found that 60 percent of the parents said they would attempt to prevent and control the premarital sexual activity of their daughters, whereas only 15 percent would

Many parents fail to adequately discuss sex with their children.

support their daughters and/or give contraceptive advice.

All investigators studying parental involvement in sex education report that mothers are much more likely than fathers to discuss sexual issues, although mothers will usually discuss only relatively impersonal topics (Gagnon & Roberts, 1983). For example, researchers noted that advice concerning menstruation was offered most often to daughters in comparison to other sex-related topics, and it was given almost exclusively by mothers (Angelino & Mech, 1955). One reason may be that mothers talk more to daughters about all topics, or perhaps menstruation is a "safe topic" that permits the opportunity for mothers to give "warnings" to daughters.

Although parents seem reluctant to discuss sex with their children, research shows that parent-child discussions about sex might be valuable. In the words of one group of researchers, "Our review of the literature . . . has consistently indicated that children whose parents talk to them about sex do in fact delay their first intercourse longer than children whose parents avoid sex education, and these children

tend to use contraception when they do have intercourse" (Gordon, Scales, & Everly, 1979, p. 164). That finding suggests that parents who do provide sex education have considerable impact. Indeed, parents may well be excellent sources of information on sex, but the problem of how to develop this source is not easily solved.

In recent years, three changes have been reported regarding the source of sex education (Gebhard, 1977). First, mothers are more involved; second, sex education in our schools has increased; and third, sex is treated more explicitly in the mass media.

Accuracy of Informally Acquired Sex Information

Many studies have documented the range and depth of people's ignorance about sexual matters. In particular, interest has focused on misinformation about birth control practices, where errors can lead to unwanted pregnancies and the serious complications that may result. For example, 20 percent of clients at a Planned Parenthood clinic thought douching was a reliable contraceptive practice (Goldsmith et al., 1972), and 66 percent of male high school students did not know that withdrawal is an unreliable method of birth control (Finkel & Finkel, 1975). One group of researchers reported that 25 percent of young women at a Planned Parenthood clinic believed that teenage boys need to have regular coitus or they will go "crazy," and 50 percent believed that masturbation may be harmful to the mind or body (Goldsmith et al., 1972). Some of these misconceptions could greatly increase the likelihood of an unwanted pregnancy. This is particularly true, since we know that "feeling safe" is a major reason for not using effective contraception (Zelnik, 1979).

Misinformation about sex knows no educational limits; even among medical students, misconceptions are common. For example, 15 percent of medical students surveyed believed that masturbation can cause medical problems (Lief and Karlen, 1976). Misinformation emanating from this sector is especially disturbing when one realizes that many people turn to physicians for what they assume is accurate information about sex.

Age of Information Acquisition

The age at which information about sex is acquired is of considerable importance because formal sex education that occurs after informal acquisition may be ignored or misinterpreted. When we examine the data relating to the age at which information is acquired, we find that it varies in at least two ways. First, people do not learn everything at once, and some types of information are learned before others. For example, young people usually learn of the existence of intercourse before they learn of the concept of sexually transmitted diseases (Gebhard, 1977; Ramsey, 1943). Second, in general, boys learn about sexual matters before girls, although that tendency appears to be lessening (Gebhard, 1977). We find that by age 15 both boys and girls have been exposed to a great deal of sex information. The data indicate, then, that if sex education is to occur before ideas have been shaped, it must begin before children reach high school age. A very strong argument therefore can be made for starting sex education programs in elementary school.

Gagnon and Roberts (1983) found that when asked about the age at which children should be exposed to sexual topics, parents of young children inevitably suggest an age later than their child's present age. That is, parents wish to delay their role as sex educators as long as possible, and many may wish to extend their children's "innocence" concerning sexuality. If parents wait for the child to question them, however, the burden of sex education falls on the child; it becomes the child's responsibility. Also, waiting until the "ideal" age will generally find parents talking to children who have learned about various aspects of sex, correctly or incorrectly, from other sources (Gagnon & Roberts, 1983). Parental sex education, by and large, can be characterized as too little, too late. Parents must face these issues if they wish to have a say about sex education.

Most early information about sex comes from one's peers.

THE SEX EDUCATION PROGRAM

A report analyzing school-based sex education programs listed the eleven most commonly covered topics (Kirby, Alter, and Scales, 1979). These topics are listed here in the order established by the people surveyed. Not all topics are covered in all courses, and the emphasis may vary from one program to another. Bear in mind that these topics are the ones generally taught, but not necessarily the ones that should be taught.

1. Human Sexuality as an Aspect of Total Personality
2. The Individual Student's Values
3. The Advantages and Disadvantages of Different Contraceptive Methods
4. Methods of Improving Communication Skills
5. The Effective Use of Different Contraceptive Methods
6. Decision-making and Problem-solving Techniques
7. Techniques for Resisting Peer Pressure to Have Unwanted Sexual Experiences
8. Premarital Sexual Activity
9. Emotional and Social Aspects of Sexual Behavior
10. Masturbation
11. Homosexuality

THE EFFECTS OF SEX EDUCATION

Some people worry that providing sex education will unleash sexual permissiveness and break down the moral fiber of our society. Others argue that without sex education there is no hope of limiting sexually transmitted diseases and unwanted pregnancies. Where lies the truth? Jacqueline Voss (1980) has provided a careful and insightful review of the effects of sex education. The next section presents Voss's four principal goals of sex education and her assessment of how well they are being met.

Goals of Sex Education

The first goal proposed by Voss is that sex education should *provide accurate information and eliminate myths and misconceptions;* of the four proposed goals, this one is the most commonly achieved. A number of studies have reported that sex education increases sex information (e.g., Mims, Brown, & Lubow, 1976; Reichalt and Werley, 1976). For example, Reichalt and Werley (1976) looked at the effects of "rap sessions" on the contraceptive knowledge of a group of young women at a Planned Parenthood center. In pretesting, only 11 percent of the questions on birth control were correctly answered, while one month after the session the percentage correct was 70. Although a control group was absent, indications are that information on contraceptives was absorbed.

Although accurate information is no guarantee that correct decisions will be made, it would seem that the lack of correct information would not be beneficial. Voss and McKillip (1979), however, reported that their control group (individuals who did not take the course) showed changes in knowledge equal to class participants in a sex education course, making the evidence supporting the value of knowledge acquisition less impressive than might otherwise be expected.

Voss's second goal of sex education is that it should *promote tolerant attitudes* and aid in participants' acceptance of others whose views and behaviors are different (Voss, 1980). Many studies indicate that attitudes of students in sex education courses are modified in a more tolerant direction (Voss & McKillip, 1979; Orlovick, 1979; Zuckerman, Tushop, & Finner, 1976). However, several qualifications must be made about these findings. First, people often will not change their attitudes about controversial topics such as abortion (Mims et al., 1976; Lamberti & Chapel, 1977); thus, if misconceptions and prejudices are strongly rooted, a single sex education course is not likely to change them. Also, a considerable difference often exists between attitude shift and behavior changes. Attitude measures may reflect only what the course participant thinks the educator wishes to hear. For example, saying, in response to a questionnaire, that one no longer views homosexuals as being perverted is much different from accepting a gay person into one's circle of friends.

Voss proposed, as the third goal, that sex education courses should be designed to promote the *solution of social problems,* such as reducing the incidence of sexually transmitted diseases and unwanted pregnancies (Voss, 1980). A search of the literature provides partial evidence that sex education can help to solve these problems. For example, Shipley (1974) found that in a college course on contraceptive use, the number of students using effective means of contraception increased 33 percent, while no use of contraceptives or their ineffective use declined 57 percent. Of particular interest, the use of contraceptives changed while attitudes toward contraception did not change.

The final goal offered by Voss suggests that sex education should *open communication* and *ease relationships* between the sexes. No researchers have tried to determine whether or not sex education has met this goal.

Does Sex Education Affect Sexual Activity?

None of the goals noted by Voss touches on the most controversial issue: Does sex education change the sexual behavior of the participants? Among anti-sex education forces, this issue is the one that most concerns them. The few studies that have examined behavioral aspects show minor changes. For example, one study of college students, which reported the greatest amount of behavioral change of any study to date, found increases only for males, and mainly in those activities already practiced (Zuckerman, Tushop, & Finner, 1976). Another study found that college students in a sex education course and those in a control group showed equal amounts of change in their sexual behavior (Bernard, 1973).

The most extensive evaluation of the effects of formal sex education was based on a national probability sample of male and female college students (Spanier, 1976, 1977, 1978). This researcher examined what kind of effect, if any, a course in sex education had on class participants' involvement

in premarital heterosexual activity. He found that having been in a sex education class did not predict or result in any increases in premarital sex. He also found that explaining birth control methods in a sex education course was unrelated to premarital heterosexual activity. Spanier's findings, then, do not suggest that formal sex education courses lead to increased sexual activity.

Sex Education for Health Professionals

Many people turn to physicians and other health professionals for information and advice concerning sexual matters. Naturally, most people assume that physicians are knowledgeable about sex since they have to learn about the body and its functions. Unfortunately, very often physicians, nurses, and other health professionals are not well educated in this area, and, therefore, their advice is based on personal biases and views and not on a foundation of solid information. Let's look at some examples of advice given by well-known and respected physicians to show how misinformed the well educated can be.

Dr. Benjamin Spock has written many articles on child care, which have been widely read and accepted. Yet when writing on nudity, he unquestioningly advocated a Freudian model, by recommending that parents should avoid being naked in front of their children (Spock, 1975). The problem is not so much whether his views are correct but the stating as fact what is, at best, an unsubstantiated theoretical hypothesis. A more extreme example can be found in the widely read bestseller, *Everything You Always Wanted to Know About Sex (But Were Afraid To Ask)* by David Reuben, M.D. (1969). That book not only contains many opinions that are presented as fact but also numerous inaccuracies. For example, Reuben states that homosexuals are doomed to a life of dissatisfaction and unhappiness. He reasons that "tragically there is no possibility of satisfaction because the formula is wrong. One penis plus one penis equals nothing" (Reuben, 1969, p. 143). Such quasi-scientific statements are not only incorrect but also help to perpetuate the myth that homosexuals are by nature unhappy and disturbed, which simply is not true. The point to be made is that physicians are as much in need of sex education as everyone else.

Many medical schools are attempting to remedy this lack by incorporating sex education into the curricula. In 1960, only three medical schools had such programs, but by 1974, 106 medical schools had included human sexuality courses in their curriculum (Lief, 1978). Most of the programs are sensitive to the fact that the health professional must be aware of his or her own anxieties, concerns, attitudes, and moral positions and how they affect decisions about and the handling of patients.

Sex education for the health professional follows a logical sequence. The American Association of Sex Educators, Counselors, and Therapists (AASECT, 1973), proposed one such program that offered the following topics:

1. The Process of Reproduction
2. Sexual Development
3. Sexual Functioning
4. Sexual Behavior
5. Sex and Gender
6. Marriage, Family, and Interpersonal Relationships
7. Sex and Health
8. The Study of Sex

Of course, many topics are covered under each of the major headings, and some of the topics overlap with the content of sex education courses in general. Of interest is that the proposed program makes no attempt to develop sex therapists. The training of a sex therapist is more complex and time-consuming than can be undertaken in the basic training of health professionals.

Physicians and other health professionals often avoid discussing sexual issues with patients, and yet clearly patients often want and need such conversations (Kolodny, Masters, & Johnson, 1979). Avoidance of sexual issues is widespread in medical training and should not continue. The health professions need to acknowledge not only the importance of sexuality in the lives of their patients, but also the effects that medical procedures often have upon sexual functioning (Geer & Messe, 1982). For example, many men assume that removal of the prostate means that orgasm in intercourse will be impossible. That is not true; furthermore, researchers have shown that information from the surgeon can alleviate fears and promote continued sexual activity on the part of the patient (Zohar et al., 1976).

"CONTINUING SEX EDUCATION" OR ADULT SEX EDUCATION

Much of what we have said concerning sex education applies only to formal programs for young people. But what about those of us who have reached adulthood and no longer have the opportunity to benefit from these programs? Does sex education stop or is it a continuing process? The obvious answer is that our education about sex and sexuality does not stop. We are continually exposed to conditions that modify our attitudes and our behavior concerning sexual matters. Many of these experiences are not designed to change attitudes and behaviors, and since they are not planned and purposeful, their effect may be great or small, positive or negative.

Private interpersonal experiences make up the most common form of sex education for all age groups, and some cultures have programmed interpersonal sex education. For example, the Trobriand and Lepcha had older and sexually experienced members of the respective tribes teach sex to the younger members by having intercourse with them (Ford & Beach, 1951). Another category of experiences that make up adult sex education include those experiences that are shared with substantial numbers of other people, such as changes in laws concerning sexuality; the media, including magazines, movies, and advertisements; marriage and/or self-help sex manuals; and sex therapy.

The media have a powerful influence on sexuality, although exactly how is not well understood. The discussion in Chapter Thirteen on erotic material describes some of the effects of public erotic material. Our only intent in this chapter is to emphasize that the constant bombardment of society with sexuality by the media is a form, for better or worse, of public sex education.

The other two categories of adult sex education, marriage and/or self-help manuals and sex therapy, deserve more detailed coverage. Much more is known about the influence of these categories in the field of adult sex education.

Marriage Manuals and Self-Help Manuals

The marriage manual has an interesting and varied history across many cultures. Designed to teach sexual skills to individuals and couples, the writings themselves were often erotic in nature and thus served to train people in some rewarding techniques while also arousing them. In the United States, however, adult sex education until quite recently was limited almost exclusively to the marriage manual. The first books on this topic were *Important Facts for Young Men* and *The Secret Habits of the Female Sex*, both written around 1850. These manuals concentrated on the "destructive" effects of masturbation (Tebbel, 1976). Marriage manuals became very popular during the twentieth century and provided a range of information and opinions on sexual matters.

Box 14–2

THE BEDCHAMBER AND PILLOW BOOKS OF OLD CHINA AND JAPAN

Many people know that the Islamic and Indian subcultures produced manuscripts and art work that dealt extensively with sexuality; the *Kama Sutra* and *The Perfumed Garden of the Sheikh Nefzaoui* are among the best-known examples of those works. It is less well known that explicit sexual materials were used in ancient China and Japan as a means of sexually educating the people.

The Chinese sex manuals were called the *fang chung,* the literal interpretation of which is "inside the bedchamber." These "bedchamber books," which were based on Taoist religious teachings, appeared very early in Chinese history, and possibly as early as the Han dynasty (206 B.C. to 220 A.D.). According to Taoist teachings, the interaction of opposing forces throughout nature, such as the rain from heaven mixing with the earth, results in the continued rebirth and revitalization of all nature. The two cosmic forces that were at work throughout the universe were given the names *yin* and *yang*. *Yin* came to mean the earth, the moon, and most importantly for our purposes, female. *Yang* became the heavens, the sun, and male.

This religious view on the dual nature of the universe and the influences and powers within it had specific implications for sexuality. For example, bearing children, and sexual intercourse as well, were very important. Children were seen as an integral part of the universe and a product of its continual process of rebirth and development. Also, it was believed that the well-being of dead ancestors in the hereafter depended on the continued sacrifices of their descendants. Thus, individuals had a responsibility to their ancestors and ultimately to themselves to reproduce so that someone would be able to continue the sacrifices.

Beyond its purpose of producing children, intercourse was believed to be crucial to the continuing health and vitality of both men and women. According to the Taoist viewpoint, the health and vitality of both sexes depend on an adequate supply and appropriate balance of *yin* and *yang*. The belief was that during intercourse the sexually aroused female produced abundant amounts of the *yin* essence, and absorbed her partner's *yang* essence released during ejaculation. Further, it was believed that high levels of *yin* in a female were beneficial for her male partner because his *yang* force was fed and nourished by absorbing *yin* from his sexual partner through the penis during intercourse. Because Taoists believed, however, that the male lost a great deal of *yang* energy during ejaculation, men withheld ejaculation as long as possible to preserve their own *yang* while at the same time producing high levels of arousal and preferably orgasm in their partner so as to absorb as much of her *yin* as possible. The ideal situation would be intercourse with many women in which the woman but not the man experienced orgasm (Bullough, 1976).

An illustration taken from a Japanese pillow book.

The Chinese "bedchamber books" were used mainly by wealthy, upper-class males. The books described thirty positions for sexual intercourse and often illustrated the positions. In addition, they offered hints on ways to improve sexual relations. Women were not permitted, however, to know the "real" reasons for or the secrets behind the suggestions. The content of the Chinese bedchamber books changed somewhat over time. For example, they offered cures for sexual problems and treatments designed to change the size or shape of the genitals. These manuals gradually became less popular, and by 1300 A.D. they were rarely found.

Apparently, the Japanese "pillow books" were adaptations from the Chinese manuals, but they were different in several important respects (Bullough, 1976). Perhaps the most important difference is that the Japanese pillow books were not as closely involved with religious teachings that promoted a form of conflict between the sexes. They also presented sex and intercourse as natural functions that were the right of everyone. Within this setting, sex education became a natural and proper direction to follow, and the pillow books became the primary form of sex education throughout Japanese history. In fact, as late as the 1930s some traditional Japanese department stores included a "pillow book" among a bride's purchases (Rawson, 1968).

The pillow books were designed to be used by marital partners during their sexual activities, giving instructions in sexual techniques as well as providing erotic stimulation. Erotic art was often included in the books, and the artists exaggerated male and sometimes female genital size to give dramatic emphasis and focus (Rawson, 1968).

The use of pillow books is an example of how a culture can approach sexuality from a direction that is dramatically different from Western society. Indeed, sex education was not considered a controversial issue, but was viewed as the right of members of the society. We have not as yet developed such an open perspective on sex education.

One of the earliest popular marriage manuals published in England and widely distributed in the United States was *Married Love: A New Contribution to the Solution of Sex Difficulties* (Stopes, 1918). This book was published through 1943. Sanger, too, wrote a widely read marriage manual, *Happiness in Marriage* (Sanger, 1926). But perhaps the most influential of all marriage manuals was written in 1926 by a Dutch gynecologist, Dr. Th. H. Van DeVelde, entitled *Ideal Marriage: Its Physiology and Technique;* the book is still available in bookstores. Van DeVelde was the first to publicly advocate oral sex, which he called the "genital kiss." He also believed mutual orgasm to be the ultimate sexual experience. Regardless of the sex bias in *Ideal Marriage,* for its time (and to many people even now) the book was more sensitive, especially to the needs of women, than was typical.

Current Marriage Manuals

Has the marriage manual disappeared? No. The modern marriage manual takes form in current books on self-help and sex. These manuals base their suggestions and views on some of the findings of current sex researchers and therapists. Several of the modern self-help or self-educational texts are basically pictorial, such as *The Sex Book: A Modern Pictorial Encyclopedia,* Goldstein & Haeberle, (1971); and *The Picture Book of Sexual Love,* Harkel (1969).

Modern marriage manuals differ from earlier texts in that they stress self-help. The popularity of many of these texts should be emphasized, as they confirm the need for sex education at all age levels. A wide range of self-help manuals are available. The development of adult sex education through such books represents an awareness of the special needs and interests of individual groups. Despite their popularity, however, the effectiveness of these new sex manuals is unknown.

Sex Therapy

Sex therapy qualifies as another form of adult sex education. A discussion of the concepts and views of sex therapy is available in Chapter Eight; we concentrate here on how sex therapy functions as a method of adult sex education.

The prototype of sex therapy is the Masters and Johnson (1973) approach to sexual problems. Sex therapy that directly treats problematic behavior by providing explicit instructions is a form of sex education. Clients are shown where they have been mistaken about certain sexual topics, and they are given specific tasks to practice. These tasks are designed to change sexual behavior directly, and they often have the effect of changing attitudes and views on sexuality. That some clinical practitioners may prefer not to view themselves as educators does not change the fact that they are teachers—teachers of adult sex education. On the other hand much of current sex therapy involves a lot more than simply giving out information. So, while sex therapy is a form of education, it has important components in addition to the dispensing of knowledge.

SUMMARY

1. People who oppose sex education programs are worried about the information content of the programs, the qualifications of teachers, and the removal of sex education from the home.

2. A number of reasons are cited in support of sex education. The President's Commission on Pornography and Obscenity suggests that sex education is necessary to guide sexual interests into "legitimate channels." Second, these programs may be effective in dealing with social ills such as unwanted pregnancy, sexually transmitted diseases, abortion, and population control. Third, because parents generally do not deal well with instructing their children about sexual matters, children need an alternative, a more dependable source, such as formal sex education programs. The final argument in support of these programs stresses the importance of teaching and developing the values of students.

3. Attitudes towards sex education have not changed much over time with most people supporting the idea.

4. Same-sex peers are the most common source of sex information. Other sources include parents, school, the mass media, books, and siblings.

5. There are a great many misconceptions about human sexual behavior. Misinformation regarding birth control practices, for example, can be serious, leading to unwanted pregnancies and the complications that can develop from them. Inaccurate information about sex knows no educational limits; teenagers as well as medical students are misinformed about sexual issues.

6. The age at which people learn about sex is important because formal education that occurs after informal acquisition may be ignored or misinterpreted. In determining the "best" age at which to educate youth about sex, certain points should be considered. First, people do not learn everything at one time and some types of information are learned first. Second, boys generally learn about sex before girls, although this trend is changing. The suggestion, therefore, is that sex education should begin prior to high school, perhaps in elementary school before ideas have been shaped.

7. One researcher, Jacqueline Voss, prepared a review of the effects of sex education; she presented its four principal goals and evaluated their success. The goals proposed are that sex education should provide accurate information and eliminate myths and misconceptions; it should promote tolerant attitudes and help participants to accept others whose views and behaviors are different; it should be designed to promote the solution of social problems, such as reducing the incidence of sexually

transmitted diseases; and finally, it should open communication and ease relationships between the sexes.

8. According to research on the effect of sex education on sexual activity, sex education appears not to have any significant effect on behavior patterns and does not corrupt our youth.

9. Interestingly, many health professionals are not well educated in sexual matters. Many medical schools have therefore incorporated sex education programs into their curriculum within the past decade.

10. People never stop learning about sex, and so adult sex education is important. Interpersonal relationships are crucial. Other important influences are the media, marriage and/or self-help manuals, sex therapy, and changes in laws regarding sexuality.

SUGGESTED READINGS

Hottois, J., & Milner, N. A. *The sex education controversy: A study of politics, education, and morality.* Lexington, Mass.: Heath, Lexington Books, 1975. A book that not only explores the issues surrounding sex education but also provides research relevant to understanding the problem.

Teenage pregnancy: The problem that hasn't gone away. New York: The Alan Gutmacher Institute, 1981. A well documented and interesting presentation of the problems involved in teenage pregnancy.

Van De Velde, T. H., *Ideal marriage: Its physiology and techniques.* New York: Random House, revised 1974. The most influential of all marriage manuals first published in 1926 and still available in bookstores.

GLOSSARY

abortion The removal of an embryo or fetus from the uterus before it can survive alone; spontaneous abortions occur from natural causes; induced abortions are deliberately induced.

abrupto placentae A complication of pregnancy that occurs when the placenta prematurely separates from the uterus; may be accompanied by shock and heavy bleeding.

agape A spiritual form of love as named by the Greeks.

aldosterone A hormone produced in both sexes by the adrenal gland that acts as an androgen.

alveoli The structures within the breast from which milk is secreted; the milk glands.

amniocentesis A procedure used to obtain a sample of the amniotic fluid from the uterus of a pregnant woman so that it may be tested to determine if genetic or biochemical disorders are present in the developing fetus.

anal intercourse The penetration of the anus by the penis.

androgens The class of hormones that promote the development and functioning of male genitals and induces the development of male's secondary sex characteristics; includes testosterone, aldosterone, and androsterone.

androsterone A hormone produced by the conversion of testosterone by the liver; acts as an androgen and is found in the urine.

anus The opening of the bowel to the exterior.

anxiety reduction A major goal of sex therapy in order to treat most dysfunctions.

areola The darkly pigmented area around the nipple.

artificial insemination Introducing semen into the vagina or uterus other than by coitus to induce pregnancy.

attempted rape Legally, if penetration does not occur for some reason, this may be the charge.

attraction Interest in and a sense of being drawn to an individual, sexual attraction is a special form in which sexual feelings clearly are involved in the allure charm.

autoeroticism Self-stimulation of the genitals, or masturbation.

autonomic branch A branch or division of the peripheral nervous system that controls smooth (involuntary) muscles and glands; it is further divided into two divisions, the sympathetic and the parasympathetic.

Bartholin's glands A pair of glands located under the labia minora, they communicate to the outside by short ducts, function unknown.

bestiality Engaging in sexual activity with an animal; also called zoophilia.

bisexual Sexual involvement with both sexes, with no strong preference between homosexual and heterosexual activity.

bondage Use of physical restraints, such as ropes and chains, for sexual arousal.

breast The milk-producing structure located on the chest; its enlargement is a female secondary sex characteristic.

breast cancer Cancer of the breast, the most common type of cancer in women.

breech presentation In childbirth when the infant begins passage to the outside in any manner other than head first.

Caesarian section Delivery of an infant through an incision made in the walls of the abdomen and uterus.

capacitation The process by which sperm during their passage through the female reproductive system become capable of penetrating an ova.

celibacy Abstaining from sexual relationships.

central nervous system (CNS) The portion of the nervous system contained within the skull and spinal column; the brain and the spinal cord.

cervical canal The passageway that extends through the cervix connecting the cavities of the vagina and the uterus; opening into the uterus is called the internal os and the opening into the vagina the external os.

cervical cap A thimble-shaped rubber cap placed over the cervix used for contraception.

cervix The lower part of the uterus that opens into the vagina.

chancroids Smooth, round, painful ulcers occurring on the genitals and sexually transmitted.

clitoris A small very sensitive organ made of erectile tissue and located between the anterior junction of the labia minora just above the urinary meatus; sole function appears to be the receipt of sexual stimulation.

cohabitation Living together and having sexual relations without being married.

coitus Sexual intercourse, in which the penis is inserted into the vagina.

coitus interruptus The withdrawal of the penis from the vagina before ejaculation.

colostrum A thin watery fluid produced by the breasts during the last weeks of pregnancy and just after birth before being replaced by milk.

coming out Refers to public acknowledgement of one's homosexual orientation.

companionate love Deep affection and involvement which can exist exclusive of passionate love.

conceptus The products of conception consisting of the embryo or fetus and all associated structures such as the placenta.

condom A contraceptive device made of thin latex worn over the penis; acts to keep sperm from being deposited in the vagina.

coprophilia Erotic interest and arousal associated with defecation or feces.

corpus luteum The small yellow body that develops at the site on the ovary where the ovum was released; acts as an endocrine gland producing large amounts of progesterone and estrogen.

corticotropin A hormone secreted by the anterior pituitary that controls the activity of the adrenal cortex, which, in turn, secretes androgens in both sexes.

counter bypassing A therapy technique in which men with retarded ejaculation express their negative feelings about sex during the sexual interaction.

courtly love Arose in twelfth century and was marked by idealism, nobleness, the elevation of the beloved (usually a married noble lady) by her lover (usually a poet or troubadour).

courtship The process of attracting and interesting a potential mate by various communication signals.

Cowper's glands Two small glands that are located on both sides of the urethra near the prostate gland; secretes mucus material that is part of the ejaculate.

cruising The homosexual term for seeking casual sexual partners in bars, parks, and gay baths.

cryptorchidism A condition in which the testes remain within the body rather than descending into the scrotum during fetal development.

cunnilingus Oral stimulation of the female genitals.

cystitis An inflammation of the urinary bladder caused by bacterial growth.

dependent love A type of love where the primary gratification is derived from reverance and submissiveness towards the loved one.

diaphragm A contraceptive device made of thin latex and shaped like a dome; fits over the cervix and prevents the travel of sperm into the uterus; should be used with spermacides.

dildo An artificial device, often in the shape of a penis, used for vaginal or anal insertion.

Down's syndrome A chromosome disorder that results in mental retardation and changes in many bodily characteristics; formerly known as Mongolism.

dysmenorrhea Painful menstruation.

dyspareunia Technically means "badly mated" but in usual therapy use refers to painful intercourse.

eclampsia A pathological condition of pregnancy characterized by elevated blood pressure, edema, excessive and rapid weight gain, convulsions, and coma.

ectopic pregnancy A pregnancy in which the fertilized ova implants somewhere other than the proper area of the uterus; usually in the fallopian tubes.

Electra complex In psychoanalytic theory, the sexual attraction of a girl for her father, and rivalrous feelings toward her mother.

embryo Early stages of development of an offspring from conception until eight weeks.

endometriosis The displacement of the endometrial tissue lining of the uterus into any abnormal place such as the ovaries.

epididymis The comma-shaped structure that is attached to the testes; is made up of a long coiled tube through which sperm slowly pass and mature.

episiotomy A surgical incision into the perineum that enlarges the vaginal opening; used to ease delivery during childbirth.

erogenous zones Areas of the body which are sensitive to sexual stimulation.

eros The carnal or physical side of love so named by the Greeks.

estrogen A class of hormones that produce female secondary sex characteristics; found in lesser amounts in males.

excitement phase The first phase of the sexual response cycle; characterized by increasing levels of myotonia and vasocongestion.

exhibitionism Exposing one's genitals to an unwilling observer.

extramarital sex Sexual activity by a married person with someone other than his or her spouse.

fallopian tubes The oviduct or egg-conducting tube that extends from each ovary to the uterus.

fantasy   A mental image, usually created and modified by a person's needs, wishes, or desires.

fellatio   Oral stimulation of the male genitals.

fetishism   Compulsive sexual interest in an inanimate object.

fetus   The developing offspring from nine weeks following conception until birth.

follicle   A small capsule near the surface of the ovary which produces and contains an ovum; after ovulation becomes the corpus luteum.

follicular stage   The first stage of the menstrual cycle, proceeds ovulation and is characterized by the development of the ovum and the buildup of the uterine wall in preparation for implantation.

foreplay   Sexual activity that precedes intercourse.

frottage   While fully clothed, rubbing one's genitals against the body of a female in a crowded place.

FSH (follicule stimulating hormone)   A hormone secreted by the anterior pituitary that stimulates the ovarian follicules to mature and produce ova and which in the male stimulates sperm production.

gay   A non-derogatory slang term for homosexual.

gender identity   The psychological sense of oneself as male or female.

gonadal hormones   Hormones produced by the ovaries and testes.

gonadotrophins   Hormones secreted by the pituitary that stimulate activity in the gonads; includes FSH and LH.

gonorrhea   One of the most common sexually transmitted diseases, caused by a bacterium.

group marriage   Several adults living together in which sexual relations are not restricted to one partner.

Halsted procedure   See radical mastectomy.

herpes   An often painful sexually transmitted disease caused by a virus; two types of virus, I and II, can occur on the genitals although Type II is more likely to occur there.

heterosexuality   Sexual preference for and sexual activity with members of the opposite sex.

homophile   Refers to homosexual organizations.

homophobia   Fear and hostility toward homosexuality; the fear of possible homosexual desires in oneself.

homosexuality   Sexual preference for, or sexual activity with, members of one's own sex.

hormone   A chemical product of endocrine glands or neural tissue that is transported to some other location where it has its effect generally by either increasing or decreasing the target tissue's activity.

hydramnois   A complication of pregnancy characterized by excessive accumulation of amniotic fluid causing damage to the developing offspring.

hymen   A thin membrane that partially closes the entrance to the vagina.

hysterectomy   Surgical removal of the uterus.

incest   Sexual relations between close relatives, such as parent and child, or siblings.

indecent assault   Legally, forced sexual activity excluding the act of intercourse, such as touching a person's breasts or genitals without their consent.

intercourse Generally refers to penile-vaginal union, or coitus.

intrauterine device (IUD) A small object placed in the uterus for the purpose of birth control.

introitus The opening of the vagina.

jealousy Feelings of rivalry regarding real or imagined competition over someone or something that is strongly desired.

klismaphilia Compulsive erotic interest in enemas.

labia majora The large outer lips of the female external genitals.

labia minora The smaller inner lips of the female external genitals.

lactation The secretion of milk by the breasts.

Lamaze method A popular alternative to the typical method of childbirth in which both the mother and father are involved as active participants.

lesbian A female homosexual.

libido Freud's term for sexual drive or desire.

limerence Passionate love, marked by several characteristics including intrusive thoughts about the loved one and extreme dependency of mood on the loved one's reactions to the limerent person.

love A difficult to define feeling which usually includes some combination of warm attachment, affection, devotion, passion, tenderness, and sexual desire.

lumpectomy Removing a tumor and a small amount of the surrounding tissues.

luteal stage The third stage of the menstrual cycle following ovulation, characterized by the corpus luteum producing high levels of progesterone and estrogen that maintain pregnancy should it occur.

LH (Luteinizing hormone) A hormone secreted by the anterior pituitary that stimulates ovulation in females and testosterone production in males.

lymphogranuloma venereum Caused by chlamydia, sexually transmitted, signalled by a blister that disappears and eventual genital swelling.

male bridge maneuver Treatment for retarded ejaculation in which the female manipulates the male's penis up to the moment of ejaculation and then inserts it into her vagina.

mammography Special X-ray technique used to identify cancerous breast tumors.

masochism Obtaining sexual pleasure from receiving pain and humiliation from another person.

masturbation The physical stimulation of one's own genitals and possibly other erogenous areas for the purpose of sexual gratification.

menarche The onset of the first menstruation.

menopause The period of cessation of menstruation in women, usually occurs between ages 45 and 55.

metastasis The process by which malignant tumors spread to other parts of the body.

monopedia An unusual sexual fetish for women with one leg amputated.

mons pubis or mons veneris A cushion of fatty tissue that in women overlays the pubic bone just above the vulva.

myotonia Muscle tension.

narcissistic love   A type of love where the primary gratification is derived from approval and adoration from the loved one.

natural selection   Proposed by Charles Darwin as the primary mechanism of evolution, in which animals who can best meet the demands of their environment (due to characteristics or behaviors) will survive and reproduce.

necrophilia   Sexual attraction to dead bodies.

neisseria gonorrhea   The bacterium causing gonorrhea.

nipple   The protuberance on the breast consisting mainly of smooth muscle fibers and nerve endings; milk is delivered through this structure.

nocturnal emissions   Involuntary male orgasm and ejaculation during sleep; Sometimes called a "wet dream."

nocturnal pollution   The historical term used to describe what are now called "wet dreams."

nongonococcol urethritis (NGU)   A frequent sexually transmitted disease in men that mimics gonorrhea symptoms. Usually signalled by burning sensation during urination.

oedipal complex   In psychoanalytic theory, the sexual attraction of a boy for his mother, and fear of retaliation from the father.

onanism   Historically used as a synonym for masturbation, based on the Biblical story of Onan, who was put to death for "spilling his seed."

oogenesis   The process of the development of a mature ova.

open marriage   A marriage in which partners agree that each may engage in sexual relationships outside the marriage.

orgasm   The intense physiological and psychological excitement which is experienced at the peak of the sexual response cycle; is almost invariably experienced as pleasurable and is followed by a relaxation of sexual tensions.

ovarectomy   Surgical removal of the ovaries.

ovaries   The female gonads; two structures located on each side of the uterus; contain and release ova and secrete hormones.

ovulatory stage   The second stage of the menstrual cycle, preceeds the luteal stage and is characterized by LH and FSH surges and the release of an ovum.

parasympathetic branch   A branch or division of the autonomic nervous system that is, in general, associated with reduced activity; is involved in genital responses during sexual arousal.

parental investment   Behaviors toward offspring which increase the chances of the offspring's survival at the expense of the parent's ability to invest in other offspring.

partialism   A sexual fetish for a portion of the body.

pederasty   Sexual activity between an adult male and an adolescent boy. Also refers to anal intercourse.

pedophilia   Sexual contact between an adult and a prepubescent child.

pelvic inflammatory disease (PID)   General infection of the pelvic organs, can be accompanied by pain or vaginal bleeding and leads to sterility in severe cases.

penile chordee   Excessive downward bowing of the penis.

penis   The male sex organ through which

semen is ejaculated and urine is discharged.

perineum The tissue and area between the posterior portion of the external genitals and the anus.

peripheral nervous system (PNS) The portion of the nervous system outside the skull and spinal column; consists of a sensory input side and a motor output side.

petting Sexual contact that stops short of coitus.

Peyronie's disease Penile erection occurs at an angle due to fibrosis of the corpora cavernosa and sometimes resulting in pain during intercourse.

pheromone A chemical secretion, usually from the glands, used to communicate within a species. Sexual pheromones released from one animal cause other animals to respond sexually.

phimosis Penile foreskin which is too tight to be fully retracted over the penis.

pimp A prostitute's agent who manages her money, and often her safety, legal arrangements, and other necessities for staying in prostitution.

placenta The structure that develops within the uterus during pregnancy that conveys nutriments to the developing offspring as well as providing for the removal of waste products.

placenta previa A complication of pregnancy in which the placenta develops, in part, over the cervical opening; is typically accompanied by bleeding.

pornography Originally a description of prostitutes and their trade, now generally defined as media (writings, pictures, etc.) intended to arouse sexual desire and response; legal definitions of this term vary.

postpartum depression Feelings of depression, blues, and fatigue that sometimes are experienced following childbirth.

pre-eclampysia A complication of childbirth; identical to eclampsia with the exception that convulsions do not occur.

premarital intercourse Sexual intercourse that occurs prior to marriage.

premature birth Birth that occurs either before thirty-seven weeks following the last menstrual cycle or in which the child weighs five and one-half pounds or less.

premature ejaculation Ejaculation which occurs too quickly, according to the definition of the male and the couple.

preorgasmic See primary anorgasmia.

priapism Continuing, long duration erection, often occuring without stimulation and can be very painful.

primary anorgasmia Lack of orgasm through any means of stimulation. Usually refers to females.

primary erectile dysfunction A sexual problem of men who have never had erections firm enough for intercourse.

progesterone A hormone produced by the corpus luteum that prepares the uterus to receive the fertilized ovum; also produced in large quantities by the placenta during pregnancy acting to maintain pregnancy.

prolactin A hormone secreted by the anterior pituitary. It is known to stimulate milk production and to be associated with stress.

promiscuous Casual or indiscriminate sexual relationships with numerous partners.

prostate gland A lobed gland located near the base of the bladder; surrounds the urethra and contributes to the seminal fluid.

prostatic cancer Cancer of the prostate gland, the leading cause of death in men over 70.

prostatectomy Surgical removal of the prostate gland.

prostitution The exchange of sexual favors for money.

prostaglandins A class of biologically active lipids produced by, among other structures, seminal vessicle, prostate gland, and the uterine walls; act to stimulate smooth muscle activity, particularly in the uterus where in sufficient quantity they can act to induce abortion.

puberty The period of time during which the body matures from that of a child to that of an adult capable of reproduction.

pubic lice (crabs) Sexually transmitted, causing severe itch, usually in the pubic hair.

pubococcygeus muscle A striate or voluntary muscle that runs from the pubic bone in front around the sex organs to the coccyx or tail bone in the rear.

radical mastectomy Surgical removal of the breast, underlying muscle, fat, and lymph nodes.

rape Legally, the act of forced sexual intercourse.

rape trauma syndrome The acute behavioral, physical, and psychological, reactions to rape or attempted rape.

recreational drugs Non-prescription street drugs that are used to alter mood.

releasing factors Hormones produced by the hypothalmus that are transported to the pituitary where they stimulate production of pituitary hormones.

reproductive isolation Describes the fact that species are only able to mate successfully with members of their own species.

resolution phase The phase of the sexual response cycle that follows orgasm and during which the body returns to the unaroused state.

retarded ejaculation The inability to ejaculate in spite of extensive stimulation and full erection.

Rh baby The developing offspring in which a disorder exists where the antibodies from the mother's blood act to destroy the red blood cells of the fetus causing anemia and other serious problems.

rhythm method A contraceptive method based on abstinence during times in the menstrual cycle when ova are not present.

sadism Deriving sexual pleasure from inflicting pain and dominance upon another person.

sadomasochism Deriving sexual pleasure from inflicting and/or receiving pain from another person.

scabies Sexually and non-sexually transmitted parasites which cause itching.

scrotum The pouch suspended below the penis that contains the testicles.

secondary erectile dysfunction A sexual problem of men who frequently lose or are unable to have erection before or during sexual activity with a partner.

secondary orgasmic dysfunction In women, infrequent orgasm or orgasm only in special circumstances. Also called situational orgasmic dysfunction.

secondary sex characteristics The physical characteristics, other than the genitals, that distinguish males from females.

self-stimulation A term sometimes used synonymously with masturbation to cover a variety of activities which include physical touching of sexual organs which produces self-generated sexual response.

Semans technique Method for increasing ejaculation latency in men with premature ejaculation, also known as the "pause" or "stop-start."

semen The whitish fluid ejaculated through the penis; made up of sperm and transporting fluids from prostate, seminal vessicles, and Cowper's gland.

seminal vessicles A pair of saclike structures near the bladder and prostate gland, contributes to the seminal fluid.

seminiferous tubules The thin coiled structures within the testes where sperm are produced.

sensate focus Graduated (usually nongenital and nonsexual in the beginning) touching exercises assigned to couples in sex therapy to decrease anxiety and increase nonverbal communication skills.

sex-change Hormonal and surgical treatment of a transsexual.

sexual abuse Legally, any forced sexual behavior in which penetration does not occur.

sexual deviation Sexual behavior that differs from the accepted norms of society.

sexual perversions Sexual behavior that is offensive and deviates from accepted norms.

sexual selection The evolution process shaping those anatomical, physiological, and behavioral characteristics which influence an animal's ability to attract successfully a mate.

sexually transmitted diseases (STDs) Diseases that can be directly transmitted through sexual contact.

shyness A tendency to feel distressed, anxious, and self-conscious in social interactions.

silent rape reaction Some women who tell no one that they were raped begin to suffer changes in mood, fears, and self-esteem.

situational orgasmic dysfunction See secondary orgasmic dysfunction.

smegma Glandular secretions, bacteria, and dirt, which can collect under the foreskin hood of the clitoris or vagina.

sodomy Usually refers to anal intercourse; also legal term which can include in its definition, anal and oral intercourse and sexual intercourse with animals.

somatic branch A branch or division of the peripheral nervous system that brings in impulses from the sense organs and sends outputs to the striate (voluntary) muscles.

sonography A diagnostic procedure using sound waves that can identify birth defects in developing fetuses.

spermatic cord The structure by which the testicle is suspended in the scrotum; contains the vas deferens, nerves, blood vessels, and the cremaster muscle.

spermatogenesis The process of the development of a mature sperm.

spermicides Chemical substances used in contraceptives that kill sperm.

spontaneous abortions A naturally occuring expulsion of a developing embryo or fetus before it can survive.

squeeze technique Method for increasing ejaculation latency as a treatment for men who complain of ejaculating too fast.

statuatory rape   Rape with a woman below the legal age of consent, regardless of whether or not both parties agree to the act.

sterilization   One of a number of procedures, usually surgical, that render an individual incapable of reproduction.

surrogate mother   Women who become pregnant from the sperm of a donating male whose spouse is sterile; resulting child is then to be given to the sperm donor and his spouse.

swinging   The practice of exchanging sex partners between consenting couples.

sympathetic branch   A division of the autonomic nervous system that is, in general, associated with increased activity; involved in orgasm.

syphilis   A serious sexually transmitted disease which occurs in three stages.

taboo   A strong prohibition based upon cultural tradition or religion.

teasing technique   A process in sex therapy exercises in which the partner stimulates a male to full erection and lets it subside.

teratogen   A substance that causes birth defects.

testes   The two male gonads located within the scrotum that produce sex hormones and sperm.

testicular failure   A condition in which the testicles fail to produce sufficient sperm.

testosterone   The principal male sex hormone or androgen that is produced by the interstitial cells of the testes; produces male secondary sex characteristics.

transsexuals   Individuals whose gender identity is contrary to their biological sex, and who desire sex-change surgery.

transvestism   Erotic preoccupation with dressing in the clothing of the other sex; cross-dressing.

trichomonas   A vaginal parasite which when too high in number produces a yellow or grey foam discharge; can be sexually transmitted.

tubal ligation   Surgical procedure whereby sterilization is accomplished by interfering with the Fallopian tubes.

tumor   A mass of new tissue which has no physiologic use and which persists and grows independently of its surrounding structures.

umbilical cord   The structure that connects the developing fetus to the placenta.

urethra   The canal through which urine passes from the bladder, semen also passes through this structure.

urinary meatus   The opening of the urethra to the exterior.

urolagnia   Sexual arousal associated with observing urination.

uterus   A hollow, pear shaped muscular organ within the pelvis in which fertilized eggs develop; the womb.

vagina   A collapsed, highly expandable muscular canal that leads from the uterus to the vulva; serves as a birth canal and receives the penis during intercourse.

varicocele   A swelling or enlargement of the veins in the spermatic cord often resulting in sterility.

vas deferens   Sperm ducts which lead from the epididymus through the body wall to the seminal vessicle there becoming the ejaculatory duct.

vasectomy   Surgical procedure whereby

sterilization is accomplished by interfering with the vas deferens.

vasocongestion The accumulation of blood in tissue; in the genitals causes erection, swelling, and color changes.

venereal disease (VD) Now called sexually transmitted diseases.

venereal warts Usually painless, these warts often itch and then disappear on their own; they can be sexually transmitted.

vertex position In childbirth when the infant begins passage to the outside head-first as is correct.

voyeurism A sexual variation, in which the individual is erotically attached to secretly observing others undressing or engaging in sexual activity.

vulva The external female sex organs; includes the labia, clitoris, mons pubis, and vaginal and urethral openings.

yeast infection (thrush) Vaginal infection with a thick white discharge.

REFERENCES

Abarbanel, A. R. Diagnosis and treatment of coital discomfort. In J. LoPiccolo & L. LoPiccolo (Eds.), *Handbook of sex therapy*. New York: Plenum, 1978.

Abel, E. L. Behavioral teratology of alcohol. *Psychological Bulletin*, 1981, *90*, 564–581.

Abel, G. *Preventing rape*. Paper presented at the Seventh Vermont Conference on the Primary Prevention of Psychopathology, June 1981.

Abel, G., Barlow, D. H., Blanchard, E. G., & Guild, D., The components of rapists' sexual arousal. *Archives of General Psychiatry*, 1977, *34*, 875–903.

Abel, G., Blanchard, E. B., & Becker, J. V. An integrated treatment program for rapists. In R. T. Rada (Ed.), *Clinical aspects of the rapist*. New York: Grune & Stratton, 1978.

Abel, G. G., Murphy, W. D., Becker, J. V., & Bitar, A. Women's vaginal responses during REM sleep. *Journal of Sex and Marital Therapy*, 1979, *5*, 5–14.

Abramson, P. R., & Mosher, D. L. An empirical investigation of experimentally induced laboratory fantasies. *Archives of Sexual Behavior*, 1979, *8*, 27–39.

Adams, G. R., & Huston, T. L. Social perception of middle-aged persons varying in physical attractiveness. *Developmental Psychology*, 1975, *11*, 657–658.

Addiego, F., Belzer, E. G., Jr., Comolli, J., Moger, W., Perry, J. D., & Whipple, B. Female ejaculation: A case study. *The Journal of Sex Research*, 1981, *17*, 13–21.

Adelman, M. R. A comparison of professionally employed lesbians and heterosexual women on the MMPI. *Archives of Sexual Behavior*, 1977, *6*, 193–201.

Aladjem, E. S. (Ed.), *Obstetrical practice*. Toronto: C. V. Mosby, 1980.

Aladjem, E. S. *Risks in the practice of modern obstetrics (2nd ed.)*. St. Louis: C. V. Mosby, 1975.

Alan Guttmacher Institute. *Teenage pregnancy: The problem that hasn't gone away*. New York, 1981.

Alexander, N. J., & Clarkson, T. B. Vasectomy increases the severity of diet-induced atherosclerosis in Macaca Fascicularis. *Science*, 1978, *201*, 568.

Allport, G. W., Vernon, P. E., & Linzey, G. *Manual for study of values*. Boston: Houghton Mifflin, 1960.

Ambroso, D. N., Brown, M., Preusse, M., Ware, E. E., & Pilkey, D. W. Erotica and social behavior: An investigation of behavioral, psychological reactions to pornographic stimuli. *Technical Reports of the Commission on Obscenity and Pornography*, 1970, 201, Washington, D.C.: U.S. Government Printing Office.

Amelar, R. D., & Dubin, L. Stimulation of fertility in men. In E. S. E. Hafez & T. U. Evans (Eds.), *Human reproduction: Conception and contraception*. New York: Harper & Row, 1973.

American Association of Sex Educators, Counselors, and Therapists. *The professional training and preparation of sex counselors*. Washington: AASECT, 1973.

American Cancer Society. *Cancer facts and figures: 1983*. American Cancer Society, 1982.

Amir, M. *Patterns in forcible rape*. Chicago: University of Chicago Press, 1971.

Amirikia, H., Zarewych, B., & Evans, T. Cesarian section: A 15-year review of changing incidence, indications, and risks. *American Journal of Obstetrics and Gynecology*, 1981, *140*, 81–90.

Anderson, C., Clancy, B. & Quirk, B. Sexuality during pregnancy. In Barnard, Clancy and Krantz, *Human sexuality for health professionals*. Philadelphia: Saunders, 1978.

Angelino, H., & Mech, E. V. Some "first" sources of sex information as reported by sixty-seven college women. *The Journal of Psychology*, 1955, *39*, 321–324.

Annobile, U., & Annobile, R. J. *Beyond open marriage*. New York: A & W Publishers, 1979.

Annon, J. S. *The behavioral treatment of sexual problems, Vol. 1*. Honolulu: Kapiolani Health Services, 1974.

Apfelbaum, B. The diagnosis and treatment of retarded ejaculation. In S. R. Leiblum and L. A. Pervin (Eds.), *Principles and practice of sex therapy*. New York: Guilford Press, 1980.

Araoz, D. L. *Hypnosis and sex therapy*. New York: Brunner/Mazel, 1982.

Ard, B. N. Premarital sexual experience: A longitudinal study. *Journal of Sex Research*, 1974, *10*, 32–39.

Aref, I., & Hafez, E. S. E. Postcoital contraceptives. In E. S. E. Hafez (Ed.) and 57 contributors, *Human reproduction: Conception and contraception*. New York: Harper & Row, 1980.

Argyle, M., & Cook, M. *Gaze and mutual gaze*. Cambridge: Cambridge University Press, 1976.

Arieff, H. J., & Rotman, D. B. One hundred cases of indecent exposure. *Journal of Nervous and Mental Disease*, 1942, *96*, 523–529.

Arkowitz, H. Measurement and modification of minimal dating behavior. In M. Hersen (Ed.), *Progress in behavior modification* (Vol. 5). New York: Academic Press, 1977.

Armstrong, L. *Kiss daddy goodnight*. New York: Pocket Books, 1979.

Aronson, E., & Linder, D. Gain and loss of esteem as determinants of interpersonal attractiveness. *Journal of Experimental Social Psychology*, 1965, *1*, 156–171.

Aronson, M. Fatal air embolism caused by bizarre sexual behavior during pregnancy. *Medical Aspects of Human Sexuality,* 1969, December, 33–39.

Athanasiou, R., Shaver, P., & Tavris, C. Sex. *Psychology Today,* July 1970, 439–52.

Bachy, V. Danish "permissiveness" revisited. *Journal of Communications,* 1976, *26,* 40–43.

Backman, C. W., & Secord, P. F. The effect of perceived liking on interpersonal attraction. *Human Relations,* 1959, *12,* 379–384.

Bakwin, H. Erotic feelings in infants and young children. *American Journal of Diseases of Children,* 1973, *126,* 52–54.

Bancroft, J. H. J. Homosexuality in the male. *British Journal of Psychiatry,* 1976, Spec. Pub. #9, 173–184.

Bancroft, J. Psychophysiology of sexual dysfunction. In van Praag (Ed.), *Handbook of biological psychiatry, Vol. II.* Netherlands: Marcel Dekker, 1980.

Bancroft, J., Tennent, G., Loucas, K., & Cass, J. The control of deviant sexual behavior by drugs. I. Behavioural changes following oestrogens and anti-androgens. *British Journal of Psychiatry,* 1974, *125,* 310–315.

Barash, D. P. *Sociobiology and behavior.* New York: Elsevier, 1977.

Barbach, L. G. Group treatment of anorgasmic women. In S. R. Leiblum & L. A. Pervin (Eds.), *Principles and practice of sex therapy.* New York: Guilford Press, 1980.

Barbach, L. G. Group treatment of preorgasmic women. *Journal of Sex and Marital Therapy,* 1974, *1,* 139–145.

Barbach, L. G. *For yourself: The fulfillment of female sexuality.* New York: Doubleday, 1975.

Barbaree, H. E., Marshall, W. L., & Lanthier, R. D. Deviant sexual arousal in rapists. *Behavior Research and Therapy,* 1979, *17,* 215–222.

Barclay, A. M. Linking sexual and aggressive motives: Contributions of "irrelevant" arousals. *Journal of Personality,* 1971, *39,* 481–492.

Barlow, D. H. Increasing heterosexual responsiveness in the treatment of sexual deviation: A review of the clinical and experimental evidence. *Behavior Therapy,* 1973, *4,* 655–671.

Barlow, D. *Sexually transmitted diseases—the facts.* New York: Oxford University Press, 1979.

Barlow, D. H., Abel, G. G., Blanchard, E. B., & Mavissakalian, M. Plasma testosterone level and male homosexuality: A failure to replicate. *Archives of Sexual Behavior,* 1974, *3,* 571–575.

Barlow, D. H., Reynolds, E. J., & Agras, W. S. Gender identity change in a transsexual. *Archives of General Psychiatry,* 1973, *28,* 569–579.

Baron, R. A. Sexual arousal and physical aggression: The inhibiting influence of "cheesecake" and nudes. *Bulletin of the Psychosomatic Society,* 1974(a), *3,* 337–339.

Baron, R. A. The aggression-inhibiting influence of heightened sexual arousal. *Journal of Personality and Social Psychology,* 1974(b), *30,* 318–322.

Bar-Tal, D., & Saxe, L. Perceptors of similarly and dissimilarly attractive couples and individuals. *Journal of Personality and Social Psychology,* 1976, *33,* 772–781.

Bart, P. Avoiding rape: A study of victims and avoiders. Springfield, Va.: National Technical Information Service, August 1979.

Bartell, G. D. Group sex among the mid-Americans. *Journal of Sex Research,* 1970, *6,* 113–130.

Bauer, G. E., Croll, F. J. T., Goldrick, R. B., Jeremy, D., Raftos, J., Whyte, H. M., & Young, A. M. Guanethidine in treatment of hypertension. *British Medical Journal,* 1961, *2,* 410–415.

Bauman, K. E. Volunteer bias in a study of sexual knowledge, attitudes, and behavior. *Journal of Marriage and the Family,* 1973, *35,* 27–32.

Beach, F. A. Cross-species comparisons and the human heritage. *Archives of Sexual Behavior,* 1976, *5,* 469–485.

Beach, F. Hormonal control of sex-related behavior. In F. Beach (Ed.), *Human sexuality in four perspectives,* pp. 247–267. Baltimore: Johns Hopkins, 1978.

Beach, F. A. Animal models for human sexuality. In F. A. Beach (Ed.), *Sex hormones and behavior. Ciba Foundation Symposium 62.* New York: Excerpta Medica, 1979.

Beck, S. B., Ward-Hull, C. I., & McLear, P. M. Variables related to women's somatic preferences of the male and female body. *Journal of Personality and Social Psychology,* 1976, *34,* 1200–1211.

Behrman, S. T. The immune response and infertility: Experimental evidence. In S. T. Behrman and R. W. Kistner (Eds.), *Progress in infertility.* Boston: Little, Brown, 1968.

Bell, A. P., & Weinberg, M. S. *Homosexualities: A study of diversity among men and women.* New York: Simon & Schuster, 1979.

Bell, R. R., & Chaskes, J. B. Premarital sexual experience among coeds, 1958 and 1968. *Journal of Marriage and the Family,* 1970, *32,* 81–84.

Bell, R. R., & Peltz, D. Extramarital sex among women. *Medical Aspects of Human Sexuality,* 1974, *5,* 10–31.

Bender, L., & Blau, A. The reaction of children to sexual

relations with adults. *American Journal of Ortho-psychiatry*, 1937, *7*, 500–518.

Benditt, J. M. Current contraceptive research. *Family Planning Perspectives*, 1980, *12*(3), 149–155.

Benedek, T. *Insight and personality adjustment.* New York: Ronald Press, 1946.

Benjamin, H. The *transsexual phenomenon.* New York: Julian Press, 1966.

Bentler, P. M. Heterosexual behavior assessment–II. Females. *Behavior Research and Therapy:* 1968*b*, *6*, 27–30.

Bentler, P. M., & Prince, C. Personality characteristics of male transvestites: III. *Journal of Abnormal Psychology*, 1969, *74*, 140–143.

Bermant, G., & Davidson, J. M. *Biological bases of sexual behavior.* New York: Harper & Row, 1974.

Bernard, H. S. *Evaluation of the impact of a sex education program.* Unpublished doctoral dissertation, University of Rochester, 1973.

Berscheid, E., & Walster, E. Physical Attractiveness. In L. Berkowitz (Ed.), *Advances in experimental and social psychology* (Vol 7). New York: Academic Press, 1974.

Berscheid, E., & Walster E. *Interpersonal Attraction* (2nd ed). Reading, Mass.: Addison-Wesley, 1978.

Berscheid, E., Dion, E., Walster, E., & Walster, G. W. Physical attractiveness and dating choice: A test of the matching hypothesis. *Journal of Experimental Social Psychology*, 1971, *7*, 173–189.

Berscheid, E., Walster, E., & Bohrnstedt, G. The body image report. *Psychology Today*, 1973, *7*, 119–131.

Berscheid, E., Walster, W., & Walster, E. Effects of accuracy and positivity of an evaluation on liking for the evaluator. Brief report in E. Berscheid & E. Walster (Eds.), *Interpersonal attraction.* Reading, Mass.: Addison-Wesley, 1969.

Bethell, M. F. A rare manifestation of fetishism. *Archives of Sexual Behavior*, 1974, *3*, 301–302.

Bibbo, M., Bartels, P. H., & Wied, G. L. Abnormal cytology and cervical neoplasia in users of oral contraceptives and IUD's. In K. S. Moghissi, *Controversies in contraception.* Baltimore: Williams & Wilkins, 1979.

Bieber, I. *Homosexuality: A psychoanalytic study.* New York: Basic Books, 1962.

Birchler, G. R., & Webb, L. A social learning formulate of discriminating interaction behaviors in happy and unhappy marriages. *Journal of Consulting and Clinical Psychology*, 1975, *45*, 494–495.

Birdwhistell, R. L. Kinesics and communication. In E. Carpenter & M. McLuhan (Eds.), *Exploration in communication.* Boston: Beacon Press, 1960.

Birdwhistell, R. L. Paralanguage: Twenty-five years after

Sapir. In *Lectures on experimental psychology.* Pittsburgh: University of Pittsburgh Press, 1961.

Birk, L., Huddleston, W., Miller, E., & Cohler, B. Avoidance conditioning for homosexuality. *Archives of General Psychiatry*, 1971, *25*, 314–323.

Blumer, D., & Walker, A. E. Sexual behavior in temporal lobe epilepsy: A study of the effects of temporal lobectomy on sexual behavior. *Archives of Neurology*, 1967, *16*, 37–43.

Blumstein, P. W., & Schwartz, P. Bisexuality: Some social psychological issues. *Journal of Social Issues*, 1977, *33*, 30–45.

Bohlen, J. G. "Female ejaculation" and urinary stress incontinence. *The Journal of Sex Research*, 1982, *18*, 360–368.

Bohlen, J. G., & Held, J. P. An anal probe for monitoring vascular and muscular events during sexual response. *Psychophysiology*, 1979, *16*, 318–323.

Bohlen, J. G., Held, J. P., & Sanderson, M. O. The male orgasm: Pelvic contractions measured by anal probe. *Archives of Sexual Behavior*, 1980, *9*(6), 503–521.

Bohlen, J. G., Held, J. P., Sanderson, M. O., & Ahlgren, A. The female orgasm: Pelvic contractions. *Archives of Sexual Behavior*, 1982, *11*, 1982.

Bolognese, R. J., & Corson, S. L. *Interruption of pregnancy —A total patient approach.* Baltimore: Williams & Wilkins, 1975.

Bossard, J. H. S. Residential propinquity as a factor in mate selection. *American Journal of Sociology*, 1932, *38*, 219–224.

Boston Women's Health Collective. *Our bodies, ourselves.* New York: Simon & Schuster, 1976.

Bracken, M. B., & Holford, T. R. Induced abortion and congenital malformation in offspring of subsequent pregnancies. *American Journal of Epidemiology*, 1979, *109*(4), 425–432.

Brady, J. P., & Levitt, E. E. The relation of sexual preferences to sexual experiences. *Psychological Record* 1965, *15*, 377–384.

Brand, J. *Observations on popular antiquities.* London: Chatto & Windus, 1877.

Brecher, E. M. *The sex researchers.* Boston: Little, Brown, 1969.

Brecher, E. M. The prevention of sexually transmitted diseases. *Journal of Sex Research*, 1975, *11*, 318–328.

Breedlove, W., & Breedlove, J. *Swap clubs.* Los Angeles: Sherborne Press, 1964.

Brenner, P. F., & Mishell, D. R. Newer developments in steroidal contraceptives: Injectables, subcutaneous implants, intravaginal rings. In K. S. Moghissi, *Controversies in contraception.* Baltimore: Williams & Wilkins, 1979.

Briddell, D., Rimm, D., Caddy, G., Krawitz, G., Sholis, D., & Wonderlin, R. Effects of alcohol and cognitive set on sexual arousal to deviant stimuli. *Journal of Abnormal Psychology*, 1978, *87*, 418–430.

Briddell, D. W., & Wilson, G. T. Effects of alcohol and expectancy on male sexual arousal. *Journal of Abnormal Psychology*, 1976, *85*, 225–234.

Brierly, H. *Transvestism: A handbook with case studies for psychologists, psychiatrists, and counsellors.* Oxford: Pergamon Press, 1979.

Broderick, C. B. Preadolescent sexual behavior. *Medical Aspects of Human Sexuality*, 1968, *2*, 20–29.

Broderick, C. B. Socio-sexual development in a suburban community. *Journal of Sex Research*, 1966, *2*, 1–24.

Brodie, H., Gartrell, N., Doering, C., & Rhue, T. Plasma testosterone levels in heterosexual and homosexual men. *American Journal of Psychiatry*, 1974, *131*, 82–83.

Brooks, J., Ruble, D., & Clark, A. College women's attitudes and expectations concerning menstrual-related changes. *Psychosomatic Medicine*, 1977, *39*, 288–98.

Brower, J. R., & Naftolin, F. The effects of estrogen on hypothalamic tissue. In Ciba Foundation Symposium 62, *Sex, hormones and behavior.* New York: Excerpta Medica, 1979.

Brown, B. A. *Crime against women alone: A system analyses of the Memphis police department sex crime squad's 1973 rape investigations, 1974.* Unpublished paper cited in Brownmiller, 1975.

Browning, D. H., & Boatman, B. Incest: Children at risk. *American Journal of Psychiatry*, 1977, *134*, 69–72.

Brownmiller, S. *Against our will.* New York: Simon & Schuster, 1975.

Bryson, J. B. *Situational determinants of the expression of jealousy.* Paper presented at the 85th annual meeting of the American Psychological Association, San Francisco, 1977.

Budoff, P. W. *No more menstrual cramps and other good news.* New York: Penguin, 1980.

Budoff, P. W. Treatment of dysmenorrhea. *American Journal of Obstetrics and Gynecology*, 1977, *129*, 232.

Buhrich, N., Theile, H., Yaw, A., & Crawford, A. Plasma testosterone, serum FSH, and serum LH levels in transvestism. *Archives of Sexual Behavior*, 1979, *8*, 49–54.

Bullough, V. I. *Sexual variance in society and history.* New York: John Wiley, 1976.

Bulpitt, C. J., & Dollery, C. T. Side effects of hypotensive agents evaluated by a self administered questionnaire. *British Medical Journal*, 1973, *3*, 485–490.

Bunker, J. P., McPherson, K., & Henneman, P. L. Elective surgery. In J. P. Bunker (Ed.), *Costs, risks, and benefits of surgery.* New York: Oxford, 1977.

Burgess, A. W., & Holmstrom, L. L. Rape trauma syndrome. *American Journal of Psychiatry*, 1974a, *131*, 981–986.

Burgess, A. W., & Holmstrom, L. L. *Victims of crisis.* Bowie: Robert J. Brady, 1974. (b)

Burgess, E. W., & Wallin, P. *Engagement and marriage.* Philadelphia: Lippincott, 1953.

Butler, C. A. New data about female sexual response. *Journal of Sex and Marital Therapy*, 1976, *2*, 40–46.

Butler, J. C., & Wagner, N. N. Sexuality during pregnancy and postpartum. In R. Green (Ed.), *Human sexuality: A health practitioner's text.* Baltimore: Williams & Wilkins, 1975.

Butler, S. *Conspiracy of silence: The trauma of incest.* New York: Bantam, 1979.

Byrne, D. Interpersonal attraction and attitude similarity. *Journal of Abnormal and Social Psychology*, 1961a, *62*, 713–715.

Byrne, D. The influence of propinquity and opportunities for interaction in classroom relationships. *Human Relations*, 1961b, *14*, 63–70.

Byrne, D., & Blaylock, B. Similarity and assumed similarity of attitudes between husbands and wives. *Journal of Abnormal and Social Psychology*, 1963, *67*, 636–640.

Byrne, D., & Lamberth, J. The effect of erotic stimuli on sexual arousal, evaluative responses, and subsequent behavior. *Technical reports of the Commission on Obscenity and Pornography* (Vol. 8). Washington, D.C.: U.S. Government Printing Office, 1970.

Byrne, D., & Nelson, D. Attraction as a linear function of proportion of positive reinforcements. *Journal of Personality and Social Psychology*, 1965, *1*, 659–663.

Calhoun, J. B. Population density and social pathology. *Scientific American*, 1962, *206*, 139–148.

Callahan, E. J. and Leitenberg, H. Aversion therapy for sexual deviation: Contingent shock and covert sensitization. *Journal of Abnormal Psychology*, 1973, *81*, 60–73.

Caprio, F. *The sexually adequate female.* New York: Citadel, 1963.

Carnegie, D. *How to win friends and influence people.* New York: Simon & Schuster, 1937.

Carver, J. R., & Oaks, W. W. Sex and hypertension. In W. W. Oaks, G. A. Melchiode, & I. Fisher (Eds.), *Sex and the life cycle.* New York: Grune and Stratton, 1976.

Casper, R. F., & Yen, S. S. C. Induction of lutealysis in the human with a long-acting analog of lutenizing hormone-releasing factor. *Science,* 1979, *205,* 408.

Cates, W., & Ory, H. IUD complication: Infection, death and ectopic pregnancy. In K. S. Moghissi, *Controversies in contraception.* Baltimore: Williams & Wilkins, 1979.

Cattrell, R. B., & Nesselroade, J. R. Likeness and completeness theories examined by 16 personality factor measures on stable and unstably married couples. *Journal of Personality and Sexual Psychology,* 1967, *7,* 351–361.

Cavallin, H. Incestuous fathers: A clinical report. *American Journal of Psychiatry,* 1966, *122,* 1132–1138.

Center for Disease Control. Gonorrhea: Recommended treatment schedule, 1979. *Annals of Internal Medicine,* 1979, *90,* 809–811.

Centers, R. Attitude similarity–dissimilarity as a correlate of heterosexual attraction and love. *Journal of Marriage and the Family,* 1975a, *37,* 305–314.

Centers, R. *Sexual attraction and love: An instrumental theory.* Springfield, Ill.: Charles C. Thomas, 1975b.

Centers, R. Evaluating the loved one: The motivational congruency factor. *Journal of Personality,* 1971, *39,* 303–318.

Centerwall, B. S. Premenopausal hysterectomy and cardiovascular disease. *American Journal of Obstetrics and Gynecology,* 1981, *139,* 58–61.

Cerny, J. Biofeedback and the voluntary control of sexual arousal in women. *Behavior Therapy,* 1978, *9,* 847–855.

Chesney-Lind, M. Judicial enforcement of the female sex role: The family court and the female delinquent. *Issues in Criminology,* 1973, *2,* 51–69.

Chevalier-Skolnikoff, S. Homosexual behavior in a laboratory group of stump-tail monkeys (Macaca arctoides): Forms, contexts, and possible social functions. *Archives of Sexual Behavior,* 1976, *5,* 511–527.

Christenson, C. V., & Gagnon, J. H. Sexual behavior in a group of older women. *Journal of Gerontology,* 1965, *20,* 351–356.

Christensen, H. T., & Gregg, C. F. Changing sex norms in America and Scandinavia. *Journal of Marriage and the Family,* 1970, *32,* 606–627.

Christianson, R. E. The relationship between maternal smoking and the incidence of congenital anomalies. *American Journal of Epidemiology,* 1980, *112,* 684–695.

Churchill, W. *Homosexual behavior among males: A cross-cultural and cross-species investigation.* New York: Hawthorn Books, 1967.

Ciba Foundation. *Size at birth, Ciba Foundation Symposium 27.* Associated Scientific Publishers, New York, 1974.

Cicero, T. J., Bell, R. D., Weist, R. G., Allison, J. H., Polakoski, K., & Robins, E. Function of the male sex organs in heroin and methadone users. *New England Journal of Medicine,* 1975, *292,* 882–887.

Cimbalo, R. S., Faling, V., & Mousan, P. The course of love: A cross-sectional design. *Psychological Report,* 1976, *38,* 1292, 1294.

Clanton, G., & Smith, L. G. The self inflicted pain of jealousy. *Psychology Today,* 1977, *10,* 44–47, 80, 82.

Clark, A. L., & Wallin, P. Women's sexual responsiveness and the duration and quality of their marriages. *American Journal of Sociology,* 1965, *71,* 187–196.

Clement, U., & Pfafflin, F. Changes in personality scores among couples subsequent to sex therapy. *Archives of Sexual Behavior,* 1980, *9,* 235–244.

Clifford, R. *Female masturbation in sexual development and clinical application.* Unpublished doctoral dissertation, State University of New York, Stony Brook, 1975.

Clifford, R. Development of masturbation in college women. *Archives of Sexual Behavior,* 1978a, *7,* 559–573.

Clifford, R. Subjective sexual experience in college women. *Archives of Sexual Behavior,* 1978b, *7,* 183–197.

Clore, G. L., & Baldridge, B. Interpersonal attraction: The role of agreement and topic agreement. *Journal of Personality and Social Psychology,* 1968, *9,* 340–346.

Clore, G. L., & Byrne, D. A reinforcement affect model of attraction. In T. L. Huston (Ed.), *Foundations of interpersonal attraction.* New York: Academic, 1974.

Clore, G. L., Wiggins, N. H., & Itkin, S. Gain and loss in attraction: Attributions from nonverbal behavior. *Journal of Personality and Social Psychology,* 1975, *31,* 706–712.

Cohen, H. D., & Shapiro, A. A method for measuring sexual arousal in the female. *Psychophysiology,* 1971, *8,* 251.

Cohen, M. L., Seghorn, T., & Calmas, W. Sociometric study of the sex offender. *Journal of Abnormal Psychology,* 1969, *74,* 249–255.

Cole, C. L., & Spanier, G. B. Comarital mate-sharing and family stability. *Journal of Sex Research,* 1974, *10,* 21–31.

Cole, P., & Berlin, J. Elective hysterectomy. *American Journal of Obstetrics and Gynecology,* 1977, *129,* 117–123.

Constantine, L. Jealousy: Techniques for intervention.

In G. Clanton & L. G. Smith (Eds.), *Jealousy*. Englewood Cliffs, N.J.: Prentice-Hall, 1977.

Constantine, L. L., & Constantine, J. M. Sexual aspects of multilateral relations. *Journal of Sex Research*, 1971, *7*, 204–225.

Cook M. *The bases of human sexual attraction*, New York: Academic Press. 1981.

Cook, M., & Howells, K. (Eds.). *Adult sexual interest in children*. New York: Academic Press, 1981.

Cook, M., & McHenry, R. *Sexual attraction*. New York: Pergamon, 1978.

Cooke, N. F. *Satan in society*. New York: Arno Press, 1974. (Originally printed in 1870.)

Coombs, L. C. Preferences for sex of children among U.S. couples. *Family Planning Perspectives*, 1977, *9*(6), 256–265.

Cooper, A. J. A factual study of male potency disorders, *British Journal of Psychiatry*, 1968, *114*, 719–731.

Cooper, A. J. Disorders of sexual potency in the male: A clinical and statistical study of some factors related to short-term prognosis. *British Journal of Psychiatry*, 1969, *115*, 709–719.

Cooper, A. J. Frigidity, treatment and short-term prognosis. *Journal of Psychosomatic Research*, 1970, *14*, 133–147.

Cooper, A. J. Diagnosis and management of "endocrine impotence." *British Medical Journal*, 1972, *2*, 34–36.

Cooper, A. J., Short-term treatment in sexual dysfunction: A review. *Comprehensive Psychiatry*, 1981, *22*, 206–217.

Cormier, B. M., Kennedy, M., & Sanjowicz, J. Psychodynamics of father-daughter incest. *Canadian Psychiatric Association Journal*, 1962, *7*, 203–211.

Costello, R., & Yalom, I. Institutional group therapy. In H. L. Resnick and M. E. Wolfgang (Eds.), *Sexual behavior: Social, clinical and legal aspects*. Boston: Little, Brown, 1972.

Coulton, G. C. *Inquisition and liberty*. London: Heinemann, 1938.

Cox, D. J., & Daitzman, R. J. (Eds.). *Exhibitionism: Description, assessment, and treatment*. New York: Garland STPM Press, 1980.

Csillag, E. R. Modification of penile erection response. *Behavior Therapy and Experimental Psychiatry*, 1976, *7*, 27–29.

Cunha, G., Discussion of Robboy et al's paper. In S. G. Silverberg & F. J. Major (Eds.), *Estrogen and cancer*. New York: John Wiley, 1978.

Curran, D., & Parr, D. Homosexuality: An analysis of 100 male cases. *British Medical Journal*, 1957, *1*, 797–801.

Curran, J. P. Skills training as an approach to the treatment of heterosexual-social anxiety: A review. *Psychological Bulletin*, 1977, *84*, 140–157.

Curran, J. P., & Lippold, S. The effects of physical attraction and attitude similarity on attraction in dating dyads. *Journal of Personality*, 1975, *43*, 528–538.

Curran, J., Neff, S., & Lippold, S. Correlates of sexual experience among college students. *Journal of Sex Research*, 1973, *9*, 124–131.

Cutright, P., & Jaffe, F. S. *Impact of family planning programs on fertility: The U.S. experience*. New York: Praeger, 1977.

Dalton, K. *The premenstrual syndrome*. Springfield, Ill.: Charles C. Thomas, 1964.

Darwin, C. *The origin of the species*. N.Y.: Modern Library, 1859. (1936 ed.)

Davenport, W. H. Sex in cross-cultural perspective. In F. A. Beach (Ed.), *Human sexuality in four perspectives*. Baltimore: Johns Hopkins University Press, 1976.

Davidson, J. M. Activation of the male rat's sexual behavior by intracerebral implantation of androgen. *Endocrinology*, 1966, *79*, 783.

Davis, A. J. Sexual assaults in the Philadelphia prison system. In J. H. Gagnon & W. Simon (Eds.), *The sexual scene*. Chicago: Aldine, 1970.

Davis, I. Nobel no-go, but still a quest for genuis. *The Times*, Friday, September 24, 1982, London, p. 10.

Davis, K. B. *Factors in the sex life of twenty-two hundred women*. New York: Harper & Brothers Publishers, 1929.

Davis, N. The prostitute: Developing a deviant identity. In J. Henslin (Ed.), *The sociology of sex*, pp. 297–322. Englewood Cliffs, N.J.: Prentice-Hall, 1971.

Davison, G. C. Homosexuality: The ethical challenge. *Journal of Consulting and Clinical Psychology*, 1976, *44*, 157–162.

de Beauvoir, S. *The second sex*. New York: Alfred A. Knopf, 1970, 1953.

DeFrancis, V., Protecting the child victim of sex crimes committed by adults. *Federal Probation*, 1971, *35*, 15–20.

Delaney, J., Lupton, M. J., & Toth, E. *The curse: A cultural history of menstruation*. New York: E. P. Dutton, 1976.

DeLeon, G., & Wexler, H. K. Heroin addiction: Its relation to sexual behavior and sexual experience. *Journal of Abnormal Psychology*, 1973, *81*, 35–38.

DeMartino, M. F. Autoeroticism: Practices, attitudes, effects. In M. F. DeMartino (Ed.), *Human autoerotic practices.* New York: Human Sciences Press, 1979.

DeMartino, M. F. *Sex and the intelligent woman.* New York: Springer, 1974.

Dement, W. An essay on dreams: The role of physiology in understanding their nature. In F. Barron (Ed.), *New directions in psychology, Vol II.* New York: Holt, Rinehart & Winston, 1965.

Denfield, D., & Gordon, M. The sociology of mate swapping, or the family that swings together, clings together. In J. R. Delora, & J. S. Delora (Eds.), *Intimate life styles.* Pacific Palisades, Calif.: Goodyear Publishing Co., 1975.

Dermer, M., & Thiel, D. L. When beauty may fail. *Journal of Personality and Social Psychology, 1975, 31,* 1168–1176.

Derogatis, L. R., & King, K. M. The coital coronary: A reassessment of the concept. *Archives of Sexual Behavior,* 1981, *10,* 325–336.

Derogatis, L. R., & Meyer, J. A psychological profile of the sexual dysfunctions. *Archives of Sexual Behavior,* 1979, *8,* 201–223.

Derogatis, L. R., Meyer, J., & King, K. M. Psychopathology in individuals with sexual dysfunction. *American Journal of Psychiatry,* 1981, *138,* 757–763.

Deutsch, H. *The psychology of women.* New York: Grune & Stratton, 1944.

Deutsch, M., & Solomon, L. Reactions to evaluations by others is influenced by self evaluations. *Sociometry,* 1959, *22,* 93–112.

Diamant, L. Premarital sexual behavior, attitudes, and emotional adjustment. *Journal of Social Psychology,* 1970, *82,* 75–77.

Diamond, M. Human sexual development: Biological foundations for social development. In F. Beach (Ed.), *Human sexuality in four perspectives,* pp. 22–61. Baltimore: Johns Hopkins, 1977.

Dickey, R. P. *Managing contraceptive pill patients* (2nd ed.). Aspen, Colo.: Creative Informatics, Inc., 1980.

Dickinson, R. L. & Beam, L. *A thousand marriages: A medical study of sexual adjustment.* Baltimore: Williams & Wilkins, 1931.

Dickoff, H. *Reactions to evaluations by another person as a function of self-evaluation and the interaction context.* Unpublished doctoral dissertation, Duke University, 1961. (Also cited in E. E. Jones, 1964)

Diekman, G., & Hassler, R. Treatment of sexual violence by stereotactic hypothalamotomy. In W. H. Sweet, S. Obrador, & J. G. Martin-Rodriguez (Eds.), *Neurosurgical treatment in psychiatry, pain, and epilepsy.* Baltimore: University Park Press, 1977.

Dion, K. L., Berscheid, E., & Walster, E. What is beau-

tiful is good. *Journal of Personality and Social Psychology,* 1972, *24,* 285–290.

Dion, K. L., & Dion, K. K. Correlates of romantic love. *Journal of Consulting and Clinical Psychology,* 1973, *41,* 51–56.

Dittes, J. R. Attractiveness of group as a function of self-esteem and acceptance by group. *Journal of Abnormal and Social Psychology,* 1959, *59,* 77–82.

Dmowski, W. P. Use of albumin gradients for X and Y sperm separation and clinical experience with male sex preselection. *Fertility and Sterility,* 1979, *31,*(1).

Doerr, P., Pirke, K. M., Kockott, G., & Dittmar, F. Further studies on sex hormones in male homosexuals. *Archives of General Psychiatry,* 1976, *33,* 611–614.

Donnerstein, E., & Barrett, G. Effects of erotic stimuli on male aggression toward females. *Journal of Personality and Social Psychology,* 1978, *36,* 180–188.

Donnerstein, E., Donnerstein, M., & Evans, R. Erotic stimuli and aggression: Facilitation or inhibition. *Journal of Personality and Social Psychology,* 1975, *32,* 237–244.

Donnerstein, E., & Hallan, J. Facilitating effects of erotica on aggression against women, *Journal of Personality and Social Psychology,* 1978, *36,* 1270–1277.

Dorman, B. W., & Schmidt, J. D. Association of priapism in phenothiazine therapy. *Journal of Urology,* 1976, *116,* 51–53.

Dörner, G., Rohde, W., Stahl, F., Krell, L., & Masius, W. G. A neuroendocrine predisposition for homosexuality in men. *Archives of Sexual Behavior,* 1975, *4,* 1–8.

Doty, R. L., Ford, M., Preti, G., & Huggins, G. R. Changes in intensity and pleasantness of human vaginal odors during the menstrual cycle. *Science,* 1975, *190,* 1316–1318.

Downing, D., & Black, D. L. Equality in survival of X and Y chromosomes bearing human spermatozoa. *Fertility and Sterility,* 1976, *27*(10), 1191–1193.

Dreikurs, R. *The challenge of marriage.* New York: Duel, Sloan & Pearce, 1946.

Driscoll, R., Davis, K., & Lipetz, M. Parental interference and romantic love: The Romeo and Juliet effect. *Journal of Personality and Social Psychology,* 1972, *24,* 1–10.

Dulton, B. G., & Aron, A. P. Some evidence for heightened sexual attraction under conditions of high anxiety. *Journal of Personality and Social Psychology,* 1974, *30,* 510–517.

Dworkin, A. *Pornography: Men possessing women.* New York: G. P. Putnam (Perigee Books), 1981.

Dymond, R. Interpersonal perception and marital happiness. *Canadian Journal of Psychology*, 1954, *8*, 164–171.

Edelman, D. A., Berger, G. S., & Keith, L. G. *Intrauterine devices and their complications*. Boston: G. K. Hall, 1979.

Edwards, A. E., & Hurted, J. R. Penile sensitivity, age, and sexual behavior. *Journal of Clinical Psychology*, 1976, *32*, 697–700.

Edwards, J. H., & Booth, A. Sexual behavior in and out of marriage: An assessment of correlates. *Journal of Marriage and the Family*, 1976, *38*, 73–81.

Edwards, R. G. *Conception in the human female*. New York: Academic Press, 1980.

Edwards, R. G., Steptoe, P. C., & Purdy, J. M. Establishing full-term human pregnancies using cleaving embryos grown in vitro. *British Journal of Obstetrics and Gynecology*, 1980, *87*, 737–756.

Efren, M. G. The effect of physical appearance in the judgement of guilt, interpersonal attraction, and severity of recommended punishment in a simulated jury task. *Journal of Research in Personality*, 1974, *8*, 45–54.

Ekman, P. Universal and cultural differences in facial expression of emotion. In J. K. Cole (Ed.), *Nebraska Symposium on Motivation*. Lincoln, Nebraska: University of Nebraska Press, 1972.

Eibl-Eibesfeldt, I. *Ethology: The biology of behavior*. New York: Holt, Rinehart & Winston, 1970.

Elias, J., & Gebhard, P. Sexuality and sexual learning in childhood. In A. M. Juhasz (Ed.), *Sexual development and behavior: Selected readings*. Homewood, Ill.: Dorsey Press, 1973.

Ellenberg, M. Sexual function in diabetic patients. *Annals of Internal Medicine*, 1980, *92*, 331–333.

Ellenberg, M. Sexual aspects of the female diabetic. *Mt. Sinai Journal of Medicine*, 1977, *44*, 495–500.

Ellis, A. *Sex without guilt*. New York: Grove, 1958.

Ellis, A. *Reason and emotion in psychotherapy*. New York: Lyle Stuart, 1962.

Ellis, A. *The art and science of love*. New York: Lyle Stuart and Bantam Books, 1969.

Ellis, A. Rational-emotive treatment of impotence, frigidity and other sexual problems. *Professional Psychology*, 1971, *2*, 346–349.

Ellis, A. The rational-emotive approach to sex therapy. *Counseling Psychologist*, 1975, *5*, 14–21.

Ellis, A. Treatment of erectile dysfunction. In S. R. Leiblum & L. A. Pervin (Eds.), *Principles and practice of sex therapy*. New York: Guilford, 1980.

Ellis, E. M., Atkeson, B. M. & Calhoun, K. S. An assessment of long-term reaction to rape. *Journal of Abnormal Psychology*, 1981, *90*, 263–266.

Ellis, A Coitus. In A. Ellis & A. Abarbanel (Eds.), *The encyclopedia of sexual behavior*. New York: Jason Aronson, Inc., 1973.

Ellis, H. *Studies in the psychology of sex*. New York: Random House, 1906.

Ellison, C. Vaginismus. *Medical Aspects of Human Sexuality*, 1972, *8*, 34–54.

Epstein, A. W. Fetishism. *Journal of Nervous and Mental Disease*, 1960, *130*, 107–119.

Epstein, L. M. *Sex laws and customs in Judaism*. New York: Bloch, 1948.

Evans, D. R. Subjective variables and treatment affects in aversion therapy. *Behavior Research and Therapy*, 1970, *8*, 147–152.

Evans, R. B. Childhood parental relationships of homosexual men. *Journal of Consulting and Clinical Psychology*, 1969, *33*, 129–135.

Evans, T. N. Female sterilization. In E. S. E. Hafez (Ed.) and 57 contributors, *Human reproduction: Conception and contraception*. New York: Harper & Row, 1980.

Farkas, G., & Rosen, R. C. Effects of alcohol on elicited male sexual response. *Quarterly Journal of Studies of Alcohol*, 1976, *37*, 265–272.

Farkas, G. M., Sine, I. F., & Evans, I. M. Personality, sexuality, and demographic differences between volunteers and nonvolunteers for a laboratory study of male sexual behavior. *Archives of Sexual Behavior*, 1978, *7*, 513–520.

Farkas, G. M., Sine, L. F., & Evans, I. A. The effects of distraction, performance demand, stimulus explicitness, and personality on objective and subjective measures of male sexual arousal. *Behavior Research and Therapy*, 1979, *17*, 25–32.

Federal Bureau of Investigation: Uniform Crime Reports. Washington, D.C.: U.S. Government Printing Office, 1973, 1974, 1979.

Feinbloom, D. H. *Transvestites and transsexuals: Mixed views*. New York: Delacorte Press, 1976.

Feisbie, L. V., & Dondis, E. H. *Recidivism among treated sex offenders. Research monograph 5*. Sacramento, California, Department of Mental Hygiene, 1965.

Feldman, M. P., and MacCulloch, M. J. *Homosexual behavior: Therapy and assessment*. Oxford, England: Pergamon Press, 1971.

Feldman, S. D. The presentation of shortness in everyday life—height and heightism in American society:

Towards a sociology of stature. Paper read to the American Sociological Association, 1971.

Feldman-Summers, S., Gordon, P., & Meagher, J. The impact of rape on sexual satisfaction. *Journal of Abnormal Psychology*, 1979, *88*, 101–105.

Felman, Y. M., & Nikitas, J. A. Nongonococcal urethritis: A clinical review. *JAMA*, 1981, *245*(4), 381–386.

Festinger, L. A theory of social comparison processes. *Human Relations*, 1954, *7*, 117–140.

Festinger, L., Schacter, S., & Back, K. *Social pressures in informal groups: A study of human factors in housing.* New York: Harper, 1950.

Finger, F. W. Changes in sex practices and beliefs of male college students over 30 years. *Journal of Sex Research*, 1975, *11*, 304–317.

Finkel, M. L., & Finkel, D. L. Sexual and contraceptive knowledge, attitudes and behavior of male adolescents. *Family Planning Perspectives*, 1975, *7*,(6), 256–260.

Finkelhor, D. *Sexually victimized children.* New York: The Free Press, 1979a.

Finkelhor, D. What's wrong with sex between adults and children? Ethics and the problem of sexual abuse. *American Journal of Orthopsychiatry*, 1979b, *49*, 692–699.

Fisher, C., Gross, J., & Zuch, J. Cycles of penile erection synchronous with dreaming (REM) sleep. *Archives of General Psychiatry*, 1965, *12*, 29–45.

Fisher, G. Psychological needs of heterosexual pedophiliacs. *Diseases of the Nervous System*, 1969, *30*, 419–421.

Fisher, K. Shess the unseen killer in AIDS. *APA Monitor*, 1983, *14*(7), p1, 20–21

Fisher, S. *The female orgasm.* New York: Basic Books, 1973.

Fitch, J. H. Men convicted of sexual offenses against children. *British Journal of Criminology*, 1962, *3*, 18–37.

Fitzpatrick, W. F. Sexual functioning in the paraplegic patient. *Archives of Physical Medicine and Rehabilitation*, 1974, *55*, 221–227.

Fjallbrant, B. Sperm antibodies and sterility in men. *Acta Obstet. Gynecology Scandinavica*, 1968, *47* (Suppl. 4).

Fletcher, G. F. Sex and the heart patient: Portable ECG finds arrythmias. *Sexual Medicine Today*, 1979, *3*, 8–9.

Fonkalsrud, E. W., & Mengel, W. (Eds). *The undescended testes.* Chicago: Year Book Medical Publishers, 1981.

Fookes, B. H. Some experience in the use of aversive therapy in male homosexuals, exhibitionists and fetishism-transvestism. *British Journal of Psychiatry*, 1969, *115*, 339–341.

Ford, C., & Beach, F. *Patterns of sexual behavior.* New York: Harper & Row, 1951.

Fox, C. A. Orgasm and fertility. In R. Gemme & C. C. Wheeler (Eds.), *Progress in sexology*, pp. 351–355. New York: Plenum, 1977.

Frank, E., Anderson, C., & Rubenstein, D. Marital role strain and sexual satisfaction. *Journal of Consulting and Clinical Psychology*, 1979, *47*, 1096–1103.

Frank, E., Anderson, C., & Rubenstein, D. Frequency of sexual dysfunction in normal couples. *New England Journal of Medicine*, 1978, *299*, 111–115.

Franklin, R. R., & Dukes, C. D. Further studies on sperm agglutinating antibody and unexplained infertility. *Journal of American Medical Association*, 1964, *190*, 682–683.

Freeman, W., & Meyer, R. G. A behavioral alteration of sexual preferences in the human male. *Behavior Therapy*, 1975, *6*, 206–212.

Freud, S. In E. Jones (Ed.), *Collected papers.* London: Hogarth, 1925.

Freud, S. *New introductory lectures on psychoanalysis.* New York: Norton, 1933.

Freud, S. Letter to an American mother, *American Journal of Psychiatry*, 1951, *107*, 252.

Freund, K. A laboratory method for diagnosing predominance of homo- or hetero-erotic interest in the male. *Behavior Research and Therapy*, 1963, *1*, 85–93.

Freund, K. Some problems in the treatment of homosexuality. In H. J. Eysenck (Ed.), *Behavior therapy and the neuroses.* Oxford, England: Pergamon Press, 1960.

Freund, M. Effect of frequency of emission on semen output and an estimate of daily sperm production in man. *Journal of Reproduction and Fertility*, 1963, *6*, 269–286.

Friday, N. *Men in love.* New York: Delacorte Press, 1980.

Friday, N. *My secret garden: Women's sexual fantasies.* New York: Simon & Schuster, 1973.

Friedlander, K. *The psychoanalytic approach to juvenile delinquency.* London: Routledge & Kegan-Paul, 1947.

Friedman, E. *Labor: Clinical evaluation and management* (2nd ed.). New York: Appleton-Century-Crofts, 1978.

Frisbie, L. Treated sex offenders and what they did. *Mental Hygiene*, 1959, *43*, 263–267.

Frisbie, L. V. Treated sex offenders who reverted to sexually deviant behavior. *Federal Probation*, 1965, *29*, 52–57.

Fromm, E. *The art of loving.* New York: Harper & Row, 1956.

Fuchs, K., Hoch, F., Paldi, E., Abramovici, H., Brandes, J. M., Timor-Tritsch, I., & Kleinhaus, M. Hypnodesensitization therapy of vaginismus: *In vitro* and *in vivo* methods. *International Journal of Clinical and Experimental Hypnosis,* 1973, *21,* 144–156.

Fullard, W., & Reiling, A. M. An investigation of Lorenz's babyness. *Child Development,* 1976, *47,* 119–123.

Gadpaille, W. J. Cross-species and cross-cultural contributions to understanding homosexual activity. *Archives of General Psychiatry,* 1980, *37,* 349–355.

Gaensbauer, T. J. Castration in the treatment of sex offenders: An appraisal. *Rocky Mountain Medical Journal,* 1973, *70,* 23–28.

Gagnon, J. Female child victims of sex offenses. *Social Problems,* 1965, *13,* 176–192.

Gagnon, J. H., & Roberts, E. J. Content and process in parental verbal communication about sexuality to preadolescent children. Unpublished manuscript, State University of New York, Stony Brook, 1983.

Gagnon, J. H., & Simon, W. E. *Sexual conduct: The social sources of human sexuality.* Chicago: Aldine, 1973.

Gagnon, J. R., Simon, W., & Berger, A. J. Some aspects of sexual adjustment in early and late adolescence. In J. Zubin & A. N. Freedman (Eds.), *Psychopathology of adolescence.* New York: Grune & Stratton, 1970.

Gardner, E. D., Gray, D. J., & O'Rahilly, R. *Anatomy, A regional study of human structure.* Philadelphia: Saunders, 1975.

Gartrell, N. K., Loriaux, D. L., and Chase, T. N. Plasma testosterone in homosexual and heterosexual women. *American Journal of Psychiatry,* 1977, *134,* 1117–1119.

Gebhard, P. Factors in marital orgasm. *Journal of Social Issues,* 1966, *22,* 88–96.

Gebhard, P. H. Fetishism and sadomasochism. *Science and Psychoanalysis,* 1969, *15,* 71–80.

Gebhard, P. H., Gagnon, J. H., Pomeroy, W. B., & Christenson, C. V. *Sex offenders: An analysis of types.* New York: Harper & Row, 1965.

Gebhard, P. H. *Incidence of overt homosexuality in the United States and Western Europe* (Final Report of NIMH Task Force on Homosexuality). Washington, D.C.: U.S. Government Printing Office, 1972.

Gebhard, P. H. The acquisition of basic information. *The Journal of Sex Research,* 1977, *13*(3), 148–169.

Gebhard, P. H. The institute. In M. S. Weinberg (Ed.), *Sex research: Studies from the Kinsey Institute.* New York: Oxford Press, 1976.

Geer, J. H. Measurement of genital arousal in human males and females. In I. Martin & P. H. Venables (Eds.), *Techniques in psychophysiology.* New York: John Wiley, 1980.

Geer, J. H., & Messe, M. R. Behavioral medicine and sexual dysfunction. In R. J. Gatchel, A. Baum, & J. Singer (Eds.), *Behavioral medicine and clinical psychology/psychiatry: Overlapping disciplines.* Hillsdale, N.J.: Lawrence Erlbaum Associates, Publishers, 1982.

Geer, J. H., Morokoff, P., & Greenwood, P. Sexual arousal in women: The development of a measurement device for vaginal blood volume. *Archives of Sexual Behavior,* 1974, *3*(6), 559–564.

Geiser, R. L. *Hidden victims: The sexual abuse of children.* Boston: Beacon Press, 1979.

Gellhorn, E., & Loofbourrow, G. N. *Emotions and emotional disorders: A neurophysiological study.* New York: Harper & Row, 1963.

George, L. K., & Weiler, S. J. Sexuality in middle and later life. *Archives of General Psychiatry,* 1981, *38,* 919–923.

Giallambardo, R. *Society of women.* New York: Wiley, 1966.

Ginder, R. *Binding with briars. Sex and sin in the Catholic church.* Englewood Cliffs, N.J.: Prentice-Hall, 1975.

Girodo, M. *Shy?* New York: Pocket Books, 1978.

Gittelson, N. L., Eacott, S. E., & Mehta, B. M. Victims of indecent exposure. *British Journal of Psychiatry,* 1978, *132,* 61–66.

Gizinski, M. N. Psychic trauma of gynecologic surgery. *Female Patient,* 1979 (Feb.), 37–39.

Glenn, N. D., & Weaver, C. N. Attitudes toward premarital, extramarital and homosexual relations in the U.S. in the 1970's. *Journal of Sex Research,* 1979, *15,* 108–118.

Gligor, A. M. *Incest and sexual delinquency: A comparative analysis of two forms of sexual behavior in minor females.* Unpublished doctoral dissertation. Case Western Reserve University, 1966.

Golde, P., & Kogan, N. A. Sentence completion procedure for assessing attitudes toward old people. *Journal of Gerontology,* 1959, *14,* 355–363.

Goldfoot, D. A., Westerborg, Van Loon, H., Groeneveld, W., & Slob, A. K. Behavioral and physiological evidence of sexual climax in the female stump-tailed macaque (*Macaca arctoides*). *Science,* 1980, *208,* 1477–1478.

Goldsmith, S., Gabrielson, M. O., Gabrielson, I., Mathews, V., & Potts, L. Teenagers, sex and contraception. *Family Planning Perspectives,* 1972, *4* (1), 32–38.

Goldstein, M., & Haeberle, E. J. *The sex book: A mod-*

ern pictorial encyclopedia. New York: Herder & Herder, 1971.

Goldstein, M. J. Exposure to erotic stimuli and sexual deviance. *Journal of Social Issues,* 1973, *29,* 197–220.

Goldstein, M.J., & Kant, H.S. *Pornography and sexual deviance.* Berkeley: University of California Press, 1973.

Gondonneau, J., Mironer, L., Dourlin-Rollier, A. M., & Simon, P. *Rapport sur le comportement sexuel des Francais.* Paris: Pierre Charron et Rene Julliard, 1972.

Goode, E. Drug use and sexual activity on a college campus. *American Journal of Psychiatry,* 1969, *128,* 92–96.

Goodlin, R. C. Orgasm and premature labor. *Lancet,* 1969, *2,* 646.

Gordon, D. C. *Self-love.* Baltimore: Penguin, 1972.

Gordon, L. *Woman's body, woman's rights: A social history of birth control in America.* New York: Grossman Publ., 1976.

Gordon, S., Scales, P., & Everly, K. *The sexual adolescent: Communicating with teenagers about sex* (2nd ed.). North Scituate, Mass.: Duxbury Press, 1979.

Gosselin, C., & Wilson, G. *Sexual variations: Fetishism, sadomasochism and transvestism.* New York: Simon & Schuster, 1980.

Grant, V. W. A case study of fetishism. *Journal of Abnormal and Social Psychology,* 1953, *48,* 141–149.

Green, R. Mythological, historical, and cross cultural aspects of transsexualism. In R. Green & J. Money (Eds.), *Transsexualism and Sex Reassignment.* Baltimore: Johns Hopkins University Press, 1969.

Green, R. *Sexual identity conflict in children and adults.* Baltimore: Penguin Books, 1974.

Green, R., Newman, L., & Stoller, R. Treatment of boyhood "transsexualism." *Archives of General Psychiatry,* 1972, *26,* 213–217.

Green, G., & Greene, C. *S—M: The last taboo.* New York: Grove Press, 1974.

Griffin, S. *Pornography and silence: Culture's revenge against nature.* New York: Harper & Row, 1981.

Grimes, D. A., & Cates, Jr., W. Abortion: Methods and complications. In E. S. E. Hafez (Ed.) and 57 contributors, *Human reproduction: Conception and contraception.* New York: Harper & Row, 1980.

Grobstein, C. *From chance to purpose: An appraisal of external human fertilization.* Don Mills, Ontario: Addison-Wesley Publishing Co., 1981.

Groth, N. A., & Birnbaum, H. J. Adult sexual orientation and attraction to underage persons. *Archives of Sexual Behavior,* 1978, *7,* 175–181.

Groth, A. N., & Birnbaum, J. J. *Men who rape: The psy-*

chology of the offender. New York: Plenum Press, 1979.

Groth, A. N., Burgess, A. W., & Holmstrom, L. L. Rape: Power, anger and sexuality. *American Journal of Psychiatry,* 1977, *134,* 1239–1243.

Guerrero, R. Association of the type and the time of insemination within the menstrual cycle with the human sex ratio at birth. *The New England Journal of Medicine,* 1974, *291*(20): 1056–1059.

Guerrero, R. Sex ratio: A statistical association with the type and time of insemination in the menstrual cycle. *International Journal of Fertility,* December 1970, *15*(4), 221–225.

Gundlach, R. H. Research project report. *The Ladder,* 1967, *11,* 2–9.

Gundlach, R. H., & Riess, B. F. Self and sexual identity in the female: A study of female homosexuals. In B. F. Riess (Ed.), *New directions in mental health.* New York: Grune & Stratton, 1968.

Guyton, A. C. *Textbook of medical physiology.* Philadelphia: Saunders, 1976.

Haas, G. G., Cines, D. B., & Schreiber, A. D. Immunologic infertility: Identification of patients with antisperm antibody. *The New England Journal of Medicine,* 1980, *303*(13), 722–727.

Hackett, T. P. The psychotherapy of exhibitionists in a court clinic setting. *Seminars in Psychiatry,* 1971, *3,* 297–306.

Hafez, E. S. E. Reproductive senescence. In E. S. E. Hafez (Ed.), *Human reproduction: Conception and contraception,* (2nd ed.). New York: Harper & Row, 1980a.

Halikas, J. A., Goodwin, D. W., & Guze, S. B. Marihuana effects—a survey of regular users. *Journal of the American Medical Association,* 1971, *217,* 692–694.

Halverson, H. Genital and sphincter behavior of the male infant. *Journal of Genetic Psychology,* 1940, *56,* 95–136.

Hamilton, G. V. *A research in marriage.* New York: Albert and Charles Boni, 1929.

Hammer, E. F., & Glueck, B. C. Psychodynamic patterns in sex offenses: A four-factor theory. *Psychiatric Quarterly,* 1957, *3,* 325–345.

Hare, E. H. Masturbational insanity: The history of an idea. *Journal of Mental Science,* 1962, *108,* 1–25.

Hariton, B. E., & Singer, J. L. Women's fantasies during sexual intercourse: Normative and theoretical implications. *Journal of Consulting and Clinical Psychology,* 1974, *42,* 313–322.

Harlap, S. Gender of infants conceived on different days of the menstrual cycle. *The New England Journal of Medicine,* 1979, *300*(26): 1445–1448.

Harlow, H. F. Sexual behavior in the Rhesus monkey. In F. Beach (Ed.), *Sex and behavior.* New York: John Wiley, 1965.

Harlow, H. F. The heterosexual affectional system in monkeys. *American Psychologist,* 1962, *17,* 1–9.

Hastings, D. W. *Impotence and frigidity.* Boston: Little, Brown, 1963.

Hatch, J. P. Vaginal photoplethysmography: Methodological considerations. *Archives of Sexual Behavior,* 1979, *8*(4), 357.

Hatch, J. P., Heiman, J. R., & Hahn, P. A photoplethysmographic device for measuring changes in penile blood volume pulse during sexual arousal in humans (Abst.). *Psychophysiology,* 1980, *17,* 287.

Hatcher, R. A., Stewart, G. K., Stewart, F., Guest, F., Schwartz, D. W., and Jones, S. A. *Contraceptive technology, 1980–1981 (10th Rev).* New York: Irvington Publishers, 1980.

Heath, R. G. Pleasure and brain activity in man. *Journal of Nervous and Mental Disease,* 1972, *154,* 3–18.

Hedblom, J. H. Dimensions of lesbian sexual experience. *Archives of Sexual Behavior,* 1973, *12,* 329–344.

Hediger, H. *The psychology and behavior of animals in zoos and circuses.* New York: Dover, 1968.

Heider, F. *The psychology of interpersonal relations.* New York: Wiley, 1958.

Heim, N., & Hursch, C. J. Castration for sex offenders: Treatment or punishment? A review and critique of recent European literature. *Archives of Sexual Behavior,* 1979, *8,* 281–303.

Heiman, J., & Hatch, J. Conceptual and therapeutic contributions of psychophysiology to sexual dysfunction. In S. Haynes and L. Gannon (Eds.), *Psychosomatic disorders: A Psychophysiological approach to etiology and treatment.* New York: Praeger, 1981.

Heiman, J. Women and sexuality: Loosening the double binds. In G. Albee, S. Gordon & H. Leitenberg (Eds.), *Promoting sexual responsibility and preventing sexual problems.* Hanover, N.H.: New England Press, in press.

Heiman, J., LoPiccolo, L., & LoPiccolo, J. *Becoming orgasmic: A sexual growth program for women.* Englewood Cliffs, N.J.: Prentice-Hall, 1976.

Heiman, J. R., LoPiccolo, L. & LoPiccolo, J. The treatment of sexual dysfunction. In A. S. Gurman and D. P. Kniskern (Eds.), *Handbook of family therapy.* New York: Brunner/Mazel, 1981.

Heiman, J. R., & LoPiccolo, J. Clinical outcome of sex therapy: Effects of daily v. weekly treatment. *Archives of General Psychiatry,* 1983, *40,* 443–449.

Heiman, J. R., & Rowland, D. Affective and physiological sexual response patterns: The effects of instructions on sexually functional and dysfunctional men. *Journal of Psychosomatic Research,* 1983, *27,* 105–116.

Heller, C. G., & Clermont, Y. Kinetics of the germinal epithelium in man: Recent progress. *Hormone Research,* 1964, *20,* 545.

Hellerstein, H. K., & Friedman, C. H. Sexual activity and the post coronary patient. *Archives of Internal Medicine,* 1970, *125,* 987–999.

Henson, D. E., Rubin, H. B., & Henson, C. Consistency of the labial temperature change measure of human female eroticism. *Behavior Research and Therapy,* 1978, *16,* 125–129.

Herbert, J. Hormones and behavior. *Proceedings of Royal Society of London (Biol.),* 1977, *199,* 425–443.

Herman, J., & Hirshman, L. Father-daughter incest. *Signs,* 1977, *2,* 735–756.

Hess, E. J. Attitude and pupil size. *American Scientist,* 1965, *212,* 46–54.

Hessellund, H. Masturbation and sexual fantasies in married couples. *Archives of Sexual Behavior,* 1976, *5,* 133–147.

Hewes, G. W. Communication of sexual interest: An anthropological view. *Medical Aspects of Human Sexuality,* 1973, (Jan.) 66–92.

Heyman, S. R. Relationship of sexual fantasies to sexual behavior and personality patterns in females and males. Paper presented at 87th Annual Convention, American Psychological Assoc., New York City, 1979.

Higgins, G. E. Aspects of sexual response in adults with spinal cord injury: A review of the literature. In J. LoPiccolo & L. LoPiccolo (Eds.), *Handbook of sex therapy.* New York: Plenum, 1978.

Himes, N. E. *Medical history of contraception.* New York: Schocken Books, Inc., 1970.

Hinde, R. A. Interpersonal relationships—in quest of a science. *Psychological Medicine,* 1978, *8,* 373–386.

Hinde, R. A. On describing relationships. *Journal of Child Psychology and Psychiatry and Allied Disciplines,* 1976, *17,* 1–19.

Hinde, R. A., & Stevenson-Hinde, J. Towards understanding relationships: Dynamic stability. In P. P. G. Bateson & R. A. Hinde (Eds.), *Growing points in ethology.* Cambridge, England: Cambridge University Press, 1976.

Hines, M. Prenatal gonadal hormones and sex differences in human behavior. *Psychological Bulletin,* 1982, *92,* 56–80.

Hirning, L. C. Genital exhibitionism, an interpretative study. *Journal of Clinical Psychopathology*, 1947, *8*, 557–564.

Hite, S. *The Hite report*. New York: Macmillan, 1976.

Hoenig, J. Freud's views on sexual disorders in historical perspective. *British Journal of Psychiatry*, 1976, *129*, 193–200.

Hoenig, J., & Kenna, J. C. The prevalence of transsexualism in England and Wales. *British Journal of Psychiatry*, 1974, *124*, 181–190.

Hoffman, M. *The gay world*. New York: Basic Books, 1968.

Hoffman, M. The male prostitute. In M. P. Levine (Ed.), *Gay men: The sociology of male homosexuality*. New York: Harper & Row, 1979.

Hogan, R. A., Fox, A. N., & Kirchner, J. H. Attitudes, opinions, and sexual development of 205 homosexual women. *Journal of Homosexuality*, 1977, *3*, 123–136.

Hohmann, G. Some effects of spinal cord lesions on experienced emotional feelings. *Psychophysiology*, 1966, *3*, 143–156.

Hollender, M. H. Women's fantasies during sexual intercourse. *Archives of General Psychiatry*, 1963, *8*, 86–90.

Holmes, K. K. Syphilis. In K. J. Isselbacher, R. B. Adams, E. Braunwald,, R. G. Petersdorf, & J. D. Wilson (Eds.), *Principles of internal medicine* (9th ed.). New York: McGraw-Hill, 1980.

Holmes, K. K., & Stamm, W. E. Chlamydial genital infections: A growing problem. *Hospital Practice*, 1979 (Oct.), 105–117.

Holmstrom, L. L., & Burgess, A. W. Sexual behavior during reported rapes. *Archives of Sexual Behavior*, 1980, *9*, 427–439.

Holstein, C. M., Goldstein, J. W., & Bem, D. J. The importance of expressive behavior, involvement, sex, and need-approval in inducing liking. *Journal of Experimental Social Psychology*, 1971, *7*, 534–544.

Hooker, E. Male homosexuals and their worlds. In J. Marmor (Ed.), *Sexual inversion: The multiple roots of homosexuality*, pp. 83–107. New York: Basic Books, 1965.

Hoon, E. F., & Hoon, P. W. Styles of sexual expression in women: Clinical implications of multivariate analysis. *Archives of Sexual Behavior*, 1978, *7*, 105–116.

Hoon, P. W., Wincze, J. P., & Hoon, E. F. The effects of biofeedback and cognitive mediation upon vaginal blood volume. *Behavior Therapy*, 1977, *8*, 694–702.

Hopkins, J. H., The lesbian personality. *British Journal of Psychiatry*, 1969, *115*, 1433–1436.

Horos, C. B. *Rape: The private crime, a social horror*. New Canaan: Tobey Publishing, 1974.

Hottois, J., & Milner, N. A. *The sex education controversy: A study of politics, education, and morality*. Lexington, Mass.: Heath, Lexington Books, 1975.

Housden, J. An examination of the biologic etiology of transvestism. *International Journal of Social Psychiatry*, 1965, *11*, 301–305.

Howard, J. L., Liptzin, M. B., & Reifler, C. B. Is pornography a problem? *Journal of Social Issues*, 1973, *29*, 133–146.

Huey, C. J., Kline-Graber, G., & Graber, B. Time factors and orgasmic response. *Archives of Sexual Behavior*, 1981, *10*, 111–118.

Humphreys, L. *Tearoom trade: Impersonal sex in public places*. Chicago: Aldine, 1970.

Hunt, M. *Sexual behavior in the 70's*. Chicago: Playboy Press, 1974.

Hunt, M. M. *The natural history of love*. New York: Funk & Wagnalls, 1959.

Huston, T. L. Ambiguity of acceptance, social desirability and dating choice. *Journal of Experimental and Social Psychology*, 1973, *9*, 32–42.

Imperato-McGinley, J., Peterson, R. E., Gautier, T. & Sturla, E. The impact of androgens on the evolution of male gender identity. In S. J. Kogan & E. S. E. Hafez (Eds.) *Pediatric andrology*. The Hague, Netherlands: Martinus Nijhoff, 1981.

Jackman, N. H., O'Toole, R., & Geis, G. The self-image of the prostitute. *Sociological Quarterly*, 1963, *4*, 150–161.

Jacobs, L. E., Berscheid, E., & Walster, E. Self-esteem and attraction. *Journal of Personality and Social Psychology*, 1971, *17*, 84–91.

Jaffe, A. C., Dynaeson, L., & Tenbensel, R. W. Sexual abuse of children: An epidemiological study. *American Journal of Diseases of Children*, 1975, *129*, 689–692.

Jaffe, Y., Malamuth, N., Feingold, J., & Feshbach, S. Sexual arousal and behavioral aggression. *Journal of Personality and Social Psychology*, 1974, *30*, 759–764.

Jain, P., Hsu, T., Freeman, R., & Chang, M. C. Demographic aspects of lactation and postpartum amenorrhea. *Demography*, 1970, *7*, 255.

James, B. B. *Women of England*. Philadelphia: Rittenhouse Press, 1908.

James, J. *A formal analysis of prostitution: Final report, part 1, basic statistical summary*. State of Washington, Department of Social and Health Services, 1971.

James, J. Two domains of the streetwalker argot. *Anthropological Linguistics*, 1972, *14*, 172–181.

James, J. Motivations for entrance into prostitution. In L. Crites (Ed.), *The female offender*, pp. 177–205. Lexington, Mass.: Lexington Books, 1976.

James, J. Women as sexual criminals and victims. In J. Laws & P. Schwartz (Eds.), *Sexual scripts*. New York: The Dryden Press, 1977, 179–216.

James, J., & Vitaliano, P. Factors in the drift toward female sex role deviance. Submitted paper, 1981.

James, J., & Meyerding, J. Early sexual experience and prostitution. *American Journal of Psychiatry*, 1977, *134*, 1381–1385.

James, W. H. The reliability of the reporting of coital frequency. *Journal of Sex Research*, 1971, *7*, 312–314.

Janda, L. H., O'Grady, K. E., & Barnhart, S. A. Effects of sexual attitudes and physical attractiveness on person perception of men and women. *Sex Roles*, 1981, *7*, 189–199.

Javert, C. T. *Spontaneous and habitual abortion*. New York: McGraw-Hill, 1957.

Jay, K., & Young, A. *The gay report*. New York: Summit Books, 1977.

Jensen, S. B., Diabetic sexual dysfunction: A comparative study of 160 insulin treated diabetic men and women and an age-matched control group. *Archives of Sexual Behavior*, 1981, *10*, 493–504.

Jochheim, K. A., & Wahle, H. A study on the sexual function in 56 male patients with complete irreversible lesions of the spinal cord and cauda equina. *Paraplegia*, 1970, *8*, 166–172.

Johnson, R. E. Some correlates of extramarital coitus. *Journal of Marriage and the Family*, 1970, *32*, 449–456.

Johnsonbaugh, R. E., O'Connell, K., Engel, S. B., Edson, M. E., Sode, J. Plasma testosterone LH and FSH after vasectomy. *Fertility and Sterility*, 1975, *26*, 329–330.

Jones, E. E. *Ingratiation*. New York: Appleton-Century-Crofts, 1964.

Jones, I. H., & Frei, D. Provoked anxiety as a treatment for exhibitionism. *British Journal of Psychiatry*, 1977, *131*, 295–300.

Jongbloet, P. H. Mental and physical handicaps in connection with over ripeness ovapathy. In J. A. Ross, & P. T. Piotrow, *Birth control without contraceptives*. Washington, D.C.: Population Reports, The George Washington Medical Center, June 1974.

Jorgensen, C. A. *A personal autobiography*. New York: Bantam Books, 1968.

Josiassen, R. C., Fantuzzo, J., & Rosen, A. C. Treatment of pedophilia using multistage aversion therapy and social skills training. *Journal of Behavior Therapy and Experimental Psychiatry*, 1980, *11*, 56–61.

Kallman, F. J. A comparative twin study of the genetic aspects of male homosexuality. *Journal of Nervous and Mental Disease*, 1952, *115*, 283–298.

Kalven, H., & Zeisel, H. *The American jury*. Boston: Little, Brown, 1966.

Kaminetzky, H. A., & Baker, H. Nutrition in human reproduction. In E. S. E. Hafez (Ed.) and 57 contributors, *Human reproduction: Conception and contraception*. New York: Harper & Row, 1980.

Kaplan, A. H., & Abrams, M. Ejaculatory impotence. *Journal of Urology*, 1958, *79*, 964–968.

Kaplan, H. S. *Disorders of sexual desire and other new concepts and techniques in sex therapy*. New York: Brunner/Mazel, 1979.

Kaplan, H. S. *The new sex therapy*. New York: Brunner/Mazel, 1974.

Kaplan, K. A., & Heuther, C. A. A clinical study of vasectomy failure and recanalization. *Journal of Urology*, 1975, *113*, 71.

Karacan, I. Diagnosis of impotence in diabetes mellitus. *Annals of Internal Medicine*, 1980, *92*, 334–337.

Karlen, A. *Sexuality and homosexuality: A new view*. New York: W. W. Norton & Co., Inc., 1971.

Kaufman, I., Peck, A. L., & Tagiuri, C. K. The family constellation and overt incestuous relations between father and daughter. *American Journal of Orthopsychiatry*, 1954, *24*, 266–277.

Kaufman, J. Organic and psychological factors in the genesis of impotence and premature ejaculation. In C. W. Wahl (Ed.), *Sexual problems: Diagnosis and treatment in medical practice*. New York: Free Press, 1967.

Kaufman, S. A. *Sexual sabotage*. New York: Macmillan, 1981.

Kegel, A. Sexual functions of the pubococcygeus muscle. *Western Journal of Surgery*, 1952, *60*, 521–524.

Keith, D., Phillips, J., Hulka, J., Hulka, B., & Keith, L. Gynecologic laparoscopy in 1975. *Journal of Reproductive Medicine*, 1976, *16*, 105–117.

Kemper, T. D. The mate selection and marital satisfaction according to sibling type of husband and wife. *Journal of Marriage and the Family*, 1966, *28*, 346–349.

Kempczinski, R. F. Role of the vascular diagnostic laboratory in the evaluation of male impotence. *American Journal of Surgery*, 1979, *138*, 278–282.

Kenyon, F. E. Studies in female homosexuality: Psychological test results. *Journal of Consulting and Clinical Psychology*, 1968, *32*, 510–513.

Kerckhoff, A., & Davis, K. E. Value consensus and need complementarity in mate selection. *American Sociological Review*, 1962, *27*, 295–303.

Kessler, I. Human cervical cancer as a venereal disease. *Cancer Research*, 1976, *25*, 783.

Keverne, B. J. Personal communication, 1982.

Keverne, E. B. Sex attractants in primates. *Journal of the Society of Cosmetic Chemists*, 1976, *27*, 257–269.

Keyes, P. L., Richards, J. S., Karsh, F. J., Midgley, Jr., A. R., & Gay, V. L. In E. S. E. Hafez (Ed.), *Human reproduction: Conception and contraception, 2nd ed.* New York: Harper & Row, 1980, pp. 287–320.

Kiesler, S., & Baral, R. The search for a romantic partner: The effects of self-esteem on romantic behavior. In K. Gergen & D. Marlow (Eds.), *Personality and social behavior.* Reading, Mass.: Addison-Wesley, 1970.

Kilpatrick, D. G., Veronen, L. J., & Resick, P. A. Assessment of the aftermath of rape: Changing patterns of fear. *Journal of Behavior Assessment*, 1979, *1*, 133–148.

King, M., & Soel, D. Sex on the college campus: Current attitudes and behavior. *Journal of College Student Personnel*, 1975, *16*, 205–209.

Kinney, J. A. Sexuality of pregnant and breastfeeding women. *Archives of Sexual Behavior*, 1973, *2*, 251–228.

Kinsey, A. C., Pomeroy, W., Martin, C., & Gebhard, P. *Sexual behavior in the human female.* Philadelphia: W. B. Saunders, 1953.

Kinsey, A. C., Pomeroy, W. B., & Martin, C. E. *Sexual behavior in the human male.* Philadelphia: W. B. Saunders, 1948.

Kipnis, D. M. Interaction between members of bomber crews as a determinant of sociometric choice. *Human Relations*, 1957, *10*, 263–270.

Kirby, D., Alter, J., & Scales, P. *An analysis of U.S. sex education programs, Vol. 1.* Atlanta: U.S. Department of Health, Education and Welfare, 1979.

Kistner, R. W. *Gynecology: Principles and practice, 3rd ed.* Chicago: Year Book Med. Pub., Inc., 1979.

Kistner, R. W. Induction of ovulation with clomiphene citrate. In S. T. Behrman & R. W. Kistner (Eds.), *Progress in infertility.* Boston: Little, Brown, 1968.

Kleinke, C. L., Staneski, R. A., & Berger, D. E. Evaluation of an interviewer as a function of interviewer gaze, reinforcement of subject gaze, and interviewer attractiveness. *Journal of Personality and Social Psychology*, 1975, *31*, 115–122.

Knutson, D. C. Homosexuality and the law. *Journal of Homosexuality*, 1979, *5*, 5–19.

Kockott, G., Feil, W., Revenstort, D., Aldenhoff, J., & Besinger, U. Symptomatology and psychological aspects of male sexual inadequacy: Results of an experimental study. *Archives of Sexual Behavior*, 1980, *9*, 457–476.

Koff, W. C. Marijuana use and sexual activity. *Journal of Sex Research*, 1974, *10*, 194–204.

Kolodny, R. C., Masters, W. E., & Johnson, V. E. *The textbook of sexual medicine.* Boston: Little, Brown, 1979.

Kolodny, R. C., Masters, W. H., Hendryx, J., & Toro, G. Plasma testosterone and semen analysis in male homosexuals. *New England Journal of Medicine*, 1971, *285*, 1170–1174.

Kolodny, R. C., Masters, W. H., Kolodny, R. M., & Toro, G. Depression of plasma testosterone levels after chronic intensive marihuana use. *New England Journal of Medicine*, 1974, *290*, 872–874.

Kolodny, R. C. Sexual dysfunction in diabetic females. *Diabetes*, 1971, *20*, 557–559.

Kotin, J., Wilbert, D., Verburg, P., & Solinger, S. Thioridazine and sexual dysfunction. *American Journal of Psychiatry*, 1976, *133*, 82–85.

Kozol, H. L., Boucher, R. J., & Garofalo, R. F. The diagnosis and treatment of dangerousness. *Crime and Delinquency*, 1972, *18*, 371–392.

Krabbe, S., Skakkebaek, N. E., Berthelsen, J. G., Eyben, F. V., Volsted, P., Mauritzen, K., Eldrup, J., & Nielsen, A. H. High incidence of undetected neoplasia in maldescended testes. *The Lancet*, May 1979, 999–1000.

Krafft-Ebing, Richard Von. *Psychopathia sexualis.* New York: Bell Publishing Co., 1965 (first published in 1886).

Krebs, D., & Adinioff, A. A. Physical attractiveness, social relations, and personality stereotype. *Journal of Personality and Social Psychology*, 1975, *31*, 245–253.

Kronhausen, P., and Kronhausen, E. *Erotic art.* New York: Bell, 1968.

Kroth, J. A. *Child sexual abuse: Analysis of a family therapy approach.* Springfield, Ill: Charles C Thomas, 1979.

Kutchinsky, B. The effect of easy availability of pornography on the incidence of sex crimes: The Danish experience. *Journal of Social Issues*, 1973, *29*, 163–182.

Kutchinsky, B. The effect of pornography—an experiment on perception, attitudes and behavior. *Technical reports of the Commission on Obscenity and Pornography* (Vol. 8). Washington, D.C.: U.S. Government Printing Office, 1970.

LaBarre, W. The Aymara indians of the Lake Titicaca

Plateau, Bolivia. *Memoirs of the American Anthropological Association,* No. 68, 1948.

Lahteenniki, P., Ylostalo, P., Sipinen, S., Tolvoner, J., Ruusuvarra, L., Pikkola, P., Nilsson, C. G., & Luukainen, T. Return of ovulation.

La Leche League International. *The womanly art of breastfeeding* (2nd ed.). Franklin Park, Ill., 1978.

Lamberti, J. W., & Chapel, J. L. Development and evaluation of a sex education program for medical students. *Journal of Medical Education,* 1977, *52,* 582–586.

Landis, J. Experiences of 500 children with adult sexual deviants. *Psychiatric Quarterly Supplement,* 1956, *30,* 91–109.

Lange, J. D., Wincze, J. P., Zwick, W., Feldman, S., & Hughes, K. Effects of demand performance, self-monitoring of arousal and increased sympathetic nervous system activity on male sexual response. *Archives of Sexual Behavior,* 1981, *10,* 443–464.

Langevin, B., Paitich, D., Freeman, R., Mann, K., & Handy, L. Personality characteristics and sexual anomalies in males. *Canadian Journal of Behavioral Science,* 1978, *10,* 222–238.

Langevin, R., Paitich, D., Ramsey, G., Anderson, C., Kamrad, J., Pope, S., Geller, G., Pearl, L., & Newman, J. Experimental studies of the etiology of genital exhibitionism. *Archives of Sexual Behavior,* 1979, *8,* 307–331.

LaRossa, R. Sex during pregnancy: A symbolic interactionist analysis. *The Journal of Sex Research,* 1979, *15,* 119–128.

Lavrakas, P. J. Female preferences for male physiques. *Journal of Research in Personality,* 1975, *9,* 324–334.

Lawrence, D. H., *Sex, literature, and censorship.* New York: Twayne, 1953.

Lawrence, D. H. *Sex, literature, and censorship.* New York, Twayne Publishers, 1953.

Laws, D. R., & Holman, M.L. Sexual response faking by pedophiles. *Criminal Justice & Behavior,* 1978, *5,* 343–356.

Lazarus, A. A. Psychological treatment of dyspareunia. In S. R. Leiblum & L. A. Pervin (Eds.), *Principles and practice of sex therapy.* New York: Guilford, 1980.

Lea, E. Instruments of autoerotic stimulation. In R. E. L. Masters (Ed.), *Sexual self-stimulation.* Los Angeles: Sherbourne Press, 1967.

Leader, A. J., Axelrod, S. D., Frankowski, R., & Mumford, S. D. Complications of 2, 711 vasectomies. *Journal of Urology,* 1974, *111,* 365.

Lear, M. W. *Heartsounds.* New York: Simon & Schuster, 1980.

Lear, M. W. Thinking about breasts. *Redbook Magazine,* August 1974.

Lebovitz, P. J. Feminine behavior in boys: Aspects of its outcome. *American Journal of Psychiatry,* 1972, *128,* 1283–1289.

Ledger, W. J. Management of postpartum caesarean section morbidity. *Clinical Obstetrics and Gynecology,* 1980, *23*(2), 621–635.

Lee, I. Y., Utidjion, H., Singh, B., Carpenter, U., & Cutler, J. C. Potential impact of chemical prophylaxis on the incidence of gonorrhea. *British Journal of Venereal Diseases,* 1972, *48,* 376–380.

Leiblum, S. R., & Pervin, L. A. (Eds.). *Principles and practice of sex therapy.* New York: Guilford, 1980*b.*

Leitenberg, H., & Slavin, L. Comparison of attitudes toward transsexuality and homosexuality. *Archives of Sexual Behavior,* 1983, *12,* 337–346.

Lentz, G. *Raping our children: The sex education scandal.* New Rochelle, N.Y.: Arlington House, 1972.

Leshner, A. I. *An introduction to behavioral endocrinology.* New York: Oxford University Press, 1978.

Lessing, D. *The summer before the dark.* New York: Bantam, 1973.

LeSueur, M. *The girl.* Cambridge, Mass.: West End Press, 1978.

Levin, R. J., & Wagner, G. Haemodynamic changes of the human vagina during sexual arousal assessed by a heated oxygen electrode. *Journal of Physiology,* 1978, *275,* 23–24.

Levinger, F. Systematic distortion in spouses' reports of preferred and actual sexual behavior. *Sociometry,* 1966, *29,* 291–299.

Levitt, E. E., & Klassen, A. D. Public attitudes toward homosexuality. *Journal of Homosexuality,* 1974, *1,* 29–43.

Levy, D. M. Finger sucking and accessory movements in early infancy. *American Journal of Psychiatry,* 1928, *7,* 881–918.

Leznoff, M., & Westley, W. A. The homosexual community. *Social Problems,* 1956, *3,* 257–263.

Libby, R. W., & Nass, G. D. Parental views on teenage sexual behavior. *The Journal of Sex Research,* 1971, *9*(3), 226–236.

Lief, H. I. Sex education in medicine: Retrospect and prospect. In N. Rosenzweig and F. P. Pearsall (Eds.), *Sex education for the health professional: A curriculum guide.* New York: Grune & Stratton, 1978.

Lief, H. I., & Karlen, A. A survey of sex education in U.S. medical schools. In H. E. Lief and A. Karlen (Eds.), *Sex education in medicine.* New York: Halsted Press, 1976.

Lipshultz, L. I., & Benson, G. S. Vasectomy. In E. S. E.

Hafez (Ed.) and 57 contributors, *Human reproduction: Conception and contraception.* New York: Harper & Row, 1980.

Lobitz, W. C., & Baker, E. L. Group treatment of men with erectile dysfunction. *Archives of Sexual Behavior,* 1979, *8,* 127–138.

LoPiccolo, J. From psychotherapy to sex therapy. *Society,* 1977, *14* (5), 60–68.

LoPiccolo, J. Direct treatment of sexual dysfunction. In J. LoPiccolo & L. LoPiccolo (Eds.), *Handbook of sex therapy.* New York: Plenum, 1978.

LoPiccolo, J., & Heiman, J. The role of cultural value in the prevention and treatment of sexual problems. In C. B. Qualls, V. P. Wincze, & D. H. Barlow (Eds.), *The prevention of sexual disorders.* New York: Plenum, 1978.

LoPiccolo, J., & Lobitz, W. C. The role of masturbation in the treatment of orgasmic dysfunction. *Archives of Sexual Behavior,* 1972, *2,* 163–172.

LoPiccolo, L. Low sexual desire. In S. R. Leiblum & L. A. Peruln (Eds.). *Principles and practice of sex therapy.* New York: Guilford, 1980.

Loraine, J. A., Adamopolulos, D. A., Kirkham, K. E., Ismail, A. A. A., & Dove, G. A. Patterns of hormone excretion in male and female homosexuals. *Nature,* 1971, *234,* 552–555.

Lowe, C. A., & Goldstein, J. W. Reciprocal liking and attributions of ability: Mediating effects of perceived intent and personal involvement. *Journal of Personality and Social Psychology,* 1970, *16,* 291–297.

Lukianowicz, N. Incest. *British Journal of Psychiatry,* 1972, *120,* 301–313.

Lundberg, P. O. Sexual dysfunction in patients with neurological disorders. In R. Gemme & C. C. Wheeler (Eds.), *Progress in sexology.* New York: Plenum, 1977.

Lustig, N., Dresser, J. W., Spellman, S. W., & Murray, T. B. Incest: A family group survival pattern. *Archives of General Psychiatry,* 1966, *14,* 31–40.

Lyle, K. C., & Segal, S. J. Contraceptive use: Effectiveness and the American adolescent. *Journal of Reproductive Medicine,* 1979, *22*(5), 225.

MacDonald, J. M. Indecent exposure. Springfield, Ill.: Charles C Thomas, 1973.

MacFadden, B. *The virile powers of supreme manhood.* New York: Physical Culture Publishing Co., 1900.

MacKeith, R., & Wood, C. *Infant feeding and feeding difficulties* (5th ed.). New York: Churchill Livingstone, 1977.

Macklin, E. D. Unmarried heterosexual cohabitation on the university campus. In J. P. Wiseman (Ed.), *The social psychology of sex.* New York: Harper & Row, 1976.

Madrone, L., Hawes, W. E., Many, F., & Hexter, A. C. A study on the effects of induced abortions on subsequent pregnancy outcome. *American Journal of Obstetrics and Gynecology,* 1981, *139*(5), 516–521.

Mahoney, E. R. Sex education in the public schools: A discriminant analysis of characteristics of pro and anti individuals. *The Journal of Sex Research,* 1979, *15*(4), 264–275.

Maisch, H. *Incest.* London: Andre Deutsch, 1975.

Makstein, N. K., McLaughlin, A. M., & Rogers, C. M. *Sexual abuse and the pediatric setting: Treatment and research implications.* Paper presented at the meeting of the American Psychological Association, New York, September 1979.

Malamuth, N., Feshbach, S., & Jaffe, Y. Sexual arousal and aggression: Recent experiments and theoretical issues. *Journal of Social Issues,* 1977, *33,* 110–133.

Malamuth, N. M. Rape fantasies as a function of response to violent sexual stimuli. *Archives of Sexual Behavior,* 1981, *10,* 33–48.

Malamuth, N. M., Haber, S., & Feshbach, S. Testing hypotheses regarding rape: Exposure to sexual violence, sex differences, and the normality of rape. *Journal of Research in Personality,* 1980, *14,* 121–137.

Malamuth, N. M., Heim, M., & Feshbach, S. Sexual responsiveness of college students to rape depictions: Inhibiting and disinhibiting effects. *Journal of Personality and Social Psychology,* 1980, *38,* 399–408.

Malamuth, N. M., Reisin, I., & Spinner, B. Exposure to pornography and reactions to rape. Paper presented at the Eighty-eighth Annual Convention of the American Psychological Association, New York, 1979.

Malamuth, N. M., & Spinner, B. A longitudinal content analysis of sexual violence in the best selling erotic magazines. *Journal of Sex Research,* 1980, *16,* 226–237.

Malatzky, B. M. Assisted covert sensitization in the treatment of exhibitionism. *Journal of Consulting and Clinical Psychology,* 1974, *42,* 34–40.

Malinowski, B. *The sexual life of savages in Northwestern Melanesia.* N.Y.: Harcourt Brace, 1929.

Malitz, S. Another report on the wearing of diapers and rubber pants by an adult male. *American Journal of Psychiatry,* 1966, *122,* 1435–1437.

Malloy, T. R., Wein, A. J., & Carpiniello, V. L. Comparison of the inflatable penile and the small carrion protheses in the surgical treatment of erectile impotence. *Journal of Urology,* 1980, *123,* 678–679.

Mangus, E. M. Sources of maternal stress in the postpartum period: A review of the literature and an alternative view. In J. E. Parsons (Ed.), *The psychology of sex differences and sex roles*. New York: Hemisphere Publishing.

Mann, J., Sidman, J., & Starr, S. Evaluating social consequences of erotic films: An experimental approach. *Journal of Social Issues*, 1973, *29*, 113–132.

Mann, J., Sidman, J., & Starr, S. Effects of erotic films in sexual behaviors of married couples. *Technical reports of the Commission on Obscenity and Pornography* (Vol. 8). Washington, D.C.: U.S. Government Printing Office, 1970.

Manosevitz, M. Early sexual behavior in adult homosexual and heterosexual males. *Journal of Abnormal Psychology*, 1970, *76*, 396–402.

Markel, G. E., & Nam, C. Sex predetermination: Its impact on fertility. *Social Biology*, 1971, *18*, 73–83.

Marks, I., & Gelder, M. Transvestism and fetishism: Clinical and psychological changes during faradic aversion. *British Journal of Psychiatry*, 1967, *113*, 711–729.

Marks, I., Gelder, M., & Bancroft, J. Sexual deviants two years after electrical aversion. *British Journal of Psychiatry*, 1970, *117*, 173–185.

Marks, I., Rachman, S., & Gelder, M. Methods for assessment of aversion treatment in fetishism with masochism. *Behavior Research and Therapy*, 1965, *3*, 253–258.

Marks, I. M. Review of behavioral psychotherapy, II: Sexual disorders. *American Journal of Psychiatry*, 1981, *138*, 750–756.

Marlatt, G. A., & Rohsenow, D. H. Cognitive processes in alcohol use: Expectancy and the balanced placebo design. In N. K. Mello (Ed.), *Advances in substance abuse: Behavioral and biological research*. Greenwich, Conn.: JAI Press, 1980.

Marmor, J. (Ed.). *Homosexual behavior: A modern reappraisal*. New York: Basic Books, 1980.

Marmor, J. "Normal" and "deviant" sexual behavior. *Journal of the American Medical Association*, 1971, *217*, 165–170.

Marshall, D. S. Sexual behavior on Mangaia. In D. S. Marshall & R. C. Suggs (Eds.), *Human sexual behavior: Variations in the ethnographic spectrum*. New York: Basic Books, 1971.

Marshall, D. S., & Suggs, R. C. *Human sexual behavior*. Englewood Cliffs, N.J.: Prentice-Hall, 1971.

Marshall, G. L. A combined treatment approach to the reduction of multiple fetish related behaviors. *Journal of Consulting and Clinical Psychology*, 1974, *42*, 613–616.

Marshall, P., Surridge, D., & Delva, N. The role of nocturnal penile tumescence in differentiating between organic and psychogenic impotence: The first stage of validation. *Archives of Sexual Behavior*, 1981, *10*, 1–10.

Martinson, F. M. Childhood sexuality. In B. B. Wolman and J. Money (Eds.), *Handbook of human sexuality*. Englewood Cliffs, N.J.: Prentice-Hall, 1980.

Maslow, A. *Motivation and personality*. New York: Harper & Row, 1954.

Maslow, A., & Sakoda, J. M. Volunteer-error in the Kinsey study. *Journal of Abnormal and Social Psychology*, 1952, *47*, 259–267.

Masters, R.E.L. *Patterns of incest*. New York: Julian Press, 1963.

Masters, W., & Johnson, V. *Homosexuality in perspective*. Boston: Little, Brown, 1979.

Masters, W., & Johnson, V. *Human sexual inadequacy*. Boston: Little, Brown, 1970.

Masters, W. H., & Johnson, V. E. *Human sexual response*. Boston: Little, Brown, 1966.

Mathes, E. W. The effects of physical attractiveness and anxiety on heterosexual attraction over a series of five encounters. *Journal of Marriage and the Family*, 1975, *37*, 769–774.

Mathes, E. W., & Kahn, A. Physical attractiveness, happiness, neuroticism and self-esteem. *Journal of Psychology*, 1975, *90*, 27–30.

Mathews, A. M., Bancroft, J. H. J., & Slater, P. The principal components of sexual preference. *British Journal of Social and Clinical Psychology*, 1972, *11*, 35–43.

Mathis, J. L., & Collins, M. Mandatory group therapy for exhibitionists. *American Journal of Psychiatry*, 1970, *126*, 1162–1166.

May, G. *Social control of sexual expression*. New York: Morrow, 1931.

McCaghy, C. Drinking and deviance disavowal: The case of child molesters. *Social Problems*, 1968, *16*, 43–49.

McConaghy, N. Aversive and positive conditioning treatments of homosexuality. *Behavior Research and Therapy*, 1975, *13*, 309–319.

McGeary, C. P. Personality profiles of persons convicted of indecent exposure. *Journal of Clinical Psychology*, 1975, *31*, 260–262.

McIntyre, J. Victim response to rape, alternative outcomes. Springfield, Va.: National Technical Information Service, October, 1979.

McGuire, L. S., & Wagner, N. N. Sexual dysfunction in women who were molested as children: One response pattern and suggestions for treatment. *Journal of Sex and Marital Therapy*, 1978, *4*, 11–15.

McGuire, R. J., Carlisle, J. M., & Young, B. C. Sexual

deviations as conditioned behavior: A hypothesis. *Behavior Research and Therapy*, 1965, *2*, 185–190.

Mead, M. *Coming of age in Samoa.* New York: Morrow, 1928 (1968).

Mead, M. *Sex and temperament: In three primitive societies.* New York: Morrow, 1935.

Meares, R., Grimwade, J., & Wood, C. A possible relationship between anxiety in pregnancy and puerperal depression. *Journal of Psychosomatic Research*, 1976, *20*, 605–610.

Meiselman, K. C. *Incest: A psychological study of causes and effects with treatment recommendations.* San Francisco: Jossey-Bass, 1978.

Melges, F. T., & Hamburg, D. A. Psychological effects of hormonal changes in women. In F. A. Beach, *Human sexuality in four perspectives.* Baltimore: Johns Hopkins, 1977.

Mendelson, J. H., Kuehnle, J., Ellinboe, J., & Babor, T. F. Plasma testosterone levels before, during, and after chronic marihuana smoking. *New England Journal of Medicine*, 1974, *290*, 1051–1055.

Menge, A. C., & Behrman, S. T. Immunologic aspects of infertility. In E.S.E. Hafez (Ed.) and 57 contributors, *Human reproduction: Conception and contraception.* New York: Harper & Row, 1980.

Menken, J. A. Teenage childbearing: Its medical aspects and implications for the United States population. In C. F. Westoff and R. Parke, Jr. (Eds.), *Demographic and social aspects of population growth.* Washington, D.C.: U.S. Government Printing Office, 1972. Commission of Population Growth and the American Future, Research Reports, Vol. 1, pp. 333–353.

Merriam, A. P. Aspects of sexual behavior among the Bala (Basongye). In D. S. Marshall & R. C. Suggs (Eds.), *Human sexual behavior: Variations in the ethnographic spectrum.* New York: Basic Books, 1971.

Messenger, T. C. Sex and repression in an Irish folk community. In D. S. Marshall and R. C. Suggs (Eds.), *Human sexual behavior: Variations in the ethnographic spectrum.* New York: Basic Books, 1971.

Meyer, J. K., & Reter, D. J. Sex reassignment: follow-up. *Archives of General Psychiatry*, 1979, *36*, 1910–1915.

Meyer, T. P. The effects of sexually arousing and violent films in aggressive behavior. *Journal of Sex Research*, 1972, *8*, 324–333.

Meyer-Bahlburg, H. F. L. Sex hormones and female homosexuality: A critical examination. *Archives of Sexual Behavior*, 1979, *8*, 101–119.

Meyer-Bahlburg, H. F. L. Sex hormones and male homosexuality in comparative perspective. *Archives of Sexual Behavior*, 1977, *6*, 297–325.

Michael, R. P. Oestrogens in the central nervous system. *British Medical Bulletin*, 1965, *21*, 87.

Miller, P. Y., & Simon, W. Adolescent sexual behavior: Context and change. *Social Problems*, 1974, *22*, 58–76.

Miller, W. R., & Lief, H. I. Masturbatory attitudes, knowledge and experience: Data from the Sex Knowledge and Attitude Test (SKAT). *Archives of Sexual Behavior*, 1976, *5*, 447–468.

Milner, C., & Milner, R. *Black players: The secret world of black pimps.* Boston: Little Brown, 1972.

Milton, J. L. *On spermatorrhea.* New York: Renshaw, 1881.

Mims, F. H., Brown, L., & Lubow, R. Human sexuality course evaluation. *Nursing Research*, 1976, *25*,(3), 187–191.

Mindel, A., Adler, M. W., Sutherland, S., & Fiddian, A. P. Intravenous aclovir treatment for primary genital herpes. *The Lancet*, 1982, *1*, 697–700.

Mintz, J., O'Hare, K., O'Brien, C. P., & Goldschmidt, G. Sexual problems of heroine addicts. *Archives of General Psychiatry*, 1974, *31*, 700–703.

Mohr, J. W., Turner, R. E., & Jerry, M. B. *Pedophilia and exhibitionism.* Toronto: University of Toronto Press, 1964.

Molnar, G., & Cameron, P. Incest syndromes: Observations in a general hospital psychiatric unit. *Canadian Psychiatric Association Journal*, 1975, *20*, 373–377.

Money, J. Preferatory remarks on outcome of sex reassignment in 24 cases of transsexualism. *Archives of Sexual Behavior*, 1971, *1*, 163–166.

Money, J. The therapeutic use of androgen-depleting hormone. In H. L. Resnick and M. E. Wolfgang (Eds.), *Sexual behaviors: Social, clinical and legal aspects.* Boston: Little, Brown, 1972.

Money, J. Use of androgen-depleting hormone in the treatment of male sex offenders. *Journal of Sex Research*, 1970, *6*, 164–172.

Money, J., & Erhardt, A. A. *Man & Woman, Boy & Girl.* Baltimore: Johns Hopkins University Press, 1972.

Mood, J. J. Consciousness. In D. C. Noel (Ed.), *Echoes of the wordless "word."* Missoula, Mont.: American Academy of Religion, 1973.

Moos, R. H. A typology of menstrual cycle symptoms. *American Journal of Obstetrics and Gynecology*, 1969, *103*, 390–402.

Morgan, A. J. Psychotherapy for transsexual candidates screened out of surgery. *Archives of Sexual Behavior*, 1978, *7*, 273–283.

Morris, D. *The naked ape.* New York: Dell, 1967.

Morokoff, P. *Female sexual arousal as a function of in-*

dividual differences and exposure to erotic stimuli. Unpublished doctoral dissertation, State University of New York at Stony Brook, 1980.

Morris, J. *Conundrum.* New York: New American Library, 1975.

Morris, N. M. The frequency of sexual intercourse during pregnancy. *Archives of Sexual Behavior,* 1975, *4,* 501–507.

Morrison, E. S., and Price, M. V. *Values in sexuality: A new approach to sex education.* New York: A & W Visual Library/Hart Publishing Co., 1974.

Morrison, I., & Olsen, V. Perinatal mortality and antipartum risk scoring. *Obstetrics and Gynecology,* 1979, *53,* 362.

Mosher, D. L., & Cross, H. J. Sex guilt and premarital sexual experiences of college students. *Journal of Consulting and Clinical Psychology,* 1971, *36,* 27–32.

Mosher, W. D. Contraceptive utilization, United States. *Vital and Health Statistics: Series 23, Data from the National Survey of Family Growth;* no 7 DHHS Publication (PHS), 1983, 81.

Moss, G. R., Rada, R. T., & Appel, J. B. Positive control as an alternative to aversion therapy. *Journal of Behavior Therapy and Experimental Psychiatry,* 1970, *1,* 291–294.

Moyer, D. L., Shaw, Jr., S. T., & Fu, J. C. Clinical aspects of inert and medical intrauterine devices. In E. S. E. Hafez (Ed.) and 57 contributors, *Human Reproduction: Conception and contraception* (2nd ed.). New York: Harper & Row, 1980.

Mrazek, P. B., & Kempe, C. H. (Eds.). *Sexually abused children and their families.* New York: Pergamon Press, 1981.

Munjack, D. Male inability to climax. *Medical Aspects of Human Sexuality,* 1975, 125–126.

Munjack, D. J., & Kanno, P. H. Retarded ejaculation: A review. *Archives of Sexual Behavior,* 1979, *8,* 139–150.

Murdock, G. P. *Social structure.* New York: Macmillan, 1949.

Murstein, B. I. Physical attractiveness and marriage adjustment in middle-aged couples. *Journal of Personality and Social Psychology,* 1976, *34,* 537–542.

Murstein, B. I. Physical attractiveness and marital choice. *Journal of Personality and Social Psychology,* 1972, *22,* 8–12.

Murstein, B. I. Stimulus-value-role: A theory of marital choice. *Journal of Marriage and the Family,* 1970, *32,* 465–481.

Murstein, B. I. *Love, sex and marriage throughout the ages.* N.Y.: Springer, 1974.

Myers, A., & Hewar, H. A. Circumstances attending 100 sudden deaths from coronary artery disease with coronors necropsies. *British Heart Journal,* 1975, *37,* 1133–1143.

Naeye, R. L. Coitus and associated amniotic fluid infections. *The New England Journal of Medicine,* 1979, *301,* 1198–1200.

Nagler, S. H. Fetishism. *Psychiatric Quarterly,* 1957, *31,* 713–741.

Nahmias, A. J. Herpes simplex virus infection of the fetus and newborn. *Progress in Clinical and Biological Research,* 1975, *3,* 63–77.

Nahmias, A. J., Dowdle, W., Josey, W., Naib, S., Painter, L., & Luce, C. Newborn infection with herpes virus hominis types 1 and 2. *Journal of Pediatrics,* 1969, *75,* 1194–1203.

Nahmias, A. J., & Sawanaburi, S. The genital herpes-cervical cancer hypothesis—10 years later. *Progress in Experimental Tumor Research,* 1978, *21,* 117–139.

National Center for Health Statistics. Final mortality statistics for 1974. *Monthly Vital Statistics Report* (Supple.), 1976, *24,* 20.

National Coordinating Group on Male Antifertility Agents. Gossypol: A new antifertility agent for males. *Chinese Medical Journal,* 1978, *4,* 417.

National Commission on the Causes & Prevention of Violence. *Crimes of violence,* Vol. II. Washington, D.C.: U.S. Government Printing Office, 1969.

Nesbitt, R. E. L. Maternal pregnancy surveillance. In S. Aldajem (Ed.), *Obstetrical practice.* St. Louis: C. V. Mosby, 1980.

Nettlebladt, P., & Uddenburg, N. Sexual dysfunction and sexual satisfaction in 58 married Swedish men. *Journal of Psychosomatic Research,* 1979, *23,* 141–149.

Newcomb, T. M. The prediction of interpersonal attraction. *American Psychologist,* 1956, *11,* 575–586.

Newman, G., & Nichols, C. R. Sexual attitudes and activities in older persons. *Journal of the American Medical Association,* 1960, *173,* 33–35.

Newman, H. F. Vibratory sensitivity of the penis. *Fertility and Sterility,* 1970, *21,* 791–793.

Nieschlag, E. The endocrine function of the human testis in regard to sexuality. In Ciba Foundation Symposium 62, *Sex, hormones and behavior,* pp. 183–208. New York: Excerpta Medica, 1979.

Nohl, J. *The black death: A chronicle of the plague.* New York: Allen & Unwin, 1926.

Norris, J., & Feldman-Summers, S. Factors related to the psychological impacts of rape on the victim. *Journal of Abnormal Psychology,* 1981, *90,* 562–567.

Nyberg, K. C. & Alston, J. P. Analysis of public attitudes

toward homosexual behavior. *Journal of Homosexuality, 1976, 2,* 99–107.

Oppenheimer, W. Prevention of pregnancy by the Grafenberg ring method. *American Journal of Obstetrics and Gynecology, 1959, 78,* 446.

Orlovick, R. H. The evaluation of a new form of adult sex education: The human sexual seminar. *Dissertation Abstract International,* January 1979, *39*(7–A), 4062–4063.

Ovesey, L., & Meyers, H. Retarded ejaculation: Psychodynamics and psychotherapy. *American Journal of Psychotherapy, 1968, 22,* 185–201.

Packard, J. *The sexual wilderness.* New York: D. McKay, 1968.

Page, E. W., Villee, C. A., & Villee, D. B. *Human reproduction: Essentials of reproductive and perinatal medicine* (3rd ed.). Philadelphia: Saunders, 1981.

Paige, K. Sexual pollution: Reproductive sex taboos in American society. *Journal of Social Issues, 1977, 33,* 144–165.

Palson, C., & Palson, R. Swinging in wedlock. In E. Goode & R. R. Troiden (Eds.), *Sexual deviance and sexual deviants.* New York: Morrow, 1974.

Pare, C. M. B. Homosexuality and chromosomal sex. *Journal of Psychosomatic Research, 1956, 1,* 247–251.

Parsons, L., & Sommers, S. C. *Psychobiology* (2nd ed.) Philadelphia: W. B. Saunders, 1978.

Paul, W., Weinreich, J. D., Gonsiorek, J. C., & Hotvedt, M. E. (Eds). *Homosexuality.* Beverly Hills, Calif.: Sage Publications, 1982.

Pauly, I. B. The current status of the change-of-sex operation. *Journal of Nervous and Mental Diseases, 1968, 147,* 460–471.

Pear, R. F.D.A. Approves New Sponge Contraceptive. *The New York Times,* April 6, 1983.

Pearlman, C. K. Frequency of intercourse in males at different ages. *Medical Aspects of Human Sexuality, 1972, 6,* 92–113.

Peel, J., & Potts, M. *Textbook of contraceptive practice.* London: Cambridge University Press, 1969.

Peele, S., & Brodsky, A. *Love and addiction.* New York: Signet, 1976.

Peplau, L. A., Rubin, Z., & Hill, C. T. Sexual intimacy in dating relationships. *Journal of Social Issues, 1977, 33,* 86–109.

Perelman, M. A. The treatment of premature ejaculation. In S. R. Leiblum and L. A. Pervin (Eds.), *Principles and practice of sex therapy.* New York: Guilford, 1980.

Perri, M. G. Behavior modification of heterosocial difficulties: A review of conceptual, treatment, and assessment considerations. *JSAS Catalogue of Selected Documents in Psychology,* 1977, 7, 75 (Ns. No. 1530).

Pervin, L. A., & Leiblum, S. R. Conclusion: Overview of some critical issues in the evaluation and treatment of sexual dysfunctions. In S. R. Leiblum and L. A. Pervin (Eds.), *Principles and practice of sex therapy.* New York: Guilford, 1980.

Peters, J. J. Children who are victims of sexual assault and the psychology of offenders. *American Journal of Psychotherapy, 1976, 30,* 398–421.

Pfeiffer, E., & Davis, G. C. Determinants of sexual behavior in middle and old age. *Journal of the American Geriatrics Society, 1972, 20,* 151–158.

Pfeiffer, E., Verwoerdt, H., & Davis, G. C. Sexual behavior in middle life. *American Journal of Psychiatry, 1972, 128,* 1282–1287.

Pickles, V. R., Hall, W. J., Best, F. A., & Smith, G. N. Prostaglandins in endometrium and menstrual fluids from normal and dysmenorrheic subjects. *British Journal of Obstetrics/Gynecology, 1965, 72,* 185–192.

Pietropinto, A., & Simenauer, J. *Beyond the male myth: A nationwide survey.* New York: Times Books, 1977.

Pillard, R. C., Rose, R. M., and Sherwood, M. Plasma testosterone levels in homosexual men. *Archives of Sexual Behavior, 1974, 3,* 453–458.

Plato. *The collected dialogues.* New York: Bollingen Foundation, 1961.

Plato, The symposium. In *The works of Plato,* B. Jowett (Translator). New York: Tudor Publishing, 1933.

Polani, P. E. General discussion in *Size at Birth, Ciba Foundation Symposium 27,* p. 386. New York: Associated Scientific Publishers, 1974.

Pomeroy, W. Some aspects of prostitution. *Journal of Sex Research, 1965, 1,* 177–187.

Pond, O. A., Ryle, A., & Hamilton, M. Marriage and neurosis in a working class population. *British Journal of Psychiatry, 1963, 109,* 592–598.

Poole, K. The aetiology of gender identity and the lesbian. *Journal of Social Psychology, 1972, 87,* 51–57.

Potts, M., Diggory, P., & Peel, J. *Abortion.* New York: Cambridge University Press, 1977.

Presidential Commission on Obscenity and Pornography. New York: Bantam Books, 1970.

Price, S., Reynolds, B. S., Cohen, B. D., Anderson, A. J., & Schochet, B. V. Group treatment of erectile dysfunction for men without partners: A controlled evaluation. *Archives of Sexual Behavior, 1981, 10,* 253–268.

Prince, V., & Bentler, P. M. Survey of 504 cases of transvestism. *Psychological Reports,* 1972, *31,* 903–917.

Proctor, F., Wagner, N., & Butler, V. The differentiation of male and female orgasm: An experimental study. In N. Wagner (Ed.), *Perspectives on human sexuality.* New York: Behavioral Publications, 1974.

Pugh, W. E., & Fernendez, F. L. Coitus in late pregnancy: A follow-up study of the effects of coitus on late pregnancy, delivery and the puperperium. *Obstetrics and Gynecology,* 1953, *2,* 636.

Queenan, J. T. *Modern management of the Rh problem* (2nd ed.). New York: Harper & Row, 1977.

Quinsey, V. L., Chaplin, T. C., & Carrigan, W. F. Sexual preferences among incestuous child molesters. *Behavior Therapy,* 1979, *10,* 562–565.

Quinsey, V. L. The assessment and treatment of child molesters: A review. *Canadian Psychological Review,* 1977, *18,* 204–220.

Rachman, S., & Hodgson, R. J. Experimentally induced sexual fetishism. *Psychological Record,* 1968, *18,* 25–27.

Rada, R. T. Alcoholism and the child molester. *Annals of the New York Academy of Science,* 1976, *273,* 492–496.

Rada, R. T., Laws, D. R., & Kellner, R. Plasma testosterone levels in the rapist. *Psychosomatic Medicine,* 1976, *38,* 257–268.

Rado, C. M. MMPI profile types of exposers, rapists, and assaulters in a court service population. *Journal of Consulting and Clinical Psychology,* 1977, *45,* 61–69.

Radzinowicz, L. *Sexual offenses.* London: MacMillan, 1957.

Rainwater, L. Some aspects of lower-class sexual behavior. *Journal of Social Issues,* 1968, *22,* 15–25.

Rainwater, L. *Family designs in marital sexuality, family planning and family limitation.* Chicago: Aldine, 1965.

Rainwater, L. Marital sexuality in four cultures of poverty, *Journal of Marriage and the Family,* 1964, *26,* 457–466.

Ramsey, G. V. The sex information of younger boys. *American Journal of Orthopsychiatry,* 1943a, *18,* 347–352.

Ramsey, G. V. The sexual development of boys. *American Journal of Psychology,* 1943b, *56,* 217–234.

Randall, J. Preoperative and postoperative status of male and female transsexuals. In R. Green and J. Money

(Eds.), *Transsexualism and sex reassignment.* Baltimore: Johns Hopkins Press, 1969.

Rasmussen, A. The importance of sexual attacks on children less than 14 years of age for the development of mental diseases and character anomalies. *Acta Psychiatrica and Neurology,* 1934, *9,* 351–434.

Rawson, P. *Erotic art of the East.* New York: G. P. Putnam's Sons, 1968.

Raymond, J. G. *The transsexual empire: The making of the She-Male.* Boston: Beacon Press, 1979.

Razini, J. Ejaculatory incompetence treated by deconditioned anxiety. *Journal of Behavior Therapy and Experimental Psychiatry,* 1972, *3,* 65–67.

Reichelt, P. A., & Werley, H. H. Sex knowledge of teenagers and the effect of an educational rap session. *Journal of Research and Development in Education,* 1976, *10*(1), 13–22.

Reid, D. E., Ryan, K. J., & Benirschke, K. *Principles and management of human reproduction* (2nd ed.). 1972.

Reik, T. A. *Psychologist looks at love.* New York: Farrar and Rinehart, 1944.

Reinberg, A., Lagouguey, M., Cesselin, F., Touitou, Y., Legrand, J. C., Delassale, A., Antreassian, J., & Lagouguey, A. Circadian and circannual rhythms in plasma hormones and other variables of five healthy young human males. *Acta Endocrinology,* 1978, *88,* 417–427.

Reiss, A. J. The social integration of queers and peers. *Social Problems,* 1961, *9,* 102–120.

Rekars, G. A., & Lovaas, O. I. Behavioral treatment of deviant sex-role behaviors in a male child. *Journal of Applied Behavior Analysis,* 1974, *7,* 173–190.

Rekars, G. A. A typical gender development and psychosocial adjustment. *Journal of Applied Behavior Analysis,* 1977, *10,* 559–571.

Renshaw, D. Impotence in diabetics. In J. LoPiccolo & L. LoPiccolo (Eds.), *Handbook of sex therapy.* New York: Plenum, 1978.

Reuben, D. *Everything you always wanted to know about sex (but were afraid to ask).* New York: D. McKay, 1969.

Reynolds, B. S. Biofeedback and facilitation of erection in men with erectile dysfunction. *Archives of Sexual Behavior,* 1980, *9,* 101–114.

Rickles, N. K. *Exhibitionism.* Philadelphia: J. B. Lippincott, 1950.

Robboy, S. J., Prat, J. & Welsch, W. R. Vaginal and cervical pathology associated with prenatal exposure to diethylstilbestrol. In S. G. Silverberg & F. J. Major (Eds.), *Estrogen and cancer.* New York: John Wiley, 1978.

Robinson, I. E., King, K., and Balswick, J. O. The premarital sex revolution among college females. *Family Coordinator,* 1972, *21,* 189–194.

Robinson, P. *The modernization of sex.* New York: Harper & Row, 1976.

Rooth, F. G. Indecent exposure and exhibitionism. *British Journal of Psychiatry,* 1976, Special publication #9, 212–222.

Rooth, F. G. Exhibitionism, sexual violence, and pedophilia. *British Journal of Psychiatry,* 1973, *122,* 705–710.

Rooth, F. G., & Marks, I. M. Persistent exhibitionism: Short-term response to aversive therapy, self-regulation, and relaxation treatments. *Archives of Sexual Behavior,* 1974, *3,* 227–248.

Rosen, R. C., & Kopel, S. The use of penile plethymography and biofeedback in the treatment of a transvestite-exhibitionist. *Journal of Consulting and Clinical Psychology,* 1977, *45,* 908–916.

Rosen, R. L. & Keefe, F. J. The measurement of human penile tumescence. *Psychophysiology,* 1978, *45,* 366–376.

Rosenberg, E. A., Marks, S. C., Howard, P. S., & James, L. P. Serum levels of follicle stimulating and luteinizing hormone before and after vasectomy.

Rosenberg, L., Hennekens, C. H., Rosner, B., Belanger, C., Rothman, K. J., & Speizer, F. E. Early menopause and the risk of myocardial infarction. *American Journal of Obstetrics and Gynecology,* 1981, *139,* 47–51.

Rosenblum, K. E. Female deviance and the female sex role. *British Journal of Sociology,* 1975, *25,* 169–185.

Rosenthal, A. M. Memoirs of a new China hand. *New York Times Magazine,* July, 1981.

Ross, I. J. The "hustler" in Chicago. *The Journal of Student Research,* 1959, *1,* 13–19.

Rossman, P. *Sexual experience between men and boys: Exploring the pederast underground.* New York: Association Press, 1976.

Rotman, M., Alderman, S., John, M., & Herskovic, T. Radiation therapy for breast cancer. *Journal of Reproductive Medicine,* 1979, *23,* 13–20.

Rougoff, N. *Prudery and passion: Sexuality in Victorian America.* New York: Putnam, 1971.

Rubin, I. Sex over 65. In I. Beigel (Ed.), *Advances in sex research.* N.Y.: Harper, 1963.

Rubin, T. *In the life.* New York: Macmillan, 1961.

Russell, D. E. H. *Rape in marriage.* New York: Macmillan, 1982.

Sagarin, E. Prison homosexuality and its effects on post-prison sexual behavior. *Psychiatry,* 1976, *39,* 245–257.

Saggs, H. W. F. *Everyday life in Babylonia and Assyria.* New York: B.T. Batsford, 1965.

Saghir, M. T., & Robins, E. *Male and female homosexuality: A comprehensive investigation.* Baltimore: Williams & Wilkins, 1973.

Salsberg, S. Is group marriage viable? *Journal of Sex Research,* 1973, *9,* 325–333.

Sanger, M. *Happiness in marriage.* New York: Brentano's Publishers, 1926.

Sanger, W. W. *The history of prostitution.* New York: Medical Publishing Co., 1910.

Santiago, L. P. A. *The children of Oedipus: Brother-sister incest in psychiatry, literature, history, and mythology.* Roslyn Heights, N.Y.: Libra, 1973.

Sarto, G. Steroidal contraceptives and congenital anomalies. In K. S. Moghissi (Ed.), *Controversies in contraception.* Baltimore: Williams & Wilkins, 1979.

Schachter, S., & Singer, J. Cognitive, social and physiological determinants of emotional states. *Psychological Review,* 1962, *69,* 379–399.

Schaefer, L. S. *Women and sex.* New York: Pantheon, 1973.

Scheflen, A. E. *Body language and social order.* Englewood Cliffs, N.J.: Prentice-Hall, 1972.

Scheflen, A. E. Significance of posture in communication systems. *Psychiatry,* 1964, *27,* 316–331.

Schmidt, G., & Sigusch, V. Psychosexual stimulation by films and slides: A further report on sex differences. *Journal of Sex Research,* 1970, *6,* 264–283.

Schmidt, G., Sigusch, V., & Shafer, A. Responses to reading erotic stories: Male female differences. *Archives of Sexual Behavior,* 1973, *2,* 181–201.

Schmidt, S. S., & Morris, R. R. Sperm granuloma: The complication of vasectomy. *Fertility and Sterility,* 1973, *24,* 941.

Schneidman, B., & McGuire, L. Group therapy for non-orgasmic women: Two age levels. *Archives of Sexual Behavior,* 1976, *5,* 239–247.

Schoedel, J., Fredrickson, W. A., & Knight, J. M. An extrapolation of the physical attractiveness and sex variables within the Byrne attraction paradigm. *Memory and Cognition,* 1975, *3,* 527–530.

Schofield, C. B. *Sexually transmitted diseases.* New York: Churchill Livingstone, 1979.

Schofield, M. *Sociological aspects of homosexuality: A comparative study of three types of homosexuals.* London: Longmans, 1965.

Schwartz, M. F., Kolodny, R. C., & Masters, W. H. Plasma testosterone levels of sexually functional and dysfunctional men. *Archives of Sexual Behavior,* 1980, *9,* 355–366.

Seeley, T. T., Abramson, P. R., Perry, L. B., Rothblatt, A. B., & Seeley, D. M. Thermographic measurement of sexual arousal: A methodological note. *Archives of Sexual Behavior*, 1980, *9*(2), 77–85.

Seemanova, E. A study of children of incestuous matings. *Human Heredity*, 1971, *21*, 108–128.

Segal, M. Impulsive sexuality: Some clinical and theoretical observations. *International Journal of Psychoanalysis*, 1963, *44*, 407–417.

Segraves, R. Pharmacological agents causing sexual dysfunction. *Journal of Sex and Marital Therapy*, 1977, *3*, 157–176.

Semans, J. H. Premature ejaculation: A new approach. *Southern Medical Journal*, 1956, *49*, 353–357.

Serber, M. Shame aversion therapy. *Journal of Behavior Therapy and Experimental Psychiatry*, 1970, *1*, 213–215.

Serber, M., & Keith, C. G. The Atascadero Project: Model of a sexual retraining program for incarcerated homosexual pedophiles. *Journal of Homosexuality*, 1974, *1*, 87–97.

Settlage, D. S. F., Motoshima, M., & Tredway, D. P. Sperm transport from the vagina to the fallopian tubes in women. In E. S. E. Hafez and G. L. Thibault (Eds.), *The biology of spermatozoa: Maturation, transport, and fertilizing ability*. Basel: S. Karger, 1975.

Sever, J. L., & Fuccillo, D. A. Perinatal infections. In R. J. Bologness & R. H. Schwartz (Eds.), *Perinatal medicine: Management of the high risk fetus and neonate*. Baltimore: Williams and Wilkins, 1977.

Seyler, L. E., Canalis, E., Spare, S., & Reichlin, S. Abnormal gonadotropin secretory responses to LRH in transsexual women after diethylstilbestrol priming. *Journal of Clinical Endocrinology Metabolism*, 1978, *47*, 176–183.

Shainess, N., & Greenwald, H. Are fantasies during sexual relations a sign of difficulty? *Sexual Behavior*, 1971, *1*, 38–54.

Sharp, H. C. Vasectomy as a means of preventing procreation in defectives. *Journal of American Medical Association*, 1909, *iii*, 1897–1902.

Shepher, J. Mate selection among second generation Kibbutz adolescents and adults. Incest avoidance and negative imprinting. *Archives of Sexual Behavior*, 1971, *1*, 293–308.

Sherfey, M. J. *The nature of and evolution of female sexuality*. New York: Vintage Books, 1973.

Shoor, M., Speed, M. H., & Bartelt, C. Syndrome of the adolescent child molester. *American Journal of Psychiatry*, 1966, *122*, 783–789.

Shope, D. F., & Broderick, C. B. Level of sexual experience and predicted adjustment in marriage. *Journal of Marriage and the Family*, 1967, *29*, 424–427.

Shover, L. R., Friedman, J. M., Weiler, S. J., Heiman, J. R., & LoPiccolo, J. Multiaxial problem-oriented system for sexual dysfunctions. *Archives of General Psychiatry*, 1982, *39*, 614–619.

Shrauger, J. S. Response to evaluation as a function of initial self-perception. *Psychological Bulletin*, 1975, *82*, 581–596.

Shrom, S. H., Lief, H. I., & Wein, A. J. Clinical profile of experience with 130 consecutive cases of impotent men. *Urology*, 1979, *13*, 511–515.

Siegelman, M. Psychological adjustment of homosexual men: A cross-national replication. *Archives of Sexual Behavior*, 1978, *7*, 1–11.

Siegelman, M. Parental background of male homosexuals and heterosexuals. *Archives of Sexual Behavior*, 1974, *3*, 3–18.

Siegelman, M. Adjustment of homosexual and heterosexual women. *British Journal of Psychiatry*, 1972, *120*, 477–481.

Sigall, H., & Landy, D. Radiating beauty: The effects of having a physically attractive partner on persons' perceptions. *Journal of Personality and Social Psychology*, 1973, *28*, 218–224.

Sigall, H., & Ostrove, N. Beautiful but dangerous: Effects of offender attractiveness and nature of the crime and juridic judgement. *Journal of Personality and Social Psychology*, 1975, *31*, 410–414.

Sigusch, V., Schmidt, G., Reinfeld, A., & Weideman-Sutor, I. Psychosexual stimulation: Sex differences. *Journal of Sex Research*, 1970, *6*, 10–24.

Singer, A., & Reid, B. Does the male transmit cervical cancer? *Contemporary Obstetrics/Gynecology*, 1979, *13*, 173–180.

Singer, J. & Singer, I. Types of female orgasm. *Journal of Sex Research*, 1972, *8*, 255–267.

Sloane, P., & Karpinski, E. Effects of incest on the participants. *American Journal of Orthopsychiatry*, 1942, *12*, 666–674.

Smith, D. D. The social context of pornography. *Journal of Communication*, 1976, *25*, 16–23.

Smith, J. R., and Smith, L. G. Co-marital sex and the sexual freedom movement. *Journal of Sex Research*, 1970, *6*, 131–142.

Smith, R. S. Voyeurism: A review of literature. *Archives of Sexual Behavior*, 1976, *5*, 585–608.

Smout, C. F. V., Jacoby, F., & Lillie, E. W. *Gynecological and obstetrical anatomy: Descriptive and applied*. Baltimore: Williams & Wilkins, 1969.

Smukler, A. J. & Schiebel, D. Personality characteristics

of exhibitionists. *Diseases of the Nervous System,* 1975, *36,* 600–603.

Solberg, O. A., Butler, J., & Wagner, N. N. Sexual behavior in pregnancy. *New England Journal of Medicine,* 1973, *228,* 1098–1103.

Solnick, R., & Birren, J. E. Age and male erectile responsiveness. *Archives of Sexual Behavior,* 1977, *6*(1), 1–9.

Sorensen, R. C. *Adolescent sexuality in contemporary America.* New York: World Publishing, 1973.

Spanier, G. B. Sex education and premarital sexual behavior among American college students. *Adolescence,* 1978, *13*(52), 657–674.

Spanier, G. B. Formal and informal sex education as determinants of premarital sexual behavior. *Archives of Sexual Behavior,* 1976, *5*(1), 36–67.

Spanier, G. B., & Cole, C. C. Mate swapping: Perceptions, value orientations, and participation in a midwestern community. *Archives of Sexual Behavior,* 1975, *4,* 143–159.

Spark, R. F., White, R. A., & Connolly, P. B. Impotence is not always psychogenic: Newer insights into hypothalamic-pituitary-gonadal dysfunction. *Journal of American Medical Association,* 1980, *243,* 750–755.

Spengler, A. Manifest sadomasochism of males: Results of an empirical study. *Archives of Sexual Behavior,* 1977, *6,* 441–456.

Speroff, L., Glass, R. H., & Case, N. G. *Clinical gynecologic endocrinology and infertility* (2nd ed.). Baltimore: Williams & Wilkins, 1978.

Spiess, W. F. J. The psycho-physiology of premature ejaculation: Some factors related to ejaculatory latency. Doctoral dissertation, State University of New York at Stony Brook, 1977.

Spock, B. What I think about nudity in the home. *Redbook,* July, 1975, pp. 29–33.

Spodak, M. K., Falck, Z. A., & Rappaport, J. R. The hormonal treatment of paraphiliacs with depo-provera. *Criminal Justice and Behavior,* 1978, *5,* 304–314.

Stegelman, M. Adjustment of male homosexuals and heterosexuals. *Archives of Sexual Behavior,* 1972, *2,* 9–25.

Stein, M. *Lovers, friends, slaves.* New York: G. P. Putnam, 1974.

Stein, M. D. Prostitution. In J. Money & H. Musaph (Eds.), *Handbook of sexology,* pp. 1069–1085. Amsterdam: Elsevier/North Holland Biomedical Press, 1977.

Stein, R. A. Sexual counseling and coronary heart disease. In S. R. Leiblum and L. A. Pervin (Eds.), *Principles and practice of sex therapy.* New York: Guilford, 1980.

Stekal, W. *Sexual aberrations: The phenomena of fetishism in relation to sex.* New York: Grove Press, 1952.

Stephan, W. E., Berscheid, E., & Walster, E. Sexual arousal and heterosexual perception. *Journal of Personality and Social Psychology,* 1971, *20,* 93–101.

Stephens, W. N. *The family in cross-cultural perspective.* New York: Holt, Rinehart & Winston, 1963.

Stewart, D., & Stewart, L. (Eds.). *Safe alternatives in childbirth.* Chapel Hill, N.C.: NAPSAC, Inc., 1976.

Stoller, R. J. *Sex and gender, Vol. II: The transsexual experiment.* New York: Jason Aronson, 1975.

Stoller, R. J. *Sex and gender, Vol. I: The development of masculinity and femininity.* New York: Jason Aronson, 1968.

Stopes, M. C. C. *Married love: A new contribution to the solution of sex difficulties.* London: A. C. Fifield, 1918.

Storaska, F. *How to say no to a rapist—and survive.* New York: Random House, 1975.

Strouse, J. To be minor and female: The legal rights of the woman under 21. *MS,* 1972, December.

Sturtevant, F. M. Oral contraceptives and liver tumors. In Moghissi (Ed.), *Controversies in contraception.* Baltimore: Williams & Wilkins, 1979.

Sue, D. Erotic fantasies of college students during coitus. *Journal of Sex Research,* 1979, *15,* 299–305.

Swanson, D. M. Adult sexual abuse of children. *Diseases of the Nervous System,* 1968, *29,* 677–683.

Symonds, C. Sexual mate-swapping: Violation of norms and reconciliation of guilt. In J. M. Henslin (Ed.), *Studies in the sociology of sex.* New York: Appleton-Century, 1971.

Symons, D. *The evolution of human sexuality.* New York: Oxford Press, 1979.

Szasz, T. S. Legal and moral aspects of homosexuality. In J. Marmor (Ed.), *Sexual inversion,* pp. 124–139. New York: Basic Books, 1965.

Szasz, T. S. *Pain and pleasure: A study of bodily feelings* (2nd ed.). New York: Basic Books, 1975 (originally published 1957).

Tannahill, R. *Sex in history.* New York: Stein & Day, 1980.

Tavris, C., & Sadd, S. *The Redbook report on female sexuality.* New York: Delacorte Press, 1975.

Taylor, G. R. *Sex in history.* New York: Vanguard, 1954. Also published New York: Harper & Row, 1970.

Tebbel, J. Today's education. *Journal of the National Education Association,* January/February, 1976.

Tennent, G., Bancroft, J., & Cass, J. The control of deviant sexual behavior by drugs: A double blind controlled study of benperidol, chlorpromazine, and placebo. *Archives of Sexual Behavior*, 1974, *3*, 261–271.

Tennov, D. *Love and limerance: The experience of being in love.* New York: Stein & Day, 1979.

Terman, L. M. Correlates of orgasm adequacy in 556 wives. *Journal of Psychology*, 1951, *32*, 115–172.

Terman, L. M. *Psychological factors in marital happiness.* New York: McGraw-Hill, 1938.

Thompson, C. Changing of concepts of homosexuality in psychoanalysis. *Psychiatry*, 1947, *10*, 183–189.

Thompson, N. C., McCandless, B. B., & Strickland, B. R. Personal adjustment of male and female homosexuals and heterosexuals. *Journal of Abnormal Psychology*, 1971, *78*, 237–240.

Thompson, N. L., Schwartz, D. M., McCandless, B. R., & Edwards, D. A. Parent-child relationships and sexual identity in male and female homosexuals and heterosexuals. *Journal of Consulting and Clinical Psychology*, 1973, *4*, 120–127.

Tietze, C. What price fertility control? Lower than that of unwanted pregnancy. *Contemporary Obstetrics and Gynecology*, 1978, *12*.

Tietze, C., & Lewit, S. Legal abortion. *Scientific American*, 1977, *236*, 21.

Tinbergen, N. *The study of instinct.* London: Oxford University Press, 1951.

Tollison, C. D., & Adams, H. E. *Sexual disorders: Treatment, theory, and research.* New York: Gardner Press, 1979.

Toobert, S., Bartelme, K., & Jones, E. Some factors related to pedophilia. *International Journal of Social Psychiatry*, 1968, *4*, 272–279.

Toppozada, M., and Hafez, E. S. E. Injectible contraceptives. In E. S. E. Hafez (Ed.), *Human reproduction: Conception and contraception* (2nd ed.). New York: Harper & Row, 1980.

Tordjman, G., Thierree, R., & Michel, J. R. Advances in the vascular pathology of male erectile dysfunction. *Archives of Sexual Behavior*, 1980, *9*, 391–398.

Townes, B. D., James, J., & Martin, D. Psychological characteristics among four groups of female offenders. *Criminology*, 1981, *18*, 471–480.

Trivers, R. L. Parental investment and sexual selection. In B. Campbell (Ed.), *Sexual selection and the descent of man.* Chicago: Aldine, 1972.

Tsai, M., Feldman-Summers, S., & Edgar, M. Childhood molestation: Variables related to differential impacts on psychosexual functioning in adult women. *Journal of Abnormal Psychology*, 1979, *88*, 407–417.

Tsai, M., & Wagner, N. N. Therapy groups for women

sexually molested as children. *Archives of Sexual Behavior*, 1978, *7*, 417–428.

Tulchinsky, D. The postpartum period. In D. Tulchinsky and K. J. Ryan (Eds.), *Maternal-Fetal endocrinology.* Philadelphia: W. B. Saunders, 1980.

Udry, J. R., Bauman, K. E., & Morris, N. M. Changes in premarital coital experiences of recent decade-of-birth cohorts of urban American women. *Journal of Marriage and the Family*, 1975, *37*, 783–787.

Udry, J. R., & Morris, N. M. Distribution of coitus in the menstrual cycle. *Nature*, 1968, *220*, 593–596.

Ueno, M. The so-called coition death. *Japanese Journal of Legal Medicine*, 1963, *17*, 333–337.

U.S. Department of Health, Education, and Welfare. *Healthy People: The Surgeon General's Report on Health Promotion and Disease Prevention.* Washington, D.C.:U.S. Government Printing Office, 1979.

United States Department of Health, Education, and Welfare: Public Health Service and Centers for Disease Control. *STD Fact Sheet, Edition 35.* Atlanta, Georgia, 1980.

Vance, E. B., & Wagner, N. N. Written descriptions of orgasm: A study of sex differences. *Archives of Sexual Behavior*, 1976, *5*(1), 87.

VanDeVelde, T. H. *Ideal Marriage: Its physiology and technique.* London: William Heinemann Medical Books, Ltd., 1926; New York, 1974 (revised).

VanDeventer, A. D., & Laws, D. R. Orgasmic reconditioning to redirect sexual arousal in pedophiles. *Behavior Therapy*, 1978, *9*, 748–765.

Van Gulik, R. H. *Sexual life in ancient China. A preliminary survey of Chinese sex and society from ca. 1500 B.C. until 1644 A.D.* Leiden, Holland: E. J. Brill, 1961.

Vaughan, E., & Fisher, E. Male sexual behavior induced by intracranial electrical stimulation. *Science*, 1962, *137*, 758.

Vaughan, V. C., McKay, R. J., & Behrman, R. E. *Nelson textbook of pediatrics* (11th ed.), Waldo E. Nelson, Sr. (Ed.). Philadelphia: Saunders, 1979.

Varni, C. A. An exploratory study of spouse-swapping. In J. R. Smith and L. G. Smith (Eds.), *Beyond monogamy.* Baltimore: Johns Hopkins University Press, 1974.

Velcek, D., Sniderman, K. W., Vaughan, E. D., Sos, T. A., & Mueckc, E. C. Penile flow index utilizing a doppler pulse wave analysis to identify penile vascular insufficiency. *Journal of Urology*, 1980, *123*, 669–673.

Verhulst, J., & Heiman, J. An interactional approach to sexual dysfunction. *American Journal of Family Therapy*, 1979, 7, 19–36.

Verwoerdt, A., Pfeiffer, E., & Wang, H. S. Sexual behavior in senescence: Changes in sexual activity and interest of aging men and women. *Journal of Geriatric Psychology*, 1967, 2, 163–180.

Vessey, M., Wiggins, P., Doll, R., Petro, R., & Johnson, B. A long-term follow-up study of women using different methods of contraception: An interim report. *Journal of Biosocial Science*, 1976, 8, 373–427.

Vierling, J. S., & Rock, J. Variations in olfactory sensitivity to exaltolide during the menstrual cycle. *Journal of Applied Physiology*, 1967, 22, 311–315.

Vilar, O. Spermatogenesis. In E. S. E. Hafez & T. N. Evans (Eds.), *Human reproduction: Conception and contraception.* New York: Harper & Row, 1973.

Vitaliano, P. P., Boyer, D., & James, J. Perceptions of juvenile experience: Females involved in prostitution versus property offenses. *Criminal Justice and Behavior*, 1981, 8, 325–342.

Voss, J. Sex education: Evaluation and recommendations for future study. *Archives of Sexual Behavior*, 1980, 9(1), 37–59.

Voss, J. R., & McKillip, J. Program evaluation in sex education: Outcome assessment of sexual awareness weekend workshops. *Archives of Sexual Behavior*, 1979, 8(6), 507–522.

Wagner, G., & Ebbehøj, J. Erectile dysfunction caused by abnormal outflow form the corpus cavernosum, Paper presented at the Third International Congress of Medical Sexology, Rome, Italy, 1978.

Walinder, J. Transsexualism: Definition, prevalence, and sex distribution. *Acta Psychiatrica Scandinavica*, 1968, *Supplement 203*, 255–258.

Walters, D. R. *Physical and sexual abuse of children: Causes and treatment.* Bloomington: Indiana University Press, 1975.

Walster E. The effect of self-esteem on romantic liking. *Journal of Experimental Social Psychology*, 1965, 1, 184–197.

Walster, E., Aronson, V., Abrahams, D., & Rottman, L. The importance of physical attractiveness in dating behavior. *Journal of Personality and Social Psychology*, 1966, 4, 508–516.

Walster, E., & Walster, G. W. *A new look at love.* Reading, Mass.: Addison-Wesley, 1978.

Walster, G. W., Walster, E., & Berscheid, E. *Equity: Theory and research.* Boston, Allyn and Bacon, 1977.

Ward, D. A., & Kassebaum, G. G. *Women's prison: Sex and social structure.* Chicago: Aldine, 1965.

Warren, C. A. B. *Identity and community in the gay world.* New York: Wiley, 1974.

Wechsler, J. Doctors and rape—a shocking story. *Good Housekeeping*, 1982, *194*, 82–87.

Weinberg, G. *Society and the healthy homosexual.* New York: St. Martin's Press, 1972.

Weinberg, M. S., & Williams, C. J. Gay baths and the social organization of impersonal sex. *Social Problems*, 1975, 23, 124–136.

Weinberg, M. S., & Williams, C. J. *Male homosexuals: Their problems and adaptations.* London: Oxford University Press, 1974.

Weinberg, S. K. *Incest behavior.* New York: Citadel Press, 1955.

Weiner, I. B. Father-daughter incest: A clinical report. *Psychiatric Quarterly*, 1962, 36, 607–632.

Weiner, I. G. On incest: A survey. *Excerpta Criminologica*, 1964, 4, 137–155.

West, D. J. *Homosexuality pre-examined.* Minneapolis: University of Minnesota Press, 1977.

Westoff, C. F. Coital frequency and contraception. *Family Planning Perspectives*, 1974, 6, 136–142.

Westermarck, E. A. *A history of human marriage.* New York: Macmillan, 1921.

Westoff, C. F., & Ryder, N. B. *The contraceptive revolution.* Princeton, N.J.: Princeton University Press, 1977.

Westwood, G. *A minority: Male homosexuality in Great Britain.* London: Longman, 1960.

Whelan, E. *Boy or girl? The sex selection technique that makes all others obsolete.* Indianapolis: Bobbs-Merrill, 1977.

Wickramasekiera, I. Aversive behavior reversal for sexual exhibitionism. *Behavior Therapy*, 1976, 7, 167–176.

Wickramasekiera, I. A technique for controlling a certain type of sexual exhibitionism. *Psychotherapy: Theory, research, and practice*, 1972, 9, 207–210.

Wieland, W. F., & Yunger, M. Sexual effects and side effects of heroine and methadone. *Proceedings of the Third National Conference on Methadone Treatment.* Public Health Service Publication, No. 2172, 1971, pp. 50–53.

Wiggins, J. D. *Childbearing: Physiology, experiences, needs.* St. Louis: C. V. Mosby, 1979.

Wiggins, J. S., Wiggins, N., & Conger, J. C. Correlates of heterosexual somatic preference. *Journal of Personality and Social Psychology*, 1968, 10, 82–90.

Williams, G. C. *Sex and evolution.* Princeton, N.J.: Princeton University Press, 1975.

Wilson, E. O. *Sociobiology: The new synthesis.* Cambridge, Mass. Harvard University Press, 1975.

Wilson, G., & Nias, D. *The mystery of love: How the science of sexual attraction can work for you.* New York: Quadrangle, 1976.

Wilson, G. T., & Lawson, D. M. Effects of alcohol on sexual arousal in women. *Journal of Abnormal Psychology,* 1976, *85,* 489–497.

Wilson, G. T., Lawson D. M., & Abrams, D. B. Effects of alcohol on sexual arousal in male alcoholics. *Journal of Abnormal Psychology,* 1978, *87,* 609–616.

Wilson, M., & Green, R. Personality characteristics of female homosexuals. *Psychological Reports,* 1971, *25,* 407–412.

Wilson, P. R. Preceptual distortion of height as function of ascribed academic status. *Journal of Social Psychology,* 1968, *74,* 97–102.

Wilson, R. J., Beecham, C. T., & Carrington, E. R. *Obstetrics and gynecology.* St. Louis: C. V. Mosby, 1975.

Wilson, W. C. Can pornography contribute to the prevention of sexual problems? In C. B. Qualls, J. P. Wincze, and D. H. Barlow (Eds.), *The prevention of sexual disorders.* New York: Plenum Press, 1978.

Wilson, W. C. The distribution of selected sexual attitudes and behaviors among the adult population of the United States. *Journal of Sex Research,* 1975, *11,* 46–64.

Wiseman, J. P. *The social psychology of sex.* New York: Harper & Row, 1976.

Witt, P. Treating the repetitive offender. *TSA News,* 1981, *4,* 1–2.

Witters, W. L. & Jones-Witters, P. *Human sexuality: A biological perspective.* New York: D. Van Nostrand, 1980.

Witzig, J. S. The group treatment of male exhibitionists. *American Journal of Psychiatry,* 1968, *125,* 179–185.

Wolchik, S. A., Beggs, V. E., Wincze, J. P., Sakheim, D. K., Barlow, D. H., & Mavissakalian, M. The effect of emotional arousal on subsequent sexual arousal in men. *Journal of Abnormal Psychology,* 1980, *89,* 595–598.

Wolfe, B. F. Behavioral treatment of childhood gender disorders: A conceptual and empirical critique. *Behavior Modification,* 1979, *3,* 550–575.

Wolff, C. *Love between women.* New York: St. Martin's Press, 1971.

Wolpe, J. *Psychotherapy by reciprocal inhibition.* Stanford: Stanford University Press, 1958.

Woodward, M. The diagnosis and treatment of homosexual offenders. *British Journal of Delinquency,* 1958, *9,* 44–59.

Wright, J., Perreault, R., & Mathieu, M. The treatment of sexual dysfunction. *Archives of General Psychiatry,* 1977, *34,* 881–890.

Yalom, I. D., Green, R., & Fisk, N. Prenatal exposure to female hormones: Effect on psychosexual development in boys. *Archives of General Psychiatry,* 1973, *28,* 554–561.

Yalom, I. D., Lunde, D. T., Moos, R. H., & Hamburg, D. A. The postpartum blues syndrome: Description and related variables. *Archives of General Psychiatry,* 1968, *18,* 16–27.

Yankelovich, D. New rules in American life. *Psychology Today,* 1981, *15,* 35–91.

Young, W. Prostitution. In J. H. Gagnon & W. Simon (Eds.), *Sexual deviance.* New York: Harper & Row, 1967.

Zander, A., & Havelin, A. Social comparison and interpersonal attraction. *Human Relations,* 1960, *13,* 21–32.

Zeiss, A. M., Rosen, G. M., & Zeiss, R. A. Orgasm during intercourse: A treatment strategy for women. In J. LoPiccolo & L. LoPiccolo (Eds.), *Handbook of sex therapy.* New York: Plenum, 1978.

Zelnick, M. Sex education and knowledge of pregnancy risk among U.S. teenage women. *Family Planning Perspectives,* 1979, *11*(6), 355–357.

Zelnick, M., & Kantner, J. F. Sexual activity, contraceptive use and pregnancy among metropolitan-area teenagers: 1971–1979. *Family Planning Perspectives,* 1980, *12.*

Zilbergeld, B. *Male sexuality.* New York: Bantam, 1978.

Zilbergeld, B., & Evans, M. The inadequacy of Masters and Johnson. *Psychology Today,* 1980, *14,* 29–43.

Zilbergeld, B., & Rinkleib, C. E. Desire discrepancies and arousal problems in sex therapy. In S. Leiblum & L. Pervin (Eds.), *Casebook of sex therapy.* New York: Guilford Press, 1980.

Zimbardo, P. *Shyness: What it is, what to do about it.* Reading, Mass.: Addison-Wesley, 1977.

Zimbardo, P., Pilkonis, R., & Norwood, R. *The silent prison of shyness.* Unpublished manuscript, Stanford University, Nov. 1974.

Zimmermann, M. K. *Passage through abortion: The personal and social reality of women's experiences.* New York: Praeger, 1977.

Zohar, J., Meiraz, D., Moaz, B., & Durst, N. Factors influencing sexual activity after prostatectomy: A prospective study. *Journal of Urology,* 1976, *116,* 332–334.

Zuckerman, M. The sensation-seeking motive. In B. Maher (Ed.), *Progress in experimental personality research;* Vol. 7. New York: Academic Press, 1974.

Zuckerman, M. Physiological measures of sexual arousal in the human. *Psychological Bulletin,* 1971, *75*(5), 297–329.

Zuckerman, M., Tushop, R., & Finner, S. Sexual attitudes and experience: Attitude and personality correlates and changes produced by a course in sexuality. *Journal of Counseling and Clinical Psychology,* 1976, *44*(1), 7–19.

Zuger, B. Effeminate behavior present in boys from early childhood. *Journal of Pediatrics,* 1966, *69,* 1098–1107.

NAME INDEX

SUBJECT INDEX

ACKNOWLEDGMENTS

Figures, tables, text

Box 1-1 Gebhard, P. H. The institute. In M. S. Weinberg (Ed.), *Sex research: Studies from the Kinsey Institute.* New York: Oxford Press, 1976.

1 Lawrence, D. H. *Sex, Literature, and Censorship.* New York: Twayne, 1953.

Box 2-1 Vance, E. B., & Wagner, N. N. Written descriptions of orgasm: A study of sex differences. *Archives of Sexual Behavior,* 1976, 5 (1), p. 87.

38 Kinsey, A. C., Pomeroy, W. B., & Martin, C. E. *Sexual behavior in the human male.* Philadelphia: W. B. Saunders, 1948, p. 158. Reprinted by permission of the Kinsey Institute for Research in Sex, Gender, & Reproduction, Inc.

Box 3-5 Adapted from Hatcher, R. A., Stewart, G. K., Stewart, F., Guest, F., Schwartz, D. W., and Jones, S. A. *Contraceptive technology, 1980-1981 (10th Rev.).* New York: Irvington Publishers, 1980.

Fig. 3-7 Source: Tulchinsky, D. The postartum period. In D. Tulchinsky and K. J. Ryan (Eds). *Maternal-Fetal endocrinology.* Philadelphia: W. B. Saunders, 1980.

Fig. 3-9 Adapted from Tietze, C. What price fertility control? Lower than that of unwanted pregnancy. *Contemporary Obstetrics and Gynecology,* 1978, 12.

Fig. 3-10 From Speroff, L., Glass, R. H., & Case, N. G. *Clinical gynecologic endocrinology and infertility.* 2nd Ed. Baltimore: Williams & Wilkins, 1978.

Fig. 3-17 From *Legalized abortion and the public health.* Institute of Medicine, National Academy of Sciences, Washington D.C. May 1975, p. 75.

Table 3-1 From E. W. Page, C. A. Villee, and B. B. Villee, *Human Reproduction: Essentials of reproductive and perinatal medicine,* 2nd ed. Philadelphia: W. B. Saunders, Co., 1976.

Table 3-2 From J. Langman, *Medical embryology: Human deveopment-normal and abnormal,* 3rd ed. Baltimore: Williams & Wilkins 1973.

Table 3-3 & 3-4 Mangus, E. M. Sources of maternal stress in the postpartum period: A review of the literature and an alternative view. In J. E. Parsons. (ed). The Psychology of sex differences and sex roles. New York: Hemisphere Publishing.

Table 3-5 This list is compiled from data from Aladjem, E. S. *Risks in the practice of modern obstetrics* (2nd Ed.). St. Louis: C. V. Mosby, 1975 and Bolognese, R. J., & Corson, S. L. *Interruption of pregnancy—A total patient approach.* Baltimore: Williams & Wilkins, 1975.

Table 3-6 From the Statistical Abstracts of the United States, 1981.

Fig. 3-17 From *Legalized abortion and the public health.* Institute of Medicine, National Academy of Sciences, Washington D.C. May 1975, p. 75.

Table 3-7 Mosher, W. D. Contraceptive utilization, United States. Vital and Health Statistics: Series 23, Data from the National Survey of Family Growth; no. 7 DHHS Publication, (PHS), 1983, 81.

Table 3-8 Adapted from Hatcher, R. A., Stewart, G. K., Stewart, F., Guest, F., Schwartz, D. W., and Jones, S. A. Contraceptive technology, 1980-1981 (10th Rev). New York: Irvington Publishers, 1980.

Table 3-9 From the Statistical Abstracts of the United States, 1981.

Box 4-2 Used by permission of the Boy Scouts of America.

Fig. 4-3 Adapted from Miller, W. R., & Lief, H. I. Masturbatory attitudes, knowledge and experience: Data from the Sex Knowledge and Attitude Test (SKAT). *Archives of Sexual Behavior,* 1976, 5, 447-468.

Table 4-1 From Hunt, M. *Sexual behavior in the '70s.* Chicago: Playboy Press, 1974.

Figure 5-1 From Alcock, John *Animal behavior: an evolutionary approach* 2nd ed. Sunderland, Mass: Sinauer Assoc., Inc. 1979.

Figure 5-2 Dutton, B. G., & Aron, A. P. Some evidence for heightened sexual attraction under conditions of high anxiety. *Journal of Personality and Social Psychology,* 1974, 30, 510-517.

Table 5-1 Adapted from Zimbardo, P., Pilkonis, R., & Norwood, R. *The silent prison of shyness.* Unpublished manuscript, Stanford University, Nov. 1974 and Zimbardo, P. *Shyness: What it is, what to do about it.* Reading, Mass.: Addison-Wesley, 1977.

179 Lessing, D. *The summer before the dark.* New York: Bantam, 1973.

195 Cook, M., & McHenry, R. *Sexual attraction.* New York: Pergamon, 1978.

Box 6-1 Messenger, T. C. Sex and repression in an Irish folk community. In D. S. Marshall and R. C. Suggs (Eds.), *Human sexual behavior: Variations in the ethnographic spectrum.* New York: Basic Books, 1971, p. 16.

Box 6-2 Sorensen, R. C. Adolescent sexuality in contemporary America. New York: World Publishing, 1973. © by Robert C. Sorensen. Reprinted by permission of Harper & Row, Pub., Inc.

Fig. 6-1 Hunt, M. *Sexual behavior in the 70's.* Chicago: Playboy Press, 1974, p. 133.

Fig. 6-3 Ibid, p. 198.

Fig. 6-8 Ibid, p. 191.

Table 6-1 Ibid, p. 166.

Table 6-2 Adapted from Kinsey et al., 1953. p. 364.

Table 6-3 Adapted from Hariton, B. E., & Singer, J. L. Women's fantasies during sexual intercourse: Normative and theoretical implications. *Journal of Consulting and Clinical Psychology*, 1974, *42*, 313-322.

Table 6-5 Adapted from Sorensen, R. C. Adolescent sexuality in contemporary America. New York: World Publishng, 1973, p. 203. © by Robert C. Sorensen. Reprinted by permission of Harper & Row, Pub., Inc.

219 Lawrence, D. H. *Sex, Literature, and Censorship.* New York: Twayne, 1953.

239 Friday, N. *My secret garden: Women's sexual fantasies.* New York: Simon & Schuster, 1973.

Box 7-1 From Hoffman, Martin, *The gay world.* New York: Basic Books, 1968. By permission of the publisher.

Figure 7-1 From Kinsey, A. C., Pomeroy, W. B., & Martin, C. E. *Sexual behavior in the human male.* Philadelphia: W. B. Saunders, 1948, p. 638. Reprinted by permission of The Kinsey Institute for Research in Sex, Gender, & Reproduction, Inc.

267 Kinsey, A. C., Pomeroy, W., Martin, C., & Gebhard, P. *Sexual behavior in the human female.* Philadelphia: W. B. Saunders, 1953.

290 Reprinted from Gagnon, J. H., & Simon, W. E. *Sexual conduct: The social sources of human sexuality.* 1973 Reprinted with permission of Aldine Publishing Co., Hawthorne, New York.

Box 8-2 Adapted from Masters and Johnson, 1970.

Table 8-1 Heiman, J., LoPiccolo, L., & LoPiccolo, J. *Becoming orgasmic: A sexual growth program for women.* Englewood Cliffs, N.J.; Prentice-Hall, 1976 and LoPiccolo, J., & Lobitz, W. C. The role of masturbation in the treatment of orgasmic dysfunction. *Archives of Sexual Behavior*, 1972, *2*, 163-172.

Table 8-2 Abridged from A. J. Cooper, Short-term treatment in sexual dysfunction; A review. Comprehensive Psychiatry, 1981, *22*, 206-217. Used by permission.

311, 326 Reprinted with permission from Kaplan, H. S. *The new sex therapy.* New York: Brunner/Mazel, 1974.

311 Reprinted with permission from *Principles and practice of sex therapy.* Leiblum, S. R., & Pervin, L. A. (Eds.). New York: Guilford, 1980.

Fig. 9-1 American Cancer Society, 1982.

347 Szasz, T. S. *Pain and pleasure: A study of bodily feelings, Second Edition.* New York: Basic Books, 1975 (originally published 1957).

353 From *Heartsounds* by Martha Weinman Lear. Copyright ©1979 by M. W. Lear. Reprinted by permission of Simon & Schuster.

Box 10-1, 393, Box 10-2 Tollison, C. D. & Adams, H. E. *Sexual disorders: Treatment, Theory, and Research.* New York: Gardner Press, 1979.

377 Gosselin, C., & Wilson, G. *Sexual variations: Fetishism, sadomasochism and transvestism.* New York: Simon & Schuster, 1980.

Box 11-1 Reprinted with permission from *Journal of Behavior Therapy & Experimental Psychiatry*, 11, Josiassen, R. C., Fantuzzo, J. & Rosen, A. C. Treatment of pedophilia using multistage aversion therapy and social skills training. Copyright 1980, Pergamon, Press, Ltd.

Box 11-2 From *Kiss daddy goodnight* by Louise Armstrong, Copyright © 1978 by L. Armstrong. Reprinted by permission of the publisher, E. P. Dutton, Inc. and Butler, S. *Conspiracy of silence: The trauma of incest.* San Francisco: Volcano Press, Inc. © 1978.

Table 11-1 Meiselman, K. C. *Incest: A psychological study of causes and effects with treatment recommendations.* San Francisco: Jossey-Bass, 1978.

409 From *Kiss daddy goodnight* by Louise Armstrong, Copyright © 1978 by L. Armstrong. Reprinted by permission of the publisher, E. P. Dutton, Inc.

Table 12-2 Holmstrom, L. L., & Burgess, A. W. Sexual behavior during reported rapes. Archives of Sexual Behavior, 1980, *9*, 427-439.

Table 12-3 Norris, J., & Feldman-Summers, S. Factors related to the psychological impacts of rape on the victim. *Journal of Abnormal Psychology*, 1981, *90*, 562-567.

439 Burgess, A. W., & Holmstrom, L. L. *Victims of crisis.* Bowie: Robert J. Brady, 1974.

463 LeSueur, M. *The girl.* Cambridge, Mass.: West End Press, 1978, p. 10.

480 Reprinted from Gagnon and Simon *Sexual Conduct,* Copyright 1973. Reprinted with permisson of Aldine Pub. Co., Hawthorne, N.Y.

489 Russell, B. Marriage and morals. New York: Liveright Pub., Corp., 1957.

492 Taken from *Raping our children* by Gloria Lentz. Copyright © 1971 by G. Lentz. Used by permission of Arlington House Publishers, Inc.

493 Reprinted by permission of A & W Publishers, Inc. from *Values in sexuality: A new approach to sex education* by Eleanor S. Morrison and Mila Underhill Price. Copyright © 1974 by Hart Publishing Co., Inc.

Photographs

3 Laimute E. Druskis **8** UPI **11** UPI **12** Austrian National Tourist Office **14** UPI **27** Multi-media Resource Center **33** Multi-media Resource Center, © Justine Hill, 1983 **62, 63** Appeared in *Atlas of Chil-*

ABOUT THE AUTHORS

James H. Geer is Professor of Psychology and Psychiatry at the State University of New York at Stony Brook. Jim received his B.S., M.S., and Ph.D. degrees from the University of Pittsburgh. He taught at the State University of New York at Buffalo and the University of Pennsylvania before coming to Stony Brook. Jim was Chairman of the Department of Psychology at Stony Brook from 1971 until 1977. He has been a visiting scholar at University College of The University of London, Cambridge University, and York University, all located in England. He has been an Associate Editor for *Cognitive Behavior Therapy* and *Psychophysiology* as well as a reviewer for many other professional publications. Jim was awarded a NATO Senior Fellowship in Science and is a Fellow of The American Psychological Association and the International Organization of Psychophysiology. He has published over sixty articles and book chapters covering topics in clinical psychology, psychophysiology, and sexual behavior and has been awarded research grants from both the federal government and private corporations.

Julia R. Heiman is Associate Professor of Psychiatry and Behavioral Sciences at the University of Washington in Seattle. After receiving her Ph.D. in Clinical Psychology from the State University of New York at Stony Brook, Julie spent 1975–1980 with SUNY's Department of Psychiatry and Behavioral Sciences, and its affiliate, Long Island Research Institute. There she was Chief of the Laboratory of Marital and Interpersonal Problems and Associate Director for Research Services at the Sex Therapy Center. She has a broad variety of publications in human sexuality, including the psychophysiology of sexual arousal, clinical outcome of sex therapy, alternative conceptualizations of sexual patterns, and a clinical self-help book and film series (co-authored with Leslie LoPiccolo and Joseph LoPiccolo), *Becoming orgasmic: A sexual growth program for women.* Currently, Julie is Research Coordinator for Harborview Community Mental Health Center, where she also does therapy and research with sex, marital, and family problems.

Harold Leitenberg is Professor of Psychology and Clinical Professor of Psychiatry at the University of Vermont. He is the Director of the Clinical Psychology Training Program and the Behavior Therapy and Psychotherapy Center. Hal received his B.A. degree from the City College of New York and his Ph.D. degree from Indiana University. He is a Fellow of the American Psychological Association and past President of the Vermont Psychological Association, and was designated University Scholar in social sciences and humanities for 1982–1983 at the University of Vermont. In addition to administration, teaching, and research, he is also a practicing psychologist. Hal is the author of over fifty research articles and chapters, and has two previous books to his credit: *Handbook of Behavior Modification and Behavior Therapy* and *Promoting Sexual Responsibility and Preventing Sexual Problems.*

James H. Geer

Julia R. Heiman

Harold Leitenberg